# FINANCIAL TRADING AND INVESTING

JOHN L. TEALL

ELSEVIER

AMSTERDAM • BOSTON • HEIDELBERG • LONDON
NEW YORK • OXFORD • PARIS • SAN DIEGO
SAN FRANCISCO • SINGAPORE • SYDNEY • TOKYO
Academic Press is an imprint of Elsevier

AP

Academic Press is an imprint of Elsevier
225 Wyman Street, Waltham, MA 02451, USA
The Boulevard, Langford Lane, Kidlington, Oxford, OX5 1GB, UK



**Library of Congress Cataloging-in-Publication Data**
Teall, John L., 1958-
Financial trading and investing / John Teall.
p. cm.
Includes index.
ISBN 978-0-12-391880-2
1. Investments. 2. Securities–Prices. 3. Speculation. I. Title.
HG4521.T36 2013
332.6—dc23
2012020467

**British Library Cataloguing-in-Publication Data**
A catalogue record for this book is available from the British Library

For information on all Academic Press publications
visit our website at http://store.elsevier.com

Ancillary materials are located at the book's companion site at
www.elsevierdirect.com/companions/9780123918802

Printed in the United States of America
Transferred to Digital Printing, 2013

**To Emily:**

Artist, Scholar

# Contents

## 3. Institutional Trading



## 4. Regulation of Trading and Securities Markets



## 5. Adverse Selection, Trading, and Spreads

## 6. Random Walks, Risk, and Arbitrage



## 7. Arbitrage and Hedging with Fixed Income Instruments and Currencies



## 8. Arbitrage and Hedging with Options

Ancillary materials are located at the book's companion site at www.elsevierdirect.com/companions/9780123918802

# Preface

There is an apocryphal story told in certain chess circles about a teenage boy that simultaneously challenged the great Russian chess champion Alexander Alekhine and the Russo-German Grandmaster Efim Bogoljubov. The boy had separately approached each of the two grandmasters to play games of correspondence chess. The two champions, without knowledge of the other's participation, accepted the boy's offers to play for money, with odds favorable to the boy. The chess greats, who happened to be friends, discovered the scheme in a much later conversation, and realized that the boy was merely acting as an intermediary between them, relaying moves between the two grandmasters. The boy, because of his favorable odds, was assured of netting a profit on the intermediation regardless of who won the match.

Intermediation is the keystone of the world financial system. While much essential financial decision-making focuses on the time and risk dimensions of investing, intermediation is the process that actually moves capital from businesses, institutions, and individuals with surplus funds to those that need them. Trading is central to this intermediation. Some traders have great expertise in valuation, quantitative analysis, or other investments tools, and serve important roles in this intermediation process. Other traders merely serve as intermediaries, quoting their prices based on the trading moves played by the experts. Their roles and opportunities are considerable as well. Regardless, all traders need to understand their markets and manage their risks. This is the objective to which *Financial Trading and Investing* strives.

Securities trading is a very broad topic, and merits far more discussion than could ever fit into a single volume. There are thousands of books on trading, all-too-many of which present their authors' opinions on "how to trade your way to riches." There are also quite a few outstanding books that focus on fairly narrow aspects of trading, such as market microstructure, algo trading, risk management or day-trading, etc. *Financial Trading and Investing* seeks to provide a broad overview to trading and investing, much as any standard investments text. However, the focus of this text is on trading, trading institutions, markets, and the institutions that participate in, facilitate, and regulate trading activities.

*Financial Trading and Investing* is intended to serve as a primary textbook for a university course focusing on trading. Most but not all students in a trading course will have already had some exposure to introductory finance or investments courses. The book should also be useful in a number of other courses, including those dealing with general investments, securities law, and classes based on student managed funds. The text discusses recent, important, newsworthy, and controversial trading tactics such as algo trading, dark liquidity pools, late trading, co-location, high frequency trading, and flash orders. It explains a number of important valuation and hedging techniques. It introduces some of the most recent market and technology advances and innovations such as Designated Market Makers (DMMs), Supplemental Liquidity Providers (SLPs), SuperMontage, ATSs, and ECNs.

While coverage in my own trading course is sequenced by the ordering of the chapters, the text is designed to be very flexible. Most chapters in this text can be presented without significant reliance on preceding chapters. For example, many instructors would prefer their class readings in behavioral finance(Chapter 10) and market efficiency (Chapter 11) to take place early in their courses. Practically any ordering of chapters is possible, though Chapter 1 is the most logical starting point and readers unfamiliar with Black-Scholes should familiarize themselves with the Appendix to Chapter 6 before proceeding to the remainder of Chapter 6 and to Chapter 8. In addition, readers might feel more comfortable reading Chapter 3 before 12. In general, the text is organized as follows:

1. Chapters 1 through 5: Introduction to trading, trading mechanisms, regulation, and markets
2. Chapters 6 through 9: Risk, arbitrage, hedging, risk management, and performance evaluation
3. Chapters 10 through 12: Behavioral aspects of trading and investing, market efficiency, and market abuses and failure

Many trading courses implement a software or internet-based trading simulation such as FTS, Interactive Brokers' IB Student Trading Lab, or TraderEx. This book was designed for use as a primary text in these learning environments. In fact, integration of simulation packages into the trading course has played a key role in the development of this book, and close to a third of class time on my own course is dedicated to simulations. The book has ancillary materials to aid in the presentation and analysis of cases and demonstrations from these simulations.

In addition to the simulation-based ancillary materials, which are located at the book's companion site at www.elsevierdirect.com/companions/9780123918802, the text has several other pedagogical features. First, each chapter provides a number of exercises, to which detailed solutions are offered at the end of the text. There are a number of appendices, both to chapters and at the end of the text. For example, text appendices review basic statistics and mathematics concepts that are most useful to traders, particularly in the measurement and management of risk. The web-based ancillary materials include additional questions and problems that can be used for in-class discussions or exams. Additional discussion on the presentations of concepts and integration with simulation packages are offered there as well.

I welcome your comments and suggestions regarding this book. I can be contacted by e-mail at tealj2@rpi.edu or by using contact information available on my web page at http://www.jteall.com.

## ACKNOWLEDGEMENTS

I am fortunate to have taught a number of excellent students who have offered many suggestions and corrections on chapter drafts for this book. Several colleagues and reviewers made helpful contributions, including T.J. Wu, Michael Goodman, Peter Knopf, Tom Coleman and Craig Holden. Stan Wakefield and editors and staff at Elsevier, including Scott Bentley, Kathleen Paoni, and Lisa Lamenzo were essential in bringing the book project to fruition. In addition, a number of anonymous reviewers, were most helpful as well. Of course, Anne, who allows me to work only one day a week and Emily, who has been a delightfully pleasant adolescent, always boost my productivity and morale.

CHAPTER

# 1

# Introduction to Securities Trading and Markets

## 1.1 TRADES, TRADERS, SECURITIES, AND MARKETS

A *trade* is a security transaction that creates or alters a portfolio position based on an investment decision. The trade action and the trade decision follow the investing decision to buy, sell, or otherwise take a position in an asset or instrument. The trade decision concerns how to execute the investment decision, in which markets, and at what prices and times and through which agents. Trade decisions are more concerned with the speed, costs, and risks associated with executing the transaction, while investing emphasizes selection of the security. The investment strategy is linked to the rationale to buy or to sell (e.g., to exploit undervaluation to provide needed liquidity). Investing is a positive sum game, allocating capital towards production and risk management. Trading is often a zero sum game, except to the extent that it facilitates investing, produces information, and improves markets by enhancing liquidity and reducing execution costs. While investing and trading activities might be distinguished from one another, there is a significant overlap between them, where high-turnover short-term investing, also generally referred to as trading, blurs the distinction between the two.

*Traders* compete to generate profits, seeking compatible counterparties in trade and seeking superior order placement and timing. *Proprietary traders* seek profits by trading on their own accounts while *agency traders* trade as commission brokers on behalf of clients. Most proprietary traders are *speculators* who focus on profits derived from price changes, *arbitrageurs* who focus on price discrepancies, and *hedgers* who seek to control risk. *Dealers*, who trade directly with clients, and *brokers*, who seek trade counterparties for clients, facilitate the trading process. Brokers act as agents for investors, buying and selling for them on a commission basis. Dealers maintain *quotes* (*bids*, which are solicitations to purchase and *offers*, which are solicitations to sell) and buy and sell on a profit basis. The typical quote specifies the security, the proposed transaction's price, and the number of units to be exchanged at this price. The spread is simply the difference between the best offer and bid. *Buy side traders* such as individual investors, mutual funds, and pension funds buy exchange or liquidity services. This means that buy side traders make investment decisions to take positions in securities and seek counterparties to buy from or sell to. *Sell side traders* such as day traders, market makers, and brokers provide liquidity and markets to buy side traders. Sell side traders stand by awaiting orders from buy side traders. One should not confuse buy side and sell side traders with buyers and sellers of securities. Regulatory definitions for traders will be discussed shortly.

## Trading Illustration

Consider a hypothetical scenario where an equities analyst working for the Flagellan Fund has recommended that the fund purchase shares of the General Engine Company. The fund's portfolio manager agreed, and placed an order for 50,000 shares with the fund's in-house trader. The in-house trader decided to transact 10,000 shares herself, and placed buy orders of 20,000 shares each with two brokers, Kanteven-Fitzgerald and Themus Trading. Counterparties for the trades will be found in various trading venues, including exchanges and alternative trading systems. Flagellan is considered a buy side market participant, not because it is buying shares, but because it is buying liquidity. Its counterparties in trade will probably be a combination of buy side and sell side market participants.

## Securities and Instruments

A security is a tradable claim on the assets of an institution or individual. Where real assets contribute to the productive capacity of the economy, securities are financial assets that merely represent claims on real assets. Many securities represent ownership (e.g., shares of stock) or creditorship (e.g., bond) of an institution (e.g., corporation). Some instruments will represent obligations to buy or sell (e.g., futures contracts) or options to buy or sell. Most corporate securities imply either fixed claims (such as bonds that typically involve fixed interest and principal repayments) or residual claims (such as common stock, whose owners receive assets remaining after creditors' and other claims have been satisfied). Most securities are marketable to the general public, meaning that they can be sold or assigned to other investors in the open marketplace. Some of the more common types of securities and tradable instruments are classified and briefly introduced in the following:

1. *Debt securities*: Denote creditorship of an individual, firm, or other institution. They typically involve payments of a fixed series of interest or amounts towards principal along with principal repayment. Examples include:
   *Bonds:* Long-term debt securities issued by corporations, governments, or other institutions.
   *Treasury securities:* Debt securities issued by the U.S. Treasury of the federal government.

2. *Equity securities (stock):* Denote ownership in a business or corporation. They typically permit for dividend payments if the firm's debt obligations have been satisfied. The two primary types of marketable equity issued by corporations are:
   *Common stock:* Security held by the residual claimant or owner of the firm
   *Preferred stock:* Stock that is given priority over common stock in the payment of dividends and liquidation; preferred stock holders must receive their dividends if common stock holders are to be paid dividends
3. *Derivative securities:* Have payoff functions derived from the values of other securities, rates, or indices. Some of the more common derivative securities are:
   *Options:* Securities that grant their owners rights to buy or sell an asset at a specific price on or before the expiration date of the security. Options on stock are among the most frequently traded. The two types of stock options are[1]:
      *Call:* A security or contract granting its owner the right to purchase a given asset at a specified price on or before the expiration date of the contract
      *Put:* A security or contract granting its owner the right to sell a given asset at a specified price on or before the expiration date of the contract
   *Futures contracts:* Instruments that oblige their participants to either purchase or sell a given asset at a specified price on the future settlement date of that contract. We will discuss later the differences between futures and options contracts. Investors may take either a long or a short position in a futures contract. A *long* position obligates the investor to purchase the given asset on the settlement date of the contract and a *short* position obligates the investor to sell the given asset on the settlement date of the contract.
   *Swaps*: Provide for the exchange of cash flows associated with one asset, rate, or index for the cash flows associated with another asset, rate, or index.
4. *Commodities*: Contracts, including futures and options on physical commodities such as oil, metals, corn, and so on. A commodity contract will be characterized by five features: the commodity (e.g., heating oil no. 2), the exchange on which the contract is traded (e.g., NYM for New York Mercantile Exchange), the size of the contract (e.g., 42,000 gallons), the settlement price per unit (e.g., $2.75 per gallon), and the settlement date or delivery month (e.g., September 2010).
5. *Currencies*: For transactions to be executed between countries with different currencies, some type of foreign exchange (also called currency exchange, FOREX or FX) must take place. Foreign exchange is simply the trading of one currency for another. Exchange rates denote the number of units of one currency that must be given up for one unit of a second currency. Exchange transactions can occur in either *spot* or *forward* markets. In the spot market, the exchange of one currency for another occurs when the agreement is made. For example, dollars may be exchanged for euro now in an agreement made now. This would be a spot market transaction. In a forward market transaction, the actual exchange of one currency for another actually occurs at a date later than that of

[1]Actually, these are "plain vanilla options." There are also a large number of exotic options with more complex terms.

the agreement. Thus, traders could agree now on an exchange rate for two currencies at a later date. Spot and forward contract participants take one position in each of two currencies:

**a.** Long: An investor has a "long" position in the currency that he will accept at the later date.

**b.** Short: An investor has a "short" position in the currency that he must deliver in the exchange.

Currency futures contracts are much like forward contracts, standardized to trade on exchanges with specified settlement prices, dates, and contract sizes. Futures contracts normally provide for margin and marking to the market.

**6.** *Indices*: Contracts pegged to measures of market performance such as the Dow Jones Industrials Average or the S&P 500 Index. These are frequently futures contracts on portfolios structured to perform exactly as the indices for which they are named. Index traders also trade options on these futures contracts.

It is important to note that this list of security types is far from complete; it only reflects some of the instruments most frequently discussed in this book. In addition, most of the instrument types will have many different variations.

Investors purchase securities for investment purposes. Their purchases may be motivated by profit motives or by risk management. As we discussed earlier, profits might be obtained through successful *speculating* (forecasting correctly the direction of security prices and payments associated with securities). Speculators are highly dependent on quality information. A second potential source of profits is *arbitrage*, the simultaneous purchase and sale of the same or substantially similar asset at different prices. Arbitrage succeeds when the price of purchased assets is less than those of sold assets. Arbitrageurs are highly dependent on low transaction costs and speed of trade execution. Profits can also be obtained through market making, that is, by providing liquidity while profiting from differences between bid and offer prices. Many investors will profit from all three types of trading motivations. Investors might also purchase securities to manage risk. For example, some securities serve as excellent hedges for others. Securities are purchased from *counterparties* and the acquisition process is referred to as trading.

## 1.2 SECURITIES TRADING

Trading occurs in securities markets, physical or virtual, where traders communicate with one another and execute transactions. The basic function of a market is to bring together buyers and sellers. Most markets also provide information in the price discovery process, and the information revealed in this process is a function of market structure. This book will focus on the process of trading and design of markets, and will discuss investing and certain investment decisions as well when appropriate.

The first component of a trade involves the *acquisition of information* and quotes. Quality information and transparency are crucial to price discovery. Traders want to know prices at which they can buy (ask or offer prices) and sell (bid prices), along with the more recent prices of actual executions (last). Real-time and time-delayed quote and price services can be purchased from data vendors such as Bloomberg, Reuters, and Interactive Data.[2] *Transparent* markets disseminate high-quality information quickly to the public. Generally, markets that communicate real-time bids, offers, and executed trade information are more transparent than dealer markets that do not. *Opaque markets* are those that lack transparency.

The second component of the trade is the *routing* of the trade order. Routing involves selecting the broker(s) to handle the trade(s), deciding which market(s) will execute the trade(s) and transmitting the trade(s) to the market(s). An individual investor might route her trade through her broker who might route it to a major exchange. The third component of the trade is its *execution*, when the security is actually bought or sold. Buys are matched and executed against sells according to the rules of that market. Rules might provide for electronic execution, telephone execution, or direct human (face-to-face) execution. Finally, the fourth component of the trade is its *confirmation*, *clearance*, and *settlement*. Clearance is the recording and comparison of the trade records, and settlement involves the actual delivery of the security and its payment. *Trade allocation* might also be a part of this final process, as large institutional orders involving many clients and many transactions are allocated to various clients.

## Algorithmic Trading: A Brief Introduction

Large orders move markets. For example, a large buy order increases security prices, which, obviously, is not good for the buyer. Typical transaction sizes in many markets such as the NYSE are very small relative to the order sizes placed by institutional traders. This means that large institutional trades can have a significant and unwanted impact on execution prices unless larger orders are broken into smaller orders. *Algorithmic trading* refers to automated trading with the use of computer programs for automatically submitting and allocating trade orders among markets and brokers as well as over time so as to minimize the price impact of large trades. Many institutional traders employ algorithmic trading (also called automated trading, black box trading, and robotrading) to break up large orders into smaller orders to reduce execution risk, preserve anonymity, and minimize the price impact of a trade. Significant portions of these orders might be withheld from public display to minimize their price impact in the market. The hidden portions of these large institutional orders are sometimes referred to as *dark liquidity pools* because they are hidden from the public. Orders are often partially revealed, in which case they are called *iceberg* or *hidden-size* orders, with brokers instructed not to reveal the full size of the order. Rooted in program trading (defined by the NYSE as computer-initiated trades involving 15 or more stocks with value totaling more than $1 million) dating back to the 1980s, algorithmic trading accounts for between 30% and 80% of trade volume in many markets.

Strategies used by algorithms vary widely. Generally, algorithmic trading results from mathematical models that analyze every quote and trade in the relevant market, identify liquidity opportunities, and use this information to make intelligent trading decisions.

[2]More details on sources of trade information will be provided later in this chapter.

Some algorithmic trading models seek to trade at or better than the average price over a day (e.g., volume weighted average price [VWAP]) and others seek to execute slowly so as to have minimal price impact. Algorithms sometimes are set to produce more volume at market opens and closes when volume is high, and less during slower periods such as around lunch. They can seek to exploit any arbitrage opportunities or price spreads between correlated securities. In addition, algorithmic trading can also account and adjust for trading costs such as commissions and taxes as well as regulatory issues such as those associated with short selling. However, algorithmic trading does have risks, such as leaks that might arise from competitor efforts to reverse engineer them. Many algorithms lack the capacity to handle or respond to exceptional or rare events. This can make algorithmic trading very risky. In addition, any malfunction, including a simple lapse in communication lines, can cause the system to fail. Thus, careful human supervision of algorithmic trading and other safeguards are crucial.

While algorithmic trading typically refers to the trade execution models referred to above, the term is also used in a more general sense to include "alpha models," which are used to make trade decisions to generate trading profits or control risk. Thus, more generally, algorithmic trading can be defined as trading based on the use of computer programs and sophisticated trading analytics to execute orders according to predefined strategies. Thus, algorithmic trading can be generalized to include program trading. Regardless, algorithmic trading is highly dependent on the most sophisticated technology and analytics.

## 1.3 BARGAINING

One of the most important aspects of the trading process is to arrive at a price agreeable to all parties of the trade. *Bargaining* is the negotiation process over contract terms that occurs between a single buyer and a single seller for a single transaction. The negotiation can be over price, quantity, security attributes, or any other factor important to one or both counterparties. More generally, bargaining occurs when two or more economic agents have in common an interest to cooperate, but have conflicting interests over the details of cooperation. Bargaining is the process used by agents to seek an agreement.

Bargaining is useful in the trading of securities when transaction sizes are large enough for the benefits of negotiation to exceed the costs of negotiation. Bargaining on prices occurs between floor brokers on the NYSE when the transaction size is large enough to justify the cost of personal interaction. *Liquidnet*, an "upstairs" market that matches institutional buyers and sellers of large blocks of equity securities, enables institutions to directly bargain and trade confidentially with one another. Liquidnet provides an electronic format for this negotiation process. Traders use the system by entering symbols for securities that they wish to buy or sell. If Liquidnet sees a potential match, it notifies the counterparties, who bargain anonymously with each other in a virtual meeting room using the Liquidnet system. In an effort to protect trader confidentiality, Liquidnet rates traders with respect to the likelihood that they will actually execute transactions that Liquidnet arranges. Traders seeking to avoid front-running and quote-matching can request that trade information be hidden from other traders who are deemed unlikely to actually successfully negotiate transactions.[3] When matched, trade counterparties negotiate directly with each other the terms of their trade. Counterparties will know prices from other markets, leaving relatively little room for significant pricing disagreements. If they come to terms, they report the transaction to Liquidnet, which arranges the transfer and takes a commission on each share. In July 2008, Liquidnet claimed that the average size of its institutional orders was approximately 198,000 shares, compared to average order sizes of less than 300 shares in the NYSE and NASDAQ markets. In the NYSE and NASDAQ markets, institutions seek to execute large orders with small counterparties, requiring them to break up orders and work them over time. It is very difficult for institutions to disguise their intents with respect to order directions and sizes, placing them at obvious disadvantage in the trading arena. Obviously, trading against smaller orders is not the most effective means of satisfying institutional liquidity needs. Bargaining is often an expensive means to discover a price, but its costs may be less than its benefits for large transactions.

Bargaining power is the relative ability of one competitor to exert influence over another. In a trading scenario, bargaining power typically reflects one trader's ability to influence the transaction price. Relative bargaining power among traders is typically a product of the following:

- Patience and liquidity, which increases bargaining power
- Risk aversion, which reduces bargaining power
- Credible alternatives and options that enhance bargaining power
- The cost of backing down, which decreases bargaining power
- Superior information, which increases bargaining power
- Reputation with respect to strength, staying power, and resolve, all of which enhance bargaining power

## 1.4 AUCTIONS

An *auction* is a competitive market process involving multiple buyers, multiple sellers, or both. An auction is the process of trading a security through bidding, and then placing it to the winning bidder.[4] Vickrey (1961) demonstrated that optimal bids are increasing in bidders' values; therefore, the auctioned object will be won by the bidder who values it the most. Auctions are a useful and cost-effective method for pricing a security with an unknown value. That is, auctions are useful price discovery processes.

[3]An example of front-running might be where a broker with information about a client's order uses this information to set a bid or offer in her own order in setting a bid or offer so as to exploit the client's order. Quote matching occurs when a small trader places an order one tick from that of a large trader so as to profit from the large trader's transaction price pressure, or to use the large trader as a counterparty should prices reverse. Both types of these often unethical transactions will be discussed in Chapter 12.

[4]Auctions have a long history. For example, the Roman Empire was sold by auction in C.E. 193 by the Praetorian Guards to Didius Julianus, who reigned as emperor for over two months before being overthrown and executed by Septimius Severus. Earlier references to auctions date back to 500 B.C.E. when the Greek historian reported that Babylonians auctioned women as wives.

A *Walrasian auction* is a simultaneous auction where each buyer submits to the auctioneer his demand and each seller submits his supply for a given security at every possible price. Theoretically, the Walrasian auctioneer conducts a series of preliminary auctions called *tâtonnement* to determine supply and demand levels at various prices. In the actual auction, supply is balanced against demand such that the resulting transaction price is set so that the total demand from all buyers equals the total supply from all sellers. Thus, the Walrasian auction finds the clearing price that perfectly matches the supply and the demand. While the Walrasian auction has been used primarily as a theoretical construct, it does closely resemble certain financial auctions, such as the London Bullion Market Association fixing process.[5] In this market, five representatives of firms meet twice each day at the offices of N.M. Rothschild where the chairman calls out prices so that firm representatives can announce their levels of supply and demand at announced prices. Until the imbalance between supply and demand clears, new prices are announced. Many markets use similar procedures to open trading for the day.

An *English auction* or ascending bid auction, used by the English art and antique auctioneers, is typically employed to sell automobiles, farm equipment, and animals as well as art. English auction participants bid openly against one another, with each successive bid higher than the previous one. Because the auction is open and involves public sequences of bids, it provides for some degree of price discovery before it concludes. The auction ends and a "winner" is declared when no participant is willing to bid higher.

The traditional *Dutch auction* or descending bid auction, used in the 17th-century Dutch tulip bulb auctions, begins with the auctioneer calling out a high offer price, which is reduced until some participant submits the first and highest bid, crying out "mine." The "winner" pays that price. Thus, the Dutch auction does reveal some information concerning a price ceiling on the auctioned object. The Dutch auction is particularly useful for matching a number of identical goods to an equal number of highest bidders. Consider the following example involving a Dutch auction of $20 billion in 91-day U.S. T-Bills, where the bids (based on yields to maturity) by financial institutions are given in Table 1.1.

**TABLE 1.1** Treasury Bids Illustration

| | |
|---|---|
| Citigroup | $2.0 billion at 3.15% |
| Wells Fargo | $4.5 billion at 3.20% |
| UBS | $5.5 billion at 3.25% |
| Deutsche Bank | $7.5 billion at 3.30% |
| JP Morgan Chase | $5.5 billion at 3.35% |
| Bank of America | $6.5 billion at 3.40% |

[5]See O'Callahan (1993) for a discussion of this market.

Obviously, the Treasury wants to sell as many bills as possible at the highest possible prices. This results in the lowest yields. The bid-to-cover ratio in this illustration is \$31.5 billion/\$20 billion = 1.525. This means that some bids will not be successful. Bids will be satisfied from the lowest yield (highest price) until \$20 billion in bills have been allocated. The stop-out price will be at a yield of 3.35% and all winners (Citigroup, Wells Fargo, UBS, Deutsche Bank, and JP Morgan Chase) will pay this same price. Actually, JP Morgan Chase will be allocated only \$0.5 billion, because its bid filled the \$20 billion total being offered. In the Yankee variation of the Dutch auction, all successful bidders would pay the prices that they bid.

Another variant of the Dutch auction was used by Filene's, a department store that was based in Boston. In the store's basement were marked-down goods, each with a price and date attached. The price paid at the register was the price on the tag minus a discount that depended on how much time elapsed since the item was tagged. The longer the item remained unsold on the shelf, the more its price was reduced.

*First-price sealed-bid* auctions have all bidders simultaneously submit sealed bids so that no bidder knows any of the other bids. The first-price sealed-bid auction does not allow for price discovery until the auction concludes. The winner submits the highest bid and pays the bid price. The winner of a bidding contest in these three auction structures faces the *"winner's curse"* problem if the auctioned item's value is not known with certainty. All bidders' bids are subject to error. The winner bids the most, and is the most likely to have bid too much for the auctioned object.

The *second-price sealed-bid auction* (Vickrey auction) is identical to the first-price sealed-bid auction, except that the winner pays the highest losing bid rather than his own winning bid. The motivation for the Vickrey auction is to encourage higher bids, in part, by reducing the winner's curse. In a second-price auction, bidders bid more aggressively because a bid raises the probability of winning without increasing the expected cost, which is determined by someone else's bid. Empirical evidence obtained from actual auctions suggests that the second-price sealed-bid auction does generate higher bids than the first-price sealed-bid structure.

*Double auctions* or *bilateral auctions* are used for the trading of most publicly traded securities in secondary (resale) markets. In double auctions, buyers submit *bids* (maximum purchase prices) and sellers submit offers (minimum selling prices; also called asks) that are ranked from best to worst. These bids and offers create demand and supply profiles for the market. Transactions occur when the highest bid and lowest offer match. A *continuous double auction*, such as that on the New York Stock Exchange, allows for many transactions on an ongoing basis as the security is continuously being auctioned.

## Auction Outcomes

The type of auction structure selected in a market can have a significant impact on submitted bids, winners, final prices, revenues realized by sellers, and information realized in the auction process. However, the *revenue equivalence theorem*, perhaps the most significant result from the game theory of auctions, states just the opposite. The revenue equivalence theorem states that, under specific restrictions, the auction type (from the listing above) will not affect the auction outcomes. Consider, for example, an environment with perfect and complete information, where all risk-neutral bidders know the values that all bidders place on the object to be auctioned. In this environment, the winner of a first-price sealed-bid auction with infinitesimal bidding increments is the participant who most highly values the auctioned object. The winner will pay a price equal to the highest price submitted by the auction losers. Note that this auction outcome is identical to the second-price sealed-bid auction. In addition, the English and Dutch auctions produce the same outcome in the perfect and complete information scenarios. The key to reconciling this conflict is that the revenue equivalence theorem is based on assumptions of perfect and complete information, with risk-neutral bidders and infinitesimal bid increments. Thus, the analysis of auction type should focus on the nature of violations of these assumptions. Actually, perfect and complete information is not a necessary assumption; it is sufficient that each bidder's value be independent and randomly drawn from a common distribution.

While the revenue equivalence theorem states that under restrictive circumstances, the auction structure will not affect revenue, experimental, statistical, and other evidence suggests otherwise. For example, evidence suggests that there is more overbidding in second-price auctions than in standard English auctions (e.g., see Kagel et al., 1987). Thus, one needs to pay close attention to how deviation from revenue equivalence theorem assumptions affects auction outcomes.

## Common Value Auctions

A *common value auction*[6] occurs when all bidders place the same value on the item to be auctioned, and that value is known with certainty. Consider the following auction example with three bidders such that each has the opportunity to bid on some random amount of cash between zero and \$1. Suppose that every monetary value between 0 and \$1 is equally likely, such that $E[V] = \$0.50$. Since each bidder has equal access to information, we will refer to this structure as a *symmetric information structure* problem. Without any additional information, risk-neutral bidders might value the random sum of cash as highly as \$0.50; risk-averse bidders will value the random sum less than \$0.50. Thus, we see here that risk aversion will affect valuation of an object of unknown value. Therefore, risk aversion will affect bids and the revenue equivalence theorem will no longer apply. The revenue equivalence theorem no longer applies because bids will not only be a function of expected value, they will also depend on information revealed in the bidding process.

Now, suppose that each of the three bidders will obtain a noisy signal, $s_1$, $s_2$, and $s_3 \in (0, 1)$, concerning the value of the bundle of cash such that the mean of the signal amounts equal the value of the bundle: $(s_1 + s_2 + s_3)/3 = V$. Now, suppose that Bidder 1's signal is $s_1 = 0.80$. Then, his estimate of the value of the bundle is $E[V_1|s_1 = 0.80] = (\$0.80 + \$0.50 + \$0.50)/3 = \$0.60$, based on his assumption that other bidders receive signals with expected values of \$0.50. If Bidder 1 is risk neutral, \$0.60 is the value that he attributes to the bundle. But, does this mean that Bidder 1 will bid \$0.60 for the bundle?

First, recall the *winner's curse* problem raised earlier. If Bidder 1 wins the auction by bidding \$0.60, this will mean that the other bidders received lower value signals than

[6]See Kagel and Levin (1986) and Thompson and Wright (2005) for discussion of this problem.

Bidder 1, indicating that \$0.80, the signal received by Bidder 1, certainly exceeded the bundle value. Thus, winning the auction is a negative signal (ex-post) as to the value of the bundle. If Bidder 1 wins the auction by bidding \$0.60, he will have overbid and will suffer from the winner's curse. This means that, from the perspective of Bidder 1 if he wins, the distribution of bundle value must range from 0 to 0.80 rather than from 0 to 1.00. This is because if Bidder 1 makes the highest bid, it is because his signal was higher than those of his competitors. Thus, the high end of his valuation range will be \$0.80. This means that the anticipated mean signal values received by other bidders should be \$0.40, since their valuation ranges will be from 0 to \$0.80, given that Bidder 1 will submit the highest bid. Thus, based on this information, Bidder 1 should revise his bid for the bundle to $[B_1|s_1 = 0.80] = (\$0.80 + \$0.40 + \$0.40)/3 = \$0.5333$.

All four auction designs will place the bundle with the same winner. However, let us consider Bidder 1 bidding strategies under different auction structures. In a second-price sealed-bid auction, \$0.5333 is an appropriate bid because there is no information revealed in the auction process. In a first-price sealed-bid auction, Bidder 1 should bid less than \$0.5333. This is also true in the Dutch auction. However, additional information is revealed in the bidding process in the English auction. This information should be used in forming the bidding strategy. Generally speaking, with more than two bidders, the highest bid or revenue realized in the English auction will be greater than or equal to that in the second-price sealed-bid auction, which will be greater than or equal to that in the Dutch auction, which will equal that obtained in the first-price sealed-bid auction. However, English auctions are often more vulnerable to manipulation by shills.

### Google's Dutch Auction Format

Google, in its widely publicized IPO 2004 offering, structured a Dutch auction process intending to sell 25.8 million shares of its stock, suggesting bids in the range of \$108 to \$135 per share. This Dutch auction searched bids for a clearing price that enabled it to finally sell 19.6 million shares at the IPO price of \$85, thereby raising \$1.67 billion. The first trade price was \$100.01, rising to over \$300 within a year and over \$500 within three years. Lead underwriters, Morgan Stanley and CS First Boston, collected a 3% commission on the offering rather than the standard 7% fee. Some observers opined that, if successful, the Google IPO could lead to a transfer of power and fees away from underwriters in favor if issuing firms. However, it is not clear just how successful the IPO was. The IPO price was not as high as anticipated or nearly as high as subsequent trading prices. A later follow-on offering was priced at \$295 per share, raising \$4.18 billion. On the other hand, the IPO created substantial favorable publicity for the firm and raised fortunes for its owners.

## 1.5 INTRODUCTION TO MARKET MICROSTRUCTURE

Investors participate in the markets for information, the markets for securities, and the markets for transaction services (Stoll, 2003). *Market microstructure* is concerned with the markets for transaction services. Market microstructure is the area of finance economics that concerns trading and market structure, market rules and fairness, success and failure, and how the design of the market affects the exchange of assets, price formation, and price discovery. Market microstructure is concerned with costs of providing transaction services along with the impact of transactions costs on the short-run behavior of securities prices (see Stoll, 2003). The market structure is the physical (or virtual) composition of the market along with its information systems and trading rules. Market microstructure examines *latency*, the amount of time that elapses between when a quote or an order is placed by a trader and when that order is actually visible to the market. Microstructure also concerns transactions costs and the impact of transactions costs on the behavior of securities prices. Transactions costs are often reflected in bid-ask spreads and in commissions paid to brokers. Generally, the best market is that which has the lowest transactions costs, facilitates the fastest trades, results in the fairest prices, disseminates price information most efficiently, and provides for the greatest liquidity. A market is said to be liquid when prospective purchasers and sellers can transact on a timely basis with little cost or adverse price impact.

The basic components of a securities market are investors, brokers, and dealers who make markets and facilitate trading, and the market facility, physical and virtual, within which trading takes place. Investors include individuals and institutions. Some market participants are price takers (typically individual investors and institutions that invest for the longer term) and others are price seekers (day traders and market makers). Brokers act as agents, processing trades on behalf of client accounts on a commission basis. Upstairs brokers deal directly with investors, and downstairs brokers execute transactions on trading floors. Dealers trade on their own accounts to secure trading profits.

## Market Execution Structures

Securities markets are categorized by their *execution systems*, that is, their procedures for matching buyers to sellers. The primary execution systems are *quote-driven markets* where dealers post quotes and participate on at least one side of every trade, *order-driven markets* where traders can trade without the intermediation of dealers, *brokered markets* where many blocks (10,000 or more shares, as defined by the NYSE or 25% of daily volume elsewhere) are broker negotiated, and *hybrid markets*. Most over-the-counter (OTC) currency and bond markets are primarily quote driven, and most stock exchange, futures, and options exchanges are primarily order driven. Quote-driven markets display quotations of specialists and market makers while order-driven markets display all quotes. In a pure quote market, dealer spreads are the source of market maker profits, whereas in a pure quote market, there are no dealers. Such distinctions have diminished in recent years.

Actually, to some extent, most markets are hybrids. For example, the NYSE uses designated market makers (formerly specialists) who can act as dealers on transactions and brokers may execute block transactions on exchanges. Stock markets around the world, with the most prominent exception being the OTC markets in the United States, are more likely to be order driven. This is because such markets require less human intervention, and tend to be cheaper to run. However, the lack of a dealer book, improved transparency, and dealer quotes tend to reduce liquidity in such markets, and may drive orders away from them to quote-driven markets.

## 1.6 ORDERS, LIQUIDITY, AND DEPTH

*Orders* are specific trade instructions placed with brokers by traders without direct access to trading arenas. The typical brokerage will accept and place a number of types of orders for clients. Among these types of orders are the following:

- *Market order*: Here, the broker is instructed to execute the order at the best price available in the market.
- *Limit order*: An upper price limit is placed for a buy order; the broker will not buy at a price above this limit. A lower price limit is placed for a sell order.
- *Stop order*: Here, the broker is instructed to place the buy order once the price has risen above a given level; in the case of the stop-sell (or stop-loss) order, the broker sells once the price of the security has fallen beneath a given level. Stop-loss orders are often intended to protect against stock price declines.
- *Day order*: If not executed by the end of the day, this order is canceled.
- *Good till canceled order*: This order is good until canceled.
- *Not held order:* Here, the broker is not obliged to execute while he is attempting to obtain a better price for his client.
- *Fill or kill* orders must be filled in their entirety immediately, or they are canceled.
- *Immediate or cancel* orders are immediately executed to the extent possible; unexecuted amounts are canceled.

This list of order types is far from complete and some brokers and exchanges will not accept all of these types of orders. Order types are not mutually exclusive; for example, a good-till-canceled, limit buy order is a legitimate order type as is a stop limit sell order. The stop limit sell order authorizes the broker to initiate the sell order once its price drops to the stop trigger, but only if the limit price can be realized for the sale.

*Liquidity* refers to an asset's ability to be easily purchased or sold without causing significant change in the price of the asset. Liquid assets can be traded quickly, with low transactions costs, at any time and with little impact on the asset's price. Markets with large numbers of active participants and few constraints on trade are more likely to have greater liquidity. Bid–offer spreads are generally considered to be good indicators of liquidity, with narrow spreads indicating that price impacts of trading will not be severe. Black (1971) described liquidity as follows:

1. There are always bid and asked prices for the investor who wants to buy or sell small amounts of stock immediately.
2. The difference between the bid and asked prices (the spread) is always small.
3. An investor who is buying or selling a large amount of stock, in the absence of special information, can expect to do so over a long period of time at a price not very different, on average, from the current market price.
4. An investor can buy or sell a large block of stock immediately, but at a premium or discount that depends on the size of the block.
5. The larger the block, the larger the premium or discount. In other words, a liquid market is a continuous market, in the sense that almost any amount of stock can be bought or sold immediately, and an efficient market, in the sense that small amounts of stock can always be bought and sold very near the current market price, and in the sense that large amounts can be bought or sold over long periods of time at prices that, on average, are very near the current market price.

**TABLE 1.2** Market Depth

| Market A | | Market B | |
|---|---|---|---|
| **# Shares** | **Offer** | **# Shares** | **Offer** |
| 1000 | 50.00 | 2000 | 50.00 |
| 2000 | 50.03 | 1000 | 50.01 |
| 1000 | 50.05 | 2000 | 50.03 |
| 2000 | 50.06 | 2000 | 50.04 |
| 3000 | 50.07 | 2000 | 50.05 |
| 1000 | 50.09 | 3000 | 50.05 |

Kyle (1985) characterized three dimensions of liquidity. The first is *width* (also known as tightness), which is simply the bid–offer spread. The second is *market depth*, which refers to a market's ability to process and execute a large order without substantially impacting its price. The third dimension of liquidity is *slippage* (also known as market impact, price impact, or market resilience), which indicates the speed with which the price pressure resulting from a noninformative trade execution is dissipated (the price returns to normal).

Normally, markets with larger numbers of active participants have more depth than thin markets. Suppose, for example, that there are two competing markets for Stock X with the following offer prices (central limit order book) for Stock X as depicted in Table 1.2. Suppose that the last transaction for Company X stock was at a price of $50.00. Further suppose that an investor places a market order to buy 5000 shares of Company X stock. In Market A, the investor will obtain 1000 shares for $50.00, 2000 for $50.03, 1000 for $50.05, and 1000 for $50.06. The final price rises to $50.06. In Market B, the investor will obtain 2000 shares for $50.00, 1000 for $50.01, and 2000 for $50.03. The final price in Market B rises to $50.03, less than Market A. Thus, Market B has more depth than Market A, at least with respect to the stated demand for the stock.

The typical double auction will have many bids and ask prices for a given security at any point in time. Whose quotations will be the next to be executed or will have priority in the next transaction? *Order precedence rules* concern which traders can place bids and offer quotations with greatest priority for execution and which can accept the quotations of other traders. In almost all cases, the primary precedence is *price priority*. The participant with the highest bid or lowest ask has priority on an execution. However, there will be many instances where multiple traders have made quotations at the same price. Which quotations receive secondary priority? Some markets give priority to the first trader to make that particular quotation if that quote improved the previous best quote. This is called *time priority*. The trader who last improved the price is normally the first to post a quote at the current best price. Time priority is intended to encourage traders to aggressively improve their quotations and is most effective when the tick size (minimum increment for quote differences) is larger. However, some markets, including the major

U.S. stock exchanges, will provide for public order precedence, meaning that orders placed by the general public will have priority over otherwise competing orders placed by exchange members. These public precedence rules are intended to enhance the credibility and perceived fairness of markets in the eyes of the general public.

Even price priority can be violated when a security trades in multiple markets. For example, consider the scenario where the best bids on a stock are $49.95 for 100 shares and $49.94 in another market for 1000. A prospective seller wishes to sell 1000 shares. In some instances, rather than break up the 1000 sell order, the broker will trade through the $49.95 order in one market, executing the entire transaction for 1000 shares at $49.94 in the second market. In most instances, this cannot be accomplished legally in a single exchange market. Sometimes time or even price priorities are violated when a broker routes an order to a market in exchange for payment for order flow. In this scenario, the broker might receive a payment from a satellite market for routing the transaction to it rather than to the principal market for the security. We will discuss payment for order flow in more detail in Chapters 4 and 12.

## 1.7 DAY TRADING

The Internal Revenue Service (IRS) defines day traders to be those who have all of the following three characteristics: (1) Traders maintain substantial trading activity. The trader buys and sells frequently (10 to 20 daily trades should be sufficient) and trading is a primary source of income for the trader. (2) The trader's trading activity is sustained on a regular and continued (one year minimum) basis. (3) The trader seeks to profit from short-term stock price fluctuations rather than dividends, capital appreciation, and interest.

The day trader should complete a year in advance IRS Form 3115 Application for a Change of Accounting Method.[7] This is crucial to avoid difficulties with the wash sale rule. The purpose for completing this form is to seek permission to use the mark-to-market accounting technique. In addition, this designation will strengthen the trader's argument that she is a for-profit day trader, allowing for better expense deduction possibilities, such as departing from the 2% miscellaneous threshold and the at-risk rules. In addition, at-home day traders should consider whether they qualify for home office and 179 depreciation deductions.

FINRA (the Financial Industry Regulatory Authority; formerly NASD, the National Association of Securities Dealers), based on its Rule 2520, defines the day trader somewhat differently. Anyone who executes buy and sell transactions on the same margin account on the same day is said to be day trading. A *pattern day trader* executes four or more of these round-trip transactions within five consecutive business days.[8] Pattern day traders are required to maintain only 25% margin requirements rather than the 50% maintained by other noninstitutional traders. Rule 2520 requires maintenance of $25,000 in the margin

[7]File Form 3115 with an income tax return prior to requesting the change of accounting method. These are not "stand-alone" forms. Consider making such a filing after forming a corporation (such as an LLC) for trading.

[8]Unless these trades summed to less than 6% or fewer of all trades made over these five days.

account to take advantage of this exception, but the pattern day trader can margin this account by four times, rather than the usual two times based on the 50% rule for other individual investors.

For other individual investors, Federal Reserve Board (FED) Regulation T requires 50% initial margin along with 25% maintenance margin. Thus, such an investor would have to put up $5000 in cash to purchase $10,000 in shares. This would give the investor $5000 in equity position in the shares, or a 50% initial margin. However, if the value of the shares were to drop to $6000, the investor's equity would drop to $1000, or 16.67% of the current investment (1000/6000), well below the 25% maintenance margin. The broker would then need to require the investor to post an additional $500 (25% × $6000 − $1000) to fulfill the margin requirement.

Brokerage clients should carefully read their *hypothecation agreements* that define terms of their margin accounts, including unauthorized liquidations of shares purchased on margin and loaning of shares to other investors who may wish to short sell them. Equally important, they should be very familiar with the requirements imposed by FED Regulation T and FINRA Rule 2520.

While the Securities and Exchange Commission (SEC) and the IRS have fairly specific definitions for day traders, other definitions exist as well. For example, some people distinguish between day traders and swing traders. Some say that swing traders usually hold a stock or a position from one day to a week and tend to concentrate on just a few selected stocks or positions. In this context, day traders neutralize their positions at the end of each trading day.

## Online Brokers and Direct Access Trading

Selection of a broker, or brokers, is a crucial decision for the day trader. *Barron's* conducts and publishes results of surveys rating the various online brokers. When making this decision, the trader should consider a number of factors, including commissions and other fees, trade execution quality, account balance minimums, margin and other interest rates, customer service and live-agent telephone access, bank services, information, research and analytical services, trading platform, level of real-time quotes, and investment selection (some brokers won't work with mutual funds, IPOs, or bonds). Other considerations might include whether the broker is or has been targeted by the SEC, FINRA, or NASD for investigation for significant and persistent violations, along with the outcomes of these investigations. How the broker routes orders and the extent to which it accepts payment for order flow might also be an important consideration.

*Full-service brokers* such as Oppenheimer, Raymond James, and UBS provide a wide array of services to their clients, including trade execution, advice, market research, and so on. They typically are compensated with commissions on securities transactions and might impose periodic account maintenance charges as well. *Discount brokers* such as Interactive Brokers, TD Ameritrade, E*Trade, and ScotTrade provide for online trade execution, and may or may not provide other services as well. *Online brokers* such as ESchwab, Thinkorswim, and Tradeking are other discount brokers that provide for online transaction order entry. For most long-term investors and some day traders, services provided by one or more of these types of brokerage firms are perfectly appropriate. Most of the firms listed here provide more than a single type or level of service to a wide array of different types of clients. However, in many instances, high-volume traders will require faster and better trade execution. *Direct access trading systems* may provide for faster and superior execution for such traders. Direct access trading through firms such as such as Interactive Brokers, Questrade, and Thinkorswim enables traders to execute transactions directly with market makers and designated market makers on the NYSE, NASDAQ, and ECNs, eliminating the broker from transaction participation. The trader may have more control over routing the transaction, avoiding issues related to payment for order flow and *slippage* (movement in the security price against the trader). While transactions through brokers can execute within a fraction of a second, most take at least seconds and some take minutes or longer. Most direct access transactions execute within fractions of a second. Direct-access trading fees are typically volume based, include exchange and other market fees, and may include fixed platform and software fees. However, total fees can actually be higher than those charged by the deepest discount brokers. In addition, more knowledge is likely to be required on the part of the trader, and high trading volume is likely to be necessary to make this method of trading cost effective.

## Trading Platforms

A trading platform is a computer system used to place or route quotes and transactions through a network to a financial intermediary or market. Trading platforms can be either software-based (e.g., TradeStation, Power E*Trade Pro, Fimat PreferredTrade, and Reuters RTEx), or web-based such as those provided by most brokers (e.g., Charles Schwab Active Trader, Thinkorswim, and E*Trade). Software-based platforms are usually integrated with analytical tools, although many web-based platforms are as well. TradeStation provides trading technology for stocks, options, futures, and forex (foreign exchange, or currencies), along with tools for creating strategies and testing, notably, including a simulation for back testing. Trading platforms can monitor markets and can often be programmed to automatically execute trading strategies based on the customer's custom trading rules. This can mean that the trading platform can be customized for the customer's own trading algorithms. As of 2011, other software trading platforms are discussed at Realtick.com, Tradestation.com, Esignal.com, and Equis.com (MetaStock).

While trading platforms are easily obtained from brokers or developers of relevant software, there are a number of advantages to the trader when creating his own platform. In fact, many brokers and trading arenas are equipped to feed data into and accept quotes and execute transactions through Excel spreadsheets. Thus, a trader can create a spreadsheet designed to receive market data such as quotes and recent transactions and program in his own trading rules or algorithms to transmit quotes and execute transactions. Such platforms can quickly analyze market data, respond to trading rules, and provide for simultaneous transmission of multiple quotes and executions. Speed, accuracy, and efficiency can be enhanced considerably with the preparation of appropriate macros. For example, macros can be created that compare bid and offer quotes for a number of different securities, complete computations, and then transmit quotes or execute transactions based on "if/then" statements reflecting trading rules. These macros can include buttons to follow rules and can scan data and execute transactions in the trader's absence. In addition, a custom spreadsheet-based trading platform is obviously very flexible and, often with little adjustment, can continue to be used when the trader switches brokers or trades new instruments. There are a number of firms that can provide assistance with developing spreadsheet-based trading platforms, although many traders should be sufficiently competent to develop platforms themselves.

## Quotations and Price Data

The day trader will need timely access price quotes. Markets where securities are traded usually retain ownership of quotation, price, and transaction data and sell these data to interested customers. In fact, in recent years, the single largest source of revenue to major exchanges such as the NYSE has been from the sale of price, volume, and quote data. Real-time quotes are available to traders as quickly as they can be transmitted and displayed; otherwise they are said to be delayed. Delayed quotations are usually less expensive than real-time quotations data. However, in a trading environment where milliseconds (thousandths of a second) or even microseconds (millionths of a second) matter, what exactly is real-time data? In theory, real-time data display exactly as quotes are placed and transactions are executed. However, quotes and transactions data cannot be made available to all traders instantaneously. Different data and vendor services provide these data using different technologies from different locations. Traders compete to obtain these data as quickly as possible and vendors compete to provide it as quickly as possible. Microsecond and even millisecond delays are to be expected, and can easily spoil many trading strategies.

More extensive real-time quotations data are more expensive than less extensive data. Level I quote access displays the best bid and offer prices (inside quote or BBO: best-bid-offer) and, in some cases, quote sizes. Level II quotes display the same along with other quotes in descending order for the best bids and ascending for the best offers along with market symbols for each (see Figure 1.1). Symbols include NBBO for the national best bid offer (best buy and sell quotations), markets, recent transactions, and so on. Market participant IDs are omitted. Level II access provides the order book (or TotalView access for all quotes) and is necessary for most trading strategies. While most brokers provide only Level I real-time quotes for free, as of 2011, ScottradeElite provides NASDAQ Level II and NASDAQ TotalView Quotes for customers with at least 15 monthly trades, while Just2Trade advertises itself as having the lowest commissions and providing free Level II quotes. Other brokers have followed suit to remain competitive. Level III quotes, offered to NASDAQ members, enable traders to have direct access to enter and revise quotes. NASDAQ's SuperMontage TotalView provides more detail on the depth of data than Level II, enabling traders to view market makers' quotes that are not as good as their best. Figure 1.2 provides a sample screen from SuperMontage TotalView. Note that multiple quotations are frequently provided by several of the MPIDs (market participant IDs).

One of the most popular sources of market information and price data is Bloomberg, which offers real-time data and news through *Bloomberg Professional* and access to these

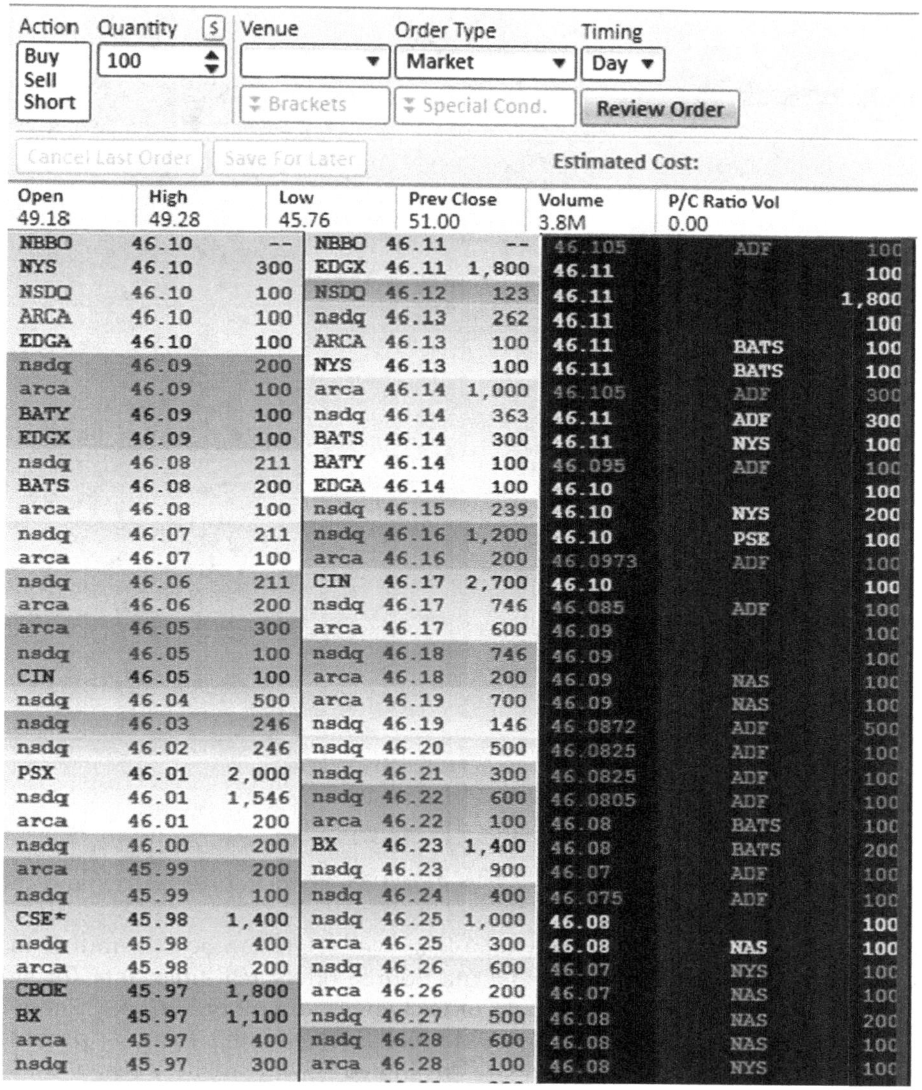


| Open | High | Low | Prev Close | Volume | P/C Ratio Vol |
|---|---|---|---|---|---|
| 49.18 | 49.28 | 45.76 | 51.00 | 3.8M | 0.00 |

| | | | | | | | | |
|---|---|---|---|---|---|---|---|---|
| NBBO | 46.10 | -- | NBBO | 46.11 | -- | 46.105 | ADF | 100 |
| NYS | 46.10 | 300 | EDGX | 46.11 | 1,800 | 46.11 | | 100 |
| NSDQ | 46.10 | 100 | NSDQ | 46.12 | 123 | 46.11 | | 1,800 |
| ARCA | 46.10 | 100 | nsdq | 46.13 | 262 | 46.11 | | 100 |
| EDGA | 46.10 | 100 | ARCA | 46.13 | 100 | 46.11 | BATS | 100 |
| nsdq | 46.09 | 200 | NYS | 46.13 | 100 | 46.11 | BATS | 100 |
| arca | 46.09 | 100 | arca | 46.14 | 1,000 | 46.105 | ADF | 300 |
| BATY | 46.09 | 100 | nsdq | 46.14 | 363 | 46.11 | ADF | 300 |
| EDGX | 46.09 | 100 | BATS | 46.14 | 300 | 46.11 | NYS | 100 |
| nsdq | 46.08 | 211 | BATY | 46.14 | 100 | 46.095 | ADF | 100 |
| BATS | 46.08 | 200 | EDGA | 46.14 | 100 | 46.10 | | 100 |
| arca | 46.08 | 100 | nsdq | 46.15 | 239 | 46.10 | NYS | 200 |
| nsdq | 46.07 | 211 | nsdq | 46.16 | 1,200 | 46.10 | PSE | 100 |
| arca | 46.07 | 100 | arca | 46.16 | 200 | 46.0973 | ADF | 100 |
| nsdq | 46.06 | 211 | CIN | 46.17 | 2,700 | 46.10 | | 100 |
| arca | 46.06 | 200 | nsdq | 46.17 | 746 | 46.085 | ADF | 100 |
| arca | 46.05 | 300 | arca | 46.17 | 600 | 46.09 | | 100 |
| nsdq | 46.05 | 100 | nsdq | 46.18 | 746 | 46.09 | | 100 |
| CIN | 46.05 | 100 | arca | 46.18 | 200 | 46.09 | NAS | 100 |
| nsdq | 46.04 | 500 | arca | 46.19 | 700 | 46.09 | NAS | 100 |
| nsdq | 46.03 | 246 | nsdq | 46.19 | 146 | 46.0872 | ADF | 500 |
| nsdq | 46.02 | 246 | nsdq | 46.20 | 500 | 46.0825 | ADF | 100 |
| PSX | 46.01 | 2,000 | nsdq | 46.21 | 300 | 46.0825 | ADF | 100 |
| nsdq | 46.01 | 1,546 | nsdq | 46.22 | 600 | 46.0805 | ADF | 100 |
| arca | 46.01 | 200 | arca | 46.22 | 100 | 46.08 | BATS | 100 |
| nsdq | 46.00 | 200 | BX | 46.23 | 1,400 | 46.08 | BATS | 200 |
| arca | 45.99 | 200 | nsdq | 46.23 | 900 | 46.07 | ADF | 100 |
| nsdq | 45.99 | 100 | nsdq | 46.24 | 400 | 46.075 | ADF | 100 |
| CSE* | 45.98 | 1,400 | nsdq | 46.25 | 1,000 | 46.08 | | 100 |
| nsdq | 45.98 | 400 | arca | 46.25 | 300 | 46.08 | NAS | 100 |
| arca | 45.98 | 200 | nsdq | 46.26 | 600 | 46.07 | NYS | 100 |
| CBOE | 45.97 | 1,800 | arca | 46.26 | 200 | 46.07 | NAS | 100 |
| BX | 45.97 | 1,100 | nsdq | 46.27 | 500 | 46.08 | NAS | 200 |
| arca | 45.97 | 400 | nsdq | 46.28 | 600 | 46.08 | NAS | 100 |
| nsdq | 45.97 | 300 | arca | 46.28 | 100 | 46.08 | NYS | 100 |

**FIGURE 1.1** BATS Level II Quotes, MSFT (Microsoft), August 17, 2011.

data through its Bloomberg terminals. Costs vary, but as of 2009, single machine access could be licensed for roughly $1800 per month, and interestingly, with only relatively insignificant volume discounts. The system provides data, news access, analytical tools, email, and trade processing systems, and is used by over a quarter million professionals worldwide. There are many, and often less expensive competitors, including Thomson Reuters, FactSet Research Systems, Jackson Terminal, Advantage Data Inc., and Dow Jones. Less

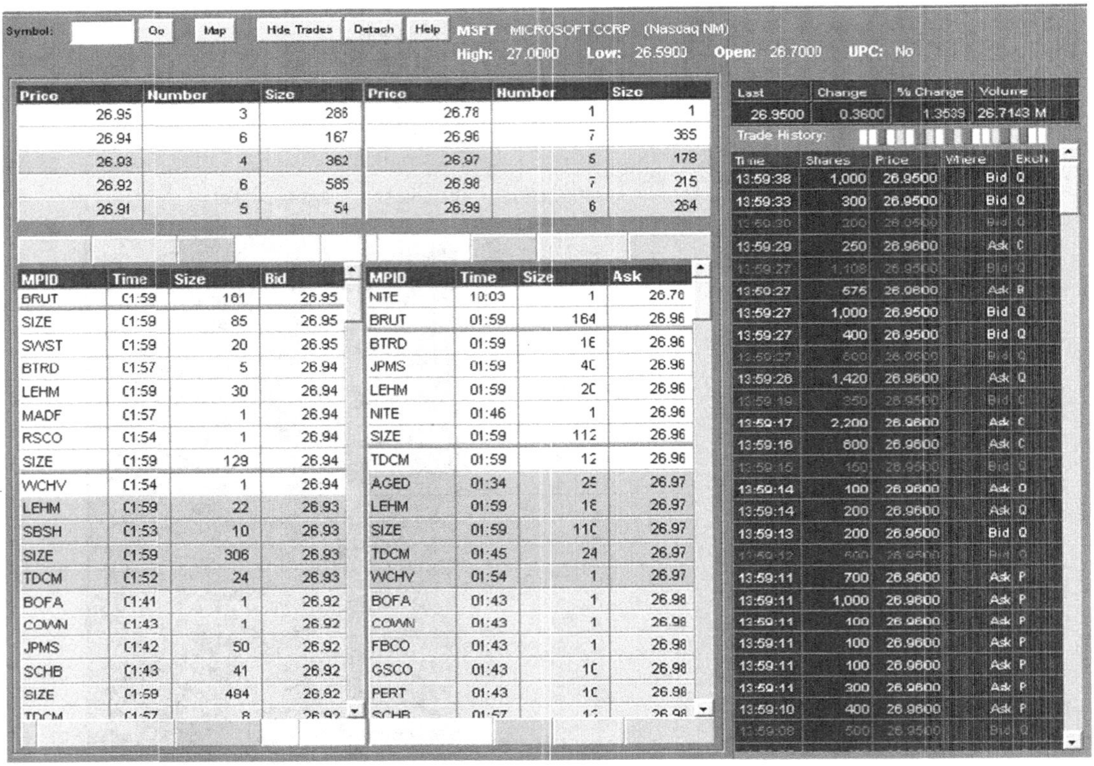


FIGURE 1.2 Screen from NASDAQ's SuperMontage TotalView.

expensive quotations systems, such as eSignal and MetaStock, offer prices and quotations for as little as $100 per month.

More specialized data systems are available as well. Data can be transmitted to day traders several ways. For example, World Data Source offers real-time data for stock, currency, and futures markets from a variety of exchanges and other markets. These data can be obtained via Internet, wireless, or satellite feeds. IQFeed and E-Signal provide quotes and recent executions to traders, and can be linked to spreadsheet-based trading platforms. For a significant fee, Dow Jones and Reuters can offer electronically "tagged" news products that can be picked up by computer algorithms to trigger programmed trading decisions.

## Trading Arcades

A *trading arcade*, sometimes referred to as a proprietary trading firm or prop shop, is a location for traders to work and trade from. The trader in the arcade might lease space, a desk, a trading platform, computers and screens, analytical services, access to market data and news services such as Bloomberg or Reuters, order routing technology, clearing and settlement services, and office facilities, in an effort to benefit from reduced expenses and economies of scale. Often, no physical space is provided; instead, traders can work from home. Some trading arcades will provide some or all of the capital to be traded, with or without interest. The trader can usually expect to receive reduced brokerage commissions and other trading costs. In addition, the arcade might charge for training services and receive payments from exchanges for order flow. Some trading arcades will provide capital to traders in exchange for a split in trading profits; firms that provide capital and receive all or most of trading profits are referred to as prop shops while true arcades simply lease facilities to traders.

Many trading arcades patronized by floor traders were rendered obsolete when their trading environments transformed. These traders transitioned from floors where size and physical ability were advantages to arenas where keystroking ability, particularly from video games provided an advantage. Some arcades have focused on working with amateur traders who have gone through periods of unemployment. In some cases, they have provided training to prospective traders, sometimes for a fee, after which some traders failed in their trading efforts. Trading arcades are frequently short-lived businesses, although some of the longer-lived arcades have included those operated by Jane Street Trading, Geneva Trading, London Golden Investments (LGI), and Maverick Trading.

## Additional Reading

Harris (2003) is certainly one of the most useful introductory books on trading, especially with respect to microstructure. However, trading mechanisms are changing so rapidly that even this excellent book will be somewhat dated. Chapters 1 to 9 are much more comprehensive than the material presented here in Chapter 1, and very much worth reading. Kim (2007) provides excellent explanations of electronic and algorithmic trading technology in Chapters 1 to 3 and 6 to 7. Elton et al. (2010) provide a brief and readable introduction to securities markets in Chapters 2 and 3, and much of the remainder of the book will be useful to traders as well. Elton et al. is among the best MBA-level texts on portfolio analysis. The two articles by Klemperer (1999) and (2002) are excellent general introductory reviews of auction mechanisms. Stoll's 2003 review on market microstructure is an excellent overview of the topic, especially from an academic perspective. There are numerous businesses with websites providing information on brokerage services, data provision, trading platforms, and trading arcades.

## References

Black, F. (1971). Towards a fully automated exchange, part I. *Financial Analysts Journal, 27*, 29–34.

Elton, E., Gruber, M., Brown, S., & Goetzmann, W. (2010). *Modern portfolio theory and investment analysis* (8th ed.). New York: Wiley.

Harris, L. (2003). *Trading and exchanges: market microstructure for practitioners.* Oxford: Oxford University Press.

Kagel, J. H., Harstad, R. M., & Levin, D. (1987). Information impact and allocation rules in auctions with affiliated private values: A laboratory study. *Econometrica, 55*, 1275–1304.

Kagel, J. H., & Levin, D. (1986). The winner's curse and public information in common value auctions. *American Economic Review, 56*(5), 894–920.

Kim, K. (2007). *Electronic and algorithmic trading technology: The complete guide.* New York: Academic Press.

Klemperer, P. (1999). Auction theory: A guide to the literature. *Journal of Economic Surveys, 13*, 227–260.

Klemperer, P. (2002). What really matters in auction design. *Journal of Economics Perspectives, 16*(1), 169–189.

Kyle, A. S. (1985). Continuous auctions of insider trading. *Econometrica, 53*(6), 1315–1336.

O'Callahan, G. (1993). *The structure of the world gold market.* Occasional Paper no. 105. Washington, DC: International Monetary Fund.

Stoll, H. R. (2003). *Market microstructure.* Working Paper. Vanderbilt University.

Thompson, R. B., & Wright, A. L. (2005). *Equilibrium bidding strategies in common-value sealed-bid auctions.* Working Paper. Department of Mathematics, University of Arizona.

Vickrey, W. (1961). Counterspeculation, auctions, and sealed tenders. *Journal of Finance, 16*, 8–37.

## 1.8 EXERCISES

1. How might long-term investors benefit from vigorous competition among short-term traders?
2. How does trading differ from speculating?
3. Suppose there was an open outcry English second-price auction. All bids are public. You are willing to bid a maximum of $100 for the auctioned item. You know that no one else will be willing to pay more than $200 for the object. The first bid by one of your competitors is for $10. What should you bid? Why?
4. An auction house has decided to sell a sculpture in an open outcry second-price auction. The auction house manager does not know the value any bidder will place on the work, but does know that every bidder will pay at least $500,000 (there is a gallery that has already announced its intent to pay at least this amount for the work, either from the gallery or from the successful bidder). Thus, the successful bidder can always sell the work for $500,000. In addition, the auction house knows that no one will be willing to pay more than $1,000,000 for the work because the only other identical sculpture (made from the same cast) is on the market for $1,000,000 and has not drawn any interest. Thus, the auction house believes that any particular bidder is willing to pay a random sum between $500,000 and $1,000,000 for the work (this random sum is the value of the work to the bidder), with an expected value of $750,000 and distributed uniformly (any value within this range is equally likely) between the minimum and maximum.
   a. Suppose that there are two bidders. What is the expected value of the second highest bid? Hint: If there are to be $n$ independent draws from a uniform distribution on the range, $[x_1, x_2]$, $E[x_{MAX}] = x_1 + (x_2 - x_1)n/(n+1)$ and $E[x_{MIN}] = x_1 + (x_2 - x_1)/(n+1)$.
   b. Now, suppose instead that there are three bidders for the sculpture. What is the expected value of the second highest bid?
   c. Suppose that there are 999 bidders for the sculpture. What is the expected value of the second highest bid?
5. There are two ways to purchase T-Bills. The first is to enter a competitive bid at the auction where the bidding institution competes for a given dollar amount of the new issue based on how much it is willing to pay. Only the approximately 2000 securities brokers and dealers that are registered to operate in the government securities market are permitted to participate directly in the competitive bidding process. However, these registered firms may participate on behalf of their clients. Second, noncompetitive bids can be tendered by anyone where the prospective purchaser states how many bills he would like to purchase at the average price of accepted competitive bids. Competitive

bidders for T-Bills generally enter their bids just before the deadline (1:00 PM Eastern Time) to participate in the auction. Noncompetitive bids are limited to $5 million and are normally due before 12:00 noon (Eastern Time) on the day of an auction. Noncompetitive bids are satisfied at the average price of successful competitive bids. The Treasury determines the dollar amount of competitive bids that it wishes to satisfy by subtracting the face values of the noncompetitive bids from the level of bills that the Treasury wishes to sell. Successful competitive bids are selected by ranking them, starting with the highest bid. Successful bidders obtain their bills at the prices that they bid; the lowest bid is referred to as the stop-out price. Consider the following example involving a Dutch auction of $20 billion in 91-day T-Bills, where the bids (based on yields to maturity) by financial institution are given as follows:

| | |
|---|---|
| Citigroup | $2.0 billion at 5.15% |
| Merrill Lynch | $4.5 billion at 5.20% |
| UBS | $5.5 billion at 5.25% |
| Deutsche Bank | $7.5 billion at 5.30% |
| JP Morgan/Chase | $5.5 billion at 5.35% |
| Bank of America | $6.5 billion at 5.40% |

Further suppose that individual investors have placed noncompetitive bids totaling $2.5 billion. What is the bid-to-cover ratio in this auction? What is the stop-out price? Which bids will be satisfied?

**6. a.** In an all-pay auction, all bidders pay the amounts that they bid for the object to be auctioned, but only the winner, that is, whoever places the highest bid, takes possession of the object. This auction process has been likened to the system of political contributions, where all lobbyists make contributions to politicians, but only the highest-contributing lobbyists can exert influence. Similarly, the all pay auction might be similar to a ticket line at a limited-seating rock concert, where each bid is reflected by the amount of time that the bidder waits in line. Other all-pay auction scenarios might involve political campaign contributions, job promotions, and R&D races. Now, consider an all-pay auction for a $1 bill. Describe how such an auction structure might realize higher revenue for the seller of the $1 bill.

**b.** Consider the entertainment shopping site, PennyCave.com (http://www.pennycave.com/). This site, as do other penny auction sites, auctions electronic items such as music players and computer screens. Items are normally sold to the highest bidder at a price that is (or seems) substantially less than the value of the auctioned item. Bidders pay a fixed amount (e.g., $1) for each bid that they place. The auction clock is set for a specific length of time (e.g., 24 hours), but a bid placed in the final seconds resets the clock for another 20 seconds. Its market structure follows (as of April 25, 2011):

- The starting price on each auction is $0.00. Bid increments are $0.01.
- Each bid costs the bidder one credit. Credits are purchased from PannyCave for costs ranging from $0.67 to $1, depending on the quantity purchased.
- The price only goes up by $0.01 with each bid placed.

- If a bid is placed in the final moments, the auction clock is reset for 20 seconds.
- How does this auction structure compare to an all-pay auction structure? What is the advantage of having bid increments set at $0.01?

7. Suppose that the last sale of Company X stock was at a price of $100.00. Further suppose that an investor wishes to place a market order to purchase 25,000 shares of Company X stock.

| Market A | | Market B | |
|---|---|---|---|
| **# Shares** | **Offer ($)** | **# Shares** | **Offer ($)** |
| 30,000 | 100.00 | 10,000 | 100.00 |
| 40,000 | 100.02 | 10,000 | 100.01 |
| 10,000 | 100.05 | 10,000 | 100.03 |
| 20,000 | 100.06 | 20,000 | 100.04 |
| 30,000 | 100.07 | 40,000 | 100.05 |
| 10,000 | 100.09 | 40,000 | 100.05 |

Which of the two markets has greater depth?

CHAPTER

# 2

# Financial Markets, Trading Processes, and Instruments

## 2.1 EXCHANGES AND FLOOR MARKETS

The Securities and Exchange Act of 1934 defined an *exchange* to be:

> any organization, association, or group of persons, whether incorporated or unincorporated, which constitutes, maintains, or provides a market place or facilities for bringing together purchasers and sellers of securities or for otherwise performing with respect to securities the functions commonly performed by a stock exchange as that term is generally understood, and includes the market place and the market facilities maintained by such exchange.

An exchange is typically a physical or virtual meeting place drawing together brokers, dealers, and traders to facilitate the buying and selling of securities. Thus, exchanges include the floor-based markets as well as many virtual meeting sites and screen-based systems provided by *electronic communications networks* (*ECNs*). In the United States and most other countries, exchange transactions are executed through some type of auction process. Exchanges in the United States are intended to provide for orderly, liquid, and continuous markets for the securities they trade. A continuous market provides for transactions that can be executed at any time for a price that might be expected to differ little from the prior transaction price for the same security. In addition, exchanges traditionally served as *self-regulatory organizations* (SROs) for their members, regulating and policing their behavior with respect to a variety of rules and requirements. However, the *Financial Industry Regulatory Authority* (*FINRA*) has provided for self-regulation of the two major U.S. stock markets since the 2007 consolidation of the *National Association of Security Dealers* (NASD) and the Member Regulation, Enforcement and Arbitration operations of the New York Stock Exchange.

### NYSE Euronext

As of August 2011, NYSE Euronext, the world's largest exchange and its first global exchange, listed over 8000 issues (excluding European structured products) from

55 countries on six equities exchanges and six derivatives exchanges in six countries. NYSE Euronext was launched on April 4, 2007, the result of a merger between the New York Stock Exchange Group and Euronext, NV. The New York Stock Exchange Group was formed by the earlier 2006 merger of the New York Stock Exchange and the Archipelago Exchange, and now operates the New York Stock Exchange (NYSE) with its now diminishing physical trading floor, the Archipelago Exchange (NYSE Arca), an electronic exchange that evolved from the Pacific Exchange, NYSE Amex, formerly the American Stock Exchange and NYSE Alternext, created in 2005 to list small and mid-sized companies. Together, these exchanges along with their European equities exchanges represent one-third of the world's equities markets. Euronext, NV was created by the merger of the Amsterdam, Brussels, and Paris bourses, and later added the Lisbon Exchange and London's International Financial Futures and Options Exchange (LIFFE). All of these markets operate under the NYSE Euronext umbrella. Figure 2.1 depicts relationships between NYSE Euronext and its affiliates as of August 2011. NYSE Euronext is a public company whose shares are listed on the New York Stock Exchange under the symbol NYX.

As of October 2008, the New York Stock Exchange, which traditionally has maintained the most stringent listing requirements, listed securities of 2,447 companies with a combined market value of over $10.3 trillion (post-crash). As of October 2008, AMEX listed 516 stocks with a combined value of $145 billion. These exchanges have since merged. At the same time, NASDAQ, which had been divested by the NASD in 2000/2001, listed 2,934 stocks with total capitalization of $2.6 trillion. By June 2011, NYSE listing capitalization had grown to $13.791 trillion and NASDAQ listing capitalization totaled $4.968 trillion. See Table 2.6 for more comparisons.

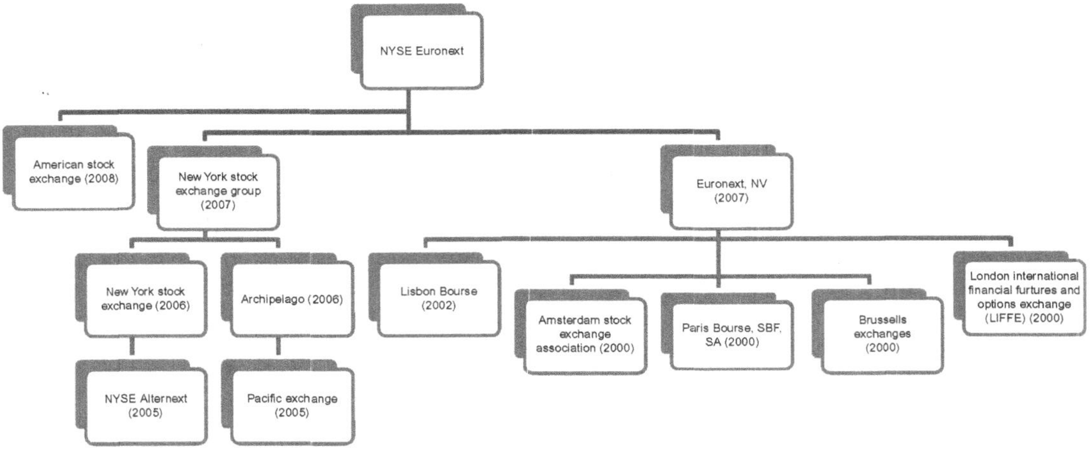


**FIGURE 2.1** NYSE Euronext family tree. (For more detail on NYSE Group ancestors, see The NYSE Group Family Tree, at www.nyse.com/pdfs/nysegrouptimeline.pdf.)

## 2.2 THE WAY IT WAS

### National and Regional Exchanges

Traditionally, the New York Stock Exchange (NYSE) and the American Exchange (ASE or AMEX) were regarded as the two national exchanges in the U.S., but the NYSE acquired the ASE in 2008, incorporating its equity business into its own. Smaller companies from the ASE traded on the NYSE Alternext market and others have been listed on NYSE Amex Equities. Until the 1990s, numerous "regional exchanges" continued to operate. Regional exchanges, a term that is now somewhat in flux, traditionally included all but the two national exchanges. Such exchanges have included those in Chicago (formerly the Midwest Exchange), Boston, and Philadelphia, the descendant of the Philadelphia-Baltimore-Washington Exchange. The Pacific Exchange, which originated as two separate regional exchanges in San Francisco and Los Angeles, maintained separate trading floors in San Francisco and Los Angeles, and was eventually acquired by Archipelago. Again, Archipelago has since merged (in 2006) with the New York Stock Exchange to form the New York Stock Exchange Group.

These and other regional exchanges traditionally listed stocks that would not qualify for national exchange listing as well as provide local or competing markets for a number of national exchange listed securities. However, many regional exchanges no longer fit this mold, and most do not consider themselves to be regional. In some instances, either lower transactions costs or better prices can be obtained for clients for dual-listed securities on the regional or smaller exchanges; to some extent, competition provided by these regional exchanges may result in lower transactions costs for investors on national exchanges. In addition, different market structures and rules might provide for unique execution opportunities for clients and investors. There also exist a number of exchanges for other securities such as the Chicago Board of Trade (CBT—for futures contracts), The Chicago Board Options Exchange (CBOE), the Kansas City Board of Trade, and the Commodities Exchange (COMEX). Finally, there are several exchanges without actual trading floors, including the National Exchange (formerly the Cincinnati Exchange, currently located in Chicago) and the International Securities Exchange (ISE). These exchanges operations are based entirely on electronic platforms. Table 2.1 provides a more comprehensive listing of exchanges as recognized by the S.E.C. as of August, 2011.[1]

### Early Ancestors to Modern Exchanges

Until recently, U.S. stock markets and many others had evolved rather slowly over the centuries, hanging on to their roots, traditions, rules, and regulations. Much of their current structures and idiosyncrasies still draw from this evolution. Understanding how markets and exchanges functioned in the past is helpful to understanding their current structures, policies, and procedures. Precursors to modern stock exchanges might have existed in Egypt as early as the 11th century, where it is believed that Jewish and Islamic

[1]These markets have registered with the SEC as exchanges, pursuant to Article 6 of the Securities Exchange Act of 1934.

**TABLE 2.1** U.S. Stock and Futures Exchanges as of August 2011

| **U.S. Stock and Options Exchanges** |
|---|
| NYSE Amex LLC (formerly the American Stock Exchange) |
| BATS Exchange, Inc. |
| BATS Y-Exchange, Inc. |
| NASDAQ OMX BX, Inc. (formerly the Boston Stock Exchange) |
| C2 Options Exchange, Incorporated |
| Chicago Board Options Exchange, Incorporated |
| Chicago Stock Exchange, Inc. |
| EDGA Exchange, Inc. |
| EDGX Exchange, Inc. |
| International Securities Exchange, LLC |
| The NASDAQ Stock Market LLC |
| National Stock Exchange, Inc. |
| New York Stock Exchange LLC |
| NYSE Arca, Inc. |
| NASDAQ OMX PHLX, Inc. (formerly Philadelphia Stock Exchange) |
| **U.S. Futures Exchanges** |
| Board of Trade of the City of Chicago, Inc. |
| CBOE Futures Exchange, LLC |
| Chicago Mercantile Exchange |
| One Chicago, LLC |
| The Island Futures Exchange, LLC |
| NQLX LLC |
| **Partially Exempt Exchanges** |
| Arizona Stock Exchange |
| SWX Europe Limited (f/k/a Virt-x) |

brokers traded a variety of credit-related instruments. Thirteenth-century Bruges (Belgium) commodity traders assembled in the van der Beurse family home (and inn), ultimately becoming the "Bruges Beurse." Additional bourses opened elsewhere in Flanders and Amsterdam. The Amsterdam Stock Exchange opened in the early 17th century, trading shares of the Dutch East India Company. The exchange continues to operate as a unit of Euronext, and is the world's longest continuously operated exchange. Several older exchanges began in coffee houses and taverns, where brokers and dealers would meet to trade securities. For example, the London Stock Exchange started operations in about 1698 in Jonathan's Coffee House on Change Alley.

The first securities exchange to operate in the United States was in Philadelphia, the second, in New York, which opened operations in 1791. The New York Stock Exchange began operations outdoors after the May 17, 1792 signing of the "Buttonwood Agreement." This contract, signed by 24 brokers under a buttonwood tree at what is now 68 Wall Street, fixed brokerage commissions among its signatories and prohibited off-board trading (i.e., traders and brokers were to trade only with each other). In earlier days, exchanges often operated outdoors so that brokers could call out their orders from their office windows to the street where transactions actually took place. In late 1793, this group of brokers obtained the Tontine Coffee House, which was used for cold weather trading until the 1880s. In 1865, the New York Stock Exchange adopted its current name. The American Stock Exchange, known as the New York Curb Exchange until 1953, did not move indoors until June 27, 1921. For most of its history, NASDAQ was not considered to be an exchange because it did not have a physical trading floor. Founded in 1971 by the National Association of Securities Dealers (NASD), NASDAQ—formerly known as the National Association of Security Dealers Automated Quotation System (NASDAQ)—has served as an electronic stock market allowing brokers and dealers to efficiently transmit bid, offer, and close prices for securities.

### Traditional New York Stock Exchange Structure

Since the New York Stock Exchange is arguably the largest and most important exchange in the world, we will first emphasize its structure and organization, first past and then present. Until 2006, the NYSE was a sort of hybrid corporation/partnership whose members faced unlimited liability.[2] At the same time, the NYSE structure was unaffected by the death or departure of any one of its 1366 members. Only members who owned or leased seats had trading privileges and there were four types of members, discussed below. Each member was an individual and most were sponsored by or associated with a brokerage firm or other organization (typically called a member firm). A membership was referred to as a seat, which was purchased (for as much as $4 million in 2005, and last sold on December 29, 2005 for $3,505,000) through a competitive market process. Full membership was limited to 1366 seats, although there had been special limited trading permits issued as well. Now, under the new structure, one can join the 1366 members by purchasing a license that permits the member to trade for one year. As of August 2011, the annual fee for a license was $40,000, billed monthly. The four types of traditional memberships were as follows:

*House Broker*: Also known as a commission broker, executed orders on behalf of clients submitting orders through brokerage firms. Until 2006, approximately half of the members on the floor were commission brokers. This and other broker roles have been taken over by "trading floor brokers."

[2]This type of organizational structure for exchanges, quite common until the 1990s, is becoming increasingly rare.

*Independent Broker*: Also called a two-dollar broker, executed orders on behalf of commission brokers when activity was high. Alternatively, sometimes commission brokers executing orders on behalf of off-floor clients were referred to as floor brokers. This type of distinct membership no longer exists.
*Floor Trader*: Executes orders on own trading accounts. As of 1992, there were approximately 40 floor traders on the NYSE and this number continued to decline through 2006. However, the NYSE has since created the "supplemental liquidity provider" role, which is intended to enhance market liquidity by allowing for proprietary trading. We will discuss this new role shortly.
*Specialist*: Was charged with the responsibility for maintaining a continuous, liquid, orderly market for the securities in which he specialized. He also kept the book (records) for unexecuted transactions and bought and sold on his own account. There were approximately 400 specialists on the NYSE in 1992. Specialists were typically selected on the basis of their performance as specialists for other securities and other qualifications. Specialists were involved in approximately 20% of NYSE transactions as a principal. Because of their dual roles in running the market for securities on behalf of the exchange and as traders buying and selling those securities at a profit, the specialist's role was particularly interesting and somewhat controversial. The specialist was expected to fulfill his obligation to maintain a continuous, orderly, and liquid market; this role may have conflicted with the desire to earn trading profits. (The specialist has been replaced by the designated market maker (DMM), to be discussed shortly.)

Traditionally, trading activity for the shares of approximately 2779 listed firms (prior to 2006) centered around trading posts located around the floor throughout various rooms. Brokers and traders would congregate about these posts and specialists who oversee trading activity. Clerks employed by the exchanges recorded trading activities and relayed records to systems that disseminated data to the investing public. However, this system has mostly given way to automated screen-based trading, DMMs who are expected to maintain liquid and orderly markets for specific stocks, and off-floor supplemental liquidity providers who are paid fees by the exchange to execute transactions.

## Transforming the NYSE

On April 20, 2005, the New York Stock Exchange dropped a bombshell on the investing public, announcing its intent to be taken over by Archipelago, the successor to the Pacific Stock Exchange. In a single sweep, the NYSE would be merged, privatized, expanded into derivatives markets, and have a springboard for its transformation to an electronic trading market. Stock markets have traditionally emphasized roles of the specialists (replaced by DMMs) who conduct auction markets and maintain liquidity for off-floor brokers and traders. Since the founding of the NYSE in the late 1700s, exchange markets have brought together widely dispersed brokers, dealers, and individual investors, creating highly organized, visible, and regulated environments intended to facilitate trading and price discovery. The traditional floor-based stock exchange in the United States centered around a specialist with a regular "trading crowd" that focused its energies on a small number of stocks. The specialist conducted an auction market for the trading crowd that gathered about. Floor brokers entered the trading crowd with orders initiated by larger off-floor traders, while smaller and routine orders were more likely to be routed to the specialist through an electronic routing system such as the now-obsolete *SuperDOT*, the "super designated order turnaround system."

The merger with Archipelago and the embrace of modern technology have completely changed the way that the NYSE conducts its markets. Now, the role of the specialist has been passed on to *designated market makers* (DMMs) whose responsibilities and rights differ somewhat from their specialist predecessors. DMMs have no trading advantages relative to other market participants, have no special access to order books, and are compensated by listing firms to provide liquidity. The NYSE has overhauled its technologies. For example, in July 2009, the SuperDOT system was replaced by the NYSE *super display book system* (SDBK) for routing and processing orders. This new system enables customers to execute orders in as quickly as five milliseconds.

Sophisticated traders are very concerned with the development of fast and efficient buy-and-sell order processing systems, order executing (clearing and settling) systems, and systems for the analysis of investments. Technology affects order processing, routing, and matching of trades, as well as valuation, hedging, and portfolio risk management techniques. The NYSE has responded with numerous enhancements to facilitate trading activity. For example, it has dramatically increased its ability to handle increasing transaction volume (averaging over 1.5 billion equity shares per day in July 2011) due to improved technology. For example, the NYSE's ECN, the SDBK permits orders to be routed electronically by brokerage firms for execution. Most program trades are also submitted through the SDBK system, accounting for over 10% of all orders. Overall, the SDBK system executes approximately 99% of all NYSE orders. For these SDBK orders, the brokerage firm need not have the order presented at the trading post by a commission broker. This means that the order can be executed faster, perhaps within 5 milliseconds. Equities orders that are executed by a broker on the floor itself average 29,000 shares. When the NYSE opens at 9:30 EST, orders that have accumulated in the *Opening Automated Report Service* (*OARS*) are matched and the DMM attempts to establish a market clearing price. The DMM will attempt to open the security through this system at a price that deviates as little as possible from the prior day's close at 4:00 PM.

As recently as the turn of the century, the majority of retail transactions were initiated with client telephone calls to their stock brokers. However, this routing process has obviously changed markedly. Figure 2.2 depicts the routing process for a typical electronic or Internet-based discount broker transaction. The process for a "brick-and-mortar" broker would be the same except that client access to the broker is by telephone, and, of course, much slower. Alternative trading system (ATS) transactions usually eliminate the broker from the process. Internalized orders are executed by the broker itself, where orders are confirmed without reaching an outside market.

## Demutualization and Governance Changes

A mutual organization is owned by members, typically employees, clients, or suppliers. Mutual stock exchanges are owned by members who have trading rights in the exchange's market. Accompanying the improvement of exchange technology in trading has been a

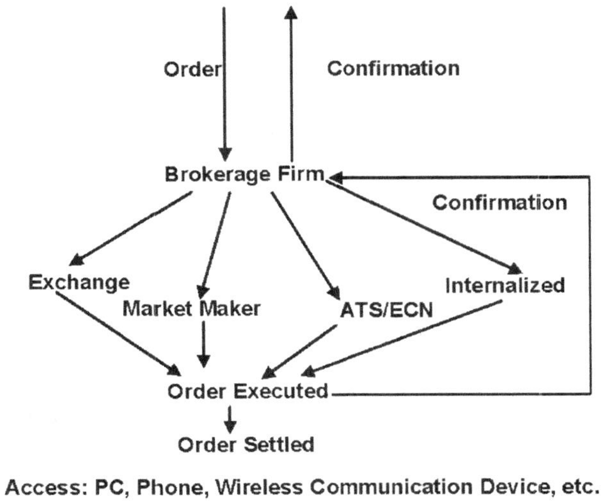


**FIGURE 2.2** Securities order routing process.

trend to demutualize exchanges. This demutualization trend has meant that many exchanges have restructured to become stockholder-owned corporations. Euronext and the Australian, Pacific, and London Exchanges were among the first to demutualize in 1997 through 1999, following the Stockholm Exchange in 1993. NASDAQ demutualized in 2000 and the NYSE in 2006. Most exchanges justified restructuring to for-profit institutions based on their needs to raise capital to finance their technology and infrastructure expenses. Exchange demutualization has also provided for more intense competition among markets. Exchange self-regulation and other regulatory issues remain important concerns for these restructured institutions. To avoid conflicts of interest, the NYSE Group created a not-for-profit corporation, NYSE Regulation, Inc., with the New York Stock Exchange LLC as its sole equity member. This new corporation performs all the SRO (self-regulatory organization, to be discussed later) regulatory responsibilities that had been conducted by the NYSE. NYSE Regulation seeks to ensure that listed companies comply with NYSE listing regulations, actively engages in the exchange rule-making process, and monitors exchange trading activity for suspicious behavior.

The NYSE merger followed on the heels of the Richard Grasso compensation quagmire, where former CEO Grasso and the NYSE were heavily criticized for his $180-million pay package. Grasso resigned in 2003 and was followed in several months by John Thain who approached Archipelago about merging. The $6 billion merger deal granted the 1366 NYSE members about 64% of the combined firm's shares and the remainder to Archipelago shareholders (30%), NYSE top management (5%), and lower-level managers and employees (1%). Interestingly, the 5% granted to NYSE CEO John Thain and other top managers was valued at approximately $300 million, more than the disputed sums paid to former CEO Richard Grasso. A number of NYSE member-seat holders, notably Kenneth Langone, former chairman of the NYSE Board of Directors, complained about the price accepted by NYSE management. However, a seat on the NYSE sold for $960,000 in January

2005, and $1.6 million on April 20, 2005, shortly before the takeover announcement, and for $3 million in July 2005, shortly after the takeover announcement. By year-end, the price of a seat had risen to $4 million before dropping to $3.505 million at year-end. In addition, some NYSE members complained about Thain's former employer, Goldman Sachs, representing both sides in the deal. Furthermore, Goldman Sachs owned several seats on the NYSE and maintained substantial holdings of Archipelago shares. However, two other investment banks, Greenhill and Lazard, did required due diligence for the deal. The deal was valued by these institutions at between $3 billion and $5 billion, a substantial discount below the value implied by the July 2005 market price of Archipelago shares.

## Diminished Floor Trading Activity

As the NYSE developed, acquired, and improved its ability to handle electronic transactions, actual in-person floor trading activity diminished. As of the end of 2006, the NYSE trading floor exceeded 43,000 square feet. During 2007, the NYSE closed trading rooms; by November 2007, slightly more than half of this trading space was available for in-person transactions. In fact, as of 2007, trading activity on the NYSE trading floor produced less than 10% of NYSE revenue. More important sources of revenue to the NYSE now include listing fees charged to firms that want their shares traded on the NYSE and from selling price, quotations, and other transactions data to the public. The trading floor crowd (including members, clerks, etc.) has diminished in numbers from over 3000 to less than 1700. Less than half of NYSE volume is executed on the floor, and DMMs (specialists) have been involved in less than 1 in 30 transactions as opposed to 1 in 7 as recently as 2002.

## Current New York Stock Exchange Equities Membership Types

In late 2008, the specialist role yielded to that of the DMM, who runs auctions for securities, has no advantageous knowledge of the order book, and does not necessarily lose trade priority over other traders. In addition, the specialist's liquidity providing function was taken over by both the DMM and supplemental liquidity providers (SLPs), outside firms that commit to maintain liquidity in specific stocks. The DMM has the obligation to maintain fair and orderly markets and facilitate price discovery in their assigned securities. The DMM opens and closes the market for its securities each day, is required to quote at the national best bid or offer (NBBO) a specified percentage of the time, provide price improvement, and match incoming orders based on a preprogrammed capital commitment schedule. DMMs for a listed security can be selected by the issuer of the listed security or the issuer can delegate authority to the NYSE to select an eligible DMM. NYSE DMM firms include BofA Merrill, Barclays Capital, GETCO Securities, LLC, Knight Capital Group, Inc., and Spear, Leeds & Kellogg Specialists, LLC.

A second type of NYSE equities membership is the *trading floor broker* who works orders on behalf of clients on an agency basis. Trading floor brokers are positioned at the point of sale during openings, closings, and unique intraday occurrences to execute trades.

The third type of NYSE equities membership is the SLP, a high-volume member trading off of her own proprietary account who adds liquidity to the NYSE. SLP members are rewarded for aggressively providing liquidity and improving markets. They are expected to maintain a bid or offer at the NBBO in each assigned security during at least 10% of the trading day. Major NYSE supplemental liquidity providing firms include Barclays Capital, Citadel Securities LLC, Goldman, Sachs & Company, HRT Financial, LLC, and Knight Capital Americas, L.P.

## Option Exchanges

Most stock options in the United States are traded on one of the options exchanges. The oldest stock options exchange is the Chicago Board Options Exchange, which also owns the C2 Options Exchange. The NYSE has grown in stature in options markets with the NYSE Amex and NYSE Arca, acquired through takeovers. NASDAQ OMX operates the NSDQ and PHLX (formerly the Philadelphia Exchange). In addition, the Boston Options Exchange (BOX, which is jointly owned by the TMX Group and seven broker dealers) and ISE (owned by Eurex) both maintain stock option markets. Table 2.2 provides volume data for all of these exchanges. The Options Clearing Corporation (OCC), jointly owned by the U.S. options exchanges, is technically the counterparty for all options transactions in the United States. This means that all option buyers own options that were written by the OCC and all option writers are obligated to the OCC. This arrangement, given the financial stability of the OCC and each of the exchanges that own and back its obligations and all of the brokerage firms that back the obligations of the exchanges have effectively eliminated default risk in listed options trading.

Options trading took place entirely over the counter until the 1973 opening of the Chicago Board Options Exchange (CBOE). The nature of options trading lends itself to technological development at every stage of the trading process. First, because of option-trading strategies' emphasis on relative valuation and stochastic processes, the valuation and portfolio analyses require mathematical analyses that are computer-based.

**TABLE 2.2** U.S. Options Exchanges (Data from January 1 through July 31, 2011)

| Exchange | Cleared Contracts | Total Premiums | Average Daily Contracts | % of Total Contracts |
|---|---|---|---|---|
| ARCA | 158,529,881 | $36,180,176,001 | 1,093,310 | 10.63 |
| BATS | 50,286,898 | $12,952,402,034 | 346,806 | 3.37 |
| BOX | 49,788,089 | $9,882,629,258 | 343,366 | 3.34 |
| C2 | 10,400,904 | $1,457,446,499 | 71,730 | 0.70 |
| CBOE | 316,112,979 | $60,812,186,839 | 2,180,090 | 21.20 |
| ISE | 259,516,879 | $45,392,864,394 | 1,789,772 | 17.40 |
| NSDQ | 69,144,416 | $16,647,189,711 | 476,858 | 4.64 |
| PHLX | 367,776,704 | $121,172,599,631 | 2,536,391 | 24.66 |
| Total | 1,491,204,897 | $340,633,377,303 | 10,284,172 | 100.00 |

*Source: The Options Clearing Corporation.*

Maintenance of these strategies requires abilities to rapidly trade in and out of multiple positions simultaneously, relying on electronic communication technologies capable of handling large amounts of data instantaneously. Technologies offered through the Internet offer these capabilities, forcing exchanges to anticipate and quickly improve on developments in order to compete.

Competition among options exchanges continues to intensify, fostered by a myriad of new technologies and the introduction of equity option multiple listings beginning in the fall of 1999. The International Securities Exchange was launched in May 2000 as the first fully electronic exchange in the United States, adding a significant dimension of competition to the then largely floor-based markets offered by the CBOE, AMEX, and PHLX. In addition, the ISE traded options with well-established markets on the other exchanges. In addition to the ISE, well-established foreign exchanges such as Eurex electronically trade contracts on U.S. equity instruments, further intensifying competitive pressures on major U.S. options exchanges. In fact, practically all European and Asian securities and derivatives exchanges have become entirely or almost entirely electronic. This increased competition has led to a number of important results, including narrowing spreads (8% between 1999 and 2000 alone according to a Securities and Exchange Commission (SEC) study; also see Battalio et al., 2004), highly uncertain futures for competitors, and the development and implementation of innovative quotations and trading systems.

Options exchanges have innovated substantial technological advances to maintain and even anticipate developments in other markets. For example, exchange-initiated technological advances include NASDAQ's automated exchange, *SuperMontage*. Options exchanges have experienced launching of the Chicago Board Options Exchange (CBOE) proprietary order routing and quotations *HyTS Terminals* (hybrid trading systems), which offer trading desks point-and-click access (CBOEdirect) to all exchanges on one screen. Such point-and-click trading systems provide for instantaneous filling and confirmation of orders at the best prices along with transparency of trades. Asset managers rely on such systems to obtain speedy access to information, route and execute orders, and obtain trade confirmations. Several exchanges are providing for off-site market makers such as the CBOE *Remote Market Makers* (RMMs). These systems facilitate trading by off-floor investors and enhance liquidity by expanding the membership of market makers. These systems offer market makers direct access to the trading floor, enabling them to participate in the provision of market liquidity and subjecting them to the same market-enhancing responsibilities without requiring their physical presence.

## 2.3 OVER-THE-COUNTER MARKETS AND ALTERNATIVE TRADING SYSTEMS

During most of the 20th century, the two national exchanges (NYSE and AMEX) along with a small number of regional exchanges hosted all U.S. exchange-based trading. All other trading was conducted either directly between counterparties or intermediated by broker dealers in what was called the *over-the-counter (OTC) markets*. The creation of the electronic bulletin board NASDAQ by NASD, followed by its evolution into a full-fledged ECN, and then its recognition as an exchange, along with the introduction of numerous alternative trading systems such as BRUT and BATS, blurred the distinction between exchange and OTC markets.

## Over-the-Counter Markets

The *OTC markets* have traditionally been defined as nonexchange markets. Where the expression applies, OTC markets are made up of broker-dealer houses that execute transactions on behalf of client accounts as well as their own. In addition, included are transactions executed directly by trading counterparties. Almost all federal, municipal, and corporate bonds are traded in the OTC markets as well as many derivative products, structured products, and shares of smaller corporations.

Brokers and dealers in the OTC markets are members of FINRA, the Financial Industry Regulatory Authority, which absorbed the National Association of Securities Dealers (NASD). FINRA is an independent, self-regulated agency cooperating with the SEC. As of 2011, approximately 4525 broker/dealer firms and 631,085 registered representatives were regulated by FINRA. FINRA also operates the largest securities dispute resolution forum in the world, processing over 8000 arbitrations and 1000 mediations per year.

OTC markets for equities are comprised of a number of venues. For example, the Over-the-Counter Bulletin Board (OTCBB) is an interdealer electronic quotation system that displays real-time quotes, last-sale prices, and volume information for many OTC equity securities. OTCBB is not an exchange; securities are not actually traded through the system. OTCBB securities include national, regional, and foreign equity issues, warrants, unit investment trust issues (UITs), American depositary receipts (ADRs), and direct participation programs issues (DPPs). Investors do not have direct access to OTCBB. In 2012, OTCBB was expected to be renamed as the Non-NMS Quotation Service (NNQS).

Another important OTC equity venue is the OTC Markets Group, Inc., informally known as "Pink Sheets." This group also facilitates trading of shares of nonlisted companies, providing quotation, messaging, and information services to broker-dealers. Pink Sheets maintains categories based on the level of financial and corporate disclosure provided by companies quoted through their systems. For example, shares quoted in OTCQX, the top tier of the OTC market, meet certain financial standards, and are subject to qualitative reviews. OTCQB tier companies (mid-tier) also provide significant disclosure to the marketplace. The OTC Pink tier, or the Speculative Trading Marketplace, is the third tier of the OTC market. OTC Pink has no financial standards or reporting requirements, and firms whose securities are traded there might not provide any public disclosure.

The OTC markets also include the so-called third and fourth markets. Third markets exist for listed securities traded between brokers off any exchange. Fourth markets are those where institutions trade securities directly among themselves in the so-called *upstairs markets*. These markets are particularly important for bank-to-bank derivatives and structured products transactions. Institutions have used these markets for block trades (transactions involving more than 10,000 shares or $200,000 of a security), particularly when such a transaction might pose liquidity problems on an exchange. The upstairs markets might account for as much as half of all stock transactions volume, although statistics are difficult to estimate and confirm.

Stock exchanges and other markets vary with respect to how orders are intermediated. For example, the NYSE permits many of its members to act as both agents (brokers) and dealers. This means that an order counterparty might be either a dealer trading on her own account or a broker representing a client. On the other hand, the OTC markets are usually dealer markets, where investors transact only with or through dealers.

## Alternative Trading Systems

An ATS might be loosely defined as a securities trading venue that is not registered with the SEC as an exchange. Alternative trading systems provide electronic forums for linking dealers with each other and with institutional investors. They also match and cross trades in the upstairs market (fourth market). We will discuss the more precise SEC definition shortly. The four primary types of ATSs are:

1. *Electronic Communication Networks (ECNs)*, which are virtual meeting places and screen-based systems for trading securities. These ECNs include Bloomberg Tradebook (which bills itself as a more comprehensive full-service agency broker), LavaFlow ECN, and ARCA Edge.
2. *Dark Pools and "Crossing Networks,"* where quotations for share blocks are matched anonymously. These ATSs include Credit Suisse Crossfinder, Goldman Sachs Sigma X, Knight Capital Link, GetMatched (Getco Execution Services), Liquidnet, Posit Marketplace (ITG), MS Pool (Morgan Stanley), and Citi Match (Citigroup). Participants in crossing markets enjoy reduced transactions costs and anonymity but often must wait for counterparty orders to accumulate before transactions can be executed.
3. *Internalization Crossing Networks* such as UBS PIN that allows brokers or firms to fill orders from that firm's own internal supply of stock.
4. *Voice-Brokered Third-Party Matching.*

A more comprehensive listing of alternative trading systems is provided in Table 2.3.

The most important of the ECNs dealing with equities have included *BRUT* (purchased by NASDAQ) *Instinet*, *REDIBook*, and *Archipelago*, with the latter two having merged in 2002. Instinet, the first of the ECNs, was founded in 1967 as Institutional Networks, became a wholly owned subsidiary of Reuters in 1987, took its shares through an IPO in 2001 and merged with Island shortly afterwards before going private again in 2005. The focus of Instinet's activities was block trading (10,000 or more shares), seeking to provide its clients with a high level of confidentiality. Major ECNs dealing with foreign exchange include Hotspot and Currenex.

The SEC defines an ATS to be an automated system that centralizes, displays, crosses, matches, or otherwise executes trading interest, but is not currently registered with the Commission as a national security exchange or operated by a registered securities association. However, the SEC redefined the term "exchange" to include "any organization, association, or group of persons that: (1) Brings together the orders of multiple buyers and sellers; and (2) uses established nondiscretionary methods (whether by providing a trading facility or by setting rules) under which such orders interact with each other, and the buyers and sellers entering such orders agree to the terms of a trade." Under this new

**TABLE 2.3** Sampling of Major Alternative Trading Systems

| Name | Host Country | Instruments | Features |
|---|---|---|---|
| Alpha | Canada | Equities | Continuous trading market platform (ECN) |
| ArcaEdge (NYSE Euronext) | U.S. | Equities | NYSE ATS |
| Bloomberg Tradebook | U.S. | Equities, FX, and derivatives | Bills itself as an integrated full-service agency broker |
| Chi-X Europe (Nomura, BoA) | U.K. | European shares | Multilateral Trading Facility |
| Citi Match (Citigroup) | U.S. | Equities | Internal Crossing Network |
| Crossfinder (Credit Suisse) | Global | Equities | Bills itself as the world's largest dark pool; internal crossing network |
| Currenex (State Street Bank) | U.S. | FX | ECN |
| Getco Execution Services | U.S. | Equities | GETMatched: dark pool ATS or dark pool and other execution services |
| Hotspot | U.S. | FX | ECN |
| Knight Link (Knight Capital) | U.S. | Equities | Largest dark pool according to Tabb Group 2008 study |
| Knight Match (Knight Capital) | U.S. | Equities | Crossing network |
| LavaFlow ECN | U.S. | Equities and derivatives | ECN |
| Level ATS | U.S. | Equities | Dark pool; crossing network |
| Liquidnet | U.S. and global | Equities | Block negotiation (crossing) |
| MidPoint Match (ISE) | U.S. | Equities | Matches executions at exchange mid-point of NBBO |
| MS Pool (Morgan Stanley) | U.S. | Equities | Dark pool |
| NASDAQ Crossing (NASDAQ) | U.S. | Equities | Crossing Network |
| NYSE Arca Europe (NYSE) | France | European shares | Multilateral trading facility, crossing network |
| Posit Marketplace (ITG) | U.S. | Equities | Crossing network |
| Sigma X (Goldman Sachs) | U.S. | Equities | Crossing network |
| Track ECN | U.S. | Equities | Suspended operations as of June 2011 |
| UBS ATF | U.S. | Equities | Crossing network |
| UBS PIN | U.S. | Equities | Internal crossing network |
| UBS MTF | U.S. | Equities | Crossing network for European stocks |

definition, at least several ATSs might be considered exchanges, even if they are not the traditional "brick-and-mortar" type. In the past few years, several large ATSs, including BATS and DirectEdge, have registered with the SEC as exchanges. Thus, consider the following definition provided by Rule 300(a) of SEC Regulation ATS:

> Alternative trading system means any organization, association, person, group of persons, or system:
>
> 1. That constitutes, maintains, or provides a market place or facilities for bringing together purchasers and sellers of securities or for otherwise performing with respect to securities the functions commonly performed by a stock exchange within the meaning of Rule 3b-16 under the Securities Exchange Act of 1934; and
> 2. That does not:
>    - i. Set rules governing the conduct of subscribers other than the conduct of such subscribers' trading on such organization, association, person, group of persons, or system; or
>    - ii. Discipline subscribers other than by exclusion from trading.

What the ATS does *not* do is what distinguishes it from an exchange. However, these sorts of distinctions might remain in flux.

The NYSE share of NYSE-listed trade executions have been steadily dropping as electronic exchanges and ATSs have grown in importance. For example, NYSE's share of trading in its own listed stocks declined to 67.3% in December 2006, down from 76.5% a year earlier.[3] ECN trading of NASDAQ-listed securities has been even more significant. Table 2.4 provides a listing of important equity markets along with their shares of daily volume as of September 2009.

**TABLE 2.4** Equity Trading Center Volume, September 2009

| | |
|---|---|
| NYSE | 14.7% |
| NYSE Arca | 13.2% |
| NASDAQ | 19.4% |
| NASDAQ OMX BX | 3.3% |
| Broker-dealer (internalization) | 17.5% |
| Direct Edge | 9.8% |
| BATS | 9.5% |
| Dark pools | 7.9% |
| Other exchanges | 3.7% |
| Other ECNs | 1.0% |

*Source: Securities and Exchange Commission, Release Number 34-61358, File Number S7-02-10, 2010, Figure 6. This table depicts trading volume for NMS shares.*

[3]Joseph Weber, "Behind the Burst of the Bourses," *Business Week*, February 5, 2007, p. 59. AMEX has since been merged into the NYSE.

## 2.4 THE DECLINE OF BRICK AND MORTAR

The natural monopoly power associated with the old exchange-based, open-outcry stock markets owes its early existence to a nearly complete absence of technology and communication systems. Investors were far too dispersed to conduct unaided securities transactions, and security traders required a central physical meeting site for competitive executions. This site or exchange enabled large networks of local broker offices to execute securities transactions on behalf of these widely dispersed investors. New York's Wall Street district provided an excellent venue for this purpose and the regional exchanges filled specific niches in the securities markets. As telecommunication technology advanced in the early decades of the 20th century offering market access to millions of investors, U.S. securities markets nearly self-destructed, only to be salvaged by regulatory authorities and intense efforts by exchanges to curb market abuse. Exchanges have since facilitated monitoring for regulatory compliance in much the same manner that they facilitate trading. Shortly after passage of the Securities Exchange Act of 1934, the SEC gained authority over the exchanges that, in turn, monitored and regulated their members.

Until the mid-1970s, brokerage firms maintained their monopoly power with a system of fixed transaction fees. All of their transactions were routed through the principal exchanges and off-floor markets. Exchanges had limited competition for securities listings. The primary sources of competition among securities brokers were in the arrays of services that they offered. After price controls were lifted in 1975, the market saw formation of a number of discount brokerage houses that unbundled nontransaction services such as research and were able to offer drastically reduced execution costs. The market segmented to an extent, with some firms offering only transaction executions and others offering the full array of brokerage house services such as client advice. However, the vast majority of transactions were still routed through the principal exchanges and off-floor markets.

More recent technological developments in telecommunications, wireless communications, the Internet, and globalization have imposed enormous competitive pressures on U.S. securities exchanges. With the electronic NASDAQ system beginning in 1971, competition from foreign fully automated exchanges trading U.S. securities (e.g., Eurex), development of fully automated exchanges in the United States (e.g., the ISE), and ECNs, such as the Instinet, Island, and Posit systems that allow direct trading between institutions, exchanges have been forced to accept and even innovate technological development to survive.

The natural monopoly enjoyed by traditional brick-and-mortar markets had been enhanced by a number of barriers to entry. Overhead outlays were required for large investments in office facilities, communications equipment, fixed exchange fees and memberships, broker training and licensing, and building client bases. Each of these overhead outlays was accompanied by significant time lags and increasing time required for recapturing initial investments (payback periods). In addition, traditional brokerage offices experienced significant returns to scale (see Stigler, 1961), making it almost impossible for smaller and newer firms to compete against larger better-established firms. Each of these barriers to entry into the securities brokerage business applies to the creation of overhead-intensive, brick-and-mortar securities exchanges and markets. For example, in the late 1990s, the Chicago Board of Trade and the New York Mercantile Exchange constructed new futures pits that cost $180 million and $228 million, respectively. However, recent electronic and other technological developments, particularly the Internet, substantially relieve these costly barriers to entry. First, most prospective clients already have Internet access and usage skills. Transaction costs are substantially reduced through use of equipment already installed in client homes. Whereas the typical U.S. customer stock transaction executed through a phone call has a variable cost of about $1, its cost is reduced to just $0.02 executed online. Similar disparities exist in open-outcry and electronic markets. For example, the open-outcry LIFFE charged about $1.50 per for long and short positions on the Bund futures contract in the late 1990s; its electronic German competitor DTB charged only $0.66 for the same contract. Open-outcry exchanges in the United States charged fees of approximately $1.50 per contract (see Cavaletti, 1997).

More significantly, overhead expenses for Internet brokers run approximately 1% of assets, as opposed to 2% to 3% for brick-and-mortar offices. Time required for Internet brokerage firm start-ups is substantially reduced relative to brick-and-mortar start-ups. In addition, the Internet and other technological advances have reduced economies of scale for brokerage firms. For example, as the Internet has largely replaced "cold calling," the fixed costs of seeking and soliciting the business of small clients have dropped significantly. Furthermore, clients of electronic brokers trade far more frequently than those of full-service brokers, with some estimates ranging to 10 to 25 times as frequent (Varian, 1998). Hence, smaller individual investors are able to play larger roles in securities markets at lower costs. The increased participation of smaller investors, acting as day traders, enables them to replace specialists and market makers, at least to some extent, in the provision of liquidity to the market. In addition, the reduction of scale economies has increased competition among brokerage firms, in large part because so many of their services (e.g., advice, loans, and cash management) could be unbundled and commoditized through automation. Some of these services require very little initial capital outlay and no unique technology.

Removal of fixed brokerage commissions has substantially increased competition in the brokerage industry as reduced costs of service provision have softened barriers to entry. Brokerage commissions and fees had fallen from an average of $52.89 per trade in early 1996 to $15.67 in mid-1998. By 2000, a few online brokerage services had temporarily reduced their commissions to zero, and most still charge less than $15 per transaction. This particular scenario is interesting and quite controversial because it seems to be in part a direct result of *payment for order flow*, where brokerage firms and other institutions receive compensation from electronic exchanges and ATSs as payment for directing their order flow to those markets. However, this practice has grown more widespread, and in 2010, even the NYSE began making payments for order flow to providers of liquidity. Barriers to entry based on ownership of physical facilities are disappearing, and existing firms are being forced to vary their product lines and merge into other institutions.

Combinations, alliances, and mergers between exchanges have also enabled previously smaller and less efficient markets to compete against larger ones. These combinations have enabled exchanges and markets to mutually benefit from one another's technological resources. Some of these combinations have been domestic such as OneChicago, LLC, an alliance created by the Chicago Board Options Exchange and Chicago Mercantile

Exchange to trade equity futures contracts and the Pacific Exchange and the Archipelago Exchange merger. On the international scene, the New York Mercantile Exchange opened a satellite open-outcry trading floor in Dublin for trading in a Brent crude oil futures contract and mergers among exchanges in other countries such as those forming Euronext and Eurex (combining the Deutsche Börse AG/SWX Swiss Exchange). Each of these latter combinations offered improvements in investors' abilities to trade on a global basis.

## Electronic versus Open Outcry

Which trading and brokerage platforms result in lower trading costs? For example, does open outcry result in superior trading performance relative to electronic execution? In an interesting study, Bakos et al. (2000), with $60,000 provided by the Salomon Brothers Center at New York University, opened a series of accounts at various full-service, discount and electronic securities brokers. Their commissions for 100-share lots averaged $7.50 for electronic brokers and $47 for full-service voice brokers. They found that full-service brokers were more likely to route orders to the principal exchanges than electronic brokers and that such orders were more likely to be improved. However, for smaller orders, these price improvement advantages are more than offset by the higher brokerage commissions. Hence, specialists and market makers on exchanges were able to provide better order executions while brokers using electronic markets charged smaller commissions. It appeared that smaller investors fared better with discount electronic brokers while larger transactions resulted in better after-commission executions on the principal exchanges.

Many of the studies of electronic versus open-outcry trading have used bid-offer spreads as a liquidity metric (e.g., Battalio et al., 1997), where wider spreads indicate lower liquidity. Shyy and Lee (1995) found that spreads appeared to be wider in electronic markets than in open-outcry markets; Pirrong (1996) found just the opposite. Pirrong argued that miscommunications and misunderstandings between trade participants reduce efficiency of open-outcry markets and that these issues are avoided in electronic markets. Regardless, time to execute trades is certainly reduced in electronic markets. In addition, screen-based trading has facilitated after-hours markets. Now, a number of exchanges are offering investors opportunities to trade after normal business hours.

The evidence concerning the provision of liquidity by open-outcry exchange markets relative to electronic markets is both ambiguous and mixed (e.g., Pirrong, 1996; Breedon and Holland, 1997). Some electronic systems have effectively eliminated driven floor-based, open-outcry markets. For example, Breedon and Holland describe how during 1997–1998, the computerized Eurex drew practically 100% of the trading in German Bund futures from the open outcry LIFFE, which had held a 70% market share only months earlier. By 2000, LIFFE had abandoned open outcry entirely for LIFFE CONNECT, a fully automated system. However, LIFFE did retain the bund options contracts, probably because of the more complicated strategies associated with them. In 1998, MATIF operated its open-outcry and electronic systems simultaneously. Within two weeks, the computerized system had taken all volume from the open-outcry markets that had to be closed. The Hong Kong Futures Exchange and the Sydney Futures Exchange both abandoned open outcry during this same period. Frino et al. (2004) found that spreads narrowed on the Sydney and Hong Kong Exchanges, whereas spreads widened on the LIFFE. In addition, according to Frino et al., bid-ask spreads on all three exchanges appear to widen in response to price volatility at a faster rate under electronic trading than with open-outcry trading, suggesting that the specialist-based system may offer better price continuity in periods of uncertainty.

One of the difficulties of screen-based trading is the inability to efficiently disseminate significant amounts of information concerning trades. While it is easy enough for screens to display bid and offer prices, open outcry participants are able to more easily verbally communicate order types and combinations as well as other more complicated trade details. Such matters grow in importance when trade sizes are larger or when, for example, an options trader is attempting to leg into a spread (execute spread transactions one at a time) or other position. While screen-based trading provides for a greater level of anonymity, many traders prefer a market where their counterparties can be identified. In addition, Sarkar and Tozzi (1998) argue that open-outcry exchanges provide for more liquidity in more active markets while newer, less active issues are less likely to be found in open-outcry markets.

One of the more troubling aspects of electronic brokerage transactions is that customers do not normally have a say in order routings and that orders need not necessarily be routed to the markets with the best prices. Many electronic markets have agreements with particular exchanges and markets to route transactions through them. These exchanges and market makers pay for order flow that might result in worse prices for clients. This practice, "payment for order flow," was pioneered by the infamous Ponzi schemer Bernard Madoff.[4] This means that a brokerage firm will receive payments from an exchange or other market for routing orders to that market. For example, in 1999, the Knight/Trimark Group paid $138.7 million for order flow, with over 10% of this sum received from Ameritrade, a large electronic brokerage firm (Bakos et al., 2000). Specialists and market makers on the major exchanges have resented this controversial practice of order flow payment and many discount brokerage clients seem unaware of it. But, as we discussed earlier (p. 41), in early 2010 even the NYSE began making payments for order flow to providers of liquidity.

## 2.5 CROSSING NETWORKS AND UPSTAIRS MARKETS

One of the most vexing problems faced by institutional traders is the price pressure, called *slippage*, associated with large transactions. For example, placing a large sell order will force prices down against the seller. In fact, merely attempting to execute a large sell order reveals negative information to the market. *Crossing networks* are alternative trading systems that match buyers and sellers with respect to agreed-upon quantities. Crossing networks do not publicly display quotations, thereby enabling participants some degree of anonymity. Trades are priced by reference to prices obtained from other markets rather than by the more traditional auction systems.[5] Traders using crossing networks announce

[4]We will discuss payment for order flow and Bernard Madoff separately in Chapter 12.

[5]The Securities and Exchange Commission (1998) defines crossing networks as "systems that allow participants to enter unpriced orders to buy and sell securities. Orders are crossed at a specified time at a price derived from another market" (i.e., a continuous market such as the NYSE).

their order sizes. The crossing network then matches buy and sell orders at prices obtained from more traditional markets such as the NYSE. This crossing procedure enables institutional traders to execute without exposing their order flow to competitors. The crossing network, by having prices determined elsewhere, also prevents the price impact or pressure typically associated with auctions of large blocks of shares. Because crossing networks do not reveal prices or client identities, and they represent nondisplayed liquidity, they are sometimes referred to as *dark pools of liquidity*.

MidPoint Match and NASDAQ Crossing provide traders with opportunities to match orders anonymously at known benchmarks (e.g., the mid-point of the spread) or closing or other prices several times a day. For example, trades can be executed after regular market hours, providing liquidity outside normal trading sessions. The match price is typically the volume weighted average price (VWAP) of all trades during the day. As of 2005, ITG's *Posit* Group was used by approximately 550 institutions and broker-dealers, crossing about 35 million U.S. shares per day.[6] Total daily market volume averaged approximately 98 million shares in 2005, compared to approximately 1.8 billion for the NYSE. Posit systems allow traders to enter order quantities that are matched during listing market trading sessions with execution prices at the midpoint of best bid and offer currently prevailing in the listing market.

We discussed *Liquidnet* in Chapter 1, which is a negotiating venue that matches institutional buyers and sellers of large blocks of equity securities, enabling them to directly bargain and trade confidentially with one another. Liquidnet provides an electronic format for this negotiation process. Traders use the system by entering symbols for securities that they wish to buy or sell. If Liquidnet finds a potential match, it notifies the counterparties, who bargain anonymously with each other in a virtual meeting room using the Liquidnet system. This facility for bargaining distinguishes Liquidnet from the other crossing systems discussed here. Thus, trade counterparties negotiate directly with each other the terms of their trade. Counterparties will know prices from other markets, leaving relatively little room for significant pricing disagreements. If they come to terms, they report the transaction to Liquidnet, which arranges the transfer and takes a commission on each share.

The New York Stock Exchange also conducts several after-hours crossing markets. First, the NYSE offers Crossing Session I from 4:15 to 5:00 PM after the NYSE closes regular floor trading. Crossing Session I, when in effect, enables traders to match single stock orders at closing price. In addition, the NYSE offers Crossing Session II from 4:00 to 6:30 PM to enable program trades for 15 or more securities, regardless of their value. Furthermore, the NYSE MatchPoint system is an electronic facility that matches aggregated orders at predetermined fixed times (up to seven times daily, as of September 2008) with prices that are derived from ongoing floor trading. NYSE MatchPoint's After-Hours Matching Session runs at 4:45 PM. This matching system uses the closing or last transaction price from NYSE trading during the day and the ATS's. NYSE MatchPoint covers all NYSE, NASDAQ, and regional stocks. It is also accessible via the Internet while crossing session orders are routed through SDBK. One market difficulty with these systems is that, like other crossing systems, they contribute little to the price discovery process.

[6]According to Degryse, van Achter, and Wuyts (2009), citing Towerwatch statistics.

### Internalization

Internalization occurs when brokers execute their own client buy orders against their own client sell orders, representing both sides of a trade and without routing them to central markets. Internalization allows brokers to execute transactions more easily and at a lower cost. Of course, internalization does present some obvious potential problems. First, internalization may inhibit the broker's ability to properly represent the client as the client's agent, particularly when the broker is also representing a client on the other side of the transaction or acting as a dealer. Second, internalization results in fewer transactions being executed in the central market, which increases market fragmentation and reduces transparency and potential price competition. These problems can lead to reduced liquidity and increased price volatility in the central market. Internalization can also lead to violations of price and time priority. Perhaps worse for the broker's clients, the transaction may be more susceptible to manipulation or may not be executed at the best possible prices, consistent with the point above concerning the broker's ability to represent the client.

Internalization of customer orders is not possible for options markets transactions because options transactions must be executed on options exchanges as per rules of each options exchange. Some customer orders may be executed by the exchange's automatic execution system, but others are subject to the options trading crowd. However, some brokerage firms will submit their own orders simultaneously with their customer orders, such that there is a reasonable possibility that they will execute against each other. On the other hand, the trading crowd might "break up" one or both sides of the orders, perhaps at better prices, such that the brokerage firm only participates in the executions of parts of one or both orders.

## 2.6 QUOTATION, INTERMARKET, AND CLEARING SYSTEMS

The Securities Act of 1975 amended the Securities Exchange Act of 1934 to facilitate development of a national market system for securities transactions. With the national system created by this Act, Congress intended to increase competition, efficiency, and price transparency in securities markets, and to promote best execution and order interaction. In this system, national and regional exchanges would list security prices simultaneously. The purpose of this national market system was to ensure that investors would receive the best possible transaction prices for their securities.

The Securities Industry Automated Corporation (SIAC) is now fully owned by NYSE Euronext, which maintains the primary systems for disseminating price and quote information to the public. The following represent some of the systems for providing price quotations and for executing and clearing trades that have arisen from this effort:

*Consolidated Tape* (CTA): High-speed electronic system maintained by SIAC for reporting transaction prices and volumes for securities on all U.S. exchanges and markets.

*Consolidated Quotations System* (CQS): Provides traders with price quotes through SIAC from the various exchanges and FINRA and calculates the NBBO. The CQS does not time delay as the Consolidated Tape can during periods of heavy volume.

*Intermarket Trading System* (ITS): Displays quotes in different markets and links markets for trade executions to facilitate investors' access to the best quotes. This system might be considered to be the centerpiece of the national market system.

Efforts to create this national market system also intended to protect investors placing limit orders from superior executions in other markets and enabling exchange members to execute off-floor transactions for exchange-listed securities. In addition to the national market systems listed above, the following quotation, intermarket, insurance, and clearing systems are important:

*Order Book*: The order book stores limit orders and might be open (visible) to floor traders and market makers as on the Tokyo Stock Exchange or NYSE (NYSE OpenBook).

*Securities Investors Protection Corporation* (SIPC): Analogous to the Federal Deposit Insurance Corporation (FDIC) in that it insures the investor's account for up to $500,000 in securities and $100,000 in cash, but only when the investor's brokerage firm fails. Thus, this coverage is very limited. SIPC does not provide protection from declines in security values nor does it provide protection for losses from securities not registered with the SEC.

## Clearing and Settlement

The general *clearing* process involves two primary tasks: trade comparison (matching of trades) and settlement (delivery of securities or book entry). Clearing refers to the set of activities resulting in settling claims of financial institutions against other financial institutions. The operations department of a financial institution, often referred to as the institution's back office, is responsible for handling or overseeing the clearing and settlement processes. Only approximately 5% of over 5000 brokerage firms are self-clearing; that is, only 5% are capable of clearing trades for themselves. Other brokers, known as correspondent firms, forward their orders to a *clearing firm*. A clearing firm is authorized by a clearing house (defined below) to manage trade comparisons and other back office operations. Leading clearing firms include Pershing, LLC, JPMorgan Clearing Corp., and National Financial Services, LLC.

A *clearing house* clears transactions for a market such as the NYSE and is typically established by that market or members of that market. A clearing house facilitates the trade settlement between two clearing firms (also called as member firms or clearing participants) and seeks to ensure that the clearing firms honor their trade settlement obligations. The clearing house will typically guarantee the obligations of its member firms, and often require collateral to ensure that settlement obligations are fulfilled. The collateral is pooled into a clearinghouse guarantee fund. The clearing house will step into a transaction to be settled by its members and assume the settlement obligations of both counterparties to the transaction, in effect becoming the counterparty to both sides of every transaction, a process known as *novation*. Thus, the clearinghouse, acting as a *central counterparty*, acts as the counterparty for each party to every transaction, and assumes all credit risk associated with each party. Option clearing houses will handle the process of option exercise.

In the United States, the *National Securities Clearing Corporation* (NSCC, a division of the Depository Trust and Clearing Corporation, described below), the successor to the combined clearing corporations of NYSE, AMEX, and NASD, is the major clearing agent for equity markets. NSCC serves as the clearing agent for these three major equity markets as well as for many bond markets. Its primary facility for clearing is the Securities Industry Automated Corporation (SIAC), which maintains the computer systems for clearing. Clearing houses clear and settle trades for most options, futures, and swap markets. The Board of Trade Clearing Corporation (BOTCC) clears and guarantees trades for the Chicago Board of Trade. All U.S. options exchange transactions are cleared through and guaranteed by the Options Clearing Corporation (OCC). The OCC clears transactions for options and futures on equity instruments, stock index contracts, currencies, and certain interest rate contracts as well as a number of contracts in other markets.

Confirmation is the first step of the clearing process. When trades are executed, buyers and sellers record trade details. Brokers and dealers receive confirmations that the trade has been executed and pass on details of the confirmation to clients. The typical confirmation document received by the client reports the security's name and CUSIP number (the security's nine-character alphanumeric identifier issued by the Committee on Uniform Security Identification Procedures), the number of units traded, the security price, and the broker commission and other fees, along with trade and settlement dates.

Trade comparison is the second step in the clearing process. Comparison matches counterparties in transactions. Trades are compared and are said to be cleared when the counterparties' records are identical. This happens for the vast majority of trades. *Out-trades* in futures markets or *DKs* (*don't knows*) in other markets, which are trade reports with discrepancies resulting from recording errors, misunderstanding, and fraud, are sent back to traders to resolve or reconcile.

The number of securities transactions that occurs each day is huge, requiring some sort of process to simplify the process of changing title to securities and moving corresponding cash proceeds between accounts. *Netting* is the simplification process used by clearing firms, and is one of the most important functions of the clearing process, and of the NSCC. Netting is the process of adding all of an institution's purchases of each security, adding the sales of each security, deducting sells from buys to determine the net change in holdings of that security for the institution and computing the net cash flows associated with all transactions. The NSCC uses an automated system through the Securities Industry Automation Corporation (SIAC) to "net down" or reduce the number of trading obligations that require financial settlement.[7] Since most brokerage firms execute large numbers of both buy and sell transactions for the securities that they trade, netting down results in only about 3% of the total reported matched or offsetting transactions actually having to be settled between financial institutions. At the end of the netting process, the NSCC delivers to each brokerage firm settlement instructions.

*Trade settlement* occurs when buyers receive their securities and when sellers receive payment for their securities. Stock ownership in most cases is evidenced by a certificate. The *Depository Trust & Clearing Corporation* (*DTCC*) holds stock certificates of member

[7]More generally, the SIAC, a subsidiary of the NYSE, runs the computer systems and communications networks on behalf of the NYSE and performs clearing functions on behalf of clearing firms.

firms, registering them in member names and maintaining computerized records of ownership and transfers.[8] As of year-end 2006, the DTCC was holding over 5.5 million stock certificates worth over $36 trillion and had processed over 8.5 billion transactions during the year. Overall, the DTCC settled more than $1.48 quadrillion in securities transactions in 2009, including equities, fixed income instruments, mutual funds, insurance products, and so on. Equity securities are held in street name, meaning that securities are held in the names of brokers (nominee names), who, in turn, maintain their own records of ownership in client accounts. Settlement of a trade is completed when the DTCC transfers the ownership of the shares from the selling firm to the buying firm in its automated book-entry recordkeeping system and transfers money between firms with net credits and net debits. Firms that have net credit after end-of-day netting are owed more by other brokers than they owe. The *National Securities Clearing Corporation* (NSCC) transfers money to banks of these net credit firms from accounts of brokers with net debits through the *Fedwire* system. Federal law requires that settlement occur within three days after the transaction. In addition, the DTCC provides cost basis information and other information services. The DTCC provides clearing services at a very low cost, averaging approximately $0.0000066 per share.

In the 1960s, securities clearing involved the physical transfer by messenger of paper securities and checks. However, by 1967, this system was failing. The *Depository Trust Corporation* (DTC) was set up in 1973 to handle the clearing business for the major stock exchanges. Since 1999, the DTCC has owned the Depository Trust Company and the National Securities Clearing Corporation. The DTCC also owns the Fixed Income Clearing Corporation and Deriv/SERV, LLC. The DTCC is owned by its customers, exchanges, and ECNs that clear through their facilities. The NSCC and the DTCC require brokerage firms to maintain collateral to ensure that they fulfill their obligations.

## 2.7 BROKERAGE OPERATIONS

Until 1975, brokerage firms in the United States functioned as a rather exclusive cartel, fixing commissions and offering clients a wide array of services ranging from providing trade executions and margin opportunities to offering advice and management services. Brokerage firms were all said to be full service, and included firms such as Merrill Lynch, E.F. Hutton, Paine Webber, and Smith Barney. The industry was forced by the federal government to break its cartel and compete with respect to brokerage commission levels. Numerous discount brokers opened operations, competing against full service brokers by offering trade executions with lower brokerage commissions. Discount brokers initiating operations in the 1970s included Quick & Reilly and Charles Schwab. The Internet's development in the 1990s and shortly afterwards created opportunities for Internet brokers such as Ameritrade, ScottTrade, and E-Trade to further reduce commissions and execute transactions for clients without actually speaking live with brokerage account representatives.

[8]In the case of direct registration systems such as dividend reinvestment plans, the issuing firm will place the security certificates with a transfer agent, which is normally a bank with an affiliate structured for this purpose.

Investors wishing to open broker accounts need to consider their trading needs and interests to properly select their brokers. Investors needing substantial advice and counsel along with other services may find their needs better fulfilled by full-service brokers such as Merrill Lynch, Raymond James, or UBS. In addition, there is some statistical evidence (discussed earlier) suggesting that larger full-service firms better provide for transaction price improvement (executing the client's transaction at a price that is better than the best bid or offering at the time of the transaction). Investors who are comfortable with their trading experience and who expect to execute smaller trades, particularly more frequent smaller trades, might prefer the lower commissions offered by an Internet broker such as ScottTrade or T.D. Ameritrade. These on-line brokers will often offer low flat-rate commissions, sometimes even dropping to zero, particularly when the brokerage firms receive payment for order flow.

J.D. Power and Associates regularly provides broker quality information based on its customer satisfaction surveys. Important evaluation criteria include commission levels, percentage of orders showing price improvement, frequency of limit order executions, margin and cash interest rates, and customer satisfaction. *Barrons* conducts similar surveys. Such surveys are useful in making broker-selection decisions.

Most stock orders in the United States are placed through stockbrokers who are compensated with commissions. These commissions are typically charged as a fraction of the dollar volume of the transaction and as a function of the number of shares associated with the order. In many instances, the broker's commission will be a function of the bid-ask spread; that is, the difference between the lowest price a trader is offering for the security and the highest price an investor is willing to bid for that security. OTC markets and particularly exchanges will provide for trading priority rules, which designate which orders will be filled or the sequence in which orders will be filled. Frequently, priority rules are designated according to transaction price, size, location of origination of order timing, and so on.

## 2.8 FIXED-INCOME SECURITIES AND MONEY MARKETS

In terms of dollar volume, the U.S. markets for debt instruments are larger than for any other type of security. Debt markets, including markets for mortgages, are more than twice as large as stock markets. Debt securities, sold for the purpose of raising capital, are IOUs issued by a variety of types of organizations, including federal, state, and local governments and their agencies, as well as by corporations and other institutions. A debt security represents a claim on the issuer for a fixed series of future payments. For example, a debt security might specify for its owner to receive a stated series of interest payments until the instrument matures. The instrument may also provide for principal repayment when the instrument matures. These securities are issued in *primary markets* and then traded in *secondary markets*, just as are other financial instruments. Debt securities will normally specify terms of payment, including amounts and dates, collateral and priority (who is to be paid first in the event of issuer financial distress). Among the various types of debt securities are bonds, notes, mortgages, and Treasury instruments. Many of the fixed income securities with shorter terms to maturity are considered to be money market instruments.

## U.S. Treasury Securities and Markets

The U.S. Treasury is the largest issuer of debt securities in the world. In 2010, the U.S. Treasury (technically, the Fed) auctioned $8.4 trillion in Treasury instruments. The federal government raises (borrows) money through the sale of U.S. Treasury issues including Treasury bills (T-Bills), Treasury notes, and Treasury bonds. By purchasing Treasury issues, an investor is loaning the government money. Notwithstanding the 2011 debt ceiling crisis, the U.S. federal government has proven to be an extremely reliable debtor (at least it has made good on all of its Treasury obligations). Treasury issues are fully backed by the full faith and credit of the U.S. government, which has substantial resources due to its ability to tax citizens, create money, and borrow more. Thus, these securities are generally expected to have the lowest default risk and should generally be safer than the safest of corporate bonds or short-term notes.

The Treasury obligations with the shortest terms to maturity are *Treasury bills*. They typically mature in less than one year (13, 26, or 52 weeks). These issues are sold as pure discount debt securities, meaning that their purchasers receive no explicit interest payments. Instead, investors purchase them at a discount from their maturity or face values. Such pure discount instruments are also known as zero-coupon issues.

One variation on the T-Bill issue is a so-called *STRIP*, issued through the U.S. Treasury's *Separate Trading of Registered Interest and Principal Securities* (STRIPS) program beginning in 1985. STRIPS are portfolios of single-payment instruments sold by the Treasury in blocks with varying maturities. For example, a single STRIP maturing at the end of five years from now would provide for a fixed payment at that time. Individual STRIPS sold in blocks can be "stripped" from the block and sold in secondary markets.

In addition to the short-term pure discount instrument issues discussed above, the Treasury also offers a number of longer-term coupon issues. For example, *Treasury notes* (T-Notes) have maturities ranging from 1 to 10 years and make semi-annual interest payments. Similarly, *Treasury bonds* (T-Bonds) typically range in maturity from 10 to 30 years and make semi-annual interest payments. These T-Bonds are frequently callable, meaning that the Treasury maintains an option to repurchase them from investors at a stated price. More than half the marketable Treasury debt outstanding as of 2000 was in the form of notes, while bills and bonds each represented about 20 percent.

The U.S. Treasury also offers nonmarketable issues such as *Series EE U.S. Savings Bonds*, *Series I U.S. Savings Bonds*, and *Series H U.S. Savings Bonds*. These savings bonds are normally issued only to individuals and cannot be traded among investors. Such issues are often subject to certain restrictions (such as a $5000 maximum level of Series EE purchases per year). These bonds can be purchased through most banks and savings institutions, and many businesses maintain plans through which their employees can purchase savings bonds through payroll deduction programs.

## Agency Issues

The U.S. federal government has created and sponsored a number of institutions known as *agencies*. These agencies enable the government to make funds available for a number of policy-related functions. Among the oldest of these agencies is the *Federal National*

*Mortgage Association* (FNMA or Fannie Mae), created in 1938 by the Federal Housing Administration (FHA) to expand the flow of money to housing markets during the Great Depression. This institution was intended to spur investment into real estate, improve employment during the depression, and to help enable people to purchase homes. The primary functions of Fannie Mae were to purchase, hold, and sell FHA-insured (and, after World War II, Veterans Administration–insured) mortgage loans originated by private lenders. Created with a congressional charter, and then privatized in 1968, FNMA was, until September 2008, one of the largest privately owned corporations in the United States with shares traded on the New York Stock Exchange and other security holders as well. However, the institution was taken over by the federal government during the financial crisis of 2008. The firm received a bail-out package from the federal government to support it until 2012.

FNMA facilitates capital acquisition in the mortgage industry through the creation of *mortgage-backed securities*, instruments denoting ownership in these pools of mortgages. Mortgage-backed securities are created by their sponsors who purchase residential mortgages from banks and thrift institutions and then create debt and other securities backed by pools of these mortgages. In effect, FNMA purchases the mortgage obligations held by banks and thrifts, repackages them as debt security portfolios, insures them, and re-sells them to the general public. The funds raised by the sale of these securities are then used to purchase additional mortgages from banks, increasing capital available to the mortgage and housing markets. These portfolios of mortgage-backed securities are also called *pass-through securities* because the interest and principal obligations associated with the mortgages are passed through to the security holders.

The *Government National Mortgage Association* (GNMA or Ginnie Mae), established by Congress in 1968 as a "spin-off" of FNMA, is a corporation owned by the U.S. federal government. GNMA guarantees mortgage-backed securities for the FHA (Federal Housing Administration), Veterans Administration (VA), and other agency mortgage issues. Many mortgages issued by these agencies are targeted towards particular groups such as lower-income or veteran families, and experience relatively high default rates. The mortgages issued by these agencies are *full faith and credit instruments*, meaning that the U.S. federal government backs them with its full ability to tax, borrow, and create money.

The *Federal Home Loan Mortgage Corporation* (FHLMC or Freddie Mac), a stockholder corporation created in 1970 by the federal government, also creates, insures, services, and sells pass-through securities related to single family and multifamily residential mortgages. Freddie Mac's creation was essentially to provide competition in the secondary mortgage market to the virtual monopoly enjoyed by Fannie Mae, thanks to federal protections enjoyed by Fannie Mae. Freddie Mac and Fannie Mae were intended to compete in a "separate but equal" regulatory framework. Freddie Mac was also placed in conservatorship by the federal government during the financial crisis of 2008–2009.

Another agency, the *Student Loan Marketing Association* (SLMA or Sallie Mae) creates, insures, and sells pass-through securities related to student loans. In addition, the company supports Section 529 education savings plans. While originally created as a government agency in 1972, the company began a privatization process in 1997 that was completed in 2004.

## Municipal Securities and Markets

The municipal securities markets owe much of their success to the U.S. federal taxation code that permits investors in municipal instruments to omit from their taxable income any interest payments received on these issues. Thus, interest received on municipal bonds need not be declared as part of income subject to federal income taxation. This feature makes municipal bonds more attractive to investors, particularly those in higher income tax brackets, enabling state and municipal issuers to offer these bonds at reduced interest rates.

Several types of municipal issues are offered by state and local governments. The first, so-called *general obligation bonds*, are full-faith and credit bonds. This means that the issuer backs the bonds to the fullest extent possible, given its assets and other obligations. However, municipal issuers usually lack the unlimited taxing and money creation abilities of the federal government. Thus, default risk analysis and ratings are important. *Limited obligation bonds* provide for the issue to be backed only by specific resources or assets. For example, a revenue bond may be backed only by the cash flows generated by a specific asset such as a toll bridge.

Most municipal issues are rated for default risk by private rating agencies such as *Fitch*. Some municipal issues are insured by private insurance institutions. This insurance is intended to reduce the default risk associated with the issue, and make them more attractive to investors. This reduced risk enables issuers to offer bonds with reduced interest rates to the public. Among the larger insurers of municipal bonds are the Ambac Financial Group, MBIA (formerly the American Municipal Bond Insurance Association), the Financial Guaranty Insurance Company (FGIC), and the Financial Security Assurance, Inc. (FSA). Collectively, these insurers are often known as "the Big Four."

## Financial Institution Instruments

Nongovernment financial institutions are obviously significant issuers and borrowers in the primary markets for debt instruments. For example, the *federal funds* markets allow banks and other depository institutions to borrow from one another to meet Federal Reserve requirements. Essentially, this market provides that excess reserves of one bank may be loaned to other banks for satisfaction of reserve requirements. The rate at which these loans are extended is referred to as the *federal funds rate*.

Normally, bank accounts are not regarded as marketable securities. One exception to this is the *negotiable certificates of deposit* (a type of jumbo CD). This is a tradable depository institution CD account with a denomination or balance exceeding $100,000. The amounts by which jumbo CDs exceed $250,000 are not subject to FDIC insurance. Negotiable CDs are often purchased by wealthy individual investors, financial institutions, corporate treasuries, and by *money market mutual funds*, which are created by banks and investment institutions for the purpose of pooling together depositor or investor funds.

*Banker's acceptances* are originated when a bank accepts responsibility for paying a client's loan or assuming some other financial responsibility on behalf of a client. Because the bank is likely to be regarded as a good credit risk, these acceptances are usually easily marketable as securities. *Repurchase agreements* (repos) are issued by financial institutions (usually securities firms) acknowledging the sale of assets and a subsequent agreement to repurchase at a higher price in the near term. This agreement is essentially the same as a collateralized short-term loan. The counterparty institution buying the securities with the agreement to resell them is said to be taking a *reverse repo*.

## Corporate Bonds and Markets

Corporations are also important issuers of debt securities. Large, well-known, credit-worthy firms needing to borrow for a short period of time may issue large denomination short-term notes frequently referred to as *commercial paper*. Well-developed markets exist for these short-term promissory notes. Firms requiring funds for longer periods of time may issue *corporate bonds*. These longer-term instruments are often issued with a variety of features, including callability, convertibility, sinking fund provisions, and so on. There are many different types of corporate bonds. The terms of the bond will be specified in a contract known as a *bond indenture*. In addition, firms may make bank commercial loans, although secondary markets for bank loans tend to be limited in size and scope.

*Callable bonds* can be *called* by the issuing institution at its option. This means that the issuing institution has the right to pay off the callable bond before its maturity date. The callable bond typically has a *call date* associated with it as well as a *call price*. The call date is the first date (and perhaps only date) that the bond can be repurchased by the issuing institution. The call price is normally set higher than the bond's par value and represents the price that the issuing institution agrees to pay the bond owners. Because the issuing institution retains the option to force early retirement of callable debt, the call provision can be expected to reduce the market value of the callable bond relative to otherwise comparable noncallable bonds.

*Convertible* bonds can be convertible by bondholders into equity or other securities. This normally means that the convertible bondholder has the right to exchange the convertible bond for a specified number of shares of common stock or some other security. The convertibility provision of such a bond enhances its value relative to otherwise comparable nonconvertible bonds.

*Debentures* are not backed by collateral. Many other bonds are either backed by collateral or have some other device such as *sinking fund* provisions to provide for additional safety for bondholders. One type of sinking fund provision has the issuing institution placing specified sums of money into a fund at specified dates that will be accumulated over time to ensure full satisfaction of the firm's obligation to bondholders. In some instances, sinking funds will be used to retire associated debt early. *Serial bonds* are issued in series with staggered maturity dates.

Many more innovative bonds have been offered in the market. *Floating rate* bonds have coupon rates that rise and fall with market interest rates; reverse floaters have coupon rates that move in the opposite direction of market interest rates. *Indexed bonds* have coupon rates that are tied to the price level of a particular commodity like oil or some other value such as the inflation rate. *Catastrophe bonds* make payments that depend on whether some disaster occurs, such as an earthquake in California or a hurricane in Florida. These catastrophe bonds provide a sort of insurance for issuers against the occurrence of the disaster. In some respects, purchasers of these bonds are providing insurance to the issuers.

The predecessor to the NYSE was established in 1792 as a venue for trading bonds. Since then, corporate and later municipal and Treasury bonds have been traded on organized exchanges and in the OTC markets, with the relative importance of these markets changing over time. While over 1000 bonds trade on "NYSE Bonds," the largest centralized corporate bond market in the United States, the majority of trades for corporate bonds occur in the OTC markets. FINRA TRACE (Trade Reporting and Compliance Engine) provides corporate bond trading data to the public, as all FINRA member broker/dealers are required to report OTC corporate bond transactions data to TRACE.

## Credit Ratings and Credit Agencies

Most publicly traded corporate bonds are rated by well-known agencies with respect to anticipated default risk. Corporations pay institutions such as Standard & Poor's and Moody's to rate the risk of their issues, although a few credit agencies still receive revenues from investor subscribers. Other U.S. rating agencies include Fitch, A.M. Best, Duff and Phelps (now merged into Fitch), Egan-Jones, and Dun and Bradstreet. Bonds without ratings assigned by these agencies can be very difficult to sell; in fact, many institutions face restrictions on purchasing bonds that are either unrated or have ratings below a given level. These constraints provide issuing companies with incentives to seek ratings from well-known agencies. In past years, particularly before the financial crisis of 2007–2009, reputations enjoyed by these rating agencies had generally been quite solid.[9] In fact, numerous international and federal government regulatory agencies including the SEC and the Fed sanction these agencies, and constrain or limit banks and other institutions' investment in low-rated instruments. For example, Basel II guidelines allow for "external credit assessment institutions" ratings for assessing bank risk. The SEC allows investment banks and broker-dealers to use credit ratings from "nationally recognized statistical rating organizations" such as the agencies listed above for similar purposes. In effect, rating agencies can serve as for-profit regulatory authorities. Federal regulatory agencies such as the FDIC can prohibit financial institutions from buying risky bonds, while credit agencies determine which bonds are risky. For example, federally chartered banks are often restricted from purchasing bonds with ratings below investment grade (BBB or higher are investment grade). Standard & Poor's and Moody's use the rating schemes depicted in Table 2.5. Other rating agencies use similar schemes.

While credit rating agencies have enjoyed many decades of strong reputation and success, many have struggled due to failures leading to the 2006–2008 U.S. housing crisis and the 2010/2011 European Union (EU) debt crisis. Many critics have argued that these agencies are often too slow in responding to dramatic shifts in market conditions and that traders are often much faster at responding to such shifts. For example, Enron bonds were

[9]Some credit rating agency reputations were marred during and after the 2007–2009 financial crisis by conflicts of interest and their apparent lack of response to the increased risk of rated issues. The problems were particularly acute with respect to mortgage-related instruments and instruments with derivative security characteristics. These conflicts and slow responses are discussed shortly here and in Chapter 12.

**TABLE 2.5** Standard & Poor's and Moody's Corporate Bond Ratings

| Description | Standard & Poor's | Moody's |
|---|---|---|
| Least likely to default | AAA | Aaa |
| High quality | AA | Aa |
| Medium-grade investment quality | A | A |
| Low-grade investment quality | BBB | Baa |
| High-grade speculative quality | BB | Ba |
| Speculative | B | B |
| Lower-grade speculative | CCC | Caa |
| Highly speculative | CC | Ca |
| Likely bankruptcy | C | C |
| Already in default | D | D |

rated triple-A by both major agencies until only a few days before the company filed for bankruptcy protection. The agencies also seemed to miss troubles brewing at WorldCom, Parmalat, and Delphi until just before their bankruptcy filings, as well as conditions leading to the 2006–2008 subprime crises. Orange County bonds were rated as investment grade until very shortly before its 1990s crisis was revealed. Nevertheless, bond rating agencies do play a crucial role in the evaluation of default risk.

Bonds rated BBB (or Baa) and higher are typically referred to as investment-grade bonds, while bonds below this level are considered speculative grade. Speculative-grade bonds are often called *junk bonds*. There is significant evidence that these bond ratings are highly correlated with incidence of default, suggesting that these agencies are least reasonably useful in forecasting default and indicating default risk. Furthermore, it is fairly unusual for ratings provided by these agencies to differ by more than one grade. Bond markets seem to agree with these statistical findings, pricing bonds such that their yields are strongly inversely correlated with bond ratings.

Bond rating agencies make extensive use of financial statement and ratio analysis to compute their ratings. Such analyses are frequently supplemented by statistical techniques such as *multidiscriminate analysis*, *probit*, and *logit* modeling. While their ratings in the past have been almost universally accepted in financial markets, even to the extent that numerous SEC, Federal Reserve, and other regulations have been based on these ratings, there have been problems with the ratings:

1. Many rating agencies are paid by the firms that issue debt instruments, creating potential conflicts of interest.
2. Rating services have provided consulting services to issuing firms, advising them on strategies to improve their ratings. However, such services have been restricted by Dodd-Frank legislation (see Chapter 4).

3. Credit agencies have been accused of strongarming clients and potential clients. For example, Moody's published an "unsolicited" rating of Hannover Re, a German re-insurance firm. It sent a letter to Hannover indicating that "it looked forward to the day Hannover would be willing to pay" (Klein, 2004). Hannover management refused payment, perhaps based on its paid use of two competing ratings agencies for its debt. Moody's continued to rate Hannover debt, which continued to pay. Over time, Moody's cut Hannover ratings to junk status, despite high ratings given by other agencies.
4. As mentioned above, rating agencies have missed major bond crises and other scenarios when bonds should have been downgraded.

## Eurocurrency Instruments and Markets

*Eurodollars* are freely convertible dollar-denominated time deposits outside the United States.[10] The banks may be non-U.S. banks, overseas branches of U.S. banks, or international banking facilities (not subject to reserve requirements). Eurodollar markets began after World War II when practically all currencies other than the U.S. dollar were perceived as unstable. Thus, most foreign trade between countries was denominated in U.S. dollars. However, the Soviet Union and Eastern European institutions were concerned that their dollars held in U.S. banks might be attached by U.S. residents in litigation with these countries. Thus, they dealt not with actual U.S. dollars, but merely denominated their debits and credits with dollars. Monies owed to them were simply offset by monies that they owed. In a sense, they dealt with "fake" eurodollars, but since their trading partners did also, and their accounts tended to "zero out" over time, this did not create significant problems. Their eurodollars were left in Western European banks. During the 1960s and 1970s, these markets thrived due to regulations imposed by the U.S. government such as Regulation Q (interest ceilings), Regulation M (reserve requirements), the Interest Equalization Tax imposed beginning in 1963 to tax interest payments on foreign debt sold in the United States, and restrictions placed on the use of domestic dollars outside the United States. More generally, eurocurrencies are loans or deposits denominated in currencies other than that of the country where the loan or deposit is created. Roughly 65% of eurocurrency loans are denominated in dollars.

Eurocredits (e.g., eurodollar credits) are bank loans denominated in currencies other than that of the country where the loan is extended. They are attractive due to very low interest rate spreads that are possible due to the large size of the loans and the lack of reserves, FDIC, and other requirements directly or indirectly affecting domestic loans and deposits. Their rates are generally tied to the LIBOR (London Interbank Offered Rate) and U.S. rates. Loan terms are usually less than five years, typically for six months. Eurocommercial paper comprises short-term (usually less than six months) notes issued by large, particularly "creditworthy" institutions. Most commercial paper is not underwritten. The notes are generally very liquid and most are denominated in dollars. Euro-medium-term notes (EMTNs), unlike eurobonds, are usually issued in installments. Again, most are not underwritten. Eurobonds are generally underwritten bearer bonds

[10]It is important to note that eurodollars and eurocurrencies are not euros, the currency used in the EU.

denominated in currencies other than that of the country where the loan is extended. Eurobonds often have call and sinking fund provisions as well as other features found in bonds publicly traded in U.S. markets.

Eurocommercial paper is the term given to short-term (usually less than six months) notes issued by large, particularly "creditworthy" institutions. Most commercial paper is not underwritten. The notes are generally very liquid (much more so than syndicated loans) and most are denominated in dollars. They are usually pure discount instruments. EMTNs are interest-bearing instruments usually issued in installments. Most are not underwritten. Eurobonds are generally underwritten bearer bonds denominated in currencies other than that of the country where the loan is extended. Eurobonds typically make annual coupon payments and often have call and sinking fund provisions.

## 2.9 MARKETS AROUND THE WORLD

As discussed above, the oldest continuously operating stock exchange is the Amsterdam Bourse, which first traded stock of the East Indies Trading Company, and now is part of the NYSE Euronext Group.[11] The NYSE started trading in the streets; the Paris Exchange, organized under Napoleon's regime, started on a bridge (Pont au Change); and the London stock market started in a tavern. Traditional brick-and-mortar exchanges since have been any one of three basic types. The first, the *public bourse*, is essentially a public institution, established by and operating under the authority of a government. However, most public bourses, including the Paris Bourse in 1990, have reorganized to become private bourses. The *private bourse*, such as the NYSE, is a private institution established by independent investors and institutions. The NYSE has evolved into a publicly traded stock institution, although it is still a private bourse in this context. These exchanges are still subject to governmental regulation. Finally, *bankers' bourses* exist where the primary dealers of securities are banks, and where commercial banking functions were not distinct from brokerage functions as was the case in the United States. In Germany, bankers' bourses have served banks who were also the primary stockbrokers.

As of early 2012, the largest stock markets in terms of monetary volume are in New York (NYSE and NASDAQ), Tokyo (TSE), and London (LSE). As of year-end 2010, the NYSE listed equities exceeding $13.39 trillion in market value (see Table 2.6). The NASDAQ and Tokyo Stock Exchanges each listed $3.8 trillion and the London Stock Exchange listed $3.6 trillion. The NYSE Euronext (Europe), with several exchanges in several countries, listed $2.9 trillion in equities and Shanghai listed $2.7 trillion.[12] The United States and United Kingdom (UK) have long histories of funding business with publicly traded equity securities, whereas commercial bank funding has played larger roles in Japan and Germany. This is one of the major reasons as to why the London stock markets are larger than those elsewhere in Europe, despite the relative small size of the UK economy relative to that of Europe.

[11]Some material in this section was adapted from Solnick (1991).

[12]Figures in this section and Table 2.6 are adapted from reports by the World Federation of Exchanges.

**TABLE 2.6** Major Exchanges of the World

| | Exchange | US$ BillionYear-end 2010 |
|---|---|---|
| 1 | NYSE Euronext (US) | 13,394 |
| 2 | NASDAQ OMX (US) | 3,889 |
| 3 | Tokyo Stock Exchange Group | 3,828 |
| 4 | London Stock Exchange Group | 3,613 |
| 5 | NYSE Euronext (Europe) | 2,930 |
| 6 | Shanghai Stock Exchange | 2,716 |
| 7 | Hong Kong Exchanges | 2,711 |
| 8 | TMX Group (Toronto) | 2,170 |
| 9 | Bombay SE | 1,632 |
| 10 | National Stock Exchange India | 1,597 |

Since 1974, China, India, and the Pacific region have produced the largest growth rates in equity markets as a percentage of world equity markets. The combined proportions of these markets as a percentage of world markets have grown from 16% to 39% by 2010 of world markets. Japan has been the most significant contributor to this figure. European equity markets as a percentage of the world total have increased from 22% to 26%. U.S. equity markets have remained fairly constant, declining from 57% to 55% of the world total.[13] Over this 37-year period, the world equity market has grown from less than $900 billion in 1974 to over $46 trillion as of 2011.

Reports from ING Baring Securities and the U.S. Census Bureau indicated that U.S. ownership of foreign stocks has increased from $41 billion in 1985 to $3.977 trillion in 2010.[14] This increased investment has been the product of a number of factors, including improved investing technology, reduced constraints on capital mobility, a greater appreciation for benefits of diversification, and a belief in the potential for higher returns from foreign investment. Historically, European and Japanese investors have maintained higher levels of international investment, but U.S. equity portfolios have significantly increased foreign holdings.

## 2.10 CURRENCY EXCHANGE AND MARKETS

For transactions to be executed between countries with different currencies, some type of foreign exchange (also called currency exchange, forex, or FX) must take place. Foreign exchange is simply the trading of one currency for another. For example, an American tourist in France can exchange her dollars for euros at an automated teller machine (ATM) in Paris.

[13]These percentage figures are estimates, drawn from somewhat different periods and sum to more than 100%.

[14]See the *Wall Street Journal*, May 28, 1996, p. R23, and U.S. Census Bureau, Table 1203, "U.S. Holdings of Foreign Stocks and Bonds by Country," 2011 Statistical Abstract.

Markets for foreign exchange are crucial for trade and the economies of most countries. The total monetary volume of foreign exchange markets is huge. The Bank for International Settlements, a major regulator and facilitator in markets for foreign exchange, estimated that the market for foreign exchange was approximately $1.2 trillion per day in 1996, growing to over $3.98 trillion daily by April 2011, making the exchange market the largest financial market in the world, larger than all world equity and bond markets combined.[15] Approximately $1.49 trillion of this volume involved spot contracts; the remainder involved forward, swap, and other derivative contracts. Almost two thirds of transactions involved counterparties trading from different countries.

Why exchange currencies? Obviously, currency exchange is needed in many international transactions for consumption and investment. For example, a Canadian automobile leasing firm purchasing a fleet of Japanese automobiles will pay the Japanese manufacturer in yen, which it purchases with Canadian dollars. In addition, investors speculate on exchange rates, buying those currencies that they believe will increase in value and selling those that they believe will decline in value. Some speculators will borrow money in low-interest rate economies and lend it in high-interest rate economies. Investors and companies exchange currencies to hedge their financial and business risks associated with international trade and financial transactions. Investors also exchange currencies to exploit *arbitrage* opportunities; that is, they buy currencies in markets where they are underpriced and sell them in markets where they are overpriced.

## Exchange Rates

*Exchange rates* denote the number of units of one currency that must be given up for one unit of a second currency. For example, the direct exchange rate of one dollar in terms of the South African rand might be SFR6, meaning that 6 rand are required to purchase one U.S. dollar. The indirect exchange rate is the inverse of the direct rate. Thus, if one U.S. dollar can be exchanged to purchase six South African rand, the direct exchange rate of rand for dollars is six. Correspondingly, the indirect exchange rate of dollars for rand is 0.1667; $0.1667 is the cost of one rand.

Foreign exchange rates are determined by supply and demand conditions. A variety of factors will affect these supply and demand conditions, including:

1. Government policies
2. Supply and demand conditions for commodities in the two countries
3. Income levels in the two countries
4. Interest rates in the two countries
5. The perceived risk of engaging in trade with the two countries

As of 2010, the most commonly traded currencies are the U.S. dollar (involved in 85% of all FX transactions), the EU euro (39%), the Japanese yen (19%), the UK pound (13%), and the Swiss franc (6%). The most common trading pair is the EUR/USD, representing approximately 28% of all FX transactions.

[15]Bank for International Settlements, "2010 Triennial Central Bank Survey."

TABLE 2.7 Cross Currency Rates, November 9, 2006

| | US $ | Ca $ | Euro | UK £ | Japan ¥ | Swiss Fr |
|---|---|---|---|---|---|---|
| US $ | 1 | 1.1317 | 0.7803 | 0.5256 | 118.27 | 1.2468 |
| Ca $ | 0.88363 | 1 | 0.68949 | 0.46443 | 104.50649 | 1.10171 |
| Euro | 1.28156 | 1.45034 | 1 | 0.67359 | 151.56991 | 1.59785 |
| UK £ | 1.90259 | 2.15316 | 1.48459 | 1 | 225.019 | 2.37215 |
| Japan ¥ | 0.00846 | 0.00957 | 0.0066 | 0.00444 | 1 | 0.01054 |
| Swiss Fr | 0.80205 | 0.90768 | 0.62584 | 0.42156 | 94.85884 | 1 |

### *Cross Rates*

Cross rates refer to the price of a currency other than the U.S. dollar in terms of the price of any other currency besides, again, the U.S. dollar. The Bretton Woods agreement following World War II provided that currencies would be pegged to the U.S. dollar. Thus, rates were normally expressed in dollars. Table 2.7 provides a listing of *cross rates* (the exchange rate or cost of one currency in terms of another) for several different major world currencies along with rates in dollars.

The price of the Swiss franc in terms of dollars is given in Table 2.7 to be \$0.80205. The price of a U.S. dollar in terms of the UK pound is £0.5256. These two rates imply that the price of a Swiss franc in terms of the UK pound is \$0.80205 × £.05256 = 0.42156, consistent with the cross rate given in Table 2.7.

## Forward Exchange Rates and Contracts

Exchange transactions can occur in either spot or forward markets. In the spot market, the exchange of one currency for another occurs when the agreement is made. For example, dollars may be exchanged for euros now in an agreement made now. This would be a spot market transaction. In a forward market transaction, the actual exchange of one currency for another actually occurs at a date later than that of the agreement. Thus, traders could agree now on an exchange rate for two currencies at a later date.

A forward exchange contract is a contract specifying delivery of one currency for another at a later date. Thus, a forward exchange contract is simply a contract providing for the exchange of currency at some future date. Forward exchange contracts involve one position in each of two currencies:

1. Long: An investor has a "long" position in that currency that she will accept at the later date.
2. Short: An investor has a "short" position in that currency that she must deliver in the exchange.

Forward exchange contracts will usually involve a third party to act as an intermediary between the exchange parties. This intermediary, generally a bank, is referred to as a market maker. The forward exchange rate, or forward rate, is the number of currency units that must be given up for one unit of a second currency at a later date. This rate may be quite different from the spot rate, which designates the number of currency units that must be exchanged for one unit of another currency now. Forward rates are likely to differ from spot rates simply because supply and demand conditions are likely to change over time. Thus, anticipated changes in the five factors listed above will cause forward rates to differ from spot rates.

There are a number of reasons for participating in forward exchange markets. Many investors participate for the purpose of speculation; they may feel that they know which directions exchange rates will change, and therefore, take positions in contracts enabling them to profit from anticipated changes. Such speculation is often regarded as quite risky. Corporations often take short positions in forward contracts to lock in exchange rates for the dates that they must deliver cash to companies in other countries. Corporations might take long or short positions in contracts to diminish their exchange rate risk. Corporations might take short positions in forward exchange contracts to lock in the exchange rates for foreign-denominated cash flows they anticipate receiving. A smaller group of investors, known as arbitrageurs, purchase forward contracts, and then invest in one of a variety of offsetting securities (including offsetting forward contracts) for the purpose of profiting from market price discrepancies.

Participants in forward exchange markets face a number of risks. Among these are:

1. Rate risk: Exchange rates may change in directions opposite to those anticipated by participants.
2. Credit risk: The other party to the contract may default by not delivering the currency specified in the contract. In many instances, an intermediary such as a large reputable commercial bank may act to ensure that one or both contracting parties will honor their agreements. Dealer reputation is key.
3. Liquidity risk: The market participant may have difficulty obtaining the currency he must deliver; he may be "stuck" with a currency that will be difficult to sell. Again, a number of intermediaries may improve liquidity by trading and making markets for various currencies.
4. Trading system risk: The trading platform, ECN, exchange, and other communication systems are all subject to malfunction or failure.

Because a forward rate specifies the prices investors will pay for currencies at a later date, one might expect that the prevailing forward rate of exchange equals the expected spot rate at the time of currency delivery:

$$F_0 = E[S_1] \tag{2.1}$$

Equation (2.1) states that the forward rate of exchange prevailing at time 0 equals the rate of exchange expected for time 1. Speculators will tend to force Equation (2.1) to hold, at least approximately, through their trading activity.

Forward markets can involve dealers executing individually negotiated transactions directly with one another through electronic trading systems or by telephone. Futures contracts are standardized transactions with standardized settlement dates on organized exchanges. While forward contracts frequently settle with delivery of the underlying asset, futures contracts typically provide for settlement by cash equivalence.

## Futures Markets

Futures contracts differ somewhat from forward contracts in that they are standardized and trade on exchanges, and typically provide for margin and marking to the market. That is, they are traded on exchanges such as the Chicago Board of Trade and the New York Mercantile Exchange. These exchanges and their associated clearing corporations eliminate much of the credit risk and some of the liquidity risk associated with futures contracts. Of course, the rate risk and other forms of risk remain. Standardization of contracts limits the numbers of contracts that can be created, thereby enhancing trader interest in those that do trade. In addition, government and exchange and brokerage houses require that futures traders maintain deposits (margin) to ensure that they will honor their obligations. Often, an investor must vary his margin, depending on the trading environment and the prices of the underlying currencies. This variance of margin, which increases as the value of the investor's obligation increases and decreases as the obligation decreases, is referred to as "marking to the market."

In the United States, a clearing house serves as the intermediary for all futures transactions. Technically, contract participants are all obligated to the clearing house to settle their contracts. Futures and options trading in the United States, including the trading of FX contracts, is regulated by the Commodities Futures Trading Commission (CFTC), which functions in a manner similar to the SEC. The forward markets, which generally include only well-known institutions, are self-regulated, and institutions that trade forward contracts are dependent on maintaining their reputations.

Futures and forward contracts are used for hedging and for speculation. Arbitrageurs help maintain an efficient pricing system by seeking situations where contracts and currencies are mispriced relative to one another. Businesses with foreign customers and suppliers frequently use futures contracts to hedge their exchange rate risk. For example, consider a Japanese firm ordering a communications system from an American manufacturer for $5,000,000 payable upon delivery in six months. The Japanese firm is obliged to pay in dollars, but has no control over the price of dollars in yen; thus, it faces the risk that the value of the dollar will increase from its current price of, say, ¥100 per dollar. Since most U.S. firms expect to be paid for their products with dollars, many foreign firms and individuals with this type of exchange rate risk would be discouraged from purchasing American products. However, there are a number of types of derivative securities to control this risk. For example, the Japanese firm could purchase in American markets put options (options to sell) on ¥500,000,000 with an exercise price of $0.01 per yen. This purchase of puts would guarantee the Japanese firm a minimum selling price for ¥500,000,000 needed to purchase $5,000,000. If the price of dollars were to decline, the Japanese would simply purchase the $5,000,000 in cash markets for fewer yen.

## Currency Trading

Professional currency traders participate in interbank and interdealer markets as well as exchange markets for various types of contracts on currencies. The most important currency trading centers are located in London, with about 37% of total volume; New York, 18%; Tokyo, 6%; and Frankfurt, Zurich, Hong Kong, and Singapore with somewhat less.

Note that the dispersion of markets implies that forex markets operate around the clock. Transactions can be executed between any two counterparties that agree to trade via the telephone or electronic network or trade through an exchange. To a large extent, currency trading is decentralized. Dealers can post or advertise their exchange rate bids and offers using an information or distribution network, such as Reuters and ICAP.

Many OTC trades proceed through a three-step process similar to the following:

1. A trader communicates by phone or electronically the currency pair and the amount he would like to trade with a given counterpart in trade.
2. The counterparty responds with both a bid and an ask quotation.
3. The trader responds to the bid and ask quotations by buying, selling, or passing on both.

The transaction is then executed if the trader agrees to buy or sell.

## Interdealer Brokers and Electronic Broking

The interbank forex markets comprise transactions directly between banks and through electronic brokering platforms. Interdealer brokers facilitate many of these transactions, as well as for those of other institutions. The largest, the UK-based ICAP Plc, is very active in both voice and electronic markets, averaging over $1.5 trillion daily in all of its brokering services.

FX dealers and certain other financial institutions are permitted to participate in the major electronic broking services. These services provide quotes, permit entry of quotes, and trade execution services. The largest of these with respect to forex trading is Electronic Broking Services (EBS), which was created as a joint venture of several of the world's major foreign exchange market–making banks, and then acquired by ICAP in 2006. It handles close to $200 billion daily in spot FX transactions as well as contracts for several commodities. Its chief competitor is Reuters Dealing 3000 Xtra, which is particularly active in sterling and Australian dollars. These services permit straight-through processing, improving speed of transactions and reduced errors.

## Futures and Other FX Markets

Currency and interest rate futures are traded on numerous exchanges throughout the world. Among the U.S. exchanges listing currency futures are the International Monetary Market (IMM), a subsidiary of the Chicago Mercantile Exchange (CME), the Philadelphia Board of Trade (PBOT), the new York Board of Trade (FINEX Division), and the MidAmerica Commodities Exchange (MIDAM). Non-U.S. exchanges trading currencies and currency futures include the London International Financial Futures Exchange (LIFFE, owned by NYSE Euronext), Euronext Paris, Eurex Frankfurt, the Singapore Stock Exchange (SGX), and the Tokyo Financial Exchange (TFX).

ECNs have made substantial headway in FX markets. For example, FXall's Accelor, fxdirect, and Hotspot FX were created for professional traders on the global FX markets. A sufficiently large and active ECN can enable institutional and individual traders to enter and trade at their own quotes, forgoing services provided by middleman dealers.

## Orders, Quotes, and Spreads

As noted above, the bid price is the maximum price a dealer is willing to pay for a currency and the ask or offer price is the minimum that she is willing to accept. Dealers typically quote both bid and offer prices, with offer prices normally somewhat higher. The difference between bid and offer prices is called the spread. Narrower spreads are usually seen in more competitive and efficient markets.

An example of a pair of bid and offer quotations on a pair of currencies, say euro/dollar, might be 0.8221/26. Here, the dealer is specifying a bid of EUR 0.8221 per dollar and an offer rate of EUR 0.8226. The spread in this example is 0.0005, or 5 basis points, sometimes called 5 pips. Interbank transactions on the order of $1 million typically quote spreads around 1 to 2 basis points while consumer exchange transactions spreads can be as high as 1000 basis points.

A variety of types of quotation types are used in the trading of currencies. Currency traders must become familiar also with the way that currencies are quoted in the particular environment in which they work. When a currency pair is quoted, the first currency or the denominator currency in the pair is typically called the base currency and the second or numerator currency is the counter or quote currency. In most quotations, the U.S. dollar is the base currency, and quotes are expressed in units of counter currency per USD (e.g., JPY/USD or CAD/USD). The normal exceptions to this convention are quotes involving the euro, the pound sterling, and the Australian dollar; these three are quoted as dollars per foreign currency. Other quotation conventions are as follows from the perspective of a U.S. trader:

1. Direct quotations (home price of foreign currency, e.g., $1.8000/£)
2. Indirect quotations (foreign price of home currency, e.g., £0.5556/$)
3. European quotations (price of USD, e.g., CHF1.8000/$)
4. American quotations (price of foreign currency, $0.5556/CHF). European quotes are more common except when trades involve the following currencies: $£_{UK}$, $\$_{AU}$, and $\$_{NZ}$.
5. Outright quotations are the price of a currency in the forward market quoted in terms of a second currency.
6. Point (or swap) quotations are quotations for a currency in forward markets in terms of the premium or discount relative to the spot price. Generally forward spreads exceed spot spreads due to higher uncertainty in forward markets.
7. Forward quotations are often made in percentage terms as follows:
   a. Forward premium or discount as a percent per annum (European terms):

$$[(\text{Spot rate} - \text{Forward rate}) \div \text{Forward rate}] \times 1200/n$$

   b. Forward premium or discount as a percent per annum (American terms):

$$[(\text{Forward rate} - \text{Spot rate}) \div \text{Spot rate}] \times 1200/n$$

8. Cross rates refer to quotations not involving the dollar. These quotations are primarily an artifact of the Bretton Woods system.
9. Eurodollar futures quotation: Stated as an index of the three-month LIBOR:

$$F = 100 - \text{LIBOR}$$

With the exception of the Japanese yen, currency quotations are expressed to four digits. As we mentioned above, the last of these four digits is referred to as a basis point, pip, or percentage in point. The yen is quoted in hundredths (e.g., JPY/USD = ¥120.07/$).

## Additional Reading

Harris (2003), Chapters 1 to 8, provides a nicely detailed introduction to securities and markets and Chapters 13 to 18 will be very useful for understanding market mechanisms and trading institutions. Schwartz (1988) provides a somewhat dated but very readable discussion focused on equity markets in Chapters 1 to 15. The NYSE website (http://www.nyse.com/), through its "About Us" and "Education" links, offered the latest developments on trading NYSE securities. Other exchanges have similar sites. The World Federation of Exchanges provided much useful information and data concerning exchanges at http://www.world-exchanges.org. Morris (2009) provides a detailed discussion of the clearing and settlement processes.

## References

Bakos, Y., Lucas, H. C., Jr., Simon, G., Viswanathan, S., Oh, W., & Weber, B. (2000). *The impact of electronic commerce on the retail brokerage industry*. Working Paper. New York: New York University.

Battalio, R., Greene, J., & Jennings, J. (1997). Do competing specialists and preferencing dealers affect market quality? *Review of Financial Studies, 10*, 969–993.

Battalio, R. J., Hatch, B., & Jennings, R. (2004). Does a national market system exist for U.S. exchange-listed equity options? *Journal of Finance, 59*, 933–962.

Breedon, F., & Holland, A. (1997). *Electronic versus open outcry markets: The case of the bund futures contract.* Working Paper. Bank of England.

Cavaletti, C. (1997). Commission rate ride. *Futures, 26*(12), 68–70.

Degryse, H., van Achter, M., & Wuyts, G. (2009). Dynamic order submission strategies with competition between a dealer market and a crossing network. *Journal of Financial Economics, 91*, 319–338.

Frino, A., Hill, A. M., Jarnecic, E., & Aitken, M. (2004). The impact of electronic trading on bid-ask spreads: Evidence from futures markets in Hong Kong, London and Sydney. *Journal of Futures Markets, 24*, 675–696.

Harris, L. (2003). *Trading and exchanges: Market microstructure for practitioners*. Oxford: Oxford University Press.

Klein, A. (2004). Credit raters' power leads to abuses, some borrowers say. *Washington Post*A01 <http://www.washingtonpost.com/wp-dyn/articles/A8032-2004Nov23.html>

Morris, V. B. (2009). *Guide to clearance & settlement*. New York: Lightbulb Press.

Pirrong, S. C. (1996). Liquidity and depth on open outcry and automated exchanges: A comparison of the LIFFE and DTB bund contracts. *Journal of Futures Markets, 15*(5), 519–543.

Sarkar, A., & Tozzi, M. (1998). Electronic Trading on Futures Exchanges. Federal Reserve Bank of New York *Current Issues in Economics and Finance 4*, no. 1 (January).

Schwartz, R. A. (1988). *Equity markets: Structure, trading and performance.* New York: Harper and Row Publishers.

Securities and Exchange Commission. (1998). Regulation of exchanges and alternative trading systems. Release Number 34-40760. December 8.

Shyy, G., & Lee, J. (1995). Price transmission and information asymmetry in bund futures markets: LIFFE vs. DTB. *Journal of Futures Markets, 15*, 87–99.

Solnick, B. (1991). *International investments* (2nd ed.). Addison-Wesley.

Stigler, G. (1961). The economics of information. *Journal of Political Economy, 49*, 213–225.

Weber, J. (2007). Behind the burst of the bourses. *Business Week*59.

# 2.11 EXERCISES

1. For a 20-year period beginning in 1986, the NYSE was regularly criticized for making less use of electronic and computer technology than most of its competitors around the

world, even less than exchanges in emerging and developing countries and than exchanges just starting business. The NYSE would argue that its specialist system required more "face-to-face" contact than other nonspecialist exchanges.

   **a.** Why would the NYSE specialist system require more face-to-face contact than its competitors?

   **b.** Assume that face-to-face contact hurt investors more through increased trading expenses and reduced trading efficiency than it helped them. That is, assume that the argument that you prepared for part (a) is simply wrong. Why might the NYSE still resist adopting improved electronic and computer technology?

**2.** How does a stop order differ from a limit order?

**3.** Exactly what does an investor expect from her broker when she places a stop limit order with a stop price to buy at 50 and a limit price of 50.10? Why might an investor place such an order?

**4.** Suppose that the Swiss franc is currently trading at 2 per U.S. dollar. The franc is expected to be revalued to CHF2.5 per dollar.

   **a.** Has the franc been devalued relative to the dollar?

   **b.** Has the dollar been devalued relative to the franc?

   **c.** What is the percentage anticipated revaluation of the franc relative to the dollar?

   **d.** What is the percentage anticipated revaluation of the dollar relative to the franc?

**5.** Assume that \$1 will purchase £0.60 and ¥108; that is, one U.S. dollar will purchase 0.6 UK pounds and 108 Japanese yen. Assume that goods in the three countries are identically priced after adjusting for currency exchange rates.

   **a.** What is the value of £1 in ¥?

   **b.** What is the value of ¥1 in £?

   **c.** If one ounce of gold costs \$1500 in the United States, what is its cost in the UK and in Japan?

CHAPTER

# 3

# Institutional Trading

## 3.1 INSTITUTIONS AND MARKET IMPACT

Institutions today own the bulk of securities traded in today's marketplace and execute the majority of trades. The Boston Consulting Group (2010) estimated that institutions managed roughly $52.1 trillion in 2009 for tens of millions of clients. Among these institutional investors are buy-side institutions such as mutual funds, pension funds, life insurance companies, trust departments of banks, and investment companies. Institutional investor transactions are frequently executed by professional traders, either as employees of the institutions or acting as their agents, and these transactions provide opportunities and risks for other traders. Institutional transactions also have important effects on security liquidity, prices, and volatility. Institutional investors play crucial and varied roles in markets and are behind conditions that affect every trader. For example, stocks with the largest proportional institutional ownership experience the most volatile swings when the market is most volatile.[1] Why is this? Is it because institutions invest in larger blocks of shares and their transactions push the market more than noninstitutional shareholders? Are institutional shareholders more informed than other traders? Regardless, understanding the link between institutional trading and security behavior is important to the trader. We will discuss such issues in this and in later chapters.

We introduced buy and sell sides of the market in Chapter 1. In this and the next two sections, we will discuss buy-side institutions before turning our attention to sell-side institutions. On the buy side, we start with the *investment company*, which is an institution that accepts funds from investors for the purpose of investing on their behalf. The investment company is compensated with fees, typically based on some combination of performance and investment portfolio size. Clients expect that the investment company will provide professional and competent management services and pass on cost advantages resulting from economies of scale. These cost advantages include reduced transactions costs and managerial costs. In addition, these scale advantages provide for more efficient

[1]See Gompers and Metrick (2001) and Dennis and Strickland (2002).

record keeping and enable improved diversification. There are a number of different types of investment companies that register with the Securities and Exchange Commission (SEC) and operate under SEC oversight. In addition, there are a variety of unregistered investment companies. We will discuss many of these shortly.

As we mentioned above, institutional traders can have dramatic impacts on security prices. Obviously, large block orders will result in dramatic price reactions. But how large will these reactions be, and what other factors will affect these reactions? Which types of institutional transactions will have the most significant price impacts? For example, numerous studies, including Kraus and Stoll (1972) and Saar (2001) have documented asymmetric reaction to block trades. In particular, institutional block buy orders result in a much larger upward effect than the downward effect caused by otherwise comparable institutional sell orders. This raises an interesting question: Why are institutional buys associated with significantly larger price impacts than institutional sells? Arguments offered by Chan and Lakonishok (1993) and Saar (2001) suggest that buy orders convey more information than sell orders because:

1. Liquidity needs drive many sales.
2. Most institutions have a much larger pool of stocks from which to buy than to sell.
3. Mutual funds are reluctant to short sell, so that they focus their research efforts on shares that they might buy and might serve as good diversification mechanisms.
5. Mutual funds cannot borrow to invest, so that they have to be particularly selective in their purchases.

Thus, if one or more of these observations are correct, there should be more information content in institutional stock purchases than stock sells, and price changes will react accordingly to institutional transactions. We will focus more on the market impact of institutional transactions later in this chapter and in Chapter 5.

## 3.2 REGISTERED INVESTMENT COMPANIES

The buy-side institutions that execute the largest volume of transactions have an enormous impact on trading for all market participants. Among the most significant of these managed investment institutions are the registered investment companies, which are required to register with the Securities and Exchange Commission (SEC) under the *Investment Company Act of 1940*. Such companies include mutual funds, unit investment trusts, and real estate investment trusts (REITs). Investment companies manage assets on behalf of clients. Managed assets usually include, but are not limited to, publicly traded financial securities such as shares of stock, bonds, and derivative instruments.

### Managed Investment Company Types

One type of managed investment company is the *closed-end investment company*, which is a corporation that issues a specified number of shares that can be traded in secondary markets such as the New York Stock Exchange. One might purchase shares through a brokerage firm. *Open-end investment companies*, typically known as *mutual funds*, frequently accept additional funds directly from investors and are willing to repurchase or redeem outstanding shares. An investor buys into a mutual fund by purchasing shares from the fund and cashes out by redeeming those shares.

The major markets in which mutual funds operate are equities, fixed income, money markets and commodities and foreign exchange markets. Fixed income funds seek to provide stable interest income for their investors. One type of income fund, the high-yield fund, seeks to provide higher income by investing in a diverse portfolio of higher-risk, higher-return (junk) bonds. Municipal bond funds purchase tax-free state and local government bonds for their investors. These funds are particularly attractive to investors in high income-tax brackets. Money market funds seek to maintain safety and liquidity for their investors, focusing their investments in short-term, highly liquid, and safe debt instruments. Such investments include U.S. Treasury bills and bonds, GNMA, FNMA, and other federal government agency issues, bank issues such as repurchase agreements and corporate issues such as commercial paper. Stock funds might be categorized according to their objectives or types of stock that they may invest in. Among the categories of stock funds are aggressive growth funds, growth funds, income funds, balanced funds, global funds, and emerging markets funds. Some larger fund management companies like Fidelity, Dreyfus, Vanguard, and T. Rowe Price manage entire families of funds with a wide variety of investment objectives ranging from aggressive growth to generating tax-free income. Commodity funds enable investors to take focused or diversified positions in a variety of commodities such as oil, gold, and agricultural products, and foreign exchange funds enable investors to take positions in the currencies and instruments of other countries.

Index funds such as those in the Vanguard family have increased in popularity in recent years. These funds employ a passive management technique where managers simply attempt to maintain a fund composition matching a particular market index (basket of stocks or other instruments) rather than attempt to "out-guess" the market. The passive management technique is also intended to keep fund management expenses low because the index strategy does not require hiring securities analysts to pick stocks in an effort to outperform the market. In addition, these funds provide investors with opportunities to achieve broad diversification at a low cost. As of April 2006, total market capitalization of index funds was approximately $1 trillion, representing approximately 17% of the total equity fund market. The share of the exchange-traded funds (ETFs) was approximately $430 billion.

## Managed Investment Company Fees and Structures

Mutual funds that accept investments directly from investors without a sales charge are called *no-load* funds; investors buy and sell funds at *net asset value*. An investor buys into a mutual fund by paying for her shares exactly the value of her proportional ownership of the fund's investments, computed at the end of the transaction date, without a sales fee or commission. Institutions that charge a sales fee are called *load* funds. The loads may be imposed when investors buy into a fund (*front-end load*), sell out of a fund (*back-end load* or redemption fee), or a combination of both. An investor should be aware that fund performance computations are frequently overstated because returns are usually calculated only on the investment net of fees. In addition, load charge percentages are generally understated in that the loads are determined as a fraction of the amount invested in the fund in addition to any loads charged.

A number of funds adopt a 12b-1 plan that enables them to use fund assets to market their shares. Such 12b-1 expenses are often included with the sum of administrative expenses when computing annual expense ratios. Funds are permitted by the SEC to call themselves no-load funds even if they charge an annual 12b-1 fee, as long as the amount is less than 0.25% of the invested amount per year. The 12b-1 fee in effect enables the fund to impose its marketing costs on investors without reporting them as loads. In addition to potential load and 12b-1 fees, both load and no-load funds normally impose an annual management fee. These fees cover management compensation and various periodic administrative expenses.

A managed investment company such as a mutual fund maintains a board of directors to oversee its operations, but normally does not have managers and employees, at least not in significant numbers. Most managed investment companies retain a separate *management company* or *advisor* to actually manage the fund's assets in accordance with the fund's prospectus. The advisor will typically hire analysts and fund managers and will pay the following types of institutions to perform certain important functions:

*Custodian*: Holds the fund assets on behalf of shareholders.
*Transfer agent*: Processes orders to purchase and redeem shares of the fund and maintains customer records. The NSCC (see Chapter 2) processes and clears most mutual funds that involve brokers and dealers.
*Distributor*: Markets shares of the fund through various channels.

Shareholders of management companies incur management fees, miscellaneous administrative expenses, and often other costs as well.

## ETFs

*Exchange-traded funds* (*ETFs*) are funds whose shares trade on exchanges. The first was the *S&P Depository Receipt* (*SPDR* or "Spider," ticker SPY) sponsored by State Street Bank and the Merrill Lynch Investment Company. The Spider fund is intended to mimic performance of the S&P 500 Index by maintaining the same portfolio of securities as is comprised by the index.

Unlike the case with most mutual funds, investors can trade shares of ETFs throughout the day at market prices that vary as the market index varies. Hence, investors can more easily trade the market portfolio throughout the day rather than have to wait for closing net asset values (NAVs) as is required for trading mutual funds. This ease of trading facilitates creation of options and other derivative contracts on the indices, which do not normally exist on mutual funds. Additionally, because an ETF is not actively managed, investors can benefit from low management expenses. On the other hand, investors typically will have to pay brokerage expenses to trade the fund and will be faced with a bid–offer spread, potentially increasing transaction costs. Some ETFs are leveraged and investors might have the opportunity to purchase ETFs on margin or even to short sell them. Most mutual funds cannot provide these opportunities.

ETFs are created by placing assets such as stocks or total return swap contracts into a trust.[2] Shares of this trust are issued and listed on an exchange in the form of ETFs. Thus, the trust underlying SPDR contracts is comprised of a portfolio of individual stocks that replicates the S&P 500. On the other hand, bear funds such as the *Short S&P 500 ProShares* (ticker SH), created to enable investors to easily short the market index, are comprised of a combination of short positions in shares of stock and short positions in swap contracts involving shares. *Ultra ETFs* (bull funds) are created to enable investors to easily leverage their investments in an index. For example, the *Ultra S&P 500 ProShares* (ticker SSO) invests in combinations of shares of stock along with long positions in shares in swap contracts to leverage its position in the market index. Funds that double leverage (2x) or triple leverage (3x) are most common among bull funds, but funds are available with as much as 50x leverage.

Other well-known ETFs include *DIA* "Diamonds" that mimic the Dow Jones Industrial Average, *QQQ* that mimics that NASDAQ 100, and a number of narrower sector and industry funds such as the *i-shares energy sector* that mimics the portfolio of Dow Jones Energy companies. These funds all provide investors opportunities to trade large or important small segments of the market and to hedge risks associated with these segments.

While different in structure from ETFs and index funds, unit investment trusts have been created to replicate indices. For example, *Diamonds* are shares of the Diamonds Trust created to replicate the Dow Jones Industrial Average (DJIA) and to sell on the former American Stock Exchange (ASE).[3] *Spiders* (Standard & Poors Depository Receipts) track the S&P 500, *Midcap Spiders* track the S&P Midcap 400 Index, and *Webs*, which track the Morgan Stanley world equity benchmark indices, were also created to trade on the ASE. Combined, these four products accounted for approximately 15% of ASE volume prior to its acquisition by the NYSE. The "Dogs of the Dow" track the 10 DJIA stocks with the highest dividend yields, and are represented by their own trust. Although each of these trusts are designed to track a particular index, their shares are often more volatile than the index itself. One explanation for this volatility is that there is substantial trading volume when the market swings. This possible explanation is interesting in that it might suggest that traders' activities tend to increase market volatility.

## 3.3 UNREGISTERED INVESTMENT COMPANIES

As we discussed, registered asset managers such as mutual funds provide investment services for tens of millions of clients, functioning under the regulatory authority of the

[2]Total return swap normally provide for one party to swap cash flows associated with a particular basket of securities for cash flows associated with an interest rate instrument. Thus, for example, a swap can provide for the exchange of profits or losses on a stock market index for cash flows realized from a treasury instrument. Sometimes, funds will substitute options, forward, futures, and reverse repo agreements for swap contracts to create leverage.

[3]Now the ASE is part of the NYSE.

SEC. But there are many asset managers that are not required to register as registered investment companies. For example, pension funds and private equity management firms are not required to register with the SEC as public investment companies. Pension fund clients cannot trade their fund investments. *Private equity* firms are alternative professionally managed equity investments in unregistered securities issued by public and private firms. Investments in private equity firms are often tightly restricted by their managers, in part, to avoid SEC reporting requirements for registered investment companies. Other unregistered asset managers include banks, bank trusts, foundations, endowments, and insurance companies. All of these institutions are important buy-side securities traders.

## Pension Funds

*Pension funds* are established by employers to facilitate and organize the investment of employees' retirement funds. *Defined benefit plans* specify payments that employees will receive when they retire and *defined contribution plans* define employer and employee contributions, but actual benefits depend on fund investment performance. In most cases, investment horizons for pension funds are long term. Many pension funds are large enough to afford more sophisticated investment techniques and managers. Pension funds in sum hold over $20 trillion in assets for their beneficiaries. More than half of working Americans participate in pension plans, representing very diverse ownership structure somewhat representative of the U.S. population. Regulators, in part due to the Employee Retirement and Security Act of 1974 (ERISA), tend to discourage pension plans from taking imprudent risks. Nevertheless, many pension funds, particularly defined benefit plans, have been criticized for being underfunded and not providing adequate capital to secure their employees' retirements (see, for example, Kwan, 2003). The Pension Benefit Guarantee Corporation, a federal corporation created by the ERISA, provides limited protection for the pensions of nearly 44 million American workers and retirees in over 30,000 private, single-employer and multiemployer, defined-benefit pension plans.

## Bank Trusts and Private Banking

Banks also provide professional asset management services, including trust management for clients. Trusts are legal entities or vehicles for enabling settlors or grantors (entities that set aside assets in trusts on behalf of beneficiaries such as heirs, charities, and others) to accomplish various financial goals. Banks in their roles as trustees or asset managers actively manage trusts on behalf of grantors and their beneficiaries. Most banks maintain trust departments to serve as trustees or perform services on behalf of trustees.

Private banking refers to financial services such as banking and investment management services provided by banks to private high-net-worth clients. Private banking services offered by major banks such as Citigroup, HSBC, Bank of America (U.S. Trust), and Wells Fargo have frequently been particularly lucrative. These personalized services tend to be rather broad-based and banks strive to provide their clients the greatest confidentiality. Private banking services frequently include specialized financing solutions to complex problems, as well as retirement and estate planning. These operations contribute to banks' trading operations.

## Private Equity

Private equity refers to asset managers who make equity investments in companies that are not publicly traded. Private equity markets provide funding for start-up firms, private middle-market firms ($25 million to $500 million in sales), management buyouts (MBOs), leveraged buyouts (LBOs), firms in financial distress, and public firms seeking buyout financing. Traditionally, private equity ownership is not publicly traded (there are a few exceptions), not liquid, and exempt from SEC registration requirements. Private equity firms frequently take active monitoring, management, and advising roles in their portfolio firms. There are a variety of types of private equity firms, ranging from venture capital (VC) firms to hedge funds.

## Hedge Funds

*Hedge funds* are unregistered private funds that allow investors to pool their investment assets. To avoid SEC registration and regulations, hedge funds usually only accept funds from small numbers (often less than 100) of *accredited* investors, typically high-net-worth individuals and institutions. Because most hedge funds have only a small number of managers, they typically focus their investment strategies on the expertise of a few key managers. Many hedge funds seek investment opportunities or niches where larger institutions are prohibited or constrained due to regulatory restrictions. For example, because many banks, pension funds, and other institutions cannot focus activities in the securities of distressed corporations facing reorganization or bankruptcy, some hedge funds will specialize in such investments. Other funds may specialize in short sales and derivatives to hedge against market downturns and others will simply focus on searches for arbitrage opportunities. Hedge fund managers typically take a proportion of assets invested (2% is a norm) and another portion of profits (20% is typical) as compensation. While hedge funds are frequently able to report results that beat the market, investors should realize that performance results do not usually include the last several months of a hedge fund's existence, which is when a fund is most likely to fail. The point here is that while the risky strategies employed by many hedge fund managers can consistently produce strong returns over long periods, many lose large sums and close down in remarkably short periods following long periods of success. Sixty consecutive months of market-beating returns followed by a single month with a return of −100% is obviously a disaster for investors. For example, consider the long-running successes of Long Term Capital Management and Amaranth, after which both suffered spectacular meltdowns (see Hosking, 2006).

## Rule 144A Markets

Rule 144A markets are specifically created for institutional traders to trade unregistered securities. The SEC adopted Rule 144A in 1990 as an amendment to the Securities Act of 1933 to set forth rules and conditions for the trading of unregistered securities. Most securities issued under Rule 144A are by public firms needing to avoid the reporting requirements and delays associated with registered offerings. In addition, some are foreign and private firms also seeking to avoid SEC reporting and registration requirements. Only "qualified institutional buyers" (QIBs: institutions with investment portfolios exceeding $100 million) can purchase securities in a Rule 144A offering. Obviously, this significantly limits the number of potential investors of these securities. Purchasers of Rule 144A offerings are restricted with respect to when and to whom they resell 144A securities. In addition, companies may have no more than 499 qualified institutional investors to retain their 144A status.

In August 2007, the NASDAQ Stock Market, Inc. announced that the SEC approved its centralized trading and negotiation system for 144A securities. This automated Web-based trading platform was developed from its 17-year-old PORTAL system. Other 144A trading platform systems and companies have included the Zealous Alternative Trading System (ZATS), the New York Private Placement Exchange (NYPPEX), the Goldman Sachs Tradable Unregistered Equity system (GSTrUE), and the Open Platform for Unregistered Securities (OPUS-5). The GSTrUE OTC program was, in part, created to sell shares of Oaktree Capital Management, LLC, a private equity firm. Oaktree, like other alternative management firms Blackstone and Fortress, prefers to operate under regulatory "radars" and with a significant degree of confidentiality. 144A trading markets give firms like these and other smaller firms opportunities to obtain public funding without SEC scrutiny, paperwork, and related delays.

## 3.4 BEST EXECUTION, EXECUTION COSTS, AND PRICE IMPROVEMENT

"*Best execution* refers to traders receiving the most favorable terms available for their trades" (Macey and O'Hara, 1997). Brokers have a responsibility to provide their clients best execution. Unfortunately, because many factors are needed to define the most favorable terms, best execution is not an easy concept to quantify, evaluate, or enforce. Suppose, for example, that the best quotes are available in one market, but trades are more likely to execute between quotes in another market. Which market will provide for the best execution? What if one market normally executes at a better price than another market, but takes longer with more risk? Regardless, execution costs are an important factor in evaluating best execution. Execution costs might be considered to be the sum of (1) order processing costs and (2) market impact costs.

Measuring *order processing costs* is normally fairly straightforward. These costs will normally include brokerage fees, which might account for other processing costs as brokers normally provide these services as well. However, *market impact* or slippage costs measurement is more problematic. The price or market impact of a transaction, the effect that a given transaction has on the market price of a security, is particularly important for a large transaction or in an illiquid market. When institutions execute large transactions, their buy or sell activities affect security prices, typically in a manner that increases execution costs. While substantial, especially for large orders, these costs are not explicit, and might be considered hidden.

### Spreads

Investors, particularly more active institutional investment managers need to track execution quality to measure the trading performance of their investment brokers. Brokerage firms have traditionally used bid–offer spreads as a basis for charging commissions to their customers. That is, buyers frequently bought at the offer and sellers sold at the bid, with brokers pocketing the difference (spread) as their commission. This tradition is one reason that spreads are an important factor for gauging transaction costs. While this commission model has changed somewhat in most markets, many studies concerned with execution costs have used the *quoted spread* (offer minus bid) or *half-spread* (quoted spread/2) to measure execution costs. However, when transactions are executed inside spreads, these measures can overstate execution costs (Macey and O'Hara, 1997). In this case, the *effective half-spread*, the difference between the actual transaction price and the mid-point of the spread may be a more accurate measure of the cost of the transaction. However, none of these measures are likely to capture the *market impact* of a transaction, often referred to as *slippage*. That is, each transaction is likely to force the price in some direction, upwards for purchases and downwards for sales. This is the market impact of the transaction. The *realized half-spread* is the difference between the security price at some future point in time and either the bid or offer quote. Suppose that the realized half-spread is computed as the difference between a subsequent transaction price and the bid quote. Then the price impact of the transaction on the subsequent transaction is captured as an execution cost for the relevant transaction. This realized half-spread might be particularly relevant when the transaction was executed as part of a series of transactions. The *perfect foresight half-spread* is the absolute value of the difference between some future price and the trade price. Here, the assumption is that the subsequent or future price is the fundamental value of the security and the prior price reflects the price impact of the transaction. Again, this perfect foresight half-spread is relevant to the trader if the trade was part of a series of trades.

Some efforts at measuring market impact have focused on examining prices of consecutive transactions. For example, what if we want to see how a series of our 80 buy orders for a stock in one day have impacted the price of that security? Presumably, each of our buy executions moved or could have moved the security price. An analysis of this series of trades with associated volumes might indicate the relationship between order sizes and market impact. We might be able to use a regression analysis of price changes on transaction sizes to infer a relationship between security price movements and transaction sizes. We might be able to improve this understanding by adding appropriate control variables to the regression analysis. We will discuss such relationships in the next section.

Numerous academic and regulatory studies have compared execution costs of different markets. Many older studies (e.g., Huang and Stoll, 1996) found that execution costs on NASDAQ were substantially higher than on the NYSE and that other equity markets did not compare favorably to the NYSE. Christie and Huang (1994) found that NYSE effective half-spreads averaged 7.9 cents compared to 18.7 cents on NASDAQ and that trading costs fall for firms that switch listings from the NASDAQ to either the AMEX or the NYSE. Similarly, Huang and Stoll (1995) found that 26.7% of trades on the NASDAQ were inside the spread, compared to 37.9% of trades on the NYSE. Thus, NYSE transactions were more likely to exhibit price improvement.

Price improvement occurs when an order is executed a price better than the prevailing bid or offer. Exchange specialists and market makers had or have an exchange responsibility to seek to improve markets for securities that they trade. Price improvement typically occurs when a specialist or market maker allows market orders to execute inside the spread, either by improving their quotes or by allowing market orders to execute against other submitted market orders inside the spread.

## Illustration: Slippage and the Perfect Foresight Half Spread

Table 3.1 depicts a series of 20 historical transaction prices that the brokerage firm paid for a given stock's purchases. Table 3.1 also depicts subsequent transaction prices, from which perfect foresight half-spreads are computed. The sizes of the purchases follow, so that the broker can analyze the relationship between the perfect foresight half-spread and the transaction size based on 20 of the broker's own purchase transactions for the same stock. For example, the first transaction has the broker purchasing 1000 shares for $50.00.

**TABLE 3.1** Transaction Size and Slippage

| Purchase | Purchase Price | Subsequent Transaction Price | Perfect Foresight Half-Spread | Transaction Size |
|---|---|---|---|---|
| 1 | 50.00 | 50.30 | 0.30 | 1000 |
| 2 | 50.26 | 50.30 | 0.04 | 200 |
| 3 | 50.26 | 50.35 | 0.09 | 400 |
| 4 | 50.17 | 50.33 | 0.16 | 600 |
| 5 | 50.32 | 50.33 | 0.01 | 100 |
| 6 | 50.41 | 50.46 | 0.05 | 300 |
| 7 | 50.51 | 50.55 | 0.04 | 200 |
| 8 | 50.44 | 50.47 | 0.03 | 300 |
| 9 | 50.71 | 51.12 | 0.41 | 1200 |
| 10 | 51.03 | 51.04 | 0.01 | 100 |
| 11 | 50.97 | 50.99 | 0.02 | 200 |
| 12 | 50.57 | 50.75 | 0.18 | 700 |
| 13 | 50.71 | 50.74 | 0.03 | 200 |
| 14 | 50.92 | 50.96 | 0.04 | 200 |
| 15 | 50.91 | 50.93 | 0.02 | 200 |
| 16 | 51.18 | 51.32 | 0.14 | 600 |
| 17 | 51.71 | 51.76 | 0.05 | 300 |
| 18 | 52.04 | 52.12 | 0.08 | 400 |
| 19 | 52.03 | 52.34 | 0.31 | 1000 |
| 20 | 52.30 | 52.34 | 0.04 | 300 |

The next transaction, by another investor, was at a price of $50.30, implying a perfect foresight half-spread of 0.30. Purchases by other investors are omitted in the "Purchase Price" column. Note that larger purchase orders tend to lead to higher perfect foresight half-spreads in Table 3.1. This suggests that larger orders lead to greater slippage, just as we would expect. What might be less apparent in Table 3.1 is that the proportional increase in slippage increases as the proportional size of the transaction increases. That is, the relationship between slippage and transaction size is concave up.

We can analyze the relationship between the perfect foresight half-spread and transaction sizes with an ordinary least square (OLS) regression. Suppose the broker expects that this relationship will not be linear because the effect of transaction size on the perfect foresight half-spread is expected to be concave up. That is, for example, the broker might expect that a single purchase transaction for 1000 shares will cause more slippage than 10 purchase transactions for 100 shares each. To analyze this nonlinear relationship, we will conduct a log-log regression of the following form:

$$log(Perfect\ \ Foresight\ \ Half\text{-}Spread)_t = logb_0 + b_1 log(Transaction\ \ Size) + \varepsilon_t$$

This implies the following estimated relationship between the perfect foresight half-spread and transaction size:

$$Perfect\ \ Foresight\ \ Half\text{-}Spread = v(Transaction\ \ Size)^m$$

where $b_0$ serves as an estimate for v and $b_1$ serves as an estimate for $m$. These parameters $b_0$ and $m$ characterize slippage, which is positive when $v$ is positive and $m$ exceeds 1. Higher values for $b_0$ and m indicate increased slippage.

Table 3.2 presents *log* values (base 10) for the perfect foresight half-spreads and transaction sizes, and depicts regression results. The log-log regression implies that $b_0 = -4.96$ and $b_1 = 1.48$; that is, $v$ is approximately equal to 0.00001 and $m$ is approximately equal to 1.5 (use anti-logs of $b_0$ and $b_1$ to obtain $v$ and $m$). Thus, slippage, $S = vc^m \approx 0.00001c^{1.5}$ where $c$ is transaction size. Regression $t$-statistics, the F-statistic, and the adjusted r-square value all suggest that these results are statistically significant.

## 3.5 ALGORITHMIC TRADING

Typical transaction sizes in many markets such as the NYSE are very small relative to the order sizes placed by institutional investors. Average transaction sizes have dropped from 1477 shares in 1998 to approximately 400 shares in 2008 to below 300 in 2011. This means that the much larger institutional trades can have a significant and unwanted impact on execution prices. This unwanted price impact, which works against the trader, is referred to as *slippage*. Slippage occurs when the market impact of a trader's buy orders forces security prices to rise and sell orders force prices down. *Algorithmic trading* refers to automated trading with the use of live market data and rule-driven computer programs for automatically submitting and allocating trade orders among markets and brokers as well as over time so as to minimize the price impact of large trades. Algorithmic trading executes orders without direct human intervention, using computers to directly interface

**TABLE 3.2** Slippage and Transaction Size Regression

| Log Perfect Foresight Half-Spread | Log Transaction Size | | | | | | |
|---|---|---|---|---|---|---|---|
| −0.522879 | 3.00000 | SUMMARY OUTPUT | | | | | |
| −1.397940 | 2.30103 | | | | | | |
| −1.045757 | 2.60206 | Regression Statistics | | | | | |
| −0.795880 | 2.77815 | Multiple R | | 0.977851577 | | | |
| −2.000000 | 2.00000 | R Square | | 0.956193706 | | | |
| −1.301030 | 2.47712 | Adjusted R Square | | 0.953760023 | | | |
| −1.397940 | 2.30103 | Standard Error | | 0.101914919 | | | |
| −1.522879 | 2.47712 | Observations | | 20 | | | |
| −0.387216 | 3.07918 | | | | | | |
| −2.000000 | 2.00000 | ANOVA | | | | | |
| −1.698970 | 2.30103 | | df | SS | MS | F | Significance F |
| −0.744727 | 2.84510 | Regression | 1 | 4.0809 | 4.0809 | 392.9 | 1.12419E-13 |
| −1.522879 | 2.30103 | Residual | 18 | 0.18696 | 0.010386651 | | |
| −1.397940 | 2.30103 | Total | 19 | 4.26787 | | | |
| −1.698970 | 2.30103 | | | | | | |
| −0.853872 | 2.77815 | | Coefficients | Std. Error | t Stat | P-value | |
| −1.301030 | 2.47712 | Intercept | − 4.96055 | 0.18957 | − 26.16 | 8.9E-16 | |
| −1.096910 | 2.60206 | X Variable 1 | 1.4805 | 0.0747 | 19.82 | 1.1E-13 | |
| −0.508638 | 3.00000 | | | | | | |
| −1.397940 | 2.47712 | | | | | | |

*The first two columns on this table are simply base 10 logs of the perfect foresight half spreads and transactions sizes, both from Table 3.1. The remainder of this table presents regression results, calculated with Excel 2007, for a test of logs of perfect half spreads as the dependent variable on logs of transaction sizes. The coefficient, X Variable 1 is the slope of this regression.*

with trading venues. Algorithmic trading models seek to determine strategies for trade amounts, prices, timing, and venues of orders, in many cases, to avoid slippage. Algorithmic trading is a response to market imperfections, and may contribute to market imperfections as well. Many institutional traders employ algorithmic trading (also called *automated trading, black box trading,* and *robotrading*) to break up large orders into smaller orders to reduce execution risk, preserve anonymity, and to minimize trade slippage. Rooted in *program trading* (defined by the NYSE as computer-initiated trades involving 15 or more stocks with value totaling more than $1,000,000), which dates back to the 1980s, algorithmic trading now accounts for between 30% and 80% of trade volume in many markets.

While algorithmic trading frequently refers to the trade execution models referred to above, the term is also used in a more general sense to include *alpha models,* which are used to make trade decisions to generate profits or control risk. More generally, algorithmic trading can be defined as trading based on the use of computer programs and sophisticated trading analytics to execute orders according to predefined strategies. Thus, algorithmic trading can be generalized to include program trading. Regardless, algorithmic trading is usually highly dependent on the most sophisticated technology and analytics.

Algorithmic trading does have risks, such as leaks that might arise from competitor efforts to reverse engineer them. Designers of algorithmic trading models seek to ensure that trading schedules and behavior cannot be predicted. However, many algorithms lack the capacity to handle or respond to exceptional or rare events. In addition, any malfunction, including a simple lapse in communication lines, can cause the system to fail. Thus, human supervision of algorithmic trading and appropriate use of filters are crucial.

## Algo Strategies

Strategies used by algorithms vary widely. Sometimes, algorithmic trading results from mathematical models that analyze every quote and trade in the relevant market, identify liquidity opportunities, and use this information to make intelligent trading decisions. This type of strategy is sometimes called *smart order routing*. Some algorithmic trading models seek to trade at or better than the average price over a day (e.g., *VWAP*, volume weighted average price, or *TWAP*, time weighted average price) and others seek to execute slowly so as to have minimal price impact. For example, with *simple time slicing*, orders are split up and sent to markets at regular time intervals. Some strategies are more competitive, such as *iceberging* where small parts of orders are revealed to determine their impact and *pegging* where orders are sent to execute at the best bid or offer to test whether the order moves the market. Algorithms sometimes are set to produce more volume at market opens and closes (e.g., *MOC*, market on close) when volume is high, and less during slower periods such as around lunch. They can seek to exploit any arbitrage opportunities or price spreads between correlated securities.

*Newsreader algorithms* employ high-speed text mining and statistical techniques to analyze news sources, blogs, tweets, and other data to obtain relevant trading information and infer its impact on security prices. Essentially, data are mined and read and content is mechanically analyzed for trading decisions. More generally, *information algorithms* search and filter information and news flow in an effort to locate trading opportunities and trigger trades. These algorithms can be structured to alert human traders or structured to execute automatically based on rules provided by the user.

In addition, some algorithms seek opportunities in options and other derivatives markets. Algorithmic trading can also account for and seek to balance trading costs such as commissions and taxes as well as regulatory issues such as those associated with short selling. An algorithm can be created to account for the relative importance of the tradeoff between the order's speed of execution and its price impact.

There are a number of vendors for algorithmic trading platforms that can feed live data into rules-based programs that can automatically place orders as per instructions. Examples of such platforms available to trading firms include Goldman Sachs's *Algorithmic Trading* and Instinet's *Sidewinder*.

## Illustration: Slicing the Large Transaction

Earlier in this chapter, we discussed best execution, slippage, and the perfect foresight half-spread. Suppose that a client of the XYZ brokerage firm seeks to have her purchase order of $X = 80{,}000$ shares completed with the best possible execution; that is, she wants to slice her 80,000-share order so as to realize the lowest possible total execution costs $B$. These execution costs $B$ will include both order processing costs $F$ per transaction and market impact (slippage) costs that are increasing in the size $c$ of each of $n$ equal-size transactions. Broker XYZ works with a market impact model that estimates the slippage cost $S$ of each of $n$ equal-sized executions $c = X/n$ with function $S = vc^m$, where the coefficient $v$ and exponent $m$ are related to the liquidity of the security to be purchased or sold.[4] In this case, the per-transaction cost $B/n$ is estimated to have a fixed component $F$ (order processing costs) and an increasing variable cost component $vc^m = v(X/n)^m$ (this is the market impact component of the execution costs):

$$B/n = F + v(X/n)^m$$

Suppose that broker analysts have estimated $F$ to be \$0.03 per order, based on knowledge of order processing costs, and $v$ and $m$ to be 0.00001 and 1.5. What are the optimal number of transactions and transaction sizes?

To answer these questions, we will set up a total transaction cost function as follows:

$$B = nF + nv\left(\frac{X}{n}\right)^m = .03n + .00001\frac{80,000^{1.5}}{n^{.5}} = .03n + 226.27n^{-.5}$$

[4]Recall that we used a log-log regression estimation procedure to determine the values of parameters $v$ and $m$. Many firms use square root, quadratic, simple linear, or other cost functions. However, significantly more sophisticated cost functions are also used, accounting for factors such as market liquidity, different markets, time of day, and the urgency of trading, and making use of more sophisticated and dynamic optimization procedures such as Euler and Bellman equations.

We find the derivative of total transaction costs $B$ with respect to the total number of transactions $n$, set this derivative equal to zero and solve for $n$ as follows:

$$\frac{dB}{dn} = \frac{d\left[nF + nv\left(\frac{X}{n}\right)^m\right]}{dn} = F - mv\frac{X^m}{n^m} = .03 - 1.5(.00001)\frac{X^m}{n^m} = .03 - \frac{339.41}{n^{1.5}} = 0$$

$$n = \sqrt[m]{\frac{mvX^m}{F}} = \sqrt[1.5]{\frac{1.5(.00001) \cdot 80000^{1.5}}{.03}} = 504$$

Thus, we find that the optimal number of stock transactions for this order is $n = 504$, each with a transaction size of $X/n$ equal to $80{,}000/504 = 159$ (subject to rounding). Thus, the broker should submit 504 purchase orders, each for 159 shares each to minimize her client's execution costs on this 80,000 share order.

The algorithm that we have just illustrated is very simple. Many potential enhancements could be used to enrich the model. For example, the model provides no guidance on spacing trades through the day or time frame. First, we might expect that the amount of time elapsing between trades executing at time $t$ and time $t+1$ would be inversely related to market impact costs. That is, as more time elapses between the broker's transactions, slippage will be reduced. Second, many securities might be expected to be more liquid during the earliest and latest parts of the day, and least liquid in the middle. That is, one might expect liquidity during the day to be "U"-shaped, and market impact costs to resemble an upside-down U. Trade urgency, competing market venues are among the many other potential factors were not considered. Clearly, the analyst developing algorithmic programs has many factors that she can consider when designing the optimal cost or trade-slicing functions.

## 3.6 DARK POOLS

Sometimes, all or parts of orders generated by algorithmic traders are hidden from the eyes of the public. These intentionally obscured portions of orders are generally referred to as *dark liquidity pools* because they are hidden from public view. These dark pools help traders with large order sizes maintain anonymity and avoid slippage while attempting to execute their large transactions. Orders are often partially revealed, in which case they are called *iceberg* (hidden-size orders are generally completely hidden), with brokers instructed not to reveal the full size of their orders. Hidden portions of orders do not contribute to the display of market depth. In many markets, the fully revealed portion of the order will normally have priority over the hidden portion. Mittal (2008) reported that dark pools represent about 7% of total market volume.

Dark pools also refer to alternative trading systems (ATSs) that do not post quotes and transaction prices in the traditional sense. In some cases, this information (often referred to as alerts) can be transmitted to certain traders such as those who can potentially provide for a match; in other cases, information is tightly restricted. These dark pools function in a parallel fashion with traditional markets, executing transactions within the national market bid/offer (NBBO) spread, usually at the NBBO mid-point. ATD (Citigroup), BIDS (NYSE),

ISE MidPoint Match, LeveL ATS, GETCO, Credit Suisse's CrossFinder ATS, Knight Link, Fidelity CrossStream, and MatchPoint (NYSE) are among the firms that offer such confidential execution services. The Investment Technology Group (ITG) and Mittal (2008) characterize five basic types of dark pools:

1. *Public Crossing Networks*: Usually created by brokerage firms to act on an agency basis for the purpose of generating trading commissions, such as POSIT, Liquidnet, Pipeline, Goldman Sachs Sigma X. They normally cross buy and sell orders, frequently at the spread mid-point.
2. *Internalization Pools*: For internalizing the broker's trade flow, such as Credit Suisse's Crossfinder, and Goldman Sach's Sigma X. Internalization of order flow means that the broker provides both the buy and sell flow from its own proprietary desk and its customers, maintaining complete control over the transaction and reducing transaction costs.
3. *Ping Destinations*: These pools, operated by hedge funds and electronic market makers, accept only immediate or cancel (fill or kill) orders. Such markets usually provide for low transaction costs and can facilitate flash trading (discussed in the upcoming section on high-frequency trading).
4. *Exchange-Based Pools*: ATSs created by exchanges, such as ISE Midpoint Match, NASDAQ Cross, and NYSE Matchpoint. In many cases, suppliers of liquidity will receive rebates for providing liquidity, while buyers of liquidity will pay higher commissions for the liquidity that they receive.
5. *Consortium-Based Pools*: Operated by multiple broker partners and function as a hybrid of public crossing networks and internalization pools, such as LEVEL and BIDS. In a sense, a consortium-based pool acts as a sort of second-step internalization pool. If a broker cannot internalize an order, it seeks to execute the order within its consortium of partners before sending it out to the public.

While anonymity is essential to the dark pool trading venues, traders have learned to game the pools. For example, in Chapter 12, we will discuss *fishing*, the practice involving gamers sending small orders to dark pools to determine whether they can be executed, in which case they often infer that larger numbers of shares await in the pool. Gamers can use this information to set their own trading strategies and game the market. Fishing activities obviously impacts market prices, as does the removal of orders from display markets to dark pools. If dark pools were to attract significantly more volume from public display markets, the price discovery process might become significantly impaired, and market efficiency (the ability for markets to fully reflect available information) might be adversely affected.

## 3.7 STEALTH AND SUNSHINE TRADING

As we discussed earlier in the context of algorithmic trading, investors with private information should trade gradually to disguise their intentions and to realize trading profits before their trades fully reveal valuable information. They fragment their orders, routing them to different markets and at different times to disguise their intentions. This is the purpose of stealth trading.

To motivate discussing the need for stealth trading to avoid slippage, consider the extent to which small, uninformed investors cause stock prices to change versus the effects of large informed traders pushing prices towards their fundamental values. Barclay and Warner (1993) argue that if informed investors' trades are the main cause of stock price changes, large trades by informed traders would reveal their information because traders can easily discern those who execute large transactions. However, small trades executed repeatedly will incur excessive transaction costs. Thus, informed traders will tend to fragment orders into medium-sized trades sufficiently small to disguise themselves but large enough to maintain fairly small transaction costs. This should lead medium-sized transactions to have the most significant impact on stock prices. Thus, medium-sized orders (500 to 9999 share orders) will be most likely to move stock prices if stealth traders are most active. Several empirical studies support this argument, including that of Barclay and Warner who find that 99.43% of the cumulative price changes on the NYSE result from medium-sized trades, which comprise 38.12% of total NYSE trades. Chakravarty (2001) confirms that the bulk of price changes are due to medium-sized trades, finds that the bulk of these price-moving trades are executed by institutions, and determines that the bulk of stealth trades are executed by institutions. Chakravarty et al. (2005) found that institutional investors appear to be more informed than individual investors, enabling them to function more appropriately as stealth traders.

In contrast, Campbell et al. (2009) found that that institutions tend to execute larger and smaller transactions rather than medium-sized transactions. This differs from earlier studies cited above that suggest that institutions execute medium-sized transactions. However, the Campbell et al. (2009) study was more recent and the exchanges have consistently been reporting smaller average transaction sizes. Perhaps significantly reduced transaction costs have made execution of smaller transactions less costly, leading institutions to execute an increased number of smaller transactions. Furthermore, Campbell et al. also found that institutions prefer medium and small size trades on high volume days and larger size trades on high volatility days. Furthermore, larger transactions move prices more on high volatility days. This suggests that stealth trading increases when liquidity is high, but when volatility is high, traders act more quickly with larger size trades, engaging less in stealth trading, causing their trades to move prices more.

Chakravarty et al. (2005) found that stealth trading occurs differently in bear markets from how it occurs in bull markets. While they did find that informed traders execute smaller trade sizes when selling than when buying, informed investors fragmented their trades more when buying in rising markets and when selling in falling markets. Furthermore, some stealth trading algorithms seek opportunities in options and other derivatives markets. In fact, Chakravarty et al. (2004) demonstrate that informed traders trade across both stock and options markets and that a significant level of price discovery occurs in options markets.

*Sunshine trading* is the opposite of stealth trading, as sunshine traders announce their intentions. The sunshine trader announces its intentions when doing so might be expected to increase the competition to act as counterparties on the same transactions, but when additional competition on the same side of the transaction won't hurt the institution.

Sunshine trading is most effective when the market for the security is elastic, that is, when a larger number of competitors on the same side of the transaction might be expected to have little long-term impact on the price of the security. Even if the announcement produces a short-term impact, in an elastic market, the price will bounce back. If information motivating a trade has already been leaked, the institution might publicize its intentions in an effort to obtain a larger number of providers of liquidity. That is, the institution might prefer to execute its transactions in a more liquid market. If forthcoming trades are not motivated by information, preannouncing the motivations of the trade may result in better trade prices than stealth trading. In fact, the signaling effect of sunshine trading might actually "scare off" potential competitors on the same side of the transaction, leading to reduced trading by competing informed traders.

Consider, for example, the 2011 scenario when the U.S. government announced its intent to sell bank shares accumulated in its efforts to mitigate the effects of the 2008 banking crisis. The market was well aware of the U.S. government's holdings and its intent to eventually sell the shares. Hence when these shares ultimately were sold, the government's announcement of the anticipated sales prevented suspicions leading to unwanted negative information effects.

## 3.8 HIGH-FREQUENCY TRADING

High-frequency trading refers to the practice of rapid executions of multiple transactions for securities followed by extremely short holding periods, perhaps as short as fractions of seconds. High-frequency traders typically use their technology to exploit market inefficiencies in market making, price effects of news, and market movements. High-frequency traders focus on small price changes and discrepancies, often "ticks." Obviously, high-frequency trading requires sophisticated technology and communications and computing resources costing millions or even tens of millions of dollars. Several studies have indicated that high-frequency trading accounts for more than half of all equities trading volume. This means that high-frequency trading can add liquidity to the marketplace. High-frequency trading obviously depends heavily on execution speed. In fact, this means that at least half of all trades are not motivated by liquidity, the need for portfolio diversification, fundamental analysis, or technical analysis. These trades are motivated by latency. Many markets measure *latency*, the delay between an order signal and its execution in milliseconds. For example, new technology put into place by the NYSE in 2009 should reduce latency to less than 10 milliseconds (0.01 seconds) for most of its high-frequency transactions. This technology was enhanced by a new data facility in Mahwah, New Jersey in 2010. BATS currently claims 0.5 millisecond latency, and other markets are beginning to make latency claims using microseconds (0.000001 seconds). Getco LLC is one of the major firms focused in the high-frequency execution services industry, and other major trading firms such as Citadel Investment Group, Renaissance Technologies LLC, and Goldman Sachs are also major participants.

A high-frequency program requires significant data, technological, and personnel resources. In addition to the ability to obtain, transmit, and analyze the most recent and complete quote and execution data, a high-frequency trader (HFT) needs to be able to develop and implement trading strategies. These strategies will require historical tick data for testing in a data repository and data-cleansing capabilities. Second, appropriate personnel and tools need to be available to develop and test appropriate trading models under real-world conditions. Such testing capabilities will include back-testing models. Third, the high-frequency trading system will require highly reliable trade-execution services that will execute on signals as prescribed by model developers.

Some HFTs, known as *liquidity rebate traders*, rely on payment for order flow. Exchanges and most electronic communications networks (ECNs) offer rebates of about ¼ penny per share to certain broker dealers that execute orders. These executed orders supply liquidity in the market, and the payments or rebates for this order flow might be regarded as payment for supplying liquidity. Brokers and traders using this liquidity might be expected to pay higher fees to the exchange or ECN. These rebate programs have led to trading strategies designed to capture these rebates. A dealer purchasing shares at 50.00 and quickly reselling them for 50.00 may still make a ½ penny profit per share from the liquidity rebate. Buy-side traders pay this fee through higher exchange/ECN fees, but these fees might be regarded as the cost of using liquidity in the market. We will discuss payment for order flow in Chapter 12.

Interestingly, high-frequency trading not only relies heavily on algorithms to provide rules and strategies for trades, but many algorithms are designed specifically to anticipate and exploit the algorithms used by other institutions. Hence, some HFT algorithms are designed to detect ("sniff out") and exploit competitors' algorithms.

High-frequency trading has gained significant importance, particularly in equity and exchange markets. Major brokerage houses, trading firms, and hedge funds often invest tens of millions of dollars into their high-frequency trading technologies and capabilities. For example, many firms engaging in high-frequency trading have co-location facilities, where they rent space from market centers, such as from the major exchange ECNs and other ATSs. The purpose of co-location where their servers are located next to the market center's data servers is to reduce latency. This co-location (also called proximity hosting) provides significant millisecond and even microsecond advantages, and enables institutions to better serve their clients.[5] However, the fairness of this high-cost practice has been questioned and remains under SEC scrutiny.

## Latency Arbitrage

Latency is concerned with the speed of quotation display or order execution after an order has been placed. Different technologies and resources (such as co-location) provide opportunities for some traders to obtain quote and order information faster than others. This speedy access to information enables them to exploit their information advantage

[5]Consider the following: In 1 microsecond, light (or, an electronic signal) can travel about 300 meters. Thus, it takes at least 200 microseconds for an electronic signal to travel 60 kilometers from the NYSE in Manhattan to a hedge fund in Greenwich, Connecticut. This calculation ignores the additional latency induced by routers, switches, and so on. Obviously, when time is of the essence, location matters. In fact, one exchange reputedly provides institutions that co-locate in its facilities with cables of identical length to connect its data feeds, regardless of how many meters the office is from the exchange computers.

over their competitors through *latency arbitrage*. Exchanges disseminate continuous updates of their best bids and offers; NBBOs on stocks are compiled from these and routed to clients. However, many dark pools, or anonymous electronic markets such as Liquidnet that don't publish bids and offers, don't contribute to the NBBO. Delays between the appearance of bids and offers on direct feeds and the processing of the NBBO provide arbitrage opportunities as do the abilities of institutions to synthesize NBBOs before they are even available. Consider the following illustration of a HFT whose automated trading facility enables it to exploit its information advantage:

1. The initial market for Stock X is 50.00 bid/offered at 50.01.
2. The HFT's superior technology and location enables it to pick up a new institutional bid for 50.01 for Stock X that is likely to be followed by more and higher bids. This bid arrives in the HFT's computer 10 microseconds before most competing traders' computers.
3. The HFT's computer buys all available shares offered at 50.01 before competing traders act.
4. The institutional buyer is unable to purchase at 50.01.
5. The market for the stock changes to 50.01 bid/offered at 50.02.
6. The HFT sells shares to the institutional buyer for 50.02, locking a 0.01 profit per share.

Consider a second example described in the *Wall Street Journal*. In July 2009, Intel, the computer chip giant, reported robust earnings and some traders considered the semiconductor company Broadcom to be a buying opportunity. Many of these traders, to disguise their interest, split their orders into small batches. Broadcom began trading that day at $26.20. HFTs with faster access to quotes were able to see that there was a strong interest in Broadcom. The HFTs began buying Broadcom shares and then reselling them to the slower investors at higher prices. The price of Broadcom quickly rose to $26.39 as HFTs began offering to sell hundreds of thousands of shares. The *Wall Street Journal* reported that slower-moving traders paid $1.4 million for about 56,000 shares, or $7800 more than if they had been able to move as quickly as the HFTs.

## HFT Strategies

Many HFT strategies are quite simple. For example, many HFT desks are largely replacing the more traditional dealers as market makers by relying on simple *passive market-making*, placing quotations in large quantities. Here, the HFT strategy seeks to profit through a simple high volume based on having its own bids and offers taken. In many instances, the firm may be using its quotations to seek liquidity rebates (payment for order flow) by providing liquidity in markets.

Other HFT desks seek profits through cross-asset or cross-market arbitrage strategies or by accessing information or executing trades more quickly than their competition. Co-location, the most rapid data feeds and trade execution abilities, are crucial here. HFT desks often seek to anticipate order flow (including sniffing out competing algorithms), and to use superior technology to trade ahead of this flow. Sometimes, order anticipators are referred to as "parasitic traders" in that they use traders' information without contributing to price discovery or enhancing liquidity. Finally, even though most HFTs seek to hedge or neutralize their positions (be flat by the end of the trading day), some do seek profits through speculation or by making other directional trades.

Trading firms can engage in high-frequency trading by obtaining direct market access (DMA) to appropriate trading venues and by obtaining hardware and software necessary for strategy implementation. Software and even strategies can be obtained through brokerage firms, purchased through consulting firms and other developers, or created in-house. For example, *InfoReach* is a provider of broker-neutral software and systems for electronic, algorithmic, and high-frequency trade analysis, management, and execution through its *HiFREQ* algorithmic engine. It is designed to enable traders to create and deploy proprietary, complex trading strategies as well as access algorithms from brokers and other third-party providers. InfoReach also supplies its internal *FIX Engine* as a routing system.[6]

## 3.9 FLASH TRADING AND SPONSORED ACCESS

The *Quote Rule,* formally referred to as SEC Rule 602 of Regulation NMS, requires that all market centers publicly disseminate their best bids and offers through the securities information processors (such as the Consolidated Tape, Consolidated Quotations System, and the Intermarket Trading System discussed in Chapter 2). However, an important exception to this Rule involves quotes that are immediately executed or canceled, defined as occurring within 500 milliseconds of the original quote. These quotes, according to many legal experts, need not be publicly displayed, and may be displayed to select clients. Such displays are referred to as *flash orders. Flash trading* refers to trading motivated by private or select market participant receipt of quotes (flash orders) in advance of the public quote stream (also called prerouting displays). NASDAQ OMX, BATS, and Direct Edge (through its Enhanced Liquidity Provider) all have facilitated flash trading, although NASDAQ OMX and BATS stopped the practice in late 2010. Flash orders, in effect, briefly (up to 500 milliseconds, but more often for as few as 30 milliseconds) display an order that is better than the national best bid or offer in order (NBBO) to solicit NBBO-priced responses. Traders requiring the fastest execution may respond, but the flash trader obtains market information regardless. In addition, by providing rather than reacting to quotes, the flash trader is enhancing the liquidity of the market, perhaps qualifying for a market trading rebate (payment for order flow).

The NYSE has argued that flash orders essentially provide private quotes for select participants competing with the public quote stream, impairing the importance of the NBBO and weakening the market by detracting the pursuit of best execution. While the NYSE did not permit flash trading prior to 2010, some observers noted that NYSE specialists had the opportunity to act on quote information in advance of the public, although this seems like less of a problem since they were replaced by designated market makers. The SEC and the U.S. Congress have considered banning flash trading. For instance, in its 2009 proposal to ban flash trading, the SEC stated that it was concerned flash orders might create a two-tiered market in which the public does not have best price information access through the consolidated quotation data streams.

[6]For details, see http://www.inforeachinc.com/aboutus.php.

On the other hand, flash orders and flash trading might provide opportunities for traders who do not want to make their interest public to participate in the market, thereby enhancing liquidity of that market. In addition to providing enhanced liquidity, the flash trader may simply be demanding immediacy. While the trader who places a limit order might be regarded as a patient provider of liquidity, the flash trader might be regarded as an impatient provider of liquidity. Either may serve to improve markets for long-term investors.

## Illustration: A Flash Trade

At 10:00.00.00, a pension fund submits a buy order for 10,000 shares of ABC stock. The NBBO at this time is 10.00–.01, both quotes on NASDAQ. The broker routes the order to Direct Edge, which flashes the order to select HFT traders for 30 milliseconds, who almost instantly purchase all available shares for 10.01, causing the NBBO to rise to 10.01–02. At 10.00.00.30, the order is routed to NASDAQ, where the HFTs sell the pension fund 10,000 shares for 10.02, netting a $100 profit in less than one second.

## Sponsored Access

Another concern to many high-frequency trade critics is the practice of registered broker-dealers providing *sponsored access*, where brokers loan their *Market Participation Identification Numbers* (MPIDs) to HFTs, enabling them to gain faster, direct access to markets by bypassing the broker's trading systems. Normally, brokers and traders must be registered members or licensed to have direct access to a trading venue such as an exchange. Sponsored access enables nonmembers to access trading venues. *Naked access*, where orders do not pass through the sponsor's pretrade risk controls, is of particular concern, since such algorithmic orders could lead to runaway executions.[7] Naked access might speed the transaction execution from as much as 750 microseconds when the trade is routed through risk controls to as little as 250 microseconds with filtered access. Tracking down destabilizing naked access trades run amok can be tricky because exchanges cannot know where they originated, and the sponsoring brokerage firm must be involved in the identification. While as much as two thirds of equities volume may involve high-frequency orders, perhaps as much as half of these trades might involve sponsored access. In 2011, the SEC implemented a ban on naked access, expressing concerns about "the potential that financial, regulatory, and other risks associated with the placement of orders are not being appropriately managed. In particular, there is an increased likelihood that customers will enter erroneous orders as a result of computer malfunction or human error, fail to comply with various regulatory requirements, or

[7]In November 2010, largely in reaction to the May 6, 2010 "flash crash" (the "flash crash" had nothing to do with flash trading), the SEC voted for a ban on naked access in stock markets, requiring brokers "to put in place risk management controls and supervisory procedures to help prevent erroneous orders, ensure compliance with regulatory requirements, and enforce pre-set credit or capital thresholds." In 2011, this ban was implemented as per Market Access Rule 15c3-5.

breach a credit or capital limit."[8] We will discuss problems originating with "unfiltered" trading in Chapter 12.

Some market observers argue that high-frequency trading enhances market liquidity, bringing into the market pools of securities when other traders need trade counterparties, and providing over half of the total volume in some markets. However, many are also concerned about risks of this high-volume, "trigger-happy" trading, perhaps fed by algorithmic, technological, or trading errors that could trigger massive one-sided order flows leading to failures, contagion, and market meltdown.

## Additional Reading

Harris (2003), Chapters 13 to 18, is a very useful guide for understanding market mechanisms and trading institutions, although it has become somewhat dated. Kim (2007) offers excellent explanations of electronic and algorithmic trading technology in Chapters 1 to 3 and 6 to 7. Schwartz (1988) provides a somewhat dated but very readable discussion focused on equity markets in Chapters 1 to 15.

## References

Arnuk, S., & Saluzzi, J. (2009, December 4). Latency arbitrage: The real power behind predatory high frequency trading. Themis Trading LLC White Paper.

Barclay, M. J., & Warner, J. B. (1993). Stealth and volatility: which trades move prices? *Journal of Financial Economics*, *34*, 281–306.

Boston Consulting Group. (2010). In search of stable growth: Global asset management 2010. Available at: <http://www.bcg.com/documents/file53448.pdf>. Accessed 26.09.11.

Campbell, J.Y., Ramadorai, T., & Vuolteenaho, T.O. (2009). Caught on tape: Predicting institutional ownership with order flow data. *Journal of Financial Economics*, *92*, 66–91.

Chakravarty, S. (2001). Stealth-trading: Which traders' trades move stock prices? *Journal of Financial Economics*, *61*, 289–307.

Chakravarty, S., Gulen, H., & Mayhew, S. (2004). Informed trading in stock and options markets. *Journal of Finance*, *59*, 1235–1257.

Chakravarty, S., Kalev, P., & Pham, L. (2005). *Stealth trading in volatile markets*. Working Paper. Department of Accounting and Finance, Monash University, Melbourne, Victoria.

Chan, L. K. C., & Lakonishok, J. (1993). Institutional trades and intraday stock price behavior. *Journal of Financial Economics*, *33*, 173–199.

Christie, W. G., & Huang, R. D. (1994). Market structures and liquidity: A transactions data study of exchange listings. *Journal of Financial Intermediation*, *3*, 300–326.

Dennis, P., & Strickland, D. (2002). Who blinks in volatile markets, individuals or institutions? *Journal of Finance*, *57*, 1923–1949.

Gompers, P., & Metrick, A. (2001). Institutional investors and equity prices. *Quarterly Journal of Economics*, *116*, 229–260.

Harris, L. (2003). *Trading and exchanges: Market microstructure for practitioners*. Oxford: Oxford University Press.

Hosking, P. (2006). Hedge fund returns 'are vastly overstated'. *The Times (London)*, February 28.

Huang, R. D., & Stoll, H. R. (1995). *Competitive trading of NYSE listed stocks: Measurement and interpretation of trading costs*. Working Paper 94–13. Financial Markets Research Center, Owen School, Vanderbilt University, Nasville, TN.

Huang, R. D., & Stoll, H. R. (1996). Dealer versus auction markets: A paired comparison of execution costs on NASDAQ and the NYSE. *Journal of Financial Economics*, *41*, 313–357.

[8]From a January 13, 2010 SEC press release, available on the SEC website, http://www.sec.gov/news/press/2010/2010-7.htm.

Kim, K. (2007). *Electronic and Algorithmic Trading Technology: The Complete Guide*. New York: Academic Press.

Kraus, A., & Stoll, H. R. (1972). Price impact of block trading on the New York stock exchange. *Journal of Finance, 27*, 569–588.

Kwan, S. (2003, June 16). Underfunding of private pension plans. *Economic Letter*, Federal Reserve Bank of San Francisco, Number 2003-16.

Macey, J., & O'Hara, M. (1997). The law and economics of best execution. *Journal of Financial Intermediation, 6*, 188–223.

Mittal, H. (2008). *Are you playing in a toxic dark pool? A guide to preventing information leakage*. Working Paper, Investment Technology Group. Available at: <http://www.itginc.com/news_events/papers/ITGResearch_Toxic_Dark_Pool_070208.pdf.> Accessed 28.07.09.

Saar, G. (2001). Price impact asymmetry of block trades: An institutional trading explanation. *Review of Financial Studies, 14*, 1153–1181.

Schwartz, R. A. (1988). *Equity markets: Structure, Trading and Performance*. New York: Harper and Row Publishers.

## 3.10 EXERCISES

1. Suppose that you are a trader at a large trading firm. You have just received a sell order from a mutual fund for 1,000,000 shares of stock that has an average daily volume of 250,000 shares. What alternatives do you have to complete this client order by the end of the trading day?
2. Suppose that a client of the ABC brokerage firm seeks to have her order of $X = 500{,}000$ shares executed within three hours with the best possible execution; that is, she wants to realize the lowest possible total execution cost B. ABC works with a market impact model that estimates the cost of each of $n$ equal-sized executions, $B/n$ to have a fixed component $F$ and a variable cost component $v(X_i/n)^2$, where $X_i/n$ is the number of shares traded in any given execution $i$:

$$B/n = F + v(X/n)^2$$

Broker analysts have estimated $F$ to be \$10, based on the order processing costs of each transaction. Market impact costs are estimated with the square root function with $v$ equal to 0.0001.

   a. What are the optimal number of equal size transactions and what are the optimal transaction sizes?
   b. What are the total market impact or slippage costs associated with the 500,000 share order?
   c. Suppose that $F$ in the market impact model is interpreted differently. Rather than representing fixed administrative costs of a transaction, $F = rn^s$, where coefficients $r = 0.1$ and $s = 0.5$ were determined as part of a new OLS regression that still determined numerical values for $v = 0.0001$ and $m = 2$, the function $F$ is now considered to reflect the total slippage associated with $n$ transactions for stock per hour. Thus, the market impact model is now estimated as follows:

$$B/n = F + v(X/n)^2 = rn^s + v(X/n)^2 = 0.1n^{.5} + 0.0001(500{,}000/n)^2$$

   Based on this new market impact model, what is the optimal number of equal-sized transactions and what are the optimal transaction sizes?

3. Sniffing algorithms attempt to discern competitors' algorithms. In some instances, mere observations of competitor trading activity can reveal information as to competitor strategies, latent demand (icebergs or dark pools), and so on. Beagle Trading is a proprietary trading company that seeks to sniff out its competitors' trading algorithms in an effort to detect their likely order flows. In an effort to sniff out trade slicing models used by brokers, Beagle intends to rely on the following market impact model estimated from an OLS based on its own trading experience:

$$B/n = F + v(X/n)^2$$

where Beagle estimates the cost of each of $n$ equal-sized executions, $B/n$ to have a fixed component $F = 10$ and a declining variable cost component $v(X/n)^2$, where $v = 0.0001$ and $X_i/n$ is the number of shares traded in any given execution $i$. Beagle observes a particular broker repeatedly placing buy orders of $c = 214$ shares of Stock GMNX in various equities marketplaces. Beagle assumes that these order sizes are optimal given its market impact model.
   a. Based on the observed order sizes $c = X/n = 214$, what can Beagle infer about the latent demand for this stock? That is, is Beagle able to sniff out the total number of shares that the broker seeks to purchase based on its market impact model and observed order sizes? Why or why not?
   b. Suppose that $F$ in the market impact model is revised to be interpreted and calculated differently. Rather than representing fixed administrative costs of a transaction, $F$ will equal $rn^s$, where coefficients $r = 0.1$ and $s = 0.5$ were determined as part of the same OLS that determined numerical values for $v = 0.0001$ and $m = 2$. The function $F$ is now considered to reflect the total slippage associated with $n$ transactions for stock per hour. Thus, this revised market impact model is now estimated as follows:

$$B/n = F + v(X/n)^2 = rn^s + v(X/n)^2 = rn^s + v(X/n)^2 = 0.1n^5 + 0.0001(X/n)^2$$

   Suppose that Beagle observes that a broker has submitted orders of $c = 214$ shares. Based on these observed order sizes, and with its revised market impact model, what can Beagle infer about the latent demand for this stock? That is, is Beagle now able to sniff out the total number of shares that the broker seeks to purchase based on its market impact model and observed order sizes? Why or why not? If Beagle can infer a latent demand, how many shares does the broker intend to purchase, including transactions already observed?

4. Critics of high-frequency trading often complain that the practice is unfair because most investors do not have the technical ability to compete with the larger, better-financed institutions. For example, some institutions pay substantial sums to co-locate trading facilities in exchange buildings to reduce latency. Exchanges argue that co-location and HFT activities are fair because the fractions of seconds shaved off order routing and execution times are not meaningful. However, Arnuk and Saluzzi (2009) point out that "some of the exchanges make sure that each co-located customer receives equal amounts of connecting cable, so that a server at the northeast corner of a facility has the

same latency as one at the southwest corner." What might this mean about the exchanges' opinions with respect to transaction speed and unfair advantages in trading?

5. What is the difference between an "immediate" or "cancel" order (described in Chapter 2) and a flash order?
6. Describe why many flash order critics regard much flash trading to be a form of front-running.

CHAPTER

# 4

# Regulation of Trading and Securities Markets

## 4.1 BACKGROUND AND EARLY REGULATION

The primary purpose of government regulation of competitive markets is to prevent market failure or collapse. Proponents of regulation argue that financial markets, left unregulated, will tend towards loss of competition, stability, efficiency, and credibility, leading to individuals and firms withdrawing from participation. This loss of participation weakens the viability of financial markets, leading to partial or complete market failure. Senator Edmund Muskie, in his 1970 introduction of what was to become the Securities Investor Protection Act to the Senate, stated[1]:

> The economic function of the securities markets is to channel individual institutional savings to private industry and thereby contribute to the growth of capital investment. Without strong capital markets it would be difficult for our national economy to sustain continued growth: indeed, the state of U.S. capital market development, more advanced than that of any other industrial country, is an important contributing factor in the rapid economic growth this country has experienced. Securities brokers support the proper functioning of these markets by maintaining a constant flow of debt and equity instruments. The continued financial wellbeing of the economy thus depends, in part, on public willingness to entrust assets to the securities industry.

The purpose of government regulation and its enforcement is to accomplish what the market on its own cannot—establishment of a set of rules intended to maintain market competition, stability, efficiency, and credibility. By the mid-1930s, the United States had developed the most comprehensive securities regulatory system in the world. Other countries and the European Union have since developed regulatory systems that resemble many aspects of the U.S. system.

[1] S. Rep. No. 91-1218.

## Regulatory Approaches

Regulatory approaches around the world can be strikingly different, despite the coordination efforts of global organizations, and the extent to which regulatory structures for securities industries seem to resemble that of the U.S. Securities regulatory authorities tend to take some combination of two basic approaches to designing a regulatory system:

- *Rules-based approach*, where authorities set forth specific and detailed prescriptive rules to which securities markets participants must adhere. Securities regulatory authorities taking this approach often focus on risk, where the authority considers whether there is a potential market failure or abuse that needs to be addressed and conducts an analysis to determine how to address the problem given the constraint of limited resources. Rules-based regulation is frequently implemented as a preventive mechanism.
- *Principles-based approach*, where authorities set forth a small number of regulatory objectives and principles, granting regulatory authorities and firm operating and compliance officers more judgment in ensuring that policy objectives are being fulfilled.

While all regulatory authorities have used some mix of these two approaches, the United States has tended to have more of a rules-based orientation while the United Kingdom (UK) has been moving towards a principles-based orientation that is more popular with the industry. Proponents of principles-based approaches argue that regulators waste less time on trivial rules-based minutiae and spend more time on meaningful deviations from appropriate practices. In addition, principles-based approaches can ease the compliance efforts of firms that engage in proper practices. On the other hand, some observers argue that principles-based regulators (such as the UK Financial Services Authority) tend to find very few violations and respond to violations with a light touch. This raises the question of whether few violations actually occur under this approach or are simply not discovered. Principles-based regulation might require more manpower and other regulatory resources to monitor and enforce, which might be in shortest supply when they are needed most. For example, such monitoring and enforcement problems might be most acute in a political environment where regulators are contemptuous of regulations or maintain close relationships with the firms that they monitor.

## Pre-1930s Securities Regulation: The Background

Securities market regulation, with some notable exceptions, is primarily a fairly recent phenomenon. However, there were a few earlier attempts to enact certain securities market regulations, and these earlier efforts provided the framework for more modern regulation. For example, under King Edward I in 1285, broker licensure was instituted after the finding that English brokers provided less satisfactory service than their Italian counterparts. The *Brokers Act of 1696* required stock brokers to be licensed and limited the number of these licenses to 100 for approximately 10 years. The *1720 Bubble Act* passed in Britain provided for the issuance of security prospectuses and prohibited certain types of trading fraud, but was ultimately repealed in 1825. The *Companies Act of 1844* provided once again for company issuances of prospectuses, and the *Companies Act of 1867* along with subsequent legislation provided for specific details in those prospectuses. This 19th-century British legislation, based largely on full disclosure of material information, served as an important conceptual foundation to 1930s U.S. securities legislation.

Securities legislation activity in the United States was very slow to start. Massachusetts enacted one of the earliest securities regulations in 1852, requiring railroad companies to certify that "responsible parties" had subscribed to their stock. The Constitution of the State of California signed in 1879 prohibited the sale of stock on margin. At the federal level, Congress made a small number of early attempts to regulate securities trading. For example, it passed and then quickly repealed the *Anti-Gold Futures Act of 1864*, intending to restrict trading in gold and exchange contracts. Congress attempted to regulate agricultural futures trading with the *Future Trading Act of 1921*, but this Act was found by the U.S. Supreme Court to be unconstitutional.

In the early 1900s, several states passed limited legislation to regulate securities markets. These earlier laws sought to prevent issuance of securities that were considered to be unfair or did not promise a "fair return." Securities were potentially subject to merit tests. For example, in response to numerous incidents of brokers having sold worthless securities of sham companies, Kansas enacted a securities law in 1911 requiring registration of brokers and securities. These worthless securities were said to be backed by "nothing but the blue skies of Kansas." This state legislation was considered to be the first of state *blue sky laws* intended to regulate securities markets.[2]

Prior to the 1930s, most regulation of U.S. securities markets was provided by these so-called blue sky laws, which critics often regarded as permitting "anything under the blue sky." The *Uniform Securities Act* was adopted by a number of states as early as 1930 in an effort to coordinate the state-based securities legislation. The Act has been revised extensively over the years, but has not been adopted by all states.

However, in recent years, and despite many criticisms and shortcomings, some observers consider the United States to have the most effective national securities regulatory system in the world. Securities market regulation and enforcement are currently provided by a web of legislation, regulatory agencies, and professional associations. This regulation is largely intended to manage systemic risk, prevent price manipulation, and protect the investing public against securities market abuses. The following are just a few of the many types of activities and abuses such regulation is intended to restrict[3]:

- *Wash sales* are transactions intended to create the appearance of sales where, in effect, no sales actually take place. Wash sales may be intended to manipulate security prices (e.g., conspirators execute transactions with one another to create records of sales prices to deceive other participants in the market). Wash sales may also involve the sale of securities for tax purposes with offsetting transactions to repurchase the securities or related instruments.
- *Corners* involve the purchase a sufficient level of a given security to obtain market power over its price.

[2]The precise meaning and origin of the term "Blue Sky Laws" is somewhat unclear. See Fleming (2011). See Loss and Cowett (1958) for more details on "Blue Sky Laws."

[3]There will be more discussion of securities markets abuses in Chapter 12.

- *Churning* occurs when a broker executes an inordinately large number of transactions on a client's account for the purpose of securing commissions.
- *Pools* exist when market participants combine their resources to obtain a large position in a security in order to manipulate its price.
- *Fraud* constitutes an intentional deception or misrepresentation for the purpose of securing a profit.
- *Inside trading* constitutes trading on the basis of material nonpublic information.

These and other market abuses might have been among the causes of the stock market crash of 1929. On September 3, 1929, the Dow Jones Industrial Average (DJIA) had reached a high of 381; by July 8, 1932, it had fallen to a low of 41. Numerous other economic and structural problems have been associated with this crash including massive unemployment, deflation, failure of over 5000 banks, and so on. Market abuses of the 1920s have often been blamed for contributing to the Great Crash and perhaps to the Great Depression as well (the causes of the Great Depression remain subject to much controversy). Nevertheless, the first major federal efforts at curbing market abuses resulted from these tumultuous events.

## 4.2 U.S. SECURITIES MARKET LEGISLATION: THE FOUNDATION

Beginning in the 1930s, a series of regulatory acts were proposed to prevent or mitigate market failures such as the Great Crash of 1929. The financial system was in shambles due to the devastated economy, and there was a clear need to restore integrity to financial markets to rebuild the economy. Government involvement was clearly needed to develop a much-needed regulatory system. The following sections discuss some of the major U.S. legislative acts intended to restrict abuses such as those discussed above and to promote fairness and transparency in the securities markets. Such sweeping legislation was made possible, in part, due to overwhelming Democrat majorities elected to both houses of Congress and the election of President Roosevelt in 1932. Twenty-five days after his inauguration in 1933, President Roosevelt asked Congress for a new law that would "put the burden of telling the whole truth on the seller" of securities, and, referring to the *caveat emptor* rule generally preferred in business circles, added: "Let the seller also beware."[4] Business leaders were in a poor position to effectively protest this imposition of regulation at the height of the Great Depression.

### The Bedrock: The Securities Act of 1933 and the Securities Exchange Act of 1934

*The Securities Act of 1933*, sometimes called the "Truth in Securities Law," deals primarily with new issues of securities. The Act requires that issuers and underwriters provide financial and other significant information concerning securities offered for public sale. In addition, the Act prohibits deceit, misrepresentations, and other fraud in the sale of

[4]See Schlesinger (1958), p. 441.

securities. Unlike most of the "blue skies laws" that focused on the merits of securities, the Securities Act focused on making reliable information available to prospective investors in securities. Its major provisions are as follows:

- All primary issues must be registered with an appropriate government agency (later to be the Securities Exchange Commission or SEC). The registration will include proper statements and documentation.
- A prospectus must accompany each new issue. This prospectus must contain a complete and accurate accounting of the firm's condition, risks, and prospects, and state how the proceeds of the new issue will be used.
- Small and private issues are exempt from the registration provisions. In addition, SEC Rule 415 (shelf registration) of 1982 allows up two years for securities to actually be issued after completing the SEC registration process.
- Firms, officers of firms, and underwriters are prohibited from making false statements regarding their new issues, and may be criminally liable for doing so.

*The Securities Exchange Act of 1934* was primarily intended to improve information availability and to prevent price manipulation. While it was signed into law shortly after the Securities Act of 1933, it was brought forth by Congress at roughly the same time and was intended to complement the Securities Act to form the framework for the new U.S. securities regulatory system. Whereas the Securities Act of 1933 dealt mainly with primary issues, the Securities Exchange Act of 1934 dealt mainly with secondary markets, accomplishing the following:

- Established the SEC as the nation's primary federal securities regulatory authority.
- Provided for annual and other periodic reporting by public companies.
- Limited insider trading activity.
- Provided rules for proxy solicitation.
- Required registration of exchanges.
- Provided for credit regulation: Regulations T (for brokerage firms) and U (for nonbroker lenders) permit the Board of Governors of the Federal Reserve to set margin requirements. Since 1974, investors have been required to post 50% margin (deposit or collateral) when purchasing stock on margin. FINRA Rule 2520 permits pattern day traders 25% initial margin requirements (subject to a $25,000 account equity balance).
- Subjected institutions to the Net Capital Rule, amended in 1975, imposing limits on broker-dealer debt-to-net capital ratios. Certain exceptions were made in 2004 to five of the largest institutions, all of which were bankrupted, merged, or otherwise suffered significant financial distress in the financial market crisis of 2008.
- Prohibited securities price manipulation.

## Additional Major Depression-Era Legislation

During the 1920s, banks were heavily engaged in trading, investments in riskier securities, and underwriting of securities. Higher risk nonbanking activities led to bank failures. The *Banking Acts of 1933 (Glass Steagall)* was motivated by the failure of thousands of banks.[5] Glass Steagall was intended to help restore faith in the banking system and prevent a similar crisis from reoccurring. This law fundamentally altered the U.S. banking system. There were three very important features of the legislation. First, the Federal Deposit Insurance Corporation (FDIC) was created to provide federal insurance on bank deposits (subject to a current $250,000 ceiling). The second provision (and most relevant to trading) of the Glass-Steagall Act was the imposition of restrictions on the activities of commercial banks. It prevented commercial banks from underwriting securities, trading with the public (excepting certain U.S. government and municipal bonds and real estate loans), and owning risky securities such as corporate stocks and bonds. These regulations separating financial functions were largely in response to the fact that many banks in 1933 had lost much of depositors' money to trading securities and in their securities underwriting services. Much of this provision was relaxed by various court decisions, regulator policy, and the Gramm-Leach-Bliley Act of 1999, with significant consequences.[6] The third important provision of the Glass-Steagall Act placed various regulations on the interest rates banks were allowed to pay (Reg Q), although most of these provisions were relaxed in the 1980s.

*The Commodity Exchange Act of 1936* provided for regulation of commodities and futures trading markets by the Department of Agriculture and required all futures and commodity options to be traded on organized exchanges. Ultimately, the Act led to the 1974 establishment of the Commodities Futures Trading Commission (CFTC).

*The Maloney Act of 1938* was essentially an amendment to Section 15.A of the Securities Exchange Act of 1934. It provided for the self-regulation of the over-the-counter (OTC) markets, leading to the establishment of the National Association of Securities Dealers (NASD, which merged into FINRA approximately 70 years later). It provided that the SEC can overrule the NASD and provided for NASD penalties. The Act has been hailed as "an especially provocative exercise of governmental power by a private organization" (see Hed-Hoffmann, 1965).

*The Trust Indenture Act of 1939* provided that issuers of bonds must clearly specify rights of their purchasers in an agreement known as a *trust indenture*, provide bond trustees with periodic financial reports, and that the trustee not impair purchasers' right or willingness to sue the issuing corporation. Essentially, this Act extended parts of the Securities Act of 1933 to primary bond markets.

*The Investment Companies Act of 1940* extended the Securities Act and the Securities and Exchange Act to investment companies such as mutual funds, which were not prevalent prior to the 1930s. This Act provided that investment companies must:

1. avoid fraudulent practices.
2. fully disclose financial statements.
3. distribute prospectuses.
4. publish statements outlining goals, which will not be changed without appropriate process.

[5]There was an earlier first Glass-Steagall Act, enacted in 1932 in reaction to deflation, dealing with the federal government's ability to trade debt securities. This act had a much smaller effect on the U.S. banking system.

[6]See Markham (2010).

5. limit issuance of debt.
6. follow uniform accounting procedures.
7. operate the fund to benefit owners, not managers.

*The Investment Advisers Act of 1940* requires advisors and certain investment institutions who provide clients with paid investment advice to register with the SEC. The Act focused more on NASD (now FINRA) and the SEC being able to identify those acting as investment advisors than on regulating and restricting their activities. However, the Act did specify certain illegal advertising practices by advisors. The Act was amended in 1996 to require only those advisers with over $25 million under management to register.

## 4.3 CRISES AND UPDATING THE REGULATORY SYSTEM

As in the 1930s, most subsequent securities market legislation was born of securities market booms and resulting crashes. This regulatory development process has often been criticized as "fighting the last war," in that much legislation seems intended to prevent the most recently occurring crisis rather than the next potential crisis.

### The 1960s Go-Go Years and Reform

The securities brokerage industry underwent another crisis in the late 1960s, with many firms failing due to their inability to handle their vastly increased volume of paperwork. Brokers struggled with their unprecedented success as the average NYSE daily trading volume increased from 3,042,000 shares in 1960 to 12,971,486 in 1968. Major firms such as Goodbody & Co., Pickard & Co., and F.I. Dupont, Glore Forgan & Co. either failed or had to be rescued. Hundreds of millions of dollars in stock certificates vanished, at least some due to organized crime, while billions of dollars in transactions failed. Senator Edmund Muskie introduced legislation to address this market failure and to restore investor confidence in markets. The *Securities Investor Protection Act of 1970* was passed, and provided for the establishment of the *Security Investors Protection Corporation* (SIPC) to insure accounts of brokerage clients. SIPC is funded with brokerage firm dues and protects clients from losses due to brokerage firm failure. The range of coverage provided by SIPC insurance should not be overestimated because it does not protect clients from trading losses or even most types of brokerage fraud. Instead, SIPC replaces missing cash, shares of stock, and other securities in the event of brokerage firm failure. SIPC generally does not provide for protection of commodity futures contracts, investment contracts (such as limited partnerships), and unregistered fixed annuity contracts.

When the auto company Studebaker Corporation failed in 1963, its pension plan was unable to fulfill its obligations. Senator Jacob Javitz introduced legislation to address failing employee pension and health plans. The eventual result was the *Employee Retirement Security Act of 1974* (ERISA), which makes provisions for preventing pension funds abuse and prohibits imprudent risks taken by fund managers. The Act provided for the use of the *prudent man rule*, but left it to the court system to clearly define it. Generally, the prudent man rule holds that a fiduciary is required to invest trust assets as a "prudent man" would invest his own property with the following factors in mind: the needs of beneficiaries, the need to preserve the estate (or corpus of the trust), and the amount and regularity of income. ERISA broadened the scope of this rule without making clear specifications, while holding fund managers personally responsible for "imprudence losses." In addition, ERISA made provisions for vesting rules and established the Pension Benefit Guarantee Corporation.

## Updating Commodities Trading Regulation and the National Market System

The *Commodity Futures Trading Commission Act of 1974* created the Commodity Futures Trading Commission (CFTC) and transferred regulatory authority over futures markets from the Department of Agriculture to the CFTC. The Act also gave the CFTC regulatory authority over nonagricultural futures and options on those futures. In 1982, the CFTS provided for the creation of the National Futures Association (NFA), a self-regulatory body for commodities and futures traders.

The brokerage crises were still worrisome to markets and legislators, and a more manageable clearance and settlement system was needed to avoid another paperwork crunch. Furthermore, many legislators were concerned about the fixed commission structure maintained by brokerage firms. As discussed in Chapter 2, The *Securities Acts Amendments of 1975* abolished this long-standing practice of fixed brokerage commissions and called for the establishment of a "national market system" (NMS) where orders would be routed to the best market. This led to efforts to establish a single CLOB (consolidated limit order book) that would list all limit orders and dealer quotes. It was expected that brokerage firms, dealers, and markets would compete with each other in a national market unhindered with unnecessary regulation. In addition, the amendments, implemented on May 1, 1975, sometimes known as "May Day" in securities markets, would lead to a national system for clearing and settlement. These amendments have led to the creation of the consolidated trade system (CTS), the consolidated quote system (CQS), and the intermarket trading system (ITS), or more generally, a national market system.

## Insider Trading Regulation

Illegal insider trading is traditionally defined as the execution of transactions on the basis of material nonpublicly available information. However, there is no comprehensive statutory definition as to precisely what constitutes impermissible insider trading or even what constitutes an insider. Regulators generally rely on several statutes to enforce prohibitions on insider trading. First, Section 14(e)-3 of the Securities Exchange Act essentially bans trading in securities of a tender offer target by anyone other than the bidder who has material, nonpublic information relating to the tender offer that he knows. The Act extends to those acting on behalf of either the target or bidder. This ban applies to trading on the basis of inside information with respect to hostile takeovers. Insider trading by officers, directors, and direct or indirect beneficial owners of more than 10% of equity is expressly prohibited in Section 16 of the Act. Section 10(b) of the Act prohibits the employment "in connection with the purchase or sale of any security registered on a national securities exchange or any security not so registered, any manipulative or deceptive device or contrivance in contravention of such rules and regulations as the Commission may prescribe as necessary or appropriate in the public interest or for the protection of investors." SEC Rule 10b-5 prohibits "any act, practice, or course of business which operates or would operate as a fraud or deceit upon any person, in connection with the purchase or sale of any security." Together, Section 10(b) and Rule 10b-5 prohibit making false statements or omitting material facts related to the purchase or sale of securities. However, while neither specifically mentions insider trading, broad court interpretations of the word "fraud" in Rule 10b-5 include breach of the personal obligation of an insider to maintain confidentiality, and extends to "tippees" of those who fail to fulfill their obligations. A 1980 Supreme Court decision (*Chiarella v. United States*) narrowed the definition of an insider to be one who maintains a relationship of trust and confidence with shareholders. This definition has been rather broadly interpreted.

Subsequent to several insider trading scandals in the early 1980s, Congress passed the *Insider Trading Sanctions Act of 1984*, which authorized penalties for illegal insider trading equal to three times the illegally obtained profits plus forfeiture of the profits. However, more scandals followed. The *Insider Trading and Fraud Act of 1988* was intended to help define exactly what constitutes an insider and to increase penalties for illegal insider trading activity. This Act increased the maximum imprisonment from 5 to 10 years, with maximum criminal fines increased from $100,000 to $1,000,000 for individuals and from $500,000 to $2,500,000 for nonindividuals. The Act also initiated a bounty program allowing the SEC to pay rewards to insider trading informants.

## 4.4 DEREGULATION, CORPORATE SCANDALS, AND THE FINANCIAL CRISIS OF 2008

After over 40 years of increasingly burdensome regulation in the financial services industries, President Ronald Reagan sought to reduce this regulatory burden, most notably in the banking industries. A near-collapse of the savings and loans industry shortly followed. Wendy Gramm (spouse of Senator Phil Gramm), as chair of the CFTC, in 1989 and 1993 exempted a number of swaps and derivative instruments from regulation. These exemptions were broadened in 2000 by the Gramm-Leach-Bliley Act. The Federal Reserve Board reinterpreted the Glass-Steagall Act several times during the 1980s and 1990s so as to ultimately permit bank holding companies to earn up to a quarter of their revenues from investment banking activities.

### Deregulation

The *Financial Modernization Act of 1999*, also known as the Gramm-Leach-Bliley Act, contributed to the consolidation of the financial services industries, allowing for the formation of "mega-banks." This act formally permitted commercial banks, investment banks, and insurance companies to consolidate, repealing the most important provisions of the Glass-Steagall Act passed in the 1930s to separate commercial banking from underwriting and other financial activities. While many combinations had already occurred before passage of this act (usually through subsidiaries), their legality was questionable. The pending combination of Citigroup (commercial banking) and Travelers (insurance, investment banking, and stock brokerage) into the world's largest financial institution accelerated and contributed to passage of this Act. Mergers that would have been impossible prior to passage of this Act might have masked severe operating and financial difficulties, simply forestalling some inevitable failures. But more importantly, this Act was not replaced with or accompanied by significant regulatory oversight.

*The Commodity Futures Modernization Act of 2000* exempted most OTC nonagricultural derivatives and transactions between "sophisticated parties" from regulation under the Commodity Exchange Act (CEA) or as "securities" under other federal securities laws. This act excluded most OTC energy trades from CFTC oversight and financial derivatives from SEC and CFTC oversight. These exemptions formed the so-called "Enron loophole" that contributed to massive fraud and the failure of the Enron company in addition to the role that credit default swaps would play in the 2008 financial crisis.[7] In part, the Act was intended to resolve disputes between the SEC and CFTC concerning overlapping jurisdictions, particularly with respect to certain types of contracts including *single equity futures* (futures contracts on shares of a single firm's stock). The Act led to retail trading of these contracts in 2003.

## Sarbanes-Oxley

*The Sarbanes-Oxley Act of 2002* (SOX) was enacted after a wave of corporate scandals (including Enron, WorldCom, and Global Crossing) in the late 1990s and early 2000s. The Sarbanes-Oxley Act, also known as the *Corporate and Criminal Fraud Accountability Act*, was passed to provide for accounting reform, improved financial reporting, reduced conflicts of interest, and increased penalties for securities fraud. The Act contained 11 sections. Among the highlights of this Act are:

- the creation of a five-member *Public Company Accounting Oversight Board* (PCAOB) to oversee public auditing firm practices (Section I)
- the requirement for CEOs and CFOs to personally certify the accuracy of their firms' periodic reports
- restricting public accounting firms from providing nonauditing services contemporaneously with auditing services to prevent certain conflicts of interest (Section II)
- limiting company loans to directors and officers (Subsection 402)
- prohibitions of share trading by officers and directors during certain "blackout" periods
- the requirement that attorneys representing reporting companies report material violations of law or breaches of contracts to appropriate corporate authorities
- Subsection 404 of the Act, which requires that companies prepare assessments of their internal controlling practices along with auditors' reports on those assessments

[7]See Sections § 2(g) and (h) of the Commodity Futures Modernization Act of 2000, and Cravath et al. (2001).

- requirement that firms to disclose material off-balance sheet transactions and relationships
- prohibitions on unfair allocations of securities in the initial public offering (IPO) process
- prohibitions on misleading research reports issued by financial advisors and advisory services
- requirements for publicly traded firms to have independent directors with financial expertise serve on their audit committees

## Post-SOX

Another crucial deregulatory action occurred in 2004 when the SEC relaxed the "net capital rule" (Rule 15c3-1) for the five largest investment banks. This enabled the largest investment banks to substantially increase their debt, both increasing their risk of failure and enabling them to invest more heavily in riskier assets. The rule was originally imposed in 1975 (updated from 1934), requiring that brokers and dealers doing business with the public value all of their tradable assets at market prices, discounting them to account for their market risk. In many respects, relaxation of this Act was consistent with the spirit with the Basel II Accord. Riskier assets were to be discounted more deeply than safer assets. The rule requires broker dealers to limit their debt-to-net capital ratios to 12:1. Broker dealers qualifying for exemptions under this 2004 relaxation were to be designated as "consolidated supervised entities" (CSEs). Goldman Sachs, Morgan Stanley, Merrill Lynch, Lehman Brothers, and Bear Stearns qualified as CSEs, enabling them to maintain debt-to-equity ratios exceeding 30:1. Four of these five firms failed or were bailed out between 2007 and 2009.

*Regulation NMS*, adopted by the U.S. SEC in 2005, was intended to modernize the regulatory structure of U.S. equity markets, reflecting the changing nature of markets due to improved technology and the increased variety of types of market centers (exchanges, crossing networks, ECNs, dark pools, etc.). An important provision of this regulation is the Order Protection Rule (Rule 611, also known as the "trade-through" rule). This rule requires that exchanges, alternative trading systems, and OTC market makers maintain and enforce policies to ensure the execution of trades at their best prices. Regulation NMS was intended to enhance client order protection and to improve client transaction executions by enhancing intermarket access. The regulation sought to reduce spreads by allowing for subpenny pricing on certain transactions and to improve public access to market data.

*The Credit Rating Reform Act of 2006* was enacted to improve competition in the credit rating industry and to reduce certain conflicts of interest and industry abuses. First, the Act abolished the SEC's authority to designate credit-rating agencies as "Nationally Recognized Statistical Rating Organizations (NRSROs)," by allowing any credit-rating agency three years of experience in fulfilling certain requirements to register with the SEC as a "statistical ratings organization." Prior to enactment of this act, only Standard & Poor's, Moody's Investors Service, Fitch Ratings (which, together controlled 95% of the market), and A.M. Best and Dominion were recognized as NRSROs. Second, the Act sought to curb the practices of sending a company unsolicited ratings along with a bill and packaging ratings with the purchase of consulting and other services. For example, the credit rating agencies had been taking fees for rating derivative instruments such as mortgage-backed securities (MBSs) and collateralized debt obligations (CDOs) after having received payments from their issuers for helping to package them. Thus, agencies would advise on structuring packages, and then rate the packages that they helped structure so as to receive their highest credit ratings. This act was intended to limit conflicts of interest that arose when MBSs, CDOs, and other securities are packaged and rated by major rating agencies. In addition, the Act required credit rating agencies to maintain policies and procedures to be in place to manage these types of conflicts when they arose.

### The 2008 Financial Crisis

In summer 2007, there were increasing reports of troubled mortgages and weakening of the securitized assets and portfolios that contained them. These reports followed on the peak of U.S. housing prices. By the end of the year, Countrywide Financial Corporation, one of the largest banks in the United States, was seeking shelter and Northern Rock in the UK was on the brink of failure. The financial system took a significant blow in March 2008 when Bear Stearns, one of the largest investment banks in the United States, collapsed, to be rescued by JP Morgan Chase with backing from the Federal Reserve. The special lending facilities of the Federal Reserve opened the discount window to investment banks to prevent an industry-wide collapse. IndyMac Bank FSB, another major depository institution, failed in July 2008. However, the crisis moved into full swing in September 2008 when Freddie Mac and Fannie Mae were placed under U.S. government conservatorship, Lehman Brothers filed for Chapter 11 bankruptcy protection, and the United States entered its worst recession since the Great Depression.

## 4.5 DODD-FRANK

Perhaps the most significant piece of securities legislation passed since the 1930s was the *Dodd–Frank Wall Street Reform and Consumer Protection Act* of 2010. Responding to the financial crisis of 2007–2009, Congress passed major reform covering and extending beyond securities markets intended to:

> promote the financial stability of the United States by improving accountability and transparency in the financial system, to end "too big to fail," to protect the American taxpayer by ending bailouts, [and] to protect consumers from abusive financial services practices.[8]

This 848-page act was intended to promote financial stability and consumer protection, and extended well beyond securities trading. Among the important reforms affecting traders are:

- Providing for the establishment of the *Financial Stability Oversight Council* (FSOC) to supervise systemic risk, promote market discipline, and respond to threats to financial

[8]Dodd-Frank Wall Street Reform and Consumer Protection Act.

stability. The Council is chaired by the U.S. Treasury Secretary and is comprised of 10 voting members and 5 nonvoting members.

- Providing new rules for transparency, independence, and accountability for credit rating agencies, and creation of the Office of Credit Ratings.
- Providing for the so-called *Volcker Rule*, regulating and limiting banks, their affiliates, and nonbank financial institutions supervised by the Fed with respect to proprietary trading and investment in and sponsorship of hedge funds and private equity funds.
- Authorizing the Federal Reserve Board or FSOC to designate clearing agents as systemically important and to oversee their activities.
- Providing for regulatory authority over swap agreements between the SEC (security-based swaps) and the CFTS (all other swaps).
- Rather than mandate that all swap contracts be traded on exchanges, Dodd-Frank provided for the creation of a swap execution facility (SEF), specifically designed to provide for trade transparency, encourage competitive execution, and ensure a complete record and audit trail of trades, all designed to enhance swaps markets.
- Requiring companies selling credit and mortgage-backed products to retain at least 5% of the instruments' credit risk unless the underlying loans meet certain standards that reduce risk.

As of early 2012, many provisions of the Dodd-Frank Act were awaiting finalization and implementation. For example, rules governing trading in the $601-trillion global swaps market were expected to be completed in the first quarter of 2012. One rule proposed by the CFTC concerning derivatives trading would set limits based on the market for the underlying commodity. One scenario was that a trader could not hold a derivatives position larger than 125% of the size of the estimated deliverable supply of the commodity, assuming that the derivatives were cash-settled and that the trader controlled no more than 25% of the physical market. Implementation of the Volcker Rule is expected to be pushed back from its original deadline of July 21, 2012. However, many of the larger U.S. banks had already sold or closed proprietary trading desks by summer 2011.

## 4.6 GOVERNMENT OVERSIGHT OF SELF-REGULATION: THE SECURITIES AND EXCHANGE COMMISSION AND COMMODITY FUTURES TRADING COMMISSION

The U.S. securities regulatory system might be characterized as a shared, cooperative coordination of industry, state, and federal systems that serve as complementary components under the authority of the U.S. federal government. However, the extent to which these systems share authority and are coordinated might be subject to some debate. Nevertheless, all these systems do play a role in the regulation of securities markets, and the U.S. government can be regarded as the "senior partner."

As discussed previously, 1930s securities legislation provided for some degree of self-regulation in securities markets. While FINRA, exchanges and other markets, and self-regulatory organizations (SROs) themselves still play a primary role in regulating and monitoring market participants, the SEC and other government agencies retain ultimate regulatory powers and frequently play oversight and technical roles in regulatory activity, and seek to "cover gaps" in self-regulation. SROs such as the NYSE have regularly pursued actions against insider trading. If markets fail to properly monitor and regulate themselves, the SEC or CFTC can take action, as might state authorities. For example, the SEC was instrumental in bringing to the forefront and terminating the so-called "odd-eighths" NASD scandal in the late 1990s. In another example of SEC oversight, after Richard Whitney, the president of the New York Stock Exchange, was discovered in 1937 to have misappropriated large sums from the NYSE "widows and orphans" fund to save his own brokerage firm, the SEC required that the NYSE to reorganize itself and strengthen the independence of its board of directors.

In some eras, the SEC has been considered to have been either lax or weak in its enforcement. In instances where the SEC has failed to take corrective action on market abuses, other regulatory authorities such as state attorneys general have done so. State "blue-sky" laws, even those predating 1930s legislation, have been used by state attorneys general to pursue abuses. For example, the former attorney general of New York, Elliot Spitzer, used the New York 1921 Martin Law prohibiting certain "boiler room" activities and securities fraud to obtain a $100 million settlement from Merrill Lynch & Co. in 2002, based on the company's alleged conflicts of interests involving its analysts. Similar pursuits by this state office led to a $1.4 billion settlement with 10 of the world's leading brokerage firms for fraudulent and/or exaggerated or unwarranted statements in analyst reports.

## The Securities and Exchange Commission

The SEC was created as an independent agency by the Securities and Exchange Act of 1934 to protect investors; to maintain fair, orderly, and efficient markets; and to facilitate capital formation, particularly in the business sectors. The SEC seeks to ensure that firms and organizations raising money by selling securities to investors disclose certain essential facts about these securities prior to their sale and while they are held. The SEC also seeks to ensure that those who trade securities are dealt with fairly and honestly.

The president of the United States, with advice and consent from the Senate, appoints the five members of the SEC, including its chair, to staggered five-year terms. No more than three can belong to any one political party. The Commission is comprised of five divisions and 16 offices, with headquarters in Washington, DC, and in 11 regional offices around the country. The Commission interprets and enforces federal securities laws, and issues and amends rules to complement, implement, and support federal legislation. In addition, the SEC monitors and sanctions securities markets (including firms, brokers, advisors, SROs, auditors, and rating agencies), oversees their inspection, and coordinates activities with state and foreign regulators.

The SEC not only investigates regulatory infractions and enforces legislation, but is an essential rule maker itself. For example, despite legislative and SEC efforts to limit trading on the basis of nonpublic information, many investors still openly did so. For example, it had been common practice for firms to assemble select securities analysts to make corporate announcements to them ahead of announcements to the general public. This type of activity certainly tilted the playing field in the favor of these analysts and their employers. In response, the SEC introduced *Regulation Fair Disclosure* (FD) in 2000, which was intended to limit this type of selective disclosure. Regulation FD requires companies to make material information public to all investors. Furthermore, if material information were to leak unintentionally, firms are required to reveal the leaked information to all investors within 24 hours.

## The Commodity Futures Trading Commission

The CFTC was created as an independent agency in 1974 after the enactment of the Commodity Futures Trading Commission Act to regulate U.S. commodity futures and option markets. Its creation was delayed in comparison to that of the SEC because most futures and options trading were related to agricultural commodities and thus were overseen by the Department of Agriculture. A number of market developments, including the 1973 opening of the Chicago Options Exchange, led to the 1974 enactment of the Commodities Futures Trading Commission Act.

In a manner similar to the SEC, the CFTC has five commissioners including its chair appointed by the president to staggered five-year terms, with no more than three commissioners from any one political party. Its mission is to protect market participants and the public from fraud, manipulation, and abusive practices related to futures and options, and to foster open, competitive, and financially sound markets. The CFTC maintains a number of essential offices and divisions[9]:

- The CFTC Office of the General Counsel is the Commission's legal advisor, represents the Commission in appellate litigation and certain trial-level cases, including bankruptcy proceedings involving futures industry professionals, and advises the Commission on the application and interpretation of the Commodity Exchange Act and other administrative statutes.
- The Office of the Executive Director formulates and implements the management and administrative functions of the CFTC and the agency's budget.
- The Division of Clearing and Risk oversees derivatives clearing organizations (DCOs), the clearing of swaps, futures, and options on futures, and market participants that may pose risk to the clearing process.
- The Division of Market Oversight is responsible for fostering markets that accurately reflect the forces of supply and demand for the underlying commodity and are free of abusive trading activity, oversees trade execution facilities, and performs market surveillance, market compliance, and market and product review functions.
- The Division of Enforcement investigates and prosecutes alleged violations of the Commodity Exchange Act and Commission regulations. Violations may involve commodity futures or option trading on U.S. futures exchanges or the improper marketing and sales of commodity futures products to the general public.

[9]Most of these CFTC operating unit descriptions were paraphrased from the Commission's website at http://www.cftc.gov/About/CFTCOrganization/index.htm.

- The Office of the Chief Economist provides economic support and advice to the Commission, conducts research on policy issues facing the agency, and provides education and training for Commission staff.

## 4.7 IMPACT OF REGULATORY ACTIVITY

Successful financial regulation prevents market failure, promotes macroeconomic stability, protects investors, and mitigates the effects of financial failures on the real economy. Financial regulation can also be used to improve market transparency and to protect investors, although these ends might simply serve to prevent market failure. However, financial regulation also imposes a variety of costs on regulated firms and the economy:

- Direct costs: Costs of regulation administration and enforcement, which might be complicated by having multiple agencies enforce regulation. These costs might be financed by some combination of taxes and fees imposed on regulated institutions and their clients. In fact, these costs might be absorbed by regulated firms through self-regulation.
- Indirect costs: Costs of compliance, such as those associated with maintaining records, hiring compliance officers, making payments to auditors and ratings agencies, and so on.
- Distortions to financial markets: Reactions to regulation often cause institutions to conduct business sub-optimally, and can cause firms to leave or restrict their entry into the marketplace. Regulated firms often seek operating jurisdictions with the least restrictive regulations.

These costs hurt profits of regulated firms, and many are ultimately passed on to the real economy. Even with the financial market crisis of 2007–2009, the U.S. financial regulatory systems are often considered to be among the most highly developed, comprehensive, effective, and mimicked in the world. But these systems are far from perfect, and numerous studies have been conducted to more closely examine the effects of financial regulation.

Since its enactment in 2002, Sarbanes-Oxley has been a source of controversy. Many observers argue that the Act did not go far enough in its requirements while many corporate managers argued that the Act imposed unduly expensive reporting and compliance requirements on them. Nonetheless, Cohen et al. (2008) found that SOX did lead to a decline in earnings management, and Gordon et al. (2006) found that SOX improved the voluntary disclosure of information security activities by firms.

While the benefits and costs associated with SOX are still being studied, U.S. regulatory actions have a number of interesting results, many of which are unintended. First, financial regulatory activity tends to impose significant burdens on business and financial institutions. Some estimates placed the compliance costs on U.S. business of Section 404 of SOX dealing with internal control quality at $6 billion per year, not counting the indirect costs associated with the impact on company operations. Accounting for the full impact of SOX, including indirect costs, Zhang (2007) estimated through stock market reactions total costs imposed on business by SOX compliance would be as high as $1.4 trillion. Within three years of the enactment of SOX, a number of European companies, including ITV and

United Business Media, had deregistered their firms' stock in the United States to avoid these costs. These and other distortions were clearly unintended by the authors of SOX. Vermont Teddy Bear, a Shelbourne, Vermont–based gift and toy company, took its shares private in a highly publicized 2005 act intended to avoid costs of complying with SOX. More generally, Chhaochharia and Grinstein (2007) argue that smaller firms suffer disproportionately from the costs of implementing Sarbanes-Oxley, particularly the costs of maintaining internal controls. In addition, smaller firms experience more difficulty attracting qualified independent directors to their boards. Chhaochharia and Grinstein found that larger firms that needed to make the most significant adjustments to comply with Sarbanes-Oxley experienced the most significant short-term benefits to their share prices.

While SOX has been blamed for causing firms to refuse to list or withdraw from listing their shares in the United States, it is important to note that companies were regularly delisted from the NYSE prior to SOX for a variety of reasons. For example, firms either delist or refuse to list their shares because they simply cannot fulfill or continue to fulfill NYSE listing requirements. Some firms that delisted might simply have found it convenient to blame SOX for being forced into exchange delisting.

Some observers (e.g., O'Hara, 2004) have noted that Regulation NMS does not account for the diverse needs of different types of traders and has led to a deterioration of liquidity. This deterioration of liquidity has led some traders seeking to bypass better quotes on the NYSE for speedier trades or more anonymous trades on an ATS. For example, some trades might have executions forced in less reliable or slower markets in order to fulfill the best price requirement. Redler (2010) and Chung and Chuwonganant (2010) argued that Regulation NMS has, contrary to its objectives, increased spreads and trading costs while reducing liquidity and depth in equity markets. In fact, Redler argued that the May 6, 2010 "flash crash was a direct result of false liquidity in the marketplace insulated by the Order Protection Rule," where HFTs retracted their orders immediately after observing the one-sided market.

Another effect of financial regulation is its encouragement of financial innovation. Numerous financial products and markets owe their creation and/or growth to financial regulation and efforts to bypass regulation. A small sampling of examples includes preferred stock, interest rate swaps, hedge funds, loan securitizations, and swap funds. A more recent innovation from SOX is markets for unregistered shares. Consider GSTRuE, the Goldman Sachs Tradable Unregistered Equity OTC Program, which was, in part, created to sell shares of Oaktree Capital Management, LLC, an alternative management firm. Oaktree, like other alternative management firms Blackstone and Fortress, prefers to operate under regulatory "radars" and with a significant degree of confidentiality. Blackstone and Fortress, as public firms, are subject to SOX and other regulation applicable to public firms. Goldman Sachs floated shares of Oaktree stock to fewer than 499 institutional investors with capital in excess of $100 million, and created GSTRuE so that these institutional investors could trade those issued shares outside of the public securities regulatory reach.

The Volcker Rule is expected to go into effect as a part of Dodd-Frank implementation. In effect, this rule withdraws federal assistance (bailout) expectations from banks undertaking risky trading activities, reducing the moral hazard problem (taking risks with the money of others). However, the banking industry has expressed much dissatisfaction with the rule because of its anticipated negative impact on an important but volatile source of bank profits. A 2011 study conducted by Oliver Wyman (a consultancy firm) on behalf of the Securities Industry and Financial Markets Association, a trade group for the securities industry, claims that the Volcker Rule could cost investors in U.S. corporate bonds as much as $315 billion, due to reductions in liquidity, increases in interest rates, and other distortions caused by the rule. However, many of these losses by banks are likely to be recaptured by other investors and institutions that fill affected banks' proprietary trading roles. In addition, some of these lost profits will be compensated by investors who receive higher interest payments, and so on.

## 4.8 REGULATION: THE INTERNATIONAL ARENA

Almost 20 years ago, Benn Stiel offered the following transaction description to illustrate the increasing globalization of securities markets:

> An American broker in London buys German "Bunds" for a Mexican client from a Japanese trading house in Paris and clears the trade in Brussels. This sort of story line is not simply plausible, but is on the verge of becoming commonplace (Stiel, 1994, p. 197).

However, most securities market regulation (other than certain instances in the European Union) is conducted at the national level, or in some cases, including Canada, even at the provincial level. Regulatory activity on the global level has been more pervasive in the banking industries than in the securities industries.

The most significant nonbanking global organization engaged in regulatory policy is the *International Organization of Securities Commissions* (IOSCO). This organization, which has no direct regulatory or legislative authority in any country, cooperates in "developing, implementing and promoting adherence to internationally recognized and consistent standards of regulation, oversight and enforcement in order to protect investors, maintain fair, efficient and transparent markets, and seek to address systemic risks."[10] Thus, the organization seeks to improve financial efficiency and transparency, protect investors, and reduce systemic risks. The Organization is comprised of representatives from over 100 national securities regulatory commissions around the world. Because of significant overlaps between the banking and securities industries, the *Basel Committee on Banking Supervision* is also a crucial global body providing for regular cooperation on securities regulation. Neither of these organizations has formal regulatory authority in any country, although their policy recommendations are regularly adopted by countries.

At a more regional level, the *European Securities and Markets Authority* (ESMA) is the European Supervisory Authorities (ESA) body that regulates EU securities markets. Unlike the IOSCO, the ESMA is the only supranational securities regulatory body that has the authority to draft legally binding technical standards and ban securities market activities likely to increase systemic risks, and has the ability to launch fast-track country-specific procedures to ensure consistent application of EU law. The ESMA can initiate investigations and request that EU member countries launch investigations and issue recommendations

[10]Taken from the IOSCO website, http://www.iosco.org/about/.

based on the results of those investigations. The ESMA also has binding mediation powers to resolve securities market conflicts among member countries.

### Selected Country Regulatory Authorities

The *Financial Services Authority* (FSA) has served as an independent regulatory body for the UK financial services industry through 2012, cooperating closely with the *Bank of England*. In 2012, the FSA, along with its securities regulatory functions, were expected to be merged into the Bank of England. The FSA has placed, and the Bank of England will continue to place a high priority on protecting retail customers, creating its Retail Distribution Review (RDR) program intended to enhance consumer confidence in the financial industry. This RDR program focuses on monitoring the delivery of services by roughly 25,000 independent financial advisers.

The *Federal Financial Supervisory Authority* (BaFin) is the German financial regulatory authority under the supervision of the *Federal Ministry of Finance*. BaFin is one of the country-specific regulators belonging to and working with ESMA.

Securities markets are regulated in Japan by its *Securities and Exchange Surveillance Commission* (SESC), established in 1992 as a commission operating under the authority of the Japanese Financial Services Agency. As is the case with the SEC in the United States, the SESC attempts to ensure that investors receive full disclosure with respect to security issues. Unlike in the United States, the SESC imposes eligibility standards on Japanese firms wishing to make public bond issues. The SESC does not have the authority to prosecute violations. The Commission files its findings and recommendations with prosecutors and the Financial Services Agency.

## 4.9 PRIVATIZATION OF REGULATION AND EXCHANGE RULES

Privatization of regulation typically refers to nongovernment creation and adoption of common guidelines to govern the behavior of participants in the system (markets). The CFA Institute (2007) stated that "the overarching purpose of any self-regulatory group is to keep industry interests aligned with the public interest so as to avoid government intervention and the possibility of more-restrictive regulation."

The Maloney Act of 1938 and the formation of the NASD launched a significant innovation leading towards some degree of privatization in the regulation of securities markets. While governmental organizations still play the dominant role in securities regulation, over time there have been wide variations in levels of privatization. NASD (now merged into FINRA), the National Futures Association, and exchanges themselves act or acted as SROs (self-regulatory organizations). However, their activity is overseen and perhaps even micromanaged by the SEC. The OTC (nonpublic) markets rely on trade associations or nonprofit corporations to prepare uniform contracts and standardized agreements among market participants. For example, in 1987 the *International Swaps and Derivatives Association* (ISDA), which sets standards for derivative contracts, prepared the then 14-page ISDA Master Agreement that has regulated the huge swaps markets. This Agreement acts as a standardized contract used among participants in these huge markets. ISDA and its early success were instrumental to the refusal by Congress to regulate derivatives markets in the 1990s. When such efforts fail to prevent market stress or failure, government regulators intervene. Major advantages to maintaining private regulatory bodies or self-regulation in securities markets might be as follows:

- Market participants have the most intimate knowledge of the markets to be regulated.
- The regulatory foci on developing best practices and effective monitoring and enforcement policies are based on economic and reputational self-interest.
- Governmental regulatory costs are reduced as they are passed on to the regulated market.

## NYSE Rules

Exchanges are established to facilitate and regulate trading, and remain important sources of securities markets regulation. Such regulations ensure that all participants remain reliable partners for trading, as well as establish exactly what is to be traded. Exchange rules are intended to ensure that markets remain active and liquid. For example, the NYSE imposes a variety of rules on trading, member firms, and listed firms. While the NYSE considers each application to list company shares for trading on its own merit, its listing standards are considered rather stringent (although standards do vary for NYSE Domestic, NYSE Worldwide, and NYSE AMEX listings). Such standards for NYSE Domestic typically include a minimum tangible asset level ($100 million in many scenarios as of 2012) and at least 1.1 million outstanding shares with at least 400 shareholders holding a minimum of 100 shares, as well as minimum historical earnings levels and restrictions concerning corporate governance. There are a number of other listing requirements in addition to requirements for delisting a security.

The NYSE imposes standards on listed firms with respect to governance, in addition to those standards imposed by SOX and other governmental regulation. Among the governance rules imposed by the NYSE are:

1. Issuers have a majority of independent directors.
2. Members of issuing firm boards meet tight standards to qualify as independent directors.
3. Nonmanagement directors conduct separate regularly scheduled meetings.
4. Issuers have a nominating/corporate governance committees and compensation committees, each of which is comprised entirely of independent directors and having their own charters listing certain minimum duties and responsibilities.
5. Audit committee members meet more stringent standards of independence and audit committees have their own charters.
6. Issuers adopt and disclose corporate governance guidelines and codes of business conduct and ethics.
7. Issuing company CEOs must certify as to compliance with NYSE corporate governance listing standards and provide written notification to the NYSE of any material noncompliance with these standards.

## NYSE Circuit Breakers

The NYSE makes significant efforts to maintain price continuity during its most volatile periods. For example, with Rule 80A, the NYSE instituted a system of "circuit breakers" following the stock market crash of 1987. This rule followed the Brady Report recommending circuit breakers as a means to limit credit risk, "level the playing field" for individual investors needing more time to obtain and react to new information, reduce the illusion of perfect liquidity in the face of one-sided volume, facilitate price discovery by giving traders additional time for analysis, inhibit panic, and publicize order imbalances. This rule required that sell (buy) orders related to *index arbitrage* in component stocks of the S&P 500 Index could be executed only on an uptick (downtick) or zero tick.[11] A 2% movement in the DJIA in a single day triggered the rule. The rule was rescinded in 2007.

NYSE Rule 80B provides for more drastic reactions to more dramatic market volatility. As revised in 1998, circuit breakers have been revised to account for the increased DJIA and increased market volatility. Now, circuit breakers will be based on the monthly average of DJIA closing values as of the most recent quarter-end month. Triggers are set quarterly as of the most recent of December 31, March 31, June 30, and September 30, and rounded to the nearest 50 points. The following circuit breakers are in effect:

1. A 10% decline in the DJIA from the previous day close prior to 2 PM will halt trading for 1 hour and for 30 minutes before 2:30 PM.
2. A 20% decline in the DJIA from the previous day close prior to 1 PM will halt trading for 2 hours, for 1 hour before 2 PM, and for the remainder of the day after 2 PM.
3. A 30% decline in the DJIA from the previous will halt trading for the remainder of the day.

Suppose that the average closing values for the Dow, rounded to the closest 50 points, were 12,000 for the prior quarter. This would mean that the point levels to trigger circuit breakers during the subsequent month are 1200, 2400, and 3600 drops from the prior day close.

In 2010, in response to the May 6 "flash crash," the SEC mandated a uniform stock-by-stock circuit breaker for most of the largest equities irrespective of marketplace, where stocks whose price moves by more than 5% in a five-minute period are subject to a five-minute (or longer) pause in trading activity. This circuit breaker was instituted on a "pilot" basis, and was extended to at least July 2012.

The extent to which these circuit breakers have actually benefited the market is not clear. First, traders complain that if market price begins to approach circuit breaker levels, their changes tend to accelerate towards the level needed to trigger the circuit breaker. Second, the extent to which the exchanges coordinate their circuit breaker activity is not clear. In addition to the circuit breaker rules described above, the NYSE may also halt trading in any specific stock on the basis of firm-specific information.

## Additional Reading

Kitch (2000) and Niemeyer (2001) are very readable and reasonably short introductions to the regulation of securities markets along with considerations for improving regulation. Fleming (2011) and the first chapter of Loss

[11]Index arbitrage involves simultaneous transactions of a large number of securities comprising a particular index, in this case, the S&P500.

and Seligman (2004) present interesting early histories of securities regulation. Websites for the NYSE, FINRA, CFTC, and SEC all provide substantial details on regulations, including the original documentation. The same is true for most of the international and private securities regulatory bodies. The FINRA site for the Series 7 Examination is a good starting point for readers interested in pursuing careers in the securities industry (http://www.finra.org/Industry/Compliance/Registration/QualificationsExams/RegisteredReps/P011051). SecLaw.com provides an extensive collection of articles on securities regulation, ranging from the very introductory to the minutiae of specific securities and markets. Ford (2008) offers a nice discussion of principles-based and rules-based securities regulation.

# References


CFA Institute. (2007). *Self-Regulation in today's securities markets: Outdated system or work in progress?* Codes, Standards and Position Papers, vol. 2007, no. 7. CFA Institute Centre For Financial Market Integrity, September.

Chhaochharia, V., & Grinstein, Y. (2007). *Corporate governance and firm value: The impact of the 2002 governance rules.* Johnson School Research Paper Series No. 23-06, AFA 2006 Boston Meetings Paper, March.

Chung, K. H., & Chuwonganant, C. (2010). *Regulation NMS and market quality.* Financial Management. doi: 10.1111/j.1755-053X.2012.01184.x.

Cohen, D., Dey, A., & Lys, T. (2008). Real and accrual-based earnings management in the pre- and post-Sarbanes Oxley periods. *Accounting Review, 82*(3), 757–787.

Cravath, Swaine and Moore. (2001). *Memorandum for ISDA members: Commodity Futures Modernization Act of 2000.* New York, New York, January 5, 2001. Available at: <http://www.google.com/url?sa=t&rct=j&q=2(h)%20and%20(g)%20of%20the%20commodity%20futures%20modernization%20act%20of%202000&source=web&cd=3&sqi=2&ved=0CDMQFjAC&url=http%3A%2F%2Fwww.isda.org%2Fspeeches%2Fpdf%2FAnalysis_of_Commodity-Exchange-Act-Legislation.pdf&ei=qiZgT9-tNIrz0gG18piyBw&usg=AFQjCNFdfROr92VJZRfKcF_G2Evyw7TKvQ> Accessed 13.03.12.

Fleming, R. A. (2011). 100 years of securities law: Examining a foundation laid in the Kansas Blue Sky. *Washburn Law Journal, 50*(3), 583–610.

Ford, C. L. (2008). New governance, compliance, and principles-based securities regulation. *American Business Law Journal, 45*(1), 1–60.

Gordon, L. A., Loeb, M. P., Lucyshyn, W., & Sohail, T. (2006). The impact of the Sarbanes-Oxley Act on the corporate disclosures of information security activities. *Journal of Accounting and Public Policy, 25*, 503–530.

Hed-Hofmann, T. (1965). The Maloney Act experiment. *Boston College Industrial and Commercial Law Review, 6*(2), 187–218.

Kitch, E. (2000). Regulation of securities markets. In B. Bouckaert, & G. De Geest (Eds.), *The regulation of contracts.* In *Encyclopedia of law and economics* (Vol. III). Cheltenham: Edward Elgar. Available at: <http://encyclo.findlaw.com/5660book.pdf> Accessed 05.01.12.

Loss, L., & Cowett, E. M. (1958). *Blue sky law.* New York: Little, Brown and Company.

Loss, L., & Seligman, J. (2004). *Fundamentals of securities regulation* (5th ed.). New York: Aspen Publishers.

Markham, J. W. (2010). The subprime crisis – a test match for the bankers: Glass-Steagall vs. Gramm-Leach-Bliley. *University of Pennsylvania Journal of Business Law, 12*(4), 1081–1134.

Niemeyer, J. (2001). *An economic analysis of securities market regulation and supervision: where to go after the Lamfalussy report?* SSE/EFI Working Paper Series in Economics and Finance No. 482. Economic Research Institute, Stockholm School of Economics, Stockholm, Sweden.

O'Hara, M. (2004). Searching for a new center: U.S. securities markets in transition. *Federal Reserve Bank of Atlanta Economic Review*, 37–52.

Oliver Wyman, Inc. (2011). *The Volcker rule: Considerations for implementation of proprietary trading regulations.* Available at: Unpublished report, <http://www.sifma.org/workarea/downloadasset.aspx?id = 22888> Accessed 04.01.12.

Redler, S., 2010. SEC Should Rethink Reg NMS to Fix HFT Liquidity Problem. MrSwing. Available at: <http://www.mrswing.com/articles/SEC_Should_Rethink_Reg_NMS_to_Fix_HFT_Liquidity_Pr.html> Accessed 04.01.12

Schlesinger, A. M., Jr. (1958). *The coming of the New Deal: 1933–1935, The Age of Roosevelt* (Vol. II). New York: Houghton-Mifflin.

Steil, B. (1994). International securities markets regulation. In B. Steil (Ed.), *International Financial Market Regulation* (pp. 197–232). West Sussex: John Wiley & Sons.
Zhang, I. X. (2007). Economic consequences of the Sarbanes Oxley Act of 2002. *Journal of Accounting and Economics*, *44*(1–2), 74–115.

## 4.10 EXERCISES

**1.** Some lawyers and economists have argued that legalizing insider trading would benefit markets by allowing insiders to disseminate information through their own trading activity. Prepare an argument to support this position.

**2.** The following was taken from the Securities Exchange Act of 1934, Section 10, amended as of January 3, 2012:

> It shall be unlawful for any person, directly or indirectly, by the use of any means or instrumentality of interstate commerce or of the mails, or of any facility of any national securities exchange.... To use or employ, in connection with the purchase or sale of any security registered on a national securities exchange or any security not so registered, or any securities-based swap agreement, any manipulative or deceptive device or contrivance in contravention of such rules and regulations as the Commission may prescribe as necessary or appropriate in the public interest or for the protection of investors.

This rule has been used as a basis to prosecute insider trading activity. Describe how regulator reliance on this rule might characterize an example of "principles-based" regulation in the United States.

**3.** This chapter discussed several of the advantages of maintaining private regulatory bodies for securities markets. What might be some of the disadvantages to this type of securities market regulation?

**4.** Some people commented that the Securities Act of 1933 was based on the "sunlight theory of regulation," which is analogous to saying that "those who are forced to undress in public will presumably pay some attention to their figures." What do these commentators mean by these expressions?

**5.** The United States has maintained a "rules-based" approach to securities regulation while the UK has been progressing to a "principles-based" system of securities regulation.

**a.** Consider the rules-based and principles-based regulatory approaches to traffic speed limits. How might speed limit regulations be phrased in either case?

**b.** Why might rules-based speed limit regulations be more difficult to implement?

**c.** Why might principles-based speed limit regulations be more difficult to enforce?

CHAPTER

# 5

# Adverse Selection, Trading, and Spreads

## 5.1 INFORMATION AND TRADING

The *economics of information* is concerned with how information along with the quality and value of this information affect an economy and economic decisions. Information can be inexpensively created, can be reliable, and, when reliable, is valuable. Some economists have suggested that more than half of the U.S. economy is currently engaged in activities that are producing and analyzing information products. In fact, revenues obtained by the New York Stock Exchange from selling trading data exceed its trading-fee based revenues. The simplest microeconomics models assume that information is costless and all agents have equal access to relevant information. But, such assumptions do not hold in reality, and costly and asymmetric access to information very much affects how traders interact with each other. Investors and traders look to the trading behavior of other investors and traders for information, which affects the trading behavior of informed investors who seek to limit the information that they reveal.

In Chapter 3, we discussed slippage and market impact models, describing how prices move against traders who execute large orders due to the perceived information content of those orders. Here, particularly in our discussion of the Bagehot (1971), Kyle (1985), and Glosten and Milgrom (1985) models, we discuss the market mechanisms causing prices to react to the information content of trades (market impact or slippage), and how traders and dealers can react to this information content to maximize their own profits (or minimize losses). This chapter is concerned primarily with problems that arise when traders and other market participants have inadequate, different (*asymmetric information availability*), and costly access to information. In this chapter, we discuss information and information asymmetries in a trading context.

### Adverse Selection

*Adverse selection* originally referred to the tendency of higher risk individuals to seek insurance coverage. More generally, adverse selection refers to precontractual

*Financial Trading and Investing*

opportunism where one contracting party uses his private information to the counterparty's disadvantage. For example, the adverse selection problem can arise when a woman planning a pregnancy purchases health insurance, when a car rental customer secretly planning a trip through a Golan Heights minefield buys comprehensive insurance on the car, or when a pyromaniac purchases fire insurance. In all three cases, the agent (insured or customer) has private information with respect to the higher anticipated costs of the insurance coverage or lease, but pays a "pooling" premium for the incident or casualty coverage. Obviously, this private information affects the behavior of insurers and other insured clients, in what might otherwise be taken to be a suboptimal manner, referred to as the adverse selection problem. In a financial trading context, adverse selection occurs when one trader with secret or special information uses that information to her advantage at the expense of her counterparty in trade. Trade counterparties realize that they might fall victim to adverse selection, so they carefully monitor trading activity in an effort to discern which trades are likely to reflect special information. For example, large or numerous buy (sell) orders originating from the same trader are likely to be perceived as being motivated by special information. Trade counterparties are likely to react by adjusting their offers (bids) upwards (downwards), resulting in slippage as we discussed in Chapter 3. This market impact or slippage is the market's reaction to the adverse selection problem. In this chapter, we will consider the impact of the adverse selection problem on order sizes, security prices, and the spread.

## 5.2 NOISE TRADERS

*Noise traders* trade on the basis of what they falsely believe to be special information or misinterpret useful information concerning the future price or payoffs of a risky asset. Noise traders make investment and trading decisions based on incorrect perceptions or analyses of the market, perhaps creating opportunities for more sophisticated investors and traders. In many models of markets, noise traders are often assumed to have no useful information or at least react inappropriately to useful information concerning a security's fundamentals. But, do noise traders distort prices? If noise traders trade in large numbers, if their trading behavior is correlated, or if their effects cannot be mitigated by informed and rational traders, they may well distort prices from fundamental values. In many models, individual investors are presumed to be noise traders and that their psychology (see Chapter 10) and poor access to information inhibit their trading success.

In 1953, the economist Milton Friedman suggested that traders who produce positive profits do so by trading against less rational or poorly informed investors who tend to move prices away from their fundamental or correct values. Fama (1965) argued that when irrational trading does occur, security prices will not be significantly affected because more sophisticated traders will react quickly to exploit and eliminate any deviations from fundamental economic values. Figlewski (1979) suggested that it might take irrational investors a very long time to lose all their money and for prices to reflect security intrinsic values, but nonetheless, those traders who choose their portfolios irrationally are doomed in the long run.

Noise traders are useful, perhaps even necessary, for markets to function. Without noise traders, markets would be informationally efficient. Prices would always fully reflect information (to the extent market frictions are absent). Even with asymmetric information access, informed traders can fully reveal their superior information through their trading activities, and prices would reflect this information and ultimately eliminate the motivation for information-based trading. That is, as Black (1986) argued, without noise traders, dealers would widen their spreads to avoid losing profits to informed traders such that no trades would ever be executed. However, noise traders do impose on other traders the risk that prices might move unpredictably, irrationally, and without reference to relevant information. In some instances, this risk imposed by noise traders might discourage arbitrageurs from acting to exploit price deviations from fundamental values. Prices can deviate significantly from rational valuations, and can remain different for long periods. In fact, arbitrageurs might sometimes need to ask themselves the following important question: "Does my ability to remain solvent exceed the asset price's ability to remain irrational?" We will discuss this issue more in Chapter 6.

## 5.3 ADVERSE SELECTION IN DEALER MARKETS

Bagehot (1971) described a market where dealers or market makers stand by to provide liquidity to every trader who wishes to trade, losing on trades with informed traders but recovering these losses by trading with uninformed, noise, or liquidity-motivated traders. The market maker sets prices and trades to ensure this outcome, on average. The market maker merely recovers his operating costs along with a "normal return." In this framework, trading is a zero-sum or neutral game. Investors with special information or superior analytical skills will earn abnormal returns; uninformed investors will lose more than they make. In fact, the more frequently an uninformed trader trades, the more he can be expected to lose, and these trading losses are reflected as informed trader profits.[1] Market makers observe buying and selling pressure on prices and set prices accordingly, often making surprisingly little use of fundamental analysis when making their pricing decisions. Kyle's (1985) theoretical model describes the trading behavior of informed traders and uninformed market makers in an environment with noise traders.

### Kyle: Informed Traders, Market Makers, and Noise Traders

#### *The Setting and Assumptions*

Suppose two rational traders have access to the same information and are otherwise identical. They have no motivation to trade. Now, suppose they have different information. Will they trade? Not if one trader believes that a second will trade only if the second has information that will enable him to profit in the trade at the first trader's expense. Rational traders will not trade against other rational traders even if their information

[1]See Barber and Odean (2000, 2001, 2002) and Barber et al. (2009) who find that more aggressive (frequent) traders underperform risk-adjusted benchmarks. We discuss these and related findings in Chapter 10.

differs. This is a variation of the Akerlof "lemon problem." So, why do we observe so much trading in the marketplace? Most of us believe that others are not as informed or rational as we are or that others do not have the same ability to access and process information that we do. Thus, Kyle examines trading and price setting in a market where some traders are informed and others (noise or liquidity traders) are not. Dealers or market makers serve as intermediaries between informed and uninformed traders, and seek to set security prices that enable them to survive even without the special information enjoyed by informed traders. Kyle models how informed traders will use their information to maximize their trading profits given that their trades yield useful information to market makers. Furthermore, market makers will seek to learn from the informed trader's trading behavior, and the informed trader's trading activity will seek to disguise his special information from the dealer and noise traders.

Consider a one-time-period single auction model involving an asset that will pay in one time period $v \sim N(p_0; \Sigma_0)$; that is, the future liquidation payoff $v$ is normally distributed with mean value $p_0$ and variance $\Sigma_0$. Thus, $p_0$ is the unconditional expected value of the asset. Variance, $\Sigma_0$, can be interpreted to be the amount of uncertainty that the informed trader's perfect information resolves, so that $\Sigma_0$ reflects the informed trader's value advantage. There are three trader types—a single informed trader with perfect information, many uninformed noise traders, and a single dealer or market maker who acts as an intermediary in all trades. All are risk neutral, there is no spread, and money has no time value. Market makers and noise traders seek to learn from the actions of the informed trader, who seeks to disguise himself and his special information in a batch market (markets accumulate orders before clearing them). Thus, the informed trader seeks to determine $x$, an appropriate share purchase (sale) volume that maximizes his trading profits based on his superior information: $\pi = E[(v-p)\ x|v]$ where $p$ is the market price of the asset. That is, the informed trader seeks to maximize his expected trading profits given his perfect knowledge of $v$ and the price $p$ that he pays (or receives) for $x$ shares of the stock. Noise traders and the market maker will observe total share purchases $X = x + u$, where $u$ reflects noise trader transactions, bidding up the price of shares $p$ as $X$ increases. The market maker cannot distinguish between informed trader demand $x$ and noise trader demand $u$, but does correctly observe total demand $X$. Nonetheless, $X$ will be correlated with $x$, hence, the informed trader needs to exercise care in deciding on his transactions volume $x$ to protect himself from price slippage (see Chapter 3). Thus, neither the dealer nor the noise traders will know which trades or traders are informed, but they seek to discern informed demand $x$ from the noisy signal $X$ representing total demand.

Noise traders submit market orders for $u$ shares randomly, such that their orders contain no useful information content. In fact, noise trader activity will obscure information provided by the informed trader, which enables informed traders to disguise the information content of their trading from the dealer and noise traders. Noise traders will demand $u$ shares, where $u$ is distributed normally with mean $E[u] = 0$ (they are as likely to sell as to buy) and variance $\sigma_u^2$: $u \sim N(0; \sigma_u^2)$. Thus, $\sigma_u^2$ is the variance of uninformed investor demand. Informed traders do not know how many shares uninformed traders will buy or sell, but the informed trader does know the parameters of the distribution of the demand. Informed and noise traders submit their order quantities $x$ and $u$ to the market maker in a batch market. The market maker observes the net market imbalance (the extent to which $X$

is positive or negative at various price levels), and sets the price $p$ at which the total order flow $X = x + u$ is executed and clears. Thus, the market maker observes $X$, and then sets the price as a function of the sum of informed and uninformed investor demand: $p = E[v|x + u]$.

### *The Informed Trader's Problem: Profit Maximization*

Kyle's Bayesian learning model assumes that informed investor demand $x$ can be expressed as a simple linear function of $v$: $x = \alpha + \beta v$, where $\alpha$ and $\beta$ are simple coefficients whose traits will be discerned and examined shortly. Similarly, the security's price $p$, set by the market maker or dealer, is also assumed to be a simple linear function of demand: $p = \mu + \lambda(x + u)$, where $\mu$ and $\lambda$ are also simple coefficients whose traits will also be examined shortly. Thus, informed investor demand $x$ is a linear function of true security value $v$ and the security price $p$ is a linear function of the sum of informed and uninformed investor demand $X = (x + u)$.[2]

Recall that the informed trader's primary problem is to determine the optimal purchase (or sale) quantity $x$ so as to maximize the expected value of his trading profits:

$$\begin{aligned} max_x\, E[\pi] &= E[(v - p)x|v] = E[(v - \mu - \lambda(x + u))x|v] \\ &= E[(vx - \mu x - \lambda x^2 - \lambda ux)] \end{aligned} \tag{5.1}$$

To maximize the informed trader's profits, find the derivative of expected trading profits $E[\pi]$ with respect to informed investor demand $x$ and set equal to zero:

$$\frac{\partial E[\pi]}{\partial x} = v - \mu - 2\lambda x - \lambda u = 0 \tag{5.2}$$

Also recall that that the distribution of $u$ implies that $E[u] = 0$ since uninformed investors randomly buy and sell. Next, note that $\lambda$ must be positive for the second-order condition (the second derivative must be negative $(-2\lambda < 0)$) to hold for maximization. We will demonstrate this later. Finally, we rearrange terms to obtain:

$$2\lambda x = v - \mu \tag{5.3}$$

$$x = -\frac{\mu}{2\lambda} + \frac{1}{2\lambda}v \tag{5.4}$$

which is linear in $v$ as Kyle proposed it would be. Now, we see that our coefficients $\alpha$ and $\beta$ are simply:

$$\alpha = -\frac{\mu}{2\lambda}, \beta = \frac{1}{2\lambda}$$

Thus, the informed trader linear demand function $x = \alpha + \beta v = -\frac{\mu}{2\lambda} + \frac{v}{2\lambda}$ is set based on the dealer pricing function.

[2]Readers who would prefer not to read this derivation might wish to skip to the numerical illustration at the end of this section.

### *Dealer Price Setting*

But, to gain insight into what the informed trader linear demand function implies, we need to better understand our coefficients $\alpha$ and $\beta$. To explore this, we will examine the trading of the dealer or market maker who observes total order flow $X = x + u$, and sets a single market clearing price $p$ or $E[v]$ as a function of total demand $p = E[v|x + u]$ where $x = \alpha + \beta v$. Note here that the dealer increases the price of the security as total demand $x + u$ increases. Since $v$ and $X$ are normally distributed, we will apply the projection theorem to $p$ as follows[3]:

$$p = E[v] + \left[\frac{COV[v, x + u]}{VAR[x + u]}\right][x + u - E[x + u]] \tag{5.5}$$

This dealer pricing function has a straightforward interpretation. First, the sensitivity of the dealer price to total share demand $x + u$ is a function of the covariance between the stock's value and total demand for the shares $COV[v, x + u]$. Thus, if the dealer believes that total demand $x + u$ for the stock increases dramatically with its intrinsic value $v$ (unknown to him, but known to the informed trader), the price that the dealer sets for shares will be very sensitive to total demand. Thus, if the informed trader is known to dominate trading in the marketplace, the dealer will set the price of the security mostly or entirely as a function of total demand for the security. This sensitivity to total demand will diminish as uninformed demand volatility increases. As total demand deviates more from expected demand, the price of shares will increase.

### *Informed Trader Demand and Dealer Price Adjustment*

Since $x = \alpha + \beta v$, and $\Sigma_0$ is the variance of or uncertainty associated with asset payoffs $v$, the variance of informed trader demand $VAR[x]$ will equal $\beta^2\Sigma_0$. This means that $VAR[x + u] = \beta^2\Sigma_0 + \sigma_u^2$, which means that we can write the dealer pricing equation as:

$$p = E[v] + \left[\frac{COV[v, x + u]}{\beta^2\Sigma_0 + \sigma_u^2}\right][x + u - \alpha - \beta E[v]] \tag{5.6}$$

Now, recall that $\beta$ is the slope of a line plotting a random dependent variable $X$ or $(x + u)$ with respect to an independent random variable $v$. That is, $\beta = COV[v, x + u]/VAR[v] = COV[v, x + u]/\Sigma_0$, which means that $COV[v, x + u] = \beta\Sigma_0$, and we can write this equation as:

$$p = E[v] + \left[\frac{\beta\Sigma_0}{\beta^2\Sigma_0 + \sigma_u^2}\right][x + u - \alpha - \beta E[v]] \tag{5.7}$$

[3]The projection theorem has many applications in finance, such as to the capital asset pricing method (CAPM) and arbitrage pricing theory (APT). Many students are first exposed to it in econometrics when seeking an unbiased estimator in an econometrics setting. Generally, the projection theorem states that the relationship between some random dependent variable $y$ and an independent random variable $x$ is

$$y = E[y] + \left[\frac{COV[y, x]}{VAR[x]}\right][x - E[x]]$$

Recall that Kyle suggested a linear relationship between the security price and its demand: $p = \mu + \lambda(x + u)$. This implies a slope $\lambda$ equal to:

$$\lambda = \left[\frac{\beta \Sigma_0}{\beta^2 \Sigma_0 + \sigma_u^2}\right] \tag{5.8}$$

which implies $\mu = p + \lambda(-x-u)$ and

$$\mu = E[v] + \lambda[-\alpha - \beta E[v]] \tag{5.9}$$

Next, we will use $\alpha$ and $\beta$ coefficients from above to demonstrate that $\mu = E[v]$:

$$\mu = E[v] + \lambda\left[\frac{\mu}{2\lambda} - \frac{1}{2\lambda}E[v]\right] = E[v] + \left[\frac{\mu}{2} - \frac{1}{2}E[v]\right] = \frac{1}{2}E[v] + \frac{\mu}{2} = E[v] \tag{5.10}$$

Now, we will rewrite $\lambda$, substituting in for $\beta$:

$$\lambda = \left[\frac{\beta \Sigma_0}{\beta^2 \Sigma_0 + \sigma_u^2}\right] = \left[\frac{\frac{1}{2\lambda}\Sigma_0}{\left(\frac{1}{2\lambda}\right)^2 \Sigma_0 + \sigma_u^2}\right] \tag{5.11}$$

We will use a bit of algebra to simplify this expression for $\lambda$, starting by multiplying $\lambda$ and the right-hand side of Equation (5.11) by the denominator of the right-hand side of the equation:

$$\lambda\left[\left(\frac{1}{2\lambda}\right)^2 \Sigma_0 + \sigma_u^2\right] = \frac{1}{2\lambda}\Sigma_0 \tag{5.12}$$

Next, we will simplify the left-hand side and then multiply both sides by $\lambda$ and simplify further by subtracting $\frac{1}{4}\Sigma_0$ from both sides:

$$\left[\left(\frac{1}{4\lambda}\right)\Sigma_0 + \lambda\sigma_u^2\right] = \frac{1}{2\lambda}\Sigma_0 \tag{5.13}$$

$$\left(\frac{1}{4}\right)\Sigma_0 + \lambda^2\sigma_u^2 = \frac{1}{2}\Sigma_0 \tag{5.14}$$

$$\lambda^2\sigma_u^2 = \frac{1}{4}\Sigma_0 \tag{5.15}$$

$$\lambda = \sqrt{\frac{1}{4}\frac{\Sigma_0}{\sigma_u^2}} = \frac{1}{2}\sqrt{\frac{\Sigma_0}{\sigma_u^2}} \tag{5.16}$$

First, we see that it is obvious that $\lambda$ is positive and that our second-order condition for profit maximization has been fulfilled. More importantly, $\lambda$ can be taken to be the dealer price adjustment for total stock demand; that is, *$\lambda$ can be considered to be the illiquidity adjustment*. The ratio $\Sigma_0/\sigma_u^2$ is the ratio of informed trader private information resolution to the level of noise trading. Thus, dealer price adjustment is proportional to the square root of this ratio, increasing as private information $\Sigma_0$ is increasing and decreasing as noise trading $\sigma_u^2$ increases. This means that if the dealer determines that the informed trader resolves a substantial level of risk relative to the amount of noise trading, the level of dealer price adjustment $\lambda$ will be large. Now, we can write our informed investor demand coefficients $\alpha$ and $\beta$ as follows:

$$\alpha = -\frac{E[v]}{\sqrt{\frac{\Sigma_0}{\sigma_u^2}}}, \ \beta = \frac{1}{\sqrt{\frac{\Sigma_0}{\sigma_u^2}}}$$

Now, we can more easily interpret our informed trader demand function:

$$x = \alpha + \beta v = -\frac{E[v]}{\sqrt{\frac{\Sigma_0}{\sigma_u^2}}} + \frac{v}{\sqrt{\frac{\Sigma_0}{\sigma_u^2}}} = \frac{(v - E[v]\sigma_u)}{\sqrt{\Sigma_0}} \tag{5.17}$$

This result indicates that informed trader transaction sizes will increase as the variance of uninformed noise demand for shares $\sigma_u^2$ increases. That is, the informed trader will trade more aggressively as noise trader volume increases. This volatility reflects noise trader demand for (or supply of) shares. Thus, informed traders will want to take larger positions in the stock or sell off more shares as uninformed trader uncertainty increases and their transaction volume increases. This increased noise volume will better enable informed traders to camouflage their information advantage over the dealer. Also note that, even with perfect information and risk neutrality, informed traders will limit their trading activity to camouflage their intentions. In fact, as the informed trader advantage $\Sigma_0$ over the market maker increases, informed trader demand for share volume will decline. That is, as the informed trader's information improves relative to the dealer, the informed trader will seek to camouflage his advantage by reducing his trade volume. This is intended to prevent the dealer from observing the increased trade volume or imbalance on buy (sell) transactions and raising the share price to balance the orders. Here, the informed trader will earn his profits by maintaining more profit on a per share basis rather than on transaction volume.

Recall from Equation (5.7) that the market maker sets the price at $p$, which we will rewrite using the result of Equation 5.16:

$$p = E[v] + \left[\frac{\beta \Sigma_0}{\beta^2 \Sigma_0 + \sigma_u^2}\right][x + u - \alpha - \beta E[v]] = E[v|x+u]. \tag{5.18}$$

$$p = \mu + \lambda(x+u) = E[v] + \frac{1}{2}\sqrt{\frac{\Sigma_0}{\sigma_u^2}}\,(x+u) \tag{5.19}$$

First, note that the dealer price $p$ is the security's expected value $E[v]$ conditioned on total demand $[x+u]$ for the security. We see here that the dealer price is linear in total demand for the security and linear in the ratio of informed trader value uncertainty to uninformed or noise trader uncertainty. Higher noise or uninformed trader uncertainty reduces the security price unless total demand $(x+u)$ is negative. The opposite is true for value or cash flow uncertainty, which increases the informed trader's informational advantage. The market maker sets the price at $p$, such that the informed trader buys (sells) whenever $v > E[v]$ $(v < E[v])$, and buys (sells) more aggressively as this difference increases.

Note that some of these implications might be clarified with the following informed trader profit function[4]:

$$E[\pi] = E[[v - E[v]]x] = E\left[[v - E[v]]\left[\frac{v}{\sqrt{\frac{\Sigma_0}{\sigma_u^2}}} - \frac{E[v]}{\sqrt{\frac{\Sigma_0}{\sigma_u^2}}}\right]\right] = \frac{\Sigma_0}{\sqrt{\frac{\Sigma_0}{\sigma_u^2}}} = \sqrt{\Sigma_0\sigma_u^2} = \sqrt{\Sigma_0}\sigma_u \qquad (5.20)$$

We see here that expected informed trader profits are linear and increasing in the quality of their information advantage $\sqrt{\Sigma_0}$ and the demand uncertainty $\sigma_u$ of noise traders. A larger value for $\Sigma_0$ implies a greater deviation in the security value $v$ (known by the informed trader) from its expected value $E[v]$ (estimated by the dealer). A larger value for $\Sigma_0$ implies a larger information advantage to the informed trader. Greater dealer price uncertainty (which arises from the combination of uninformed demand variability and value uncertainty) increases informed trader trading profits. Increased uninformed trader uncertainty and its associated increase in transactions $\sigma_u$ mean that the informed trader is better able to disguise from the market maker his information advantage $\Sigma_0$ and trading activity through the increased noise trader volume $\sigma_u$. This ability to camouflage means that the informed trader can trade more aggressively, taking larger positions ($x$ or $-x$) and profits in the stock without accurately revealing his transactions to the market maker. While the market maker does observe order imbalances $X$, he cannot distinguish between informed trader demand $x$ and noise trader demand $u$. The market maker responds by setting a competitive price $p$ such that informed traders earn their profits indirectly from noise traders. The market maker loses on trades with informed traders and earns profits on trades with noise traders. The market maker merely earns a competitive profit as long as informed traders successfully camouflage their intentions at the ultimate expense of noise traders. Kyle continues his model in a multiperiod framework to demonstrate that analogous implications arise in sequential and continuous auctions.

### *Illustration: Kyle's Adverse Selection Model*

Traders rely on the market and each other for information. Suppose, for example, that the unconditional value of a stock in a Kyle (1985) framework is normally distributed with an expected value equal to $E[v] = \$50$ and a variance of $\Sigma_0 = 30$. However, the informed trader has private information that the value of the stock is actually $v = \$45$ per share. Uninformed investor trading is random and normally distributed with an ex-ante expected net share demand of zero (negative net demand represents net selling activity or net supply) and a variance $\sigma_u^2$ equal to 5,000. The dealer can observe the total level of order volume $X = x + u$ where $u$ reflects noise trader transactions and $x$ reflects informed demand, but the dealer cannot distinguish between $x$ and $u$. The dealer's problem is to set a market clearing price for the security such that losses on transactions with informed traders are offset by profits from trading with noise traders.

In the context of the Kyle model, what gives the informed trader the ability to camouflage his trades and have them appear to blend in with noise traders? Quite simply, it is the level of random noise trader activity indicated by $u$ and anticipated to be related to $\sigma_u^2$

[4]Note that by definition of variance $\Sigma_0$, $E[[v-E[v]][v-E[v]]]^2 = \Sigma_0$.

along with the informed trader's level of trading $x$. Perfect camouflage would be indicated by an infinite $\sigma_u^2$ and/or a zero $x$. Unfortunately, the second allows the informed trader no profits. Nevertheless, the ability of the informed trader to camouflage his activity is directly related to $\sigma_u^2$ and inversely related to $x$.

Under the market and trading circumstances set forth above, what would be the level of informed trader demand for the stock? We solve for $x$ as follows, using Equation 5.17:

$$x = -\frac{E[v]}{\sqrt{\frac{\Sigma_0}{\sigma_u^2}}} + \frac{v}{\sqrt{\frac{\Sigma_0}{\sigma_u^2}}} = -\frac{50}{\sqrt{\frac{30}{5{,}000}}} + \frac{45}{\sqrt{\frac{30}{5{,}000}}} = \frac{-5}{.07746} = -64.5497$$

Thus, the informed trader will provide a net supply of 64.5497 shares to sell in the marketplace. Note that an increase in either the variance of uninformed trader demand $\sigma_u^2$ or the expected value of the asset without special information $E[v]$ would increase the number of shares that the dealer informed trader would supply. On the other hand, an increase in either the amount of information that the informed trader's special information resolves $\Sigma_0$ or the true value of the asset would reduce the supply that the informed trader would supply.

The informed trader would wish to sell an infinite number of shares to earn a \$5 profit on each, but cannot because the dealer would correctly infer that his share sales convey meaningful information, and the dealer's price revisions would lead to slippage. Thus, at what level does the dealer set his price, given the total demand $X = [x + u] = -64.5497 + 0$ that he observes? First, we solve for parameters in the dealer pricing equation using Equations 5.4 and 5.16, and then solve for the price level using either Equations 5.18 or 5.19 as follows:

$$\alpha = -\frac{E[v]}{\sqrt{\frac{\Sigma_0}{\sigma_u^2}}} = -\frac{50}{\sqrt{\frac{30}{5{,}000}}} = -645.49$$

$$\beta = \frac{1}{\sqrt{\frac{\Sigma_0}{\sigma_u^2}}} = \frac{1}{\sqrt{\frac{30}{5{,}000}}} = 12.91$$

$$\lambda = \frac{1}{2}\sqrt{\frac{\Sigma_0}{\sigma_u^2}} = \frac{1}{2}\sqrt{\frac{60}{10{,}000}} = .0387$$

Next, we calculate the price set by the dealer:

$$p = E[v] + \left[\frac{\beta\Sigma_0}{\beta^2\Sigma_0 + \sigma_u^2}\right][x + u - \alpha - \beta E[v]]$$

$$= 50 + \left[\frac{12.91 \cdot 30}{12.91^2 \cdot 30 + 5{,}000}\right][-64.5497 + 0 + 645.49 - 12.91 \cdot 50]$$

$$= 50 - .0387 \cdot 64.5497 = 47.50$$

Note that the final expression above, $p = \mu + \lambda(x + u) = E[v] + \lambda(x + u)$ is the same as Equation 5.19.

## 5.4 ADVERSE SELECTION AND THE SPREAD

Walrasian markets assume perfect and frictionless competition where supply of and demand for securities are simultaneously apparent. Market microstructure is, in large part, concerned with how imperfect competition, frictions, and the nonsynchronous arrival of supply and demand impact markets. Walrasian markets are perfectly efficient; market microstructure is concerned with inefficiencies and their impact on the market. In security markets, imperfect competition, bid–offer imbalances, and frictions often reveal themselves in bid–offer spreads. Here, we are concerned with the determinants of the bid–offer spread. First, the evolution of prices through time should provide insight as to what affects the spread. Consider, for example, frictions such as transaction costs and taxes. If these were the only factors affecting the spread, we should expect that in the absence of new information, execution prices would tend to bounce between bid and ask prices. For example, after a trade at the bid price, the next trade would be either at the same price or at the offer. After a trade at the offer, the next trade would be either at the same price or the bid. That is, price changes would tend to be either zero or at the opposite side of the spread. Thus, execution prices will tend to be either unchanged or to change in the opposite direction from the most recent transaction. Thus, transaction costs tend to induce negative serial correlation in asset prices.

On the other hand, asymmetric information tends to produce positive serial correlation in asset prices. Now, suppose that asymmetric information is the only source of the spread, such that transaction prices reflect information communicated by transactions. Transactions executed at bid prices would cause permanent drops in prices to reflect negative information and transactions executed at offer prices would cause permanent increases in prices to reflect positive information. However, the extent to which information arrives randomly will induce a random element in price changes. Thus, if price changes are solely a function of random news arrival, price changes will be random. If the distribution of information is asymmetric, prices will exhibit positive serial correlation as informed traders communicate their information through their trading activity (recall that this is what informed traders try to avoid in the Kyle model). Thus, the extent to which information distribution is asymmetric will affect the serial correlation of asset prices.

Inventory costs (such as unsystematic risk from the dealer's inability to diversify) will tend to cause negative serial correlations in price quotes. Transactions at the bid will tend to cause risk averse dealers to reduce their bid quotes as they become more reluctant not to overdiversify their inventories. Similarly, transactions at the ask will tend to cause dealers to raise their quotes as they become more reluctant not to underdiversify their inventories. Thus, inventory costs and transaction costs will tend to lead towards negative serial correlation in security prices. Asymmetric information availability will lead towards positive serial correlation in security prices as transactions communicate new information.

### The Demsetz Immediacy Argument

As we discussed earlier, trader bids and offers do not arrive to markets simultaneously. Order imbalances impose waits on impatient traders requiring immediacy. The costs of providing immediacy to liquidity traders include order processing costs (transaction costs), information and adverse selection costs, inventory holding costs, costs of absorbing inventory risks, and costs of providing trading options. The bid–offer spread provides the dealer compensation for assuming these costs on behalf of the market. Each of these costs is examined in the following sections. But first, in the Demsetz (1968) analysis, buyers and sellers of a security are each of two types, one of which who wants an immediate transaction and a second who wants a transaction, but can wait. Buy and sell orders arrive to the market in a nonsynchronous fashion, causing order imbalances. An imbalance of traders demanding an immediate trade forces the price to move against himself, causing the less patient trader to pay for immediacy. The greater the costs of trading, and the greater the desire for immediacy, the greater the market spread.

## Glosten and Milgrom Information Asymmetry Model

The Glosten and Milgrom (1985) adverse selection model assumes that dealer spreads are based on the likelihood $\pi$ ($\pi$ is a probability, not a profit level in this scenario) that an informed trader (one who knows the value of the asset) will trade. Trades arrive to the market maker, each with some random chance of originating from either an informed or uninformed trader. Suppose that the asset can take on one of two prices, a high price $P_H$ and a low price $P_L$, each with probability 1/2. The informed trader originates the trade with probability $\pi$ and knows which price the asset will take on. Liquidity or uninformed traders will not pay more than $P_H$ for the asset and they will not sell for less than $P_L$. Thus, the informed trader will sell only when the asset is worth $P_L$ and will buy only when the asset is worth $P_H$. Risk-neutral liquidity traders value the asset at $(P_H + P_L)/2$. When setting his quotes, the dealer needs to account for the probability that an informed trader will transact at his quote, and will set his bid price $P_b$ and ask price $P_a$ as follows:

$$P_b = \pi P_L + (1 - \pi)(P_H + P_L)/2$$
$$P_a = \pi P_H + (1 - \pi)(P_H + P_L)/2$$

The spread is simply the difference between the ask and bid prices:

$$P_a - P_b = \pi(P_H - P_L)$$

Thus, in the single-period Glosten and Milgrom model, the spread is a function of the likelihood that there exists an informed trader in the market and uncertainty in the value of the traded asset. The greater the uncertainty in the value of the traded asset as reflected by $(P_H + P_L)/2$, and the greater the probability $\pi$ that a trade has originated with an informed trader, the greater will be the spread.

## The Stoll Inventory Model

A dealer needs to maintain inventories in assets in which he makes a market to sell to investors as well as cash to purchase assets from investors. Suppose that a dealer currently without inventory in a particular asset $P$ trades so as to maximize the expected utility level that he associates with his uncertain level of wealth $W$.[5] We assume here that the dealer's wealth level could be subject to some uncertain normally distributed security return represented by $r$ whose expected value is zero. This security produces an uncertain profit equal to $rP$ and a variance of profits equal to $\sigma^2$.[6] The dealer is willing to quote a bid price $P_b$ to purchase this security whose consensus value or price is $P$. Our problem here is to determine the maximum price that a risk averse dealer would be willing to bid; we show that the level of this bid is a function of the dealer's level of risk aversion. First, we note that the maximum bid that the dealer is willing to quote would be that which equates the expected utility associated with his current uncertain level of wealth after purchasing the risky security with the level of utility he would realize if he opted not to purchase the risky security and its associated risk:

$$E[U(W - P_b + (1 + r)P)] = U(W)$$

Rewriting to adjust expected utility for the expected trading profit against the bid and return over time on the asset consensus value:

$$E[U(W + (P - P_b) + rP)] = U(W)$$

Thus, the dealer's expected utility after the security purchase is a function of his current level of wealth $W$, his bid price $P_b$, and his uncertain return. If the security is not purchased, the dealer's utility will be a function of his current wealth level. Our problem is to solve this equality for $P_b$. We start by performing a Taylor series expansion around the left side of the equality:

$$E[U(W) + (P - P_b + rP)(U'(W)) + 1/2(P - P_b + rP)^2(U''(W)) + \ldots] = U(W)$$

Since $E[r] = 0$, $E[rP])U'(W)$ can be dropped from the equality and $\sigma^2 = E[(P - P_b + rP)^2]$:

$$E[U(W) + (P - P_b)(U'(W)) + 1/2(\sigma^2)U''(W) + \ldots] = U(W)$$

We will approximate by dropping all of the left-hand-side higher-order terms not explicitly stated in the above equality, which is quite reasonable if we are willing to assume that the risk is normally distributed, meaning, for example, that $E[z^3]$ will equal 0. Our pricing equation simplifies as follows:

$$(P - P_b)(U'(W)) \approx -1/2(\sigma^2)U''(W)$$
$$(P - P_b) \approx -1/2(\sigma^2)U''(W)/U'(W)$$
$$(P - P_b) \approx 1/2(\sigma^2)ARA$$

where $-U''(W)/U'(W)$ is the dealer's *Arrow-Pratt absolute risk aversion coefficient* (ARA). The ARA indicates the dealer's aversion to a given risk $\sigma^2$, based on his utility of wealth function $U(w)$ and his current level of wealth. Thus, the greater the dealer's risk aversion,

[5]See Stoll (1978). In this discussion, we will assume that the cumulative consensus value of shares traded is $P$.

[6]Assume that $P$ represents the total investment into asset $P$. We will not concern ourselves with individual share prices and numbers of shares; we will use $P$ to reflect investment into the tradable asset.

or the greater the uncertainty associated with the asset, the greater will be the discount associated with his bid.

Now, suppose that the dealer maintains an initial inventory $W_p$ of securities constituting his initial wealth level $W_p = W_0$. The dealer is free to borrow and lend at the riskless rate $r$, for sake of simplicity, assumed to be zero. This initial inventory of securities $W_p$ is an optimal portfolio that maximizes the dealer's utility associated with his uncertain level of terminal wealth $W$ subject to his initial wealth constraint:

$$E[U(W_p(1 + r_p) - (P - P_b) + rP)] = U(W)$$

where $r$ is the uncertain return on the tradable asset $i$ and $r_p$ is the uncertain return on the optimal portfolio $W_p$. As we did above, we will expand the left side of this equation around $E[U(W_p)])$, and assuming that $E[r] = E[r_p] = 0$, and after dropping higher-order terms, we have:

$$E[U(W_p) + (P - P_b)(U'(W_p)) + 1/2(\sigma^2)U''(W_p) + 2 \times 1/2 \times E[rP \times r_p W_p] \times U''(W_p)]) \approx U(W)$$

The covariance of cash flows between profits on the optimal portfolio and the tradable asset $i$ is $2 \times 1/2 \times E[rP \times r_p W_p] = \sigma_{i,P}$. Simplifying and solving for $(P - P_b)$, we find that the dealer's bidding discount from the consensus price is:

$$(P - P_b) = \sigma_{I,P} ARA + 1/2(\sigma^2) ARA$$

In addition to the discount components described above, the dealer will increase his bid discount as his inventory of securities increases and as the covariance between his inventory returns and the asset returns increases. Similarly, the premium based the dealer's ask or offer price $P_a$ is obtained as follows:

$$(P_a - P) = -\sigma_{I,P} ARA + 1/2(\sigma^2) ARA$$

Thus, the dealer will increase his offer premium as his inventory of securities decreases and as the covariance between his inventory returns and the asset returns decreases. The bid–offer spread is simply the sum of the bid discount and offer premium:

$$(P_a - P_b) = (\sigma^2) ARA$$

Thus, the greater the dealer's risk aversion, or the greater the uncertainty associated with the asset, the greater will be the dealer's spread. Interestingly, the dealer's inventory level does not affect the size of the spread, although it will symmetrically affect both of the two price quotes from which the spread is determined.

## The Copeland and Galai Options Model

Copeland and Galai (1983) reasoned that a bid provides prospective sellers a put on the asset, with the exercise price of the put equal to the bid. For as long as the bid is quoted, other traders (at least the first to exercise) have the right to sell the asset at the quoted price. Similarly, an offer provides a call to other traders. Thus, when the dealer posts both bid and offer quotes, the spread is, in effect, a short *strangle* provided to the market.[7] Increases in underlying asset risk increase both the values of call options and the values of put options. Both legs of this strangle are more valuable when the risk of the underlying security is higher. The value of this short strangle is directly related to the volatility of the asset and inversely related to how quickly it can be revoked or revised.

An options pricing model can be used to value this dealer spread. When the dealer posts quotes, she provides other traders free long and short positions on short-term calls and puts. Thus, dealer posting of quotes is a costly activity. Essentially, a dealer can value each leg of the short strangle as individual options, and add the two to value the short strangle position associated with her quotes. The dealer will then widen the spread to capture this lost value. Ultimately, this "implied premium" associated with this dealer spread is paid by liquidity (uninformed, as in Glosten and Milgrom) traders who trade without information. Informed traders make money at the expense of the dealer, who ultimately earns it back at the expense of uninformed traders. Unlike some of the other models we discussed, the Copeland and Galai model, as presented here, does not have a mechanism to allow trading activity to convey information from informed traders to dealers and uninformed traders. Nonetheless, in the Copeland and Galai option-based model, the spread widens as the uncertainty with respect to the security price increases.

## Additional Reading

Chapters 10 to 12 in Harris (2003) offer good introductions to several models presented in this chapter, and O'Hara (1998) offers a somewhat more rigorous introduction. Stoll (2003) and Madhavan (2000) provide excellent reviews of relevant literature as of their publication dates and all four offer broader discussions of market microstructure and related literature. Amihud et al. (2005) provide a slightly more technical discussion of liquidity and its effects on security prices.

## References

Amihud, Y., Mendelson, H., & Pedersen, L. H. (2005). Liquidity and asset prices. *Foundations and Trends in Finance, 1*(4), 269–364.

Bagehot, W. (1971). The only game in town. *Financial Analysts Journal, 27*(12–14), 22.

Barber, B., Lee, Y. -T., Liu, Y. -J., & Odean, T. (2009). Just how much do investors lose from trade? *Review of Financial Studies, 22*, 151–186.

Barber, B., & Odean, T. (2000). Trading is hazardous to your wealth: The common stock investment performance of individual investors. *Journal of Finance, 55*, 773–806.

Barber, B., & Odean, T. (2001). Boys will be boys: Gender, overconfidence, and common stock investment. *Quarterly Journal of Economics, 116*(1), 261–292.

Barber, B., & Odean, T. (2002). On-line investors: Do the slow die first? *Review of Financial Studies, 15*(2), 455–487.

Barclay, M. J., & Warner, J. B. (1993). Stealth and volatility: Which trades move prices? *Journal of Financial Economics, 34*, 281–306.

Black, F. (1986). Noise. *Journal of Finance, 41*(3), 529–543.

Copeland, T. C., & Galai, D. (1983). Information effects of the bid-ask spread. *Journal of Finance, 38*, 1457–1469.

[7]As we shall discuss in Chapter 6 (see Chapter 1 and the appendix to Chapter 6 for an introduction to options and options pricing), a call is an option to buy the underlying asset and a put is an option to sell the underlying security. A straddle is a combination of put and call options on the same underlying asset; a strangle has different exercise prices.

Demsetz, H. (1968). The cost of transacting. *Quarterly Journal of Economics, 82*, 33–53.
Fama, E. (1965). The behavior of stock market prices. *Journal of Business, 38*, 34–105.
Figlewski, S. (1979). Market "efficiency" in a market with heterogeneous information. *Journal of Political Economy, 86*, 581–597.
Friedman, M. (1953). The case for flexible exchange rates. In M. Friedman (Ed.), *Essays in positive economics*. Chicago: University of Chicago Press.
Glosten, L. R., & Milgrom, P. R. (1985). Bid, ask and transactions prices in a specialist market with heterogeneously informed traders. *Journal of Financial Economics, 14*(1), 71–100.
Harris, L. (2003). *Trading and exchanges: Market microstructure for practitioners*. Oxford: Oxford University Press.
Kyle, A. S. (1985). Continuous auctions of insider trading. *Econometrica, 53*(6), 1315–1336.
Madhavan, A. (2000). Market microstructure: A survey. *Journal of Financial Markets, 3*, 205–258.
O'Hara, M. (1998). *Market microstructure theory*. New York: Blackwell Publishers.
Stoll, H. R. (1978). The supply of dealer services in securities markets. *Journal of Finance, 33*, 1133–1151.
Stoll, H. R. (2003). Market microstructure. In G. M. Constantinides, M. Harris, & R. Stulz (Eds.), *Handbook of the economics of finance*. Elsevier Science, 553–604.

## 5.5 EXERCISES

1. Members of tribal fishing societies generally undertake efforts to share information on where the fish are biting. Modern fishermen often purchase information identifying locations of schools of fish obtained from remote sensing satellite data. However, this information is often kept secret. Why do members of tribal societies share this information and modern fishermen opt not to share?
2. The model of demand in the Kyle (1985) assumes that perfectly informed trader demand $x$ increases linearly in his expected value of the traded stock. This assumption is important to Kyle's results. Demonstrate that perfectly informed trader demand $x$ in the Kyle model increases linearly in the difference between his expected value of the traded stock and the price $p$ set by the dealer. (This difference, $v-p_0$, is the profit per share to the informed trader.)
3. An informed trader has private information that the value of a stock is \$100 per share. Without this information, the variance of payoffs on the stock would be \$60; this is the level of payoff uncertainty faced by uninformed investors. The variance associated with uninformed investor trades is 10,000 shares.
   a. If the value of the stock were to be \$100 without the private information, what would be the level of informed trader demand for the stock?
   b. If the value of the stock were to be \$90 without the private information, what would be the level of informed trader demand for the stock?
   c. What will be the informed trader's expected profits from purchasing the number of shares computed in part b?
   d. Suppose that actual uninformed demand for the stock were zero. Based on your computations from part b, at what level would the dealer set the stock price?
4. We saw in Chapter 3 that in a statistical study of stock market data, Barclay and Werner (1993) found that very small trades and the very large trades did not have a significant impact on stock prices. They found that medium-sized trades had the greatest impact on the security process. Describe how this empirical finding might be consistent with the theoretical results of Kyle (1985).

5. In the Glosten and Milgrom (1985) model, dealer spreads will tend to be smaller when arrivals of buy and sell orders are balanced. Why do such balanced order arrivals tend to produce smaller dealer spreads?
6. Based on his estimates of the risk of a security, a trader believes that the price of a stock traded in a dealer market will fall within a $3 range, with potential prices being uniformly distributed. The trader knows that there are a substantial number of informed traders trading this stock, and that these informed traders will know with certainty the value of the stock. The dealer's bid–offer quotations are 12.9 and 14.1, respectively. Based on these quotes provided by the dealer, what is the probability that the trader will estimate that any given trade will have originated with an informed trader?
7. Describe how transaction costs will tend to increase inverse correlations between trade-to-trade transaction prices.
8. Suppose that dealer inventory costs were the sole source of the dealer spread. Further suppose that a transaction was executed at the bid. Would subsequent bid and offer quotes tend to be higher or lower? Why? Now, suppose that a transaction was executed at the offer. Would subsequent bid and offer quotes tend to be higher or lower? Why? In either scenario, would transaction prices tend to exhibit positive, negative, or zero autocorrelation? Why?
9. This exercise is related to a trading practice called *quote matching* (see Chapter 12), which occurs when a small trader places an order one uptick (downtick) from that of a large trader so as to profit from the large trader's transaction upward (downward) price pressure, or to use the large trader as a trade counterparty should prices decrease (increase). Suppose that Stock X has just sold for $10.05. An institutional investor places a limit order to purchase 1 million shares at $10.00, which is now the best bid. The best offer is currently $10.10. A trader, who reasons that the stock is equally likely to have an intrinsic value (true worth) of either $10.00 or $10.00 ($E[V] =$ $10.05), places a limit order to buy 200,000 shares of the stock for $10.01.
   a. Describe how the trader is attempting to exploit the options provided by the spread.
   b. How might the institutional investor be losing wealth as a result of his limit order?
10. Based on models described in this chapter, why does the dealer spread widen as the uncertainty associated with the relevant security increases?

CHAPTER

# 6

# Random Walks, Risk, and Arbitrage

## 6.1 MARKET EFFICIENCY AND RANDOM WALKS

Market efficiency exists when market prices reflect all available information. Price changes in an efficient market occur when information is disseminated or changes. Since information dissemination (news) occurs randomly, security price changes might be expected to occur randomly. Thus, an efficient market leads to random security price changes. Back tests for market efficiency are concerned with which types of information are reflected in security prices and the length of time required for new information to be reflected in prices. We will discuss market efficiency extensively in Chapter 11; we will introduce random walks here.

### Random Walks and Submartingales

A *stochastic process* is a sequence of random variables $x_t$ defined on a common probability space $(\Omega,\Phi,P)$ and indexed by time $t$.[1] In other words, a stochastic process is a random series of values $x_t$ sequenced over time. The values of $x_t(\omega)$ define the sample path of the process leading to state $\omega\in\Omega$. The terms $x(\omega,t)$, $x_t(\omega)$, and $x(t)$ are synonymous. A *discrete time process* is defined for a finite or countable set of time periods. This is distinguished from a *continuous time process* that is defined over an interval of an infinite number of infinitesimal time periods. The *state space* is the set of values in process $\{x_t\}$:

$$S=\{x\in X_t(\omega) \text{ for } \omega\in\Omega \text{ and some } t\}$$

[1]A probability space consists of three types of elements: a sample space $\Omega$ of all potential outcomes $\omega$ (e.g., government policy announcements that affect security prices), events $\phi$ (e.g., security price levels), which are subsets of $\omega$ taken from $\Omega$ and are elements of the set of events $\Phi$, and their associated probabilities $P$ mapped from $\Phi$ to [0,1]. Random variable $x$ is simply a mapping from set $\Omega$ of events. In our example, the random variable $x$ simply represents the security price resulting from a specific event $\phi$ comprised of outcomes $\omega$. Readers are likely to encounter this sort of somewhat formal notation in financial mathematics books, but understanding this section is not essential for the remainder of this text.

The state space can be discrete or continuous. For example, if a bond price changes in increments of eighths or sixteenths, the state space for prices of the bond is said to be discrete. The state space for prices is continuous if prices can assume any real value.

Consider an example of a particular stochastic process, a discrete time *random walk*, also known as a discrete time *Markov* process. A Markov process or random walk is a stochastic process whose increments or changes are independent over time; that is, the Markov process is without memory. The change in the variable to any point in time is unrelated to previous changes in the variable. A random walk is a process whose future behavior, given by increments of independent random variables, is independent of its past.[2] Let $z_i$ be a random variable associated with time $i$ and let $S_t$ be a state variable (e.g., stock price) at time $t$ such that $S_t = S_0 + z_1 + z_2 + \ldots + z_t$. Assume that random variables $z_i$ are independent. The discrete time random walk is described as follows:

$$E[S_t | S_0, z_1, z_2, \ldots, z_{t-1}] = S_{t-1} + E[z_t]$$

It is important to note that $E[S_t]$ is a function only of $S_{t-1}$ and $z_t$; the ordering of $z_i$ where $i < t$ (the price change history) is irrelevant to the determination of the expected value of $S_t$. A specific type of Markov process, the discrete *martingale process* with $E[z_i] = 0$, is defined with respect to probability measure $P$ and history or *filtration* $\Im_{t-1} = \{S_0, z_1, z_2, \ldots, z_{t-1}\}$ as follows:

$$E_P[S_t | S_0, z_1, z_2, \ldots, z_{t-1}] = E_P[S_t | \Im_{t-1}] = S_{t-1}$$

which implies:

$$E_P[S_t | S_0, z_1, z_2, \ldots, z_i] = E_P[S_t | \Im_i] = S_i \ \forall i < t$$

Note that $E[z_i] = E[z_t] = 0$. Thus, a martingale is a process whose future variations cannot be predicted with respect to direction based on the process history $\Im_i$.[3] A martingale is said to have no memory and will not exhibit consistent trends. A *submartingale* is defined as:

$$E[S_t | S_0, z_1, z_2, \ldots, z_{t-1}] \geq S_{t-1}$$

A submartingale will tend to trend upward over time such that $E[z_i] > 0$, and a *supermartingale* will tend to trend downward over time.[4] Stock prices are often modeled as submartingales because they trend upwards due to time value of money and investor risk aversion.

[2]Pearson (1905) described the optimal search process for finding a drunk left in the middle of a field. Left to stagger in an entirely unpredictable fashion, he is more likely to be found where he was left than in any other position on the field.

[3]A martingale has increments whose expected values equal zero.

[4]A submartingale has increments whose expected values exceed zero; expected values of increments from a supermartingale are less than zero.

## Brownian Motion Processes

One particular version of a continuous time/space random walk is a *Brownian motion process* $dS_t = bdz_t$. Now, define $z$ to be a stochastic process whose changes over infinitesimal periods of time are $dz_t$. A process $z$ is a standard Brownian motion process if:

1. changes in $z$ over time are independent; $COV(dz_t, dz_{t-i}) = 0$.
2. changes in $z$ are normally distributed with $E[dz] = 0$ and $E[(dz)^2] = 1$; $dz \sim N(0,1)$.
3. $z$ is a continuous function of $t$.
4. the process begins at zero, $z_0 = 0$.

Brownian motion has a number of unique and very interesting traits. First, it is continuous everywhere and differentiable nowhere under Newtonian calculus; the Brownian motion process is not smooth and does not become smooth as time intervals decrease. We see in Figure 6.1 that Brownian motion is a *fractal*, meaning that regardless of the length of the observation time period, the process will still be Brownian motion. Consider the Brownian motion process represented by the top graph in Figure 6.1. If a short segment is cut out and magnified as in the middle graph in Figure 6.1, the segment itself is a Brownian motion process; it does not smooth. Further magnifications of cutouts as in the bottom graph continue to result in Brownian motion processes. Many other processes smooth as segments covering shorter intervals are magnified and examined such that they can be differentiated under Newtonian calculus. Once a Brownian motion hits a given value, it will return to that value infinitely often over any finite time period, no matter how short. Over a small finite interval, we can express the change in $z$ (i.e., $\Delta z$) over a finite period as follows:

$$\Delta z = dz\sqrt{\Delta t} \sim N(0, \ \Delta t)$$

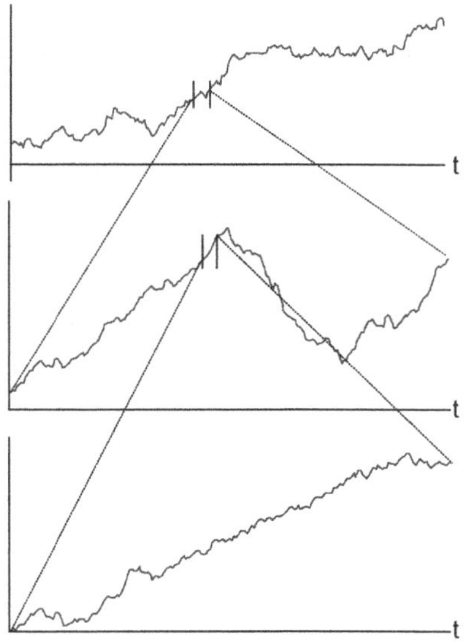


**FIGURE 6.1** Brownian Motion, A Fractal.

### Weiner Processes

A more general continuous time/space random walk is a *Wiener process*. A Weiner process is a generalized form of a *Brownian motion process*. The Weiner process may allow for drift $a$; the standard Brownian motion process does not. A *Wiener process* is defined as follows:

$$dS_t = adt + bdz$$

where $a$ represents the drift tendency in the value of $S_t$, $dz$ is a standard Brownian motion process, and b is a scaling factor for this process. In a sense, $b$ can represent the standard deviation of returns for a stock whose returns follow this Weiner Process. Because prices of many securities such as stocks tend to have a predictable drift component in addition to randomness, generalized Wiener processes might be more practical for some modeling purposes than standard Brownian motion, which only includes a random element.[5] The generalized Wiener process expression can be applied to stock returns as follows:

$$dS_t/S_t = \mu dt + \sigma dz$$

The drift term, $\mu$, represents the instantaneous expected rate of return for the stock per unit of time and $\sigma$ is the instantaneous stock return standard deviation. We shall later derive the Black-Scholes option pricing model from this Weiner process. Over a small finite interval, we can express $\Delta S_t$ as follows:

$$\Delta S_t = a\Delta t + bdz\sqrt{\Delta t} \sim N(a\Delta t,\ b^2\Delta t)$$

This expression can be applied to stock returns as follows:

$$\frac{\Delta S_t}{S_t} = \mu\Delta t + \sigma dz\sqrt{\Delta t} \sim N(\mu\Delta t,\ \sigma^2\Delta t)$$

Over a continuous or infinitesimal interval, this finite return can be written as an infinitesimal return:

$$\frac{dS_t}{S_t} = \mu dt + \sigma dz\sqrt{dt} \sim N(\mu dt,\ \sigma^2\ dt)$$

This geometric Weiner process can be interpreted in a stock environment as a return-generating process. Unfortunately, the Brownian path $dz\sigma\sqrt{dt}$ of this process is not Newtonian differentiable. This means that the path does not smooth, so that we cannot draw tangent lines that we associate with derivatives.

## 6.2 RISK

Definitions of risk vary based on context. Measuring risk can be rather difficult when it is difficult to define risk or to capture all of its characteristics. One perspective on the risk

[5]A Weiner process is a continuous time-space Markov process with normally distributed increments. A positive drift would be consistent with time value of money and investor risk aversion.

of an investment is that it is simply the uncertainty associated with investment returns or cash flows. However, uncertainty can be a complex quality. Analysts often attempt to quantify risk with absolute measures such as variance or relative risk measures such as beta. Although return variance is a quite simple mathematical concept with many desirable characteristics, its estimation is hampered by the lack of ideal data. Suppose, for example, that we wish to estimate the risk or variance associated with a stock's returns over the next year. Consider the following discrete expression for ex-ante variance $\sigma_F^2$ that considers all potential return outcomes $R_i$ and associated probabilities $P_i$:

$$\sigma_F^2 = \sum_{i=1}^{n} (R_i - E[R_i])^2 P_i \tag{6.1}$$

While this expression for variance is by definition correct, its computation requires that we identify all potential returns for the security (which might range from minus infinity to positive infinity) along with their associated probabilities. This is actually practical when the list of potential returns is small or when we can ascertain a specific return generating process (such as Brownian motion). However, associating probabilities with these returns is a particularly difficult problem. For example, what is the probability that the return for a given stock will range between 5% and 6%? In many instances, we will be forced to either make probability assignments of a somewhat subjective nature or define a joint return and probability generating process for the security. Availability of historical price data can makes risk estimation based on historical variances more practical.[6]

## Historical Volatility Indicators

Because it is frequently difficult to estimate the inputs necessary to estimate security ex-ante variance, analysts often use the volatility of ex-post or historical returns as a surrogate for ex-ante risk:

$$\sigma_H^2 = \sum_{t=1}^{n} \frac{(R_t - \overline{R_t})^2}{n-1} \tag{6.2}$$

where $R_t$ represents the return realized during period $t\,(R_t = [(P_t - P_{t-1})/P_{t-1}])$ in this $n$ time period framework. Table 6.1 presents sample monthly historical price data for a stock along with returns computed from these prices. The traditional sample monthly variance estimator for this stock based on these 23 returns equals 0.012. If we were to assume that returns follow a Brownian motion process (or at least assume that stock returns are uncorrelated over time), the annualized variance would be $0.144 = 0.012 \times 12$. Use of the traditional sample estimator to forecast variance requires the assumption that stock return variances are constant over time, or more specifically, that historical return variance is an appropriate indicator of future return variance. While this can often be a reasonable assumption, firm risk conditions can change and it is well documented that price volatility does fluctuate over time (see, for example, Officer, 1971). In addition, note that the sample

[6]See section A.1. in the Appendix at the end of the text for a review of elementary statistics and Appendix 6.A on page 154 for a discussion of estimating risk on a spreadsheet.

**TABLE 6.1** Traditional Sample Estimators for GM Stock, October 2000 to September 2002

| Date | Close | $R_t$ | Date | Close | $R_t$ |
|---|---|---|---|---|---|
| 3-Sep-02 | 38.9 | −0.187212704 | 4-Sep-01 | 41.66 | −0.216475456 |
| 1-Aug-02 | 47.86 | 0.028141783 | 1-Aug-01 | 53.17 | −0.132343342 |
| 1-Jul-02 | 46.55 | −0.12909261 | 2-Jul-01 | 61.28 | −0.011612903 |
| 3-Jun-02 | 53.45 | −0.13998391 | 1-Jun-01 | 62 | 0.130767828 |
| 1-May-02 | 62.15 | −0.024026382 | 1-May-01 | 54.83 | 0.047573558 |
| 1-Apr-02 | 63.68 | 0.061156474 | 2-Apr-01 | 52.34 | 0.05716017 |
| 1-Mar-02 | 60.01 | 0.141091462 | 1-Mar-01 | 49.51 | −0.027690495 |
| 1-Feb-02 | 52.59 | 0.046567164 | 1-Feb-01 | 50.92 | 0.001967729 |
| 2-Jan-02 | 50.25 | 0.052135678 | 2-Jan-01 | 50.82 | 0.054138146 |
| 3-Dec-01 | 47.76 | −0.022113022 | 1-Dec-00 | 48.21 | 0.029028815 |
| 1-Nov-01 | 48.84 | 0.217044605 | 1-Nov-00 | 46.85 | −0.195984211 |
| 1-Oct-01 | 40.13 | −0.036725876 | 2-Oct-00 | 58.27 | N/A |

variance estimator rather than the population estimator is proposed in Equation (6.2). This difference becomes more significant with smaller samples.

$$\sigma_H^2 = \sum_{t=1}^{n} \frac{(R_t - \overline{R_t})^2}{n-1} = 0.012$$

Using Equation (6.2) to estimate security variance requires that the analyst choose a sample series of prices (and dividends, if relevant) at $n$ regular intervals from which to compute returns. Two problems arise in this process:

1. Which prices should be selected and at what intervals?
2. How many prices should be selected?

First, since each of the major stock markets tend to close at regular times on a daily basis, closing prices will usually reflect reasonably comparable intervals, whether selected on a daily, weekly, monthly, annual, or other basis. Those prices closer to the date of computation will probably better reflect security risk (e.g., price volatility of a security 30 years ago hardly seems relevant today). On the other hand, longer-term returns, such as those computed on a monthly or annual basis, might more closely follow a normal distribution than returns computed on a daily or shorter-term basis. This is a highly desirable quality, since many of the statistical estimation procedures used by analysts assume normal (or lognormal) distribution of inputs; the characteristics of most non-normal distributions are not well known.

Generally speaking, more prices or data points used in the computation process will increase the statistical significance of variance estimates. However, this leads to a dilemma: more data points, particularly pertaining to longer-term returns, will require prices from the more distant, but less relevant past. On the other hand, shorter estimation intervals may result in non-normal return distributions as well as autocorrelation issues. Hence, the analyst must balance the needs for a large sample to ensure statistical significance, recent data for relevance, and longer-term data for independence and normality of distribution. These conflicting needs call for compromise. One convention that has developed over the years both in academia and in the industry is based on computations of five years of monthly returns.

Nonetheless, numerous difficulties still remain with this estimation procedure. For example, as we discussed above, variances are not necessarily stable over time. In our numerical illustration, higher-volatility periods are clustered together as are lower volatility periods, in a manner similar to actual return variances. Second, returns themselves might not be independently distributed. In our numerical illustration, returns are somewhat inversely correlated, potentially leading to significant differences in our variance estimates. Thus, both problems arise in our numerical illustration data in Table 6.1. In addition, nontrading may omit returns data for computations, creating more problems with historical variance estimations.

## Extreme Value Estimators

Two difficulties associated with the traditional sample estimator procedure, time required for computation and arbitrary selection of returns from which to compute volatilities might be dealt with by using extreme value estimators. Extreme value estimators are based on high and low values (and sometimes other parameters) realized by the security's price over a given time period.

For example, consider the Parkinson extreme value estimator (Parkinson, 1980). This estimating procedure is based on the assumption that underlying stock returns are lognormally distributed without drift. Given this distribution assumption, the underlying stock's realized high and low prices over a given period provide information regarding the stock's variance. Thus, if we are willing to assume that the return distribution is to be the same during the future period, Parkinson's estimate for the underlying stock return variance is determined as follows:

$$\sigma_p^2 = .361 \cdot \left[\ln\left(\frac{HI}{LO}\right)\right]^2 \tag{6.3}$$

where *HI* designates the stock's realized high price for the given period and *LO* designates the low price over the same period. The high and low prices for GM in October 2002 were 47.51 and 38.11 for October 2002, the most recent month listed in Table 6.1. The extreme value estimator for this month would be calculated as follows

$$\sigma_p^2 = .361 \cdot \left[\ln\left(\frac{HI}{LO}\right)\right]^2 = .361 \cdot \left[\ln\left(\frac{47.51}{38.11}\right)\right]^2 = 0.017546$$

Alternatively, we could obtain an average monthly variance for the 24-month period covered in the table (ignoring the possibility of intraday highs and lows that differ from closing prices).[7] Since our price data cover 24 months, we will divide this figure by 24 to obtain our monthly variance. The Parkinson measure results in a monthly variance estimate equal to 0.007414 for GM over the period October 2000 to September 2002 in Table 6.1:

$$\sigma_p^2 = .361 \cdot \left[\ln\left(\frac{HI}{LO}\right)\right]^2 / m = .361 \cdot \left[\ln\left(\frac{63.68}{38.9}\right)\right]^2 / 24 = 0.007414$$

Clearly, the Parkinson variance estimate will be easy to obtain when periodic high and low prices for a stock are regularly published as they are for the NYSE and many other stocks. Furthermore, the econometric efficiency of the Parkinson procedure is several times higher than the traditional sample estimation procedure. Using the extreme value estimator might be as simple as inserting into Equation (6.3) the 52-week high and low prices. Note that the Parkinson estimate is significantly smaller than the monthly historical estimate. This difference draws largely from the negative autocorrelation in the returns series.

## Implied Volatilities[8]

A problem shared by both the traditional sample estimating procedures and the extreme value estimators is that they require the assumption of stable variance estimates over time; more specifically, that future variances equal or can be estimated from historical variances. A third procedure first suggested by Latane and Rendleman (1976) is based on market prices of options that might be used to imply variance estimates. For example, the Black-Scholes option pricing model and its extensions provide an excellent means to estimate underlying stock variances if call prices are known. Essentially, this procedure determines market estimates for underlying stock variance based on known market prices for options on the underlying securities. Consider our stock example from Table 6.1 on September 3, 2002 when GM stock closed at \$38.9. Suppose that a one-month ($T = 1$) call on GM stock with a striking price equal to \$40 was at the same time trading for $c_0 = \$1.16$:

$$T = 1 \quad r_f = 0.005 \quad c_0 = \$1.16 \quad X = \$40 \quad S_0 = \$38.9$$

[7]Accuracy of the Parkinson measure can be improved if the sample period can be subdivided into $n$ equal sub-periods such that variance is estimated as follows:

$$\sigma_p^2 = \frac{.361}{n} \cdot \left[\sum_{t=1}^{n} \ln\left(\frac{HI_t}{LO_t}\right)\right]^2$$

This is the more general form of the Parkinson estimator. We should obtain an intraday highs and lows for each of the 24 months, and then square the sum of their logs. The constant, 0.361, is the normal density function constant, $1/\sqrt{2\pi}$.

[8]See's section 6.A.2 in this chapter's Appendix for a review of options and the Black-Scholes option pricing model and section 6.A.3 for additional discussion and examples of estimating implied volatilities.

**TABLE 6.2** Basic Risk Measures

| Measure | Best Used When |
|---|---|
| Ex-ante measure based on probabilities | (1) Ex-ante or future-oriented measure is needed such as when: a. The asset's historical volatility does not properly indicate its future risk. b. The asset's risk characteristics have recently changed. c. The asset has no price or returns history. (2) All potential future return or cash flow outcomes can be specified. (3) Probabilities can be associated with each potential return or cash flow outcome. (4) Instead of (2) & (3), there is a specific return generating process with known parameters. |
| Traditional sample estimator | (1) Variances are expected to be constant between historical and future time periods. (2) There are an appropriate number of sampling intervals where: a. More periods increase statistical significance. b. More periods increase reliance on older, less relevant historical data. (3) Appropriate interval lengths can be determined; longer periods approach normality. |
| Parkinson extreme value estimator | (1) The computationally simplest measure based on a minimum of data is desired. (2) Asset returns are lognormally distributed without drift. (3) Historical volatility is a good indicator of future risk. |
| Implied volatility: analytical procedures | (1) Option prices on relevant underlying asset are readily available. (2) Option pricing model assumptions hold in the relevant market. (3) Can be used when historical volatility does not indicate future risk. (4) User is able to use the appropriate analytical procedures. (5) The market can be assumed capable of assessing risk. |

where $r_f$ equals the monthly riskless return rate and $X$ is the option striking price. If investors use the Black-Scholes option pricing model to value calls, the following must hold:

$$\begin{aligned} 1.16 &= 38.9 \cdot N(d_1) - 40e^{-r_f T} \cdot N(d_2) \\ d_1 &= \frac{\ln\left(\frac{38.9}{40}\right) + (.005 + .5\sigma^2) \cdot 1}{\sigma\sqrt{1}} \\ d_2 &= d_1 - \sigma\sqrt{1} \end{aligned} \tag{6.4}$$

We find that this system of equations holds when $\sigma^2 = 0.01$. Thus, the market prices this call as though it expects that the variance of anticipated monthly returns for the underlying stock is 0.01. The annualized variance would be 0.12 (12 times the monthly variance).

Unfortunately, the system of equations required to obtain an implied variance has no closed form solution. That is, we will be unable to solve Equation (6.4) explicitly for variance; we must search, iterate, and substitute for a solution. You can substitute trial values for $\sigma^2$ until one is found that solves the system. A significant amount of time can be saved by using one of several well-known numerical search procedures such as the method of bisection or the Newton-Raphson method.[9]

Table 6.2 presents, describes, and compares basic risk measures discussed in this chapter. There is no consensus as to which measure is clearly best, although some measures perform better under some circumstances. Risk measures need to be evaluated on the basis of the availability of appropriate data and appropriateness of underlying assumptions. In addition, all of the measures that we have discussed in this chapter are incomplete in that they do not account for factors such as skewness (unequal concentrations of potential outcomes unequally distributed below and above the mean) and fat tails (kurtosis or high probabilities of extreme events). No single risk measure can serve adequately to capture all sources of security risk. Hence, the trader or securities analyst needs to use judgment in the application and interpretation of risk measures.

## 6.3 ARBITRAGE

Arbitrage, perhaps the single most important pricing tool in modern finance, is defined as the simultaneous purchase and sale of assets or portfolios yielding identical cash flows. Assets generating identical cash flows (certain or risky cash flows) should be worth the same amount. This is known as the *Law of One Price*. If assets generating identical cash flows sell at different prices, opportunities exist to create a profit by buying the cheaper asset and selling the more expensive asset. The ability to realize a profit from this type of transaction is known as an *arbitrage opportunity*. Rational investors in such a scenario will seek to purchase the underpriced asset, financing its purchase by simultaneously selling the overpriced asset. The *arbitrageur* will execute such arbitrage transactions, continuing to earn arbitrage profits in increasing quantities until the arbitrage opportunity is eliminated. If markets are competitive, the arbitrageur's purchases of the underpriced asset will bid its price up while the arbitrageur's selling transactions will force down the price of the overpriced asset. These arbitrage transactions should continue until no assets are over- or under- priced. Hence, arbitrageurs should force assets that produce identical cash flow structures to have identical prices.

*Classic arbitrage* is the simultaneous purchase and sale of the same asset at a profit. For example, if gold is selling in London markets for $1,600 per ounce and in New York markets for $1,620 per ounce, a classic arbitrage opportunity exists. An investor could purchase gold in London for $1,600 per ounce and simultaneously sell it in New York for $1,620. This results in a $20 profit per "round-trip" transaction. The transactions involve no risk since both the selling and purchase prices are known and are executed simultaneously. Furthermore, no initial net investment is required because the transactions offset each other; the proceeds of the sale are used to finance the purchase. Thus, if a classic arbitrage opportunity exists, an investor will have the opportunity to make a riskless profit

[9]These and other numerical procedures for estimating implied volatilities are discussed in section 6.A.3 in the Appendix to this chapter. More discussion of the Black-Scholes and other option pricing models is available in Chapter 8.

without investing any of his own money. If the laws of supply and demand are not impeded by market inefficiencies, investors will flock to exploit this opportunity. Their buying pressure in London markets will force the London price to rise; their selling pressure in New York markets will force the New York price down. Buying and selling pressure will persist until the prices in the two markets are equal. Thus, significant classic arbitrage opportunities are not likely to persist long in unimpeded free markets. Perhaps an even simpler form of arbitrage opportunity exists in a *crossed market*, where a bid exceeds an offer price. This can occur when a slow trader's quote is not withdrawn quickly enough, enabling a prospective buyer to purchase a security at the lower offer price and immediately sell it at the higher bid price.

More generally, arbitrage refers to the near simultaneous purchase and sale of portfolios generating similar cash flow structures. For example, the cash flow structure of a long position in a forward contract can be replicated by a portfolio consisting of a long position in a call and short position in a put. Although the contracts in the options portfolio are different from the forward contract, the anticipated cash flows are identical. Thus, if the portfolio produces a lower initial cash flow, it can be sold (shorted) while a long position is taken in the forward contract. These positions in sum comprise an arbitrage portfolio. Future cash flows are offset because they are identical, and net sales proceeds from the options portfolio will exceed those of the futures contract. Similarly, arbitrage can refer to offsetting trades of securities whose payoff structures are strongly correlated. For example, the cash flow structure of an automobile industry stock can be nearly replicated with the cash flow structure of a portfolio of other securities designed to be strongly correlated with the stock. When prices of the portfolio and the stock diverge, arbitrage opportunities might arise. Sometimes, these opportunities are referred to as *quasi-arbitrage* in that they are not necessarily completely riskless or that their transactions are not necessarily executed simultaneously.

The principle of arbitrage is the foundation underlying relative securities valuation. That is, we are able to price securities relative to one another or relative to replicating portfolios when arbitrageurs are able to exploit violations of the *law of one price*. The no-arbitrage price of a security is the value of the portfolio constructed to replicate the security. When the law of one price does not hold, one (or both) of the following will hold:

1. There exist opportunities to secure riskless arbitrage opportunities by buying underpriced assets while selling overpriced assets.
2. There exists some sort of market imperfection such as high transactions preventing arbitrageurs from exploiting arbitrage opportunities.

## Pairs Trading and Stat-Arb

As with other arbitrage strategies, *pairs trading* involves the simultaneous purchase and sale of similar securities. Pairs trading involves taking offsetting positions two different stocks (perhaps options or index contracts) with strong returns correlations, one long and one short, such that gains in one position are expected to more than offset losses in the other position. One simple strategy illustration might involve taking a long position in GM stock based on recent price decreases along with a short position in Ford based on recent price increases. If the investor generally expects that automobile stock prices ought to be strongly correlated, and should have been performing similarly, she might expect that future short term performance of the underperforming stock will exceed the performance of the stock with the stronger current price level. Pairs trading is essentially an arbitrage strategy anticipating that the deviation of a recent pricing relation between two securities is only temporary. Holding periods for most pairs trading strategies tend to be quite short, ranging from seconds to days. Pairs traders typically focus either on the ratio between prices of two securities or the difference between their prices. One cannot expect to consistently earn high returns based on such strategies, so that many pairs traders execute many such trades over many different pairs of stocks with the expectation that their strategies will be correct more often than they are wrong. Furthermore, many pairs traders will seek to hold "portfolios of pairs" whose expected returns will tend to be uncorrelated with those of the market as a whole. Such "beta-neutral" portfolios might be expected to be insulated from large losses related to stock market swings.

In a manner similar to pairs trading, *stat-arb* (statistical arbitrage) strategies seek to exploit mispricing opportunities while minimizing risk. Stat-arb strategies focus on statistical or historical relationships among securities and seek to exploit price divergences as portfolios of securities diverge from "normal" pricing relationships. Khandani and Lo (2007) refer to stat-arb as a set of "highly technical short-term mean-reversion strategies involving large numbers of securities (hundreds to thousands, depending on the amount of risk capital), very short holding periods (measured in days to seconds), and substantial computational, trading, and IT infrastructure." There is no single stat-arb strategy; there are many types, all of which involve large sets of securities whose statistical price relationships relative to each other diverge from what the investor expects.

## 6.4 LIMITS TO ARBITRAGE

Arbitrage opportunities are the traders' "pot of gold at the end of the rainbow." Once found, they are free sources of money. In theory, arbitrage is riskless because offsetting asset cash flows are known to be offsetting in the future and because initial transactions are executed simultaneously at known prices. Unfortunately, the reality is often quite different. For example, *implementation risk* arises because transactions might not be executed or be executed at prices that differ from what the arbitrageur anticipated. Perhaps even worse, one leg of the arbitrage transaction might fail to execute, leaving the arbitrageur unhedged in an undesirable portfolio. Arbitrageur profit opportunities should cause markets to respond more efficiently to new information and mispricing of securities. However, sometimes arbitrageurs simply don't fully understand or appreciate the models that they trade on. This misunderstanding is called *model risk*. In many instances, model risk arises from a simple failure to appreciate the differences between model assumptions and reality. Despite potential profit opportunities, some markets are slow to react to arbitrage opportunities and some do not react at all. In fact, some markets may move opposite to the arbitrageur's expectations, at least in the short run. This might render traders unable to survive in the long run. This risk is called *basis risk*. If trading is difficult or expensive, perhaps due to high transaction costs, price adjustments to arbitrage may be delayed, prevented, or again, move further in the unanticipated direction. Furthermore, the arbitrageur is subject to margin calls, forced sell-outs and forced buy-ins, potentially shortening her time horizon to recover from the unanticipated price change. Basis risk is mitigated if the arbitrageur is able to count on a known terminal liquidation position (such as with short-term options, futures, and Treasury bills) and maintain her portfolio hedge until that date. Thus, short-lived securities such as options tend to have smaller basis risk than long-lived securities such as common stock. An additional source of arbitrage risk, particularly when instruments are not exchange-traded, is *counterparty risk*, which is the potential that a trade counterparty fails to fulfill his side of a transaction.

De Long et al. (1990) argue that the short investment horizons of arbitrageurs can prevent them from taking advantage of errors or noise in market prices. If it appears that price deviations from fundamental values might persist, arbitrageurs might avoid potentially profitable opportunities, causing even greater risk and deviations from fundamental values. This might enable noise traders to earn even higher returns from their pricing errors, causing pricing bubbles to form. For example, consider the case of Long Term Capital Management (LTCM), which was founded in the early 1990s by John Meriwether, formerly head of the fixed income unit of Salomon Brothers, Inc. He brought in famed academics Myron Scholes and Robert Merton, developers of some of the most important derivatives and arbitrage strategies of the time, and the fund focused much of its trading activity on derivatives and fixed income. LTCM realized enormous returns and growth until 1998, when it lost over $4 billion in one spectacularly disastrous quarter, forcing the fund into liquidation and threatening contagion throughout financial markets and potential market meltdown. In many instances as we will discuss shortly, LTCM took appropriate positions in arbitrage portfolios, but the fund was so highly leveraged that it could not withstand short-term market moves against their positions.

Among the most important strategies to LTCM was to exploit *convergence trades*, which often involved taking long positions in cheaper foreign debt and short positions in more expensive U.S. Treasury securities. The foreign debt instruments were generally cheaper because they were not as liquid; thus they had higher yields. However, holding positions over the long term meant that the cheaper foreign debt would eventually rise in prices relative to the more expensive U.S. Treasury securities. LTCM, with its less than $5 billion in equity capital, controlled over $100 billion in assets and approximately $1.25 trillion notional in derivative contracts. Unfortunately for LTCM, the Southeast Asian financial crisis in 1997–1998 followed by the Russian financial crisis of 1998 caused a "flight to liquidity," meaning in this case that investors sold non-U.S. debt, forcing down non-U.S. debt prices, and purchased U.S. Treasury securities, forcing U.S. debt prices up. LTCM's equity capital was wiped out within days, and the fund was bailed out by a consortium of financial institutions under the supervision of the U.S. Federal Reserve System. While LTCM's strategy may well have been correct had it been able to survive for an extended period of time, the fund was too highly leveraged to survive extreme short-term volatility.

One of LTCM's equity market arbitrage ventures involved the Royal Dutch/Shell Group, a dual-listed company independently incorporated in the Netherlands and the UK. This arrangement originated from a 1907 alliance agreement between Royal Dutch and Shell Transport in which the two companies agreed to merge their interests on a 60/40 basis.

Royal Dutch trades primarily in the United States and the Netherlands while Shell trades primarily in London. After adjusting for foreign exchange rates, shares of the two firms' stock should trade at a 1.5:1 ratio. However, this anticipated trading ratio has deviated by more than 35%, well beyond levels of tax differentials and transaction costs. In the summer of 1997, Royal Dutch traded at an 8% to 10% premium over its 1.5 expected level relative to Shell. To exploit this differential, LTCM had taken significant arbitrage positions on the two stocks. As the differential widened to 20% in 1998, LTCM increased its positions until financial distress caused by trading activities elsewhere in the fund (related to the economic crisis in Russia) forced the firm to liquidate. The positions taken in Royal Dutch/Shell by LTCM were ultimately proven correct, but not until 2001 when the fund was no longer in existence. Rosenthal and Young (1990) argue that significant mispricing in dual-listed companies has prevailed over long periods of time without satisfactory explanations. Nevertheless, arbitrage can sometimes take significant amounts of time to equalize prices, causing arbitrageurs to maintain positions longer than they are able.

In another well-publicized failure of arbitrage, dating from a March 2000 equity carve-out, 3Com spun off its Palm division, a maker of handheld computers. 3Com retained 95% of the shares of Palm and announced that each 3Com shareholder would ultimately receive 1.5 shares of Palm for each share of 3Com. The remaining 5% of Palm shares were issued at $38 per share, increasing to $165 by its first day of trading before closing at $95.06 (see Lamont, 2002). Remember that ownership of one 3Com share implied ownership of 1.5 shares of Palm stock. The stocks of the two companies should have moved in tandem, but on the date of the IPO, 3Com actually decreased by 21% to $81.81 as Palm increased. This $81.81 is substantially less than the $142.59 price implied by the 1.5 shares of Palm stock due to each 3Com shareholder ($1.5 \times \$95.06 = \$142.59$), implying that the remainder of 3Com, on a per share basis, was worth negative $60.78. This negative stub value (the whole is worth less than the sum of the parts; in particular, the parent and the subsidiary are worth less than the subsidiary alone) seems particularly unlikely, since 3Com had about $10 per share in cash and marketable securities alone. In other words, what happened wasn't rational, given the numbers, or just could not have been sustainable had investors been able to arbitrage. However, prospective arbitrageurs found themselves unable to short sell shares because the two stocks were under different national regulatory authorities. Thus, arbitrage and price correction could not be implemented because the short selling mechanism was not available for the Palm IPO.

Such negative stub values are not uncommon. For example, in 1923, Benjamin Graham chronicled his purchase of shares of stock in Du Pont, a well-established firm that had negative stub value given its investment in the new company General Motors. Lamont and Thaler (2001) identified five other 1990s technology equity carve-outs with negative stub values: UBID, Retek, PFSWeb, Xpedior, and Stratos Lightwave. Arbitrage in each of these cases was impeded by the inability to short sell. Mitchell et al. (2002) found 82 similar instances in U.S. markets between 1985 and 2000. But in most cases, arbitrage was impeded by inability to short sell, high transaction costs, and difficulty in getting reliable price quotes or other information. But, Mitchell et al. found that approximately 30% of negative stub values were never eliminated through arbitrage. Some of the spin-offs failed, and others may have faced this risk. But, even this probably cannot explain particularly large negative stub values.

There are even more obvious limits on many arbitrage opportunities. Restrictions on trading and transaction costs can be major barriers to arbitrage. For example, Han and Wang (2004) found that upper and lower fractional ownership bounds on the holdings of a stock can limit institutional arbitrage and contribute to the momentum of returns for that stock. For example, many countries such as China restrict proportional ownership and even the United States imposes insider trading regulations on major shareholders (e.g., the Williams Amendment). Pontiff (1996) argued that large differences in prices and net asset values in closed end funds result when fund portfolios are more difficult to replicate, when trading costs are high for the stocks in fund portfolios, and when stocks in the funds paid dividends. Thus, difficulties in replicating assets do limit arbitrage opportunities. Similarly, traders know well that Treasury instruments regularly trade at lower yields than nearly identical "off-the-run Treasuries." Violations of the simple put-call parity relation regularly arise when there are restrictions on short-selling underlying securities. Transaction costs often require that the arbitrageur set upper and lower bounds on security purchase and selling prices, essentially determining the interval within which the no-arbitrage security price must be.

## Additional Reading

Pearson (1905) provides a nice, 100-year-old nontechnical discussion of the random walk process. Lamont (2002) is a very readable case study referred to in this chapter concerning the anomalous behavior of the Palm and 3-Com shares following their takeover scenario. The case is important because it depicts the failure of the market to provide rational relative pricing for the two firms. Lamont and Thaler (2002) provide a listing of other firms demonstrating negative stub values. Lowenstein's 2000 book *When Genius Failed: The Rise and Fall of Long-Term Capital Management* is an excellent history of the rise and fall of LTCM.

## References

Brenner, M., & Subrahmanyam, M. G. (1988). A simple formula to compute the implied standard deviation. *Financial Analysts Journal, 5*, 80–83.

Corrado, C., & Miller, T. W. (1996). A note on a simple, accurate formula to compute implied standard deviations. *Journal of Banking and Finance, 20*, 595–603.

DeLong, J. B., Shleifer, A., Summers, L. H., & Waldman, R. J. (1990). Noise trader risk in financial markets. *Journal of Political Economy, 98*(4), 703–738.

Han, B., & Wang, Q. (2004). *Institutional investment constraints and stock prices*. Dice Center Working Paper No. 2004-24. Available at: <http://ssrn.com/abstract = 628683> Accessed 12.01.12.

Khandani, A. E., & Lo, A. W. (2007). What happened to the quants in August 2007? *Journal of Investment Management, 5*(4), 5–54.

Lamont, O. (2002). The curious case of Palm and 3 Com. In J. Pickford (Ed.), *Mastering investment* (pp. 261–266). New York: Prentice Hall.

Lamont, O., & Thaler, R. (2001). *Can the market add and subtract? Mispricing in tech stock carve-outs*. CRSP Working Paper No. 528. Chicago: University of Chicago.

Latane, H., & Rendleman, R. (1976). Standard deviations of stock price ratios implied by option prices. *Journal of Finance, 31*, 369–381.

Lowenstein, R. (2000). *When genius failed: The rise and fall of long-term capital management*. New York: Random House.

Mitchell, M., Pulvino, T., & Stafford, E. (2002). Limited arbitrage in equity markets. *Journal of Finance, 57*(2), 551–584.
Officer, R. A. (1971). *A time series examination of the market factor of the new york stock exchange.* Ph.D. diss. University of Chicago.
Parkinson, M. (1980). The extreme value method for estimating the variance of the rate of return. *Journal of Business, 57,* 61–65.
Pearson, K. (1905). The problem of the random walk. *Nature, 72,* 342.
Pontiff, J. (1996). Costly arbitrage: Evidence from closed end funds. *Quarterly Journal of Economics, 111,* 1135–1152.
Rosenthal, L., & Young, C. (1990). The seemingly anomalous price behavior of Royal Dutch/Shell and Unilever N.V./PLC. *Journal of Financial Economics, 26,* 123–141.

## 6.5 EXERCISES

**1.** Historical *percentage* stock returns for the Robinson and Boyer Companies are listed in the following chart along with percentage returns on the market portfolio:

| Year | Robinson | Boyer | Market |
|---|---|---|---|
| 2008 | 4 | 19 | 15 |
| 2009 | 7 | 4 | 10 |
| 2010 | 11 | −4 | 3 |
| 2011 | 4 | 21 | 12 |
| 2012 | 5 | 13 | 9 |

Calculate the following based on the preceding table:

**a.** mean historical returns for the two companies and the market portfolio.
**b.** variances associated with Robinson Company returns and Boyer Company returns as well as returns on the market portfolio.
**c.** Forecast a variance and a standard deviation of returns for both the McCarthy and Alston Companies based on your calculations in parts a and b.

**2.** The following table represents outcome numbers, probabilities, and associated returns for Stock A:

| Outcome ($i$) | Return ($R_i$) | Probability ($P_i$) |
|---|---|---|
| 1 | 05 | 10 |
| 2 | 15 | 10 |
| 3 | 05 | 05 |
| 4 | 15 | 10 |
| 5 | 15 | 10 |
| 6 | 10 | 10 |
| 7 | 15 | 10 |

| | | |
|---|---|---|
| 8 | 05 | 10 |
| 9 | 15 | ? |
| 10 | 10 | 10 |

Thus, there are 10 possible return outcomes for Stock A.

**a.** What is the probability associated with outcome 9?
**b.** What is the standard deviation of returns associated with Stock A?

**3.** The Nettles Company management projects an expected return level of 15% for the upcoming year. Assuming that returns are normally distributed with a standard deviation equal to .1, what is the probability that the actual return level will:
**a.** fall between 5% and 25%?
**b.** fall between 15% and 25%?
**c.** exceed 25%?
**d.** exceed 30%?

**4.** What would each of the probabilities in problem 3 be if Nettles Company management were certain enough of its forecast to associate a 5% standard deviation with its returns projection?

**5.** The following table presents sample daily historical price data for a stock whose returns are given in the third column.

| **Time** | **Price$_t$** | **Return$_t$** |
|---|---|---|
| 0 | 30.000 | N.A. |
| 1 | 30.125 | 0.00417 |
| 2 | 30.250 | 0.00415 |
| 3 | 30.125 | −0.00413 |
| 4 | 32.000 | 0.06224 |
| 5 | 34.000 | 0.06250 |
| 6 | 31.000 | −0.08824 |
| 7 | 32.000 | 0.03226 |
| 8 | 30.500 | −0.04688 |
| 9 | 30.750 | 0.00820 |
| 10 | 30.875 | 0.00407 |
| 11 | 31.000 | 0.00405 |
| 12 | 30.875 | −0.00403 |
| 13 | 31.000 | 0.00405 |
| 14 | 31.125 | 0.00403 |

| | | |
|---|---|---|
| 15 | 30.250 | −0.02811 |
| 16 | 33.000 | 0.09091 |
| 17 | 30.000 | −0.09091 |
| 18 | 35.125 | 0.17083 |
| 19 | 33.000 | −0.06050 |
| 20 | 32.125 | −0.02652 |
| 21 | 32.250 | 0.00389 |
| 22 | 32.375 | 0.00388 |
| 23 | 32.125 | −0.00772 |
| 24 | 32.250 | 0.00389 |
| 25 | 34.250 | 0.06202 |
| 26 | 36.375 | 0.06204 |
| 27 | 38.500 | 0.05842 |
| 28 | 34.375 | −0.10714 |
| 29 | 33.875 | −0.01455 |
| 30 | 33.625 | −0.00738 |

**a.** Based on a traditional sample estimator, calculate a daily variance estimator for this stock.

**b.** Assume that returns follow a Brownian motion process (at least that stock returns are uncorrelated over time) and that there are 30 trading days per month. What would be the monthly variance for this stock?

**c.** What would be the Parkinson extreme value estimated daily returns variance for this stock?

**6.** The following daily prices were collected for each of three stocks over a 12-day period.

| Company X | | Company Y | | Company Z | |
|---|---|---|---|---|---|
| **Date** | **Price** | **Date** | **Price** | **Date** | **Price** |
| 1/09 | 50.125 | 1/09 | 20.000 | 1/09 | 60.375 |
| 1/10 | 50.125 | 1/10 | 20.000 | 1/10 | 60.500 |
| 1/11 | 50.250 | 1/11 | 20.125 | 1/11 | 60.250 |
| 1/12 | 50.250 | 1/12 | 20.250 | 1/12 | 60.125 |
| 1/13 | 50.375 | 1/13 | 20.375 | 1/13 | 60.000 |
| 1/14 | 50.250 | 1/14 | 20.375 | 1/14 | 60.125 |
| 1/15 | 52.250 | 1/15 | 21.375 | 1/15 | 62.625 |
| 1/16 | 52.375 | 1/16 | 21.250 | 1/16 | 60.750 |

| | | | | | |
|---|---|---|---|---|---|
| 1/17 | 52.250 | 1/17 | 21.375 | 1/17 | 60.750 |
| 1/18 | 52.375 | 1/18 | 21.500 | 1/18 | 60.875 |
| 1/19 | 52.500 | 1/19 | 21.375 | 1/19 | 60.875 |
| 1/20 | 52.375 | 1/20 | 21.500 | 1/20 | 60.875 |

Based on the data given above, calculate the following:

**a.** Returns for each day on each of the three stocks. There should be a total of 10 returns for each stock–beginning with the date 1/10.
**b.** Average daily returns for each of the three stocks.
**c.** Daily return standard deviations for each of the three stocks.

**7.** Torre Company stock realized a 52-week high of \$50 per share and a 52-week low of \$25. What is the Parkinson extreme value estimate for variance for this stock? What would be the corresponding standard deviation estimate?

**8.** Suppose that there is a six-month call currently trading for \$8.20 while its underlying stock is currently trading for \$75. Other details for this example are as follows:

$$T = 0.5 \quad r_f = 0.10 \quad c_0 = 8.20 \quad X = 80 \quad S_0 = 75$$

What is the volatility (standard deviation) implied by the market price of this call?

**9.** Santo Company stock currently trades for \$50 per share. The current riskless return rate is 0.06. Under the Black-Scholes framework, what would be the standard deviations implied by six-month (0.5 year) European calls with current market values based on each of the following striking prices?

**a.** $X = 40$; $c_0 = 11.50$
**b.** $X = 45$; $c_0 = 8.25$
**c.** $X = 50$; $c_0 = 4.75$
**d.** $X = 55$; $c_0 = 2.50$
**e.** $X = 60$; $c_0 = 1.25$

# APPENDIX 6.A

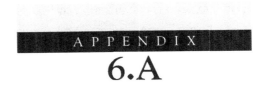

## 6.A.1 RETURN AND RISK SPREADSHEET APPLICATIONS

Table 6.A.1 contains spreadsheet entries for computing stock variances, standard deviations, and covariances. The table lists daily closing prices for Stocks X, Y, and Z from January 9 to January 20 in cells B3:B14, E3:E14, and H3:H14. From these prices, we compute returns in Cells B19:B29, E19:E29, and H19:H29. Variance, standard deviation, and covariance statistics in rows 30 to 38 are computed from formulas displayed in Table 6.A.2.

Formulas for computing returns are given in rows 19 to 29 in Table 6.A.2. Means, variances, standard deviations, covariances, and correlation coefficients are computed in rows 30 to 38. Row 30 computes the arithmetic mean return for each of the three stocks. Table 6.A.2 lists formulas associated with the values in cells A30:H38. The = (Average) function may be typed in directly as listed in Table 6.A.2 row 30 or obtained from the Paste Function button ($f_x$) menu under the Statistical submenu. Entry instructions are given in the dialogue box obtained when the Average function is selected. The variance formulas in row 31 are based on the sample formula; the variance (P) formulas in row 32 are based on the population formula. Standard deviation sample and population results are given in rows 33 and 34. Covariances and correlation coefficients are given in rows 35 to 38.

TABLE 6.A.1 Stock Prices, Returns, Risk, and Co-Movement

| | A | B | C | D | E | F | G | H |
|---|---|---|---|---|---|---|---|---|
| 1 | CORP. X | | | CORP. Y | | | CORP. Z | |
| 2 | DATE | PRICE | | DATE | PRICE | | DATE | PRICE |
| 3 | 9-Jan | 50.125 | | 9-Jan | 20 | | 9-Jan | 60.375 |
| 4 | 10-Jan | 50.125 | | 10-Jan | 20 | | 10-Jan | 60.5 |
| 5 | 11-Jan | 50.25 | | 11-Jan | 20.125 | | 11-Jan | 60.25 |
| 6 | 12-Jan | 50.25 | | 12-Jan | 20.25 | | 12-Jan | 60.125 |
| 7 | 13-Jan | 50.375 | | 13-Jan | 20.375 | | 13-Jan | 60 |

| | | | | | | |
|---|---|---|---|---|---|---|
| 8 | 14-Jan | 50.25 | 14-Jan | 20.375 | 14-Jan | 60.125 |
| 9 | 15-Jan | 52.25 | 15-Jan | 21.375 | 15-Jan | 62.625 |
| 10 | 16-Jan | 52.375 | 16-Jan | 21.25 | 16-Jan | 60.75 |
| 11 | 17-Jan | 52.25 | 17-Jan | 21.375 | 17-Jan | 60.75 |
| 12 | 18-Jan | 52.375 | 18-Jan | 21.5 | 18-Jan | 60.875 |
| 13 | 19-Jan | 52.5 | 19-Jan | 21.375 | 19-Jan | 60.875 |
| 14 | 20-Jan | 52.375 | 20-Jan | 21.5 | 20-Jan | 60.875 |
| 15 | | | | | | |
| 16 | **CORP. X** | | **CORP. Y** | | **CORP. Z** | |
| 17 | **DATE** | **RETURN** | **DATE** | **RETURN** | **DATE** | **RETURN** |
| 18 | 9-Jan | N/A | 9-Jan | N/A | 9-Jan | N/A |
| 19 | 10-Jan | 0 | 10-Jan | 0 | 10-Jan | 0.00207 |
| 20 | 11-Jan | 0.002494 | 11-Jan | 0.00625 | 11-Jan | −0.00413 |
| 21 | 12-Jan | 0 | 12-Jan | 0.006211 | 12-Jan | −0.00207 |
| 22 | 13-Jan | 0.002488 | 13-Jan | 0.006173 | 13-Jan | −0.00208 |
| 23 | 14-Jan | −0.00248 | 14-Jan | 0 | 14-Jan | 0.002083 |
| 24 | 15-Jan | 0.039801 | 15-Jan | 0.04908 | 15-Jan | 0.04158 |
| 25 | 16-Jan | 0.002392 | 16-Jan | −0.00585 | 16-Jan | −0.02994 |
| 26 | 17-Jan | −0.00239 | 17-Jan | 0.005882 | 17-Jan | 0 |
| 27 | 18-Jan | 0.002392 | 18-Jan | 0.005848 | 18-Jan | 0.002058 |
| 28 | 19-Jan | 0.002387 | 19-Jan | −0.00581 | 19-Jan | 0 |
| 29 | 20-Jan | −0.00238 | 20-Jan | 0.005848 | 20-Jan | 0 |
| 30 | Mean | 0.004064 | Mean | 0.006694 | Mean | 0.00087 |
| 31 | Variance | 0.000145 | Variance | 0.00022 | Variance | 0.000266 |
| 32 | Variance (P) | 0.000132 | Variance (P) | 0.0002 | Variance (P) | 0.000241 |
| 33 | St.D. | 0.01204 | St.D. | 0.014842 | St.D. | 0.016296 |
| 34 | St.D. (P) | 0.011479 | St.D. (P) | 0.014151 | St.D. (P) | 0.015538 |
| 35 | COV(X,Y) = | | 0.0001494 | COV(Y,Z) = | 0.000192 | |
| 36 | COV(X,Z) = | | 0.000139 | | | |
| 37 | CORR(X,Y) = | | 0.9196541 | CORR(Y,Z) = | 0.8733657 | |
| 38 | CORR(X,Z) = | | 0.7791748 | | | |

**TABLE 6.A.2** Stock Returns, Risk, and Co-Movement: Formula Entries

| | A | B | C | D | E | F | G | H |
|---|---|---|---|---|---|---|---|---|
| 1 | CORP. X | | | CORP. Y | | | CORP. Z | |
| 2 | DATE | RETURN | | DATE | RETURN | | DATE | RETURN |
| 18 | 9-Jan | N/A | | 9-Jan | N/A | | 9-Jan | N/A |
| 19 | 10-Jan | = B4/B3-1 | | 10-Jan | = E4/E3-1 | | 10-Jan | = H4/H3-1 |
| 20 | 11-Jan | = B5/B4-1 | | 11-Jan | = E5/E4-1 | | 11-Jan | = H5/H4-1 |
| 21 | 12-Jan | = B6/B5-1 | | 12-Jan | = E6/E5-1 | | 12-Jan | = H6/H5-1 |
| 22 | 13-Jan | = B7/B6-1 | | 13-Jan | = E7/E6-1 | | 13-Jan | = H7/H6-1 |
| 23 | 14-Jan | = B8/B7-1 | | 14-Jan | = E8/E7-1 | | 14-Jan | = H8/H7-1 |
| 24 | 15-Jan | = B9/B8-1 | | 15-Jan | = E9/E8-1 | | 15-Jan | = H9/H8-1 |
| 25 | 16-Jan | = B10/B9-1 | | 16-Jan | = E10/E9-1 | | 16-Jan | = H10/H9-1 |
| 26 | 17-Jan | = B11/B10-1 | | 17-Jan | = E11/E10-1 | | 17-Jan | = H11/H10-1 |
| 27 | 18-Jan | = B12/B11-1 | | 18-Jan | = E12/E11-1 | | 18-Jan | = H12/H11-1 |
| 28 | 19-Jan | = B13/B12-1 | | 19-Jan | = E13/E12-1 | | 19-Jan | = H13/H12-1 |
| 29 | 20-Jan | = B14/B13-1 | | 20-Jan | = E14/E13-1 | | 20-Jan | = H14/H13-1 |
| 30 | Mean | = AVERAGE (B19:B29) | | Mean | = AVERAGE (E19:E29) | | Mean | = AVERAGE(H19:H29) |
| 31 | Variance | = VAR(B19: B29) | | Variance | = VAR(E19: E29) | | Variance | = VAR(H19:H29) |
| 32 | Variance (P) | = VARP(B19: B29) | | Variance (P) | = VARP(E19: E29) | | Variance (P) | = VARP(H19:H29) |
| 33 | St.D. | = STDEV(B19: B29) | | St.D. | = STDEV(E19: E29) | | St.D. | = STDEV(H19:H29) |
| 34 | St.D. (P) | = STDEVP(B19: B29) | | St.D. (P) | = STDEVP(E19: E29) | | St.D. (P) | = STDEVP(H19:H29) |
| 35 | | COV(X,Y) = | | = COVAR(B19:B29,E19:E29) | COV(Y,Z) = | | = COVAR(E19:E29,H19:H29) | |
| 36 | | COV(X,Z) = | | = COVAR(B19:B29,H19:H29) | | | | |
| 37 | | CORR(X,Y) = | | = CORREL(B19:B29,E19:E29) | CORR(Y,Z) = | | = CORREL(E19:E29,H19:H29) | |
| 38 | | CORR(X,Z) = | | = CORREL(B19:B29,H19:H29) | | | | |

## 6.A.2 A PRIMER ON BLACK-SCHOLES OPTION PRICING

### Calls and Puts

First, we will introduce a few option basics. A *stock option* is a legal contract that grants its owner the right (not obligation) to either buy or sell a given stock. There are two types of stock options: puts and calls. A *call* grants its owner to purchase stock (called underlying shares) for a specified exercise price (also known as a striking price or exercise price) on or before the expiration date of the contract. In a sense, a call is similar to a coupon that one might find in a newspaper enabling its owner to, for example, purchase a roll of paper towels for one dollar. If the coupon represents a bargain, it will be exercised and the consumer will purchase the paper towels. If the coupon is not worth exercising, it will simply be allowed to expire. The value of the coupon when exercised would be the amount by which value of the paper towels exceeds one dollar (or zero if the paper towels are worth less than one dollar). Similarly, the value of a call option at exercise equals the difference between the underlying market price of the stock and the exercise price of the call.

Suppose, for example, that there is a call option with an exercise price of $90 on one share of stock. The option expires in one year. This share of stock is expected to be worth either $80 or $120 in one year, but we do not know which at the present time. If the stock were to be worth $80 when the call expires, its owner should decline to exercise the call. It would simply not be practical to use the call to purchase stock for $90 (the exercise price) when it can be purchased in the market for $80. The call would expire worthless in this case. If, instead, the stock were to be worth $120 when the call expires, its owner should exercise the call. Its owner would then be able to pay $90 for a share that has a market value of $120, representing a $30 profit. In this case, the call would be worth $30 when it expires. Let $T$ designate the options term to expiry, $S_T$ the stock value at option expiry, and $c_T$ be the value of the call option at expiry determined as follows:

$$c_T = MAX[0, S_T - X] \tag{6.A.2.1}$$

$$\text{When } S_T = 80,\ c_T = \text{MAX}[0,\ 80 - 90) = 0$$

$$\text{When } S_T = 120,\ c_T = \text{MAX}[0,\ 120 - 90) = 30$$

A put grants its owner the right to sell the underlying stock at a specified exercise price on or before its expiration date. A put contract is similar to an insurance contract. For example, an owner of stock may purchase a put contract ensuring that he can sell his stock for the exercise price given by the put contract. The value of the put when exercised is equal to the amount by which the put exercise price exceeds the underlying stock price (or zero if the put is never exercised).

To continue the above example, suppose that there is a put option with an exercise price of $90 on one share of stock. The put option expires in one year. Again, this share of stock is expected to be worth either $80 or $120 in one year, but we do not know which yet. If the stock were to be worth $80 when the put expires, its owner should exercise the put. In this case, its owner could use the put to sell stock for $90 (the exercise price) when it can be purchased in the market for $80. The put would be worth $10 in this case. If, instead, the stock were to be worth $120 when the put expires, its owner should not exercise the put. Its owner should not accept $90 for a share that has a market value of \$120. In this case, the put would be worth nothing when it expires. Let $p_T$ be the value of the put option at expiry, determined as follows:

$$p_T = \text{MAX}[0,\ X - S_T) \tag{6.A.2.2}$$

$$\text{When } S_T = 80,\ p_T = \text{MAX}[0,\ 90 - 80) = 10$$

$$\text{When } S_T = 120,\ p_T = \text{MAX}[0,\ 90 - 120) = 0$$

The owner of the option contract may exercise his right to buy or sell; however, he is not obligated to do so. Stock options are simply contracts between two investors issued with the aid of a clearing corporation, exchange, and broker, which ensure that investors honor their obligations to each other. The corporation whose stock options are traded will probably not issue and does not necessarily trade these options.

For each owner of an option contract, there is a seller or "writer" who creates the contract, sells it to a buyer, and must satisfy an obligation to the owner of the option contract. The option writer sells (in the case of a call exercise) or buys (in the case of a put exercise) the stock when the option owner exercises. The owner of a call is likely to profit if the stock underlying the option increases in value sufficiently over the exercise price of the option (he can buy the stock for less than its market value); the owner of a put is likely to profit if the underlying stock declines in value sufficiently below the exercise price (he can sell stock for more than its market value). Since the option owner's right to exercise represents an obligation to the option writer, the option owner's profits are equal to the option writer's losses. Therefore, an option must be purchased from the option writer; the option writer receives a "premium" from the option purchaser for assuming the risk of loss associated with enabling the option owner to exercise.

## The Black-Scholes Model

The Black-Scholes option pricing model provides a simple mechanism for valuing calls under certain assumptions (see Chapter 8 for more detail on the Black-Scholes model and its assumptions). If circumstances are appropriate to apply the Black-Scholes model, call options can be valued with the following:

$$c_0 = S_0 N(d_1) - \frac{X}{e^{r_f T}} N(d_2) \tag{6.A.2.3}$$

$$d_1 = \frac{\ln(S_0/X) + (r_f + \sigma^2/2)T}{\sigma\sqrt{T}} \tag{6.A.2.4}$$

$$d_2 = d_1 - \sigma\sqrt{T} \tag{6.A.2.5}$$

where $N(d^*)$ is the cumulative normal distribution function for (d*). This function might be referred to in a statistics setting as the "z" value for ($d^*$). From a computational perspective, one would first work through Equation (6.A.2.4) and then Equation (6.A.2.5) before valuing the call with Equation (6.A.2.3). $N(d_1)$ and $N(d_2)$ are areas under the standard normal distribution curves (z-values). Simply locate the z-value on an appropriate table (see Table A.1 in the text appendix) corresponding to the $N(d_1)$ and $N(d_2)$ values.

Consider the following simple illustration of a Black-Scholes model application: An investor has the opportunity to purchase a six month call option for \$7.00 on a stock that is currently selling for \$75. The exercise price of the call is \$80 and the current riskless rate of return is 10% per annum. The variance of annual returns on the underlying stock is 16%. At its current price of \$7.00, does this option represent a good investment? First, we note the model inputs in symbolic form:

$$T = 0.5 \quad r_f = 0.10 \quad \sigma = 0.4 \quad S_0 = 75$$

$$X = 80 \quad \sigma^2 = 0.16 \quad e = 2.71828$$

Our first steps are to find $d_1$ and $d_2$ from Equations (6.A.2.4) and (6.A.2.5):

$$d_1 = \frac{\ln(75/80) + (.1 + .5 \cdot .16) \cdot .5}{.4 \cdot \sqrt{.5}} = \frac{\ln(.9375) + .09}{.2828} = .09$$

$$d_2 = d_1 - .4 \cdot \sqrt{.5} = .09 - .2828 = -.1928$$

Next, by either using a z-table (see Table A.1 in the text Appendix) or by using an appropriate estimation function from a statistics manual, we find normal density functions for $d_1$ and $d_2$:

$$N(d_1) = N(.09) = .536 \quad N(d_2) = N(-.1928) = .420$$

Finally, we use $N(d_1)$ and $N(d_1)$ in Equation (6.A-3) to value the call:

$$c_0 = 75 \cdot (.536) - (80 \cdot .9512) \cdot (.420) = 8.23$$

Since the 8.23 estimated value of the call exceeds its 7.00 market price, the call should be purchased.

## Appendix Exercises

1. Call and put options with an exercise price of \$30 are traded on one share of Company X stock.
   - **a.** What are the value of the call and the put if the stock is worth \$33 when the options expire?
   - **b.** What are the value of the call and the put if the stock is worth \$22 when the options expire?
   - **c.** What is the value of the call writer's obligation if the stock is worth \$33 when the options expire? What is the value of the put writer's obligation if the stock is worth \$33 when the options expire?
   - **d.** What is the value of the call writer's obligation if the stock is worth \$22 when the options expire? What is the value of the put writer's obligation if the stock is worth \$22 when the options expire?

e. Suppose that the purchaser of a call in part a paid \$1.75 for his option. What was his profit on his investment?
f. Suppose that the purchaser of a call in part b paid \$1.75 for his option. What was his profit on his investment?

2. Evaluate calls for each of the following European stock option series:

| Option 1 | Option 2 | Option 3 | Option 4 |
|---|---|---|---|
| $T = 1$ | $T = 1$ | $T = 1$ | $T = 2$ |
| $S = 30$ | $S = 30$ | $S = 30$ | $S = 30$ |
| $\sigma = 0.3$ | $\sigma = 0.3$ | $\sigma = 0.5$ | $\sigma = 0.3$ |
| $r_f = 0.06$ | $r_f = 0.06$ | $r_f = 0.06$ | $r_f = 0.06$ |
| $X = 25$ | $X = 35$ | $X = 35$ | $X = 35$ |

## Appendix Exercise Solutions

1. a. $c_T = \$33 - \$30 = \$3;\ p_T = 0$
   b. $c_T = 0;\ p_T = \$30 - \$22 = \$8$
   c. $c_T = -\$3;\ p_T = 0$
   d. $c_T = 0;\ p_T = -\$8$
   e. $\$3 - \$1.75 = \$1.25$
   f. $\$0 - \$1.75 = -\$1.75$
2. The options are valued with the Black-Scholes model in a step-by-step format in the following table:

| | Option 1 | Option 2 | Option 3 | Option 4 |
|---|---|---|---|---|
| $d(1)$ | 0.957739 | −0.163836 | 0.061699 | 0.131638 |
| $d(2)$ | 0.657739 | −0.463836 | −0.438301 | −0.292626 |
| $N[d(1)]$ | 0.830903 | 0.434930 | 0.524599 | 0.552365 |
| $N[d(2)]$ | 0.744647 | 0.321383 | 0.330584 | 0.384904 |
| Call | 7.395 | 2.455 | 4.841 | 4.623 |

## 6.A.3 ESTIMATING IMPLIED BLACK-SCHOLES VARIANCES

Analysts often employ historical return variances to estimate the volatility of securities. However, one cannot always assume that variances will be constant over time or that historical data properly reflects current conditions. An alternative procedure to estimate security variances is based on the assumption that investors price options based on consideration of the underlying stock risk. If the price of the option is taken to be correct, and if the Black-Scholes option pricing model is appropriate for valuing options, then one can infer the underlying stock standard deviation based on the known market price of the option and the option pricing model. Consider the following example pertaining to a six-month call currently trading for \$8.20 and its underlying stock currently trading for \$75:

$$T = 0.5 \quad r_f = 0.10 \quad c_0 = 8.20$$

$$X = 80 \quad S_0 = 75$$

If investors have used the Black-Scholes option pricing model to evaluate this call, the following must hold:

$$8.20 = 75 \times N(d_1) - 80 \times e^{-0.1 \times 0.5} \times N(d_2)$$

$$d_1 = \{\ln(75/80) + (0.1 + 0.5\sigma^2) \times 0.5\} \div \sigma\sqrt{0.5}$$

$$d_2 = d_1 - \sigma\sqrt{0.5}$$

Thus, we wish to solve the above system of equations for $\sigma$. This is equivalent to solving for the root of:

$$f(\sigma^*) = 0 = 75 \times N(d_1) - 80 \times e^{-0.1 \times 0.5} \times N(d_2) - 8.20$$

based on equations above for $d_1$ and $d_2$. There exists no closed form solution for $\sigma$. Thus, we will use the method of bisection to search for a solution. We first arbitrarily select endpoints $b_1 = 0.2$ and $a_1 = 0.5$ such that $f(b_1) < 0$ and $f(a_1) > 0$. Since these endpoints result in $f(\sigma)$ with opposite signs, our first iteration will use $\sigma_1 = 0.5(0.2 + 0.5) = 0.35$. We find that this estimate for sigma results in a value of $-1.30009$ for $f(\sigma)$. Since this $f(\sigma)$ is negative, we know that $\sigma^*$ is in the segment $b_2 = 0.35$ and $a_2 = 0.5$. We repeat the iteration process, finding after 19 iterations that $\sigma^* = 0.411466$. Table 6.A.3 details the process of iteration.

The Newton-Raphson method can also be used to more efficiently iterate for an implied volatility. Consider the following example where we wish to estimate the volatility implied by a six-month option with an exercise price of \$80 currently selling for \$8.20. Assume that the underlying stock price is currently \$75 and that the riskless return rate is 0.10. We shall solve for the implied standard deviation using the Newton-Raphson method, with an arbitrarily selected initial trial solution of $\sigma_1 = 0.6$. First, we need the derivative of the Black-Scholes model with respect to the underlying stock return standard deviation[10]:

$$\frac{\partial C}{\partial \sigma} = S\sqrt{t}\frac{e^{\frac{-(d_1^2)}{2}}}{\sqrt{2\Pi}} > 0 \quad Vega^{\nu} \tag{6.A.3.1}$$

We see from Table 6.A.4 that this standard deviation results in a value of $f(\sigma_0) = 3.950117$. Plugging 0.6 into Equation (6.A.3.1) for $\sigma$, we find that $f'(\sigma_1) = 20.82508$. Thus, our second trial value for $\sigma$ is determined by: $\sigma_2 = 0.6 - (3.950117 \div 20.82508) = 0.410319$. This process continues until we converge to a solution of approximately 0.411466. Note

[10]See Chapter 8 for additional details and discussion concerning vega.

**TABLE A.3** Using the Bisection Method to Estimate Implied Volatility

Initial Equation: $SN(d_1) - Xe^{-r_f T}N(d_2)$

$a_1 = 0.5$ $b_1 = 0.2$ $\sigma_1 = 0.35$
$r_f = 0.1$ $S_0 = 75$ $X = 80$
$c_0 = 8.2$ $T = 0.5$

| | | | $d_1(\sigma_n)$ | $d_2(\sigma_n)$ | $N(d_1)$ | $N(d_2)$ | $N(d_1)$ | $N(d_2)$ | $f(\sigma_n)$ |
|---|---|---|---|---|---|---|---|---|---|
| $f(a_1) =$ | 1.860465 | 0.5 | 0.1356555 | −0.2178978 | 0.553953 | 0.41375 | 0.553953 | 0.413754 | 1.860465 |
| $f(b_1) =$ | −4.46788 | 0.2 | −0.0320922 | −0.1735135 | 0.487199 | 0.431122 | 0.487199 | 0.431124 | −4.46788 |

| $n$ | $a_n$ | $b_n$ | $\sigma_n$ | $d_1(\sigma_n)$ | $d_2(\sigma_n)$ | $N(d_1)$ | $N(d_2)$ | $N(d_1)$ | $N(d_2)$ | $f(\sigma_n)$ |
|---|---|---|---|---|---|---|---|---|---|---|
| 1 | 0.5 | 0.2 | 0.35 | 0.06499919 | −0.1824882 | 0.525913 | 0.427597 | 0.525913 | 0.4276 | −1.29619 |
| 2 | 0.5 | 0.35 | 0.425 | 0.10188237 | −0.198638 | 0.540575 | 0.42127 | 0.540575 | 0.421273 | 0.284948 |
| 3 | 0.425 | 0.35 | 0.3875 | 0.08394239 | −0.1900615 | 0.533449 | 0.424628 | 0.533449 | 0.424630 | −0.50501 |
| 4 | 0.425 | 0.3875 | 0.40625 | 0.09302042 | −0.1942417 | 0.537056 | 0.42299 | 0.537056 | 0.422993 | −0.10987 |
| 5 | 0.425 | 0.40625 | 0.41562 | 0.09747658 | −0.1964147 | 0.538826 | 0.42214 | 0.538826 | 0.422143 | 0.087583 |
| 6 | 0.41562 | 0.40625 | 0.41093 | 0.09525501 | −0.1953217 | 0.537944 | 0.42256 | 0.537944 | 0.422571 | −0.01113 |
| 7 | 0.41562 | 0.41093 | 0.41328 | 0.09636739 | −0.1958666 | 0.538386 | 0.42235 | 0.538386 | 0.422357 | 0.038229 |
| 8 | 0.41328 | 0.41093 | 0.41210 | 0.09581161 | −0.1955937 | 0.538165 | 0.42246 | 0.538165 | 0.422464 | 0.01355 |
| 9 | 0.41210 | 0.41093 | 0.41152 | 0.09553341 | −0.1954576 | 0.538054 | 0.42251 | 0.538054 | 0.422517 | 0.00121 |
| 10 | 0.41152 | 0.41093 | 0.41123 | 0.09539424 | −0.1953896 | 0.537999 | 0.42254 | 0.537999 | 0.422544 | −0.00496 |
| 11 | 0.41152 | 0.41123 | 0.41137 | 0.09546383 | −0.1954236 | 0.538027 | 0.42252 | 0.538027 | 0.422531 | −0.00188 |
| 12 | 0.41152 | 0.41137 | 0.41145 | 0.09549862 | −0.1954406 | 0.538041 | 0.42252 | 0.538041 | 0.422524 | −0.00033 |
| 13 | 0.41152 | 0.41145 | 0.41148 | 0.09551602 | −0.1954491 | 0.538048 | 0.42251 | 0.538048 | 0.422521 | 0.000438 |
| 14 | 0.41148 | 0.41145 | 0.41146 | 0.09550732 | −0.1954449 | 0.538044 | 0.42251 | 0.538044 | 0.422522 | 0.000053 |
| 15 | 0.41146 | 0.41145 | 0.41145 | 0.09550297 | −0.1954427 | 0.538042 | 0.42252 | 0.538042 | 0.422523 | −0.00014 |
| 16 | 0.41146 | 0.41145 | 0.41146 | 0.09550514 | −0.1954438 | 0.538043 | 0.42252 | 0.538043 | 0.422523 | −0.00004 |
| 17 | 0.41146 | 0.41146 | 0.41146 | 0.09550623 | −0.1954443 | 0.538044 | 0.42252 | 0.538044 | 0.422523 | 0.000004 |
| 18 | 0.41146 | 0.41146 | 0.41146 | 0.09550569 | −0.1954441 | 0.538043 | 0.42252 | 0.538043 | 0.422523 | −0.00002 |
| 19 | 0.41146 | 0.41146 | 0.41146 | 0.09550596 | −0.1954442 | 0.538044 | 0.42252 | 0.538044 | 0.422523 | 0.00000 |
| 20 | 0.41146 | 0.41146 | 0.41146 | 0.09550610 | −0.1954443 | 0.538044 | 0.42252 | 0.538044 | 0.422523 | 0.00000 |
| 21 | 0.41146 | 0.41146 | 0.41146 | 0.09550616 | −0.1954443 | 0.538044 | 0.42252 | 0.538044 | 0.422523 | 0.00000 |
| 22 | 0.41146 | 0.41146 | 0.41146 | 0.09550613 | −0.1954443 | 0.538044 | 0.42252 | 0.538044 | 0.422523 | 0.00000 |
| 23 | 0.41146 | 0.41146 | 0.41146 | 0.09550615 | −0.1954443 | 0.538044 | 0.42252 | 0.538044 | 0.422523 | 0.00000 |

**TABLE 6.A.4** Newton-Raphson Method and Implied Volatilities

| $n$ | $\sigma_n$ | $f'(\sigma_n)$ | $d_1(\sigma_n)$ | $d_2(\sigma_n)$ | $N(d_1)$ | $N(d_2)$ | $N(d_1)$ | $N(d_2)$ | $f(\sigma_n)$ |
|---|---|---|---|---|---|---|---|---|---|
| 1 | 0.600000 | 20.82508 | 0.177864 | −0.2463997 | 0.57058527 | 0.40268 | 0.570585 | 0.402686 | 3.950117 |
| 2 | 0.410319 | 21.06193 | 0.094961 | −0.1951785 | 0.53782718 | 0.42262 | 0.537827 | 0.422627 | −0.024150 |
| 3 | 0.411466 | 21.06084 | 0.095506 | −0.1954443 | 0.53804365 | 0.42252 | 0.538044 | 0.422523 | 0.000000 |
| 4 | 0.411466 | 21.06084 | 0.095506 | −0.1954443 | 0.53804365 | 0.42252 | 0.538044 | 0.422523 | 0.000000 |
| 5 | 0.411466 | 21.06084 | 0.095506 | −0.1954443 | 0.53804365 | 0.42252 | 0.538044 | 0.422523 | 0.000000 |
| 6 | 0.411466 | 21.06084 | 0.095506 | −0.1954443 | 0.53804365 | 0.42252 | 0.538044 | 0.422523 | 0.000000 |

that the rate of convergence is much faster by using the Newton-Raphson method than by using the method of bisection.

$$\text{Initial Equation: } S_0N(d_1) - Xe^{-r_fT}N(d_2)$$

$$r_f = 0.1 \quad S_0 = 75 \quad X = 80$$

$$c_0 = 8.20 \quad T = 0.5 \quad \sigma_0 = 0.6$$

## Simple Closed-Form Procedures

The implied volatilities described above have the desirable characteristic of having an ex-ante orientation. However, their use is somewhat complicated by the frequently time-consuming methodology of iterating for solutions. Spreadsheet file and even computer program solutions packages can sometimes be cumbersome. This section provides two methodologies for obtaining simple closed form solutions for implied underlying asset volatilities.

Brenner and Subrahmanyam (1988) provide a simple formula to estimate an implied standard deviation (or variance) from an option whose striking price equals the current market price of the underlying asset. As the market price differs more from the option striking price, the estimation accuracy of this formula will worsen:

$$\sigma_{BS}^2 = \frac{2\pi c_0^2}{tS_0^2} \tag{6.A.3.2}$$

The accuracy of Equation (6.A.3.2) when the option strike and underlying asset market prices are unequal can be improved with use of a quadratic procedure proposed by Corrado and Miller (1996). Their formula makes use of a second-order approximation of the cumulative normal density function and an approximation for $ln(S_0/X)$ as $2(S_0 - X)/(S_0 + X)$. Several additional simplifications and approximations lead to the following formula for $\sigma$:

$$\sigma^2_{CM} = \frac{2\pi}{t(S_0+X)^2} \times \left[c_0 - \frac{S_0-X}{2} + \sqrt{\left(c_0 - \frac{S_0-X}{2}\right)^2 - \frac{(S_0-X)^2}{\pi}}\right]^2 \tag{6.A.3.3}$$

While the accuracy of this formula is improved when the market price of the underlying asset is close to the striking price of the option, it is not nearly as sensitive to differences between these prices as is the Brenner-Subrahmanyam formula.

## Aggregating Procedures

A difficulty arising with estimating implied variances results from the fact that there will typically be more than one option trading on the same stock. However, what if the short- and long-term uncertainty of a stock differs? Each option's market price will imply its own underlying stock variance, and these variances are likely to differ. Worse, what if the implied volatility of option contracts differs with respect to exercise prices? (This is called a volatility smile.) How might we use this conflicting information to generate the most reliable variance estimate? Each of our implied variance estimates is likely to provide some information, yet has the potential for having measured with error. We can preserve much of the information from each of our estimates and eliminate some of our estimating error if we use for our own implied volatility a value based on an average of all of our estimates. However, because volatility might be expected to vary over time, one should average only those variances implied by options with comparable terms to expiration. The following suggests two methods for averaging implied standard deviation estimates:

1. Simple average: Here, the final standard deviation estimate is simply the mean of the standard deviations implied by the market prices of the calls.
2. Average based on price sensitivities to $\sigma$: Calls that are more sensitive to $\sigma$ as indicated by $\partial c_j/\partial \sigma_j$ are more likely to imply a correct standard deviation estimate. Suppose we have $n$ calls on a stock and each of which implies a stock standard deviation $\sigma_j$. Each call price will have a sensitivity to its implied underlying stock standard deviation $\partial c_j/\partial \sigma_j$. The sensitivities can be summed, and a weighted average standard deviation estimate for the underlying stock can be computed from the following weighting scheme:

$$w_i = \frac{\dfrac{\partial C_{O,i}}{\partial \sigma_i}}{\displaystyle\sum_{j=1}^{n} \frac{\partial C_{O,j}}{\partial \sigma_j}} \tag{6.A.3.4}$$

where $w_i$ represents the weight for the implied standard deviation estimate for call option $i$. Thus, the final standard deviation estimate for a given stock $k$ based on all of the implied standard deviations from each of the call prices is:

$$\sigma_k = \sum_{i=1}^{n} w_i \sigma_i \tag{6.A.3.5}$$

CHAPTER

# 7

# Arbitrage and Hedging with Fixed Income Instruments and Currencies

## 7.1 ARBITRAGE WITH RISKLESS BONDS

As we discussed in Chapter 6, riskless arbitrage involves the simultaneous purchase and sale of identical cash flows. The most easily arbitraged financial instruments are often those with guaranteed payments or with payments that are perfectly correlated with other instruments. Consider a set of riskless bonds whose coupon payments and redemption values are guaranteed. Such riskless bonds might be replicated with portfolios of other riskless bonds if their payments are similarly guaranteed and are to be made on the same dates. For example, consider the illustration provided in Table 7.1, which consists of three priced riskless bonds, all making payments on the same dates until they mature. The cash flow structure of any one-, two-, or three-year bond (e.g., Bond D) added to the market can be replicated with some portfolio of bonds A, B, and C, as long as all the cash payments to investors on Bond D are on the same dates as those made by at least one (in this example, two) of the three bonds A, B, and C. For example, assume that there now exists Bond D, a three-year, 20% coupon bond selling in this market for $1360. This bond will make payments of $200 in years 1 and 2 in addition to a $1200 payment in year 3. We will demonstrate that a portfolio of bonds A, B, and C can be assembled to generate the same cash flow series as Bond D.

Thus, as we will demonstrate, Bond D can be replicated by a portfolio of our first three bonds in the following quantities: $b_A = 0$, $b_B, = 3\frac{1}{3}$, and $b_C = -2\frac{1}{3}$, which are determined by the following system of equations:

$$
\begin{aligned}
200 &= 40b_A + 60b_B + 0b_C \\
200 &= 1040b_A + 60b_B + 0b_C \\
1200 &= 1060b_B + 1000b_C
\end{aligned}
$$

This system sets the cash flows each year from Bond D equal to those of a portfolio comprising specific numbers of Bonds A, B, and C. There are many ways to solve this

**TABLE 7.1** Coupon Bonds A, B, and C

| Bond | Current Price | Face Value | Coupon Rate | Years to Maturity |
|---|---|---|---|---|
| A | 1000 | 1000 | 0.04 | 2 |
| B | 1055.5 | 1000 | 0.06 | 3 |
| C | 889 | 1000 | 0 | 3 |

system for the numbers ($b$) of Bonds A, B, and C to place in this replicating portfolio. One such way is to start by subtracting the first equation from the second equation, obtaining the following:

$$0 = 1000b_A$$

This is easily solved for $b_A = 0$. Now, substitute $b_A = 0$ into our original second equation:

$$200 = 1040b_A + 60b_B$$

Now, we see that $b_B = 3\frac{1}{3}$. Substitute this result into our original third equation:

$$1200 = 1060b_B + 1000b_C$$

$$1200 = 3533.33 + 1000b_C$$

Now, solve this to obtain $b_C = -2\frac{1}{3}$.

Thus, we find from this system that $b_A = 0$, $b_B = 3\frac{1}{3}$, and $b_C = -2\frac{1}{3}$. We determine the value of the portfolio replicating Bond D by weighting their current market prices: $(0 \times \$1000) + (3\frac{1}{3} \times \$1055.5) + (-2\frac{1}{3} \times 889) = \$1444$. Based on the portfolio's price, the value of Bond D is \$1444, although its current market price is \$1360. Thus, a trader can gain an arbitrage profit from the purchase of this bond for \$1360 financed by the sale of the portfolio of Bonds B and C at a price of \$1444. Shorting the portfolio implies selling $3\frac{1}{3}$ Bonds B and purchasing $2\frac{1}{3}$ Bonds C. Our cash flows in years 1, 2, and 3 will be zero, although we receive a positive cash flow now or time zero equal to $\$1444 - 1360 = 84$. This is a clear arbitrage profit. This arbitrage opportunity will persist until the value of the portfolio equals the value of Bond D.

Using matrix notation from text Appendix A.2, we have the following system to replicate Bond D:

$$\begin{bmatrix} 200 \\ 200 \\ 1200 \end{bmatrix} = \begin{bmatrix} 40 & 60 & 0 \\ 1040 & 60 & 0 \\ 0 & 1060 & 1000 \end{bmatrix} \begin{bmatrix} b_A \\ b_B \\ b_C \end{bmatrix}$$

$$\mathbf{cf_d} = \mathbf{CF} \qquad \mathbf{b}$$

To solve this system we first invert matrix **CF**, then use it to premultiply vector $\mathbf{cf_D}$ to obtain vector **b**:

$$\begin{bmatrix} 0 \\ 3.333333 \\ -2.33333 \end{bmatrix} = \begin{bmatrix} b_A \\ b_B \\ b_C \end{bmatrix} = \begin{bmatrix} -.001 & .001 & 0 \\ .0173333 & -.0006667 & 0 \\ -.018373 & .00070667 & .001 \end{bmatrix} \begin{bmatrix} 200 \\ 200 \\ 1200 \end{bmatrix}$$

$$\mathbf{b} \quad = \quad \mathbf{CF^{-1}} \quad \mathbf{cf_d}$$

This simple matrix system yields the same results as our system above. Cash flows, starting with time zero generated by the four-bond arbitrage portfolio, are represented in the following system:

$$\begin{bmatrix} -1000 & -1055.5 & -889 & -1360 \\ 40 & 60 & 0 & 200 \\ 1040 & 60 & 0 & 200 \\ 0 & 1060 & 1000 & 1200 \end{bmatrix} \begin{bmatrix} 0 \\ -3.33333 \\ 2.33333 \\ 1 \end{bmatrix} = \begin{bmatrix} 84 \\ 0 \\ 0 \\ 0 \end{bmatrix}$$

Thus, by buying Bonds C and D at quantities $2\frac{1}{3}$ and 1, respectively, and shorting Bond B in quantity $3\frac{1}{3}$, the arbitrageur locks in a profit of 84 in time zero, and zero profits in the subsequent three years. The arbitrage portfolio is riskless because all bonds are presumed to be default risk-free and are presumed to be held to maturity, thereby eliminating interest rate and liquidity risk.

## 7.2 FIXED INCOME HEDGING

Fixed income instruments provide for fixed interest payments at fixed intervals and principal repayments. In the absence of default and liquidity risk (and hybrid or adjustable features), uncertainties in interest rate shifts are the primary source of pricing risk for many fixed income instruments. In this section, we will define a few terms used in the analysis of fixed income instruments and discuss how to manage interest rate uncertainty.

### Bond Yields and Sources of Risk

Assume that we wish to analyze a bond maturing in n periods with a *face value* (or principle amount) equal to $F$ paying interest annually at a rate of $c$. The annual interest payment is rate c multiplied by face value $F$ (or $cF$) and the bond makes a single payment in time $n$ equal to $F$. Using a standard *present value* model discounting cash flows at a rate of $k$, the bond is evaluated as follows:

$$PV = \sum_{t=1}^{n} \frac{cF}{(1+k)^t} + \frac{F}{(1+k)^n} \tag{7.1}$$

For example, let $c$ equal 0.10, $F$ equal \$1000, $k$ equal 0.12, and $n$ equal 2. The present value of this bond is computed as follows:

$$PV = \frac{100}{(1+.12)^1} + \frac{100}{(1+.12)^2} + \frac{1000}{(1+.12)^2} = 966.20$$

Present value is used to determine the economic worth of a bond; the return of a bond measures the profit relative to the investment of a bond. There are several measures of bond return including current yield and yield to maturity. One such simple measurement, *current yield*, measures the annual interest payments relative to the initial investment required by the bond and is measured as follows:

$$\frac{cF}{P_0} \tag{7.2}$$

If the bond used in the example above might be purchased for \$986.48, its current yield is simply 10.14%.

An analyst encounters two problems when using current yield as a return measure. First, the current yield does not account for any capital gain or loss ($F - P_0$) that may accrue when the bond matures. Second, current yield does not account for the time value of money or compounding of the cash flows associated with the bond. Hence, the analyst might wish to compute the bond's internal rate of return, which is generally referred to as *yield to maturity* ($y$):

$$PV = \sum_{t=1}^{n} \frac{cF}{(1+y)^t} + \frac{F}{(1+y)^n} \tag{7.3}$$

Yield to maturity is that value for $y$ that satisfies Equation (7.3) (or $k$ in Equation (7.1)). Usually, a solution must be obtained through an iterative process. The yield to maturity (or internal rate of return) for the bond described above has a yield to maturity of 12%, computed as follows:

$$P_0 = 966.20 = \frac{100}{(1+.12)^1} + \frac{100}{(1+.12)^2} + \frac{1000}{(1+.12)^2}$$

Thus, yield to maturity may be interpreted as that discount rate which sets the purchase price of a bond equal to its present value.

The *yield to call* for a callable bond differs from yield to maturity in two respects. First, cash flows are assumed to cease at the call date rather than the maturity date. Second, the call price is used for the yield computation as the bond's final cash flow rather than the face value of the bond.

In general, bond risk might be categorized as follows:

1. *Default or credit risk*: The bond issuer may not fulfill all of its obligations.
2. *Liquidity risk*: An efficient market for investors to resell their bonds may not exist.
3. *Interest rate risk*: Market interest rate fluctuations affect values of existing bonds.

U.S. Treasury issues are generally regarded as being practically free of default risk. Furthermore, there exists an active market for Treasury issues, particularly those maturing within a short period. Thus, Treasury issues are regarded as having minimal liquidity risk. However, all bonds are subject to interest rate risk. Longer-term bonds are subject to increased interest rate risk due to the increased periods that the yields on longer-term bonds are likely to differ from newly issued bonds. We will discuss hedging this interest risk shortly.

## Fixed Income Portfolio Dedication

Fixed income funds seek to ensure relatively stable income levels over given periods of time. Typically, a fixed income fund must provide payments to its creditors, clients, or owners for the given period. For example, a pension fund is often expected to make a series of fixed retirement payments to pension fund participants. Such funds must invest their assets to ensure that their liabilities are paid. In many cases, fixed income funds will purchase assets such that their cash flows exactly match the liability payments that they are required to make. This exact matching strategy is referred to as dedication or laddering and is intended to minimize the risk of the fund. The process of dedication is much the same as the arbitrage transactions discussed above; the fund manager merely determines the cash flows associated with his liability structure and replicates them with a series of default risk-free bonds. For example, assume that a pension fund manager needs to make payments to pension plan participants of $12,000,000 in one year, $14,000,000 in two years, and $15,000,000 in three years. The manager wishes to match these cash flows with a portfolio of Bonds A, B, and C whose characteristics were given above in Table 7.1. These three bonds must be used to match the cash flows associated with the fund's liability structure. For example, in year 1, Bond A will pay $40, B will pay $60, and C will pay $0. These payments must be combined to total $12,000,000. Cash flows must be matched in years 2 and 3 as well. Only one exact matching strategy exists for this scenario. The following system can be solved for $b_A$, $b_B$, and $b_C$ to determine exactly how many of each of the bonds are required to satisfy the fund's cash flow requirements:

$$12,000,000 = 40b_A + 60b_B + 0b_C$$
$$14,000,000 = 1040b_A + 60b_B + 0b_C$$
$$15,000,000 = 1060b_B + 1100b_C$$

Note the similarity of this system to the system presented in the previous section. There are many ways to solve this system for the numbers ($b$) of Bonds A, B, and C to dedicate to the institution's portfolio of liabilities. One way to start is by subtracting the first equation from the second equation, obtaining the following:

$$2,000,000 = 1000b_A$$

This is easily solved for $b_A = 2000$. Now, substitute $b_A = 2000$ into our original second equation:

$$14,000,000 = 1040b_A + 60b_B$$

At this juncture, we see that $b_B = 198{,}666\{2/3\}$. Substitute this result into our original third equation:

$$\begin{aligned}15,000,000 &= 1060b_B + 1000b_C\\ 15,000,000 &= 210,586,670 + 1000b_C\end{aligned}$$

Now, solve this to obtain $b_C = -195{,}586\{2/3\}$.

Thus, we find from this system that $b_A = 2{,}000$, $b_B = 198{,}666.67$, and $b_C = -195{,}586.67$. We can determine the value of the portfolio of liabilities by weighting their current market prices: $(2000 \times \$1000) + (198{,}666.67 \times \$1055.5) + (-198{,}586.67 \times 889) = \$37{,}816{,}120$. Using matrix notation from Appendix section A.2 starting on page 358, we have the following system to replicate the portfolio of liabilities:

$$\begin{bmatrix}12,000,000\\14,000,000\\15,000,000\end{bmatrix} = \begin{bmatrix}40 & 60 & 0\\1040 & 60 & 0\\0 & 1060 & 1000\end{bmatrix}\begin{bmatrix}b_A\\b_B\\b_C\end{bmatrix}$$

$$\mathbf{cf_L} \qquad = \qquad \mathbf{CF} \qquad \mathbf{b}$$

To solve this system, we first invert matrix **CF**, and then use it to premultiply vector $\mathbf{cf_L}$ to obtain vector **b**:

$$\begin{bmatrix}2000\\198666.67\\-195586.67\end{bmatrix} = \begin{bmatrix}b_A\\b_B\\b_C\end{bmatrix} = \begin{bmatrix}-.001 & .001 & 0\\.0173333 & -.0006667 & 0\\-.018373 & .00070667 & .001\end{bmatrix}\begin{bmatrix}12,000,000\\14,000,000\\15,000,000\end{bmatrix}$$

$$\mathbf{b} \quad = \qquad \mathbf{CF^{-1}} \qquad \mathbf{cf_L}$$

This simple matrix system yields the same results as our system above.

Exact matching or dedication programs can be very effective when liquidity is sufficient to secure appropriately priced bonds with appropriate cash flow structures when needed. However, what if a portfolio manager needs to lock in a cash flow from her portfolio of bonds equal to, say, \$1,000,000 on a specific date exactly 12 years, 3 months, and 2 days into the future? If no bonds are available on that date, some sort of approximation must be acceptable. Alternatively, what if such bonds are available, but overpriced? Again, the manager must work with an approximation or accept investment in overpriced bonds. In any case, dedication programs can limit managers with respect to what bonds they can purchase and in what quantities they must be purchased. Next, we will discuss portfolio immunization, which is not always as effective as an interest-rate hedging tool, but does allow for more flexibility.

## 7.3 FIXED INCOME PORTFOLIO IMMUNIZATION

As discussed earlier, bonds and certain other debt instruments issued by the U.S. Treasury are often regarded to be practically free of default risk and of relatively low liquidity risk. However, these bonds, particularly those with longer terms to maturity, are subject to market value fluctuations after they are issued, primarily due to changes in interest rates offered on new issues. Generally, interest rate increases on new bond issues decrease values of bonds that are already outstanding; interest rate decreases on new bond issues increase values of bonds that are already outstanding. Immunization models such as the duration model are intended to describe the proportional change in the value of a bond induced by a change in interest rates or yields of new issues.

## Bond Duration

Many analysts use present value models to value Treasury issues, frequently using yields to maturity of new Treasury issues to value existing issues with comparable terms. It is important for analysts to know how changes in new-issue interest rates will affect values of bonds with which they are concerned. Bond *duration* measures the proportional sensitivity of a bond to changes in the market rate of interest. Consider a two-year 10% coupon Treasury issue which is currently selling for \$966.20. The yield to maturity $y$ of this bond is 12%. Default risk and liquidity risk are assumed to be zero; interest rate risk will be of primary importance. Assume that this bond's yield or discount rate is the same as the market yields of comparable Treasury issues (which might be expected in an efficient market) and assume that bonds of all terms to maturity have the same yield. Further assume that investors have valued the bond such that its market price equals its present value; that is, the discount rate $k$ for the bond equals its yield to maturity $y$. If market interest rates and yields were to rise for new Treasury issues, then the yield of this bond would rise accordingly. However, since the contractual terms of the bond will not change, its market price must drop to accommodate a yield consistent with the market. Assume that the value of an $n$-year bond paying interest at a rate of $c$ on face value $F$ is determined by a present value model with the yield $y$ of comparable issues serving as the discount rate $k$:

$$PV = \sum_{t=1}^{n} \frac{cF_t}{(1+y)^t} + \frac{F}{(1+y)^n} \tag{7.4}$$

Assume that the terms of the bond contract, $n$, $F$, and $c$ are constant. Just what is the proportional change in the price of a bond induced by a proportional change in market interest rates (technically, a proportional change in $[1+y]$)? This can be approximated by the bond's *Macaulay simple duration formula* as follows:

$$\frac{\Delta PV}{PV} \div \frac{\Delta(1+y)}{(1+y)} \approx Dur = \frac{dPV}{PV} \div \frac{d(1+y)}{(1+y)} = \frac{dPV}{d(1+y)} \times \frac{(1+y)}{PV} \tag{7.5}$$

Equation (7.5) provides a reasonable approximation of the proportional change in the price of a bond induced by an infinitesimal proportional change in $(1+y)$. To derive this measure of a bond's interest rate sensitivity (Equation (7.5)), we first rewrite Equation (7.4) in polynomial form (to take derivatives later) and substitute $y$ for $k$ (since they are assumed to be equal):

$$PV = \sum_{t=1}^{n} \frac{cF}{(1+y)^t} + \frac{F}{(1+y)^n} = \sum_{t=1}^{n} cF(1+y)^{-t} + F(1+y)^{-n} \tag{7.6}$$

Next, we find the derivative of $PV$ with respect to $(1 + y)$:

$$\frac{dPV}{d(1+y)} = \sum_{t=1}^{n} -tcF(1+y)^{-t-1} - nF(1+y)^{-n-1} \tag{7.7}$$

Equation (7.7) can be rewritten:

$$\frac{dPV}{d(1+y)} = \frac{\sum_{t=1}^{n} -tcF(1+y)^{-t} - nF(1+y)^{-n}}{(1+y)} \tag{7.8}$$

Since the market rate of interest is assumed to equal the bond yield to maturity, the bond's price $P_0$ will equal its present value $PV$. Next, multiply both sides of Equation (7.8) by $(1 + y) \div P_0$ to obtain the bond's proportional interest rate sensitivity, which is often more practical for portfolio purposes:

$$Dur = \frac{dPV}{d(1+y)} \times \frac{(1+y)}{P_0} = \frac{\sum_{t=1}^{n} -tcF(1+y)^{-t} - nF(1+y)^{-n}}{P_0} \tag{7.9a}$$

Equation (7.9a) is equivalent to the right side of Equation (7.5). Thus, duration is defined as the proportional price change of a bond induced by an infinitesimal proportional change in $(1 + y)$ or 1 plus the market rate of interest:

$$Dur = \frac{dPV}{d(1+y)} \times \frac{(1+y)}{P_0} = \frac{\sum_{t=1}^{n} \frac{-tcF}{(1+y)^t} + \frac{-nF}{(1+y)^n}}{P_0} \tag{7.9b}$$

Since the market rate of interest will likely determine the yield to maturity of any bond, the duration of the bond described above is determined as follows from Equation (7.9b):

$$Dur = \frac{\frac{-1 \cdot .1 \cdot 1000}{(1+.12)} + \frac{-2 \cdot .1 \cdot 1000}{(1+.12)^2} + \frac{-2 \cdot 1000}{(1+.12)^2}}{966.20} = -1.907 \tag{7.10}$$

This duration level of $-1.907$ suggests that the proportional decrease in the value of this bond will equal 1.907 times the proportional increase in market interest rates. This duration level also implies that this bond has exactly the same interest rate sensitivity as a *pure discount bond* (a bond making no coupon payments) that matures in 1.907 years.

Application of the simple Macaulay duration model does require several important assumptions. First, it is assumed that yields are invariant with respect to maturities of bonds; that is, the yield curve is flat. Furthermore, it is assumed that investors' projected reinvestment rates are identical to the bond yields to maturity. Any change in interest rates will be infinitesimal and will also be invariant with respect to time. The accuracy of this model will depend on the extent to which these assumptions hold.

## Portfolio Immunization

Earlier, we discussed bond portfolio dedication, which is concerned with matching terminal cash flows or values of bond portfolios with required payouts associated with liabilities. This process assumes that no transactions will take place within the portfolio and that cash flows associated with liabilities will remain as originally anticipated. Clearly, these assumptions will not hold for many institutions. Alternatively, one may hedge fixed income portfolio risk by using *immunization* strategies, which are concerned with matching the present values of asset portfolios with the present values of cash flows associated with future liabilities. More specifically, immunization strategies are primarily concerned with matching asset durations with liability durations. If asset and liability durations are matched, it is expected that the net fund value (equity or surplus) will not be affected by a very small shift in interest rates; asset and liability changes offset each other. Again, this simple immunization strategy is dependent on the following:

1. Changes in $(1 + y)$ are infinitesimal.
2. The yield curve is flat (yields do not vary over terms to maturity).
3. Yield curve shifts are parallel; that is, short- and long-term interest rates change by the same amount.
4. Only interest rate risk is significant.

The first assumption, because it allows us to use derivatives to measure sensitivities, can only be an approximation when interest rates change by finite amounts. We will discuss bond convexity shortly as a correction for this scenario. Assumptions requiring flat yield curves and parallel yield curve shifts are useful in that we do not have to distinguish between different rates (e.g., short- and long-term rates) over the term of the bond. Immunization becomes significantly more complicated when we need to analyze fixed income risks such as those related to liquidity and default.

### *Immunization Illustration*

Let us revisit our portfolio dedication illustration discussed in the Fixed Income Hedging section. We note here that our illustration allows for a flat yield curve, such that all yields to maturity equal 4%. In this illustration, the pension fund manager still has anticipated cash payouts of \$12,000,000, \$14,000,000, and \$15,000,000 over the next three years 1, 2, and 3. Now, suppose that the manager seeks to immunize interest rate risk associated with this liability stream with a portfolio. Rather than exactly match the liability outflow streams with bond inflows, the manager will match durations of the liability stream with the duration of the bond investment portfolio. This will ensure that changes in the value of the liability stream induced by interest rate changes are approximately the same as changes in the value of the bond portfolio. This will minimize fluctuations in the net value (assets minus liabilities) of the fund as interest rates vary. Bond details are given in Table 7.1. In addition, given the flat yield curve of 4%, the value of the liability stream is \$37,816,120.

We calculate bond and liability stream durations as follows:

$$\mathrm{Dur_A} = \frac{\dfrac{40}{1+0.04} + 2\times\dfrac{1040}{(1+0.04)^2}}{-1000} = -1.96$$

$$\mathrm{Dur_B} = \frac{\dfrac{60}{1+0.04} + 2\times\dfrac{60}{(1+0.04)^2} + 3\times\dfrac{1060}{(1+0.04)^3}}{-1055.5} = -2.84$$

$$\mathrm{Dur_C} = \frac{3\times\dfrac{1000}{(1+0.04)^3}}{-889} = -3$$

$$\mathrm{Dur_L} = \frac{\dfrac{12,000,000}{1+0.04} + 2\times\dfrac{14,000,000}{(1+0.04)^2} + 3\times\dfrac{15,000,000}{(1+0.04)^3}}{-37,817,193.9} = -1.97$$

Portfolio immunization is accomplished when the duration (weighted average duration) of the portfolio of bonds equals the duration (−1.97) of the liability stream:

$$\begin{aligned} Dur_A \times w_A + Dur_B \times w_B + Dur_C \times w_C &= Dur_L \\ w_A + \quad w_B + \quad w_C &= 1 \\ -1.96 \times w_A - 2.84 \times w_B \; - 2.84 \times w_C &= -1.97 \\ w_A + \quad w_B + \quad w_C &= 1 \end{aligned} \qquad (7.11)$$

There is an infinity of solutions to this two-equation, three-variable system. Any solution that both satisfies these two equations and satisfies any other of the manager's other constraints and/or preferences is acceptable. Next, suppose that the manager already has invested \$3,781,612 (10% of the total liability value) into Bond A and wants to hold this investment in Bond A constant at $w_A = 0.1$. We solve for investment weights as follows:

$$\begin{aligned} -1.96 \times w_A - 2.84 \times w_B - 2.84 \times w_C &= -1.97 \\ w_A + \quad w_B + \quad w_C &= 1 \\ w_A = 3,781,612/37,816,120 &= 0.1 \end{aligned}$$

Solving this $3 \times 3$ system reveals that the immunized portfolio will have the following weights: $w_A = 0.1$, $w_B = 5.064$, and $w_C = -4.164$. Consider the following system:

$$\begin{bmatrix} -1.97486 \\ 1 \\ 0.1 \end{bmatrix} = \begin{bmatrix} -1.9615 & 2.837 & -3 \\ 1 & 1 & 1 \\ 1 & 0 & 0 \end{bmatrix} \begin{bmatrix} w_A \\ w_B \\ w_C \end{bmatrix}$$

$$\mathbf{s} \quad = \quad \mathbf{Dur} \quad \mathbf{w}$$

We can solve this system by first inverting matrix **Dur**, then using it to pre-multiply vector **s** to obtain vector **w**:

$$\begin{bmatrix} .1 \\ 5.064 \\ -4.164 \end{bmatrix} = \begin{bmatrix} w_A \\ w_B \\ w_C \end{bmatrix} = \begin{bmatrix} 0 & 0 & 1 \\ 0.171321 & .513963 & -.17792 \\ -.17132 & .486037 & -.82208 \end{bmatrix} \begin{bmatrix} -1.97486 \\ 1 \\ 0.1 \end{bmatrix}$$

$$\mathbf{w} \quad = \quad \mathbf{Dur}^{-1} \quad \mathbf{s}$$

This simple matrix system yields the same results as our system above.

Duration-immunized portfolios are most effective when interest rate changes are infinitesimal. Since interest rate changes are likely to be finite, immunization strategies will be improved if we correct for finite interest rate movements by using convexity. Duration is based on the first derivative of a bond's price with respect to interest rates. This first derivative, or first order approximation, would be accurate only if the relationship were linear, which it is not. To correct for nonlinearities in this relationship, we match asset and liability portfolio convexities as well as durations to correct for finite interest rate changes. We will discuss convexity calculations next.

## Convexity

We used duration to determine the approximate change in a bond's value induced by a change in interest rates $(1 + y)$. However, the accuracy of the duration model is reduced by finite changes in interest rates, as we might expect. Duration may be regarded as a first order approximation (it only uses the first derivative) of the change in the value of a bond induced by a change in interest rates. *Convexity* is determined by the second derivative of the bond's value with respect to $(1 + y)$. The first derivative of the bond's price with respect to $(1 + y)$ is given:

$$\frac{\partial P_0}{\partial(1+y)} = \sum_{t=1}^{n} - tcF(1+y)^{-t-1} - nF(1+y)^{-n-1} \tag{7.12}$$

We find the second derivative by determining the derivative of the first derivative as follows:

$$\begin{aligned} \frac{\partial^2 P_0}{\partial(1+y)^2} &= \left[\sum_{t=1}^{n} - t(-t-1)cF(1+y)^{-t-2}\right] - \left[n(-n-1)F(1+y)^{-n-2}\right] \\ &= \left[\sum_{t=1}^{n} \frac{(t^2+t)cF}{(1+y)^{t+2}}\right] + \left[\frac{(n^2+n)F}{(1+y)^{n+2}}\right] \end{aligned} \tag{7.13}$$

Convexity is merely the second derivative of $P_0$ with respect to $(1 + y)$ divided by $P_0$:

$$Convexity = \frac{\left[\sum_{t=1}^{n} \frac{(t^2 + t)cF}{(1+y)^{t+2}}\right] + \left[\frac{(n^2 + n)F}{(1+y)^{n+2}}\right]}{P_0} \tag{7.14}$$

The first two derivatives can be used in a second-order Taylor series expansion to approximate new bond prices induced by changes in interest rates as follows:

$$P_1 \approx P_0 + f(1 + y_0) \cdot [\Delta(1 + y)] + \frac{1}{2!} \cdot f''(1 + y_0) \cdot [\Delta(1+y)]^2 \tag{7.15}$$

$$\begin{aligned} P_1 \approx P_0 &+ \left[\sum_{t=1}^{n} \frac{-tcF}{(1+y_0)^{t+1}} - \frac{nF}{(1+y_0)^{n+1}}\right][\Delta y] \\ &+ \frac{1}{2}\left[\sum_{t=1}^{n} \frac{(t^2 + t) \cdot cF}{(1+y_0)^{t+2}} + \frac{(n^2 + n) \cdot F}{(1+y_0)^{n+2}}\right] \cdot [\Delta y]^2 \\ &= P_0 + Dur \cdot \frac{P_0}{1 + y_0} \cdot [\Delta y] + \frac{1}{2} \cdot P_0 \cdot convexity \cdot [\Delta y]^2 \end{aligned} \tag{7.16}$$

Consider a five-year, 10%, \$1000-face-value coupon bond currently selling at par (face value). We might compute the present yield to maturity of this bond as $y_0 = 0.10$. The first derivative of the bond's value with respect to $(1 + y)$ at $y_0 = 0.10$ is found from Equation (7.11) to be 3790.78 (duration is $3790.78 \times 1.1 \div 1000 = 4.1698$); the second derivative is found from Equation (7.14) to be 19,368.34 (convexity is $19{,}368.34 \div 1000 = 19.36834$). If bond yields were to drop from 0.10 to 0.08, the actual value of this bond would increase to 1079.85, as determined from a standard present value model. If we were to use the duration model (first-order approximation from the Taylor expansion, based only on the first derivative), we estimate that the value of the bond increases to 1075.8157. If we use the convexity model second-order approximation from Equation (7.16), we estimate that the value of the bond increases to 1079.6894.

Note that this second estimate with the second-order approximation generates a revised bond value that is significantly closer to the bond's actual value as measured by the present value model. Therefore, the duration and immunization models are substantially improved by the second order approximations of bond prices (the convexity model). The fund manager wishing to hedge portfolio risk should not simply match durations (first derivatives) of assets and liabilities, he should also match their convexities (second derivatives).

Now, let us reconsider our portfolio dedication illustration from Section B and the portfolio immunization illustration from above. In this illustration, the pension fund manager has anticipated cash payouts of \$12,000,000, \$14,000,000, and \$15,000,000 over the next three years. We calculate bond A, B, and C convexities along with that for the liability stream as follows:

$$\text{Conv}_\text{A} = \frac{2 \times \dfrac{40}{(1+0.04)^3} + 6 \times \dfrac{1040}{(1+0.04)^4}}{1000} = 5.41$$

$$\text{Conv}_\text{B} = \frac{2 \times \dfrac{60}{(1+0.04)^3} + 6 \times \dfrac{60}{(1+0.04)^4} + 12 \times \dfrac{1060}{(1+0.04)^5}}{-1055.5} = 10.30$$

$$\text{Conv}_\text{C} = \frac{12 \times \dfrac{1000}{(1+0.04)^5}}{-889} = 11.09$$

$$\text{Conv}_\text{L} = \frac{2 \times \dfrac{12,000,000}{(1+0.04)^3} + 6 \times \dfrac{14,000,000}{(1+0.04)^4} + 12 \times \dfrac{15,000,000}{(1+0.04)^5}}{-37,816.120} = 6.38$$

Portfolio immunization is accomplished when the weighted averages of the duration and the convexity of the portfolio of bonds equals the duration and convexity (6.38) of the liability stream:

$$\begin{aligned}
Dur_A \times w_A + Dur_B \times w_B + Dur_C \times w_C &= Dur_o \\
Conv_A \times w_A + Conv_B \times w_B + Conv_C \times w_C &= Conv_o \\
w_A + w_B + w_C &= 1 \\
-1.962 \times w_A - 2.837 \times w_B - 3 \times w_C &= -1.975 \\
5.41 \times w_A + 10.30 \times w_B + 11.09 \times w_C &= 6.38 \\
w_A + w_B + w_C &= 1
\end{aligned} \tag{7.17}$$

The single solution to this $3 \times 3$ system of equations is $w_A = -0.481$, $w_B = 9.358$, and $w_C = -7.877$. This system provides an improved immunization strategy when interest rate changes are finite.

## 7.4 TERM STRUCTURE, INTEREST RATE CONTRACTS, AND HEDGING

Thus far in this chapter, we have discussed fixed income arbitrage and hedging without use of derivative instruments such as forward and futures contracts. In addition, we assumed that yield curves were flat, and that shifts in the yield curve are parallel. Here, we will discuss long-term interest rates as a function of short-term rates, both originating at time zero (spot rates, originating on loans originating now) and short-term rates originating in the future (forward rates, originating in the future at rates locked in now). In fact, we will argue that long-term interest rates are related to a combination of short-term rates on loans originating now (spot rates) and on loans originating in the future (forward rates). More specifically, the long-term spot rate will be expressed as a geometric mean of short-term spot and forward interest rates. In addition, we will discuss how to use forward and futures contracts to arbitrage fixed income instruments and to hedge fixed income portfolios.

## The Term Structure of Interest Rates

The *term structure of interest rates* is concerned with interest rates on debt securities and how these rates vary with respect to varying dates of maturity. For example, term structure might be concerned with why the interest rate on debt maturing in one year is 2% versus 5% for debt maturing in 20 years. Generally at a given point in time, we observe longer-term interest rates exceeding shorter-term rates, although this is not always the case (e.g., the years 1980–1983).

The *pure expectations theory* states that long-term spot rates (interest rates on loans originating now) can be explained as a product of short-term spot rates and short-term forward rates (interest rates on loans committed to now but actually originating at later dates). Where $y_{t,m}$ is the rate on a loan originated at time $t$ to be repaid at time $m$, the pure expectations theory defines the relationship between long- and short-term interest rates as follows:

$$(1+y_{0,n})^n = \prod_{t=1}^{n}(1+y_{t-1,t}) \tag{7.18}$$

Thus, the long-term spot rate $y_{0,n}$ is defined as $n$-th root of the product of the one-period spot rate $y_{0,1}$ and a series of one-period forward rates $y_{t-1,t}$ minus one. In other words, the long-term spot rate $y_{0,n}$ can be determined based on the short-term spot rate $y_{0,1}$ and a series of one-period forward rates $y_{t-1,t}$ as follows:

$$y_{0,n} = \sqrt[n]{\prod_{t=1}^{n}(1+y_{t-1,t})} - 1 \tag{7.19}$$

Consider an example where the one-year spot rate $y_{0,1}$ is 5%. Investors are expecting that the one-year spot rate one year from now will increase to 6%; thus, the one-year forward rate $y_{1,2}$ on a loan originated in one year is 6%. This means that investors can lock in an interest rate of 6% on a one-year loan originating in one year and maturing in two years. Furthermore, assume that investors are expecting that the one-year spot rate two years from now will increase to 7%; thus, the one-year forward rate $y_{2,3}$ on a loan originated in two years is 7%. Based on the pure expectations hypothesis, what is the three-year spot rate? This is determined with Equation (7.21) as follows:

$$y_{0,n} = \sqrt[n]{\prod_{t=1}^{n}(1+y_{t-1,t})} - 1 = \sqrt[3]{(1+y_{0,1})(1+y_{1,2})(1+y_{2,3})} - 1 = \sqrt[3]{(1+.05)(1+.06)(1+.07)} = .05997$$

## Term Structure Estimation with Coupon Bonds

The *spot rate* is the yield at present prevailing for zero coupon bonds of a given maturity. The $t$ year spot rate is denoted here by $y_{0,t}$, which represents the interest rate on a loan to be made at time zero and repaid in its entirety at time $t$. Spot rates can be estimated from bonds with known future cash flows and their current prices. We can obtain spot rates from yields implied from series of coupon bonds if the law of one price holds.

These next few sections are concerned with how interest rates or yields vary with maturities of bonds. The simplest bonds to work with from an arithmetic perspective are *pure discount notes*, that is, notes that make no interest payments. Such notes make only one payment at one point in time—on the maturity date of the note. Determining the relationship between yield and term to maturity for these bonds is quite trivial. The return obtained from a pure discount note is strictly a function of capital gains; that is, the difference between the face value of the note and its purchase price. Short-term U.S. Treasury bills are an example of pure discount (or zero coupon) notes. Coupon bonds are somewhat more difficult to work with from an arithmetic perspective because they make payments to bondholders at a variety of different periods.

## Bootstrapping the Yield Curve

The yield curve can be obtained empirically by examining the payoffs associated with a bond simultaneously with the bond's purchase price. Let $D_t$ be the discount function for time $t$; that is, $D_t = 1/(1 + y_{0,t})^t$. This means that a coupon payment $cF$ or payment to face value $F$ made at time $t$ will be discounted by multiplying it by the discount function $D_t$:

$$PV = \sum_{t=1}^{n} cF \times D_t + FD_n = \sum_{t=1}^{n} cF/(1+y_{0,t})^t + F/(1+y_{0,t})^n \tag{7.20}$$

A little algebra produces the following spot rate:

$$y_{0,t} = (1/D_t)^{1/t} - 1 \tag{7.21}$$

Thus, one can obtain spot rates $y_{0,t}$ from the bond's current purchase price $P_0$ and expected future cash flows from coupon payments $cF$ and face value $F$. Thus, consider a \$1000 face value bond making a single interest payment at an annual rate of 5% (see Table 7.2). Suppose this bond is currently selling for 102 (actually meaning 102% of its face value, or 1020) and that it matures in one year when its coupon payment is made. The one-year spot rate implied by this bond is determined as follows:

$$1020 = (50 + 1000) \times D_1 = (1050)/(1+y_{0,1})^1$$
$$D_1 = 1020/1050 = (0.9714286)^{1/1};\quad 1/0.9714286 - 1 = y_{0,1} = 0.0294$$

The one-year spot rate is 2.94%. However, a difficulty arises when the bond has more than one cash flow. As spot rates may vary over time, there may be a spot rate for each period, hence, a spot rate for each cash flow. Now, consider a \$1000 face value, two-year, bond-making interest payments at an annual rate of 5% (again, see Table 7.2). Suppose that this bond is currently selling for 101.75 (meaning 101.75% or 1017.5) and that it matures in two years when its second coupon payment is made. The two-year spot rate implied by this bond is bootstrapped from the one-year bond as follows:

$$1017.5 = 50 \times 0.9714286 + (50 + 1000) \times D_2$$
$$D_2 = [1017.5 - (50 \times 0.9714286)]/[50 + 1000] = 0.9227891$$
$$(1/.9227891)^{1/2} - 1 = y_{0,2} = 0.0410$$

Bootstrapping simply means to make use of the rate (the one-year rate) or information that is already known to obtain the desired result (the two-year rate). The three-year spot rate $y_{0,3}$ implied by the three-year bond from Table 7.2 is bootstrapped from the one-year and two-year bonds as follows:

$$1015.0 = 50 \times 0.9714286 + 50 \times 0.9227891 + (50 + 1000) \times D_3$$
$$D_3 = [1015 - (50 \times 0.9714286) - (50 \times 0.9227891)]/[50 + 1000] = 0.8764658$$
$$(1/.8764658)^{1/3} - 1 = y_{0,3} = 0.0449$$

Bootstrapping to map out the $n$-year yield curve requires that there be one bond maturing in each year $t$ for $t = 1$ to $n$ so that its $D_t$ can be used to determine (bootstrap) the $D_t$ for the bond maturing in one-year subsequent (Figure 7.1). Thus, one starts by determining $D_1$, then $D_2$ and so on until all $D_t$ values have been determined through year $n$.

**TABLE 7.2** Bootstrapping Spot Rates

| Maturity | % Coupon | Ask Price | $D_t$ | Spot Rate |
|---|---|---|---|---|
| 1 | 5.00 | 102 | 0.9714286 | 2.94% |
| 2 | 5.00 | 101-3/4 | 0.9227891 | 4.10% |
| 3 | 5.00 | 101-1/2 | 0.8764658 | 4.49% |
| 4 | 5.00 | 101-1/4 | 0.8323484 | 4.69% |
| 5 | 5.00 | 101-1/4 | 0.7927128 | 4.76% |
| 6 | 5.00 | 101-1/4 | 0.7549645 | 4.80% |
| 7 | 5.00 | 101-1/4 | 0.7190138 | 4.83% |
| 8 | 5.00 | 101-1/4 | 0.6847751 | 4.85% |
| 9 | 5.25 | 102-1/4 | 0.6445500 | 5.00% |
| 10 | 5.25 | 102-1/4 | 0.6123990 | 5.03% |
| 11 | 5.25 | 102-1/4 | 0.5818518 | 5.05% |
| 12 | 5.25 | 102-1/4 | 0.5528283 | 5.06% |
| 13 | 5.50 | 104 | 0.5193962 | 5.17% |
| 14 | 5.50 | 104 | 0.4923187 | 5.19% |
| 15 | 5.50 | 104 | 0.4666528 | 5.21% |
| 16 | 5.75 | 105-3/4 | 0.4331835 | 5.37% |

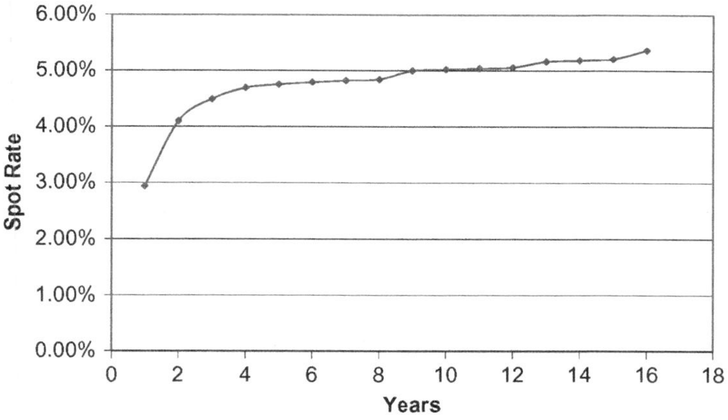


**FIGURE 7.1** Mapping the yield curve.

If we accept the Pure Expectations Theory for the term structure of interest rates, we can obtain forward rates from spot rates. Any $i$-year forward rate, $y_{t-i,t}$, from year $t-i$ to year $t$ is determined from $(D_t/D_{t-i})^{1/i}-1$. For example, the two-year spot rate is a function of the one-year spot rate and the one-year forward rate on a loan originating in one year as follows:

$$y_{0,2} = .0410 = \sqrt{(1+y_{0,1})(1+y_{1,2})} - 1 = \sqrt{(1+.0294)(1+y_{1,2})} - 1$$

We can use this relationship to solve for the one-year forward rate on a loan originating in one year as follows:

$$(1+.0410)^2 = (1+.0294)(1+y_{1,2})$$
$$y_{1,2} = \frac{(1+.0410)^2}{(1+.0294)} - 1 = .052731$$

Similarly, we can solve for the one-year forward rate on a loan originating in two years, forward rate $y_{2,3}$, as follows:

$$(1+.0449)^3 = (1+.0294)(1+.052731)(1+y_{2,3})$$
$$y_{2,3} = \frac{(1+.0449)^3}{(1+.0294)(1+.052731)} - 1 = .052744$$

The two-year forward rate on a loan originating in one year, forward rate $y_{1,3}$, is determined as follows:

$$(1+.0449)^3 = (1+.0294)(1+y_{1,3})^2$$
$$y_{1,3} = \sqrt{\frac{(1+.0449)^3}{(1+.0294)}} - 1 = .052737$$

**TABLE 7.3** Coupon Bonds E, F, and G

| Bond | Current Price | Face Value | Coupon Rate | Years to Maturity |
|---|---|---|---|---|
| E | 947.376 | 1000 | 0.05 | 2 |
| F | 904.438 | 1000 | 0.06 | 3 |
| G | 981 | 1000 | 0.09 | 3 |

which is identical to

$$y_{1,3} = \sqrt{(1 + .052731)(1 + .052744)} - 1 = .052737$$

## Simultaneous Estimation of Discount Functions

A coupon bond might be treated as a portfolio of pure discount notes, with each coupon payment being treated as a separate note maturing on the date the coupon is paid. Consider an example involving three bonds whose characteristics are given in Table 7.3. The three bonds are trading at known prices with a total of eight annual coupon payments among them (three for bonds E and F and two for bond G). Bond yields or spot rates must be determined simultaneously to avoid associating contradictory rates for the annual coupons on each of the three bills.

Let $D_t$ be the discount function for time $t$; that is, $D_t = 1/(1 + y_{0,t})^t$. Since $y_{0,t}$ is the spot rate or discount rate that equates the present value of a bond with its current price, the following equations may be solved for discount functions then spot rates:

$$947.376 = 50D_1 + 1050D_2$$
$$904.438 = 60D_1 + 60D_2 + 1060D_3$$
$$981 = 90D_1 + 90D_2 + 1090D_3$$

This system of equations might be represented by the following system of matrices:

$$\begin{bmatrix} 50 & 1050 & 0 \\ 60 & 60 & 1060 \\ 90 & 90 & 1090 \end{bmatrix} \begin{bmatrix} D_1 \\ D_2 \\ D_3 \end{bmatrix} = \begin{bmatrix} 947.376 \\ 904.438 \\ 981 \end{bmatrix}$$
$$\mathbf{CF} \qquad \mathbf{d} = \mathbf{P_0}$$

To solve this system we first invert matrix CF, and then use this inverse to premultiply vector $P_0$ to obtain vector $d$:

$$\begin{bmatrix} -.001 & -.03815 & .0371 \\ .001 & .00181667 & -.00177 \\ 0 & .003 & -.002 \end{bmatrix} \begin{bmatrix} 947.376 \\ 904.438 \\ 981 \end{bmatrix} = \begin{bmatrix} D_1 \\ D_2 \\ D_3 \end{bmatrix} = \begin{bmatrix} .943377 \\ .85734 \\ .751316 \end{bmatrix}$$
$$\mathbf{CF^{-1}} \qquad \mathbf{P_0} = \mathbf{d}$$

Thus, we find from solving this system for vector $d$ that $D_1 = 0.943377$, $D_2 = 0.85734$, and $D_3 = 0.751316$. Since $D_t = 1/(1+y_{0,t})^t$, $1/D_t = (1+y_{0,t})^t$, and $y_{0,t} = 1/D^{1/t} - 1$. Thus, spot rates are determined as follows:

$$\frac{1}{D_1} - 1 = .06 = y_{0,1}$$

$$\frac{1}{D_2^{1/2}} - 1 = .08 = y_{0,2}$$

$$\frac{1}{D_3^{1/3}} - 1 = .10 = y_{0,3}$$

Note that there exists a different spot rate (or discount rate) for each term to maturity; however, the spot rates for all cash flows generated by all bonds at a given period in time are the same. Thus, $y_{0,t}$ will vary over terms to maturity, but will be consistent for all bonds in a given time period. Thus, for example, the values of the three bonds are determined as follows:

$$947.376 = 50D_1 + 1050D_2 = \frac{50}{(1+.06)^1} + \frac{1050}{(1+.08)^2}$$

$$904.438 = 60D_1 + 60D_2 + 1060D_3 = \frac{60}{(1+.06)^1} + \frac{60}{(1+.08)^2}\frac{1060}{(1+.10)^3}$$

$$981 = 90D_1 + 90D_2 + 1090D_3 = \frac{90}{(1+.06)^1} + \frac{90}{(1+.08)^2}\frac{1090}{(1+.10)^3}$$

Any other bond with cash flows paid at the ends of some combination of years one, two, and three must have a value that is consistent with these three spot rates. For example, a three-year 2% coupon Bond H must be valued as follows:

$$P_H = 20D_1 + 20D_2 + 1020D_3 = \frac{20}{(1+.06)^1} + \frac{20}{(1+.08)^2}\frac{1020}{(1+.10)^3} = 802.36$$

A different market price for Bond H will lead to an arbitrage opportunity. In addition, prices for Bonds E, F, and G above will lead to the following forward rates:

$$y_{1,2} = \frac{(1+.08)^2}{(1+.06)} - 1 = .10$$

$$y_{2,3} = \frac{(1+.10)^3}{(1+.06)(1+.10)} - 1 = .14$$

$$y_{1,3} = \sqrt{\frac{(1+.10)^3}{(1+.06)}} - 1 = .12$$

Again, contract or bond contracts that are inconsistent with these rates lead to arbitrage opportunities.

## 7.5 ARBITRAGE WITH CURRENCIES

Currency arbitrage can exist when currency prices are not consistent with respect to other currencies or with respect to goods or financial instruments in different countries. Thus, there exist many potential types of currency (foreign exchange or FX) arbitrage opportunities. Here, we discuss triangular arbitrage and absolute purchase power parity (PPP), scenarios that often do not require derivative securities to exploit. When no-arbitrage conditions force prices to retain consistency, triangular arbitrage and PPP can be used to hedge currency risk.

### Triangular Arbitrage

*Triangular arbitrage* exploits the relative price difference between one currency and two other currencies. Suppose, for example, the buying and selling prices of EUR1.0 is USD1.2816. However, another currency, the South African Rand (SFR), has a price (buying or selling) equal to USD0.2000 or EUR0.1600. Is there a triangular arbitrage opportunity? There is if there is a price discrepancy for SFR in terms of USD and EUR. Note that the price of SFR in terms of both dollars and euro imply that 1 EUR is worth 1.25 USD:

$$\text{SFR1} = \text{USD0.2000} = \text{EUR0.1600}$$

Since USD0.20 = EUR0.16, dividing both figures by 0.16 implies that USD1.25 = EUR1. But, this is inconsistent with the currency price information given above, which states that USD1.2816 = EUR1.0. Even without knowing which pair of currencies is relatively mispriced, we can exploit an arbitrage opportunity taking advantage of the price inconsistencies. So, we will start rather arbitrarily with one pair, the SFR and USD. In terms of the SFR, it appears that the USD is too strong relative to the EUR, so we will start by selling USD0.20 for SFR1 as per the price given above. We will cover the short position in USD by selling EUR0.16, which actually nets us 0.16 × USD1.2816 = USD0.2051. We will cover our short position in EUR by selling SFR at the price listed above. Positions from our three transactions are summarized and totaled in Table 7.4.

**TABLE 7.4** Triangular Arbitrage

| | USD | SFR | EUR |
|---|---|---|---|
| Sell USD0.20 for SFR1 | −0.2000 | +1.0000 | |
| Sell EUR0.16 for USD0.2051 | +0.2051 | | −0.1600 |
| Sell SFR1.0 for EUR0.16 | | −1.0000 | +0.1600 |
| Totals | +0.0051 | 0 | 0 |

Because of our price inconsistency, we will earn USD0.0051 every time that we execute this series of transactions. Existence of such arbitrage profits should be exploited by arbitrageurs, whose arbitrage transactions will ultimately force down the price SFR in terms of USD and force up the price of SFR in terms of EUR until the discrepancy is eliminated.

## Purchase Power Parity, Arbitrage, and Hedging in FX Markets

In a world economy characterized by free trade, complete certainty and no market frictions (such as transactions costs), we would expect that exchange rates will be regulated by *purchase power parity* (PPP). PPP is an example of the *law of one price*, which simply states that securities offering the same cash flow characteristics or baskets offering the same commodities must sell for the same price. PPP states that the values of currencies relative to each other are determined by the quantity of goods they will purchase. This condition holds both in spot markets and forward markets (we will discuss forward markets in the next section). Currency traders creating arbitrage portfolios should force the PPP to hold. Violations of this parity condition should lead traders to purchase the less expensive currency sell the more expensive currency.

One well-known (though somewhat tongue in cheek) test of PPP is the "Big Mac standard" popularized by *The Economist*. MacDonald's Corporation's Big Mac hamburgers are generally regarded to be more or less identical all over the world. Given PPP, then the Big Mac should sell for the same price in each country. For example, suppose that the Big Mac cost \$4.60 in a U.S. restaurant and costs £3.62 in the UK; Further suppose that the dollar/pound exchange rate is \$1.46/£; that is, GBP1 has the same value as USD1.46. At this exchange rate of \$1.46/£, the British pound appeared overvalued by approximately 15% relative to the U.S. dollar. However, we need to recognize that Big Macs are not easily exported from countries where they are underpriced, which might prevent absolute PPP from holding in this instance. Nor does this relationship among prices account for differences in taxes, subsidies, labor, and other production costs.

### *Purchase Power Parity in Spot Markets*

Purchase power parity states that two commodities must sell for the same price (after adjusting for relative currency values). PPP is the primary basis for international comparisons of prices, income and expenditures. In spot markets, the price of a commodity in a foreign market (e.g., $P_{UK0}$ – the price in the UK) multiplied by the exchange rate at present ($S_0$ – the dollars per pound exchange rate) should equal the price of the commodity in domestic markets (e.g., $P_{US0}$ – the price in the United States):

$$P_{US0} = S_0 \times P_{UK0}$$

This condition is known as PPP in spot markets or absolute PPP. In the absence of market frictions in both commodity and exchange markets, and with the ability to freely transport commodities between markets, the potential for arbitrage should force absolute PPP in spot markets to hold. For example, if the spot price of gold in U.S. markets is USD1400 per ounce and EUR1000 in German markets, the spot exchange rate must be USD1.400/EUR.

Any single deviation from these rates will lead to an arbitrage opportunity. We will discuss changes in exchange rates and forward markets for exchange in the next section.

## 7.6 ARBITRAGE AND HEDGING WITH CURRENCY FORWARD CONTRACTS

In frictionless markets, currency arbitrage opportunities exist when forward currency exchange rates are inconsistent given prices of commodities or rates associated with financial instruments in different countries. Here, we will discuss triangular arbitrage in forward markets and relative PPP, scenarios that do require certain derivative securities.

### Parity and Arbitrage in FX Markets

In a world economy characterized by free trade, complete certainty, and no market frictions (such as transactions costs), we can argue that the following conditions will hold in equilibrium:

1. Purchase power parity (PPP)
2. Interest rate parity (IRP)
3. Forward rates equal expected spot rates
4. The Fisher effect
5. The international Fisher effect

Collectively, these conditions are often referred to as the *international equilibrium model*. Violations of these conditions imply either arbitrage opportunities or frictions that prevent the exploitation of arbitrage opportunities.

#### ***Purchase Power Parity***

We argued above that PPP states that two commodities must sell for the same price (after adjusting for relative currency values). In forward markets, as in spot markets, the price of a commodity in a foreign market (e.g., $P_{UK1}$ – the forward price in the UK) multiplied by the forward exchange rate ($F_1$ – the dollars per pound forward exchange rate) should equal the price of the commodity in domestic markets (e.g., $P_{US1}$ – the forward price in the United States):

$$P_{US1} = F_1 \times P_{UK1}$$

This condition is known as PPP in forward markets. In the absence of market frictions in both commodity and exchange markets, and with the ability to freely transport commodities between markets, the potential for arbitrage should force absolute PPP in spot or forward markets to hold.

The combination of PPP conditions in both spot and forward markets leads to the *relative PPP* condition. Consider a basket of groceries in the United States, which costs 20 dollars ($P_{US0} = \$20.00$). Assume that the same basket of groceries can be purchased in the United Kingdom for 12.50 pounds ($P_{UK0} = £12.50$). Further assume that the exchange rate of dollars for British pounds ($S_0$) is 1.6; that is, 1.6 dollars buys one pound. Purchase power parity holds here in the spot market, since an American can exchange 20 dollars for 12.5 pounds in the foreign exchange market and purchase the same basket of commodities as he could in the United States.

If in one year, the price of the basket were to increase by 10% to USD22 (perhaps due to inflation) in the United States, and increase by 8% in the United Kingdom, what would we expect to see happen to the exchange rate of dollars for pounds ($F_1$)? Recall that the PPP Theorem states that the same basket of commodities must cost the same in any two economies, given relevant exchange rates. Furthermore, changes in price levels in one economy will be matched by either offsetting changes in its currency value (exchange rates), changes in prices in the second economy, or some combination of the two. Thus, since the price of goods in the United States increased by 10% and the price of goods in the United Kingdom increased by 8%, the exchange rate should increase by 1.8512% to 1.6296 dollars for one pound ($F_1 = 1.6296$). Thus, the change in the exchange rate ($\Delta S$) under PPP must be:

$$\Delta S = \frac{F_1}{S_0} - 1 = \frac{1.6296}{1.6000} - 1 = \frac{P_{US1}/P_{US0}}{P_{UK1}/P_{UK0}} - 1 = \frac{22.00/20.00}{13.50/12.50} - 1 = 0.01851. \quad (7.22)$$

Note that the country with the higher inflation rate will have its currency devalued relative to the country with the lower inflation rate. More generally, if ($\pi_{US}$) represents the U.S. inflation rate and ($\pi_{UK}$) represents the UK inflation rate, then the following holds:

$$\frac{(1 + \pi_{US})}{(1 + \pi_{UK})} = \frac{F_1}{S_0} \quad (7.23)$$

Equation 7.23 is the general mathematical definition or statement of PPP. It provides the relationship between forward and spot rates of exchange as a function of relative inflation rates in relevant countries.

### *Example 1: Purchase Power Parity Violation and Arbitrage*

Consider the following violation of PPP. The exchange rates of dollars for pounds are 1.6000 and 1.6296 in the spot and one-year forward markets, respectively. Assume that gold is selling for \$400 per ounce in American spot markets and for £250 in British spot markets. The one-year forward price of gold is \$440 in American markets and £280 in British markets. We might wish to assume that inflation rates in the United States and the UK are, respectively, 10% and 12%. In this case, we should be able to demonstrate an arbitrage opportunity. Consider the following transactions in forward markets (future prices are locked in now by taking positions in forward contracts):

| Transaction Number | Transaction |
|---|---|
| 1 | Long forward contract for one ounce of gold in United States |
| 2 | Short forward contract for £270 at $F = 1.6296$ |
| 3 | Short forward contract for one ounce of gold in UK |

| Transaction Number | Time-One Gold Position | Time-One Pound Position | Time-One Dollar Position |
|---|---|---|---|
| 1 | +1 ounce | | −$440 |
| 2 | | −£270 | +$440 |
| 3 | −1 ounce | +£280 | |
| Totals | 0 | +£10 | |

Because all prices are locked in by spot and forward contracts, we are able to lock in a profit of £10 by engaging the above transactions. The change in exchange rates does not coincide appropriately with the countries' relative gold price changes. You should be able demonstrate for yourself that Equation (7.23) does not hold for this example. Whenever Equation (7.23) does not hold, we should either be able to exploit an arbitrage opportunity or a identify a constraining market friction.

How do we know that we should purchase gold in the United States at time one? Consider the following:

$$\frac{(1+\pi_{us})}{(1+\pi_{uk})} = \frac{(1+0.10)}{(1+0.12)} < \frac{F_1}{S_0} = \frac{1.6296}{1.6} \tag{7.24}$$

The forward price of the pound ($1.6296) increased relative to the dollar while the inflation rate affecting the dollar is less than for the pound. This means that the forward price of gold in the United States is too low relative to the UK, the forward price of gold in the UK is too high relative to the United States, and the forward price of pounds is too high relative to dollars.

### *Interest Rate Parity*

*Interest rate parity* states that anticipated currency exchange rate shifts will be proportional to countries' relative interest rates. Continuing the above example, assume that the current nominal interest rate in the United States is 12%, and the spot exchange rate of dollars for pounds is 1.6. Based on these rates, what must be the nominal interest rate in the UK? To avoid arbitrage opportunities in the market for interest bearing securities, interest rate parity must hold:

$$\frac{(1+i_{US})}{(1+i_{UK})} = \frac{F_1}{S_0} = \frac{(1+0.12)}{(1+i_{UK})} = \frac{1.6296}{1.600} \tag{7.25}$$

Thus, the interest rate in the UK must be 9.9636%. If the British interest rate were lower, arbitragers would borrow at the lower British rate, exchange pounds for dollars, and then loan at the higher American interest rate. Thus, interest rate parity holds that a strategy of borrowing money in one currency, immediately exchanging that currency for a second that is immediately loaned, will enable the investor to break even on the loans if futures contracts are used to lock in future exchange rates.

### *Example 2: Interest Rate Parity Violation and Arbitrage*

Here, we continue to assume that exchange rates of dollars for pounds are 1.6 and 1.6296 in the spot and one-year forward markets, respectively. Assume that nominal interest rates are 12.5% in the United States and 12% in the United Kingdom. Again, we should be able to demonstrate an arbitrage opportunity. Consider the following transactions in markets for interest bearing securities and forward exchange (forward prices are locked in now by contracts):

| Transaction Number | Transaction |
|---|---|
| 1. | Borrow \$1000 now in the United States at 12.5%; repay at Time One |
| 2. | Buy £625 now for \$1000 |
| 3. | Loan £625 at 12%; Collect proceeds at Time One |
| 4. | Sell £700 at Time One at $F_1 = 1.629629$ for \$1140.74 |

Time Zero Positions

| Transaction Number | Time Zero Pound Position | Time Zero Dollar Position |
|---|---|---|
| 1 | | +\$1000 |
| 2 | +£625 | −\$1000 |
| 3 | −£625 | |
| 4 | —— | —— |
| Totals | 0 | 0 |

Time One Positions

| Transaction Number | Time One Pound Position | Time One Dollar Position |
|---|---|---|
| 1 | | −\$1125.00 |
| 2 | | |
| 3 | +£700 | |
| 4 | − £700 | + \$1140.74 |
| Totals | 0 | +15.74 |

Here, we are able to lock in a profit of \$15.74 by engaging the above transactions. The change in exchange rates did not coincide appropriately with the countries' relative interest rates. You should be able demonstrate for yourself that Equation (7.24) does not hold for this example. Whenever Equation (7.24) does not hold, we will be able to locate an arbitrage opportunity or a friction that prevents its exploitation.

### *Exchange Rate Expectations*

The third of the four parity relations states that the prevailing forward rate of exchange equals the expected spot rate at the time of delivery:

$$F_1 = E[S_1] \tag{7.26}$$

Speculators will force Equation (7.26) to hold, at least approximately, through their trading activity. However, its violation does not necessarily represent an arbitrage opportunity.

### *The Fisher Effect*

The *Fisher effect* within a given country states that the relationships among the nominal interest rate ($i$), the real interest rate ($i'$) and the expected inflation rate $E(\pi)$ are given by Equation (7.27):

$$(1 + i) = (1 + i')(1 + E(\pi)) \tag{7.27}$$

The Fisher effect provides a definition for the real rate $i'$ of inflation within an economy in terms of the nominal rate $i$ and the inflation rate $\pi$. Equation (7.27) provides a definition, but does not necessarily indicate an arbitrage opportunity.

### *The International Fisher Effect*

The international counterpart to the Fisher effect is the final parity condition—the *international Fisher effect*. The international fisher effect draws from the Fisher effect and purchase and interest rate parity. For example, the following states the international fisher effect for the United States, the United Kingdom:

$$\frac{(1 + i_{US})}{(1 + i_{UK})} = \frac{(1 + E[\pi_{US}])}{(1 + E[\pi_{UK}])} \times \frac{(1 + i'_{US})}{(1 + i'_{UK})} \tag{7.28}$$

Thus, the Fisher effect specifies the relationships among real and nominal interest rates and inflation rates. The international Fisher effect extends this relation among countries, indicating that real interest rates among countries will be identical. If this condition were not to hold, arbitrageurs would borrow in countries with low real interest rates and lend in countries with higher nominal interest rates. Alternatively, they might be able to exploit arbitrage opportunities arising from violations in PPP. Please take time to notice the relationships among Equations (7.23) through (7.28) and how additional equalities can be created from them.

## 7.7 HEDGING EXCHANGE EXPOSURE

Multinational companies face a number of risks not experienced by companies operating in only one country. Among the most significant of these risks is exchange rate uncertainty and fluctuations. Transaction exposure is a firm's risk arising from settlement of obligations denominated in foreign currencies. The following are sources of transaction exposure:

1. Purchasing or selling goods or services on foreign-denominated credit
2. Borrowing or lending with foreign-denominated notes
3. Taking positions in forward exchange contracts
4. Buying or selling assets denominated in foreign currencies

The corporate treasurer is responsible for managing these risks. The treasurer will either employ traders or engage agency traders to take exchange and derivative positions to manage these risks. The following are strategies that treasurers and traders employ to contend with transactions exposure:

1. Do nothing—accept the risk
2. Hedge in forward markets
3. Hedge in money markets: take offsetting position in local currency debt instruments
4. Hedge in option markets: incomplete hedge with puts or complete hedge with conversions

We use illustrations to examine the first three of these strategies for dealing with transactions exposure. We will discuss the options strategies in the next chapter.

### *Illustration: Managing Transactions Exposure*

Consider an example regarding the management of transactions exposure. The Dayton Company of America invested in a British construction project and expects to receive a payoff of £1,000,000 in three months. The company seeks to realize its revenues in dollars. The problem is that management does not know the dollar amount of the payoff due to exchange rate uncertainty. Assume relevant data as follows:

Spot exchange rate: $1.7640/£
Three-month forward exchange rate: $1.7540/£
UK borrowing interest rate: 10.0%
U.S. borrowing interest rate: 8.0%
UK lending interest rate: 8.0%
U.S. lending interest rate: 6.0%
Forward contract settlement price: $1.75 per £
Transactions cost on £1,000,000 forward contract: $500

The treasurer's problem is to evaluate non-options–based methods of managing the transaction risk associated with this extension of credit and the implications of each. We will determine which hedging strategy is likely to be optimal and why. First, we consider the alternative of doing nothing.

### UNHEDGED ALTERNATIVE

The unhedged alternative simply means to accept the risk. The strategy is simply to wait 3 months, then sell £1,000,000 for dollars at the then prevailing spot rate. The result of this strategy is that all £1,000,000 is at risk. The expected value of the transaction is \$1,754,000 based on the forward rate of exchange used as a predictor for the future spot rate. However, all funds are at risk.

### FORWARD MARKET HEDGE

The *forward market hedge* strategy is to sell £1,000,000 forward for dollars at once. The result is that, in the absence of default risk, \$1,754,000 will certainly be received in three months. Transactions costs at time zero will total \$500. Forgone interest on this \$500 over three months totals $\$7.50 = 0.06 \times 0.25 \times \$500$. The total amount (net of forgone interest) to be received in three months is \$1,753,492.50. This amount is certain.

### MONEY MARKET HEDGE

The *money market hedge* strategy is to borrow £975,609.76 in UK for three months at an annual rate of 10%, exchange the £975,609.76 for \$1,720,975.60 now at the spot exchange rate, and then invest \$1,720,975.60 for three months at an annual rate of 6%. The result of this strategy is that the UK pound loan is repaid by receipts from sale in three months. \$1,746,790.20 is obtained from the U.S. investment. This amount is certain in the absence of default risk. Note that this strategy in this example is inferior to the forward market hedge.

### *Other Hedging Strategies:*

The hedging strategies described in the above examples and in the next chapter are more effective when firms can easily enter into forward, money market and options contracts. This is normally quite easily accomplished in countries with major currencies. However, in many instances, firms will need to hedge exchange rate volatility in countries where such opportunities are not available. For example, it is often very difficult to employ the above strategies in smaller African, Asian, or Latin American countries. In many instances, firms might modify these strategies with cross-hedges. Typically, these cross-hedging strategies involve the use of contracts denominated in currencies strongly correlated with the currency to be hedged. For example, rather than attempt to directly hedge exchange rate risk involving Philippine pesos, a firm might use contracts denominated in yen, which are fairly highly correlated with pesos. An alternative cross hedging strategy is to hedge currency risk with commodity contracts whose values are strongly correlated with that of the currency. For example, the price of oil is strongly correlated with the value of the Saudi Arabia riyal (SAR). The firm needing to hedge risk associated with the riyal can use futures contracts on oil as an imperfect substitute for the currency itself.

## Additional Reading

Elton et al. (2010), chapters 21 and 22, offer good coverage of yield curves, fixed income arbitrage, and hedging. Chapter 18 in Neftci (2000) extends the material in this chapter to continuous time. Chapters 1 through 6 in Neftci comprise good background reading for Chapter 18. Shapiro (2006) and Grabbe (1996) discuss parity conditions along with currency exposure and hedging. Chapter 9 in Saunders and Cornett (2009) provides a concise overview of FX markets, instruments, and analysis.

## References

Elton, E., Gruber, M., Brown, S., & Goetzmann, W. (2010). *Modern portfolio theory and investment analysis* (8th ed.). New York: Wiley.

Grabbe, J. O. (1996). *International financial markets* (3rd ed.). Englewood Cliffs, NJ: Prentice Hall.

Neftci, S. N. (2000). *An introduction to the mathematics of financial derivatives* (2nd ed.). San Diego: Academic Press.

Saunders, A., & Cornett, M. M. (2009). *Financial markets and institutions: A modern perspective*. Irwin, Boston: McGraw-Hill.

Shapiro, A. C. (2006). *Multinational financial management* (8th ed.). New York: Wiley.

## 7.8 EXERCISES

1. There are two three-year bonds with face values equaling $1000. The coupon rate of bond A is 0.05 and 0.08 for bond B. A third bond C also exists, with a maturity of two years. Bond C also has a face value of $1000; it has a coupon rate of 11%. The prices of the three bonds are $878.9172, $955.4787, and $1055.419, respectively. Find a portfolio of bonds A, B, and C that would replicate the cash flow structure of bond D, which has a face value of $1000, a maturity of three years, and a coupon rate of 3%.
2. A $1000 face value bond is currently selling at a premium for $1200. The coupon rate of this bond is 12% and it matures in three years. Calculate the following for this bond assuming that its interest payments are made annually:
   **a.** Annual interest payments
   **b.** Current yield
   **c.** Yield to maturity
3. Work through each of the calculations in Problem 2 assuming that interest payments are made semiannually.
4. A life insurance company expects to make payments of $30,000,000 in one year, $15,000,000 in two years, $25,000,000 in three years, and $35,000,000 in four years to satisfy claims of policyholders. These anticipated cash flows are to be matched with a portfolio of the following $1000 face value bonds:

| Bond | Current Price | Coupon Rate | Years to Maturity |
|---|---|---|---|
| 1 | 1000 | 0.10 | 1 |
| 2 | 980 | 0.10 | 2 |
| 3 | 1000 | 0.11 | 3 |
| 4 | 1000 | 0.12 | 4 |

   How many of each of the four bonds should the company purchase to exactly match its anticipated payments to policyholders?
5. Find the duration of the following pure discount bonds:
   **a.** $1000 face value bond maturing in one year currently selling for $900
   **b.** $1000 face value bond maturing in two years currently selling for $800

   c. \$2000 face value bond maturing in three years currently selling for \$1400
   d. Portfolio consisting of one of each of the three bonds listed in parts a, b, and c of this problem
6. What is the relationship between the maturity of a pure discount bond and its duration?
7. Find the duration of each of the following \$1000 face value coupon bonds assuming coupon payments are made annually:
   a. Three-year 10% bond currently selling for \$900
   b. Three-year 12% bond currently selling for \$900
   c. Four-year 10% bond currently selling for \$900
   d. Three-year 10% bond currently selling for \$800
8. Based on duration computations, what would happen to the prices of each of the bonds in Question 8 if market interest rates $(1 + r)$ were to decrease by 10%?
9. What is the duration of a portfolio consisting of one of each of the bonds listed in problem 7?
10. Find durations and convexities for each of the following bonds:
    a. 10% five-year bond selling for \$1079.8542 yielding 8%
    b. 12% five-year bond selling for \$1000 yielding 12%
11. a. Use the duration (first-order) approximation models to estimate bond value increases induced by changes in interest rates (yields) to 10% for each of the bonds in Problem 10 above.
    b. Use the convexity (second-order) approximation models to estimate bond value increases induced by changes in interest rates (yields) to 10% for each of the bonds in Problem 10 above.
    c. Find the present values of each of the bonds in Problem 10 above after yields (discount rates) change to 10%.
12. Consider an example where we can borrow money today for one year at 5%; $y_{0,1} = 0.05$. Suppose that we are able to obtain a commitment to obtain a one-year loan one year from now at an interest rate of 8%. Thus, the one-year forward rate on a loan originated in year equals 8%. According to the pure expectations theory, what is the two-year spot rate of interest $y_{0,2}$?
13. Suppose that the one-year spot rate $y_{0,1}$ of interest is 5%. Investors are expecting that the one-year spot rate one year from now will increase to 6%; thus, the one-year forward rate $y_{1,2}$ on a loan originated in one year is 6%. Furthermore, assume that investors are expecting that the one-year spot rate two years from now will increase to 7%; thus, the one-year forward rate $y_{2,3}$ on a loan originated in two years is 7%. Based on the pure expectations hypothesis, what is the three-year spot rate?
14. Suppose that the one-year spot rate $y_{0,1}$ of interest is 5%. Investors are expecting that the one-year spot rate one year from now will increase to 7%; thus, the one-year forward rate $y_{1,2}$ on a loan originated in one year is 7%. Furthermore, assume that the three-year spot rate equals 7% as well. What is the anticipated one-year forward rate $y_{2,3}$ on a loan originated in two years based on the pure expectations hypothesis?

**15.** Consider the following four bonds:

| $F$ | $n$ | $c$ | $P_0$ |
|---|---|---|---|
| 1000 | 1 | 0.01 | 1005 |
| 1000 | 2 | 0.05 | 1040 |
| 1000 | 3 | 0.04 | 1020 |
| 1000 | 4 | 0.04 | 990 |

Based on the cash flows and prices associated with these bonds, determine the following:

**a.** Spot rates $y_{0,n}$ for each of four years 1 through 4. These are interest rates on loans originating at time 0.

**b.** Forward rates $y_{1,t}$ for each of three periods beginning with year 1. These are interest rates on loans originating at time 1.

**c.** Forward rates $y_{2,t}$ for each of two periods beginning with year 2. These are interest rates on loans originating at time 2.

**d.** Forward rates $y_{3,n}$ for the period beginning with year 3. This is the interest rates on loans originating at time 3.

**16.** Bond A, a three-year 7% issue, currently sells for 964.3227. Bond B is a two-year 8% issue currently selling for 1010.031. Bond C is a three-year 6% issue currently selling for 938.4063. Based on this information, answer the following:

**a.** What are the one-, two-, and three-year spot rates of interest?

**b.** What are the one- and two-year forward rates on loans originating one year from now?

**c.** What is the one-year forward rate on a loan originated in two years?

**17.** Assume that there are two three-year bonds with face values equaling \$1000. The coupon rate of Bond A is 0.05 and 0.08 for Bond B. A third Bond C also exists, with a maturity of two years. Bond C also has a face value of \$1000; it has a coupon rate of 11%. The prices of the three bonds are \$878.9172, \$955.4787, and \$1055.419, respectively.

**a.** What are the spot rates implied by these bonds?

**b.** Find a portfolio of Bonds A, B, and C which would replicate the cash flow structure of Bond D, which has a face value of \$1000, a maturity of three years, and a coupon rate of 3%.

**18.** Suppose we expected that PPP should hold between the United States and Canada. Assume that the exchange rate between U.S. dollars and Canadian dollars is CAD1/USD0.64. That is, one Canadian dollar will purchase USD0.64. If USD2.30 purchases one Big Mac in the United States, how much should a Big Mac cost in Canada?

**19.** Consider a case involving three currencies concerning cross rates of exchange. Assume that 1.5 Swiss francs are required to purchase 1 U.S. dollar and that 0.64 U.S. dollars are required to purchase 1 Canadian dollar.

**a.** How many Canadian dollars are required to purchase 10 Swiss francs?
**b.** Assuming that PPP holds, how many Swiss francs are required to purchase one Big Mac?

**20.** Assume that $1 will purchase £0.60 and ¥108; that is, 1 U.S. dollar will purchase 0.6 UK pounds and 108 Japanese yen. Assume that goods in the three countries are identically priced after adjusting for currency exchange rates.
**a.** What is the value of £1 in ¥?
**b.** What is the value of ¥1 in £?
**c.** If one ounce of gold costs $300 in the United States, what is its cost in the United Kingdom and in Japan?

**21.** Consider the following exercise concerned with management of transactions exposure. The Smedley Company has sold products to a Japanese client for ¥15,000,000. Payment is due six months later. Relevant data is as follows:
Spot exchange rate: ¥105/$
Six-month forward exchange rate: ¥104/$
Japanese borrowing interest rate: 9.0%
U.S. borrowing interest rate: 7.0%
Japanese lending interest rate: 7.0%
U.S. lending interest rate: 5.0%
Size of futures contracts: ¥1,000,000
Term to settlement of contracts: six months
Transactions cost on ¥15,000,000 forward contract: $500
Discuss the implications associated with each of the non-options–based methods for managing the transactions exposure risk associated with this extension of credit. Determine which hedging strategy is likely to be optimal and why.

CHAPTER

# 8

# Arbitrage and Hedging with Options

## 8.1 DERIVATIVE SECURITIES MARKETS AND HEDGING

As discussed earlier, a *derivative security* is simply a financial instrument whose value is derived from that of another security, financial index, or rate. A large number of different types of derivative securities have become increasingly important for management and hedging a variety of different types of risks. There exist a huge variety of derivative securities. Some of the more frequently traded derivatives follow:

*Futures contracts*, which provide for the transfer of a given asset at an agreed-to price at a future date.
*Options*, which confer the right but not obligation to buy or sell an asset at a prespecified price on or before a given date. Options are introduced with more detail in the appendix to Chapter 6.
*Swaps*, which provide for the exchange of one set of cash flows for another set of cash flows.
*Hybrids*, which combine features of two or more securities (e.g., a convertible bond).

Risk factors frequently hedged with derivatives include, but are not limited to, uncertainties associated with underlying and related asset price movements, interest and exchange rate variability, debtor default, and economy-wide and sector-specific output levels. Markets for explicit insurance policies on such a wide array of risks do not exist largely due to contracting costs. Most insurance policies are fairly standardized (e.g., health, life, and many casualty policies), while customized insurance contracts are expensive and time consuming to write. Businesses must be able to act quickly to manage their risks in this environment of rapid change. Flexibility and liquidity along with low contracting and transactions costs are key to the success of the risk management operations of a firm. An active and efficient market for derivative securities can help firms hedge and manage a variety of different types of risks.

Business firms and individual investors desiring to hedge risks are not the only participants in markets for derivatives. A second type of market participant is the speculator who takes a position in a security based on his expectation regarding future price movement. Although the speculator is essentially concerned with his own trading profits, he plays an important role in maintaining liquidity in derivative markets, affording business and individual investors the opportunity to hedge risks quickly and efficiently. The speculator is often the counterparty to a hedger's trade, selling or purchasing derivatives as required by hedgers.

The arbitrageur, who exploits situations where derivatives are mispriced relative to one another, not only provides additional liquidity to derivative markets, but plays an important role in their pricing. By constantly seeking price misalignments for a variety of types of securities, and by understanding the payoffs of securities relative to one another, arbitragers help ensure that derivative securities are fairly priced. This activity reduces price volatility and uncertainty faced by hedgers. In addition, the presence of arbitrageurs provides liquidity to other market participants.

Derivative securities are traded in the United States either on exchanges or over the counter (OTC) markets. Substantial market interest is required for exchange listing, whereas securities with smaller followings or even customized contracts can be traded OTC, including trading between banks and other major participants. The role of the derivatives dealer is essentially the same as that for other security dealers: to facilitate transactions for clients at competitive prices. Derivative dealers match counterparties for derivative contracts, act as counterparty for many of their own custom contracts, and provide an array of support services including expert advice and carefully engineered customized risk management products. It is necessary that the dealer providing full support services have a proper understanding of his client and the client's business and needs. Since some clients do not have an understanding of the technical terms used in the industry, the dealer must be an effective communicator. It is equally important for the dealer to understand the nature of the securities with which he deals and how serving as a market maker for derivatives affects the risk structure of his employer. This understanding usually requires strong analytical skills.

Many stock options in the United States and Europe are traded on exchanges. The largest U.S. stock options exchanges are the Chicago Board Options Exchange and the NASDAQ OMX Group. The latter operates the NASDAQ Options MarketSM (NOM) and the options markets at the former Philadelphia Exchange. The NYSE operates the options markets of the former American Exchange and the International Stock Exchange (taken over by Eurex) maintains an options market. Options are also traded on numerous commodities, futures contracts, currencies, and other financial instruments such as Treasury instruments and index contracts.

Options can be classified into either the European variety or the American variety. European options may be exercised only at the time of their expiration; American options may be exercised any time before and including the date of expiration. Most option contracts traded in the United States (and Europe as well) are of the American variety. American options can never be worth less than their otherwise identical European counterparts. In fact, because most call options have time value in addition to their intrinsic or exercise value (calls on stocks that go ex-dividend before the call expires can be an important exception to this), we usually do not exercise American calls before exercise. This means that we can often value American call options (on non-dividend–paying stock) as though they are European calls.

## 8.2 PUT–CALL PARITY

First, since the call (put) owner has the right to buy (sell) the underlying stock at a price of $X$, the terminal payoff functions for calls and puts are written as follows:

$$c_T = MAX[0,\ S_T - X] \tag{8.1}$$

$$p_T = \mathrm{MAX}[0,\ X - S_T] \tag{8.2}$$

If we subtract Equation (8.2) from Equation (8.1) we obtain the terminal value *put–call relation*:

$$c_T - p_T = \mathrm{MAX}[0,\ S_T - X] - \mathrm{MAX}[0,\ X - S_T] = S_T - X \tag{8.3}$$

A slight rewrite of this terminal put–call relation allows us to write the terminal or exercise value a put given the terminal value of a call with identical exercise terms:

$$p_T = c_T + X - S_T \tag{8.4}$$

Since the terminal value of a put is always given by Equation (8.4), the time-zero value of a put must be given by Equation (8.5):

$$p_0 = c_0 + Xe^{-r_f T} - S_0 \text{ in continuous time; } p_0 = c_0 + X/(1+r_f)^T - S_0 \text{ in discrete time} \tag{8.5}$$

This arbitrage-free relationship allows us to value a put based on the price knowledge of a call with exactly the same exercise terms. The put–call parity function holds regardless of the stochastic process generating stock prices, but assumes that the underlying stock pays no dividends during the lives of the options.

### Illustration: Hedging with a Call, a Put, and a Collar

Suppose that an investor has 1000 shares of stock that are currently worth $50 per share each. The investor wishes to lock in his gains on the stock, but does not want to sell at this time for tax reasons. The current two-year riskless return rate is 5%. The investor could write two-year calls on these shares, with an exercise price of $50 per share, receiving $8 for each share that he owns. That is, he could receive $8 per share by selling covered calls. He could also purchase two-year puts on each share which would enable him to eliminate downside risk. What are the potential hedging strategies available to the investor? What are the costs and benefits of each?

First, the investor could simply write covered calls. This strategy offers no downside risk protection, but it does provide the investor with $8 (or $8000 total) in immediate cash flows. The strategy also limits the investor's upside potential on the shares, locking out any gains should the share price rise above \$50. This is because the investor would be obliged to sell the stock to the owner of the call should its price rise above \$50 per share. The owner of the call would not exercise this option if the share price remains below \$50. While the covered call strategy does reduce portfolio volatility, it is more significant to the investor as a means of generating short-run income at the expense of potential stock profits.

A second potential strategy for the investor is to purchase puts. We can use put–call parity to value these puts. Since the riskless rate is $r_f = 0.05$, the exercise price is $X = \$50$, the current share price is $S_0 = \$50$, and the $T =$ two-year call price is $c_0 = \$8$, we can use Equation (8.5) to value the put:

$$p_0 = 8 + 50e^{-0.05\times 2} - 50 = 3.24$$

Each put will protect the investor from downside stock price movements below \$50 per share, and, based on the data given, a fair price for each put is \$3.24. Thus, for \$3.24, the investor can lock in a minimum selling price of \$50 for each share. The puts will not require the investor to give up any gains above \$50.

What if the investor objects to paying \$3.24 to eliminate downside price risk? Another possibility is to simultaneously purchase a put and write a call, in effect financing the cost of the put with proceeds from selling the call. One such strategy is to create a *collar*, which is a package consisting of a long position in a put and a short position in a call. Here, if the investor purchases a put for \$3.24 and sells a call for \$8, he nets \$4.76 per share. If the share price drops below \$50 in two years, he puts his shares to the put writer for \$50. If the share price rises above \$50 in two years, his shares are called away from him at \$50 per share. Thus, for a net cash flow today of \$4.76, the investor gives up all potential profits and losses on his shares, locking or "collaring" in a price of \$50 today.

## 8.3 OPTIONS AND HEDGING IN A BINOMIAL ENVIRONMENT

The *binomial option pricing model* is based on the assumption that the underlying stock follows a binomial return generating process. This means that for any period during the life of the option, the stock's value will be only one of two potential constant values. For example, the stock's value will be either $u$ (multiplicative upward movement) times its current value or $d$ (multiplicative downward movement) times its current value.

Consider a stock currently selling for 100 and assume for this stock that $u$ equals 1.2 and $d$ equals 0.8. The stock's value in the forthcoming period will be either 120 (if outcome $u$ is realized) or 80 (if outcome $d$ is realized). Suppose that there exists a European call trading on this particular stock during this one-time period model with an exercise price of 90. The call expires at the end of this period when the stock value is either 120 or 80. Thus, if the stock were to increase to 120, the call would be worth 30 ($c_u = 30$), since one could exercise the call by paying 90 for a stock which is worth 120. If the stock value were to decrease to 80, the value of the call would be zero ($c_d = 0$) since no one would wish to exercise by paying 90 for shares that are worth only 80. Furthermore, suppose that the current riskless return rate is 0.10. Based on this information, we should be able to determine the value of the call.

Note that we have not specified probabilities of a stock price increase or decrease during the period prior to option expiration. Nor have we specified a discount rate for the option or made inferences regarding investor risk preferences. We will value this call based on the fact that during this single time period, we can construct a riskless hedge portfolio consisting of a position in a single call and offsetting positions in $\alpha$ shares of stock. This means that by purchasing a single call and by selling $\alpha$ shares of stock, we can create a portfolio whose value is the same regardless of whether the underlying stock price increases or decreases. Let us first define the following terms:

$S_0$ = Initial stock value
$u$ = Multiplicative upward stock price movement
$d$ = Multiplicative downward stock price movement
$c_u$ = MAX[0,u$S_0$ − $X$]; value of call if stock price increases
$c_d$ = MAX[0,d$S_0$ − $X$]; value of call if stock price decreases
$\alpha$ = Hedge ratio
$r_f$ = Riskless return rate

In our numerical example offered above, we use the following to determine the value of the call in the binomial framework:

$S_0 = 100$
$u = 1.2$
$d = 0.8$
$c_u = 30$
$c_d = 0$
$r_f = 0.10$
$X = 90$

Our first step in determining the value of the call is to determine $\alpha$, the *hedge ratio*. The hedge ratio defines the number of shares of stock that must be sold (or short sold) in order to maintain a riskless portfolio. This riskless portfolio will be comprised of one call option along with a short position in $\alpha$ shares of stock. In this case, the riskless hedge portfolio made up of one call option and $-\alpha$ shares of stock will have the same value whether the stock price increases to $uS_0$ or decreases to $dS_0$. If we were to purchase one call and sell $\alpha$ shares of stock, our riskless hedge condition is given as follows:

$$c_u + \alpha u S_0 = c_d + \alpha d S_0 \tag{8.6}$$

$$30 + \alpha \cdot 120 = 0 + \alpha \cdot 80$$

We defined $\alpha$ to be the number of shares to sell for every call purchased. This value is known as a hedge ratio. By maintaining this hedge ratio, we maintain our hedged portfolio. Solve for the hedge ratio $\alpha$ as follows:

$$\alpha = \frac{c_u - c_d}{S_0(d - u)}$$

$$\alpha = \frac{30 - 0}{100(.8 - 1.2)} = -.75 \tag{8.7}$$

In our example, $\alpha = -0.75$, meaning that the investor should sell 0.75 shares of underlying stock for each call option that he purchases to maintain a riskless portfolio. If the investor shorts 0.75 shares for each call purchased, the riskless portfolio will be worth −60 regardless of whether the stock rises to 120 or drops to 80. Similarly, if the investor purchased 0.75 shares for each call sold or written, the riskless portfolio will be worth 60 regardless of whether the stock rises to 120 or drops to 80. Thus, as long as the investor can confirm that there are only two potential outcomes for the underlying stock price, and determine what these prices are, he can create a hedge or riskless portfolio comprised of the option and $\alpha$ shares of the underlying stock. Since this hedge portfolio is riskless, it must earn the riskless rate of return for arbitrage opportunities to be avoided:

$$c_u + \alpha u S_0 = c_d + \alpha d S_0 = (c_0 + \alpha S_0)(1 + r_f) \tag{8.8}$$

Thus, our problem now is to value the call, $c_0$. From here, we can work equally well with either with outcome $u$ or outcome $d$; since it makes no difference we can choose outcome $d$. Note that the time-zero option value $c_0$ can be solved for by rearranging Equation (8.8). If Equation (8.8) does not hold, or if the current price of the option is inconsistent with Equation (8.8), a riskless arbitrage opportunity will exist. Thus, we will rewrite equation 8 to solve for the zero NPV condition that eliminates positive profit arbitrage opportunities:

$$c_0 + \alpha S_0 = \frac{c_d + \alpha d S_0}{(1 + r_f)} \tag{8.9}$$

It is now quite simple to solve for the call value $c_0$ by rewriting Equation (8.9):

$$c_0 = \frac{-(1 + r_f)\alpha S_0 + c_d + \alpha d S_0}{(1 + r_f)} \tag{8.10}$$

$$c_0 = \frac{(1 + .10) \cdot .75 \cdot 100 + 0 - .75 \cdot .8 \cdot 100}{(1 + .10)} = 20.4545$$

Equation (8.10) is quite appropriate for evaluating a European call in a one-time period framework. That is, in the model presented thus far, share prices can either increase or decrease once by a prespecified amount or percentage. Thus, there are only two potential prices that the stock can assume at the expiration of the stock. This binomial option pricing model can easily be extended to cover as many potential outcomes and time periods as necessary for a particular scenario.

### *Arbitrage in the One-time Period Case*

We found the arbitrage-free value of the call in the above example to be 20.4545. What if its price in the marketplace were 19? In this scenario, since the call is undervalued, we will purchase it, along with taking a short position in 0.75 shares of the underlying stock at \$100. This initial investment will be − \$56, which we will loan at the riskless rate of 10%. Our initial and time-one cash flows are computed as follows:

$$\text{Time-zero cash flow: } 1 \times -19.00 - 0.75 \times -100 - 56 = 0$$
$$\text{Time-one cash flow: } 1 \times 30.00 - 0.75 \times 120 + 56(1.1) = 1 \times 0 - 0.75 \times 80 + 56(1.1) = 1.6$$

Thus, the time-zero cash flow nets to zero. If the stock price rises to 120 in time one, the call pays \$30, the short position requires \$90 to settle, and the loan repays \$61.60. If the stock price drops to 80 in time one, the call pays 0, the short position requires \$60 to settle and the loan repays \$61.60. Regardless, the time−one net cash flow is \$1.60, representing a time-one arbitrage profit.

## Extending the Binomial Model to Two Periods

As we stated above, Equation (8.10) is appropriate for evaluating a European call in a one-time-period framework. That is, in the model presented thus far, share prices can either increase or decrease once by a prespecified percentage. Thus, there are only two potential prices that the stock can assume at the expiration of the stock. Our next step in the development of a more realistic model is to extend the framework to two time periods. One complication is that the hedge ratio only holds for the beginning of the first time period. After this period, the hedge ratio must be updated to reflect price changes and movement through time. Thus, our first step in extending the model to two time periods is to substitute for the hedge ratio based on Equation (8.10):

$$c_0 = \frac{(1 + r_f)\frac{(c_u - c_d)}{(S_0(u - d))}S_0 + c_d - \frac{(c_u - c_d)}{(S_0(u - d))}dS_0}{(1 + r_f)} \tag{8.11}$$

The next two steps of our development are to simplify Equation (8.11):

$$c_0 = \frac{\frac{(1 + r_f)(c_u - c_d) + c_d(u - d) - d(c_u - c_d)}{(u - d)}}{(1 + r_f)} \tag{8.12}$$

$$c_0 = \frac{c_u\frac{(1 + r_f) - d}{(u - d)} + c_d\frac{(u - (1 + r_f))}{(u - d)}}{(1 + r_f)} \tag{8.13}$$

Assume for the moment that $r_f$ can be regarded as a riskless discount rate and that investors will discount cash flows derived from the call based on this riskless rate; that is, for the moment, assume that investors are risk neutral. This assumption is reasonable if investors investing in options behave as though they are risk neutral; in fact they will evaluate options as though they are risk neutral because they can eliminate risk by setting appropriate hedge ratios. Their extent of risk aversion will already be reflected in the current value that they associate with underlying stock given its potential future values. Note that Equation (8.13) defines the current call value in terms of the two potential call prices $c_u$ and $c_d$ and this riskless return rate. Since it is reasonable to assume that investors behave towards options as though they are risk neutral, the numerator of Equation (8.13) might be regarded as an expected cash flow. Hence, the terms which $c_u$ and $c_d$ are multiplied by might be regarded as probabilities. Define $p$ to be the probability that the risk neutral investor associates with the stock price changing to $uS_0$ and $(1-p)$ as the probability $p$ that the stock price changes to $dS_0$:

$$p = \frac{((1+r_f)-d)}{(u-d)} \qquad (1-p) = \frac{(u-(1+r_f))}{(u-d)} \tag{8.14}$$

We simplify Equation (8.13) by substituting in Equations (8.14):

$$c_0 = \frac{c_u p + c_d(1-p)}{(1+r_f)} \tag{8.15}$$

Equation (8.15) represents a slightly simplified version of the one-time period option pricing model. However, it is easily extended to a two-period model if we assume that $u$ and $d$ are constant over the periods. Let $c_{u^2}$ be the call's expiration value after two time periods assuming that the stock's price has risen twice; $c_{d^2}$ is the value of the call assuming the stock price declined twice during the two periods and $c_{ud}$ is the value of the call assuming the stock price increased once and decreased once during these two periods. Thus, our two-time-period model becomes:

$$c_0 = \frac{c_{u^2}p^2 + 2p(1-p)c_{ud} + (1-p)^2 c_{d^2}}{(1+r_f)^2} \tag{8.16}$$

### *Illustration: Two-Time-Period Hedges*

Now, we will extend our illustration above from a single period to two periods, each with a riskless return rate equal to 0.10. As before, the stock currently sells for 100 and will change to either 120 or 80 in one time period ($u = 1.2$, $d = 0.8$). However, in the second period, the stock will change a second time by a factor of either 1.2 or 0.8, leading to potential values of either 144 (up then up again), 96 (up once and down once), or 64 (down twice). The lattice (tree) associated with this stock price process is depicted in Figure 8.1. Call option prices are also given for the second period. The probability of upward and downward movements are computed with the Equation (8.14) set as follows:

$$p = \frac{((1+.1)-.8)}{(1.2-.8)} = .75 \qquad (1-p) = \frac{(1.2-(1+.05))}{(1.2-.8)} = .25$$

The time-zero call value in this two-period binomial framework is computed with Equation (8.16) as follows:

$$c_0 = \frac{(144-90)\times .75^2 + 2\times .75(1-.75))\times(96-90) + (1-.75)^2\times 0}{(1+.10)^2} = 26.96281$$

Because the call is priced relative to the stock and riskless asset, any deviation of the market price of the call from this theoretical binomial price creates an arbitrage opportunity for investors, just as in the one-time period illustration above.

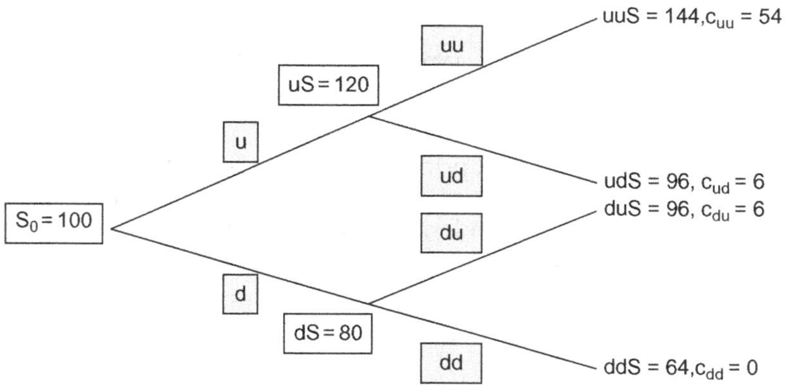


**FIGURE 8.1** Two-time-period binomial model.

We calculate the hedge ratio for time zero to be −0.75 from Equation (8.7) and the hedge ratio in time one to be either −.875 or −1, depending on whether the share price increases or decreases in the first period:

$$\alpha_0 = \frac{30 - 0}{100(.8 - 1.2)} = -.75$$

$$\alpha_u = \frac{54 - 6}{120(.8 - 1.2)} = -1 \quad \alpha_d = \frac{6 - 0}{80(.8 - 1.2)} = -.1875$$

Thus, the investor will hedge by shorting 0.75 shares for each long call in the first period, and will update his hedge ratio to either 1 or 0.1875 short shares in the second period. Also, note the change in time perspectives for $u$ and $d$ in the second period after one period has elapsed.

## Extending the Binomial Model to *n* Time Periods

The binomial model is easily extended to $n$ time periods (evenly split within the interval $T$) by implementing the binomial theorem to obtain the following[1]:

$$c_0 = \frac{\sum_{j=0}^{n} \frac{n!}{j!(n-j)!} p^j (1-p)^{n-j} MAX\left[0, u^j d^{n-j} S_o - X\right]}{(1+r_f)^n} \tag{8.17}$$

Computing Equation (8.17) might be simplified by using Equation (8.18), where $a$ is determined by Equation (8.19)[2]:

$$c_0 = \frac{\sum_{j=a}^{n} \frac{n!}{j!(n-j)!} p^j (1-p)^{n-j} \left[u^j d^{n-j} S_o - X\right]}{(1+r_f)^n} \tag{8.18}$$

[1]See Appendix 8.A for details on the application of this model and its relationship to the Black-Scholes model.

[2]See Appendix 8.A for a derivation of Equation (8.19).

$$a = MAX\left[INT\left(\frac{\ln\left(\frac{X}{S_0 d^n}\right)}{\ln\left(\frac{u}{d}\right)} + 1\right), 0\right] \tag{8.19}$$

The binomial option pricing model prices calls and puts relative to the pricing of underlying securities and the riskless return. That is, the binomial model prices an option against a portfolio comprising the underlying security and the riskless asset. Any deviation in the market prices from their binomial prices suggests one or both of the following:

1. The binomial option pricing model does not apply to this market.
2. There is an arbitrage opportunity in this market.

### *Illustration: Three Time Periods*

Now, we will extend our illustration above from two periods to three, each with a riskless return rate equal to 0.10. By the third period, potential stock values are $1.2^3 \times 100 = 172.8$, $1.2^2 \times 0.8 \times 100 = 115.2$, $0.8^2 \times 1.2 \times 100 = 76.8$, or $0.8^3 \times 100 = 51.2$. The time-zero call value in this three-period binomial framework is computed with Equations (8.19) and (8.18) as follows:

$$a = MAX\left[INT\left(\frac{\ln\left(\frac{90}{100 \times .8^3}\right)}{\ln\left(\frac{1.2}{.8}\right)} + 1\right), 0\right] = 2$$

$$c_0 = \frac{3 \times .75^2 \times .25 \times (1.2^2 \times .8 \times 100 - 90) + 1 \times .75^3 \times (1.2^3 \times 100 - 90)}{(1+.10)^3}$$
$$= \frac{10.63125 + 34.93125}{1.331} = 34.23178$$

Put–call parity still applies[3]:

$$p_0 = 34.23178 + 90/(1.1)^3 - 100 = 1.85$$

## Obtaining Multiplicative Upward and Downward Movement Values

One apparent difficulty in applying the binomial model as it is presented above is in obtaining estimates for $u$ and $d$ that are required for $p$; all other inputs are normally quite easily obtained. There are several methods that are used to obtain parameters for the binomial method from the actual security returns generating process. For example, following

[3]We will discount the exercise money with a discrete discount function since the binomial model is a discrete time model.

Cox et al. (1979), derive the following to estimate probabilities of an uptick $p$ and downtick $(1-p)$:[4]

$$p = \frac{e^{r_f} - d}{u - d} \quad (1-p) = \frac{u - e^{r_f}}{u - d} \tag{8.20}$$

Cox et al. also proposes the following to estimate $u$ and $d$ in the binomial approximation to the Weiner process, where $\sigma$ is the standard deviation of stock returns:

$$u = e^{\sigma} \quad d = \frac{1}{u} \tag{8.21}$$

or, if $n$ and $T$ differ from 1:

$$u = e^{\sigma\sqrt{\frac{T}{n}}} \quad d = \frac{1}{u} \tag{8.22}$$

Suppose, for example, that for a particular Weiner process, $\sigma = 0.30$ and $r_f = 0.05$. Using Equations (8.20) and (8.22), we estimate $p$, $u$, and $d$ for a single-time-period binomial process as follows:

$$u = e^{.3} = 1.3498588$$

$$d = \frac{1}{u} = .7408182$$

## Binomial Model: An Illustration

Suppose that we wished to evaluate a call and a put with an exercise price equal to \$110 on a share of stock currently selling for \$100. The underlying stock-return standard deviation equals 0.30 and the current riskless return rate equals 0.05. If both options are of the European variety and expire in six months, what are their values?

First, we will compute the call's value using the binomial model. We will vary the number of jumps in the model as the example progresses. First, let $n = 1$ and use Equations (8.20) and (8.22) to compute $p$, $u$, and $d$:

$$u = e^{.3 \times \sqrt{.5}} = 1.2363111$$

$$d = \frac{1}{1.2363111} = .8088578$$

$$p = \frac{e^{r_f T} - d}{u - d} = 0.5063881$$

Thus, in a risk-neutral environment, there is a 0.5064 probability that the stock price will increase to 123.63 and a 0.4936 probability that the stock price will be 80.88678. Similarly, in a risk-neutral environment, there is a 0.5064 probability that the call will be

[4]See Appendix 8.A for derivations of $p$, $u$, and $d$. Regardless, notice the somewhat minor deviation from the probability estimates given by the Equation (8.14) set. The difference between the Equation (8.14) and (8.20) sets is that Equation (8.20) allows interest ($r_f$) to be continuously compounded, whereas Equation (8.14) is based on discrete compounding. This distinction is not important for our purposes here.

worth 13.63; therefore, its current value is $6.73 = 0.5064 \times 13.63 \times e^{-05 \times .5}$. The call value is determined by the binomial model as follows where $n = a = 1$[5]:

$$c_0 = \frac{\sum_{j=a}^{n} \frac{n!}{j!(n-j)!} p^j (1-p)^{n-j} \left[u^j \times d^{n-j} S_o - X\right]}{(1+r_f)^T}$$

$$c_0 = \frac{.506388^1 \times .4936119^{1-1} \times [1.236311^1 \times .8088578^{1-1} \times 100 - 110]}{(1+.05)^5} = 6.73$$

We can also use the binomial model to value the put with identical exercise terms on the underlying stock[6]:

$$p_0 = \frac{\sum_{j=0}^{a-1} \frac{n!}{j!(n-j)!} p^j (1-p)^{n-j} \left[X - u^j d^{n-j} S_o\right]}{(1+r_f)^T}$$

$$p_0 = \frac{.506388^0 \times .4936119^1 \times [110 - 1.23631^0 \times .8088578^1 \times 100]}{(1+.05)^5} = 14.08$$

Now, revise the illustration by dividing the single six-month interval into two three-month intervals; that is, $n = 2$. We will now use a two-period binomial model to evaluate calls and puts on this stock. First, we use Equations (8.20) and (8.22) to compute $p$, $u$, and $d$[7]:

$$u = e^{\sqrt{\frac{3}{2}}} = 1.1618342$$

$$d = \frac{1}{1.1618342} = .8607079$$

$$p = \frac{e^{r_f T/n} - d}{u - d} = .5043415$$

Thus, there is a $0.5043^2$ probability that the stock price will increase to 134.98, a 0.5 probability that the stock price will remain unchanged at 100, and a $0.4957^2$ probability that the stock price will decline to 74.08. Thus, there is a 0.2543 probability that the call will be exercised, in which case, it will be worth 24.98. Therefore, the call's current value is $6.20 = 0.2543 \times 24.98 \times e^{-.05 \times 0.5}$. Call and put values are determined by the binomial model as follows where $n = a = 2$:

$$c_0 = \frac{\sum_{j=a}^{n} \frac{n!}{j!(n-j)!} p^j (1-p)^{n-j} \left[u^j d^{n-j} S_o - X\right]}{(1+r_f)^T}$$

[5]$a$ is determined by Equation (8.16) and is the first positive integer where $u^j d^{n-j} S_0 > X$. That is, the minimum number of up-jumps required for exercise of the call option equals $a$. Any smaller number of stock up-jumps produces a terminal call value equal to zero, and need not be considered.

[6]Recall that put–call parity, demonstrated in the Options and Hedging in a Binomial Environment section, can be used to value puts. We verify this for this example by using Equation (8.3) as follows: $14.08 = 6.73 + 110e^{-.05 \times .5} - 100$.

[7]When there are multiple jumps per period ($n > 1$), and/or when $T$ does not equal 1, $p = \frac{e^{r_f(T/n)} - d}{u - d}$ and $(1 - p) = \frac{u - e^{r_f(T/n)}}{u - d}$.

**TABLE 8.1** Convergence of Binomial Model to Black-Scholes Model

| $n$ | $c_0$ | $p_0$ |
|---|---|---|
| 1 | 6.73 | 14.02 |
| 2 | 6.20 | 13.48 |
| 3 | 5.47 | 12.72 |
| 4 | 6.04 | 13.30 |
| 5 | 5.18 | 12.44 |
| 6 | 5.91 | 13.17 |
| 7 | 5.43 | 12.68 |
| 8 | 5.81 | 13.06 |
| 9 | 5.57 | 12.82 |
| 10 | 5.73 | 12.98 |
| 50 | 5.63 | 12.89 |
| 100 | 5.59 | 12.85 |
| $\infty$ | 5.59 | 12.85 |
| Volatility | $\sigma = 0.30$ | |
| Riskless rate | $r_f = 0.05$ | |
| Exercise price | $X = 110$ | |
| Initial stock price | $S_0 = 100$ | |
| Term to expiration | $t = 0.5$ | |

$$c_0 = \frac{.5043^2 \times .4957^{2-2} \times [1.16185^2 \times .8607^{2-2} \times 100 - 110]}{(1+.05)^{.5}} = 6.20$$

$$p_0 = \frac{\sum_{j=0}^{a} \frac{n!}{j!(n-j)!} p^j (1-p)^{n-j} \left[X - u^j d^{n-j} S_o\right]}{(1+r_f)^T}$$

$$p_0 = \frac{.5043^{2-2} \times .4957^2 \times [110 - 1.1618^{2-2} \times .8607^2 \times 100] + 2 \times .5043 \times .4957 \times [110 - 100]}{(1+.05)^{.5}}$$

$$= 6.20 + 110e^{-.05 \times 5} - 100 = 13.48$$

As the six-month period is divided into more and finer subintervals, the values of the call and put will approach their Black-Scholes values. Table 8.1 extends this example to more than two subintervals.

## 8.4 THE GREEKS AND HEDGING IN A BLACK-SCHOLES ENVIRONMENT

As the number of trials $n$ in a binomial distribution approaches infinity, the binomial distribution approaches the normal distribution. Black and Scholes (see Appendix 8.B) provide a derivation for an option pricing model based on the assumption that the natural logs of stock price relatives will be normally distributed.[8] We introduced the Black-Scholes model in the appendix to Chapter 6. The assumptions on which the *Black-Scholes options pricing model* and its derivation are based are as follows:

1. There are no restrictions on short sales of stock or writing of call options.
2. There are no taxes or transactions costs.
3. There exists continuous trading of stocks and options.
4. There exists a single constant riskless interest rate that applies for both borrowing and lending.
5. The range of potential stock prices is continuous. This means that a stock's price can take on any real value.
6. The underlying stock will pay no dividends during the life of the option.
7. The option can be exercised only on its expiration date; that is, it is a European option.
8. Shares of stock and option contracts are infinitely divisible.
9. Stock prices follow an Îto process; that is, they follow a continuous time-random walk in two-dimensional continuous space. This simply means that stock prices are randomly distributed and can take on any positive value at any time.

From an applications perspective, one of the more useful aspects of the Black-Scholes model is that it only requires five inputs. All of these inputs, with the exception of the variance of underlying stock returns, is normally quite easily obtained[9]:

1. The current stock price ($S_0$): Use the most recent quote.
2. The variance of returns on the underlying stock ($\sigma^2$): Several methods for estimating stock volatilities were discussed in Chapter 6.
3. The exercise price of the option ($X$) is given by the contract.
4. The time to maturity of the option ($T$) is given by the contract.
5. For the risk-free return rate ($r_f$), use a Treasury instrument rate with an appropriate term to maturity.

It is important to note that the following less easily obtained factors are not required as model inputs:

1. The expected or required return on the stock or option.
2. Investor attitudes toward risk.

[8]The stock price relative for a given period $t$ is defined as $S_t \div S_{t-1}$. Thus, the log of the stock price relative is defined as $\ln[S_t \div S_{t-1}]$.

[9]These five inputs are the only ones necessary if the assumptions underlying the model hold.

If the assumptions given above hold, the Black-Scholes model specifies that the value of a call option is as follows:

$$c_0 = S_0 N(d_1) - \frac{X}{e^{r_f T}} N(d_2) \tag{8.23}$$

$$d_1 = \frac{\ln(S_0/X) + (r_f + .5\sigma^2)T}{\sigma\sqrt{T}} \tag{8.24}$$

$$d_2 = d_1 - \sigma\sqrt{T} \tag{8.25}$$

where $N(d^*)$ is the cumulative normal distribution function for $(d^*)$.[10]

## Black-Scholes Model Sensitivities

Options can be very volatile instruments, and hedging is crucial for traders' management of options portfolios. Sources of sensitivity, or the "Greeks," are key to this management process. The Black-Scholes model can provide much useful information concerning options and underlying shares. First, assuming that investors behave as though they are risk neutral and that other Black-Scholes assumptions hold, $N(d_2)$ might be interpreted as the probability that the stock price will be sufficiently high at the expiration date of the option to warrant its exercise. Thus, $N(d_2)$ might be regarded as the probability that investors assign to $S_T$ exceeding X. A second particularly useful point is that $N(d_1)$ might be interpreted as a hedge ratio, although it must be updated at every period. This means that $N(d_1)$ can be interpreted as the number of shares to short for every purchased call, but, as the option's time to maturity diminishes, and as share prices change, this hedge ratio will change. In addition, $N(d_1)$ is the sensitivity of the option value to changes in the stock price. This sensitivity means that the option's value will change by $N(d_1)$ for each unit of change in the underlying stock price. In the finance industry, this value is often referred to as the call *delta*.

Option traders find it very useful to know how the values of their option positions will change as the various factors used in the pricing model change. Knowledge of these sensitivities (sometimes called *Greeks*) is particularly useful to investors holding portfolios of options and can often be extended to weighted averages for the portfolios. For example, we mentioned above that the sensitivity of the call's value to the stock's price is Delta:[11]

$$\frac{\partial c}{\partial S} = N(d_1) > 0 \quad \textit{Delta} \quad \Delta \tag{8.26}$$

Thus, a small increase in the value of the underlying stock would lead to approximately $N(d_1)$ times that increase in the price of the call option. A call investor can hedge his portfolio risk associated with infinitesimal share price changes by shorting $N(d_1)$ shares of underlying stock for each purchased call option. Thus, the hedged portfolio would consist of an offsetting position of $N(d_1)$ underlying shares for each call option in the portfolio.

[10]See the appendices to Chapter 6 for an introduction to the Black-Scholes model.

[11]Applying the Chain Rule when finding this derivative yields two additional terms that cancel each other.

In addition, the trader can offset this delta risk with multiple positions in options and the underlying stock. For example, if the trader was long a single call option with a delta of 0.5, this risk could be neutralized with offsetting positions in a portfolio of stock and one or more other option contracts on that stock. Thus, in our example, the stock delta could be offset with a portfolio whose weighted average delta was −0.5, comprised of a single short position in a call option with a delta equal to 0.25 and a short position in 0.25 shares of the underlying stock. Any portfolio whose weighted average delta is 0.5 could be comprised to offset the original call option delta risk.

There is a major caveat to the application of this hedge ratio. In addition to the Black Scholes assumptions, this sensitivity or delta measure worsens as the change in the stock price increases. Furthermore, a large change in the stock price will lead to a change in the value of the *delta neutral portfolio* because delta is based on a derivative or "point slope," and applies only to infinitesimal changes in the stock price. Thus, because this delta is based on a partial derivative with respect to the share price, it holds exactly only for an infinitesimal change in the share price; it holds only approximately for finite changes in the share price. This delta only approximates the change in the call value resulting from a change in the share price because any change in the price of the underlying shares would lead to a change in the delta itself:

$$\frac{\partial^2 c}{\partial S^2} = \frac{\partial \Delta}{\partial S} = \frac{\partial N(d_1)}{\partial S} = \frac{\frac{e^{\left(\frac{-(d_1^2)}{2}\right)}}{\sqrt{2\pi}}}{S\sigma\sqrt{T}} > 0 \quad Gamma \quad \Gamma \tag{8.27}$$

This change in delta resulting from a change in the share price is known as *gamma*. Since gamma is positive, an increase in the share price will lead to an increase in delta. However, again, this change in delta resulting from a finite share price change is only approximate. Each time the share price changes, the investor must update his portfolio to reflect the changing delta.

Gamma is very useful to traders that want to hold delta neutral portfolios. With a fairly large number of puts and calls on the same underlying stock to choose from, traders will be able to discern an infinity of portfolios (in theory with an infinity of potential stock price changes) that maintain delta neutrality. That is, with a single option and shares of its underlying stock, there will normally be a single hedge ratio that provides for portfolio delta neutrality. This delta neutrality means that fairly small changes in the underlying stock's price will have a negligible impact on the value of the portfolio of shares and options. With two different options contracts, for example, contracts with different exercise prices, there may be an infinity of portfolios that maintain delta neutrality. However, there will probably be only one of these portfolios that simultaneously maintains delta and gamma neutrality (select portfolio weights appropriately because all gammas are positive) will minimize adjustments necessary to accommodate stock price changes in the hedged portfolio. At least two different options contracts along with underlying shares will be needed to maintain both delta and gamma neutrality. With two different options contracts and underlying shares, there will normally be a single combination of portfolio weights that simultaneously maintains delta and gamma neutrality; more than two different options contracts and underlying shares will allow for an infinite number of delta/gamma neutral portfolios.

Since each call and put option has a date of expiration, calls and puts are said to amortize over time. As the date of expiration draws nearer ($T$ gets smaller), the value of the European call (and put) option might be expected to decline as indicated by a positive *theta*:

$$\frac{\partial c}{\partial T} = r_f X e^{-r_f T} N(d_2) + S \frac{\sigma}{\sqrt{T}} \frac{e^{\left(\frac{-(d_1^2)}{2}\right)}}{2\sqrt{2\pi}} > 0 \quad Theta \quad \theta \tag{8.28}$$

Many traders seek to maintain portfolios that are simultaneously neutral with respect to delta, gamma, and theta. Be certain that the units of time for theta are consistent with those used in the calculation of the option value. Some option traders calculate option prices based on numbers of years (fractions of years) prior to option expiry, but prefer to calculate theta in days. This is acceptable, but divide the annual theta by 365 (or the number of trading days in the year) to obtain the daily theta.

*Vega*, which actually is not a Greek letter, measures the sensitivity of the option price to the underlying stock's standard deviation of returns. One might expect the call option price to be directly related to the underlying stock's standard deviation:

$$\frac{\partial c}{\partial \sigma} = S\sqrt{T} \frac{e^{\left(\frac{-(d_1^2)}{2}\right)}}{\sqrt{2\pi}} > 0 \quad Vega \quad \nu \tag{8.29}$$

Although the Black-Scholes model assumes that the underlying stock volatility is constant over time, in reality, volatility can and does shift. Vega provides an estimate for the impact of a volatility shift on the option's value. Vega is also useful in calculating option implied volatilities when the iteration process is made more efficient with the use of the Newton-Raphson method.

A trader should expect that the value of the call would be directly related to the riskless return rate and inversely related to the call exercise price:

$$\frac{\partial c}{\partial e^{r_f}} = T X e^{-r_f T} N(d_2) > 0 \quad Rho \quad \rho \tag{8.30}$$

$$\frac{\partial c}{\partial X} = -\, e^{-r_f T} N(d_2) < 0 \tag{8.31}$$

The option rho can be very useful in economies with high or volatile interest rates, though most traders of "plain vanilla options" do not concern themselves much with call value sensitivities to exercise prices.

## Illustration: Greeks Calculations for Calls

In the appendix to Chapter 6, we worked through the Black-Scholes model to value a call. We summarize details as follows:

$$T = 0.5 \quad r_f = 0.10$$

$$X = 80 \quad \sigma^2 = 0.16$$

$$\sigma = 0.4 \quad S_0 = 75$$

$$d_1 = \frac{\ln(75/80) + (.1 + .5 \cdot .16) \cdot .5}{.4 \cdot \sqrt{5}} = \frac{\ln(.9375) + .09}{.2828} = .09$$

$$d_2 = d_1 - .4 \cdot \sqrt{.5} = .09 - .2828 = -.1928$$

$$N(d_1) = N(.09) = .536 \quad N(d_2) = N(-.1928) = .420$$

$$c_0 = 75 \cdot .536 - (80 \cdot .9512) \cdot .420 = 8.23$$

Sensitivities (Greeks) for this call option are computed as follows:

$$\frac{\partial c}{\partial S} = N(d_1) = \Delta = .536$$

$$\frac{\partial^2 c}{\partial S^2} = \frac{\partial \Delta}{\partial S} = \frac{\partial N(d_1)}{\partial S} = \frac{\dfrac{e^{\left(\frac{-(d_1^2)}{2}\right)}}{\sqrt{2\pi}}}{S\sigma\sqrt{T}} = \Gamma = .0187$$

$$\frac{\partial c}{\partial T} = -r_f X e^{-r_f T} N(d_2) - S \frac{\sigma}{\sqrt{T}} \frac{e^{\left(\frac{-(d_1^2)}{2}\right)}}{2\sqrt{2\pi}} = \theta = -11.6522 \quad \textit{Daily} \quad \textit{Theta} = -.032$$

$$\frac{\partial c}{\partial \sigma} = S\sqrt{T} \frac{e^{\left(\frac{-(d_1^2)}{2}\right)}}{\sqrt{2\pi}} = \nu = 21.06$$

$$\frac{\partial c}{\partial e^{r_f}} = T X e^{-r_f T} N(d_2) = \rho = 16.1156$$

$$\frac{\partial c}{\partial X} = -e^{-r_f T} N(d_2) = -.4028$$

Sometimes thetas are expressed in daily terms and sometimes vegas and rhos are expressed in terms based on one percentage point increases in standard deviation or interest rates.

## Illustration: Hedging with Delta and Gamma Neutral Portfolios

In our numerical example above, we can establish a delta neutral portfolio by purchasing a single call and shorting 0.536 shares of stock. The portfolio delta is the weighted average of its component security deltas, and one call has already been purchased:

$$delta_S \times \#_S + delta_C \times \#_C = delta_{port}$$

$$\#_C = 1$$

The portfolio delta is to be set equal to zero for delta neutrality, and the delta of shares is 1.

$$1 \times \#_S + 0.536 \times \#_C = 0$$
$$\#_C = 1$$

Clearly the solution to this system is $\#_S = -0.536$, implying that delta neutrality requires an offsetting position in 0.536 shares of underlying stock.

Next, suppose instead that we have purchased a single share of underlying stock and that we wish to maintain both delta and gamma neutrality ($\Delta$ and $\Gamma$ equal zero) for our portfolio. These two criteria cannot simultaneously be accomplished with only a single option with our single share. Suppose that we can take positions in a second call option, with the same exercise terms as the first except that the exercise price equals 75 rather than 80. We calculate the delta and gamma of our second option to be 0.62483 and 0.0178, respectively. Stock deltas are 1 and stock gammas are zero. Now, we will seek to solve the following system:

$$\begin{bmatrix} delta_{port} \\ gamma_{port} \\ \#_S \end{bmatrix} = \begin{bmatrix} delta_S & delta_{C1} & delta_{C2} \\ gamma_S & gamma_{C1} & gamma_{C2} \\ 1 & 0 & 0 \end{bmatrix} \begin{bmatrix} \#_S \\ \#_{C1} \\ \#_{C2} \end{bmatrix}$$
$$\mathbf{r} = \mathbf{Y} \quad \#$$

$$\begin{bmatrix} delta_{port} \\ gamma_{port} \\ \#_S \end{bmatrix} = \begin{bmatrix} 0 \\ 0 \\ 1 \end{bmatrix} = \begin{bmatrix} 1 & .53586 & .62483 \\ 0 & .0187 & .0178 \\ 1 & 0 & 0 \end{bmatrix} \begin{bmatrix} \#_S \\ \#_{C1} \\ \#_{C2} \end{bmatrix}$$
$$\mathbf{r} = \mathbf{Y} \quad \#$$

$$\begin{bmatrix} \#_S \\ \#_{C1} \\ \#_{C2} \end{bmatrix} = \begin{bmatrix} 1 \\ 8.42 \\ -8.82 \end{bmatrix} = \begin{bmatrix} 0 & 0 & 1 \\ -8.42 & 294.27 & 8.42 \\ 8.82 & -252.37 & 8.42 \end{bmatrix} \begin{bmatrix} 0 \\ 0 \\ 1 \end{bmatrix}$$
$$\# = \mathbf{Y}^{-1} \quad \mathbf{r}$$

Thus, for each underlying share of stock purchased, a delta-gamma neutral portfolio requires a long position in 8.42 calls with \$80 exercise prices and a short position in 8.82 calls with \$75 exercise prices. The availability of additional option contracts would increase flexibility with respect to maintaining delta-gamma neutrality. On the other hand, simultaneous maintenance of theta neutrality along with delta-gamma neutrality would require at least one additional different option contract.

## Put Sensitivities

If put-call parity holds along with Black-Scholes assumptions given above, the Black-Scholes put value is computed as follows:

$$p_0 = -S_0 N(-d_1) + \frac{X}{e^{r_f T}} N(-d_2) \tag{8.32}$$

$$d_1 = \frac{\ln(S_0/X) + (r_f + .5\sigma^2)T}{\sigma\sqrt{T}} \tag{8.24}$$

$$d_2 = d_1 - \sigma\sqrt{T} \tag{8.25}$$

In our numerical example, the put is worth 9.05 if its exercise terms are identical to those of the call in the same example. We can use these put sensitivities to hedge and manage portfolio risk in the same manner that we used the call sensitivities. Put sensitivities formulas and calculations for our example are as follows:

$$\frac{\partial p}{\partial S} = N(d_1) - 1 = \Delta_p = -.464$$

$$\frac{\partial^2 p}{\partial S^2} = \frac{\partial \Delta_p}{\partial S} = \frac{\partial N(d_1) - 1}{\partial S} = \frac{\frac{e^{\left(\frac{-(d_1^2)}{2}\right)}}{\sqrt{2\pi}}}{S\sigma\sqrt{T}} = \Gamma_p = .0187$$

$$\frac{\partial p}{\partial T} = r_f X e^{-r_f T} N(-d_2) - S\frac{\sigma}{\sqrt{T}}\frac{e^{\left(\frac{-(-d_1^2)}{2}\right)}}{2\sqrt{2\Pi}} = \theta_p = -4.110; \quad \textit{Daily} \quad \textit{Theta} = -.011$$

$$\frac{\partial p}{\partial \sigma} = S\sqrt{T}\frac{e^{\left(\frac{-(d_1^2)}{2}\right)}}{\sqrt{2\pi}} = \nu_p = 21.06$$

$$\frac{\partial p}{\partial e^{r_f}} = -TXe^{-r_f T}N(-d_2) = \rho_p = 21.93$$

$$\frac{\partial p}{\partial X} = -e^{-r_f T}N(d_2) = -21.93$$

## 8.5 EXCHANGE OPTIONS

In this section, we discuss a variation of the Black-Scholes model provided by Garman and Köhlagen (1983) and Grabbe (1983) for the valuation of currency options. The stock option pricing model is based on the assumption that investors price calls as though they expect the underlying stock to earn the risk free rate of return. However, when we value currency options, we acknowledge that interest rates might differ between the foreign and domestic countries, and that money might be borrowed in one country and loaned in another. Hence, we quote two interest rates—one each for the foreign and domestic currencies. In this scenario, we value currency options as follows:

$$c_0 = S_0 e^{-r(f)T} N(d_1) - \frac{X}{e^{r(d)T}} N(d_2) \tag{8.33}$$

$$d_1 = \frac{\ln\left(\frac{S_0 e^{-r(f)T}}{Xe^{-r(d)T}}\right) + \left(r(d) - r(f) + \frac{\sigma^2}{2}\right)T}{\sigma\sqrt{T}} \tag{8.34}$$

$$d_2 = d_1 - \sigma\sqrt{T} \tag{8.35}$$

where $r(d)$ is the domestic riskless rate (the rate for the currency that will be given up if the option is exercised), $r(f)$ is the foreign riskless rate (the rate for the currency that might be purchased). The spot rate for the currency is $S_0$. The standard deviation of proportional exchange rates for the foreign currency to be purchased in terms of the domestic currency is $\sigma$. The exercise price of the option, $X$, represents the number of units of the domestic currency to be given up for each unit of the foreign currency. The following variation of put–call parity will apply to the valuation of currency puts:

$$p_0 = c_0 + Xe^{-r(d)T} - S_0 e^{-r(f)T} \tag{8.36}$$

## Illustration: FX Option Valuation

Consider, for example, a currency option series on Swiss francs (CHF) denominated in U.S. dollars. Suppose that a six-month (0.5 years) call option is available on francs with an exercise price equal \$0.5556. The domestic and foreign riskless rates are 0.1. The current exchange rate is \$0.5556/CHF and the standard deviation associated with the exchange rate is 0.4. What is the value of this currency call?

To answer this question, we first calculate $d_1$:

$$d_1 = \frac{\ln\left(\frac{.5556e^{-.1 \cdot .5}}{.5556e^{-.1 \cdot .5}}\right) + \left(.1 - .1 + \frac{.4^2}{2}\right) \cdot .5}{.4\sqrt{.5}} = \frac{.04}{.2828} = .1414$$

Next we calculate $d_2$:

$$d_2 = d_1 - \sigma\sqrt{T} = .1414 - .2828 = -.1414$$

Next, find cumulative normal density functions (z-values) for $d_1$ and $d_2$:

$$N(d_1) = N(0.1414) = 0.556$$
$$N(d_2) = N(-0.1414) = 0.443$$

Finally, we value the call as follows:

$$c_0 = (\$0.5556 \times 0.556) - [\$0.5556 \times 0.9512] \times 0.443 = \$0.05943$$

We can evaluate a European put for CHF using Equation (8.36) as follows:

$$p_0 = c_0 + Xe^{-r(d)T} - S_0 e^{-r(f)T} = 0.05943 + 0.5556e^{-0.1 \times 0.5} - 0.5556e^{-0.1 \times 0.5} = 0.05943$$

TABLE 8.2 Currency Option Illustration

| Option 1 | Option 2 | Option 3 | Option 4 |
|---|---|---|---|
| $T = 1$ | $T = 1$ | $T = 0.5$ | $T = 2$ |
| $r(f) = 0.1$ | $r(f) = 0.1$ | $r(f) = 0.1$ | $r(f) = 0.1$ |
| $r(d) = 0.05$ | $r(d) = 0.05$ | $r(d) = 0.05$ | $r(d) = 0.05$ |
| $S_0 = 2$ | $S_0 = 2$ | $S_0 = 2$ | $S_0 = 2$ |
| $\sigma = 0.3$ | $\sigma = 0.3$ | $\sigma = 0.3$ | $\sigma = 0.3$ |
| $X = 1.8$ | $X = 2$ | $X = 2.2$ | $X = 2.2$ |

TABLE 8.3 Currency Option Values

| | Option 1 | Option 2 | Option 3 | Option 4 |
|---|---|---|---|---|
| $d_1$ | 0.1679 | −0.1833 | −0.5789 | −0.4839 |
| $d_2$ | −0.1321 | −0.4833 | −0.7911 | −0.9081 |
| $N(d_1)$ | 0.5666 | 0.4272 | 0.2813 | 0.3142 |
| $N(d_2)$ | 0.4474 | 0.3144 | 0.2144 | 0.1819 |
| Call | 0.2594 | 0.1750 | 0.07504 | 0.1524 |

Consider the next example where four call options are traded on CHF (Swiss Francs) with exercise prices $X$ expressed in U.S. dollars. One U.S. dollar is currently worth 2 Swiss francs ($S_0 = 2$). We wish to evaluate calls for each of the following European currency option series depicted in Table 8.2.

We will work through Equations (8.33) through (8.35) to value the calls. Final solutions are given in the bottom line of Table 8.3.

We use a currency-specific variation of the put–call parity relation (Equation (8.36)) to value the puts:

$$p_0 = c_0 + Xe^{-r(d)T} - S_0e^{-r(d)T}$$

Thus, put options with terms identical to those of the calls in Tables 8.2 and 8.3 have the following values:

| | Option 1 | Option 2 | Option 3 | Option 4 |
|---|---|---|---|---|
| Put | 0.1619 | 0.2678 | 0.3183 | 0.5056 |

## 8.6 HEDGING EXCHANGE EXPOSURE WITH CURRENCY OPTIONS

Based on the example from Chapter 7, Hedging Exchange Exposure section, suppose that the Dayton Company of America expects to receive a payoff of £1,000,000 in three months, and intends to convert its cash flows to dollars. Continue to assume relevant data as follows:

Spot exchange rate: $1.7640/£
Three-month forward exchange rate: $1.7540/£
U.K. borrowing interest rate: 10.0%
U.S. borrowing interest rate: 8.0%
U.K. lending interest rate: 8.0%
U.S. lending interest rate: 6.0%

Also assume that there exist call and put options and forward contracts with the following terms, and that their premiums might not reflect formula values:

Term to options expiration: 3 months
Exercise price: $1.75/£
Put premium: $0.025/£
Call premium: $0.065/£
Brokerage cost per options contract on £31,250: $50

Our problem is to evaluate methods of managing the transaction risk associated with this extension of credit and the implications of each.

We will consider two options-based hedging strategies here. The first is the put hedge (partial hedge) strategy which involves the purchase of a put on pounds, enabling the firm to protect itself against devaluation of pounds. If the value of pounds increases, the firm realizes a greater profit. However, the firm must pay the full cost of the put. With the conversion or call and put hedge strategy, the proceeds from the sale of a call are used to offset the purchase price of the put. This strategy acts as a collar, locking in the value of pounds at the originations of the options contracts. Hence, the firm would not benefit from any appreciation in the value of the pound.

First, we consider the put hedge strategy. We will purchase three month put options on £1,000,000 with an exercise price of $1.75/£ with a total premium of $25,000. Time-zero brokerage costs total $1600 (32 contracts at $50 per contract). Thus the total time-zero cash outlay is $26,600. Forgone interest on the sum of the premium and brokerage costs totals $399. Expressed in terms of future value, the total cash outlay is $26,999. The result of this strategy is that the firm receives one of the following in three months:

1. An unlimited maximum less the $26,999 premium, forgone interest and brokerage fees. The dollar value of this strategy increases as the value of the dollar drops against the pound. Since cash flows are not certain, this hedge is considered partial.
2. A minimum of $1,750,000 less $26,999 for a net of $1,723,001. This minimum value to be received might be unacceptably low; however, there is upside cash flow potential.

Alternatively, the firm can employ the conversion or the call and put hedge. This strategy involves the combination of calls and puts, such that total risk can be eliminated.

Consider the writing of a call with an exercise price of $1.75 expiring in three months along with the purchase of a put with the same terms. The time-zero net cash flows are summarized as follows:

| | |
|---|---|
| Put premium − $25,000 | Call premium + $65,000 |
| Put brokerage fee − $1,600 | Call brokerage fee − $1,600 |
| Net time-zero cash flows + $36,800 | |

The result of this conversion is that the interest earned on the net time-zero outlay is $552. If the three-month exchange rate is less than $1.75/£, the exchange rate of $1.75/£ is locked in by the put. If the exchange rate exceeds $1.75/£, the obligation incurred by the short position in the call is activated. Thus, the firm's exchange rate of $1.75/£ is locked in no matter what the market exchange rate is. The cash flows in three months are summarized as follows:

Put cash flows (£1,000,000 × MAX[1.75 − $S_1$,0])
Call cash flows (£1,000,000 × MIN[1.75 − $S_1$,0])

Total of option transactions:

£1,000,000 × (1.75 − $S_1$) = $1,750,000 − (£1,000,000 × $S_1$)
Exchange of currency = (£1,000,000 × $S_1$)
Time zero cash flows = $36,800
Interest on time zero flows = $552
Total time one cash flows = $1,787,352

This cash flow of $1,787,352 is assured in the absence of default risk.

## Additional Reading

Elton et al. (2010), chapters 21 to 24, offer good coverage of fixed income, options and futures arbitrage and hedging. Grabbe (1996) discusses currency option pricing and hedging. Jarrow and Rudd (1983), while dated, provide a very useful overview of options pricing, hedging and arbitrage. The industry standard reading for options and derivatives is Hull (2011), going far beyond the material in this chapter. Neftci (2000) provides excellent background reading in the mathematics of financial derivatives, again, going far beyond the scope of this chapter.

## References

Cox, J., Ross, S., & Rubinstein, M. (1979). Option pricing: A simplified approach. *Journal of Financial Economics, 7*, 229–263.

Elton, E., Gruber, M., Brown, S., & Goetzmann, W. (2010). *Modern portfolio theory and investment analysis* (8th ed.). New York: Wiley.

Garman, M., & Köhlagen, S. (1983). Foreign currency option values. *Journal of International Money and Finance, 2*, 231–237.

Grabbe, J. O. (1983). The pricing of call and put options on foreign exchange. *Journal of International Money and Finance, 2*, 239–253.

Grabbe, J. O. (1996). *International financial markets* (3rd ed.). Englewood Cliffs, NJ: Prentice Hall.

Hull, J. C. (2011). *Options, futures and other derivatives* (8th ed.). Englewood Cliffs, NJ: Prentice Hall.

Jarrow, R., & Rudd, A. (1983). *Option pricing*. Homewood, IL: Dow Jones-Irwin.
Jarrow, R. A., & Turnbull, S. M. (1999). *Derivative securities* (2nd ed.). South-Western College Publishers.
Neftci, S. N. (2000). *An introduction to the mathematics of financial derivatives* (2nd ed.). San Diego: Academic Press.

## 8.7 EXERCISES

**1.** Consider a one-time-period, two potential outcome framework where there exists Company Q stock currently selling for $50 per share and a riskless $100 face value T-Bill currently selling for $90. Suppose Company Q faces uncertainty, such that it will pay its owner either $30 or $70 in one year. Further assume that a call with an exercise price of $55 exists on one share of Q stock.
   **a.** What are the two potential values the call might have at its expiration?
   **b.** What is the riskless rate of return for this example? Remember, the Treasury bill pays $100 and currently sells for $90.
   **c.** What is the hedge ratio for this call option?
   **d.** What is the current value of this option?
   **e.** What is the value of a put with the same exercise terms as the call?

**2.** Rollins Company stock currently sells for $12 per share and is expected to be worth either $10 or $16 in one year. The current riskless return rate is 0.125. What would be the value of a one-year call with an exercise price of $8?

**3.** A stock currently selling for $50 has an annual returns variance equal to 0.36. The riskless return rate equals 0.08 per year. Under the binomial framework, what would be the value of nine-month (0.75 year) European calls and European puts with striking prices equal to $80 if the number of tree steps ($n$) were
   **a.** two?
   **b.** three?
   **c.** eight?

**4.** Ibis Company stock is currently selling for $50 per share and has a multiplicative upward movement equal to 1.2776 and a multiplicative downward movement equal to 0.7828. What is the value of a nine-month (0.75 year) European call and a European put with striking prices equal to $60 if the number of tree steps were two? Assume a riskless return rate equal to 0.081.

**5.** Kestrel Company stock is currently selling for $40 per share. Its historical standard deviation of returns is 0.5. The one-year Treasury bill rate is currently 5%. Assume that all of the standard Black-Scholes option pricing model assumptions hold.
   **a.** What is the value of a put on this stock if it has an exercise price of $35 and expires in one year?
   **b.** What is the implied probability that the value of the stock will be less than $30 in one year?

**6.** Evaluate each of the European options in the series on ABC Company stock. Prices for each of the options are listed in the table. Determine whether each of the options in the series should be purchased or sold at the given market prices. The current market price of ABC stock is 120, the August options expire in nine days, September options in 44 days, and October options in 71 days. The stock return standard deviations prior to expirations are projected to be 0.20 prior to August, 0.25 prior to September, and 0.20 prior to October. The Treasury bill rate is projected to be 0.06 for each of the three periods prior to expiration. Do not forget to convert the number of days given to fractions of 365-day years.

Calls

| $X$ | Aug | Sep | Oct | |
|---|---|---|---|---|
| 110 | 9.500 | 10.500 | 11.625 | $\sigma = 0.20$ for Aug |
| 115 | 4.625 | 7.000 | 8.125 | $\sigma = 0.25$ for Sep |
| 120 | 1.250 | 3.875 | 5.250 | $\sigma = 0.20$ for Oct |
| 125 | 0.250 | 2.125 | 3.125 | $r = 0.06$ |
| 130 | 0.031 | 0.750 | 1.625 | $S = 120$ |

Puts

| $X$ | Aug | Sep | Oct |
|---|---|---|---|
| 110 | 0.031 | 0.750 | 1.500 |
| 115 | 0.375 | 1.750 | 2.750 |
| 120 | 1.625 | 6.750 | 4.500 |
| 125 | 5.625 | 6.750 | 7.875 |
| 130 | 10.625 | 10.750 | 11.625 |

Prices for five calls and five puts are given in the left columns. Expiration dates are given in column headings and current market prices are given in the table interiors.

7. What is the gamma of a long position in a single futures contract? Why?
8. Tanker Company stock currently sells for 30 per share and has an anticipated volatility (annual return standard deviation) equal to 0.6. Three month (0.25 year) call options are available on this stock with an exercise price equal to 25. The current riskless return rate equals 0.05.
   a. Calculate the call's value.
   b. Calculate the call's delta, gamma, theta, vega, and rho.
   c. What is the Black-Scholes implied probability that the stock price will exceed 25 three months from now?
   d. What is the value of a put with the same exercise terms as the call?
   e. What are the Greeks for the put in part d?
9. Tanker Company stock, which currently sells for 30 per share and has an anticipated volatility (annual return standard deviation) equal to 0.6, also has a three-month (0.25 year) call option with an exercise price equal to 30. The current riskless return rate equals 0.05.

**a.** Calculate this second call's value.
**b.** Calculate this call's delta, gamma, theta, vega, and rho.
**c.** What is the Black-Scholes implied probability that the stock price will exceed 30 three months from now?
**d.** What positions in these calls and the calls from Question 8 should be taken for each long share of stock to maintain a delta-gamma neutral portfolio?
**e.** What is the theta of the portfolio in part d?

**10.** A currency option series on Australian dollars (AUD) denominated in U.S. dollars. Suppose that a two-year call option is available on AUD with an exercise price equal USD0.65. The U.S. interest rate is 0.04 and the Australian rate is 0.06. The current exchange rate is USD0.7/AUD and the standard deviation associated with the exchange rate is 0.3. What is the value of this currency call? What is the value of a put with the same exercise terms?

**11.** Consider an extension of the Exercise 21 from Chapter 7 concerned with the management of transactions exposure. The Smedley Company sold products to a Japanese client for ¥15,000,000. Payment is due six months later. Relevant data are as follows:

Spot exchange rate: ¥105/$
Japanese borrowing interest rate: 9.0%
U.S. borrowing interest rate: 7.0%
Japanese lending interest rate: 7.0%
U.S. lending interest rate: 5.0%
There exist currency call and put options with the following terms:
Size of options contracts: ¥1,000,000
Term to expiration of options contracts: six months
Exercise price of put and call: $0.009/¥
Put premium: $0.00001/¥
Call premium: $0.0001/¥
Brokerage cost per options contract: $50

Discuss the implications associated with each of the options-based methods for managing the transactions exposure risk associated with this extension of credit.

# APPENDIX 8.A

## 8.A.1 THE BINOMIAL MODEL: ADDITIONAL CONSIDERATIONS

### A Computationally More Efficient Version of the Binomial Model

Here, we simply discuss a computationally more efficient version of the $n$-time-period binomial model Equation (8.17):

$$c_0 = \frac{\sum_{j=0}^{n} \frac{n!}{j!(n-j)!} p^j (1-p)^{n-j} MAX\left[0, u^j d^{n-j} S_0 - X\right]}{(1+r_f)^n} \tag{8.17}$$

The number of computational steps required to solve Equation (8.17) is reduced if we eliminate from consideration all of those outcomes where the option's expiration date price is zero. Thus, the smallest non-negative integer for $j$ where $S_n > X$ is the smallest integer that exceeds the following (Equation (8.19):

$$a = MAX\left[\frac{\ln\left(\frac{X}{S_0 d^n}\right)}{\ln\left(\frac{u}{d}\right)}, 0\right] \tag{8.19}$$

This result is obtained by first determining the minimum number of price increases $j$ needed for $S_n$ to exceed $X$:

$$S_n = u^j d^{n-j} S_0 > X \tag{8.A.1.1}$$

We then solve this inequality for the minimum non-negative integer value for $j$ such that $u^j d^{n-j} S_0 > X$. Take logs of both sides to obtain:

$$\begin{gathered} j \cdot \ln(u) + n \cdot \ln(d) - j \cdot \ln(d) + \ln(S_0) > \ln\ X \\ j \cdot \ln\left(\frac{u}{d}\right) > \ln(X) - n \cdot \ln(d) - \ln(S_0) \end{gathered} \tag{8.A.1.2}$$

Next divide both sides by In$(u/d)$ and simplify to obtain Equation (8.19), where $a$ is the smallest non-negative integer for $j$ for which $S_n > X$. Finally, we substitute Equation (8.19) into Equation (8.7) to obtain *the binomial option pricing model*:

$$c_0 = \frac{\sum_{j=a}^{n} \frac{n!}{j!(n-j)!} p^j (1-p)^{n-j} \left[u^j d^{n-j} S_o - X\right]}{(1+r_f)^n} \tag{8.18}$$

Or

$$c_0 = S_0\left[\sum_{j=a}^{n}\frac{n!}{j!(n-j)!}\frac{(pu)^j[(1-p)d]^{n-j}}{(1+r_f)^n}\right] - \frac{X}{(1+r_f)^n}\left[\sum_{j=a}^{n}\frac{n!}{j!(n-j)!}p^j(1-p)^{n-j}\right] \qquad (8.18a)$$

In short-hand form:

$$c_0 = S_0B_1[a, n, p'] - X(1+r_f)^{-n}B_2[a, n, p] \qquad (8.18b)$$

where $p' = pu/(1+r_f)$. There are two more points regarding Equation (8.18b). First, assuming that investors behave as though they are risk neutral, $B_2[a, n, p]$ can be interpreted as the probability that the stock price will be sufficiently high at the expiration date of the option to warrant its exercise. Second, $B_2[a, n, p']$ can be interpreted as a hedge ratio, although it must be updated at every period.

## Obtaining Multiplicative Upward and Downward Movement Values

One apparent difficulty in applying the binomial model as it is presented above is in obtaining estimates for $u$ and $d$ that are required for $p$; all other inputs are normally quite easily obtained. There are several methods that are used to obtain parameters for the binomial method from the actual security returns generating process. For example, following Cox et al. (1979), we can begin the process of estimating the mean and variance to be used in the binomial distribution by first approximating the mean and variance for the binomial process from the historical Weiner process as follows:

$$E[S_T] = S_0e^{\mu T+\frac{1}{2}\sigma^2 T} \approx puS_0 + (1-p)dS_0 \qquad (8.A.1.3)$$

$$\sigma_s^2 T = S_0^2(e^{\sigma^2 T}-1)(e^{2\mu T+\sigma^2 T}) \approx [pu^2S_0^2 + (1-p)d^2S_0^2] - [puS_0 + (1-p)dS_0]^2 \qquad (8.A.1.4)$$

Approximation 2 approaches equality as $T$ approaches zero. Scaling $S_0$ to one such that we work with returns rather than actual security prices, the following can be used for returns variance of a binomial process:

$$\sigma^2 = [pu^2 + (1-p)d^2] - [pu + (1-p)d]^2 \qquad (8.A.1.5)$$

We will rewrite Equation (8.A.1.5) as follows[12]:

$$\sigma^2 = p(1-p)(u-d)^2 \qquad (8.A.1.6)$$

[12]The following are algebraic steps to obtain Equation (8.A.1.6) from Equation (8.A.1.5):

$$\sigma^2 = \lfloor pu^2 + (1-p)d^2\rfloor - [pu + (1-p)d]^2 = \lfloor pu^2 + d^2 - pd^2\rfloor - \lfloor p^2u^2 + (1-p)^2d^2 + 2pu(1-p)d\rfloor$$

$$\sigma^2 = \lfloor pu^2 + d^2 - pd^2\rfloor - \lfloor p^2u^2 + d^2 + p^2d^2 - 2pd^2 + 2pud - 2p^2ud\rfloor$$

$$\sigma^2 = |pu^2| - |p^2u^2 + p^2d^2 - pd^2 + 2pud - 2p^2ud|$$

$$\sigma^2 = p(u^2 - pu^2 - pd^2 + d^2 - 2ud + 2pud) = p(1-p)(u^2 + d^2 - 2ud)$$

Assume that the binomial process will lead to expected return for a security equaling the riskless rate:

$$e^{\mu T+\frac{1}{2}\sigma^2 T} = e^{r_f} \approx pu + (1-p)d \tag{8.A.1.7}$$

Solving Equation (8.A.1.7) for p enables us to estimate probabilities of an uptick $p$ and downtick $(1-p)$ as:

$$p = \frac{e^{r_f} - d}{u - d} \quad (1-p) = \frac{u - e^{r_f}}{u - d} \tag{8.A.1.8}$$

If we define $d$ as $1/u$ such that $ud = 1$, we can rewrite Equation (8.A.1.6), the variance of returns, as follows:

$$\sigma^2 = p(1-p)(u-d)^2 = p(1-p)(e^{\delta} - e^{-\delta})^2 \tag{8.A.1.9}$$

Thus, we have simply substituted some constant $e^{\delta}$ for $u$. Substituting $\sigma$ for $\delta$ will provide a good approximation for variance (improving as the number of jumps in the binomial process, $n$ approaches infinity):

$$\sigma^2 = p(1-p)(e^{\delta} - e^{-\delta})^2 = p(1-p)(e^{\sigma} - e^{-\sigma})^2 \tag{8.A.1.10}$$

Thus, we can use the following to estimate $u$ and $d$ in the binomial approximation to the Weiner process:

$$u = e^{\sigma} \qquad d = \frac{1}{u} \tag{8.A.1.11}$$

or, if $n$ and $T$ differ from 1,

$$u = e^{\sigma\sqrt{\frac{T}{n}}} \quad d = \frac{1}{u} \tag{8.A.1.12}$$

Suppose, for example, that for a particular Weiner process, $\sigma = 0.30$ and $r_f = 0.05$. Using Equations (8.A.1.7) and (8.A.1.10), we estimate $p$, $u$, and $d$ for a single time period binomial process as follows:

$$u = e^{.3} = 1.3498588$$

$$d = \frac{1}{u} = .7408182$$

We can verify our estimates with Equations (8.A.1.6) and (8.A.1.9) as follows:

$$e^{.005+\frac{1}{2}\times .3^2} = e^{.05}$$

$$= .5097409 \times 1.3498588 + (1 - .5097409) \times .7408182 = 1.0512$$

$$\sigma^2 = p(1-p)(e^{\delta} - e^{-\delta}) \approx .5097409 \times (1 - .5097409)(e^{.3} - e^{-.3})^2 = .0926974$$

As discussed above, there are several procedures for getting parameters $\sigma$, $u$, $d$, and $p$ for the binomial distribution. This procedure is probably the most commonly used, in part, because it provides a relatively straightforward method for estimating option Greeks. The primary difficulty with the one presented above is that it may result in negative probabilities. An additional methodology for estimating binomial distribution parameters is given in Jarrow and Turnbull (1996: 136–138).

## 8.A.2 DERIVING THE BLACK-SCHOLES MODEL

For this derivation, we shall assume that all standard Black-Scholes assumptions (see The Greeks and Hedging in a Black-Scholes Environment section) hold and that investors behave as though they are risk neutral. That is, investors price options as though they are risk neutral because they can always construct riskless hedges comprising options and their underlying securities, and that the returns of these hedged portfolios must be the riskless rate. The law of one price dictates that the current value of a call $c$ on stock can be found from constructing a hedge portfolio:

$$c = \#sS + \#bB$$

$S$ is the current value of its underlying stock and $B$ is the current value of a riskless Treasury instrument. Let $\#s$ be the number of shares of stock to purchase and $\#b$ be the number of Treasury instruments to short in order to replicate the cash flow structure of the call. Similarly, we can replicate the cash flow structure of a single bond as follows:

$$B = \#sS + c \tag{8.A.2.1}$$

Let $V_h = B$ represent the value of a perfectly hedged portfolio. We can rewrite the above equation in terms of $V_H$ as follows:

$$V_h = c + \#sS \tag{8.A.2.2}$$

Since the hedge is riskless, its return should equal the riskless rate:

$$dV_h = r_f V_h dt = dc + \#sdS \tag{8.A.2.3}$$

The hedge requires that we short sell $\#s$ shares of stock for each call that we purchase. The sensitivity of the call price to the stock price is $\partial c/\partial S$. Thus, the hedge will require that we short $\partial c/\partial S$ shares for each purchased call. We write the value of the hedge portfolio and rewrite its differential equation as follows:

$$V_h = c - \frac{\partial c}{\partial S} S \tag{8.A.2.4}$$

$$r_f V_h dt = dc - \frac{\partial c}{\partial S} dS \tag{8.A.2.5}$$

We rearrange the above differential equation by substituting for $V_h$ and solving for $dc$:

$$dc = r_f\left[c - \frac{\partial c}{\partial S}S\right]dt + \frac{\partial c}{\partial S}dS \tag{8.A.2.6}$$

which is rewritten as follows:

$$dc = r_f c dt - r_f \frac{\partial c}{\partial S} S dt + \frac{\partial c}{\partial S}dS \tag{8.A.2.7}$$

We shall assume that the instantaneous price change for the stock follows an Itô process:

$$dS = \mu S dt + \sigma S dz \tag{8.A.2.8}$$

which requires us to use Itô's lemma to solve for $dc$. Substituting this Weiner process for $dS$ into the preceding equation, we obtain the following:

$$dc = r_f c dt - r_f \frac{\partial c}{\partial S} S dt + \frac{\partial c}{\partial S}(\mu S dt + \sigma S dz) \tag{8.A.2.9}$$

We will rewrite Equation (8.A.2.9) separating out the term in the parentheses as follows:

$$dc = r_f c dt - r_f \frac{\partial c}{\partial S} S dt + \frac{\partial c}{\partial S}\mu S dt + \frac{\partial c}{\partial S}\sigma S dz \tag{8.A.2.10}$$

$$dc = \mu S \frac{\partial c}{\partial S}dt + \frac{\partial c}{\partial t}dt + \frac{1}{2}S^2\sigma^2\frac{\partial^2 c}{\partial S^2}dt + \sigma S\frac{\partial c}{\partial S}dz \tag{8.A.2.11}$$

Note that the first and fourth terms in Equation (8.A.2.11) are identical to the third and fourth terms in Equation (8.A.2.10). Furthermore, Equations (8.A.2.10) and (8.A.2.11) solve for $dc$. This means that the second and third terms in Equation (8.A.2.11) are identical to the first and second terms in Equation (8.A.2.10):

$$r_f c dt - r_f \frac{\partial c}{\partial S} S dt = \frac{\partial c}{\partial t}dt + \frac{1}{2}S^2\sigma^2\frac{\partial^2 c}{\partial S^2}dt \tag{8.A.2.12}$$

which, after dividing by $dt$, is rewritten:

$$\frac{\partial c}{\partial t} = r_f c - r_f \frac{\partial c}{\partial S} S_t - \frac{1}{2}S^2\sigma^2\frac{\partial^2 c}{\partial S^2} \tag{8.A.2.13}$$

This is the Black-Scholes differential equation. Its particular solution, subject to the *boundary condition* $c_T = MAX[0, S_T - X]$, is given by Equations (8.A.2.14) through (8.A.2.16):

$$c_0 = S_0 N(d_1) - \frac{X}{e^{r_f T}}N(d_2) \tag{8.A.2.14}$$

$$d_1 = \frac{\ln\left(\frac{S_0}{X}\right) + \left(r_f + \frac{1}{2}\sigma^2\right)T}{\sigma\sqrt{T}} \tag{8.A.2.15}$$

$$d_2 = d_1 - \sigma\sqrt{T} \tag{8.A.2.16}$$

where $N(d^*)$ is the cumulative normal distribution function for $(d^*)$. This function is frequently referred to in a statistics setting as the z-value for $(d^*)$. This solution to the Black-Scholes differential equation can be verified by finding the derivative of $c_0$ in the Black-Scholes model with respect to $t$. From a computational perspective, one would first work through Equation (8.A.2.15) and then Equation (8.A.2.16) before valuing the call with Equation (8.A.2.14).

CHAPTER

# 9

# Evaluating Trading Strategies and Performance

## 9.1 EVALUATING INVESTMENT PORTFOLIO PERFORMANCE

A goal of every investor is to find an investment system that generates large profits. An investment system is simply a security selection and combination strategy. Huge numbers of systems are used by investors, ranging from making purchase decisions based on moving averages to selling securities based on sunspot cycle theories. Many of these systems have made millions of dollars for investors. It should be noted that while perhaps each of these systems have worked well in the past, or at least have been lucky in the past, they might not perform well in the future. With thousands of investment systems in practice at any point in time, at least one might be expected to perform well over a period of time in any market, in as much as at least one out of thousands of randomly selected portfolios might be expected to perform well.

Among the simplest of investment systems is the simple buy and hold into a diversified portfolio strategy. A large randomly selected portfolio or index portfolio might be used as a benchmark portfolio for comparison of any other investment system. Proper evaluation of an investment system does require consideration of a number of factors and statistical concerns. Perhaps, the most important and difficult of these to account for is risk. One should note that higher-risk portfolios would be expected to generate higher returns over extended periods of time. Furthermore, the evaluator might also wish to account for investor risk preferences or objectives when evaluating an investment system.

One problem that we encounter when evaluating trading strategies and performance is separating the portfolio selection from the trading decisions. Many traders make both decisions simultaneously. In this section, we will focus first on the portfolio decision performance aspect of the trading decision, leaving trade execution aspects to later sections. The first step in the evaluation of portfolio decision performance is to measure the increase in asset or portfolio value relative to the initial asset value during a given time frame.

*Financial Trading and Investing*

These returns can then be adjusted by or compared to a relevant benchmark. In addition, the trader will want to evaluate the trading component of performance. This trading decision is often more difficult to evaluate than the overall portfolio performance.

## Computing Net Asset Value and Returns

Again, investment portfolio performance can be rather difficult to assess. First, standardization of performance measures and selection of benchmarks are crucial for evaluations and portfolio comparisons. In the case where we evaluate a hypothetical mutual fund, we begin by valuing its net assets at the end of a given trading period, typically at the end of a day, with $NAV_t$ computed as follows:

$$NAV_t = \frac{\text{Market value of assets minus liabilities at the end of time t}}{\text{\# Shares Outstanding at time t}} \tag{9.1}$$

Obviously, NAV depends more on the initial investment amount than on portfolio performance. Thus, it is useful to evaluate returns, which are NAV levels measured relative to initial investment amounts or prior NAV levels. If no capital is added or withdrawn from the fund between times $t-1$ and $t$, the fund's return $r_t$ for time $t$ is computed from the change in its NAV during the period $t$:

$$r_t = \frac{NAV_t - NAV_{t-1}}{NAV_{t-1}} \tag{9.2}$$

Equation 9.1 provides a one-year return for the portfolio. Now, let's consider the performance of a fund held for $n$ years. It will be convenient to express returns on an annual basis, as is the convention for most institutions. The measurement of a geometric mean annual return $r_g$ for a portfolio held for $n$ years is fairly straightforward when there are no funds added to or withdrawn from the portfolio:

$$\bar{r}_g = \sqrt[n]{\frac{NAV_n}{NAV_0}} - 1 \tag{9.3}$$

However, matters can become more complicated when the fund's investment base is changing. For example, fund investors might deposit and withdraw funds each day. When there is a cash flow $CF_t$ moving in (a deposit to the fund would be represented by a positive value) or out of the portfolio (such as a withdrawal or redemption) at the beginning of each time period $t$ for $n$ periods, one might measure the n-period return with a variation of the internal rate of return ($r$), solving the following for $r$:

$$NAV_n = NAV_0(1+r)^n - \sum_{t=1}^{n} CF_t(1+r)^{n-t} \tag{9.4}$$

A return computed in this manner is called a *dollar-weighted return*. For example, consider the case where a given cash flow ($CF_t$) was positive because the portfolio received a deposit from an investor. This increases the investment base of the portfolio, reducing the portfolio's return if no compensating increase in the terminal asset value ($NAV_n$) is realized. This dollar-weighted return accounts for the addition (or subtraction) of cash flows to (or from) the fund. However, it does not fully account for compounding of returns over time. Bear in mind that computing this dollar-weighted return can be time consuming because substitution is usually required to obtain r and there can be instances when more than one $r$ value will solve this equation.

A second method for computing a return, the *time-weighted average return*, requires periodic return computations each time a change to the investment base occurs:

$$\bar{r}_{g,p} = \sqrt[n]{\prod_{t=1}^{n}(1+r_t)} - 1 \tag{9.5}$$

where $r_t$, adjusted for dividends, is the fund return for a single period $t$ and $CF_t$ represents capital moving in (positive) or out of (negative) the fund at the start of each period $t$ for $n$ periods:

$$r_t = \frac{NAV_t - NAV_{t-1} + DIV_t - CF_t}{NAV_{t-1}} \tag{9.6}$$

Generally, the time-weighted return will be a more meaningful measure because the returns on funds initially deposited into the portfolio will not be affected by future deposits or withdrawals.

## Net Asset Value and Returns Illustration

In Table 9.1, we illustrate NAVs and returns for a hypothetical Fund A for each of 10 days starting on January 3, 2013. Note that January 4 is a Friday, and that the fund will not trade over the weekend of January 5 and 6. A three-day return is calculated for January 9; the returns for January 4, 5, and 6 will be −3.92%/3 or −1.31% each day.

On January 2, the fund initiates activities with a contribution of $10,000,000 by investors. No return is computed. On January 3, the fund realizes $200,000 in trading profits, increasing its total assets to $10,200,000, yielding a return of 2.00% for the day. On January 4, the fund incurred $400,000 in trading losses, ending the day with $9,800,000 in total assets, $9.8 in NAV and a return of −3.92% for the day, or −1.31% for Friday, Saturday, and Sunday. Trading profits for January 7 were $200,000; the return was 2%. On January 8, the fund realized $200,000 in trading profits, but paid a dividend of $200,000. NAV remained constant at $10.00 because the trading profits exactly offset the dividends. The return for the day was 2%. On January 9, the fund realized trading profits of $200,000, and investors redeemed 19,608 shares at a value of $10.20 for a total of $200,000. This withdrawal did not affect NAV or returns. On January 10, investors purchased 19,037 shares for $10.51 each, totaling $200,000, which combined with trading profits of $300,000 increasing total assets to $10,500,000. The investor contributions to the fund did not affect its 3% return for the day. On January 11, investor share purchases exceeded share redemptions by 9,703. Trading losses for the day totaled $200,000, producing a return of −1.9%. The time-weighted average return for the fund is computed as follows:

$$\bar{r}_{g,p} = \sqrt[n]{\prod_{t=1}^{n}(1+r_t)} - 1 = \sqrt[9]{(1.02)(.9969)^3(1.0204)(1.02)(1.02)(1.03)(.981)} - 1 = .0056$$

One minor note: The average daily weekend return of −1.31% was computed as an arithmetic average; had it been computed as a geometric mean, it would have been −1.325%.

**TABLE 9.1** Net Asset Value and Return Calculations

| Date | Investor Contributions | Investor Withdrawals | Fund Dividends | Total Assets | Number of Shares | *NAVt* | $r_t$ |
|---|---|---|---|---|---|---|---|
| 1/2/2013 | 10,000,000 | 0 | 0 | 10,000,000 | 1,000,000 | 10.00 | N/A |
| 1/3/2013 | 0 | 0 | 0 | 10,200,000 | 1,000,000 | 10.20 | 2.00% |
| 1/4/2013 | 0 | 0 | 0 | 9,800,000 | 1,000,000 | 9.80 | −3.92% |
| 1/7/2013 | 0 | 0 | 0 | 10,000,000 | 1,000,000 | 10.00 | 2.04% |
| 1/8/2013 | 0 | 0 | 200,000 | 10,000,000 | 1,000,000 | 10.00 | 2.00% |
| 1/9/2013 | 0 | 200,000 | 0 | 10,000,000 | 980,392 | 10.20 | 2.00% |
| 1/10/2013 | 200,000 | 0 | 0 | 10,500,000 | 999,429 | 10.51 | 3.00% |
| 1/11/2013 | 300,000 | 200,000 | 0 | 10,400,000 | 1,009,132 | 10.31 | −1.90% |

## Portfolio Benchmarking

Higher returns are generally associated with higher risk. Proper risk-adjusted benchmarks for comparison need to be established when evaluating portfolio returns. Portfolio risk can be measured by portfolio standard deviation $\sigma_p$. This portfolio standard deviation measures the risk of the portfolio as a function of the risk levels of individual securities, the investment proportions in the individual securities, and the level of diversification of the portfolio. Portfolio risk can also be measured by the sensitivity of the portfolio's return to returns on the market portfolio, captured by the portfolio's beta, $\beta_p$, a measure of undiversifiable risk as per the capital asset pricing model (CAPM).[1] The following are three well-known risk adjusted measures for portfolio performance evaluation (see Elton et al., 2010):

$$S_p = \frac{r_p - r_f}{\sigma_p} \qquad T_p = \frac{r_p - r_f}{\beta_p}$$

*Sharpe ratio* *Treynor ratio*

$$\textit{Jensen measure: } J_p = [r_p - r_f] - [\beta_p(r_m - r_f)]$$

The *Sharpe and Treynor ratios* calculate the portfolio's reward to risk ratio, as a function of overall portfolio risk and as a function of portfolio sensitivity to the market. The *Jensen measure* (Jensen, 1968) is often referred to as the portfolio alpha. Alpha

[1]A security beta, $\beta_i$ or portfolio beta, $\beta_p$, can be computed as the slope term from a simple OLS regression of risk premiums on the security $(r_i - r_f)$ or portfolio $(r_p - r_f)$ against risk premiums of the market $(r_m - r_f)$. See text Appendix section A.1 for a brief review of the simple OLS.

measures the excess return of a portfolio beyond the time value of money and risk. A host of other measures have been described in the public literature, including the Sortino coefficient (Sortino, 1996) and the M-square measure (Modigliani and Modigliani, 1997).

However, each of these measures has difficulties in addition to the proper computation of returns. For example, what exactly is the riskless rate of return for a given period? Analysts often use the six-month Treasury bill rate as a proxy, but what if the investor has a much longer investment horizon? The Jensen and Treynor measures require computation of market portfolio returns. What is the appropriate index for the market? Roll (1977) shows that different indices (even if highly correlated) will lead to very different performance rankings. Note that the Sharpe ratio does not require a market proxy. Once returns have been computed, exactly how are portfolio betas computed? This may be a significant problem, given that the composition of the portfolio is likely to constantly be in transition. Should portfolio beta be computed as a "time-weighted" average of individual security betas, or based on historical portfolio returns?

The following represent additional issues for investment institutions regarding the difficulties of using the above risk-adjusted portfolio performance measures:

1. Given that portfolio managers change jobs rather frequently, is it reasonable to measure fund performance rather than manager performance?
2. How frequently are we able to obtain enough data to obtain statistically significant measures of performance?
3. The CAPM, a model that decomposes return into compensation for time value of money and compensation for risk, serves as the basis for the Treynor and Jensen measures:

$$\text{CAPM: } E[r_p] = r_f + [\beta_p(r_m - r_f)]$$

   where $E[r_p]$, $r_f$, and $r_m$ are the expected return on the portfolio, the riskless Treasury bill, and the market as a whole. However, the CAPM is only a single-time-period model. Multiple time periods and multiple cash flows cause problems in its application. In addition, many analysts will be concerned about the many assumptions that underlie the CAPM, as well as certain statistical tests that cast doubt on the empirical validity of the CAPM.
4. Investors holding funds representing only market segments might find that any measure based on the CAPM is inappropriate.
5. The Sharpe ratio will understate portfolio performance of undiversified portfolios in a setting where investors, in sum, hold numerous undiversified portfolios. That is, much of the risk captured in the Sharpe ratio can be diversified away.
6. Errors in computing returns will bias measured betas downwards and will "slop" over into unsystematic variances (the part of risk that is unrelated to the market). Even seemingly minor problems can significantly bias beta measures.
   However, reasonably good correction procedures for betas measured with error do exist.

## Portfolio Performance Benchmarking Illustration

Here, we will use the Jensen alpha measure to evaluate the performance of a portfolio:

$$J_p = \alpha_p = [r_p - r_f] - [\beta_p(r_m - r_f)]$$

Presumably, a positive alpha ($\alpha_p$) that is statistically significant will indicate that the portfolio outperforms the market on a risk-adjusted basis. Consider Table 9.2, which records returns over a 20-year period for a hypothetical portfolio ($p$) and the market along with riskless return rates.

To compute the Jensen alpha measure, we first convert returns to risk premiums by subtracting riskless rates from returns on the portfolio and the market. We then run a regression of portfolio risk premiums against market risk premiums. The following represent the regression results and diagnostics:

$$[r_{p,t} - r_{f,t}] = \alpha_p + \beta_p(r_{m,t} - r_{f,t}) + e_t = \underset{(8.5056)}{0.073509} + \underset{(10.7452)}{0.951512}(r_{m,t} - r_{f,t}) + e_t \quad r\text{-squared} = 0.865127 \quad \text{d.f.} = 18$$

The regression $t$-statistics are reported in parentheses below the regression coefficients. First, we can conclude that the portfolio beta (0.951512) is statistically significant at the 1% level. The portfolio has slightly less systemic (market-related) risk than the market itself. The $r$-squared value suggests that slightly more than 86% of this fund's risk premiums are driven by market risk premiums. But most importantly, we can conclude that Jensen's alpha is positive and statistically significant at the 1% level. Thus, the fund outperformed the market on a risk-adjusted basis for the reported period. Although we have concluded statistical significance for alpha, we should question the relevance of data as old as 20 years to evaluation of current fund management. Figure 9.1 provides a pictorial display of our results.

**TABLE 9.2** Portfolio p and Market Performance

| Year | $r_p$ | $r_m$ | $r_f$ | $r_p - r_f$ | $r_m - r_f$ | Year | $r_p$ | $r_m$ | $r_f$ | $r_p - r_f$ | $r_m - r_f$ |
|---|---|---|---|---|---|---|---|---|---|---|---|
| 1991 | 0.14 | 0.05 | 0.03 | 0.11 | 0.02 | 2001 | 0.11 | 0.07 | 0.05 | 0.06 | 0.02 |
| 1992 | 0.11 | 0.03 | 0.02 | 0.09 | 0.01 | 2002 | 0.22 | 0.17 | 0.06 | 0.16 | 0.11 |
| 1993 | 0.04 | 0.01 | 0.02 | 0.02 | 0.03 | 2003 | 0.22 | 0.16 | 0.07 | 0.15 | 0.09 |
| 1994 | 0.16 | 0.11 | 0.03 | 0.13 | 0.08 | 2004 | −0.01 | −0.05 | 0.06 | −0.07 | −0.11 |
| 1995 | 0.03 | −0.12 | 0.02 | 0.01 | −0.14 | 2005 | 0.04 | −0.08 | 0.05 | −0.01 | −0.13 |
| 1996 | 0.14 | 0.09 | 0.03 | 0.11 | 0.06 | 2006 | 0.28 | 0.21 | 0.06 | 0.22 | 0.15 |
| 1997 | 0.26 | 0.13 | 0.04 | 0.22 | 0.09 | 2007 | 0.22 | 0.11 | 0.07 | 0.15 | 0.04 |
| 1998 | 0.26 | 0.18 | 0.05 | 0.21 | 0.13 | 2008 | 0.21 | 0.11 | 0.08 | 0.13 | 0.03 |
| 1999 | 0.13 | 0.04 | 0.05 | 0.08 | −0.01 | 2009 | −0.04 | −0.11 | 0.07 | −0.11 | −0.18 |
| 2000 | −0.08 | −0.11 | 0.04 | −0.12 | −0.15 | 2010 | 0.18 | 0.12 | 0.05 | 0.13 | 0.07 |

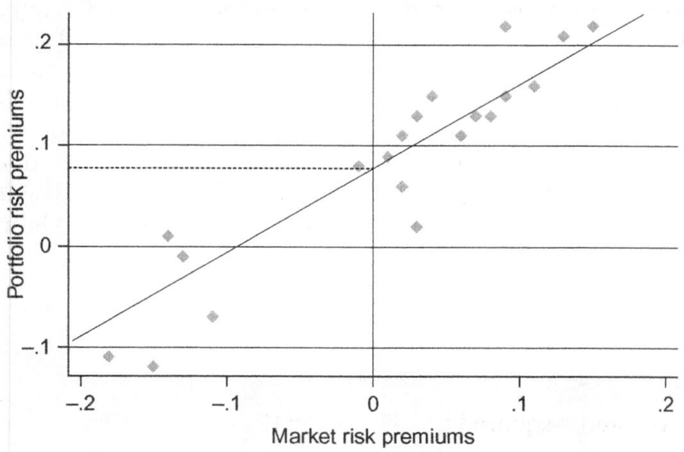


FIGURE 9.1 Jensen's alpha scatter diagram.

## 9.2 MARKET TIMING VERSUS SELECTION

Why might an investment portfolio earn consistently exceptional returns? First, higher risk portfolios tend to earn higher returns. This is why we benchmarked portfolios in the previous section. Second, strong portfolio performance might be due to simple luck. This is why we attempt to examine performance over many time periods and examine the statistical significance of our indicators. If an investment portfolio consistently earns higher than normal returns, it is useful to understand why. An important step in this process is to distinguish between skill at "security selection" versus "market timing skill." Suppose, for example, an analyst is able to discern the future direction of the market. In periods before anticipated market upswings, the analyst should recommend increasing the beta of her portfolio to exploit this upswing. In the case of an anticipated market downturn, the analyst should recommend decreasing the beta of the portfolio.

### The Quadratic Variable Approach

The CAPM concludes that there is a linear relationship between the risk premiums of well-diversified portfolios and risk premiums of the market portfolio, as in Figure 9.1. However, investors who correctly time the marker will shift their portfolios to lower betas during market downturns, shifting returns to be closer to the riskless rate. During market upturns, investors with strong timing ability will increase portfolio betas. Thus, for investors with strong market timing ability, the relationship between portfolio risk premiums and market risk premiums will be concave up.

We return to our portfolio and market data from Table 9.2 in the previous section. We create an additional column for $(r_{m,t} - r_{f,t})^2$, which will serve as a second explanatory variable (see Treynor and Mazuy, 1966). This new testing variable accounts for the concave up relationship between portfolio and market risk premiums that strong timers will observe. We now run a multiple regression to examine $[r_{p,t} - r_{f,t}]$ relative to $(r_{m,t} - r_{f,t})$ and $(r_{m,t} - r_{f,t})^2$. Our coefficient $\gamma_p$ for $(r_{m,t} - r_{f,t})^2$ reflects timing ability on the part of the manager. A positive coefficient $\gamma_p$ reflects the extent to which the manager shifts portfolios to reduce betas during periods of low market returns and the extent to which managers shift portfolio weights to increase beta during periods of high market returns. Since $\gamma_p$ below is not statistically significant, this manager does not exhibit significant market timing ability. However, because Jansen's alpha is still positive and statistically significant, we conclude that this portfolio manager exhibits portfolio timing ability.

$$\begin{aligned} r_{p,t} - r_{f,t} &= \alpha_p + \beta_p(r_{m,t} - r_{f,t}) + \gamma_p(r_{m,t} - r_{f,t})^2 + e_t \\ &= \underset{(5.158)}{0.0713} + \underset{(9.472)}{0.9605}(r_{m,t} - r_{f,t}) + \underset{(0.201)}{0.2148}(r_{m,t} - r_{f,t})^2 + e_t \end{aligned}$$

Multiple adjusted $r$-squared = 0.85 d.f. = 17

Consider a second portfolio $q$ with returns given in Table 9.3. Market returns and riskless rates are identical; however, we will see that returns for this second portfolio reflect beta shifting in particularly strong and weak markets. A similar quadratic regression is run for this second portfolio to check for this apparent timing ability, and results reveal significant timing ability. The plot for the second regression is pictured in Figure 9.2. Regression parameters are given by the following equation:

$$\begin{aligned} r_{q,t} - r_{f,t} &= \alpha_q + \beta_q(r_{m,t} - r_{f,t}) + \gamma_q(r_{m,t} - r_{f,t})^2 + e_t \\ &= \underset{(4.350)}{0.0580} + \underset{(10.230)}{1.0004}(r_{m,t} - r_{f,t}) + \underset{(1.990)}{2.0425}(r_{m,f} - r_{f,t})^2 + e_t \end{aligned}$$

Multiple adjusted $r$-squared = 0.85 d.f. = 17

**TABLE 9.3** Portfolio $q$ and Market Performance

| Year | $R_q$ | $R_m$ | $r_f$ | $R_q - r_f$ | $R_m - r_f$ | Year | $R_q$ | $R_m$ | $r_f$ | $R_q - r_f$ | $R_m - r_f$ |
|---|---|---|---|---|---|---|---|---|---|---|---|
| 1991 | 0.14 | 0.05 | 0.03 | 0.11 | 0.02 | 2001 | 0.11 | 0.07 | 0.05 | 0.06 | 0.02 |
| 1992 | 0.05 | 0.03 | 0.02 | 0.03 | 0.01 | 2002 | 0.22 | 0.17 | 0.06 | 0.16 | 0.11 |
| 1993 | 0.04 | 0.01 | 0.02 | 0.02 | 0.03 | 2003 | 0.22 | 0.16 | 0.07 | 0.15 | 0.09 |
| 1994 | 0.16 | 0.11 | 0.03 | 0.13 | 0.08 | 2004 | −0.01 | −0.05 | 0.06 | −0.07 | −0.11 |
| 1995 | 0.03 | −0.12 | 0.02 | 0.01 | −0.14 | 2005 | 0.04 | −0.08 | 0.05 | −0.01 | −0.13 |
| 1996 | 0.14 | 0.09 | 0.03 | 0.11 | 0.06 | 2006 | 0.34 | 0.21 | 0.06 | 0.28 | 0.15 |
| 1997 | 0.26 | 0.13 | 0.04 | 0.22 | 0.09 | 2007 | 0.22 | 0.11 | 0.07 | 0.15 | 0.04 |
| 1998 | 0.26 | 0.18 | 0.05 | 0.21 | 0.13 | 2008 | 0.21 | 0.11 | 0.08 | 0.13 | 0.03 |
| 1999 | 0.13 | 0.04 | 0.05 | 0.08 | −0.01 | 2009 | −0.01 | −0.11 | 0.07 | −0.08 | −0.18 |
| 2000 | −0.02 | −0.11 | 0.04 | −0.06 | −0.15 | 2010 | 0.18 | 0.12 | 0.05 | 0.13 | 0.07 |

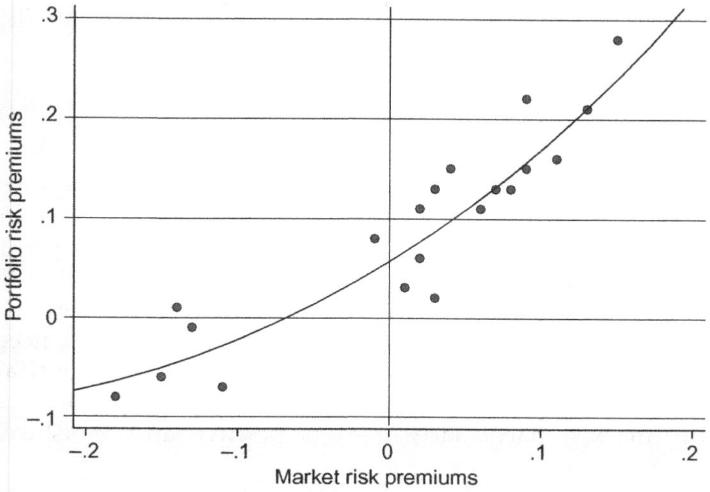


**FIGURE 9.2** Jensen's alpha and timing ability.

Coefficients $\alpha_q$ and $\beta_q$ are statistically significant at the 1% level and coefficient $\gamma_q$ is significant at the 6% level. Thus, portfolio q reflects superior overall performance ($\alpha_q = 0.0580$) and likely superior timing ability ($\gamma_q = 2.0425 > 0$). The upward concavity of the relationship between $(r_{q,t} - r_{f,t})$ and $(r_{m,t} - r_{f,t})$ suggests that the investor tends to shift her portfolio beta down (and portfolio returns up towards the riskless return rate) in weak markets, and that she tends to shift her portfolio beta up (and portfolio returns up further away from the riskless return rate) in strong markets. However, in a quadratic regression such as this, the analyst needs to be careful about interpreting $\alpha_q$. For example, a negative or statistically insignificant $\alpha_q$ in this quadratic regression should not be interpreted to imply investment performance inferior to or on par with the market, particularly if $\gamma_q$ is positive and statistically significant.

## The Dummy Variable Approach

An alternative indicator of market timing is based on a regression including an interaction term, which is a combination of a dummy variable $D$ (takes on a value of 0 or 1) and market risk premiums:

$$r_{q,t} - r_{f,t} = \alpha_q + \beta_q(r_{m,t} - r_{f,t}) + \gamma_q D(r_{m,t} - r_{f,t}) + e_t$$

$$\text{where:}\quad \text{If } (r_{mt} - r_{ft}) \geq 0,\ D = 0$$

$$\text{If } (r_{mt} - r_{ft}) < 0,\ D = 1$$

Thus, if the market return equals or exceeds the riskless return, $\beta_q$ is the portfolio beta; that is, $\beta_q$ can be taken to be the up-market beta. If the market return is less than the riskless return, $\beta_q - \gamma_q$ can be taken to be the portfolio beta; that is, $\beta_q - \gamma_q$ is the down-market beta. The portfolio's shift in beta is $\gamma_q$, so that a negative and statistically significant $\gamma_q$ is indicative of market timing ability. For our numerical illustration for portfolio $q$, multiple regression results are reported as follows:

$$R_{q,t} - r_{f,t} = \alpha_q + \beta_q(r_{m,t} - r_{f,t}) + \gamma_q D(r_{m,t} - r_{f,t}) + e_t$$

$$\begin{aligned} &= \underset{(2.931)}{0.050} + \underset{(5.853)}{1.311}(r_{m,t} - r_{f,t}) - \underset{(-1.928)}{0.672}D(r_{m,t} - r_{f,t}) + e_t \end{aligned}$$

Coefficients $\alpha_q$ and $\beta_q$ once again are statistically significant at the 1% level and coefficient $\gamma_q$ is significant at the 6% level. Thus, portfolio $q$ reflects superior overall performance ($\alpha_q = 0.050$) and likely superior timing ability ($\gamma_q = -0.672 < 0$). It appears that the portfolio manager shifts the beta of her portfolio down by 0.672 in down markets relative to up markets. Again in this regression with the interactive term, the analyst needs to be careful about interpreting $\alpha_q$. For example, a negative or statistically insignificant $\alpha_q$ in this type of regression should not be interpreted to imply investment performance inferior to or on par with the market, particularly if $\gamma_q$ is positive and statistically significant.

## 9.3 TRADE EVALUATION AND VOLUME-WEIGHTED AVERAGE PRICE

The tools that we discussed in the previous two sections are particularly appropriate for evaluating portfolios and portfolio strategies over longer periods of time. Their focus is on overall portfolio performance, without distinguishing the trading aspect of the investment decision from the selection and timing aspects. Evaluating trader performance independently of portfolio performance is important for trading firms, portfolio managers, funds, and other financial institutions. Unfortunately, evaluating trader performance is not a simple task. The trading decision is different from the investing or portfolio management decision, and needs to be evaluated accordingly. We discussed portfolio benchmarking earlier; here, we discuss trade benchmarking. Trade benchmarking is generally based on comparing a trade or series of trades against the hypothetical results of a series of trades based on a specific or benchmark strategy.

Traders are expected to seek the "best execution" for their transactions. But what is best execution? As we discussed earlier in the book, this concept is rather vague. The Chartered Financial Analyst (CFA) Institute's trade-management guidelines (CFA, 2004) characterize best execution "as the trading process firms apply that seeks to maximize the value of a client's portfolio within the client's stated investment objectives and constraints." Obviously, this characterization is ambiguous and difficult to quantify and its complexity leads to many problems. More generally, deciding on an appropriate evaluation metric or benchmarking strategy is a difficult decision. Many firms use one or more of the following:

- *Volume-Weighted Average Price* (VWAP, introduced by Berkowitz et al., 1988): Calculated by dividing the dollar volume of trading in a stock by the share volume over a given period of time, typically one day.

- *Arrival Price*: The midpoint of the bid–offer spread at the time the order is received (bid-ask midpoint or BAM). See also Section 5.4, Adverse Selection and the Spread.
- *Market-on-Close* (MOC): The last price obtained by a trader at the end of the day relative to the last price reported by the exchange.
- *Implementation shortfall*: The performance difference between the hypothetical profits realized by a paper or theoretical portfolio replicating an actual portfolio ignoring friction costs and the profits realized by the actual portfolio.

## VWAP

VWAP, introduced by Berkowitz et al. (1988) and popularized by the trading consulting firm Abel/Noser, is the most commonly used of the trading evaluation metrics and benchmarks. VWAP is the average price at which a stock trades in a given period, weighted by the volume traded at each price. Suppose that a customer engaged a broker to purchase a large number of shares. Since the customer has already made the decision to invest in the shares, the broker should be evaluated only on the trade execution. VWAP can be used as a benchmark to evaluate the quality of the execution provided by the broker. If the brokerage firm's purchases were made at a lower VWAP than the market VWAP for the relevant period, we might infer that the firm handled the order well for the customer. VWAP, either for the trader or for the market, is calculated as follows:

$$VWAP = \frac{\sum_j Q_j P_j}{\sum_j Q_j} \tag{9.7}$$

where $Q_j$ represents the number of shares executed in a given order $j$ at a price of $P_j$. Thus, VWAP is the transaction execution average price of over a given period of time. While VWAP is usually computed for the day of the trade, sometimes traders use multiday VWAP. This is likely when orders broken up for execution over several days. In addition, intraday VWAPs can be used for orders executed entirely within a given trading day or some portion thereof. A trader (broker) might be regarded to have abnormal trading performance if she can consistently beat the market or other relevant VWAP on her trades.

One criticism of VWAP cost is that trader's own trades will be included in the benchmark price. This is corrected by excluding from VWAP the trader's own transactions, although it can cause problems when the trader's own trades account for a significant portion of the total. Suppose, for example, that the trader was counterparty to all security trades for that period. Obviously, VWAP would not be useful. But, this issue can arise whenever any illiquid security is being traded. One problem with performance evaluation based on daily VWAP benchmarks is that this benchmark can encourage traders to spread their trades out over the day simply avoid the risk of trading at the high or low prices for the day.

VWAP is quick and easy to compute, understand, and compare. This simplicity is VWAP's main strength. In addition, VWAP is also useful for securities that trade in different markets. However, VWAP becomes less meaningful when the security's price trends up or down over the course of the trading period. In addition, VWAP does not account for costs related to trade delays, trade cancellations or failures to execute trades. In fact, VWAP is not useful when completing the transaction immediately is urgent. An immediate execution requirement does not allow the trader any discretion on which to be evaluated. Nor does VWAP account for slippage, the trader's price impact on the security. Executing a large transaction at once can certainly impact the security price, but this impact will not necessarily adversely affect the broker's apparent performance against VWAP. In fact, a trader might even be able to manipulate this price impact and VWAP by increasing the volume of his trades along with the impact on VWAP.

Traders can practically always match VWAP by merely executing their transactions at the same prices and with the same proportional shifts in volume as the market over the transaction period. Forecasting volume is important for traders benchmarking against VWAP. For example, in U.S. markets, stock trade volume tends to be higher earlier in the morning and later in the afternoon sessions with lower volumes around midday. In European markets, volumes tend increase in afternoon hours when U.S. markets are open.

## VWAP: A Simple Illustration

Suppose that a broker has been instructed to purchase 600 shares at the market. She does so, purchasing them for a total price of 30,011. Market transactions over the security's intraday execution period are listed in Table 9.4. The broker's executed transactions were the second through fourth transactions in the table. The total volume of shares exchanged was 2500, with a total value of 125,098. Hence, VWAP for these transactions was 125,098/2500 = 50.0392. The broker purchased 100 shares in the second transaction at \$50.01, 400 shares in the third transaction at \$50.02, and 100 shares in the fourth transaction at \$50.02. The average share price paid by the broker was 30,011/600 = 50.0183. Our calculations suggest that the broker beat the market VWAP. However, note that she did so by purchasing early or quickly in a rising market.

**TABLE 9.4** Price and Volume for VWAP Calculations

| Price (\$) | Volume | $P \times Q$ |
|---|---|---|
| 50.01 | 200 | 10002 |
| 50.01 | 100 | 5001 |
| 50.02 | 400 | 20008 |
| 50.02 | 100 | 5002 |
| 50.03 | 200 | 10006 |
| 50.05 | 600 | 30030 |
| 50.06 | 400 | 20024 |
| 50.05 | 500 | 25025 |
| Totals | 2500 | 125098 |

## 9.4 IMPLEMENTATION SHORTFALL

A trader or portfolio manager makes a decision to buy or sell a security based on its current price, referred to here as its decision price. In many instances, the broker might treat this decision price as the arrival price (e.g., bid/ask midpoint), the price of the security when the broker receives the order. However, the actual implementation of an investment strategy by the trader or portfolio manager leads to four primary types of friction costs:

1. Broker, exchange, and other explicit fees and commissions. Frequently, brokers bundle exchange, SEC, and other fees into their own commissions. Small transactions tend to have higher proportional explicit transactions costs.
2. Delay costs, based on the price difference between the portfolio manager's decision price and the broker's arrival price.
3. Price impact costs associated with transaction executions (slippage). Buy orders will exert upward price pressure on the security; sell orders will exert downward pressure. Larger transactions will tend to have larger impact costs.
4. Opportunity costs associated with transactions; that is, the opportunities and profits were forgone prior to the trade's completed execution. Opportunity costs can also include the portion of an order that was canceled due to a limit order restriction.

To an extent, the costs of market impact, which increase as the execution speed of the transaction increases, balances against opportunity costs, which increase as complete execution of the transaction is delayed. When paper portfolios are created for back-testing and other purposes, prices for transactions are taken from actual bid and offer quotations or from actual transactions taken from market data. These paper transactions do not normally include the costs of implementing the portfolio strategies. *Implementation shortfall* is the performance difference between the hypothetical profits realized by a paper or theoretical portfolio replicating an actual portfolio ignoring friction costs and the profits realized by the actual portfolio. That is, implementation shortfall is the difference between the decision or order arrival price and the realized price of the execution, including broker and exchange fees, slippage, and transaction opportunity costs.

### Illustration: Implementation Shortfall

Suppose that a portfolio manager makes a decision to purchase 10,000 shares of stock one hour before its open based on its $50.00 closing price the prior day (the decision price) and places a limit order at 50.45. The stock opened at 9:30 at a price of 50.20, and 1000 shares are purchased at 9:31 at a price of 50.25. At 9:32, 5000 shares are purchased for 50.40, and 1000 more for 50.30 at 10:03. An additional 1000 shares are purchased for 50.30 at 12:15, the market price quickly rises to 50.48 and closes at 50.50 with 2000 shares in the order unexecuted. These transactions are represented in Table 9.5. The commissions, including all explicit fees, were $0.01 for each of 8,000 shares.

The total implementation cost is $3,830. First, the delay to the first execution cost 0.25 per share, affecting all 10,000 shares. The 10:03 transaction had additional per share opportunity

**TABLE 9.5** Implementation Shortfall Executions

| $t$ | Volume | $Price_t$ |
|---|---|---|
| Close | | 50.00 |
| Open | | 50.20 |
| 9:31 | 1000 | 50.25 |
| 9:32 | 5000 | 50.40 |
| 10:03 | 1000 | 50.30 |
| 12:15 | 1000 | 50.35 |
| Close | | 50.50 |

**TABLE 9.6** Implementation Shortfall

| | |
|---|---|
| Commissions | 80 |
| Delay cost | 2500 |
| Price Impact | 1250 |
| Opportunity costs | 900 |
| Total costs | 4730 |

costs of 0.05, and the 12:15 transaction had additional opportunity costs of \$0.10 per share, for a total of \$150. The transaction executed at 9:32 was particularly large and seemed to exert upward price pressure. Potential price pressure is ignored on other transactions because it did not seem pronounced. The price impact cost of this transaction might be estimated at $5000 \cdot (50.40 - 50.25) = \$750$. Finally, 2000 shares failed to execute, with a "virtual" opportunity cost of $2000 \times (50.50 - 50.00 - 0.25) = \$500$, where 0.25 is the associated delay cost already accounted for. Thus, Table 9.6 sums the implementation shortfall of the executions. This breakdown of the explicit and implicit implementation costs illustrates the typical magnitude of the implicit costs relative to the explicit transaction costs.

## 9.5 VALUE AT RISK

Value at risk (VaR) is a standard tool for risk management in financial institutions. It measures the worst loss for a given time frame, with a given set of distributional assumptions at a given confidence level. Thus, for example, if asset values are distributed normally with a given variance, the analyst can calculate a "worst case scenario" at a given confidence level, typically 95% or 99%. For example, for a confidence level of $\alpha = 99\%$, one can be 99% certain that at the end of the given risk horizon there will be no greater loss than just the VaR—as long as the model's assumptions hold true. Thus, the *VaR model* concerns the probability that a loss of a given size will not be exceeded over a given period of time:

$$VaR = Asset\ Value \times Daily\ Return\ Standard\ Deviation \times Confidence\ Interval\ Factor \times the\ Square\ Root\ of\ Time \quad (9.8)$$

$$VaR = Asset\ Value \times \sigma \times z \times \sqrt{t}$$

Asset value is the total value of the institution, or its relevant unit, which might even be the portfolio of a single trader or desk. The daily (or some other time interval) return standard deviation applies to this asset value, the confidence interval factor represents the maximum acceptable probability that this loss will be exceeded (typically a z-value such as 1% from a normal distribution), and time is measured in days or some other period. Suppose a bank with $1 billion in its derivative asset portfolio experiences a 0.5% standard deviation in its normally distributed daily returns. The one-tailed z-value corresponding with the 1% confidence interval is 2.326. The bank seeks to determine the size of a loss that has a 1% probability of being incurred over a five-day week:

$$\text{VaR} = \$1{,}000{,}000{,}000 \times 0.005 \times 2.326 \times \sqrt{5} = \$26{,}005{,}471$$

Thus, assuming that daily asset returns are normally distributed (this is an extremely important assumption) with a standard deviation of 0.005, there is a 1% probability that the bank will experience a loss exceeding $26,005,471. While this figure is fairly small compared to the total asset level, its importance is enhanced by the bank's borrowing levels. For example, if the bank were 30-to-1 debt financed, its initial equity level would be $33,333,333, and this loss would wipe out almost 80% of the bank's equity stake. Thus, if bank profits are normally distributed, 99% of the time, losses realized by the institution will be less than the computed five-day VAR figure. However, if the bank's profits were not normally distributed as assumed, but instead were subject to a distribution with more extreme observations than implied by normal distributions (fat tails), equity capital might have a significantly higher probability of being wiped out after five days.

Calculating, using, and interpreting VaR for a single asset with a known volatility and normal distribution of returns is fairly straightforward. As we will demonstrate shortly, the same is true for a portfolio of similarly "well-behaved" assets. However, portfolios of derivative securities or significantly different assets can be more of a problem. For example, the returns of put and call options are not normally distributed. Calculating VaR for a larger mix of options, even on a single security, can be quite difficult. Some traders will focus on deltas and gammas of portfolio components, but even these are problematic when underlying security variances are large. Recall from Chapter 8 that the "Greeks" only apply when underlying security price changes are small. But changes required to be consistent with 95% or 99% confidence intervals are normally large. In such instances, VaR calculations can be facilitated with the use of Monte-Carlo simulations. Again, as we alluded to above, working with appropriate and realistic distributions is essential to interpreting VaR.

**TABLE 9.7** Portfolio Weights and Security Characteristics

| $i$ | $w_i$ | $\sigma_i$ | $\sigma_{1,i}$ | $\sigma_{2,i}$ | $\sigma_{3,i}$ |
|---|---|---|---|---|---|
| 1 | 0.20 | 0.20 | 0.04 | 0.01 | 0.02 |
| 2 | 0.50 | 0.40 | 0.01 | 0.16 | 0.04 |
| 3 | 0.30 | 0.60 | 0.02 | 0.04 | 0.36 |

## Equity Portfolio VaR: Illustration

Here, we illustrate a simple VaR calculation for an equity portfolio made up of three stocks. For sake of simplicity, we will assume that portfolio returns are normally distributed. The trader has "borrowed" \$900,000 from his employer and invested \$100,000 of his "own" money, for a total of \$1,000,000. This trader's employer requires that the trader's one-week portfolio VaR not exceed his trading capital of \$100,000, with a 99% degree of confidence. We will examine the trader's portfolio and its three component stocks to determine whether he is within his risk limits.

Table 9.7 lists the three securities, 1, 2, and 3, along with their portfolio weights, annualized return variances, and covariances with each other. We calculate the portfolio variance with Equation (9.9), (9.10), or (9.11). We find that portfolio variance equals 0.0904, and its standard deviation of returns is 0.3. Weekly VaR is calculated with Equation 9.8 within a 99% confidence interval, using a "z" value of 2.236, and $t = \sqrt{1/52}$ years. This VaR calculation suggests that the trader's portfolio does lie within his 99% confidence interval VaR risk limits for one week.

$$\sigma_p^2 = \sum_{i=1}^{n}\sum_{j=1}^{n} w_i\, w_j\, \sigma_{ij} \tag{9.9}$$

$$\begin{aligned}\sigma_p^2 &= (w_1^2 \cdot \sigma_1^2) + (w_2^2 \cdot \sigma_2^2) + (w_3^2 \cdot \sigma_3^2) + 2(w_1 \cdot w_2 \cdot \sigma_{1,2}) + 2(w_1 \cdot w_3 \cdot \sigma_{1,3}) + 2(w_2 \cdot w_3 \cdot \sigma_{2,3}) \\ &= (.04 \cdot .04) + (.25 \cdot .16)(.09 \cdot .36) + 2(.2 \cdot .5 \cdot .01) + 2(.2 \cdot .3 \cdot .02) + 2(.5 \cdot .3 \cdot .04) = .0904\end{aligned} \tag{9.10}$$

$$\sigma_p^2 = [w_1 \quad w_2 \quad w_3]\begin{bmatrix}\sigma_1^2 & \sigma_{1,2} & \sigma_{1,3}\\ \sigma_{2,1} & \sigma_2^2 & \sigma_{2,3}\\ \sigma_{3,1} & \sigma_{3,2} & \sigma_3^2\end{bmatrix}\begin{bmatrix}w_1\\ w_2\\ w_3\end{bmatrix} = [.2 \quad .5 \quad .3]\begin{bmatrix}.04 & .01 & .02\\ .01 & .16 & .04\\ .02 & .04 & .36\end{bmatrix}\begin{bmatrix}.2\\ .5\\ .3\end{bmatrix} = .0904 \tag{9.11}$$

$$VaR = Asset\ Value \times \sigma \times z\sqrt{t} = \$1{,}000{,}000 \times \sqrt{.0904} \times 2.326 \cdot \sqrt{1/52} = \$96{,}996.84$$

## Additional Reading

The CFA Institute's (2004) *Trade Management Guidelines* is helpful for better understanding of the ambiguous concept of "best execution," and the need for and how to establish trade execution policies, disclosures, and record-keeping. In addition, issues related to trade performance have appeared on recent CFA Level III exams. The portfolio management textbook by Elton et al. (2010) provides an excellent introduction to portfolio evaluation techniques in chapter 25. Perold (1988) provides a readable practitioner-oriented introduction to implementation shortfall, and Hasbrouck (2007) discusses implementation shortfall and trading costs in chapters 14 and 15. Jorion (1997) is a standard introduction to VaR. Harris (2003) offers excellent reading on transaction costs and performance evaluation in chapters 21 and 22. Wagner (2008) wrote a highly readable account of his personal experiences as a consultant in performance evaluation and with transaction costs.

## References


Berkowitz, S. A., Logue, D. E., & Noser, E. A. (1988). The total costs of transacting on the NYSE. *Journal of Finance, 43*, 97–112.

CFA Institute. (2004). *Trade management guidelines*. Available at: <http://www.cfapubs.org/doi/pdf/10.2469/ccb.v2004.n3.4007> Accessed 25.03.11.

Elton, E., Gruber, M., Brown, S., & Goetzman, W. (2010). *Modern portfolio theory and investment analysis* (8th ed.). New York: John Wiley.

Hasbrouck, J. (2007). *Empirical market microstructure: The institutions, economics and econometrics of securities trading*. New York: Oxford University Press.

Jensen, M. (1968). The performance of mutual funds in the period 1945–1964. *Journal of Finance, 23*(2), 389–416.

Jorion, P. (1997). *Value at Risk*. Chicago: Irwin Press.

Modigliani, F., & Modigliani, L. (1997). Risk-adjusted performance. *Journal of Portfolio Management, Winter*, 45–54.

Perold, A. (1988). The implementation shortfall: Paper versus reality. *Journal of Portfolio Management, 14*(3), 4–9.

Roll, R. (1977). A critique of the asset pricing theory's tests, part I: On past and potential testability of the theory. *Journal of Financial Economics, 4*(2), 129–176.

Sortino, F. (1996). On the use and misuse of downside risk. *Journal of Portfolio Management, 22*(2), 35–42.

Treynor, J. L, & Mazuy, M. (1966). Can mutual funds outguess the market? *Harvard Business Review, 44*(4), 131–136.

Wagner, W. H. (2008). The incredible story of transaction cost management: A personal recollection. *Journal of Trading, 3*(3), 8–14 Available at: <http://www.scribd.com/doc/6419002/Incredible-Story-of-Transaction-Cost-Measurement> Accessed 25.03.11


## 9.6 EXERCISES

1. On February 1, a hedge fund initiated activities with a trading account of $1,000,000 and 20,000 outstanding shares of stock. On January 2, the fund realized $30,000 in trading profits. On February 3, the fund again realized $30,000 in trading profits, but paid a dividend of $30,000. On February 4, the fund incurred $50,000 in trading losses. Trading profits for February 5 were $10,000. In addition, on February 5, investors redeemed 1000 shares at the NAV.
   a. What were NAVs for the fund for each day of the week beginning February 1?
   b. What were daily returns for February 2 through February 5?
   c. What was the time-weighted average return for this four-day period?
2. Suppose that we wished to compute monthly returns for Fund A over a period of five months. We collect relevant end-of-month NAVs along with any dividends. The following table lists NAV's and dividends collected for Fund A from June 30 to November 30. Following the NAV data are sample return calculations:

| Date | | $NAV_t$ | $NAV_{t-1}$ | $DIV_t$ |
|---|---|---|---|---|
| June 30 | 1 | 50 | — | 0 |
| July 31 | 2 | 55 | 50 | 0 |
| Aug. 31 | 3 | 50 | 55 | 0 |
| Sep. 30 | 4 | 54 | 50 | 0 |
| Oct. 31 | 5 | 47 | 54 | 2 |
| Nov. 30 | 6 | 51 | 47 | 0 |

**a.** Calculate returns for each month starting with July.
**b.** The following lists NAVs for Fund B. Calculate monthly returns for Fund B.

Fund B

| Date | $t$ | $NAV_t$ | $NAV_{t-1}$ | $DIV_t$ |
|---|---|---|---|---|
| June 30 | 1 | 50 | — | 0 |
| July 31 | 2 | 80 | 50 | 0 |
| Aug. 31 | 3 | 40 | 80 | 0 |
| Sep. 30 | 4 | 60 | 40 | 0 |
| Oct. 31 | 5 | 30 | 60 | 0 |
| Nov. 30 | 6 | 45 | 30 | 0 |

**c.** Calculate geometric mean returns for Funds A and B.
**d.** Calculate time-weighted average returns for Funds A and B.

**3.** The following table provides historical *percentage* returns for the Patterson and Liston Funds along with percentage returns on the market portfolio (index or fund):

| Year | Patterson | Liston | Market |
|---|---|---|---|
| 2007 | 4 | 19 | 15 |
| 2008 | 7 | 4 | 10 |
| 2009 | 11 | −4 | 3 |
| 2010 | 4 | 21 | 12 |
| 2011 | 5 | 13 | 9 |

Suppose that the riskless rate of return (or T-Bill rate) was 3% for each year. Calculate the following based on the preceding table:
**a.** Mean historical returns for the two funds and the market portfolio.

**b.** Variances associated with Patterson Fund returns and Liston Fund returns along with returns on the market portfolio.
**c.** The historical covariance and coefficient of correlation between returns of the Patterson Fund and returns on the market portfolio.
**d.** The historical covariance and coefficient of correlation between returns of the Liston Fund and returns on the market portfolio.
**e.** Historical betas for Patterson and Liston Funds, based on five years of returns data. (Note that the data sets are too limited in size to be considered very reliable.)
**f.** Suppose that a market return of 8% was obtained in the year 2012, and that the riskless return for 2012 was 3%. Further suppose that the Patterson and Liston Funds earned 10% and 14%, respectively, over 2012. Based on a Treynor Index, how did each of these funds perform relative to the market?
**g.** Comment on the 2012 risk-adjusted performance for each of the two funds based on Treynor Index results.

**4.** Historical returns for the Ripco Fund and the market portfolio along with Treasury bill (T-Bill) rates ($r_f$) are summarized in the following table:

| Year | Ripco | Market | T-Bill | Year | Ripco | Market | T-Bill |
|---|---|---|---|---|---|---|---|
| 1 | 0.35 | 0.28 | 0.05 | 11 | −0.07 | −0.15 | 0.05 |
| 2 | 0.04 | 0.05 | 0.05 | 12 | −0.11 | −0.21 | 0.05 |
| 3 | 0.10 | 0.09 | 0.05 | 13 | 0.42 | 0.26 | 0.05 |
| 4 | −0.01 | −0.02 | 0.05 | 14 | 0.01 | 0.04 | 0.05 |
| 5 | 0.38 | 0.32 | 0.05 | 15 | 0.05 | 0.08 | 0.05 |
| 6 | 0.31 | 0.25 | 0.05 | 16 | 0.07 | 0.11 | 0.05 |
| 7 | 0.33 | 0.26 | 0.05 | 17 | −0.01 | −0.03 | 0.05 |
| 8 | 0.42 | 0.30 | 0.05 | 18 | −0.12 | −0.37 | 0.05 |
| 9 | 0.07 | 0.14 | 0.05 | 19 | 0.33 | 0.30 | 0.05 |
| 10 | −0.02 | −0.06 | 0.05 | 20 | 0.05 | 0.13 | 0.05 |

**a.** Calculate the fund beta over the 20-year period.
**b.** Calculate Jensen's alpha for the fund over the 20-year period. Did the fund outperform the market during this period based on Jensen's alpha?
**c.** Based on a squared market risk premium term, does the Ripco Fund demonstrate market timing ability?
**d.** Based on an appropriate interaction term, does the Ripco Fund demonstrate market timing ability?

**5.** Suppose that the market for Stock X on a given date consisted of the transactions listed in the following table. The left two columns represented transactions for Stock X, excluding the broker's orders. The right two columns consisted of the broker's orders only, all of which were orders to buy. What was the VWAP for shares of X stock for that day? What was the VWAP excluding the broker's own orders? How did the broker perform relative to the market for his buy transactions?

| **Market for X Excluding Broker's Transactions** | | **Broker's Transactions for X** | |
|---|---|---|---|
| # Shares | Price | # Shares | Price |
| 30,000 | 100.00 | 10,000 | 100.00 |
| 40,000 | 100.02 | 10,000 | 100.01 |
| 10,000 | 100.05 | 10,000 | 100.03 |
| 20,000 | 100.06 | 20,000 | 100.04 |
| 30,000 | 100.07 | 40,000 | 100.05 |
| 10,000 | 100.09 | 40,000 | 100.05 |

CHAPTER

# 10

# The Mind of the Investor

## 10.1 RATIONAL INVESTOR PARADIGMS

Many financial models assume that all investors and all corporate managers are rational individuals who prefer more money to less and seek to maximize their wealth. Rational investors process information efficiently and use it to maximize their wealth. But, do investors really behave this way? Should they? The theories and models of efficient capital markets all draw from the assumption that investors are greedy, rational, and can access and exploit new information efficiently. By greedy, we mean that investors will strive to maximize their wealth. By rational, we mean that investors can efficiently process and use all information to maximize their wealth. Such assumptions may be quite reasonable—at least to an extent, and allow for simpler and more straightforward model building. The efficient market theories are attractive, in part, because they facilitate financial model building. Financial model-builders can treat investors as participants in a mathematical game if investors' behavior is rational. Models based on rational behavior are usually less contrived, easier to create, and more believable than theories based on irrational behavior. Rational investors should maintain better survival rates in the marketplace, control more dominant wealth levels, and be more influential in price setting. However, ask yourself how many investors you know that are truly rational. As reasonable as the rationality assumption might seem, and as compelling as the models that it leads to are, does the rationality assumption really reflect the mind of the investor? This chapter explores the extent to which investors might or might not be rational and how such deviations from rationality might affect financial markets. Experiments by psychologists (and perhaps our own observations of market behavior) suggest that the "rational man" assumption is not fully justified. Behavioral finance is concerned with the actual behavior and thinking of individuals who make financial decisions.

*Financial Trading and Investing*

## The St. Petersburg Paradox and the Expected Utility Paradigm

In 1713, the mathematician Nicholas Bernoulli reasoned that a rational gambler should be willing to buy a gamble for its expected value. For example, it seemed rational for a gambler to invest up to $1 for a gamble that paid either $2 or zero based on the toss of a coin. He extended his reasoning to a series of coin tosses, continuing to reason that the ultimate value of the more complex gamble should still be its expected value. His cousin, Daniel Bernoulli, presented his paradigm in 1738 at a conference of mathematicians in St. Petersburg.[1] His extended problem, commonly referred to as the St. Petersburg Paradox, was concerned with why gamblers would pay only a finite sum for a gamble with an infinite expected value. Suppose, in Bernoulli's paradigm, the coin lands on its head on the first toss, the gamble payoff is $2. If the coin lands tails, it is tossed again. If the coin lands heads on this second toss, the payoff is $4; otherwise, it is tossed a third time. If the coin lands heads on the third toss, the payoff doubles again to $8; otherwise, it is tossed again for a potential payoff of $16. The process continues until the payoff is determined by the coin finally landing heads. Where $n$ equals infinity, the expected value of this gamble is determined by the following equation:

$$E[V] = (0.5^1 \times 2^1) + (0.5^2 \times 2^2) + (0.5^3 \times 2^3) + \cdots + + (0.5^\infty \times 2^\infty)$$

This equation is based on the expectation that the probability of the coin landing heads on the first (or any) toss equals 0.5. If the coin lands heads on the first toss, the payoff equals $\$2 = 2^1$. Since there is a 50% chance that the coin will land tails on the first toss and a 50% chance the coin will land heads on the second toss, the probability of achieving a payoff of $\$4 = 2^2$ on the second toss is $0.5 \times 0.5 = 0.5^2$. Thus, the payoff $2^n$ is realized with probability equal to $0.5^n$. The expected value of the gamble equals the sum of all potential payoffs times their associated probabilities. So, exactly what is the expected value of this gamble? We simplify the equation above as follows:

$$E[V] = (0.5^1 \times 2^1) + (0.5^2 \times 2^2) + (0.5^3 \times 2^3) + \cdots + (0.5^n \times 2^n)$$
$$E[V] = (0.5 \times 2) + (0.5 \times 2) + (0.5 \times 2) + \cdots + (0.5 \times 2)$$
$$E[V] = (1) + (1) + (1) + \cdots + (1)$$

It appears, since there is some possibility that the coin is tossed tails an infinity of times ($n = \infty$), the expected or actuarial value of this gamble is infinite. This seems quite obvious from a mathematics perspective. Paradoxically, Bernoulli found that none of the esteemed mathematicians at the conference would be willing to pay an infinite sum (or, in most cases, even a large sum) of money for the gamble with infinite actuarial value. Were the mathematicians simply irrational? Or, should the worth or market value of a gamble or investment be less than its actuarial or expected value?

[1]Nicholas Bernoulli first proposed this problem in a letter to Pierre Raymond de Montmort dated September 9, 1713, who then published it in his book later that year. The Swiss mathematician Gabriel Cramer actually proposed an essentially identical solution 10 years before Daniel. Correspondence between Nicholas Bernoulli and Cramer is available at http://www.cs.xu.edu/math/Sources/Montmort/stpetersburg.pdf#search=%22Nicolas%20Bernoulli%22. Daniel further argued in his essay that risk-averse investors should diversify.

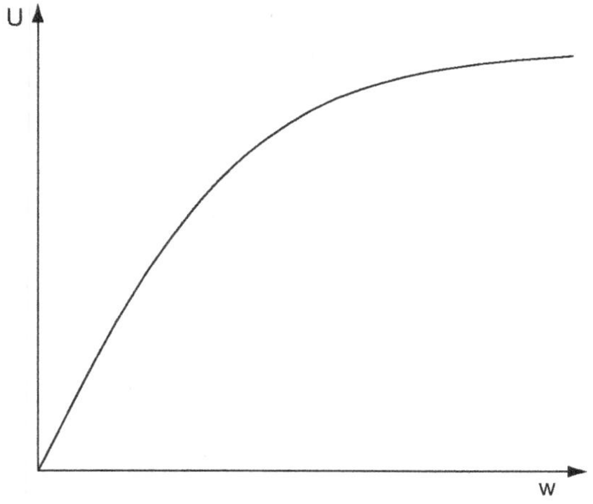


**FIGURE 10.1** Utility of wealth $U = ln(w)$.

Bernoulli opined that the resolution to this paradox is the now commonly accepted notion of "diminishing marginal utility," which holds that as a person's wealth increases, the satisfaction that she derives increases, but at a lesser rate (see Figure 10.1). More money produces more satisfaction, but the rates of increase in satisfaction are less than the rates of increase in wealth. So the worth of a gamble to an investor is less than its expected value because the utility derived from each dollar of potential gains is less than the utility of each dollar potentially lost. Bernoulli proposed a log-utility function where an individual's level of satisfaction derived from wealth is related to the log of her wealth level. The key to this utility function is that satisfaction increases as wealth increases, but at a lesser rate. This means that an investor stands to lose more satisfaction in an actuarially fair gamble than she stands to gain. The potential loss in a "double-or-nothing" bet is more significant than the potential gain. Thus, investors will reject actuarially fair gambles because, on average, they lose satisfaction or utility.

The implication of the utility function is that rational investors should seek to maximize the expected utility of their wealth, not expected wealth itself. Furthermore, this theory of utility can serve as the theoretical foundation for risk aversion. Thus, rational investors can be motivated not only by greed, but by fear as well.

## Von Neuman and Morgenstern: Axioms of Choice

In their seminal treatise on game theory, John von Neumann and Oscar Morgenstern (1947) present a set of behavioral assumptions (axioms) that we will adapt and use to derive the expected utility hypothesis. We shall start by assuming that investors make investment selection $x_i$ from a convex subset $\mathbf{x}$ of the $n$-dimensional Euclidian space $\mathbb{R}^n$.[2]

[2]Don't worry about any complicated-looking math terms here if you don't understand them. We are simply using some language from game theory to describe the set of investment choices.

The element $x_i$ represents the number of units of investment $i$ that can be selected by the investor from the $n$ elements of vector $\mathbf{x} = [x_1, x_2, \ldots x_n]^T$. Convexity of this subset means that the investor can form linear combinations of any elements in $\mathbf{x}$ to obtain new elements in $\mathbf{x}$; that is, for any $\alpha \in [0,1]$, $\alpha x_j + (1-\alpha)x_k \in \mathbf{x}$. The first three axioms ensure investor rationality:

1. *Reflexivity*: For an entire set $\mathbf{x}$ of investment alternatives $x_i$, $x_j \succsim x_j$ ($x_j$ is at least as desirable as $x_j$). This axiom might be regarded as merely a mathematical necessity. This formal axiom is of little intuitive importance for our purposes.
2. *Completeness (or Comparability)*: For an entire set of investment alternatives $x_i$, either $x_j \succ x_k$ ($x_j$ is preferred to $x_k$), $x_j \prec x_k$ ($x_j$ is less desirable than $x_k$) or $x_j \sim x_k$ ($x_j$ is equally desirable to $x_k$) for all $j$ and $k$. Thus, the investor can fully specify his preferences over the entire set of investments.
3. *Transitivity*: For any $x_i$, $x_j$, $x_k$, if $x_i \succ x_j$ and $x_j \succ x_k$, then $x_i \succ x_k$. This axiom ensures consistency among choices.

While the three axioms listed above are sufficient to ensure investor rationality, working with such preference relations is difficult at best when $n$ is very large. Hence, it is useful to develop and apply a rule that assigns values to choices. Such a rule is known as a cardinal utility function. A cardinal utility function assigns a unique number (utility level) to each and every choice (e.g., wealth level, risk/return combination, etc.). Three more axioms are needed to establish a cardinal utility function:

1. *Strong Independence*: If $x_i \sim x_k$, then for any $\alpha \in [0,1]$, $\alpha x_i + (1-\alpha)x_j \sim \alpha x_k + (1-\alpha)x_j$. It may be useful to interpret $\alpha$ as a probability. This axiom implies that preference rankings are not affected by inclusion in more complicated arrangements.
2. *Measurability (or Intermediate Value)*: If $x_i \succ x_j \succ x_k$, then there exists some $\alpha$ such that $\alpha x_i + (1-\alpha)x_k \sim x_j$. This implies nonexistence of lexicographic (dictionary) orderings. Lexicographic orderings imply discontinuities in utility functions.
3. *Ranking*: Assume that $x_i \succ x_j \succ x_k$ and $x_i \succ x_m \succ x_k$, and $x_j \sim \alpha x_i + (1-\alpha)x_k$ and $x_m \sim \gamma\, x_i + (1-\gamma)x_k$ where $\gamma \in [0,1]$. Then it follows that if $\alpha > \gamma$, $x_j \succ x_m$ or if $\alpha = \gamma$, $x_j \sim x_m$.

These six axioms are sufficient to construct a cardinal utility function where utility can be represented with numbers. We shall usually add two more assumptions to this list:

1. Greed: Investors prefer more to less wealth.
2. Risk aversion: Investors prefer certainty to uncertainty. (This assumption need not always apply, but it does seem realistic.)

While seemingly complicated, these axioms of choice are the basis for the microeconomics of investment theory. Positive economics is typically based on the assumption that investors behave consistently with these axioms so as to maximize the utility associated with expected wealth. Perhaps more importantly, these axioms illustrate the mindset of economists analyzing the behavior of investors. The question we pose in the next section is whether and the actual extent to which investor behavior is consistent with these axioms.

## 10.2 PROSPECT THEORY

In the late 1970s, an experimental psychologist named Amos Tversky began to find evidence that investors and gamblers might not behave in a manner consistent with maximizing utility. Tversky, in collaboration with others, including Daniel Kahneman (Nobel Prize winner for this body of work), have conducted numerous experiments on subjects testing decision-making characteristics. Generally, these experiments suggest that most subjects are quite irrational and inconsistent in their decision making. They have also written on applications of their results to financial decision making, suggesting that investors may actually be quite different from the theoretical "rational economic man." Kahneman and Tversky (1979) were particularly interested in how people made decisions when faced with uncertainty calling their new perspective *prospect theory* (with no particularly good reason). While expected utility maximization focuses on levels of wealth, prospect theory focuses on changes in wealth. Consider, for example, the following very simple illustration. Investor A has $1,000,000 right now, having doubled his money over the past 24 hours. Investor B has $1,500,000 right now, having lost 50% of his wealth over the past 24 hours. Which investor is happier now? Is more wealth always preferred to less? Do people make decisions as though this is true? Now, consider some slightly more complex scenarios.

### Losses and Inconsistency

Consider the following example choice of gambles:

**Gamble A:** 0.33 probability of receiving 2500, 0.66 of receiving 2400, and 0.01 of receiving 0
**Gamble B:** 100% probability of receiving 2400

Kahneman and Tversky found that 82% of their experiment participants preferred Gamble B to Gamble A. However, they offered the same set of participants the following second set of gambles:

**Gamble A*:** 0.33 probability of receiving 2500, 0.67 of receiving 0
**Gamble B*:** 0.34 probability of receiving 2400 and 0.66 of receiving 0

In the second part of this experiment, 83% of participants preferred Gamble A* to B*. The same change was made to both gambles in moving from the first to second sets; 0.66 probability was shifted from Gambles A and B to A* and B* from winnings of 2400 to zero. The gamble shifts were identical, but many participants reversed their preferences. Yet from the first to second sets of choices, the changes to both gambles were identical; losses of 2400 were imposed on both gambles from the first set to the second set with probability 0.34.[3] Since the losses were identical, participants should not have reversed their decisions, but, clearly, the majority did. Kahneman and Tversky surmised that people

[3]See Exercise 6 at the end of this chapter for a more detailed discussion concerning the equivalence of these two gambles.

are risk averse when evaluating positive outcomes (winnings), but risk-seeking when evaluating losses. Hence, people have diminishing utility of wealth functions with respect to winnings, but increasing marginal utility when faced with wealth decreases. Investors seem to exhibit similar reactions to reductions in wealth.

Consider a very simple variation on this problem. One group of subjects was presented with this problem:

1. In addition to whatever you own, you have been given $1000. You are now asked to choose between:
   A: A sure gain of $500
   B: A 50% chance to gain $1000 and a 50% chance to gain nothing
   A second group of subjects was presented with another problem.
2. In addition to whatever you own, you have been given $2000. You are now asked to choose between:
   A*: A sure loss of $500.
   B*: A 50% chance to lose $1000 and a 50% chance to lose nothing.

In the first group 84% chose A. In the second group 69% chose B*. The two problems are identical in terms of terminal wealth to the subject. However, the phrasing of the question causes the problems that invoke different emotional responses. This leads to the following framing versus substance problem.

***Frames versus substance***

Determining the preferences of individuals is complicated by their apparently inconsistent responses to questions that are presented to them. These inconsistencies not only make it more difficult to study investor behavior, they make the problem of offering financial advice rather problematic. For example, Kahneman and Tversky (1981, 1986) describe how various individuals form decisions when identical questions are phrased differently. In particular, consider the following example when individuals are asked from two different perspectives to select from radiation or surgery for cancer treatment:

*Survival Frame*
Surgery: Of 100 people having surgery, 90 live through the postoperative period, 68 are alive at the end of the first year, and 34 are alive at the end of five years.
Radiation: Of 100 people having radiation therapy, all live through the treatment, 77 are alive at the end of the first year, and 22 are alive at the end of five years.
*Mortality Frame*
Surgery: Of 100 people having surgery, 10 die during surgery or the postoperative period, 32 die by the end of the first year, and 66 die by the end of five years.
Radiation: Of 100 people having radiation therapy, none die during treatment, 23 die by the end of one year, and 78 die by the end of five years.

Although the information presented in the "survival frame" is identical to that presented in the "mortality frame," 18% of respondents preferred radiation therapy when presented with the "survival frame," compared with 44% when presented with the "mortality frame." Interestingly, physicians and statistically trained business students did not react differently from other respondents when surveyed.

Consider an even simpler example suggested by Ritter (2003). How would you feel about paying a "peak-period surcharge" to dine in a restaurant? Next, consider how this surcharge pricing scheme differs from an "early bird" or "after-theatre" discount. Presentation does matter. In any case, not only do we have evidence that individual decision making is inconsistent, but preferences may be inconsistent and individuals irrational as well. Consider this problem in an investments context. How can an investment advisor assess her client's level of risk aversion when the framing of the question affects the investor's response? Can we really expect investors to behave consistently when their risk attitudes change depending how their situations are addressed?

The framing issue presents itself regularly in promotional literature distributed by investment advisors, mutual funds, and other financial institutions, who regularly exploit investors' inability to contend with fallacious arguments. Consider the following description concerning corporate annual reports by Beattie and Jones (2000); "measurement distortion can occur through graphical devices such as a nonzero axis or a broken axis, which cause the rate of change in trend lines to appear greater than is actually warranted." Their paper argues that graphs are frequently used selectively and graph formats exploit measurement distortions, implying inaccurate depictions of financial performance. Diacon and Hasseldine (2007) find evidence that investors are regularly misled by such distorted displays when selecting investment funds.

### *Maintaining the Status Quo: Joe and His Opera Tickets*

The following story was taken from the *Wall Street Journal*[4]:

> On the way to the opera, Joe loses his pair of $50 tickets. Most likely, he will not buy another pair—spending [a total of] $200 [including $100 on the lost tickets] to hear "La Boheme" seems a bit much. But suppose, instead, he arrives at the theater tickets-in-hand, but discovers he has lost a $100 bill. He could sell his tickets, which would net him the same result as in the first case—out $100 and out the tickets. But he probably won't sell.... Joe may think he is entirely rational, but he leans consistently toward the status quo.

This particular type of bias to maintain the status quo is sometimes referred to as the *endowment effect*. This effect causes losses or what is given up to weigh more heavily in the decision-making process than gains or what is acquired. This effect seems to manifest itself in investing through a seeming reluctance to sell stocks, particularly stocks that have lost value. Numerous studies (e.g., Shefrin and Statman, 1985) have documented investors' reluctance to sell their "losers" to capture tax write-offs. The tax write-off implications of selling a stock that has lost value are enhanced when "losers" are sold before year's end. Tax loss write-offs captured on that year's return filings have more value than delayed loss write-offs. However, most investors demonstrate a pronounced reluctance to sell their losers to capture their write-offs. Investors seem intent on maintaining their status quo even when changing their portfolios would result in increased wealth. Some observers refer to this phenomenon as "fear of regret." More generally, studies have suggested that

[4]This article entitled, "Intrinsic Value: Outsider who Challenged Dismal Science," by Roger Lowenstein in the June 6, 1996 issue of the *Wall Street Journal* provided a number of examples of the work of Amos Tversky, the Stanford psychologist who studied irrational consumer and investor behavior.

this endowment effect or disposition effect might lead stock markets to underreact to news (Frazzini, 2006) and exacerbate momentum effects in stock prices (Grinblatt and Han, 2005).

### *Anchoring*

A similar sort of problem exists with "anchoring," where the decision maker places undue emphasis on some factor, number, or measure. For example, Kahneman and Tversky asked participants in an experiment to spin a roulette wheel with numbers from 1 to 100 and then estimate the number of countries in Africa. They found that participants' estimates were unduly influenced by the result of the roulette wheel spin result. Low roulette wheel outcomes were followed by lower estimates of the numbers of African countries. Similarly, Genesove and Mayer (2001) found that sellers of houses and apartments tend to be unduly influenced by purchase prices of their homes. There is similar evidence suggesting that investors may be unduly biased by purchase prices of their securities. Studies have found that amateur traders are more affected by endowment and anchoring effects than professionals.

## 10.3 BEHAVIORAL FINANCE

Behavioral finance, largely rooted in prospect theory, is concerned with the impact of human emotions and cognitive impairments on investment decision making. Economists have used expected utility maximization for over two centuries as the presumed objective of the rational investor. Expected utility maximization has served and still serves as the "industry standard" for modeling investor behavior. In this section, we review a number of studies concerning individual and investor rationality. Many of these studies were conducted by experimental psychologists while most of the remainder are based on statistical analyses of financial data.

The case for assuming capital markets efficiency when developing financial models is strong. Models based on rationality tend to be simple and one can argue that rational investors generate market prices despite a large contingent of irrational investors. However, regardless of their intuitive appeal, theoretical models should not be accepted without consideration for empirical evidence. There exists much controversy in academia and in the profession regarding the extent to which models of market efficiency reflect reality. The following sections represent a sampling of this literature.

### The Monty Hall Judgment Error

One very interesting experimental study of investor irrationality, failure to learn, and market rationality is presented in Kluger and Wyatt (2004). This problem is adapted from the well-known Monty Hall problem, based on the late 1960s game show "Let's Make a Deal." In the show, Monty Hall, its host, would offer contestants an opportunity to choose one prize hidden behind one of three identical doors. Prizes hidden behind two of three doors were worthless (if the contestant selected either of these doors, she was "zonked") but the prize hidden behind the third was valuable. The contestant would choose the door behind which his prize was to be hidden. At this stage in the game, the contestant had a one-third probability of winning the valuable prize. Before allowing the contestant to see whether she had won the valuable prize, and with increasing audience anticipation, Hall would then typically show the contestant the worthless prize behind one of the two doors that the contestant did not select. He would then offer the contestant an opportunity to switch her selection to the prize behind the third door. Thus, the contestant's problem is whether to stick with her original selection or to switch her selection to the prize hidden behind the third door.

To summarize, the valuable prize is behind one of the three doors. The probability of the contestant having selected the door with the valuable prize was initially 1/3. But, once one of the two worthless prizes is revealed behind a second door, can the contestant improve his odds of obtaining a valuable prize by switching his decision to select the other unopened door?

Regardless of what prize remains behind the first door selected by the contestant, Mr. Hall will reveal the worthless prize behind a second door. Hence, the probability of a valuable prize behind the first door remains 1/3. We know that Mr. Hall will not reveal the prize behind the selected door, so its probability of being the desirable prize is unchanged. The door that Mr. Hall will select to open will have a worthless prize with probability one. This door will not have a valuable prize behind it. What is the probability that the valuable prize is behind the third door? This probability must be $1 - 1/3 - 0 = 2/3$. Why? Remember that Mr. Hall will not open a second door with a valuable prize behind it. This doubles the probability that the valuable prize is behind the third door. Hence, the contestant should always switch his selection to maximize his probability of obtaining the valuable prize.[5] Most contestants did not. In fact, most experimental subjects, when provided a description of this problem announce that they would not switch (Friedman, 1998). When asked to calculate probabilities, many people will say that the valuable prize is equally likely to be behind the first and third doors, despite the additional information realized when Mr. Hall reveals the prize behind the second door.

Most people have no difficulty estimating that the initial probability of 1/3 for the prize behind any one of the three doors. This heuristic has served most people well for years. However, people tend to use the same heuristic when a "zonk" is revealed behind one of

[5]If you are not convinced that this solution to the Monty Hall problem is correct, consider the following table. The contestant has three choices to start with, followed by two choices after each of the first three. Thus, there are six possible outcomes, including three that result from switching doors. In two of the three switching outcomes, the contestant gets the car, compared to only one out of the three if the contestant keeps his original door selection.

| Choose a door with a car behind it | | Choose a door with a goat behind it | | Choose a door with a goat behind it | |
|---|---|---|---|---|---|
| Keep Door | Switch Door | Keep Door | Switch Door | Keep Door | Switch Door |
| Get a Car | **Get a Goat** | Get a Goat | **Get a Car** | Get a Goat | **Get a Car** |

the doors, leading them to conclude that there is a 50/50 probability that the prize is behind one of them. This heuristic is difficult to abandon when the nature of the problem changed, as the problem solution shifts from an unconditional probability regime to a less intuitive conditional probability. Most people refuse to accept this shift.

Perhaps, more interestingly, most subjects refuse to accept the validity of mathematical proofs offered to demonstrate the wisdom of switching doors. Furthermore, most subjects continue to refuse to switch doors after being permitted to watch repeated trials of this experiment where the third door leads to the valuable prize with a frequency of approximately 2/3. Hence, subjects seem to either never learn from their errors or learn very slowly.

Kluger and Wyatt (2004) conducted experiments to determine how a market might behave in such a scenario. Kluger and Wyatt gathered subjects in a laboratory setting and had them compete to select investments whose payoffs were "behind doors." "Investors" participated in repeated trials, were offered opportunities to select doors, and then compete to pay to either retain or switch their selections. If investors were rational and understood the nature of the Monty Hall problem, market prices to switch should be twice the levels of prices to retain original selections. Kluger and Wyatt found that when all investors mispriced the selections, prices of original selections remained roughly comparable to prices to switch. Hence, misinformed or irrational investors consistently mispriced the investments. However, when as few as two "rational investors" who correctly estimated the probabilities were included in the trials, prices to switch were roughly double the prices to retain original selections. Hence, it seemed that competition between only two rational investors out of many were necessary for market prices to reflect rational probabilities.

Similarly, traders all have good reason to question their abilities to beat the market. First, at least 50% of traders are likely to be "below average," even without transaction costs. Transaction costs worsen traders' abilities to outperform random "buy-and-hold" strategies. The market efficiency hypotheses provide ample rationale to avoid the attempt to "out trade" the market. Statistical evidence demonstrating the inability to outperform the market is overwhelming.

## Dumb, Dumber, and Dead

The Monty Hall illustration result is quite counterintuitive and has caused confusion even among trained mathematicians. However, investors are susceptible to even more basic errors. For example, Rashes (2001) documents numerous cases of strong correlations between stocks with similar ticker symbols. For example, shares of stock for Massmutual Corporate Investors (ticker: MCI), an NYSE listed fund that did not hold shares of any major telecommunications companies, were strongly correlated with those of MCI Communications (ticker: MCIC), realizing particularly high volume and price during the period of merger discussions and activity involving the telecommunications firm. Massmutual's returns were far more correlated with MCI's than with AT&T or any of the other telecommunications firms. In fact, there is evidence that investors bought shares of Massmutual and held them for long periods of time, believing that they had invested in

MCI. Similarly, the most volatile trading day for the Castle Convertible Fund (ticker: CVF) was April 15, 1997, after an article appeared in the *Financial Times* about investments in fraudulent companies by the Czech Value Fund (abbreviated as CVF in the article). In a 22-minute span, the stock price dropped from 24.75 to 16.75 before closing the day's session at 23. On June 24, 1998, an AT&T bid for shares of Tele-Communications Inc. led to a 4.3% increase in the price of Transcontinental Reality Investors Inc. (ticker: TCI). In fact, the highest trading volume ever experienced by Transcontinental Reality shares to that date was on October 13, 1993, when Bell Atlantic announced its intent to purchase Tele-Communications.

Even options markets exhibit evidence of uninformed or perhaps even irrational behavior. Studies have found that more than half of outstanding long-call-option positions that should have been exercised on the day before the ex-dividend date went unexercised, costing investors approximately $491 over 10 years.[6] While approximately half of this failure to exercise can be attributed to transaction costs, the remainder seems to be due to lack of awareness of the early exercise decision, inability to monitor their option positions, or irrationality. Furthermore, early exercises of CBOE call options seem to be irrational, where customers of both full-service and discount brokers seem to exhibit irrational exercise behavior, while traders in large investment houses did not.

Perhaps the most notorious of underperforming funds during the 1990s bull market was the Steadman Technology & Growth Fund. Its returns during part of this decade were −5% in 1992, −8% in 1993, −37% in 1994, −28% in 1995, −30% in 1996, and −28% in 1997. Market returns were positive in each of these years. Only one of the four Steadman funds had a positive long-term return, although it was quite small. Why were returns so dismal? Portfolio turnover rates and transaction costs were extremely high, expense ratios were frequently in the 6% to 7% range, and Steadman seemed not to have a coherent investment strategy, indiscriminately investing in stocks and other securities. The SEC forced the fund to stop accepting money from new investors in 1989. Why did other investors keep money invested throughout the dismal performance of the early 1990s? When the Technology & Growth Fund was finally shut down, about 30% of the redemption checks were returned, presumably because the shareholders were dead.

## Myopia and Overreaction

Several studies have suggested that investors react more to the most recent information than they should, and that they are too influenced by short-term price swings than they should be. In addition, Griffin and Tversky (1992) and Sorescu and Subramanyam (2006) find that investors tend to overreact to dramatic upgrade recommendations of less experienced and less reputable analysts while they under-react to less dramatic upgrade recommendations to more experienced and more reputable analysts. Furthermore, there is some empirical evidence (to be detailed later) that stocks that experience wide short-term price swings reverse those swings in the intermediate term. This behavior suggests that investors may overreact to information. In addition, there is much evidence in the

[6]See Pool, Stoll, and Whaley (2008) and Barraclough and Whaley (2011) for failure to exercise early and Poteshman and Serbin (2003) for irrational early exercise.

psychology and investments literature that people tend to be overconfident in their own judgments, perhaps, oddly enough, even enabling certain overconfident traders to generate higher profits than their more rational competitors under limited conditions. While, in general, overconfident investors seem to trade more frequently and realize reduced returns, in more professional trading settings, more confident traders may realize higher profits by more frequently exploiting bid–offer spreads. There is also evidence that experts tend to be more prone to overconfidence than novices. Overconfident professional traders also tend to be more aggressive in their trading strategies, and in some instances, improving their returns.

### *Myopia*

Consider a paper by Benartzi and Thaler (1995) that examines the widespread large differences between bond and stock returns. From 1925 to 1997, intermediate term government bond returns have averaged approximately 5.2% while stock returns have averaged approximately 10.7%. This spread indicates reluctance on the part of investors to buy stock, even though for practically every intermediate- to long-term period over the 75 years prior to 1997, investors could have expected to earn more in stock markets.[7] Benartzi and Thaler argue that even long-term investors have a myopic outlook, causing them to make every effort to avoid short-term losses and risks. This aversion to losses is often referred to as *myopic loss aversion* and is frequently offered as the cause for the equity return premium relative to bonds. For example, their experiments conducted on university employees indicated that when shown only the 30-year returns on stocks and bonds, employees preferred to hold more stock in their pension accounts. Thus, when employees see how much money will be available in their retirement accounts in 30 years, they prefer the higher returns associated with stocks. However, when shown additional information reflecting the entire year-by-year return path over the 30-year period, employees preferred less stock in their accounts, even though they still would have more money at the end of the period with stock investment. Thus, investors with a long-run orientation to investment still maintain a myopic aversion to risk because they care not only about how much money they will have available when they retire, but their gains and losses en route to their retirements. A number of financial institutions, such as Bank Hapoalim, the largest manager of mutual funds in Israel, reduced the frequency with which they issue financial statements to their investors, citing investors' myopic risk aversion as their rationale (see Gneezy et al., 2003). They expected that their investor-clients would be less likely to move money out of their funds if they received reports of balances less frequently.

Jeremy Siegel, in his book titled *Stocks for the Long Run* (1994), lends support for this myopic loss aversion argument, arguing that, "It is widely known that stock returns on average, exceed bond returns in the long run. But it is little known that in the long run, the risks in stocks are less than those found in bonds or even bills!" While this statement might overstate the risk/return point, it does seem that most investors overemphasize short-term risk at the expense of long-term returns. On the other hand, Dimson et al. (2002) note that the long run can be very long. For example, the Italian stock market failed

[7]Note that their study period did not include the slumping stock market period 2000 to 2009. The same is true of Siegel's study, discussed in the next paragraph.

to keep pace with inflation from 1915 to 1978 and communist takeovers closed down Russian and Chinese stock markets in the 20th century.

Numerous experiments reported in the psychology literature have indicated that individuals in their decision making tend to overemphasize recent information and trends and underemphasize prior information. For example, Shiller (1996) found that at the peak of the Japanese market, 14% of Japanese investors expected a crash. However, just after the market did crash, 32% expected another crash. Even professional analysts tend to overreact to new information. Excessive dependence on recent information may lead the market to overreact to new information, and may even explain the so-called price-to-earnings ratio anomaly (discussed in Chapter 11). In an important paper, Shiller (1981) examines empirical data and argues that the volatility in stock markets cannot be explained by the volatility of cash flows (dividends) associated with stocks, suggesting that investors may overreact to risk. Market prices are extremely sensitive to potential future earnings anticipation, and in fact, are too sensitive, so that they vary far more than the actual dividends.

### *Hyperbolic Discounting*

Suppose that you just won the lottery. Would you rather be paid $500,000 in five years or $1,000,000 in ten years? Many, but not all people would opt for the larger sum delayed by an additional five years. Now, change the payout dates. Would you rather have $500,000 now or $1,000,000 in five years? Many more people would opt for the smaller sum now. That is, at least a few people would reverse their preferences by advancing the payoff dates by five years. Similarly, as cash flow dates approach, some investors will reverse their preferences toward preferring smaller cash flows sooner.

The time value principle holds that preferences should not depend on the decision date. That is, if an investor prefers Investment A to B today based on its current time value of money, she would still prefer A to B at a later date given that the cash flow dates do not change. For example, suppose that an investor (consumer) prefers alternative A to alternative B (A≻B, or $CF_Ae^{-rT_A} > CF_Be^{-rT_B}$ with $r > 0$, where alternative A has a higher nominal value or cash flow ($CF_A > CF_B$), but is delayed longer ($T_A > T_B$). Thus, the investor (consumer) decides now that she prefers to consume the larger amount $CF_A$ at the later date $T_A$ to the smaller $CF_B$ sooner at date $T_B$. However, if both alternative investment payoff levels were advanced by the same increments in time $T_B$ (e.g., alternative A now pays at time $(T_A - T_B)$ and B now pays at time $T_B - T_B$ or time zero – now), many decision makers would reverse their preferences. That is, even though they might initially prefer the larger awards even if delayed longer, if the smaller reward were offered now, they would prefer it to the larger reward with a shorter delay. That is:

$$CF_Ae^{-rT_A} > CF_Be^{-rT_B}$$

$$CF_Ae^{-r(T_A-T_B)} < CF_Be^{-r(T_B-T_B)}$$

These two statements are mutually inconsistent, and illustrate temporal myopia. Consider the following example, with cash flow present values set forth in Table 10.1. An investor has the opportunity to decide between receiving $50 five years from now and $100 ten years from now. If she discounted cash flows at an annual rate of 10% ($PV = CFe^{-0.10T}$), she would prefer to have $100 ten years from now. Suppose that the

**TABLE 10.1** Hyperbolic Discounting

| $t$ | $CF_A$ | $CF_B$ | $PV(CF_A)$, $r=0.1$ | PV($CF_B$), $r=0.1$ | PV($CF_A$), Hyperbolic Discounting | PV($CF_B$), Hyperbolic Discounting |
|---|---|---|---|---|---|---|
| 0 | | | 36.7879445 | 30.32653314 | 36.78647301 | 24.28315774 |
| 1 | | | 40.65696636 | 33.51600244 | 38.88817407 | 25.67051386 |
| 2 | | | 44.93289679 | 37.04091115 | 41.10995044 | 27.13713301 |
| 3 | | | 49.65853074 | 40.93653774 | 43.45866232 | 28.6875437 |
| 4 | | | 54.88116395 | 45.24187095 | 45.94156184 | 30.32653314 |
| 5 | | 50 | 60.65306629 | 50 | 48.56631548 | 50 |
| 6 | | | 67.03200488 | | 51.34102771 | |
| 7 | | | 74.0818223 | | 54.27426602 | |
| 8 | | | 81.87307548 | | 57.37508741 | |
| 9 | | | 90.4837419 | | 60.65306629 | |
| 10 | 100 | | 100 | | 100 | |

investor had "impulse issues," and that her discount rate were 50% for one year immediately prior to consumption and 5.556% for all other years: $PV = CFe^{-(0.05556+\cdots+0.05556+0.5)}$. Still, the investor would prefer to receive \$100 in 10 years to receiving \$50 in five years. However, if the investor were permitted to make her decision in the fifth year, her preference ranking would reverse: $PV_A = 48.47 < PV_B = 50$.

This investor uses a form of hyperbolic discounting to discount her cash flows. The discounting functions are based on a constant discount rate $r = .10$ from above and can be easily generalized to accommodate time-varying discount rates:

$$CF_A e^{-(r_1+r_2+\cdots+rT_B+\cdots+rT_A)} > CF_B e^{-(r_1+r_2+\cdots+rT_B)}$$

$$CF_A e^{-(r_1+\cdots+r_{(T_A-T_B)})} < CF_B e^{-(r_{(T_B-T_B)})} = CF_B$$

which is still inconsistent unless $r_1$ (along with, perhaps other $r_t < r_{TB}$) is sufficiently high. This type of hyperbolic discounting was proposed by Strotz (1956) and Laibson (1997).

Thus, Table 10.1 suggests that the consumer will prefer option A in every period except when the consumption of option B is imminent. The preference ranking changes because immediate consumption is considered (discounted) differently from deferred consumption. However, this impulse typically applies only when one of the options is immediate.

Neuroeconomics might offer an explanation for this effect.[8] Consider a scenario where experimental subjects in a laboratory experiment are offered a choice between \$10 now and \$15 in one month. MRI analysis shows that both the separate limbic (which governs

[8]We will discuss neurofinance (which is concerned with the physiological effects of financial decision making) in greater detail shortly.

intuitive, affective, and emotional cognition) and analytic (which govern analytical, computational, and strategic cognition) systems show blood flow activity. Next, change the offer terms such that only two future award alternatives exist: $10 two weeks from now and $15 in one month. The MRI imaging changes such that only the analytic system shows activity. Subjects are more willing to accept the delayed, but larger rewards. Thus, when the choices include a current reward, the limbic system seems to allow the temptation of immediate gratification to dominate the otherwise apparently more rational decision (Eat, drink and be merry, for tomorrow, we may die). Hence, precommitment (policy, monetary deposits, contracts, etc.) to more rational decisions might help overcome this effect. Similarly, reliance on others for decision making may also be useful when their analytical systems are more involved in this process.

Consider, for example, that Dr. Edward Miller, dean of the Johns Hopkins University Medical School and chief executive officer of its hospital, claims that over half a million people undergo coronary-artery bypass graft surgery every year in the United States, but only about 10% of these patients make lifestyle changes needed to prevent future surgeries, chest pains, and premature death. It is well known that employees regularly opt not to participate in employer retirement savings plans, even when employers match their contributions. One might argue that contractual precommitment or government intervention might play a role in regulating human behavior. For example, O'Donoghue and Rabin (2006) suggest that willpower weaknesses might be remedied by taxing potato chips and subsidizing carrots. The U.S. federal government provides for tax deferral subsidies to encourage employer-sponsored retirement accounts.

### *Overreaction*

Stocks that experience wide short-term price swings may have a tendency to reverse those swings in the intermediate term. This behavior suggests that investors may overreact to information. As we will discuss later, DeBondt and Thaler (1985) argue that the market overreacts to information and that abnormal returns can be realized by buying losers and selling winners. Their study indicated that buying stocks that performed poorly in a prior three- to five-year period and selling those that performed well would have generated higher than normal returns in subsequent three- to five-year periods. Most significant mean reversion tendencies seem to hold for the month of January.

### *Overconfidence*

How many investors believe that they are better than average traders? How many drivers think that they are better than average?[9] How many people think that they are dumb (less intelligent than average)? Half? Certainly, no one begins trading stocks thinking that he will perform worse than the market or the average trader.[10] Yet, it is likely that half

[9]Svenson (1981) found in his survey of 22-year-old drivers that 82% considered themselves to be among the 30% safest.

[10]For example, Itô (1990) finds in surveys of foreign exchange traders that most are more optimistic about how rate changes will affect them than they are about how rate changes will affect their competitors.

of all traders are below average. But, how do typical investors actually fare? And how do they fare relative to professionals? Russo and Schoemaker (1992) wrote:

> Good decision-making requires more than knowledge of facts, concepts and relationships, it also requires metaknowledge—an understanding of the limits of our knowledge. Unfortunately, we tend to have a deeply rooted overconfidence in our beliefs and judgments.

To test for overconfidence and compare results across professions, Russo and Schoemaker created and administered a 10-question test similar to the Trivia Quiz provided in Table 10.2.[11] Before discussing the results of their study, take the test yourself. Since you will probably not know the exact answers for each of these questions, your objective is to guess by setting minimum and maximum bounds for each of the questions such that you are 80% confident that the actual answer will be within the 80% confidence interval that you set. Obviously, if your range is from 0 to infinity for each question, the

**TABLE 10.2** Trivia Quiz: Enter the Range (Minimum and Maximum) for Which You Are 80% Certain the Answer Lies Within

| | Min | Max |
|---|---|---|
| **1.** What was the population of the city of San Diego according to the 2010 census? | | |
| **2.** In what year did Michelangelo complete his painting of the Sistine Chapel ceiling? | | |
| **3.** What was the maximum weight in pounds of President William Howard Taft (the heaviest U.S. president)? | | |
| **4.** What is the height in feet (3.3 feet per meter) of Mount Kosciuszko, the highest peak in Australia? | | |
| **5.** As of 2013, how many years have elapsed since the birth of the Carthaginian military commander, Hannibal? | | |
| **6.** What is the maximum heart rate in beats per minute of the blue throated hummingbird? | | |
| **7.** In nautical miles (1.1 miles or 1.8 km per nautical mile), what is the maximum flight range of a Boeing 747-8? | | |
| **8.** Excluding amendments and signatures, how many words are in the U.S. Constitution? | | |
| **9.** What is average distance in miles of the earth's orbit around the sun from the planet Saturn's orbit? | | |
| **10.** What is the weight in grams of the Hope Diamond? | | |

[11]The actual test administered by Russo and Schoemaker is over 15 years old and has been replaced here by another set of 10 questions. A few readers will have some difficulty converting figures either into or from the metric system; the reader should adjust confidence intervals for these difficulties.

correct answers will all fall within your confidence intervals. But, again, your goal is to answer only with 80% certainty, so narrow your ranges accordingly. Take this test before reading further.

The answers to this test are provided in Table 10.3. Since takers of this test were to establish 80% confidence intervals for each of the question estimates, each person taking this test should have gotten eight questions correct—at least on average. Answering a question correctly simply means that the actual answer will fall within the 80% confidence interval. Thus, correctly answering eight questions indicates correct "calibration" of the confidence ranges. More than eight correct may indicate underconfidence and excess conservatism; less than 80% correct indicates overconfidence. Thus, the real purpose of this test is to examine the test-taker's ability to calibrate her confidence range. The vast majority of test takers find that their answers fall within 80% confidence intervals far less than 80% of the time; in fact 20% to 50% scores are typical. Russo and Schoemaker administered a test similar to this to members of many professions, finding that most members of most professions exhibit significant overconfidence. In fact, securities analysts performed poorly relative to members of other professions, receiving scores of only 36% when asked to set 90% confidence intervals. Test subjects in most professions simply fail consistently to calibrate their certainty levels.

To test whether experiment subjects function better with respect to their areas of expertise, they were administered similar types of tests focusing on issues more relevant to their professions. The majority of professionals in most fields failed to perform much better. Interestingly, only two of the tested professions exhibited calibration skills failing to exhibit overconfidence: accountants on tests related to auditing and climatologists when forecasting weather.

**TABLE 10.3** Trivia Quiz Answers

| | |
|---|---|
| **1.** What was the population of the city of San Diego according to the 2010 census? | 1,307,402 |
| **2.** In what year did Michelangelo complete his painting of the Sistine Chapel ceiling? | 1512 |
| **3.** What was the maximum weight in pounds of President William Howard Taft? | 355 |
| **4.** What is the height in feet of Mount Kosciuszko, the highest peak in Australia? | 7,310 |
| **5.** As of 2013, how many years have elapsed since the birth of the Carthaginian military commander, Hannibal? | 2,195 |
| **6.** What is the maximum heart rate in beats per minute of the blue throated hummingbird? | 1,250 |
| **7.** In nautical miles, what is the maximum flight range of a Boeing 747-8? | 8,000 |
| **8.** Excluding amendments and signatures, how many words are in the U.S. Constitution? | 4,543 |
| **9.** What is average distance in miles of the earth's orbit around the sun from the planet Saturn's orbit? | 800,000,000 |
| **10.** What is the weight in grams of the Hope Diamond? | 9.1 |

What does this mean for stock market behavior? First, several studies show that trading activity increases when traders are overconfident. Overconfident traders tend to be more aggressive in their trading strategies. Overconfident traders under react to the information content of trades by rational traders, causing positive serial correlation in returns. Odean (1998a, 1998b) and Barber and Odean (2000, 2001), in studies of trading in 10,000 and over 60,000 discount-brokerage accounts from 1987 to 1993 and from 1991 to 1996, found that trading by investors reduced their levels of wealth below what they would have realized with simple buy-and-hold strategies. For example, they found that stocks these investors sold beat the market while those they bought did worse than the market. By one year after the trades, the average investor ended up over 9% worse off than if had he done nothing. In another study of 1,607 investors, Barber and Odean (2001) found that investors that had switched from phone-based trading to internet systems increased their portfolio turnover rates from 70% per year to 120%. They outperformed the market on average by 2.35% before switching and were outperformed by the market by 3.5% after switching. Amateur traders clearly underperformed the market and the most active traders experienced the worst performance. While commissions certainly hurt these traders, the data suggested that bid-ask spreads hurt them even more. However, their trading activity would have reduced their wealth levels even if trading costs had been zero. Interestingly, investors who traded the least actually beat market indices.

Overconfidence extends beyond the individual investor. For example, Hilary and Menzly (2006) argue that professional stock analysts who have outperformed their peers in the recent past tend to become overconfident and underperform their peers in subsequent periods. In another line of inquiry, Lichtenstein et al. (1982) argue that people tend to be overconfident in their own judgments. Griffin and Tversky (1992) argue that experts tend to be more prone to overconfidence than novices. Taylor and Brown (1988) argue that overconfidence leads "to higher motivation, greater persistence, more effective performance and ultimately more success." Perhaps, according to Kyle and Wang (1997), more aggressive trading behavior of overconfident professional traders them to generate higher profits than their more rational competitors.

## Overconfidence, Gender, Entertainment, and Testosterone

The relationship between overconfidence and performance is rather complicated. First, experimental evidence presented by Deaves et al. (2009) suggest that overconfidence, as measured by degree of miscalibration (perhaps indicated by performance on the trivia quiz above) leads to increased trading activity. However, they did not find a correlation between gender and degree of miscalibration. Nonetheless, other studies have suggested that men are more prone to overconfidence than women, particularly in male-dominated realms such as finance. Dorn and Huberman (2005) found that investors who believe that they are better than average trade more frequently. Using account data from over 35,000 accounts from a discount brokerage firm, Barber and Odean (2001) find that men trade 45% more frequently than women, reducing their returns relative to market indices by 2.65% compared to 1.72% for women. Differences between men and women in the trading realm are so striking that one might ask whether people trade for entertainment in addition to wealth creation.

Evolutionary biologists have argued that males of many species tend to take more risks than their female counterparts (e.g., Gat, 2000). They suggest that males take increased risks to enhance their status in order to create more opportunities to reproduce, knowing that prospective mates prefer higher-status males.

Science has demonstrated that testosterone and cortisol, hormones more abundant in the male body than in the female, have clear cognitive and behavioral effects. For example, testosterone is well known to be more prevalent in the bodies of winning male athletes than in losing athletes, and cortisol is known to increase in situations characterized by uncontrollability, novelty, and uncertainty. But, what is the relationship between these hormones and trading behavior? Coates and Herbert (2008) sampled, under real working conditions, endogenous steroids from a group of male London traders in the City of London. They found that a trader's morning testosterone level predicts his day's trading profitability. More specifically, they found that on mornings when testosterone levels were high, 14 of the 17 traders in their study realized higher trading profits. They also found that a trader's cortisol rises with both the variance of his trading results and the volatility of the market. Thus, Coates and Herbert found that that higher testosterone levels seem to contribute to trading returns while cortisol levels increased as risk and risk-taking increase.

Coates and Herbert expressed concern that chronically elevated testosterone levels could have negative effects on returns, because testosterone has also been found to lead to impulsivity and sensation seeking and to harmful risk taking. For example, in one study, testosterone administered to players of a gambling game led to their accepting irrational risk–reward tradeoffs. However, elevated cortisol levels accompanying elevated risk levels are likely to decrease traders' risk-taking behavior.

If individual traders, particularly aggressive individual traders, lose money relative to the market, who makes money? Consider a study by Barber et al. (2009) covering the entire Taiwanese stock market from 1995 to 1999. They documented that individual investor trading results in consistently large losses averaging approximately 3.8%. These individual investor losses amount to 2.2% of Taiwan's GDP, almost as much as total private expenditures on clothing and footwear. These losses are attributable to aggressive trading behavior. On the other hand, institutional investors outperform the market by 1.5% (after commissions and taxes, but before other costs). Both aggressive and passive trades of institutions are profitable. Perhaps aggressive trading behavior leads to wealth transfers from amateurs to professional traders.

### *Sensation Seeking*

Aggressive trading behavior does seem related to overconfidence, but there is also good reason to think that it can be related to sensation or thrill seeking, just as gambling might be. In a paper linking thrill-seeking behavior with aggressive trading, Grinblatt and Keloharju (2009) demonstrate that aggressive trading is directly related to the number of speeding tickets that traders receive. In earlier research, Zuckerman (1994) and Jonah (1997) suggest that driving behavior is an excellent observable behavior for assessing thrill seeking. Furthermore, the finding that men trade more aggressively may be rooted in the same quality that leads them to more frequently violate speed limits. Men may simply enjoy the thrill of trading and the thrill of speeding more than women do.

## Investor Moods, the Weather, and Investment Returns

There is some evidence that investor moods might significantly affect market performance. For example, Kramstra et al. (2003) found that seasonal disorder, a medical condition where the shorter days in fall and winter lead to depression for many people, is associated with reduced stock market returns after adjusting for a variety of other factors. They found that stock market returns are higher during the spring quarter than in the fall quarter. Seasonally related factors can be captured by examining cyclical ties in markets with varying latitudes, paying attention to variations in behavior near solstices and equinoxes. Northern and southern hemisphere returns seem six months out of phase.

Several studies have found that weather might affect market returns. For example, Hirshleifer and Shumway (2003) found that cloud cover in the city of a country's major stock exchange is negatively correlated with daily stock index returns in 18 of 26 national exchanges for the period of 1982 to 1997. Stock market performance was simply worse on cloudy days. In New York City, there was a 24.8% annualized return for all days forecast to be perfectly sunny, and an 8.7% average return occurred on cloudy days. There seems to be evidence in the psychology literature indicating that sunshine improves investor moods, and may collectively increase investor willingness to accept risk. Limpaphayom et al. (2007) obtained consistent results using wind and the traders on the Chicago Mercantile Exchange, with windy days seeming to increase bid-ask spreads.

However, despite these dramatic return differences, the evidence on the relationship between investor behavior and weather is not entirely clear. For example, Goetzmann and Zhu (2005) analyzed trading accounts of 79,995 investors from 1991 to 1996, finding that individual investors' trading behavior is no different on sunny days than on cloudy days. Nevertheless, market-maker behavior was significantly affected by cloud cover in one important respect: cloudy days were associated with wider bid-ask spreads, suggesting that investors (or market makers) were more risk averse on these days.

Edmans et al. (2006) find evidence of a strong link between soccer outcomes and mood, using international soccer results as their primary mood variable. They found that markets experienced significant decline after soccer losses, such as losses in the World Cup elimination stage leading to next-day abnormal stock returns of 0.49%. These loss effects were stronger in small stocks (more likely to be traded by individual investors) and for more important games. They also documented loss effects after international cricket, rugby, and basketball games. They controlled for effects of related business revenues resulting from contest outcomes. While sports losses were clearly related to stock returns, they did not find that sports wins had any significant effects on returns.

Scientific evidence is clear that lunar cycles are related to tides, animal behavior, and other natural phenomena. In related research drawing on inconsistent research results indicating that homicide rates, hospital admissions, and crisis incidents all peak in the days around full moons, Dichev and Janes (2001) find evidence that stock returns around new moons nearly double those around full moons. The effects arise in U.S. stock markets over 100 years and in other markets over the past 30 years. Are there good explanations for this? Should we suspect that eventually anything can be proved or disproved with careful statistical analysis?

## Simplifying the Decision Process

Even if investors were able to efficiently and rationally process small information sets for simple decisions, are they capable of processing larger sets of information for more complex decisions? Consider the following case illustrated by Bently MacLeod and presented by Andrew Lo in TIAA-CREF's Investment Forum:

> [C]onsider the simple task of getting dressed in the morning: For a typical male wardrobe of 5 jackets, 10 pants, 20 ties, 10 shirts, 10 pairs of socks, 4 pairs of shoes and 5 belts, there are two million different combinations to evaluate, and if we allow one second to evaluate each outfit, it would take about 23 days to select the "best" outfit. . . . Yet we all seem to get dressed in just a few minutes—how?

Even fairly simple problems such as getting dressed require heuristics or rules of thumb. However, all too often, these rules of thumb simply do not work for more complex problems such as selecting stocks. In his paper on stock market noise, Black (1986) wrote:

> Because there is so much noise in the world, people adopt rules of thumb. They share their rules of thumb with each other, and very few people have enough experience with interpreting noisy evidence to see that the rules are too simple.

Nevertheless, rules of thumb are important. Without them, many people would be simply unable to invest (or, even get dressed in the morning).

## Rational Investors and Diversification

Perhaps the single most important lesson from modern finance is the importance of diversification and its role in the management of risk. Investors can create more efficient portfolios by investing in broader arrays of investments. However, many studies suggest that investors do not diversify efficiently. For example, investors tend to concentrate their holdings in shares of their employers, in domestic shares, and even in the shares of companies located near their residences. While many investors certainly have lost substantial portfolio efficiency due to this sort of myopia, a smaller number of investors have been able to outperform the market by under diversifying. For example, Coval et al. (2005) document strong persistence in the performance of trades made by skillful individual investors who seem able to exploit market inefficiencies and information advantages to earn abnormal profits. Ivković and Weisbenner (2005) corroborate this result, finding that households exhibit a strong preference for local investments. Ivković and Weisbenner demonstrate that individuals' investments in local stocks outperform their investments in nonlocal stocks. They find that this effect is more pronounced for their investments in smaller companies outside of the S&P 500. Similarly, Massa and Simonov (2005) found that Swedish investors also exhibited strong preferences for holding stocks to which they are geographically or professionally close. They also found that such apparent information advantages enabled these investors to earn excess returns on their more "familiar" investments. In fact, Ivković et al. (2005) found that investors holding smaller, less diverse portfolios and concentrating their holdings in local companies actually outperformed their more "efficient" counterparts who held more diverse portfolios. Coval and Moskowitz (1999 and 2001) found similar results for professional fund managers: professionals tend to invest more heavily in shares of companies located nearby and earn higher returns on the holdings of these local companies.

## 10.4 NEUROFINANCE: GETTING INTO THE INVESTOR'S HEAD

While neoclassical economics has given us excellent tools to understand market behavior, behavioral finance has enabled us to better understand how financial markets might behave when its participants are irrational. Behavioral finance uses methods and results from cognitive psychology to better understand financial decision making. *Neurofinance*, in its infancy stages, is concerned with understanding the neurological processes in the investor's brain as she or he makes financial decisions. We already discussed studies concerning potential physiological causes of hyperbolic discounting and concerning the effects of testosterone on trading. In another well-publicized paper, Shiv et al. (2005) studied the relative abilities of brain-damaged study participants to make gambling decisions. This study gathered 19 subjects who had incurred damage (stable focal lesions) to parts of their brains impairing their abilities to process emotions. The subjects were asked to participate in a series of gambles along with two control groups, one that had experienced no brain damage and a second group that had experienced some other type of brain damage. Each study participant was asked to participate in a sequential series of 20 gambles, betting $1 against a 50/50 chance at either 0 or $2.50. The expected value of each gamble was $1.25, $0.25 higher than its cost. The subjects experiencing damage to their emotional circuitry bet more consistently than their "normal" counterparts and earned more money. The performance differences were more pronounced after nonimpaired subjects experienced losses, making them even more reluctant to take advantage of expected wealth-increasing gambles. The performance of the emotionally damaged group compared favorably to the control group of participants who had experienced no brain damage and to the second control group who had experienced unrelated types of brain damage.

A contrasting study by Naqvi et al. (2006) found that subjects with similar brain damage (in the ventromedial prefrontal cortex) impairing their abilities to experience emotion seem unable to learn from mistakes in everyday life decisions, leading to repeated impairment of their well-being. Similarly, when faced with repeated losses in "rigged" gambling scenarios, subjects with impaired ability to experience emotions seemed unable to learn from negative experiences. Perhaps, in sum, this and the previous studies suggest that emotions are useful in reacting to negative experiences but can lead to irrational overreactions.

Other neurofinance studies have focused on brain imaging tools, including the EEG, PET scans and, most importantly, fMRI. These imaging techniques allow researchers to examine the activity in the subject's brain as the subject experiences various stimuli, such as facing risk. For example, Knutson and Peterson (2005) discuss the application of fMRI technology to map expected utility while Kuhnen and Knutson (2005) focus directly on financial risk taking. In one study of professional foreign exchange traders, Lo and Repin (2002) used fMRI to find that more experienced traders experienced significantly less emotional reactions to dramatic market changes than did their less experienced counterparts. Essentially, they "wired" traders to examine their physiological reactions to changes in market conditions.[12] Other studies have made use of intra- and extra-cellular recording of electrical activity, which involves inserting electrodes into the cell bodies of neurons.

Neurofinance seems to be a very promising approach to understanding the way investors make decisions. Most financial research is based on the methodologies from classical economics where economists model how investors ought to behave in order to maximize their wealth, and then examine statistical and case data to determine whether they do behave in the manners that the models predict. While this study methodology has proven to be very successful in most respects, it leaves many important questions unanswered. Behavioral finance research often examines how investors make decisions in experimental or laboratory settings. Neurofinance pursues the same questions by examining the physical biological reactions of subjects to stimuli.

## 10.5 THE CONSENSUS OPINION: STUPID INVESTORS, SMART MARKETS?

Is it possible for a market comprised of irrational investors to actually, in sum, behave rationally? Is it likely that rational or educated investors play a greater role in the price-setting process than less rational or poorly educated investors? Could poorly educated or irrational investors be driven out of the price-setting process as their wealthier investors gain more power as they accumulate more wealth at the expense of their irrational counterparts? Consider a hypothetical market where professional analysts and competing investors are attempting to secure and employ all information that would enable them to evaluate stocks more accurately. However, none of the analysts have perfect information, and cannot know with certainty what stock values are. Further assume that each analyst may have some information (or method for analyzing this information) not available to other analysts. However, each analyst may be lacking some information or technique known to his competitors. Thus, information sets available to different analysts are not perfectly correlated. Given a reasonably large number of analysts, one might expect their errors to offset or cancel to some extent and that their "average" or consensus projections to outperform any given analyst's forecasts. In this scenario, the market prices generated by the large number of analysts and investors may be closer to the true security prices estimated by any individual analyst or investor. It would be very difficult for the individual investor to beat the market in this scenario.

Surowiecki (2004) described the popular TV show *Who Wants To Be a Millionaire?* to demonstrate the "wisdom of crowds" relative to individual decision makers. In this show, a contestant was asked multiple-choice questions, which, if answered correctly, could result in winnings of as much as $1 million. The contestant had the option ("lifeline") of seeking each of three types of assistance should he require it. The contestant could request

[12]Zak (2004) provides a very readable introduction to neuroeconomics methodology and literature and Peterson (2007) provides an introduction more specific to finance literature.

to have two of three incorrect answers eliminated from the answer set, call a friend or relative to ask for help, or poll the studio audience to vote on the correct answer. Eliminating incorrect answers should produce correct answers at least 50% of the time. Phone calls to friends or relatives produced the correct answer almost 65% of the time. However, the studio polls produced the correct answers 91% of the time, suggesting that crowd wisdom did seem superior to individual opinions, even the potentially expert opinions offered by the phone calls.

Surowiecki proposed conditions under which collective wisdom works well, including diversity, independence, and aggregation. For example, investors have diverse decision rules and may well make investment decisions independently of one another. They absorb information from their environments, combine it with their own interactions with their environments, and then formulate decision rules. Their effective decision rules survive, adapt, and are maintained. Securities markets provide the mechanism for aggregating the diverse rules and opinions of investors. De Figueiredo and de Figueiredo (2002) demonstrated with experimental evidence that while individual managers are able to effectively resolve less complicated problems, markets provide better settings for the resolution of more complex issues.

Numerous experiments have demonstrated that averages of classroom estimates of temperatures are more accurate than individual student estimates. Similarly, average estimates provided by surveys produce better estimates of numbers of jellybeans in jars than individual estimates. Such experiments do suggest that the crowd may compile information to produce better estimates than individuals acting alone.

## The Football Pool

Sports forecasting and betting provide excellent opportunities for testing market efficiency in that true outcomes are revealed after games are played. Consider data in Table 10.3 based on a paper by Beaver (1981) to describe how football reporters might find it difficult to outperform consensus forecasts made by a group of their colleagues.[13] The *Chicago Daily News* recorded the college football predictions of its sports staff for the last weekend of November during the 1966 to 1968 seasons. While the results of this "study" are not intended to be suitable for scientific purposes, they do illustrate the difficulty faced by forecasters attempting to outperform their peers.

While results reported in Table 10.4 do suggest that a consensus generates better football predictions than a single analyst, to what extent might this result hold in the stock market? An individual analyst might be regarded as able to generate superior forecasts if his returns consistently outperform those of the market on a risk-adjusted basis. While it is certain that at least a small number of investors consistently outperform the market, it is likely that a much larger number simply claim to do so. Furthermore, in a market with millions of investors, many would consistently outperform the market even if all selected their investments randomly. Perhaps, one should be somewhat skeptical when reviewing reports of superior investment performance.

[13]This example was described in Foster (1986).

**TABLE 10.4** The Football Pool

| | 1966 | 1967 | 1968 |
|---|---|---|---|
| Total forecasters (including consensus) | 15 | 15 | 16 |
| Total forecasts made per forecaster | 180 | 220 | 219 |
| Rank of consensus forecast | 1-tie | 2 | 2 |
| Median rank of forecasters | 8 | 8 | 8.5 |
| Rank of best forecasters | | | |
| J. Carmichael (1966) | 1-tie | 8 | 16 |
| D. Nightingale (1966) | 1-tie | 11 | 5 |
| A. Biondo (1967) | 7 | 1 | 6 |
| H. Duck (1968) | 8 | 10 | 1 |

*Sources: Beaver (1981), figure 6.1, 162; Foster (1986), table 9.1, 325.*

## Analyst Estimates

Because earnings forecasts are such an integral part of the typical analyst's stock valuation process, a number of studies have been performed to determine analysts' abilities to forecast earnings per share (EPS). Studies have indicated that consensus forecasts for EPS are superior to those of a randomly selected analyst (e.g., Fried and Givoly, 1982). By combining a large number of forecasts, individual analyst idiosyncratic errors will tend to offset one another. Several firms make consensus forecasts available to the public, including Lynch, Jones & Ryan's Institutional Brokers Estimate System (IBES), First Call (a subsidiary of Thomson Corporation), and Zacks Investment Research, Inc. Furthermore, as one might expect, studies suggest that EPS forecasts become more accurate as announcement dates approach (e.g., Brown and Chen, 1990). However, a number of studies have demonstrated that analysts' EPS forecasts tend to be overly optimistic, perhaps by as much as 20%. A number of hypotheses have been offered to explain this phenomenon, including interests of the underwriting divisions of investment banks. Nonetheless, there is evidence that investors account for this bias and are able to sift through a huge volume of other information (and misinformation) to price securities. The extent to which investors and the market are able to price securities appropriately represents the extent to which the market is efficient.

## Rational Investors and Price Setting

Consider again our example with a minimum of two rational traders and many other irrational investors (as in Kluger and Wyatt, 2004). The two rational traders competing against others can force prices up to rational levels as they compete to buy. They will force prices down to rational levels as they compete to sell. As irrational buyers buy at high prices, rational sellers will sell, competing to keep prices down to rational levels. As irrational buyers sell at low prices, rational sellers will compete to buy, competing to keep prices up to rational levels. A somewhat similar finding by Schwartz (2008) that firms forced to compete for the business of both sophisticated and naïve customers are less likely to exploit less sophisticated customers than firms that don't compete. In addition, List (2003) found that, in markets for sports memorabilia, the "endowment effect" (such as those experienced by "Joe and his opera tickets" or the roulette wheel experiments) disappears as dealers' levels experience increase.

Observations of the behavior of individuals and a variety of experiments have indicated that apparently irrational decision making frequently governs actions of consumers and investors, particularly in cases that involve potential losses. Nonetheless, might one expect that rational investors will outperform irrational investors in the market? Might rational investors tend to better preserve their capital, and even that of other investors (e.g., as professional money managers)? Perhaps, the market will tend to drive out (or bankrupt) irrational investors or at least, in time, reduce their impact on the market? Perhaps the rational investors, always driving to exploit an opportunity at the expense of irrational investors, will force market prices to properly reflect information whenever a deviation occurs? That is, might rational investors through their own efforts to secure profits, dominate the market and force prices to fully and rationally reflect available information? Furthermore, people observing the actions of others may be all too eager to note apparent irrational behavior. One is usually not able to observe the actual rationale or basis for the actions of others, and hence, may not be in a strong position to determine whether the resulting behavior truly is rational.

## Herds and Swarms

Stock markets are key mechanisms for planning and allocating economic resources for society. However, unlike governments, military organizations, and corporations, they function without formal leadership or hierarchies. No one is in charge of price setting in stock markets and determining who owns what securities in the investment arena. In fact, some observers have compared stock markets to swarms of bees and ant colonies. Miller (2007, 130) wrote that "Ants aren't clever little engineers, architects, or warriors after all—at least not as individuals." He quotes the biologist Deborah Gordan, "If you watch an ant try to accomplish something, you'll be impressed by how inept it is. Ants aren't smart. Ant colonies are." Ants collectively decide how, when, and where to forage for food. As Miller writes, they are "simple creatures following simple rules, each one acting on local information. No ant tells any other ant what to do.... No leadership is required. Even complex behavior may be coordinated by relatively simple interactions." Each ant has a tiny sliver of information that is communicated in a very rudimentary fashion to other ants, but no ant comes close to understanding the "big picture" and no ant can direct the activities of the colony as a whole. Nevertheless, a huge ant colony with hundreds of thousands of ants can thrive, feed itself, reproduce, take care of its young, fight, and even enslave other species.

The stock market may function quite similarly. Individual traders, each with a tiny subset of relevant information communicates bids and offers. Most traders do not reveal their rationale for their quotations, only their quotes. Through this process, the market collectively sets prices and allocates productive resources throughout the economy. All of this is accomplished without formal leadership or without anyone really understanding exactly why stock prices behave as they do. Ivković and Weisbenner (2007) find evidence of herding in an examination of 35,000 brokerage accounts detailing investor zip codes. They found that investors were substantially more likely to invest in securities if their neighbors had already done so. The likelihood of investing in a given stock dropped substantially as the distance to other investors who had already done so increased. To deal with the potential problem of investors simply buying stocks or in industries important to the local economy, Ivković and Weisbenner used a "social interaction barometer" developed by Putnam (2000) and found that the herding tendency was greatest in states with higher levels of social interaction. However, markets (and ant colonies as well) may be capable of committing enormous collective blunders, which might be termed bubbles and crashes.

An *information cascade* might be characterized as a sequential decision process in which each decision maker bases his decision on those made by previous decision makers and then follow what their predecessors did in the decision-making queue did rather than use his own information. This information cascading may form the basis for *herd behavior*, where decision makers pursue the same action without collaborative planning. In an information cascade, decision makers earlier in the queue have information relevant to subsequent decision makers, so this herding might be rational. The sequential nature of this decision making and its information flow is what characterizes information cascading. But, herd behavior need not be the result of sequential decision making. Members of a herd merely need to exhibit the same behavior without collaborative planning. In fact, herding behavior may seem consistent with collective irrationality. Herding behavior has been blamed for stock market bubbles and crashes as well as bank runs.

## Additional Reading

Nofsinger's 2004 book on the psychology of investing is interesting reading and very accessible to a beginner. Kahneman and Tversky (1982) contains a collection of their classic essays (other authors contributed as well) that serve as foundation classic reading for this field. Shiv et al.'s 2005 scientific article on the role of emotion in investment decision making drew substantial coverage in the popular and financial press, and Zak (2004) provides a review of academic literature in the neurofinance field. Hirshleifer and Teoh (2003) provide an excellent review of the herding literature, including discussions of herding in stock markets, bank runs, creditor runs, analyst herding, and herding in accounting reports. More generally, Surowiecki's 2004 book is highly readable, very entertaining, and offers striking examples concerning crowd wisdom, both in and outside the finance field. Statman (1997) and Ritter (2003) provide good overviews of the academic literature in behavioral finance, while Shefrin's 2002 book is an excellent and very readable introduction to the field. Miller's 2007 article is a highly readable and thoroughly entertaining discussion of swarm behavior in the insect kingdom, and describes parallels between swarm behavior in the insect kingdom and the stock market.

## References

Barber, B., Lee, Y. T., & Liu, Y.-J. (2009). Just how much do investors lose from trade? *Review of Financial Studies*, *22*, 609–632.

Barber, B., & Odean, T. (2000). Trading is hazardous to your wealth: The common stock investment performance of individual investors. *Journal of Finance, 55*, 773–806.

Barber, B., & Odean, T. (2001). Boys will be boys: Gender, overconfidence, and common stock investment. *Quarterly Journal of Economics, 116*(1), 261–292.

Barber, B., & Odean, T. (2001). On-line investors: Do the slow die first? *Review of Financial Studies, 15*(2), 455–487.

Baron, J. (2000). *Thinking and deciding* (3rd ed.). Cambridge: Cambridge University Press.

Barraclough, K., & Whaley, R. E. (2012). Early exercise of put options on stocks. *Journal of Finance* (forthcoming).

Beattie, V., & Jones, M. (2000). Impression management: The case of inter-country financial graphs. *Journal of International Accounting, Auditing & Taxation, 9*, 159–183.

Beaver, W. H. (1981). *Financial reporting: An accounting revolution*. Englewood Cliffs, NJ: Prentice-Hall.

Benartzi, S., & Thaler, R. (1995). Myopic loss-aversion and the equity premium puzzle. *Quarterly Journal of Economics, 110*, 73–92.

Black, F. (1986). Noise. *Journal of Finance, 41*, 529–544.

Block, S., & Stanley, M. (1980). The financial characteristics and price movement patterns of companies approaching the unseasoned securities market in the late 1970s. *Financial Management, 9*(4), 30–36.

Brown, L. D, & Chen, D. M. (1990). Composite analysts earnings forecasts: The next generation. *Journal of Business Forecasting, 9*, 11–15.

Coates, J. M., & Herbert, J. (2008). Endogenous steroids and financial risk taking on a London trading floor. *Proceedings of the National Academy of Sciences of the United States of America, 105*, 6167–6172.

Coval, J. D., Hirshleifer D., & Shumway T. (2005). Can individual investors beat the market? Unpublished working paper No. 04-025, School of Finance, Harvard University.

Coval, J., & Moskowitz, T. (1999). Home bias at home: Local equity preference in domestic portfolios. *Journal of Finance, 54*, 2045–2074.

Coval, J., & Moskowitz, T. (2001). The geography of investment: Informed trading and asset prices. *Journal of Political Economy, 109*, 811–841.

Deaves, R., Lüders, E., & Luo, G. Y. (2009). An experimental test of the impact of overconfidence and gender on trading activity. *Review of Finance, 13*(3), 555–575.

DeBondt, W. F. M., & Thaler, R. (1985). Does the market overreact? *Journal of Finance, 40*, 793–805.

De Figueiredo, J., & de Figueiredo, R. J., Jr. (2002). Managerial decision-making in non-market environments: A survey experiment. *Advances in Strategic Marketing*, 67–96.

Diacon, S., & Hasseldine, J. (2007). Framing effects and risk perception: The effect of prior performance presentation format on investment fund choice. *Journal of Economic Psychology, 28*, 31–52.

Dichev, I. D., & Janes, T. D. (2001). *Lunar cycle effects in stock returns*. Working Paper Series. Available at <http://ssrn.com/abstract = 281665> or <http://dx.doi.org/10.2139/ssrn.281665>.

Dimson, E., Marsh, P., & Staunton, M. (2002). *Triumph of the optimists: 101 years of global investment*. Princeton, NJ: Princeton University Press.

Edmans, A., García, D., & Norli, Ø. (2007). Sports sentiment and stock returns. *Journal of Finance, 62*(4), 1967–1998.

Foster, G. (1986). *Financial statement analysis*. Englewood Cliffs, NJ: Prentice-Hall.

Friedman, D. (1998). Monty Hall's three doors: Construction and deconstruction of a choice anomaly. *American Economic Review, 88*, 933–946.

Gat, A. (2000). The human motivational complex: Evolutionary theory and the causes of hunter-gatherer fighting. *Anthropological Quarterly, 73*, 20–34.

Genesove, D., & Mayer, C. (2001). Loss aversion and seller behavior: Evidence from the housing market. *Quarterly Journal of Economics, 116*(4), 1233–1260.

Gneezy, U., Kapteyn, A., & Potters, J. (2003). Evaluation periods and asset prices in a market experiment. *Journal of Finance, 58*, 821–837.

Goetzmann, W. N., & Zhu, N. (2005). Rain or shine: Where is the weather effect? *European Financial Management, 11*, 559–578.

Griffin, D., & Tversky, A. (1992). The weighing of evidence and the determinants of confidence. *Cognitive Psychology, 24*, 411–435.

Grinblatt, M., & Han, B. (2005). Prospect theory, mental accounting, and momentum. *Journal of Financial Economics, 78*, 311–339.

Grinblatt, M., & Keloharju, M. (2009). Sensation seeking, overconfidence, and trading activity. *Journal of Finance, 64*(2), 549–578.
Hirshleifer, D., & Shumway, T. (2003). Good day sunshine: Stock returns and the weather. *Journal of Finance, 58*, 1009–1032.
Hirshleifer, D., & Teoh, T. H. (2003). Herd behavior and cascading in capital markets: A review and synthesis. *European Financial Management, 9*(1), 25–66.
Hess, A., & Frost, P. A. (1982). Tests for price effects of new issues of new securities. *Journal of Finance, 36*, 11–25.
Hilary, G., & Menzly, L. (2006). Does past success lead analysts to become overconfident? *Management Science, 52*, 489–500.
Holloway, C. (1981). A note on testing an autoregressive investment strategy using value line ranks. *Journal of Finance, 36*, 711–719.
Ito, T. (1990). Foreign exchange expectations: Micro survey data. *American Economic Review, 80*, 434–449.
Ivković, Z., Poterba, J., & Weisbenner, S. (2005). Tax-motivated trading by individual investors. *American Economic Review, 95*(5), 1605–1630.
Ivković, Z., & Weisbenner, S. (2005). Local does as local is: Information content of the geography of individual investors' common stock investments. *Journal of Finance, 60*, 267–306.
Ivković, Z., Sialm, C., & Weisbenner, S. (2005). *Portfolio concentration and the performance of individual investors.* Working Paper, University of Illinois. AFA 2006 Boston Meetings.
Ivković, Z., & Weisbenner, S. (2007). Information diffusion effects in individual investors' common stock purchases: Covet thy neighbors' investment choices. *Review of Financial Studies, 20*(4), 1327–1357.
Jonah, B. A., Thiessen, R., & Au-Yeung, E. (2001). Sensation seeking, risky driving and behavioral adaptation. *Accident Analysis & Prevention, 33*(5), 679–684.
Kahneman, D., & Tversky, A. (1979). Prospect theory: An analysis of decision under risk. *Econometrica, 47*(2), 263–291.
Kahneman, D., & Tversky, A. (1982). Intuitive prediction: Biases and corrective procedures. In D. Kahneman, P. Slovic, & A. Tversky (Eds.), *Judgment under uncertainty: Heuristics and biases.* Cambridge: Cambridge University Press, 414–421.
Kamstra, M. J., Kramer, L. A., & Levi, M. D. (2003). Winter blues: A SAD stock market cycle. *American Economic Review, 93*(1), 324–343.
Kluger, B. D., & Wyatt, S. B. (2004). Are judgment errors reflected in market prices and allocations? Experimental evidence based on the Monty Hall problem. *Journal of Finance, 59*(3), 969–997.
Knutson, B., & Peterson, R. (2005). Neurally reconstructing expected utility. *Games and Economic Behavior, 52*, 305–315.
Kuhnen, C., & Knutson, B. (2005). The neural basis of financial risk taking. *Neuron, 47*, 763–770.
Kyle, A. S., & Wang, F. A. (1997). Speculation duopoly with agreement to disagree: Can overconfidence survive the market test? *Journal of Finance, 52*(5), 2073–2089.
Laibson, D. (1997). Golden eggs and hyperbolic discounting. *Quarterly Journal of Economics, 112*, 443–477.
Lichtenstein, S., Fischhoff, B., & Phillips, L. D. (1982). Calibration of probabilities: The state of the art to 1980. In D. Kahneman, P. Slovic, & A. Tversky (Eds.), *Judgment under uncertainty: Heuristics and biases.* Cambridge: Cambridge University Press, 306–334.
Limpaphayom, P., Locke, P. R., & Sarajoti, P. (2007). Gone with the wind: Chicago's weather and futures trading. *Review of Futures Markets, 16*, 1.
List, J. A. (2003). Does market experience eliminate market anomalies? *Quarterly Journal of Economics, 118*(1), 41–71.
Lo, A. W., & Repin, D. V. (2002). The psychophysiology of real-time financial risk processing. *Journal of Cognitive Neuroscience, 14*(3), 323–339.
Loewenstein, G., & Prelec, D. (1993). Preferences over outcome sequences. *Psychological Review, 100*(1), 91–108.
Massa, M., & Simonov, A. (2006). Hedging, familiarity, and portfolio choice. *Review of Financial Studies, 19*(2), 633–685.
Miller, P. (2007). Swarm theory. *National Geographic*, 126–147.
Myers, S. C., & Majluf, N. S. (1984). Corporate financing and investment decisions when firms have information that investors do not have. *Journal of Financial Economics, 13*, 187–221.
Naqvi, N., Shiv, B., & Bechara, A. (2006). The role of emotion in decision-making: A neuroscience perspective. *Current Directions in Psychological Science, 15*(4), 260–264.

Nofsinger, J. (2004). *The psychology of investing* (2nd ed.). Englewood Cliffs, NJ: Prentice Hall.
Odean, T. (1998a). Are investors reluctant to realize their losses? *Journal of Finance, 53*(5), 1775–1798.
Odean, T. (1998b). Volume, volatility, price and profit when all traders are above average. *Journal of Finance, 53*(6), 1887–1934.
O'Donoghue, T., & Rabin, M. (2006). Optimal sin taxes. *Journal of Public Economics, 90*(10–11), 1825–1849.
Peterson, R. (2007). Affect and financial decision-making: How neuroscience can inform market participants. *Journal of Behavioral Finance, 8*(2), 1–9.
Pool, V. K., Stoll, H. R., & Whaley, R. E. (2008). Failure to exercise call options: An anomaly and a trading game. *Journal of Financial Markets, 11*, 1–35.
Poteshman, A. M., & Serbin, V. (2003). Clearly irrational financial market behavior: Evidence from the early exercise of exchange traded stock options. *Journal of Finance, 58*, 37–70.
Putnam, R. D. (2000). *Bowling Alone*. New York: Simon and Schuster.
Rashes, M. S. (2001). Massively confused investors making conspicuously ignorant choices (MCI-MCIC). *Journal of Finance, 56*(5), 1911–1928.
Ritter, J. (2003). Behavioral finance. *Pacific Basin Finance Journal, 11*(4), 429–437.
Russo, J. E., & Schoemaker, P. J. H. (1992). Managing overconfidence. *MIT Sloan Management Review, 33*(2), 7–17.
Schwartz, A. (2008). How much irrationality does the market permit? *Journal of Legal Studies, 37*, 131.
Shefrin, H. (2002). *Beyond greed and fear: Understanding behavioral finance and the psychology of investing*. Oxford: Oxford University Press.
Shefrin, H., & Statman, M. (1985). The disposition to sell winners too early and ride losers too long: Theory and evidence. *Journal of Finance, 40*, 777–790.
Shiller, R. J. (1981). Do stock prices move too much to be justified by subsequent changes in dividends? *American Economic Review, 71*, 421–436.
Shiller, R. J., Kon-Ya, F., & Tsutsui, Y. (1996). Why did the Nikkei crash? Expanding the scope of expectations data collection. *Review of Economics and Statistics, 78*(1), 156–164.
Shiv, B., Lowenstein, G., Bechara, A., Damasio, H., & Damasio, A. (2005). Investment behavior and the negative side of emotion. *Psychological Science, 16*(6), 435–439.
Sorescu, S., & Subramanyam, A. (2006). The cross section of analyst recommendations. *Journal of Financial and Quantitative Analysis, 41*(1), 139–168.
Statman, M. (1997). Behavioral finance. *Contemporary Finance Digest, 1*(1), 5–21.
Strotz, R. H. (1956). Myopia and inconsistency in dynamic utility maximization. *Review of Economic Studies, 23*, 165–180.
Surowiecki, J. (2004). *The Wisdom of crowds: Why the many are smarter than the few and how collective wisdom shapes business, economics, societies, and nations*. New York: Doubleday.
Svenson, O. (1981). Are we all less risky and more skilled than our fellow drivers? *Acta Psychologica, 47*, 143–148.
Taylor, S., & Brown, J. (1988). Illusion and well-being: A social psychological perspective on mental health. *Psychological Bulletin, 103*, 193–210.
Tversky, A., & Kahneman, D. (1981). The framing of decisions and the psychology of choice. *Science, 211*, 453–458.
Tversky, A., & Kahneman, D. (1986). Rational choice and the framing of decisions. *Journal of Business, 59*(4), 251–278.
von Neumann, J., & Morgenstern, O. (1947). *The Theory of Games and Economic Behavior* (2nd ed.). Princeton, NJ: Princeton University Press.
Zak, P. (2004). Neuroeconomics. *Philosophical Transactions of the Royal Society B, 359*, 1737–1748.
Zuckerman, M. (1994). *Behavioural Expressions and Biosocial Bases of Sensation-Seeking*. Cambridge: Cambridge University Press.

## 10.6 EXERCISES

1. Suppose that an investor with \$2 in capital has a logarithmic utility of wealth function: $U = ln(w)$. The investor has the opportunity to buy into the gamble described in the

St. Petersburg paradox. Assume that the investor can borrow without interest and that the gamble payoff is $2^i$ where $i$ is the number of tosses or outcomes realized before the first head is realized.

**a.** What is the investor's current utility of wealth level?

**b.** How much would the investor be willing to pay for the gamble described in the St. Petersburg paradox?

**c.** How much would the investor be willing to pay for the gamble described in the St. Petersburg Paradox if his initial wealth level were $1000 rather than $2?

**d.** What would be your answer to part b if the gamble payoff were to change to $2^{2i-1}$ where $i$ is the number of tosses or outcomes realized before the first head is realized?

**2.** Three traders are at lunch and must decide on a dessert that they will share. Consider the following table, which compares trader preferences for three types of desserts, all ranked according to preferences one through three for each trader. Individual trader preferences are rational. There are three possible desserts, and thus three possible preference rankings. The traders have determined that if they vote on which dessert they will order, each of the three desserts will receive one vote, resulting in a tie. Thus, the traders decided to hold pairwise votes on combinations of two desserts. That is, they will eliminate desserts one at a time in three votes, with the winning dessert being matched against the next dessert. Thus, ice cream will be matched against cake, and then against cookies and then cookies against cake. Demonstrate that a pairwise vote (one dessert option against another) on any combination of two desserts would ultimately result in a "social" selection that will violate the principle of transitivity.

| | *Voter* 1 | *Voter* 2 | *Voter* 3 |
|---|---|---|---|
| *Ice Cream* | 1 | 3 | 2 |
| *Cake* | 2 | 1 | 3 |
| *Cookies* | 3 | 2 | 1 |

**3.** A car with a replacement value of $20,000 can be insured against a total loss with an insurance policy sold for a premium of $1200. The insurance company selling the policy and the consumer purchasing the policy agree that there is a 5% probability that the car will be destroyed.

**a.** What is the actuarial (fair or expected) value of the policy?

**b.** If the insurance maintains a large, well-diversified portfolio of such policies, what is its expected profit from the sale of this policy?

**c.** What is the expected profit (or gain or loss) to the consumer from the purchase of this policy?

**d.** Under what circumstances is the sale of this policy a rational transaction for the insurance company?

**e.** Under what circumstances is the purchase of this policy a rational transaction for the consumer?

**4.** Suppose that you were to perform an experiment on subjects to determine whether they prefer to have coffee mugs or money. You plan to use a large representative sampling of individuals and endow half of the participants in your experiment with coffee mugs and then ask those to whom mugs were given what would be the lowest price at which they would sell. Those subjects who were not given mugs were asked how much they would pay for a mug.

**a.** If participants are rational and consistent in their preferences, how should purchase prices differ from selling prices?

**b.** Assume that the endowment effect described by Kahneman and Tversky is true for individuals. How should purchase prices differ from selling prices?

**c.** What would be the relevance of this type of experiment to stock markets?

**5.** For each of the following three scenarios, would you rather:

**a.** Receive \$100 in one month or \$100 in two months (most people prefer the former)?

**b.** Be given an excellent meal at a nice restaurant in one month or in two months (most people prefer the former)?

**c.** Be given a mediocre meal at a mediocre restaurant in one month and then an excellent meal at a nice restaurant in two months or an excellent meal at a nice restaurant in one month followed by mediocre meal at a mediocre restaurant in two months (most people prefer the former)?

Assume that you respond as do most people. Explain any inconsistency in your preferences.

**6.** Churches, schools, and other nonprofit institutions have held jelly bean counting contests where contestants compete for a prize by estimating the number of jelly beans in a large jar. There is evidence suggesting that averages of contestant estimates tend to be superior to specific individual estimates. Why might this be true?

**7.** In our discussion of prospect theory, we considered the following choice of gambles:

Gamble A: 0.33 probability of receiving 2500, 0.66 of receiving 2400 and 0.01 of receiving 0

Gamble B: 100% probability of receiving 2400

and

Gamble A*: 0.33 probability of receiving 2500, 0.67 of receiving 0

Gamble B*: 0.34 probability of receiving 2400 and 0.66 of receiving 0

Demonstrate that if an investor is indifferent between Gambles A and B, he must be indifferent to A* and B* in order to fulfill the *strong independence axiom* identified by von Neumann and Morgenstern.

**8.** Suppose that the United States is preparing for the outbreak of an Asian viral disease, which, if a vaccine is not developed, is expected to kill 600 people. Two alternative vaccination programs have been proposed. The benefits of the two vaccination programs are described as follows:

Program A: 200 lives are saved

Program B: 1/3 probability that 600 lives are saved

Tversky and Kahneman (1981, 1986) find that most people prefer Program A. Now, consider the following descriptions:

Program A: 400 die

Program B: 2/3 probability that 600 die

Kahneman and Tversky find that most people prefer Program B. (See also Baron, 2000.) Since the first set of descriptions is identical to the second, choices seem to be inconsistent.

**a.** How does this example relate to the framing problem discussed by Kahneman and Tversky?

**b.** How do the descriptions presented here pertain to risk-aversion and risk-seeking preferences?

**9.** Suppose that an investor has the opportunity (and funding ability) to pay $100,000 for a 50% chance to win $300,000 and a 50% chance of winning nothing.

**a.** What is the expected value of the gamble?

**b.** What is the standard deviation of payoffs for this gamble?

**c.** Suppose that you have the opportunity (and funding ability) to repeat participation in this gamble for a total of five gambles. Each wager's outcome is independent of the outcomes of all other wagers (the correlation coefficient between wager payoffs is zero). What is the expected value of this set of five wagers?

**d.** What is the standard deviation for this set of five wagers?

**e.** Which set of wagers has a higher expected payoff—that described in parts a and b of this question or that described in parts c and d of this question?

**f.** Which set of wagers has a lower risk as measured by standard deviation—that described in parts a and b of this question or that described in parts c and d of this question?

**g.** Which set of wagers seems to be preferable based on your answers to parts a through f—the single wager or the set of five wagers?

**h.** Devise an argument that if an individual finds the gamble described in parts a and b unacceptable, he will also find the gambles described in parts c and d unacceptable.

CHAPTER

# 11

# Market Efficiency

## 11.1 INTRODUCTION TO MARKET EFFICIENCY

An efficient capital market is defined as a market where security prices reflect all available information. More formally, one can state that in an efficient market, the expected price $E[\tilde{P}]$ of a tradable asset, given the information $\phi$ available to the market and the information $\phi_k$ available to any investor $k$, equals the expected price based on the information available to the market for all investors $k$:

$$E[\tilde{P}|\phi, \phi_k] = E[\tilde{P}|\phi] \ \forall k$$

Thus, the price of the asset reflects the consensus evaluation of the market based on the information available to the market, regardless of private information held by investor $k$. This statement implies that a given individual $k$'s information set $\phi_k$ not shared with the market does not improve his estimate of expected price in an efficient market; the market price already reflects all relevant information $\phi$ including investor $k$'s special information $\phi_k$. In a perfectly efficient market where security prices fully reflect all available information, all security transactions will have zero net present value.

While we cannot realistically expect markets to be perfectly efficient, it is interesting to study the extent to which markets approach efficiency. For example, what type of information is reflected in security prices? What is the speed of information flow? How much time is required for a particular type of information to be reflected in security prices? Does market reaction to new information (or lack thereof) reflect rational self-serving behavior on the part of investors? If markets were perfectly efficient with regard to a given type of information, investors could not use this type of information to gain higher than normal returns; the information would already be reflected in security prices. Thus, investors might be able to earn abnormal returns if markets were slow to react to new information. Slow reactions to new information suggest that prices are predictable after new information is available.

If markets are perfectly efficient, then, by definition, securities reflect all available information. One might argue that security prices will fluctuate only as new information

*Financial Trading and Investing*

is realized by the market. New information should be expected to occur randomly; otherwise, it is not really new. Thus, one should expect prices in an efficient market to fluctuate randomly. Samuelson (1965) formalizes this argument in his paper entitled "Proof that Properly Anticipated Prices Fluctuate Randomly." This means that many tests of market efficiency are concerned with the extent to which security prices fluctuate randomly. Furthermore, since prices in an efficient market properly reflect all that investors know about securities, all transactions, on an ex-ante basis, will have zero net present value. Investors pay for securities exactly what they are worth.

While one might argue that market efficiency is the necessary product of rationality and greed, and that market survival requires these characteristics of investors who determine price-setting, we already suggested (in Chapter 5, concerning the importance of noise traders) that perfect market efficiency would cause financial markets to fail. Furthermore, we will present arguments later that predictable prices might be perfectly consistent with market efficiency when investors are risk-averse and in certain other circumstances.

## 11.2 WEAK FORM EFFICIENCY

As discussed in the previous section, a capital market is efficient when security prices reflect all available information. One type of relevant information might be historical price sequences or trends. *Technical analysis* is concerned with finding situations where historical price sequences can be used to forecast price movements. *Weak form efficiency tests* are concerned with whether an investor might consistently earn higher than normal returns based on knowledge of historical price sequences and other trading information. One can never prove weak form efficiency because there are an infinite number of potential ways to forecast future returns from past returns. However, one might argue that certain tests imply efficiency (or inefficiency) with regard to a specific sequence or pattern of prices. An investor armed with the knowledge of a test indicating a market inefficiency might expect to earn a higher than normal return, or face a market impediment preventing him from doing so. On the other hand, any test of market inefficiency is actually a joint test for that particular inefficiency and of some model describing normal returns in an efficient market. Thus, market efficiency cannot be fully rejected unless one is certain that the correct model for normal returns has been selected for that market. Furthermore, Grossman and Stiglitz (1980) argue that the existence of costly information retrieval and processing must lead to abnormal return sequences. Thus, markets cannot be fully or perfectly efficient. In any case, some of the more significant weak form efficiency tests are described in the following paragraphs.

### Price Sequences, Momentum and Mean Reversion

Statisticians and economists with an interest in statistics have long been fascinated by the tremendous amounts of financial data made available by the various data services. For example, Cowles (1933), Working (1934) and Kendall (1953) studied weak form markets efficiency, or more specifically, the random movement of stock prices.

Their results indicated that stock prices seemed to fluctuate randomly, without being influenced by their histories. Such processes are called random walks (see Chapter 6).

Another of the earlier weak form efficiency tests (Granger (1968)) found a very slight, but statistically significant relationship between historical and current prices: 0.057% of a given day's variation in the log of the price relative is explained by the prior day's change in the log of the price relative:

$$\ln\left(\frac{P_{i,t}}{P_{i,t-1}}\right) = \hat{b}_0 + \hat{b}_1 \cdot \ln\left(\frac{P_{i,t-1}}{P_{i,t-2}}\right) + \hat{\varepsilon}_{i,t}$$

The r-square value from this regression was 0.00057, where $P_{i,t}$ represents price of stock $i$ on a given day $t$, $P_{i,t-1}$ the price on the day immediately prior, $\hat{b}_0$ and $\hat{b}_1$ regression coefficients, and $\hat{\varepsilon}_{i,t}$ the error terms in the regression.[1] On the other hand, Fama and MacBeth (1973), after adjusting for risk, found no correlation in daily capital asset pricing model (CAPM) residuals. A typical testing format assumed that stock returns were produced by the CAPM (or single index model), but that residuals from such a model were uncorrelated with prior day residuals:

$$r_{i,t} = r_f + \beta_i(r_{m,t} - r_f) + \hat{\varepsilon}_{i,t}$$

$$\hat{\varepsilon}_{i,t} = \hat{a} + \hat{b}_i\hat{\varepsilon}_{i,t-1} + \hat{\eta}_{i,t}$$

where $r_{i,t}$ represents the return on stock $i$ on a given day $t$, $\beta_i$ its CAPM beta, and $r_f$ the riskless return rate. Error terms (residuals or excess returns) $\hat{\varepsilon}_{i,t}$ are then regressed against their prior day values $\hat{\varepsilon}_{i,t-1}$. The sign of the $\hat{b}_i$ coefficient here would be key. A negative value for $\hat{b}_i$ suggests that sequential returns or price changes are inversely correlated, indicating that stock prices are more likely to drift towards their historical mean values than drift away. Positive values for $\hat{b}_i$ suggest that directions of sequential price changes are likely to be sustained, indicating that price changes might carry momentum. Fama and MacBeth found no (or very little) evidence for either mean reversion or momentum in stock prices.

Regardless of the analyst's findings concerning evidence for mean reversion or momentum in stock prices, it is important to note that correlation coefficients can be unduly influenced by extreme observations. This is because returns (or logs of one plus returns) and residuals are not normally distributed as required by CAPM and OLS regression assumptions. One way to deal with such assumption violations is to construct a simple runs test. For example consider the following daily price sequence: 50, 51, 52, 53, 52, 50, 45, 49, 54, and 53. The price changes might be represented by the following: $(+++---++-)$, indicating four price runs. That is, there were four series of positive or negative price change runs. The expected number of runs in a runs test if price changes are random is (MAX + MIN)/2, where MAX is the largest number of possible runs (equals the number of prices in the series minus 1) and MIN is the minimum number (1). The number of runs consistent with random sequences in our example is $10 = (9 + 1)/2$. More runs than this number suggests price reversals (mean reversion), and a smaller number of runs suggests

[1]See text Appendix A.1 for a review of basic statistics topics. We will illustrate a mean reversion/momentum test in the Testing Momentum and Mean Reversion Strategies section of this chapter.

positive correlations between sequential price changes (momentum). Thus, our example might be consistent with slight evidence of momentum, but the sample set is too small to suggest significance. The actual levels of returns are unimportant; only the signs of returns are important, so that extreme observations will not unduly bias tests. In one test of daily price changes, Fama (1965) expected 760 runs based on the assumption that price changes were randomly generated, but only found 735 runs. This indicated a small positive correlation in daily stock price changes. Granger and Morgenstern (1972) found that high transactions costs seem to be related to runs—investors are unable to exploit a series because of brokerage commissions.

Niederheffer and Osborn (1966) found two to three times as many reversals of price trends as continuations based on transaction-to-transaction price data. This might be because of unexecuted limit orders—for them to be executed the price has to reverse itself. For example, suppose that a market purchase order has just been executed at an uptick. All of the limit sell orders at this most recent execution price have to be executed for the price to increase again. This means that a purchase is more likely to be followed by a downtick (−) or no change at all (0) than an uptick (+).

## Relative Strength

Relative strength trading rules are concerned with the current price of a stock relative to a historical price or the prices of other securities or indices. For example, one relative strength rule compares the current price of a stock to its average price over a given period of time. Levy (1967), conducting a test of many such rules, found the following rule to be profitable:

1. Rank stocks based on the ratio ($P_t/P_{avg}$) where $P_t$ is the current price and $P_{avg}$ is the average price over the prior 27 weeks.
2. Buy the stocks in the highest fifth percentile and sell the stocks in the lowest 70th percentile.

This rule might suggest that the stocks with the strongest performance over the past 27 weeks will outperform the market. However, this rule might simply mean we buy the riskiest securities (high expected returns) and sell the lowest risk securities. Thus, perhaps, this rule simply means that investors purchasing higher risk stocks are merely compensated with higher returns for bearing this risk. Jensen and Bennington (1970) found that relative strength rules worked no better than random purchases of stocks after adjusting for transaction costs and even worse given risk adjustments. They suggest that the success of the rule suggested by Levy is due merely to selection bias, in that Levy had tested 68 different trading rules. That is, one of the 68 trading rules must surely work in his limited size sample of prices.

## Filter Rules and Market Overreaction

A filter rule states that a transaction for a security should occur when its price has changed by a given percentage over a specified period of time. For example, Alexander (1961), in a study of stock prices from 1897 to 1959, suggested that certain price increases of given proportions indicated upward trends, and should serve as purchase signals. He concluded that there were identifiable trends in security prices, but that these trends varied over time. Other early studies (e.g., Fama and Blume (1966)) found that when filter rules did seem to work (however slightly), they were not able to cover transactions costs. Profitability of these rules seems to be related to daily correlations. Such correlation and filter rules seemed to work slightly better in Norway, where stronger correlations tended to exist. However, these markets were less liquid and transactions costs were significantly higher in Norwegian markets than in American markets (See, for example, Jennergren and Korsvold (1975).). None of the tested rules seemed to work well enough to cover the particularly high transactions costs. Regardless, the apparent profitability of the filter rules seem directly related to transactions costs, and failed to cover them.

A few statistical studies suggest that market overreactions to information and abnormal returns can be realized by buying losers and selling winners. DeBondt and Thaler (1985) argued that buying stocks that performed poorly in a prior three- to five-year period and selling those that performed well would have generated abnormally high returns in subsequent three- to five-year periods. Apparently, longer-term stock-price mean reversion seems due to market overreactions over these longer periods. Richards (1997) found similar results for market indices in various countries.

On the other hand, Jegadeesh and Titman (1993) found results that conflicted with DeBondt and Thaler based on shorter holding periods (3 to 12 months). Their study suggested that the market is slow to react to firm-specific information. Lo and MacKinlay (1988) found that the level of short-term momentum effects displayed by stocks is inversely related to firm size. Apparently, smaller firms experience more momentum effects than do larger firms. If smaller firms have smaller investor followings and more restricted information availability, this apparent momentum might suggest that the market is relatively slow to react to information.

The findings of both DeBondt and Thaler and Jegadeesh and Titman that seem to contradict weak form market efficiency are not universally accepted. For example, Richardson and Stock (1988) argued that these momentum results of DeBondt and Thaler were due largely to their statistical methodology, as did Jegadeesh (1991), who argued that these mean reversion effects seemed to hold only in January.

## Moving Averages

*Moving average* techniques consolidate shorter series of observations into longer series, are commonly used for smoothing data variability, and are frequently used as a reference point to gauge daily fluctuations. A simple q−period moving average is computed as follows:

$$MA_{q,t} = \frac{x_t + x_{t-1} + \cdots + x_{t-q-1}}{q} = \sum_{i=1}^{q} x_{t-i}/q$$

For example, daily stock prices are compared to a moving average of a specified number of historical prices. Trading strategies might be based on these moving averages.

For example, if current prices rise above a falling moving average, they might be expected to drop back towards the moving average; selling is suggested. The movement above the moving average might suggest that the current high price is due to random error or noise. Buying is suggested when the moving average flattens out and the stock's price falls below the moving average. There are numerous other moving average rules, and they can be thoroughly contradictory with one another.

Moving averages can be computed for any number of price data points. For example, consider the following sequence of daily closing prices for a given stock over a period of time:

| | | | | | | | | | | | |
|---|---|---|---|---|---|---|---|---|---|---|---|
| 12 | 14 | 17 | 13 | 14 | 19 | 22 | 17 | 11 | 18 | 16 | 22 |
| $t = 1$ | $t = 2$ | $t = 3$ | $t = 4$ | $t = 5$ | $t = 6$ | $t = 7$ | $t = 8$ | $t = 9$ | $t = 10$ | $t = 11$ | $t = 12$ |

The following represents the sequence of simple three-day moving averages for the above price sequences:

| | | | | | | | | | | | |
|---|---|---|---|---|---|---|---|---|---|---|---|
| NA | NA | 14.3 | 14.7 | 14.7 | 15.3 | 18.3 | 19.3 | 16.7 | 15.3 | 15.0 | 18.7 |
| $t = 1$ | $t = 2$ | $t = 3$ | $t = 4$ | $t = 5$ | $t = 6$ | $t = 7$ | $t = 8$ | $t = 9$ | $t = 10$ | $t = 11$ | $t = 12$ |

A study by Brock et al. (1992) demonstrated evidence suggesting that certain moving average rules and rules based on resistance levels produced higher than normal returns when applied to daily data for the Dow Jones Industrial Average from 1897 to 1986. However, Sullivan et al. (1997) tested their findings on updated data and found "that the best technical trading rule does not provide superior performance when used to trade in the subsequent 10-year post-sample period."

## The January Effect

Numerous studies including Rozeff and Kinney (1976), Roll (1981), Keim (1983), and Reinganum (1983) have confirmed a "January effect." This effect is that returns for the month of January tend quite consistently to exceed returns for any other of the eleven months. This January effect seems most pronounced during the first five trading days in January and the last trading day in December. However, the January effect continues to persist throughout the month. Additionally, this January effect seems to have a greater effect on the shares of smaller companies (which are frequently held by individual investors) than on the shares of larger firms (frequently held by institutional investors).

Roll (1983), Keim (1989), and Griffiths and White (1993) argued that much of the January effect can be explained by the tendency for December transactions to be seller initiated and execute at bid prices, while January transactions are buyer initiated and execute at offer prices. However, the latter two papers argue that the January effect is large enough that it would exist even if all transactions executed at bid prices. None of these papers explains the full size of the January effect.

### *The January Effect and Tax-Driven Selling*

One explanation for this January effect is year-end tax selling—investors sell their "losers" at the end of the year to capture tax write-offs. This year-end tax selling forces down prices at the end of the year. They recover early in the following year, most significantly during the first five trading days in January (and the last trading day in December). Branch (1977) finds evidence suggesting this explanation. He found that stocks selling at their annual low at year's end outperformed the market in January by 8%. However, he concluded that this increase barely covered transaction costs for investors wishing to exploit this price increase (he assumed a high transaction cost). Nonetheless, an investor wishing to purchase securities in late December might benefit from this knowledge. Dyl (1977) supports the year-end selling hypothesis by reporting that abnormally high trading volume exists in December. Adding further credibility to the year-end tax selling hypothesis, other studies, including Givoly and Ovadia (1983), have also found that "losers" outperform "winners" in January of the subsequent year and that firm returns in January are directly related to losses in the prior year. Furthermore, Chan et al. (1985) and Chang and Pinegar (1986) report January effects for low-grade corporate bonds and in shares of companies that issue these bonds. This effect does not seem to hold for high-grade corporate bonds or for the shares of the companies that issue these bonds. This, they argue, supports the tax-loss selling hypothesis for the January effect.

Contrasting the tax explanations for the January effect are studies demonstrating that this effect exists in markets whose tax years differ from the calendar year. That is, if tax-loss selling explains the January effect, the January effect should not hold in countries whose tax years differ from calendar years. Nonetheless, the January effect does appear in Australia and other countries where the fiscal and calendar years differ. Furthermore, the January effect in Canada existed before the introduction of a capital gains tax. Why should a country experience a tax-related January effect if there is no tax-driven selling?

However, some observers have argued that U.S. markets are sufficiently influential in world markets that year-end tax selling in the U.S. might simply drive prices in other markets. On the other hand, studies have demonstrated a January effect in U.S. markets during the 1877–1916 period, prior to the introduction of U.S. income taxes–again, a January effect with no tax-driven selling. Furthermore, Kihn (1996) presents evidence that municipal bond issues, which are free from federal taxation, experience a significant January effect. Thus, despite the popularity of the tax explanation, there still remain serious doubts regarding its ability to explain the January effect.

### *The January Effect and Window Dressing*

Some market observers have also suggested that funds will "window dress" at year-end by buying winners (stocks that performed well earlier in the year) and by selling losers. These transactions occur at the end of the year so that their clientele can see from year-end financial statements that their funds held high-performing stocks and did not hold losers. The buy pressure on winners and sell pressure on losers might be expected to cause losers to underperform winners during the period of window dressing; in January after the period of window dressing losers will outperform winners. However, most institutions will report their holdings to their clients more than once per year and some will report based on fiscal years other than from January 1 to December 31. But, this effect does not appear in any other month. Furthermore, winners still realize higher January returns than in any other month, just not as high as losers. If the "window-dressing" hypothesis explains the January effect better than the tax-selling hypothesis, one should expect that shares held by institutions should outperform shares held by individuals during the month of January. First, we note that the January effect is more pronounced for smaller firms than for larger firms (smaller firms are more likely to be held by individual investors). Second, another study found that the January effect is far more pronounced for companies with significant numbers of individual shareholders than those companies with significant numbers of institutional investors. Thus, the tax-selling hypothesis seems to explain the January effect better than the "window-dressing" hypothesis. However, since there are still many holes in the tax-selling hypothesis, it appears that the January effect remains an anomaly.

## The Small Firm and Price/Earnings Effects

There also exists substantial evidence that smaller firms outperform larger firms (e.g., Banz (1981)). For example, if one were to rank all NYSE and Nasdaq firms by size, one is likely to find that those firms that are ranked as smaller will outperform those that are ranked larger. This effect holds after adjusting for risk as measured by beta. However, other measures of risk may be more appropriate for smaller firms that may not have well-established trading records due to market thinness or due to "newness" when compared to typical larger firms. Furthermore, transactions costs for many smaller firms may exceed those for larger firms, particularly when they are thinly traded. There is also evidence that these abnormally high returns for smaller firms are most pronounced in January. Although Fama and French (1992) find a significant size effect in their study of the CAPM over a 50-year period, they do not find a size effect during the period between 1981 and 1990. This *might* suggest that the size effect either no longer exists or was merely a statistical artifact prior to 1981. Two studies found that abnormal returns in January are more related to share price effects than to firm size; in fact, after controlling for share prices (and noting the higher proportional transactions costs on lower priced shares), the size effect disappears as a partial explanation of the January effect.

Basu (1977) and Fama and French (1992) find that firms with low P/E ratios outperform firms with higher P/E ratios. Fama and French find that the P/E ratio, combined with firm size, predicts security returns significantly better than the CAPM.

## The Initial Public Offering Anomaly

The initial public offering (IPO) anomaly refers to three unusual pricing patterns associated with IPOs of equities:

1. Short-term IPO returns are abnormally high.
2. IPOs seem to underperform the market in the long run.
3. Abnormal IPO returnperformance seems to be cyclical.

IPOs have been shown to generate significant short-term returns. These returns are most substantial on the day of the new issue. The abnormal returns exist after adjusting for risk (see, for example, McDonald and Fisher, 1972, Ibbotson and Jaffee, 1975, and Ritter, 1984). Thus, it seems that unseasoned offerings with no trading histories do generate abnormally high short-term returns. However, the longer-term returns on IPOs do not seem nearly so high; in fact, several studies report IPO returns to be negative over the period 20 days to two years after the IPO (see, for example, Ritter, 1991). Some evidence suggests that these IPO returns are due to the provision of useful price-setting information by IPO market participants and by price supports in the IPO aftermarket. The third part of the IPO anomaly is that the first two are cyclical, being more pronounced during strong stock market periods.

## Sports Betting Markets

Sports betting markets potentially have much in common with stock markets. There is some evidence of persistent inefficiencies in sports betting markets. For example, Thaler and Ziemba (1988) note that favorites in horse races outperform long shots while Woodland and Woodland (1994) find the opposite is true for baseball betting. Brown and Sauer (1993) find that several observable variables in addition to the spread can be used to improve the outcomes of professional basketball games. Gray and Gray (1997), Golec and Tamarkin (1991), Sauer et al. (1988), and Gandar et al. (1988) find evidence that certain strategies can be used to improve professional football betting.

## Summary

Generally, statistical studies seem to indicate that stock markets are efficient with respect to historical price sequences. However, one must realize that an infinite number of possible sequences can be identified with any series of prices. Clearly, many of these series must be associated with higher than normal future returns. Statistical studies have certainly found evidence of predictability in stock prices, normally referring to such findings as anomalies.[2] However, when research finds a sequence that leads to higher than normal returns, one must question whether the abnormal return result is merely a statistical artifact due to data mining. According to William Schwert (2003):

> These [research] findings raise the possibility that anomalies are more apparent than real. The notoriety associated with the findings of unusual evidence tempts authors to further investigate puzzling anomalies and later try to explain them. But even if the anomalies existed in the sample period in which they were first identified, the activities of practitioners who implement strategies to take advantage of anomalous behavior can cause the anomalies to disappear (as research findings cause the market to become more efficient).

Richard Roll (1992), in a blunt comment, stated:

> I have personally tried to invest money, my client's and my own, in every single anomaly and predictive result that academics have dreamed up. That includes the strategy of DeBondt and Thaler (that is, sell

[2]Most notably, the IPO effect, calendar effects, size effects, and momentum/reversion effects.

short individual stocks immediately after one-day increases of more than 5%), the reverse of DeBondt and Thaler which is Jegadeesh and Titman (buy individual stocks after they have decreased by 5%), etc. I have attempted to exploit the so-called year-end anomalies and a whole variety of strategies supposedly documented by academic research. And I have yet to make a nickel on any of these supposed market inefficiencies.

Clearly, technical analysis has its share of critics. For example, Warren Buffet was quoted saying, "I realized technical analysis didn't work when I turned the charts upside down and didn't get a different answer." In any case, most apparent incidences of mispricing seem eliminated by transactions costs. The primary exceptions to weak form market efficiency seem to be IPO effect, probably the January effect, perhaps the small firm effect, and perhaps the P/E effect. There seems to be little agreement as to why these effects persist or even whether the latter two exist; they remain anomalies.

## 11.3 TESTING MOMENTUM AND MEAN REVERSION STRATEGIES

In this section, we provide an illustration of a momentum/mean reversion test. Essentially, this means that we will test whether the return for a stock on a given day can be used to predict the return on that stock for the subsequent day. (See the discussion on price sequences and relative strength in the previous section.) If returns seem to be positively correlated from one day to the next, this would evidence momentum in stock prices over time. A negative correlation would evidence mean reversion. Consider the sequence of daily closing prices in Table 11.1 for a hypothetical stock Q, from which we compute returns. The prices given in this table assume that the stock traded each day, including

**TABLE 11.1** Stock Price and Return Data

| Date | $t$ | $\text{Price}_t$ | $\text{Return}_t$ | $\text{Return}_{t-1}$ |
|---|---|---|---|---|
| 02/01/12 | 1 | 49 | | |
| 02/02/12 | 2 | 50 | 0.020408 | |
| 02/03/12 | 3 | 51 | 0.020000 | 0.020408 |
| 02/04/12 | 4 | 52 | 0.019607 | 0.020000 |
| 02/05/12 | 5 | 55 | 0.057692 | 0.019607 |
| 02/06/12 | 6 | 57 | 0.036363 | 0.057692 |
| 02/07/12 | 7 | 58 | 0.017543 | 0.036363 |
| 02/08/12 | 8 | 59 | 0.017241 | 0.017543 |
| 02/09/12 | 9 | 58 | −0.016949 | 0.017241 |
| 02/10/12 | 10 | 55 | −0.051724 | −0.016949 |
| 02/11/12 | 11 | 53 | −0.036363 | −0.051724 |
| 02/12/12 | 12 | 52 | −0.018867 | −0.036363 |

**TABLE 11.2** Stock Price Data

| $t$ | $\text{Return}_t$ | $\text{Return}_{t-1}$ | $a + br_{t-1}$ | $\varepsilon_i$ | $\varepsilon_i^2$ |
|---|---|---|---|---|---|
| 3 | 0.020000 | 0.020408 | 0.013735 | 0.00626 | 0.000039239 |
| 4 | 0.019607 | 0.020000 | 0.013420 | 0.00618 | 0.000038278 |
| 5 | 0.057692 | 0.019607 | 0.013118 | 0.04457 | 0.001986848 |
| 6 | 0.036363 | 0.057692 | 0.042510 | −0.00614 | 0.000037788 |
| 7 | 0.017543 | 0.036363 | 0.026049 | −0.00850 | 0.000072353 |
| 8 | 0.017241 | 0.017543 | 0.011525 | 0.00571 | 0.000032673 |
| 9 | −0.016949 | 0.017241 | 0.011291 | −0.02824 | 0.000797554 |
| 10 | −0.051724 | −0.016949 | −0.015095 | −0.03662 | 0.001341651 |
| 11 | −0.036363 | −0.051724 | −0.041934 | 0.00557 | 0.000031029 |
| 12 | −0.018867 | −0.036363 | −0.030079 | 0.01121 | 0.000125692 |
| | | | | SSE = | 0.004503110 |

weekends. We will attempt our test illustration based on an extremely small sample to simplify our computations.

Although there are many ways to determine the nature of the relationship between the return on a security and its prior day's return, we will examine whether there exists a linear relationship based on a simple ordinary least squares (OLS) regression of the form: $\hat{r}_{i,t} = \hat{a} + \hat{b}_i\hat{r}_{i,t-1} + \hat{\varepsilon}_{i,t}$. We report regression results as follows:

$$\hat{r}_{i,t} = -.0020142 + .7717758 \cdot \hat{r}_{i,t-1} \quad r^2 = 0.57$$

$$(-0.25959) \; (3.259325) \qquad \text{SSE} = 0.00450311$$

$$n = 10 \quad d.f. = 8$$

Note that $t$-statistics are given in parentheses. The slope term $\hat{b}_i$ is 0.7717758, positive and statistically significant at the 5% level. We will return shortly to explain and interpret these results. However, we will first work through the details on obtaining the results of our simple OLS regression. First, our $\hat{a}_i$ and $\hat{b}_i$ coefficients are determined following the simple OLS method as follows:

$$\hat{b}_i = \frac{\sum(r_t - \bar{r}_t)(r_{t-1} - \bar{r}_{t-1})}{\sum(r_{t-1} - \bar{r}_{t-1})^2} = \frac{.000775}{.001004} = .7717758 \tag{11.1}$$

$$\hat{a}_i = \bar{r}_t - \hat{b}_i\bar{r}_{i,t-1} = -.0020142 \tag{11.2}$$

To obtain regression diagnostics, we compute squared error-term values as in Table 11.2.

We are able to compute regression standard errors from calculations in Table 11.2:

$$se(\hat{b}_i) = \sqrt{\frac{\frac{SSE}{n-2}}{\sum (r_t - \bar{r}_t)^2}} = \sqrt{\frac{.000562888}{.01003}} = \sqrt{.056069} = .23679$$

$$se(\hat{a}_i) = \sqrt{\frac{\frac{\sum_{i=1}^{n} \varepsilon_i^2}{n-2} \cdot \sum_{i=1}^{n} x_i^2}{n \cdot \sum_{i=1}^{n} (x_i - \bar{x})^2}} = \sqrt{\frac{.000562888 \cdot .0107417}{10 \cdot .01003911}} = \sqrt{.000060228} = .007760684$$

Given our standard error estimates $se(\hat{a}_i) = 0.007760684$ and $se(\hat{b}_i) = 0.05606069533$, we find our $t$-statistics to be $t(\hat{a}_i) = -.25959$ and $t(\hat{b}_i)$ to be 3.2593. Suppose our tests were expressed formally as follows:

$$H_0: \hat{a}_i = 0 \quad H_0: \hat{b}_i = 0$$

$$H_A: \hat{a}_i \neq 0 \quad H_A: \hat{b}_i \neq 0$$

Since we will assume that $a$ and $b$ follow student $t$-distributions, we will compare our $t$-statistic to critical values found in the $t$-distribution table, given the appropriate level of confidence and degrees of freedom. We are performing two-tail tests for significance. Suppose we test for significance at a level of 0.95 (0.025 on each side of the tail). In this case, the significance of our test is $\alpha = 0.025$ and the number of degrees of freedom $k$ equals $10 - 2 = 8$. Our critical value for the test is found:

$$t^{8}_{.025} = 2.306$$

While we fail to reject our first null hypothesis that $\hat{a}_i = 0$ (not an important finding here), we reject our second null hypothesis that $\hat{b}_i = 0$. Thus, our test does provide evidence that the returns for this security are linearly related to returns on prior days, and for a momentum effect in stock prices.

## 11.4 SEMISTRONG FORM EFFICIENCY

Investors acquire information for input to their valuation models. If markets are efficient, their valuation results will reflect the information that is available for them to acquire. *Semistrong form efficiency* tests are concerned with whether security prices reflect all publicly available information. For example, how much time is required for a given type of information to be reflected in security prices? What types of publicly available information might an investor use to generate higher than normal returns? The majority of studies of semistrong form market efficiency suggest that the tested publicly available information and announcements cannot be used by the typical investor to secure significantly higher than normal returns. A few of the exceptions to this rule are included in the following paragraphs. In addition, investors able to react within a few minutes to event news may be able to secure higher than normal returns.

## Early Tests

Garfield Cox (1930) found no evidence that professional stock analysts could outperform the market. Similarly, and more rigorously, Cowles (1933) performed several tests of what was later to be known as the efficient market hypothesis (EMH). He examined the forecasting abilities of 45 professional securities analysis agencies (including fire insurance companies, financial services companies, and financial publications). He compared the returns that might have been generated by professionals' recommendations to actual returns on the market over the same period. He found that the average returns generated by professionals were less than those generated by the market over the same periods. He found that the best performing fund was not an outlier; that is, it did not exhibit unusually high performance at a statistically significant level. Cowles also tested whether analyst recommendations were correct an unusually high number of times; that is, he tested whether analyst picks were profitable relative to the market more frequently than might be expected with random picks. Analyst picks were not more profitable.

Cowles also examined the abilities of analysts to predict the direction of the market as opposed to selecting individual stocks. He found that a buy and hold strategy was at least as profitable as following "average" advice of professionals as to when to be long or short in the market. He performed a simulation study using a deck of cards (since there were no computers capable of generating random numbers at the time). Based on reports of analyst recommendations, he computed the average number of times analysts change their recommendations over a year (33 times). He then randomly selected 33 dates, using cards numbered 1 to 229 (the number of weeks the study covered) to make simulated random recommendations. Draws were taken from a second set of randomly selected cards numbered 1 to 9, each with a certain recommendation (long, short, half stock, and half cash, etc.) for a given date. Cowles then compared the results distribution of the 33 recommendations based on randomly generated advice to the advice provided by the actual advisors. He found that the professionals generated the same return distributions as did the random recommendations. Thus, he concluded that the best-informed analysts would perform no better than the uninformed investor making random investing decisions. Cowles also examined 255 editorials by William Peter Hamilton, the fourth editor of the *Wall Street Journal*, who had gained a reputation for successful forecasting. Between 1902 until his death in 1929, Hamilton forecast 90 changes in the market; 45 were correct and 45 were incorrect.

If experts are unable to distinguish between strong and weak stock market performers, and investors are well aware of this lack of ability, why do market forecasters still exist and investors still purchase and follow their advice? One possible explanation for reliance on unreliable "expert" forecasters is that investors are less interested in accuracy than in avoiding responsibility for their selections. Investors who rely on advice from experts seek to avoid blame when the forecasts are inaccurate. Avoidance of responsibility in another field is illustrated by Cocozza and Steadman (1978) in their study of New York psychiatrists who were asked to predict whether mental patients were dangerous and required involuntary confinement. Although numerous studies have consistently shown that psychiatrists cannot predict which patients are dangerous, the expert diagnoses were accepted by 87% of the courts in their study. Such "expert" advice seemed to relieve courts of further responsibility for the patients.

## Stock Splits

In a particularly important seminal test of semistrong form market efficiency, Fama et al. (1969) examined the effects of stock splits on stock prices. Because it seems logical that stock splits should be cosmetic in nature, and that Fama et al. generally reached this empirical conclusion, the results of this paper are somewhat less important than the methodology used in the study. This paper was the first to use the now classic event study methodology. Although stock prices did change significantly before announcements of stock splits (and afterwards as well), Fama et al. argued that splits were related to more fundamental factors (such as dividends), and that it was actually these fundamental factors that affected stock prices. The splits themselves were unimportant with respect to subsequent returns.

Fama et al. identified the month in which a particular stock split occurred, calling that event month time zero for that stock. Thus, each stock had associated with it a particular month zero ($t = 0$), and months subsequent to the split were assigned positive values. They then estimated expected returns for each month $t$ for the stocks in their sample with single index model: $r_{i,t} = a + b_i r_{m,t} + e_{i,t}$ where the expected residual ($e_{i,t}$) value was zero. Fama et al. tested 940 splits occurring between from 1956 to 1960, excluding from their beta computations returns data 15 months before and after splits. They then examined residuals ($e_{i,t}$) for each security $i$ for each month $t$ then averaged the residuals ($AR_t$) for each month across securities. Afterwards, they calculated cumulative average residuals ($CAR_t$) starting 30 months before splits ($t = -30$). Cumulative average residuals increased dramatically starting 30 months before split. Fama et al. regarded it unlikely for this increase to occur because a split was anticipated, but reasoned that splits occur after significant price growth. They found that after splits, residuals ($AR_t$) again average zero. Finally, Fama et al. split their sample of companies into those increasing dividends after a split versus companies not increasing dividends. Companies splitting stock and then increasing dividends had continued increasing CARs after the split announcement date; those splitting stock then decreasing dividends experienced decreasing CARs. Thus, dividends might indicate fundamental strengths; splits do not appear to be relevant. On average, once the split is announced, positive residuals (CARs) no longer exceed zero.

Subsequent tests on stock splits have not been entirely consistent with the results of Fama et al. For example, it has been argued that splits increase the proportional trading costs of stocks. Investors should require higher returns to compensate for these higher trading costs. Later studies have documented positive residuals on split announcements.

Nonetheless, the Fama et al. study provided the framework for future event studies and semistrong efficiency tests. Consider the following general notes regarding testing the semistrong form efficiency hypothesis:

1. Use daily price and returns data since information is incorporated into prices within days (or much shorter periods).

2. Announcements are usually more important than events themselves.
3. Base security performance on estimated expected returns.
4. When using the market model (standard single index model), we estimate slopes from historical data. Normally, we find them biased forecasters for future values, so we may adjust them towards one.
5. One way to deal with slope measurement error is to use moving windows for the period whose excess return is being determined, estimate slope based on time periods preceding and following the testing period, excluding the testing period itself.
6. An alternative to adding to determine cumulative excess returns is adding them to 1, then multiplying them to compute *buy and hold abnormal residuals* as follows: $BHAR_t = \Pi(1 + e_t) - 1$.

## Corporate Merger Announcements, Annual Reports, and Other Financial Statements

Thousands of other tests of semistrong form efficiency have been reported in the academic literature, covering wide varieties of events. For example, Firth (1976) considered market efficiency when an announcement is made for purchase of more than 10% of a firm. Presumably, an announcement indicates a potential merger. Firth calculated CAR starting 30 days prior to announcements; the bulk of CAR is realized between last trade before and first trade after announcements, though it still increases slightly after an announcement. Thus, a large block purchaser can still make excess returns. An insider obviously can make excess returns; one without inside information cannot (except very shortly after the announcement). Since returns change almost immediately, Firth suggested that there is semistrong efficiency with respect to merger announcements.

Ball and Brown (1968) study the usefulness of the information content of annual reports. With a primary focus on EPS, they find that security prices already reflect 85% to 90% of information contained in annual reports; security prices show no consistent reactions to annual report releases. They conclude that analysts obtain more timely information from other sources.

## Information Contained in Publications and Analyst Reports

Davies and Canes (1978) considered information analysts sell to clients then publish in the "Heard on the Street" column in *The Wall Street Journal*. They used the market model to measure the relationship among the market, risk, and the security. Information in this column was frequently sold by investment firms to clients before publication in the journal. Prices seemed to rise significantly after information was sold to clients, then even more when it was published in the *Wall Street Journal*. Davies and Canes tested to see whether these large residuals on the *Wall Street Journal* publication day were significant by standardizing each day's return and then checking to see how many standard deviations from zero the excess or abnormal return lies.

Other studies (e.g., Black (1973), Holloway (1981), and Huberman and Kandel (2002)) have been performed on the ability to use information provided by *Value Line Investment Surveys* to generate profits. Although they are not consistent, many studies, particularly those before 1990, seem to suggest that *Value Line* reports can be used to generate higher than normal returns. However, the excess returns based on *Value Line* analyses may not have been sufficient to cover trading costs and may have been due to systematic risk. A number of later studies have been unable to identify abnormal returns from following *Value Line* recommendations.

More general studies on the value of analyst reports are somewhat mixed. The earlier study by Cowles (1933) found no evidence of value in analyst reports. On the other hand, Green (2005) found in his study of 7000 recommendation changes from 16 brokerage firms from 1999 to 2002 that, after controlling for transaction costs, purchasing (selling) quickly following upgrades (downgrades) resulted in average two-day returns of 1.02% (1.50%). He found that short-term profit opportunities persisted for two hours following the premarket release of new recommendations.

Womack (1996) found that analysts' mean postevent drift averages 2.4% on buy recommendations and is short-lived. However, sell recommendations result in average losses of 9.1% that are longer lived. These price reactions seem more significant for small-capitalization firms than for larger capitalization firms. Also, consider that sell recommendations may be particularly costly to brokerage firms, potentially damaging investment banking relationships and curtailing access to information in the future. Clearly, buy recommendations far outnumber sell recommendations and an incorrect sell recommendation may be particularly damaging to an analyst's reputation.

### *Analyst Reports and Conflicts of Interest*

Michaely and Womack (1999) studied after-market returns of 391 firms going public in 1990 and 1991, attempting to discern whether analysts working for firms underwriting the IPOs provided buy recommendations that were superior to those of investment institutions not participating in the underwriting efforts. Results suggest that if the analysts worked for an institution that did not participate in the underwriting, they were more likely to recommend a stock that had performed well in the recent past and would continue its strong performance. However, if the analysts worked for a firm that participated in bringing the IPO to the market, it was more likely to have recorded poor performance both before and after the analysts' recommendation. This evidence suggests that analysts working for investment banks are likely to attempt to prop up the prices of their underwritten securities with their recommendations.

In response to these apparently biased and unethical analyst recommendations, the Securities and Exchange Commission (SEC) announced in 2003 the *Global Research Analyst Settlement* with 10 of the industry's largest investment banks. This settlement resulted from investigations by Congress, the Office of New York Attorney General Elliot Spitzer, the SEC, and other regulators into apparent conflicts of interest among security analysts working for investment banks. The settlement required the 10 investment banks to pay $875 million in penalties and profit disgorgement, $80 million for investor education, and $432.5 million to fund independent research. In addition to these payments, the investment banks were required to separate their investment banking and research departments and add certain disclosures to their research reports. Nevertheless, Barber et al. (2007) found that between February 1996 and June 2003, buy recommendations of independent research firms outperformed those of investment banks by an average of 3.1 basis points per day. Investment bank hold/sell recommendations, in contrast, outperformed those of the independent research firms by an average of 1.8 basis points daily. Thus, investment bank buy opinions still underperform those of independent analysts, despite their other recommendations outperforming those of their independent competitors.

## Discounted Cash Flow Analysis and Price Multiples

In their study of 51 highly leveraged transactions (management buyouts and leveraged recapitalizations), Kaplan and Ruback (1995) found that discounted cash flow (DCF) analysis provided better estimates of value than did price-based multiples. The free cash flow estimates used by Kaplan and Ruback were provided by management to the public as required by SEC regulation in going private transactions. Discount rates were estimated with CAPM (ands other methods were used as well). Kaplan and Ruback found that between 95% and 97% of firm value was explained by (as indicated by r-square) DCF and slightly less was explained by price-based multiples. The price-based multiples did add useful information to the valuation process. In addition, analysts may be able to improve on DCF estimates by refining those provided by management. Regardless, the high r-squares do suggest that reasonably reliable information and analytical techniques are available in the marketplace for analysts and investors to use in company valuations.

## Political Intelligence Units

Investors with money at stake have obvious incentives to access and quickly exploit information. Many investors and institutions are able to access and exploit important information before it can be gathered and disseminated by the news agencies. Consider the case of USG Corporation, whose shares increased by 5.4% over two days prior to November 16, 2005 when Senate Republican Majority Leader Bill Frist announced that there would be a full Senate vote on a bill to create a $140 billion public trust for asbestos liability claims (see Mullins and Scannell, 2006). This fund would pay medical expenses and resolve lawsuits involving thousands of cancer victims who blamed USG, W.R. Grace, and Crown for their illnesses. Share prices of all these firms increased over the two days prior to November 16. However, the price increases clearly preceded the trust fund announcement. Returns for these firms over the two-day period exceeded those of the market. In addition, returns experienced by these particular firms far exceeded returns of their peer firms that were not involved in asbestos litigation. On the date that the actual announcement was finally made, these three firms showed no substantial reaction.

The SEC initiated an informal investigation to determine whether and how information might have been leaked to investors prior to its announcement. While staff members for Senator Frist claim to have been careful not to leak information prior to the announcement, the bill's authors, Senators Spector and Leahy, had held extensive discussions with lobbyists. Several law firms, including Sonnenschein Nath & Rosenthal, LLP and DLA Piper, have operated "political intelligence" units enabling their clients to obtain public policy information from lobbyists operating in Washington. These firms and political intelligence units include hedge funds as clients. Several hedge funds holding substantial stakes in affected companies belonged to the Financial Institutions for Asbestos Reform, an industry advocacy group, giving them additional opportunities to access information provided by lobbyists. While it is not yet clear whether any laws have been broken, it does appear that hedge funds may have successfully gained an information edge in their trading.

### Market Volatility

If security price changes are purely a function of information arrival, then security price volatility should be the same when markets are closed as when they are open. For example, stock return variances should be three times as high over a weekend as over a 24-hour period during weekdays. However, Fama (1965) and French (1980) found that return variances were only around 20% higher during weekends. On the other hand, one might argue that the arrival of new information over weekends is slower. But another study by French and Roll (1986) found that agricultural commodity futures prices (orange juice concentrate) were substantially more volatile during trading days than during weekends. Agricultural commodity futures prices are primarily a function of weather, news about which occurs over the weekend just as efficiently as during trading days. This suggests that volatility, to some extent, is caused by trading itself. More generally, Shiller (1981) found that the volatility of stock prices significantly exceeded the level that might be explained by the volatility of dividends.

## 11.5 THE EVENT STUDY METHODOLOGY

An event study is concerned with the impact of a given firm-specific corporate event on the prices of the company's securities. For example, an event study might be conducted for the purpose of determining the impact of corporate earnings announcements on the stock price of the company. Event studies are used to measure market efficiency and to determine the impact of a given event on security prices. More important, from a trading perspective, event studies are used to back-test price data to determine the usefulness and reliability of trading strategies.

A number of studies have suggested a relatively high degree of efficiency in capital markets. If this suggestion is true, then one would expect that security prices would continuously reflect all available information. If security prices are a function of all available information, and new information occurs randomly (otherwise, it would not be new information), then one would expect that security prices would fluctuate randomly as randomly generated news is impounded in security prices. Thus, the "purchase or sale of any security at the prevailing market price represents a zero NPV transaction" (Brown and Warner, 1980). In a perfectly efficient market, any piece of relevant new information would be immediately reflected in security prices. One should be able to determine the relevance of a given type of information by examining the effect of its occurrence on security prices. Thus, nonrandom performance of security prices immediately after a given event suggests that news of the event has a significant effect on security values. The degree of efficiency in a market to a given type of information may be reflected in the speed that the market reacts to the new information.

At any given point in time, security prices might be affected by a large number of randomly generated pieces of new information or events. An event study is concerned with the impact of a specific type of new information of a security's price. Given that more than one piece of news may be affecting the security's price at any point in time, one will probably need to study more than one firm to determine how the given type of information will affect securities. Thus, a population or sampling of firms experiencing the given event will be gathered; the impact of the event on each of the firms' securities will be studied simultaneously. Thus, the first step in conducting an event study is to gather an appropriate sample of firms experiencing the event.

The impact of the event on security prices is typically measured as a function of the amount of time that elapses between event occurrence and stock price change. In a relatively efficient market, one might expect that the effect of the event on security prices will occur very quickly after the first investors learn of the event. Event studies are usually based on daily, hourly, or even trade-to-trade stock price fluctuations. However, we frequently are forced to study only daily security price reactions when more frequent data are not readily available.

In addition, if markets are relatively efficient, one should obtain security price information as soon as possible after the event is known, although determining when the information is known may be problematic. For example, analysts are often able to predict with a reasonably high degree of accuracy the earnings of firms and trade securities on the basis of their predictions (See, for example, Firth (1876) and Jaffee et al. (1989).). Thus, the impact of corporate earnings changes may be realized in security prices long before earnings reports are officially released. Consequently, one may need to study the impact of a given event, news item, or announcement by considering security price reactions even before the event occurs. One should also take care in deciding on the precise nature of the event. For example, a dividend announcement may be of much greater interest than actual payment of the dividend.

Event studies typically standardize security price reactions by measuring the timing of security price reactions relative to the date of the event. For example, suppose that Company X announced its earnings on January 15 and Company Y announced its earnings on February 15. Let the base period time ($t = 0$) for Company X be January 15 and the base period time ($t = 0$) for Company Y be February 15. January 16 and February 16 (one day after the events) will be denoted as ($t = 1$) for the respective companies. Thus, the timing of the corporate events are standardized and we are able to measure average security price reactions 1, 2, etc., days after (and before) the event occurs.

Although stock return generating processes might be modeled as a random walk if capital markets are efficient, one should expect a long-term general drift in returns; that is, one might expect that investors will earn a "normal" return on their securities. Thus, excess or abnormal return randomness is observed when markets are efficient, except for a very short period after relevant new information is available. The abnormal return or residual in a given period for security $i$, $\varepsilon_{i,t}$, for a security is the difference between its total, actual, or ex-post return $r_{i,t}$ and its expected, normal, or ex-ante return $E[r_{i,t}]$: $\varepsilon_{i,t} = r_{i,t} - E[r_{i,t}]$. To measure the impact of an event on security returns, one must have a consistent means of measuring normal returns. Brown and Warner (1980, 1985), in their classic studies of event study methodologies, suggest three models of normal returns:

1. *Mean Adjusted Returns*: The normal return for a security $i$ equals a constant $K_i$. Typically, the mean return for the security over a sampling of time periods outside of

the testing period serves as the constant $K_i$. The expected return for the security is assumed to be constant over time, though ex-ante returns will vary among securities. Thus, the abnormal return for the security is found: $\varepsilon_{i,t} = r_{i,t} - K_i$.

2. *Market Adjusted Returns*: The normal return for a security at a given point in time equals the market return for that period. The expected returns for all securities are assumed to be the same during a given period, though they vary over time. Abnormal returns are found: $\varepsilon_{i,t} = R_{i,t} - R_{m,t}$.
3. *Market and Risk Adjusted Returns*: Here, normal returns are assumed to be generated by a single index model. Typically, security returns are linearly related to market returns through stock betas. These risk-adjusted returns vary across securities and over time. Abnormal returns can be determined: $\varepsilon_{i,t} = R_{i,t} - \beta_i(R_{m,t} - r_{f,t})$.

One might test the significance of an event by averaging the abnormal performance for the sampling of securities around the event dates. If abnormal returns are not statistically significantly different from zero during the relevant testing period, one may conclude that the test did not provide evidence indicating the significance of the event. If either no abnormal performance is detected around the event date or abnormal performance rapidly disappears, we have evidence of market efficiency with respect to that type of information.

## Illustration: Event Studies and Takeovers

Numerous firms have been targets of takeover attempts in recent years. There is good reason to expect that targets of takeover attempts experience significant positive abnormal returns. This suggests that investors with prior knowledge (or strong suspicion) of an impending takeover can realize abnormal returns by purchasing shares of the target firm prior to the takeover announcement. Is this true? We will conduct our own event study to test the following hypotheses:

1. Takeover targets experience positive stock price reactions to takeover announcements.
2. Markets react efficiently to takeover announcements.

The event that we will study is takeover announcements. We need to locate an appropriate sampling of companies to study. Suppose we wish to base our study on the three targets of takeover attempts listed in Table 11.3.[3]

Obviously, an actual statistical study would certainly require a much larger sampling of firms, but for sake of computational ease, we will focus on only three firms here. Suppose that we establish a 21-day testing period (event window) for returns around the event dates, the event date plus 10 days before and 10 days after. Table 11.4 provides our three target firm stock prices during 21-day periods around merger announcement dates. We standardize event dates (merger announcements occur on the 11th date, standardized at day 0) and compute returns for each stock during each of the days in the testing period as

[3]A sample size of three for our study is absurdly small to be able to reach meaningful conclusions. We will examine only three companies merely for ease in computations and illustration.

**TABLE 11.3** Takeover Targets

| Target Firm | Symbol | Announcement Date |
|---|---|---|
| Fleet Boston | FBF | 10/27/2003 |
| Disney | DIS | 02/11/2004 |
| AT&T Wireless | AWE | 01/18/2004 |

Note: The successful takeover of Fleet Boston by Bank of America was consummated in 2004. Comcast's bid for Disney failed. AT&T Wireless, the target of competing offers from Vodafone and Cingular, was acquired by Cingular in 2004.

**TABLE 11.4** Target Company Stock Prices

| Day | Calendar Date | FBF Price | Calendar Date | DIS Price | Calendar Date | AWE Price |
|---|---|---|---|---|---|---|
| 10 | 10–Nov–03 | 39.69 | 26–Feb–04 | 26.73 | 3–Feb–04 | 11.08 |
| 9 | 7–Nov–03 | 39.84 | 25–Feb–04 | 26.30 | 2–Feb–04 | 11.16 |
| 8 | 6–Nov–03 | 40.26 | 24–Feb–04 | 25.96 | 30–Jan–04 | 11.05 |
| 7 | 5–Nov–03 | 39.89 | 23–Feb–04 | 26.75 | 29–Jan–04 | 11.03 |
| 6 | 4–Nov–03 | 39.60 | 20–Feb–04 | 26.55 | 28–Jan–04 | 11.02 |
| 5 | 3–Nov–03 | 39.86 | 19–Feb–04 | 27.00 | 27–Jan–04 | 11.17 |
| 4 | 31–Oct–03 | 39.73 | 18–Feb–04 | 26.71 | 26–Jan–04 | 10.93 |
| 3 | 30–Oct–03 | 39.45 | 17–Feb–04 | 26.90 | 23–Jan–04 | 10.61 |
| 2 | 29–Oct–03 | 38.90 | 13–Feb–04 | 26.92 | 22–Jan–04 | 10.56 |
| 1 | 28–Oct–03 | 38.17 | 12–Feb–04 | 28.00 | 21–Jan–04 | 10.99 |
| 0 | 27–Oct–03 | 38.56 | 11–Feb–04 | 27.60 | 20–Jan–04 | 10.39 |
| −1 | 24–Oct–03 | 31.28 | 10–Feb–04 | 24.08 | 16–Jan–04 | 9.99 |
| −2 | 23–Oct–03 | 31.54 | 9–Feb–04 | 23.77 | 15–Jan–04 | 9.81 |
| −3 | 22–Oct–03 | 31.47 | 6–Feb–04 | 23.35 | 14–Jan–04 | 9.99 |
| −4 | 21–Oct–03 | 31.88 | 5–Feb–04 | 23.20 | 13–Jan–04 | 8.55 |
| −5 | 20–Oct–03 | 32.17 | 4–Feb–04 | 23.19 | 12–Jan–04 | 8.13 |
| −6 | 17–Oct–03 | 32.08 | 3–Feb–04 | 23.26 | 9–Jan–04 | 8.15 |
| −7 | 16–Oct–03 | 32.31 | 2–Feb–04 | 23.80 | 8–Jan–04 | 8.24 |
| −8 | 15–Oct–03 | 31.99 | 30–Jan–04 | 24 | 7–Jan–04 | 8.21 |
| −9 | 14–Oct–03 | 32.10 | 29–Jan–04 | 24.45 | 6–Jan–04 | 8.29 |
| −10 | 13–Oct–03 | 31.87 | 28–Jan–04 | 23.67 | 5–Jan–04 | 8.03 |

TABLE 11.5 Target Company Stock Returns

| Date | PRICES | | | RETURNS | | |
|---|---|---|---|---|---|---|
| | FBF | DIS | AWE | FBF | DIS | AWE |
| 10 | 39.69 | 26.73 | 11.08 | −0.004 | 0.016 | −0.01 |
| 9 | 39.84 | 26.30 | 11.16 | −0.010 | 0.013 | 0.01 |
| 8 | 40.26 | 25.96 | 11.05 | 0.009 | −0.03 | 0.002 |
| 7 | 39.89 | 26.75 | 11.03 | 0.007 | 0.008 | 0 |
| 6 | 39.60 | 26.55 | 11.02 | −0.007 | −0.02 | −0.01 |
| 5 | 39.86 | 27.00 | 11.17 | 0.003 | 0.011 | 0.022 |
| 4 | 39.73 | 26.71 | 10.93 | 0.007 | −0.01 | 0.03 |
| 3 | 39.45 | 26.90 | 10.61 | 0.014 | −0 | 0.005 |
| 2 | 38.90 | 26.92 | 10.56 | 0.019 | −0.04 | −0.04 |
| 1 | 38.17 | 28.00 | 10.99 | −0.010 | 0.014 | 0.058 |
| 0 | 38.56 | 27.60 | 10.39 | 0.233 | 0.146 | 0.04 |
| −1 | 31.28 | 24.08 | 9.99 | −0.008 | 0.013 | 0.018 |
| −2 | 31.54 | 23.77 | 9.81 | 0.002 | 0.018 | −0.02 |
| −3 | 31.47 | 23.35 | 9.99 | −0.013 | 0.006 | 0.168 |
| −4 | 31.88 | 23.20 | 8.55 | −0.009 | 0 | 0.052 |
| −5 | 32.17 | 23.19 | 8.13 | 0.003 | 0 | 0 |
| −6 | 32.08 | 23.26 | 8.15 | −0.007 | −0.02 | −0.01 |
| −7 | 32.31 | 23.80 | 8.24 | 0.010 | −0.01 | 0.004 |
| −8 | 31.99 | 24.00 | 8.21 | −0.003 | −0.02 | −0.01 |
| −9 | 32.10 | 24.45 | 8.29 | 0.007 | 0.033 | 0.032 |
| −10 | 31.87 | 23.67 | 8.03 | N/A | N/A | N/A |

Note: Table calculations will reflect rounding errors.

in Table 11.5. The return for a particular day is simply the closing price for that day divided by the closing price for the prior day minus one: $(P_t/P_{t-1}) - 1$.

The next step in this study is to determine normal or expected returns for each of the securities for each date. We could use any of the three adjustment methods discussed above (with more information). Suppose that we have decided to use the Market Adjusted Return method. In this case, we compute daily returns for the market index for each day in our 21-day testing period for each stock. Table 11.6 lists adjusted S&P index values for each of the 21 dates affecting each of the three stocks along with returns for the index for each of those dates.

TABLE 11.6 Returns on the S&P 500

| Calendar Date | Adj. Close | Return | DIS | AWE | Calendar Date | Adj. Close | Return | FBF | AWE | Calendar Date | Adj. Close | Return | FBF |
|---|---|---|---|---|---|---|---|---|---|---|---|---|---|
| 26–Feb–04 | 1,144.91 | 0.00108 | 10 | | 27–Jan–04 | 1,144.05 | −0.0098 | | 5 | 3–Nov–03 | 1,059.02 | 0.00791 | 5 |
| 25–Feb–04 | 1,143.67 | 0.00402 | 9 | | 26–Jan–04 | 1,155.37 | 0.01211 | | 4 | 31–Oct–03 | 1,050.71 | 0.0036 | 4 |
| 24–Feb–04 | 1,139.09 | −0.0017 | 8 | | 23–Jan–04 | 1,141.55 | −0.0021 | | 3 | 30–Oct–03 | 1,046.94 | −0.0011 | 3 |
| 23–Feb–04 | 1,140.99 | −0.0027 | 7 | | 22–Jan–04 | 1,143.94 | −0.0032 | | 2 | 29–Oct–03 | 1,048.11 | 0.00126 | 2 |
| 20–Feb–04 | 1,144.11 | −0.0026 | 6 | | 21–Jan–04 | 1,147.62 | 0.00777 | | 1 | 28–Oct–03 | 1,046.79 | 0.01519 | 1 |
| 19–Feb–04 | 1,147.06 | −0.0041 | 5 | | 20–Jan–04 | 1,138.77 | −0.0009 | | 0 | 27–Oct–03 | 1,031.13 | 0.00216 | 0 |
| 18–Feb–04 | 1,151.82 | −0.0045 | 4 | | 16–Jan–04 | 1,139.83 | 0.00687 | | −1 | 24–Oct–03 | 1,028.91 | −0.0047 | −1 |
| 17–Feb–04 | 1,156.99 | 0.00976 | 3 | | 15–Jan–04 | 1,132.05 | 0.00135 | | −2 | 23–Oct–03 | 1,033.77 | 0.00331 | −2 |
| 13–Feb–04 | 1,145.81 | −0.0055 | 2 | | 14–Jan–04 | 1,130.52 | 0.00829 | | −3 | 22–Oct–03 | 1,030.36 | −0.015 | −3 |
| 12–Feb–04 | 1,152.11 | −0.0049 | 1 | | 13–Jan–04 | 1,121.22 | −0.0053 | | −4 | 21–Oct–03 | 1,046.03 | 0.00129 | −4 |
| 11–Feb–04 | 1,157.76 | 0.01067 | 0 | | 12–Jan–04 | 1,127.23 | 0.00479 | | −5 | 20–Oct–03 | 1,044.68 | 0.00516 | −5 |
| 10–Feb–04 | 1,145.54 | 0.00503 | −1 | | 9–Jan–04 | 1,121.86 | −0.0089 | | −6 | 17–Oct–03 | 1,039.32 | −0.0102 | −6 |
| 9–Feb–04 | 1,139.81 | −0.0026 | −2 | | 8–Jan–04 | 1,131.92 | 0.00496 | | −7 | 16–Oct–03 | 1,050.07 | 0.00316 | −7 |
| 6–Feb–04 | 1,142.76 | 0.01256 | −3 | | 7–Jan–04 | 1,126.33 | 0.00237 | | −8 | 15–Oct–03 | 1,046.76 | −0.0026 | −8 |
| 5–Feb–04 | 1,128.59 | 0.00184 | −4 | | 6–Jan–04 | 1,123.67 | 0.00129 | | −9 | 14–Oct–03 | 1,049.48 | 0.00395 | −9 |
| 4–Feb–04 | 1,126.52 | −0.0084 | −5 | | 5–Jan–04 | 1,122.22 | 0.0124 | | −10 | 13–Oct–03 | 1,045.35 | N/A | −10 |
| 3–Feb–04 | 1,136.03 | 0.00068 | −6 | 10 | 10–Nov–03 | 1,047.11 | −0.0058 | 10 | | | | | |
| 2–Feb–04 | 1,135.26 | 0.00365 | −7 | 9 | 7–Nov–03 | 1,053.21 | −0.0046 | 9 | | | | | |
| 30–Jan–04 | 1,131.13 | −0.0026 | −8 | 8 | 6–Nov–03 | 1,058.05 | 0.00593 | 8 | | | | | |
| 29–Jan–04 | 1,134.11 | 0.00499 | −9 | 7 | 5–Nov–03 | 1,051.81 | −0.0014 | 7 | | | | | |
| 28–Jan–04 | 1,128.48 | −0.0136 | −10 | 6 | 4–Nov–03 | 1,053.25 | −0.0054 | 6 | | | | | |

TABLE 11.7 Target Firm Stock Residuals

| Date | Abnormal Returns | | | Average |
|---|---|---|---|---|
| | FBF | DIS | AWE | Residuals (ARs) |
| 10 | 0.002 | 0.0153 | −0.0078 | 0.003149 |
| 9 | −0.006 | 0.0091 | 0.0063 | 0.003174 |
| 8 | 0.0033 | −0.028 | 0.00444 | −0.006695 |
| 7 | 0.0087 | 0.0103 | −0.0041 | 0.004956 |
| 6 | −0.001 | −0.014 | 0.00018 | −0.004996 |
| 5 | −0.005 | 0.015 | 0.03176 | 0.014036 |
| 4 | 0.0035 | −0.003 | 0.01805 | 0.006319 |
| 3 | 0.0153 | −0.011 | 0.00682 | 0.00386 |
| 2 | 0.0179 | −0.033 | −0.0359 | −0.017053 |
| 1 | −0.025 | 0.0194 | 0.04998 | 0.014683 |
| 0 | 0.2306 | 0.1355 | 0.04097 | 0.135687 |
| −1 | −0.004 | 0.008 | 0.01148 | 0.005316 |
| −2 | −0.001 | 0.0206 | −0.0194 | 0 |
| −3 | 0.0021 | −0.006 | 0.16013 | 0.052052 |
| −4 | −0.01 | −0.001 | 0.05699 | 0.015093 |
| −5 | −0.002 | 0.0054 | −0.0072 | −0.00141 |
| −6 | 0.0031 | −0.023 | −0.002 | −0.007428 |
| −7 | 0.0068 | −0.012 | −0.0013 | −0.002151 |
| −8 | 0 | −0.016 | −0.012 | −0.009543 |
| −9 | 0.0033 | 0.028 | 0.03109 | 0.020772 |
| −10 | N/A | N/A | N/A | N/A |

Next, based on actual returns computed in Table 11.5 and normal returns from the S&P 500 Index from Table 11.6, we compute periodic residuals $\varepsilon_{i,t}$ (abnormal returns) for each stock during each date in the testing period along with the average residual over the sample for each date as in Table 11.7.

One of our objectives is to determine whether any daily residual is statistically significantly different from zero. Following standard hypotheses testing techniques reviewed in the text appendix A.1.a, standard deviations for each of the average daily residuals are computed along with normal deviates or test statistics ($[\varepsilon_t - 0] \div \sigma_{\varepsilon i}$) as in Table 11.8.

Our test for each daily average residual ($AR_t$) is structured more formally as follows:

$$H_0\colon AR_t \leq 0 \quad H_A\colon AR_t > 0$$

**TABLE 11.8** Target Firm Average Residuals and Standard Deviations

| Day | Average Residuals (ARs) | σ Residuals | Normal Deviate |
|---|---|---|---|
| 10 | 0.003149 | 0.0116 | 0.2715 |
| 9 | 0.003174 | 0.00794 | 0.39957 |
| 8 | −0.006695 | 0.01834 | −0.3649 |
| 7 | 0.004956 | 0.00787 | 0.63007 |
| 6 | −0.004996 | 0.0079 | −0.6321 |
| 5 | 0.014036 | 0.01821 | 0.77059 |
| 4 | 0.006319 | 0.01061 | 0.59555 |
| 3 | 0.00386 | 0.01313 | 0.29393 |
| 2 | −0.017053 | 0.03027 | −0.5633 |
| 1 | 0.014683 | 0.03786 | 0.38784 |
| 0 | 0.135687 | 0.0948 | 1.43123 |
| −1 | 0.005316 | 0.00786 | 0.67597 |
| −2 | 0 | 0.01999 | 0.00187 |
| −3 | 0.052052 | 0.09369 | 0.55561 |
| −4 | 0.015093 | 0.03656 | 0.41285 |
| −5 | −0.00141 | 0.00635 | −0.2219 |
| −6 | −0.007428 | 0.01404 | −0.5289 |
| −7 | −0.002151 | 0.00944 | −0.2278 |
| −8 | −0.009543 | 0.00777 | −1.2279 |
| −9 | 0.020772 | 0.01524 | 1.36292 |
| −10 | N/A | N/A | N/A |

We shall assume the residuals follow a t-distribution and we will perform a one-tailed test with a 95% level of significance. Given a sample size of three firms such that we work with $1 = 3 - 2$ degrees of freedom, the critical value for each test will be 6.314. Based on our computations above, we find that none of the residual *t*-statistics (normal deviates or test statistics) exceed 6.314. Thus, we may not conclude with a 95% level of confidence that any residual differs from zero. Based on the confines of the test that we established here, we may not conclude that markets appear inefficient with respect to merger announcements. Perhaps, in part due to our small sample with such a small number of degrees of freedom, we cannot conclude that merger announcements have any effect on security returns. Note that this example was structured so as to facilitate computations; it is unlikely that a realistic test would be structured with a sample set of only three firms.

The tests performed above were concerned with whether merger announcements significantly affected stock prices in any given date around the time of the announcement.

TABLE 11.9 Target Firm Cumulative Average Residuals

| Day | Average Residuals (ARs) | CAR |
|---|---|---|
| 10 | 0.003149 | 0.22986 |
| 9 | 0.003174 | 0.22671 |
| 8 | −0.006695 | 0.22354 |
| 7 | 0.004956 | 0.23023 |
| 6 | −0.004996 | 0.22527 |
| 5 | 0.014036 | 0.23027 |
| 4 | 0.006319 | 0.21623 |
| 3 | 0.00386 | 0.20991 |
| 2 | −0.017053 | 0.20606 |
| 1 | 0.014683 | 0.22311 |
| 0 | 0.135687 | 0.20843 |
| −1 | 0.005316 | 0.07274 |
| −2 | 3.74E − 05 | 0.06742 |
| −3 | 0.052052 | 0.06739 |
| −4 | 0.015093 | 0.01533 |
| −5 | −0.00141 | 0.00024 |
| −6 | −0.007428 | 0.00165 |
| −7 | −0.002151 | 0.00908 |
| −8 | −0.009543 | 0.01123 |
| −9 | 0.020772 | 0.02077 |
| −10 | N/A | N/A |

We found no significant effect for any single-day returns. In some other instances, we might find that while no effect is found on the residual for any particular date, the effect might be realized over a period of days. This might be expected if market reactions are slow, that is, if the market is somewhat inefficient. Perhaps, we may even wish to broaden our test to determine whether some of the effect might be realized over a period of time before the date of the announcement. We can compute cumulative average residuals to determine cumulative effects over time:

$$CAR_t = \sum_{i}^{t} AR_i \qquad (11.3)$$

Cumulative average residuals are computed in Table 11.9 from average residuals taken from Table 11.8. Cumulative average residuals can also be computed by summing individual firm residuals and dividing by the number of firms in the sample as in Table 11.10.

**TABLE 11.10** Target Firm Cumulative Average Residuals

| Day | CR FBF | CR DIS | CR AWE | CAR | CR σ | Normal Deviate |
|---|---|---|---|---|---|---|
| 10 | 0.241609 | 0.1196 | 0.328365 | 0.229858 | 0.104878 | 2.191678 |
| 9 | 0.239582 | 0.104334 | 0.336212 | 0.226709 | 0.116474 | 1.946444 |
| 8 | 0.24544 | 0.095258 | 0.329908 | 0.223535 | 0.118849 | 1.880836 |
| 7 | 0.242097 | 0.123125 | 0.325467 | 0.23023 | 0.101692 | 2.263999 |
| 6 | 0.233407 | 0.112865 | 0.329549 | 0.225274 | 0.108571 | 2.074906 |
| 5 | 0.234481 | 0.12696 | 0.329368 | 0.23027 | 0.10127 | 2.273827 |
| 4 | 0.239118 | 0.11197 | 0.297613 | 0.216234 | 0.094913 | 2.278221 |
| 3 | 0.235621 | 0.114565 | 0.279559 | 0.209915 | 0.085448 | 2.456643 |
| 2 | 0.220366 | 0.125065 | 0.272735 | 0.206055 | 0.074868 | 2.752261 |
| 1 | 0.202502 | 0.158168 | 0.308654 | 0.223108 | 0.07733 | 2.885135 |
| 0 | 0.227803 | 0.138796 | 0.258678 | 0.208426 | 0.062246 | 3.348411 |
| −1 | −0.00278 | 0.003284 | 0.217708 | 0.072739 | 0.125584 | 0.579205 |
| −2 | 0.000767 | −0.00473 | 0.206232 | 0.067423 | 0.120244 | 0.560715 |
| −3 | 0.001852 | −0.0253 | 0.225603 | 0.067385 | 0.137692 | 0.489392 |
| −4 | −0.00027 | −0.01921 | 0.065477 | 0.015333 | 0.044446 | 0.34498 |
| −5 | 0.010039 | −0.0178 | 0.008485 | 0.00024 | 0.015645 | 0.01535 |
| −6 | 0.012391 | −0.02317 | 0.015725 | 0.00165 | 0.021555 | 0.076564 |
| −7 | 0.009272 | 0.000202 | 0.01776 | 0.009078 | 0.008781 | 1.033889 |
| −8 | 0.002431 | 0.012187 | 0.019069 | 0.011229 | 0.00836 | 1.343124 |
| −9 | 0.003266 | 0.027964 | 0.031086 | 0.020772 | 0.015241 | 1.362916 |
| −10 | N/A | N/A | N/A | N/A | N/A | N/A |

Do any of the CARs in Tables 11.9 or 11.10 exceed zero? A quick glance reveals that all do. Do any CARs exceed zero at a statistically significant level? We need a little more analysis to examine this second question. We begin to test for the statistical significance of cumulative average residuals by computing standard deviations of the cumulative residuals of the firms for each day and computing normal deviates. For example, the sample standard deviation of cumulative residuals for day −5 is computed based on the following:

$$\sigma = \sqrt{\frac{(.010039 - .00024)^2 + (-.0178 - .00024)^2 + (.008485 - .00024)^2}{3 - 1}} = .015645$$

These one-day standard deviations measure the spread or variability of residuals for that day. In Table 11.9, the normal deviate for a given date is simply the cumulative average residual for that date divided by the standard deviation applicable to that date. Daily standard deviations of cumulative residuals along with their normal deviates are given in Table 11.10. Larger normal deviates are consistent with larger positive and statistically significant stock price reactions.

The largest normal deviate is for day zero, the merger announcement date. In a realistic scenario, this would not be a surprise if prices rapidly adjusted to new information. However, we need a benchmark for statistical significance for these normal deviates. Because our sample set numbers only 3, we have $3 - 2 = 1$ degrees of freedom. For a one-tail test with 95% certainty, we find from a $t$-table that our benchmark for statistical significance is 6.314. Note that none of our normal deviates exceed this critical value of 6.314. Thus, if our hypotheses concerning each date t in our testing period were given as follows:

$$H_0: CAR_t \leq 0 \quad H_A: CAR_t > 0,$$

we would not be able to reject the null hypothesis that $CAR_t \leq 0$ with 95% confidence for any date in our event period. However, we note that the sample set for our illustration was particularly small.

## 11.6 STRONG FORM EFFICIENCY AND INSIDER TRADING

Strong form market efficiency tests are concerned with whether any information, publicly available or private, can be used to generate abnormal returns. We generally take it for granted that insiders are capable of generating higher than normal returns on their transactions. There have been many well-publicized cases of insiders generating abnormal returns—and being prosecuted for their trading. There is even some evidence that insiders are able to generate abnormal returns on apparently legal transactions that are duly registered with the SEC (see Jaffee, (1974). Jaffee examined SEC insider transaction filings and determined that stock performance relative to market performance after months when insider purchases exceed insider sales. When insiders sell, shares that they sold are outperformed by the market.

Why do insiders appear to outperform the market on their duly registered insider transactions? Are insiders trading on the basis of their private information or do they actually have superior trading ability? A study by Givoly and Palmon (1985) suggests that transactions generating these superior returns are not related to subsequent corporate events or announcements. Givoly and Palmon examined insider transactions and then searched for subsequent announcements in the business press for that might have explained the superior returns on their investments. They found that insider superior returns were not explained by the published announcements. This may suggest that these insiders may either simply have superior investing ability or may generate higher returns for themselves on the basis of information that is not later announced.

On the other hand, perhaps insiders are trading on the basis of insider information that is not subsequently released on a specific date. Furthermore, managers are not obliged to announce most types of inside information according to any particular schedule. In addition, many insiders participate in plans to regularly buy (without liability, as per SEC Rule 10b5-1) or sell shares. Managers can obtain 10b5-1 protection for trades if they create the plan at a time when they don't have nonpublic information and they announce their transactions schedule in advance. For example, Kenneth Lay was said to have protected $100 million in his own wealth by selling shares of Enron stock through a 10b5-1 plan. In addition, insiders always have the right to abstain from trading on the basis of inside information. Thus, it is not illegal to *not buy* shares on the basis of inside information.[4] How would investigators determine whether one declined to trade solely on the basis of inside information? Regardless, Jagolinzer (2005) found that insider trading within the 10b5-1 plans outperforms the market by 5.6% over six-month periods.

## 11.7 ANOMALOUS EFFICIENCY AND PREDICTION MARKETS

Sometimes markets seem so efficient that prices can be used to predict nonfinancial events. For example, French and Roll (1986) found that prices of orange juice concentrate futures can be used to forecast temperature conditions in central Florida better than the National Weather Service. In other instances, the market incorporates relevant information so efficiently that it is difficult to understand how the process worked.

### The *Challenger* Space Shuttle Disaster

On January 28, 1986, at 11:38 AM Eastern Standard Time, the space shuttle *Challenger* was launched in Florida and exploded 74 seconds later ten miles above ground on national television. The stock market reacted within minutes of the event, with investors dumping shares the four major contractors contributing to building and launching the *Challenger*. The four primary contractors, Rockwell International, builder of the shuttle and its main engines, Lockheed, manager of the ground support, Martin Marietta, manufacturer of the vessel's external fuel tank, and Morton Thiokol, builder of the solid-fuel booster rocket. Less than a half-hour after the disaster, Rockwell's stock price had declined 6%, Lockheed 5%, Martin Marietta 3%, and Morton Thiokol had stopped trading because of the flood of sell orders. By the end of trading for the day, the first three companies' share prices closed down 3% from their open prices, representing a slight recovery from their initial reactions. However, Morton Thiokol stock resumed trading and continued to decline, finishing the day almost 12% down from its open price. These reactions suggested that the market believed that Morton Thiokol would suffer the greatest losses from the disaster, despite the fact that no reports surfaced in the public media identifying Morton Thiokol as the cause of the disaster. Even news reports of rumors in the media failed to single out the firm as the cause of the disaster.

However, many months after the disaster, Richard Feynman, the charismatic and brilliant physicist, in dramatic testimony to a congressional hearing on the explosion, dropped O-rings into ice water, causing them to become brittle and easily break, thereby demonstrating that

[4]The decision to retain stock cannot be a violation of Rule 10b-5. See Condus v. Howard Savings Bank, 781 F. Supp. 1052 (D.N.J. 1992). However, failure to trade can be a violation of U.K. insider trading regulations.

they were the cause of the explosion. Morton had used the O-rings in its construction of the booster rockets, which failed in the uncharacteristically cold weather that morning and leaked explosive fumes when the launch temperatures were less than could be tolerated by the O-rings. Yet, there were no announcements of such failures on the dates of the disaster or even within weeks of the explosion. Nonetheless, the market had reacted within minutes of the disaster as though Morton Thiokol would be held responsible.

In their study of this event, Maloney and Mulherin (2003) found no evidence that Morton Thiokol corporate officers and other insiders sold shares on the date of the disaster. How is it that no individual seemed to know that Morton Thiokol would ultimately be held responsible for the disaster, yet the market would react as though everyone knew? It may be useful to note that Morton Thiokol engineers were aware of the potential for failure of the O-rings in cold weather, but were overruled by company managers concerning their use. But, again, Maloney and Mulherin found no evidence of unusual insider trading activity. This scenario suggests that the information marketplace does quickly sift through and identify relevant information used for the valuation of company shares.

## Prediction Markets

Price discovery is one of the most important functions of trading, particularly in more transparent markets such as the NYSE. This price discovery is of vital importance to investors and business decision making. What is the essence of trading that produces this information? Several of the models that we have discussed in this chapter allow for market frameworks where informed traders communicate information (perhaps reluctantly) through their trading activities. Might gambling serve the same essential purpose as trading in the price discovery and information production processes? Similarly, what might gambling be able to teach us about information dissemination in financial markets? Consider the 1988 to 2008 presidential elections, where an increasing number of online betting markets offered tradable securities on election outcomes.[5] The most visible of these markets have been Intrade, accessed at www.intrade.com, and the Iowa Electronic Markets at the Tippie School of Business, University of Iowa. Intrade and the Iowa Electronic Markets (http://www.biz.uiowa.edu/iem/index.cfm) have created "futures" contracts that can be purchased and sold by "investors," whose values fluctuated as perceived election chances of various candidates and referendums varied. Thus, a contract that pays \$1 if a given candidate is elected might sell for a price less than \$1. Thus, if a contract sells for \$0.50, one might guess that the market believes that the candidate has a 50% chance (ignoring discount factors and other complications) of getting elected. In effect, futures contract prices might have been interpreted as the market's assessment of the probability that a given candidate would be elected. Hence, such a site might serve as a *prediction market*. Prediction markets are markets created for the purpose of making

[5]Organized betting markets in political elections preceded the Internet, even on Wall Street. Although such gambling has recently been either illegal or prohibited by NYSE and AMEX rules (but not always, as we will discuss shortly), well-organized "underground" markets have existed for over a hundred years on the major U.S. exchanges.

predictions or benefiting from correct predictions. The Iowa Electronic Markets and Intrade have been more successful at predicting election outcomes than most opinion polls. Consider, for example, the report by *Time Magazine* (Saporito, 2005) of Intrade's contract making payment contingent on the capture of Saddam Hussein suddenly moving two days before he was captured on December 13, 2003. Other prediction markets such as Cantor Fitzgerald's Hollywood Stock Exchange, Centrebet, Goldman Sach's, and Deutsche Bank's Economic Derivatives and TradeSports have served as useful prediction devices in other arenas, and have been very useful in making nonfinancial predictions. A number of research papers have discussed use of prediction markets for a variety of types of predictions (e.g., Wolfers and Zitzewitz, 2004 and 2007).[6]

Security markets are excellent aggregators of information. Security prices have been used for many years to estimate a variety of types of probability distributions. For example, currency traders have for many years used futures prices to estimate future currency exchange rates. Similarly, commodity traders have used commodity futures prices to predict commodity prices. Latane and Rendleman (1976) proposed used market prices of put and call options to estimate implied volatilities (return standard deviations) for underlying stocks (discussed in Chapter 6). Bodurtha and Shen (1995) and Campa and Chang (1998) used similar statistical methods to estimate implied correlations between two underlying variables such as exchange rates using derivative contracts written on each underlying currency as well as contracts written on both currencies.

Prediction markets, even with respect to political wagering, did not originate with Intrade and the Iowa Electronic Markets. The Curb Exchange (the precursor to the American Stock Exchange) operated wagering markets for presidential markets during much of the late 19th century. Such wagering frequently involved large sums of money, with daily volume that often exceeded presidential campaign budgets. More recent prediction markets have been quite successful, including the North American Derivatives Exchange (Nadex), a Commodity Futures Trading Commission (CFTC)-registered futures exchange that got its start as HedgeStreet prediction market.

We close this section with several questions. Is the information provided by markets of use to traders? Clearly, derivative markets do provide useful information for forecasting risk, futures rates, and so on. Is the information provided by markets of use to decision-making entities in business and government? Consider an example from the 1990s where CERN, the European laboratory for particle physics, needed to estimate whether the probability of discovering the Higgs boson was sufficiently high to justify extending the operation of its collider.[7] Traders at the Foresight Exchange website (http://www.ideosphere.com/) took positions on whether the Higgs boson would be discovered by 2005, setting a contract price of 0.77 as of 2001. We close this section with a few rhetorical questions:

[6]Wolfers and Zitzewitz (2004) was the source for much of the information in this section.

[7]The boson is a hypothesized subatomic particle (such as a quark or leptons) that seems to impart mass on other bosons, quarks, and leptons. While there is strong theoretical and some empirical evidence for the existence for the Higgs boson, as of June 2010, the Higgs boson's existence had not been empirically confirmed. There is some debate as to whether this is still true as of early 2012.

Should markets provide information aggregation services to the public? If so, at what cost to traders? Consider the following excerpt from Looney (2003)[8]:

> The Defense Advanced Research Projects Agency (DARPA) was born in the uncertain days after the Soviets launched Sputnik in 1958. Its mission was to become an engine of technological change that would bridge the gap between fundamental discoveries and their military use (Bray, 2003). Over the last five decades, the Agency has efficiently gone about its business in relative obscurity, in many cases not getting as much credit as it deserved. The Agency first developed the model for the internet as well as stealth technology. More recently, DARPA innovations have spanned a wide array of technologies. To name a couple: computers that correct a user's mistakes or fix themselves when they malfunction and new stimulants to keep soldiers awake and alert for seven consecutive days.
>
> Because DARPA is mandated to take on risky projects, failures have occurred. For the most part, however, the Agency's low profile has protected it from inaccurate scare stories cropping up in the popular press. However, in 2003 DARPA has managed to make the front pages twice, both times with disastrous results. Earlier in the year Congress moved to scale back the agency's Terrorism Information Awareness Program (TIA). In an effort to spot patterns of terrorist activity, this program proposed the development of advanced computer systems capable of scanning commercial databases containing information on millions of Americans.
>
> Then, in late July, the Agency backed off a plan to set up a kind of futures market (Policy Analysis Market or PAM) that would allow investors to earn profits by betting on the likelihood of such events as regime changes in the Middle East. Critics, mainly politicians and op-ed writers, attacked the futures project on the grounds that it was unethical and in bad taste to accept wagers on the fate of foreign leaders and the likelihood of terrorist attacks. The project was canceled a day after it was announced. Its head, retired Admiral John Poindexter, has resigned.

One addition to this excerpt: Poindexter's resignation followed the creation of a contract by Tradesports.com that would pay $100 if he resigned. In any case, can markets trading terrorism-based contracts aid in the prediction of terrorist strikes and dealing with the effects of such strikes? If so, should such contracts be traded? For example, might the risk associated with investment in military or private security companies be managed with contracts on specific terrorist actions? Should such contracts be traded even in the light of potential moral hazard consequences?

## 11.8 EPILOGUE

In his presidential address to the American Finance Association, Richard Roll (1988) discussed the ability of academics to explain financial phenomena:

> The maturity of a science is often gauged by its success in predicting important phenomena. Astronomy, the oldest science, is able to predict the positions of planets and the reappearance of comets with a high degree of accuracy.... The immaturity of our science [finance] is illustrated by the conspicuous lack of predictive content about some of its most intensely interesting phenomena, particularly changes in asset prices. General stock price movements are notoriously unpredictable and financial economists have even developed a coherent theory (the theory of efficient markets) to explain why they should be unpredictable.

The theories of capital market efficiency are quite powerful in that they are quite simple and do explain much of the behavior that is observed in capital markets. However, much

[8]Excerpted from http://www.au.af.mil/au/awc/awcgate/nps/pam/si_pam.pdf on April 12, 2012.

empirical evidence exists that refutes capital markets efficiency. It should be noted that much of this evidence is contradictory and often reflects investors' desire to discover money-making strategies, investment advisors' needs to sell their services, and academicians' needs for publications. Furthermore, some evidence of market inefficiencies may simply be the result of data mining; one can always find or "demonstrate" an interesting pattern or relationship given enough data. An even greater difficulty for the opponents of capital market efficiency is that they are not able to offer a reasonably coherent and robust set of competing theories of capital markets behavior. Thus, it is reasonable to conclude based on prevailing theoretical and empirical research that the verdict is still out regarding the extent to which capital markets are efficient.

## Additional Reading

Perhaps the single most important book for any investor or trader to read is Burton Malkiel's still-relevant classic *A Random Walk Down Wall Street* (2003). It is a nontechnical easy read and provides a rather skeptical discussion of a wide variety of trading strategies. Lo and MacKinlay's (1999) more technical response, *A Non-Random Walk Down Wall Street,* is a more academic collection of essays depicting the nonrandom nature of stock prices. Chapter 17 of Elton et al. (2010) provides a nice review of the market efficiency literature and discusses the methodology of event studies. Chapters 2 and 4 of Campbell et al. (1997) discuss the econometrics of testing stock return randomness and event studies. Wolfers and Zitzewitz (2004, 2007) offer very useful and readable introductions to prediction markets. Surowiecki's 2004 well-written book on crowd wisdom provides good insight on how divergent and largely uninformed individual opinions are aggregated into a highly efficient market. Boudoukh et al. (1994) offer an interesting synthesis of the literature on mean reversion and momentum trading rules.

## References

Alexander, S. (1961). Price movements in speculative markets: Trends or random walks. *Industrial Management Review, 2,* 7–26.

Ball, R., & Brown, P. (1968). An empirical evaluation of accounting income numbers. *Journal of Accounting Research, 6,* 159–178.

Banz, R. (1981). The relationship between return and market value of common stock. *Journal of Financial Economics, 9,* 3–18.

Barber, B., Lehavy, R., & Truman, B. (2007). Comparing the stock recommendation performance of investment banks and independent research firms. *Journal of Financial Economics, 85,* 490–517.

Basu, S. (1977). Investment performance of common stocks in relation to their price-earnings ratios. *Journal of Finance, 32,* 663–682.

Black, F. (1973). Yes Virginia, there is hope: Tests of the *Value Line* ranking system. *Financial Analysts Journal, 29,* 10–14.

Bodurtha, J. N., & Shen, Q. (1995). *Historical and implied measures of "value at risk": The DM and yen case.* Working paper. Ann Arbor: University of Michigan.

Boudoukh, J., Richardson, M., & Whitelaw, R. (1994). A tale of three schools: Insights on autocorrelations of short-horizon stock returns. *Review of Financial Studies, 7,* 539–573.

Branch, B. (1977). A tax loss selling rule. *Journal of Business, 50,* 198–207.

Bray, H. (2003, August 3). In defense of DARPA programs. Boston Globe.

Brock, W., Lakonishok, J., & LeBaron, B. (1992). Simple technical trading rules and the stochastic properties of stock returns. *Journal of Finance, 47,* 1731–1764.

Brown, S., & Warner, J. (1980). Measuring security price performance. *Journal of Financial Economics, 8,* 205–258.

Brown, S., & Warner, J. (1985). Using daily stock returns: The case of event studies. *Journal of Financial Economics, 14,* 3–31.

Brown, W. O., & Sauer, R. D. (1993). Fundamentals or noise? Evidence from the professional basketball betting market. *Journal of Finance, 48*, 1193–1209.

Campaa, J. M., & Chang, P. H. K. (1998). The forecasting ability of correlations implied in foreign exchange options. *Journal of International Money and Finance, 17*, 855–880.

Campbell, J. Y., Lo, A. W., & MacKinlay, A. C. (1997). *The econometrics of financial markets*. Princeton, NJ: Princeton University Press.

Chan, K. C., Chen, N. F., & Hsieh, D. (1985). An exploratory investigation of the firm size effect. *Journal of Financial Economics, 14*, 451–471.

Chang, E. C., & Pinegar, J. M. (1986). Return seasonality and tax-loss selling in the market for long term government and corporate bonds. *Journal of Financial Economics, 17*, 391–415.

Cowles, A., 3rd (1933). Can stock market forecasters forecast? *Econometrica, 1*, 309–324.

Davies, P. L., & Canes, M. (1978). Stock prices and the publication of second hand information. *Journal of Business, 51*, 43–56.

DeBondt, W. F. M., & Thaler, R. (1985). Does the market overreact? *Journal of Finance, 40*, 793–805.

Dyl, E. (1977). Capital gains taxation and year-end stock market behavior. *Journal of Finance, 32*, 165–175.

Elton, E., Gruber, M., Brown, S., & Goetzman, W. (2010). *Modern portfolio theory and investment analysis* (8th ed.). New York: Wiley.

Fama, E. (1965). The behavior of stock market prices. *Journal of Business, 38*, 34–105.

Fama, E., & Blume, M. (1966). Filter rules and stock market trading profits. *Journal of Business, 39*, 226–241.

Fama, E., Fisher, L., Jensen, M. C., & Roll, R. (1969). The adjustment of stock prices to new information. *International Economic Review, 10*, 1–21.

Fama, E., & French, K. (1992). The cross-section of expected stock returns. *Journal of Finance, 47*, 427–465.

Fama, E., & MacBeth, J. (1973). Risk, return, and equilibrium: Empirical tests. *Journal of Political Economy, 71*, 607–636.

Firth, M. (1976). The impact of earnings announcements on the share price behaviour of similar type firms. *Economics Journal, 86*, 296–306.

French, K. (1980). Stock returns and the weekend effect. *Journal of Financial Economics, 8*, 55–69.

French, K., & Roll, R. (1986). The arrival of information and the reaction of traders. *Journal of Financial Economics, 13*, 547–559.

Gandar, J., Zuber, R., O'Brien, T., & Russo, B. (1988). Testing rationality in the point spread betting market. *Journal of Finance, 43*, 995–1008.

Givoly, D., & Ovadia, A. (1983). Year-end induced sales and stock market seasonality. *Journal of Finance, 38*, 171–185.

Givoly, D., & Palmon, O. (1985). Insider trading and the exploitation of inside information: Some empirical evidence. *Journal of Business, 58*, 69–87.

Golec, J., & Tamarkin, M. (1991). The degree of inefficiency in the football betting markets. *Journal of Financial Economics, 30*, 311–323.

Granger, C. W. (1968). Some aspects of the random walk model of stock prices. *International Economic Review, 9*, 253–257.

Granger, C. W., & Morgenstern, O. (1972). *Predictability of stock market prices*. Boston: Heath.

Gray, P., & Gray, S. F. (1997). Testing market inefficiency: Evidence from the NFL sports betting market. *Journal of Finance, 52*, 1725–1737.

Griffiths, M., & White, R. (1993). Tax-induced trading and the turn of the year anomaly: An intraday study. *Journal of Finance, 48*, 575–598.

Grossman, S., & Stiglitz, J. (1980). On the impossibility of informationally efficient markets. *American Economic Review, 70*, 393–408.

Holloway, C. (1981). A note on testing an autoregressive investment strategy using value line ranks. *Journal of Finance, 36*, 711–719.

Huberman, G., & Kandel, S. (1982). Market efficiency and value line record. *Journal of Business, 63*, 187–216.

Ibbotson, R., & Jaffee, J. (1975). Hot Issue Markets. *Journal of Finance, 30*(2), 1027–1042.

Jaffee, J. (1974). Special information and insider trading. *Journal of Business, 47*, 410–428.

Jaffee, J., Keim, D. H., & Westerfield, R. (1989). Earnings yields, market values, and stock returns. *Journal of Finance, 44*, 135–148.

Jagolinzer, A.D. (2005). *An analysis of insiders' information-based trade within the SEC Rule 10b5-1 safe harbor*. Unpublished Working paper, Stanford University.

Jegadeesh, N. (1991). Seasonality in stock price mean: Evidence from the U.S., the U.K. *Journal of Finance, 46*, 1427–1444.

Jegadeesh, N., & Titman, S. (1993). The returns to buying winners and selling losers: Implications for stock market efficiency. *Journal of Finance, 48*, 65–91.

Jennergren, P., & Korsvold, P. (1975). The non-random character of Norwegian and Swedish stock market prices. In E. J. Elton, & M. J. Gruber (Eds.), *International Capital Markets* (pp. 37–54). Amsterdam: North-Holland.

Jensen, M., & Bennington, G. (1970). Random walks and technical theories: Some additional evidence. *Journal of Finance, 25*, 469–482.

Kaplan, S. N., & Ruback, R. S. (1995). The valuation of cash flow forecasts: An empirical analysis. *The Journal of Finance, 50*(4), 1059–1093.

Keim, D. B. (1983). Size-related anomalies and stock return seasonality: Further empirical evidence. *Journal of Financial Economics, 12*, 13–32.

Keim, D. B. (1989). Trading patterns, bid-ask spreads, and estimated security returns: The case of common stock at calendar turning points. *Journal of Financial Economics, 25*, 75–97.

Kendall, M. (1953). The analysis of economic time series. *Part I: Prices, Journal of the Royal Statistical Society, 96*, 11–25.

Kihn, J. (1996). The financial performance of low-grade municipal bond funds. *Financial Management, 25*, 52–73.

Latane, H., & Rendleman, R. (1976). Standard deviations of stock price ratios implied in option prices. *Journal of Finance, 31*, 369–381.

Levy, R. (1967). Relative strength as a criterion for investment selection. *Journal of Finance, 22*, 595–610.

Lo, A. W., & MacKinlay, A. C. (1988). Stock market prices do not follow random walks: Evidence from a simple specification test. *Review of Financial Studies, 1*, 41–46.

Lo, A. W., & MacKinlay, A. C. (1999). *A non-random walk down wall street*. Princeton, NJ: Princeton University Press.

Looney, R. (2003). DARPA's policy analysis market for intelligence: Outside the box or off the wall? *Strategic Insights, 2*. Available at <http://www.au.af.mil/au/awc/awcgate/nps/pam/si_pam.pdf>. Accessed 12.04.12.

Malkiel, B. (2003). *A random walk down wall street*. New York: W.W. Norton and Company.

Maloney, M., & Mulherin, J. H. (2003). The complexity of price discovery in an efficient market: The stock market reaction to the Challenger crash. *Journal of Corporate Finance, 9*, 453–479.

McDonald, J., & Fisher, A. K. (1972). New issue stock price behavior. *Journal of Finance, 27*, 97–102.

Michaely, R., & Womack, K. (1999). Conflict of interest and the credibility of underwriter recommendations. *Review of Financial Studies, 12*, 653–686.

Neiderhoffer, V., & Osborne, M. F. M. (1966). Market making and reversal on the stock exchange. *Journal of the American Statistical Association, 61*, 897–916.

Reinganum, M. (1983). The anomalous stock market behavior of small firms in January: Empirical tests for tax-loss selling effects. *Journal of Financial Economics, 12*, 89–104.

Richards, A. J. (1997). Winner-loser reversals in national stock market indices: Can they be explained? *Journal of Finance, 52*, 2129–2144.

Richardson, M., & Stock, J. H. (1988). Inferences drawn from statistics based on multiyear asset returns. *Journal of Financial Economics, 25*, 323–348.

Ritter, J. R. (1984). The "hot issue" market of 1980. *Journal of Business, 57*, 215–240.

Ritter, J. (1991). The long-run performance of initial public offerings. *Journal of Finance, 46*, 3–28.

Roll, R. (1981). A possible explanation of the small firm effect. *Journal of Finance, 36*, 879–888.

Roll, R. (1988). $R^2$. *Journal of Finance, 43*, 541–566.

Rozeff, M. S., & Kinney, W. R., Jr. (1976). Capital markets seasonality: The case of stock returns. *Journal of Financial Economics, 3*, 379–402.

Samuelson, P. (1965). Proof that properly anticipated prices fluctuate randomly. *Industrial Management Review, 6*, 41–49.

Saporito, B. (2005). Place your bets!. *Time Magazine*, October 24, 76.

Sauer, R., Brajer, V., Ferris, S. P., & Marr, M. W. (1988). Hold your bets: Another look at the efficiency of the gambling market for NFL games. *Journal of Political Economy, 96*, 206–213.

Schwert, W. G. (1983). Size and stock returns and other empirical regularities. *Journal of Financial Economics, 12*(1), 3–12.

Shiller, R. J. (1981). Do stock prices move too much to be justified by subsequent changes in dividends? *American Economic Review, 71*, 421–436.

Sullivan, R., Timmerman, A., & White, H. (1997). Data-snooping, technical trading rule performance, and the bootstrap. *Journal of Finance, 54*, 1647–1691.
Surowiecki, J. (2004). *The wisdom of crowds: Why the many are smarter than the few and how collective wisdom shapes business, economics, societies, and nations*. New York: Doubleday.
Thaler, R. H., & Ziemba, W. T. (1988). Anomalies: Parimutuel betting markets: Racetracks and lotteries. *Journal of Economic Perspectives, 2*, 161–174.
Wolfers, J., & Zitzewitz, E. (2004). Prediction markets. *Journal of Economic Perspectives, 18*, 107–126.
Wolfers, J., & Zitzewitz, E. (2007). *Interpreting prediction market prices as probabilities*. Working paper, University of Pennsylvania. Available at <http://bpp.wharton.upenn.edu/jwolfers/Papers/InterpretingPredictionMarketPrices.pdf>.
Womack, K. L. (1996). Do brokerage analysts' recommendations have investment value? *Journal of Finance, 51*, 137–167.
Woodland, L. M., & Woodland, B. M. (1994). Market efficiency and the favorite-longshot bias: The baseball betting market. *Journal of Finance, 49*, 269–279.
Working, H. (1934). A random difference series for use in the analysis of time series. *Journal of the American Statistical Association, 29*, 11–24.

## 11.9 EXERCISES

1. If price changes reflect new information, why should returns fluctuate randomly?
2. Consider the following stock price sequence:

| $t$ | $P_t$ |
|---|---|
| 1 | 50 |
| 2 | 51 |
| 3 | 52 |
| 4 | 58 |
| 5 | 56 |

   Compute three-day moving averages for days 3, 4, and 5. If one assumes that the three-day moving average price represents the true value of the stock because of the elimination of noise, should the investor buy or sell shares on days 3, 4, and 5?
3. Compute five-day moving averages for each date of the following series, assuming that 5 is the price for day 1 and 18 is the price for day 12:

| | | | | | | | | | | | |
|---|---|---|---|---|---|---|---|---|---|---|---|
| 5 | 6 | 5 | 6 | 8 | 10 | 9 | 12 | 15 | 12 | 16 | 18 |

4. Toy stores have very clear seasonal patterns in their revenue flows. Should toy store company share prices exhibit similar seasonality?
5. An analyst has tested the effect of spin-off announcements on share prices using event study methodology. The analyst's procedure proceeded as follows:
   **a.** Ten spin-offs were obtained from the most recent year.
   **b.** Announcement dates were standardized with 30 days of prices collected from both before and announcement dates.

c. Returns were computed and averaged for each company in the spin-off sample. Standard deviations and normal deviates were computed for the sample for each date. Appropriate tests for statistical significance were conducted.
d. Cumulative average residuals were computed for each date and tested for statistical significance.

Test results suggested that spin-offs were associated with 30-day returns of 8%. Why might an investor be skeptical of this test? How can the test be improved?

6. Which is worth more?
   a. A market forecasting service that correctly predicts the direction of the market portfolio with 100% consistency every month for extended periods of time and can be expected to continue to do so in the future.
   b. A market forecasting service that incorrectly predicts the direction of the market portfolio with 100% consistency every month for extended periods of time and can be expected to continue to do so in the future.
7. Suppose that we wished to conduct an event study on whether acquiring firms experience share price reactions to takeover announcements. For our event study, we will use for our sample the following three acquiring firms:

   Company X: Merger announcement date January 15, 2012
   Company Y: Merger announcement date February 15, 2012
   Company Z: Merger announcement date April 10, 2012

   Suppose we establish an 11-day testing period for returns around the event dates, the event date plus five days before and five days after. The following table provides our three acquiring firm stock prices during 12-day periods around merger announcement dates:

| Company X | | Company Y | | Company Z | |
|---|---|---|---|---|---|
| Date | Price | Date | Price | Date | Price |
| 1/09 | 50.125 | 2/09 | 20.000 | 4/04 | 60.375 |
| 1/10 | 50.125 | 2/10 | 20.000 | 4/05 | 60.500 |
| 1/11 | 50.250 | 2/11 | 20.125 | 4/06 | 60.250 |
| 1/12 | 50.250 | 2/12 | 20.250 | 4/07 | 60.125 |
| 1/13 | 50.375 | 2/13 | 20.375 | 4/08 | 60.000 |
| 1/14 | 50.250 | 2/14 | 20.375 | 4/09 | 60.125 |
| 1/15 | 52.250 | 2/15 | 21.375 | 4/10 | 60.625 |
| 1/16 | 52.375 | 2/16 | 21.250 | 4/11 | 60.750 |
| 1/17 | 52.250 | 2/17 | 21.375 | 4/12 | 60.750 |
| 1/18 | 52.375 | 2/18 | 21.500 | 4/13 | 60.875 |
| 1/19 | 52.500 | 2/19 | 21.375 | 4/14 | 60.875 |
| 1/20 | 52.375 | 2/20 | 21.500 | 4/15 | 60.875 |

**a.** Compute one-day returns for each of 11 days for each of the three stocks.

**b.** Suppose that we have decided to use the mean adjusted return method to compute excess or abnormal stock returns. Here, we will compute mean daily returns for each security for a period outside of our 11-day testing period. Suppose we compute average daily returns and standard deviations for each of the stocks for 180-day periods prior to the testing periods (the raw returns data are not given here). Suppose that we have found normal or expected daily returns along with standard deviations as follows:

| Stock | Normal Return | Standard Deviation |
|---|---|---|
| X | 0.000465 | 0.00415 |
| Y | 0.000520 | 0.00637 |
| Z | 0.000082 | 0.00220 |

Compute excess returns for each stock for each of the 11 days.

**c.** For each of the 11 days in the analysis, compute average residuals for the three stocks. Then, for each day, compute a standard deviation of residuals for the three stocks. Finally, compute normal deviates for each of the 11 dates based on the averages and standard deviations for the three stocks.

**d.** Are average residuals for any of the dates statistically significant at the 95% level?

**e.** Compute cumulative average residuals for each of the 11 dates.

**f.** Compute standard deviations and normal deviates for each of the 11 dates.

**g.** Does there appear to be statistically significant evidence of abnormal acquiring firm returns around announcement dates?

**8.** The following table reflects abnormal returns for each of 10 stocks over a seven-day period about day zero, which is the standardized date of the sudden death of the CEO for each of the 10 firms. An analyst wants to determine whether the death announcement date represents a significant event and make appropriate portfolio adjustments when CEOs suddenly die in the future.

| Day | Stock 1 | Stock 2 | Stock 3 | Stock 4 | Stock 5 | Stock 6 | Stock 7 | Stock 8 | Stock 9 | Stock 10 |
|---|---|---|---|---|---|---|---|---|---|---|
| −3 | 0.003279 | −0.00814 | 0.008945 | −0.00255 | 0.011395 | −0.00797 | 0.011223 | 0.014037 | 0.020344 | 0.015708 |
| −2 | 0.004440 | −0.01997 | 0.017064 | 0.003790 | 0.048419 | 0.017966 | −0.01098 | −0.02468 | 0.023697 | 0.031806 |
| −1 | 0.031991 | 0.022567 | −0.01350 | 0.026311 | 0.069986 | 0.047213 | 0.012632 | 0.038042 | 0.015502 | 0.002453 |
| 0 | 0.091624 | 0.086352 | 0.088165 | 0.077971 | 0.128351 | 0.112391 | 0.069263 | 0.089396 | 0.107763 | 0.102206 |
| 1 | 0.043105 | 0.028967 | 0.027764 | 0.006769 | −0.04901 | −0.01061 | 0.010702 | −0.00974 | 0.005449 | 0.009521 |
| 2 | 0.006715 | 0.011545 | 0.014355 | 0.013281 | −0.02619 | −0.03346 | 0.026330 | 0.003409 | 0.015373 | 0.006225 |
| 3 | −0.01942 | −0.00453 | −0.00708 | −0.00114 | −0.00493 | 0.02925 | −0.00783 | −0.03250 | 0.024930 | 0.030536 |

**a.** What are the average residuals, their standard deviations, and normal deviates for each of the seven dates?

**b.** What are the cumulative average residuals, their standard deviations, and normal deviates for each of the seven dates?

**c.** On which days are average residuals statistically significant at the 1% level? On which days are cumulative average residuals statistically significant at the 1% level?

**9.** The Hollywood Stock Exchange (www.hsx.com) describes itself as "the world's leading entertainment stock market." The site is owned by Cantor Fitzgerald, one of the world's leading trading firms. "Investors" at the HSX.trade virtual shares of celebrities and movies with virtual money called the Hollywood Dollar. For example, "investors" can trade "stock" on a new major movie release. Although the site is still considered an entertainment website, how might information concerning the price of this "stock" be of use to investors in the actual stock market? Similarly, how might information concerning the price of this "stock" be of use to managers of firms that produce and distribute films?

CHAPTER

# 12

# Trading Gone Awry

## 12.1 ILLEGAL INSIDER TRADING

Unfair markets fail to draw customers; unfair capital markets fail to draw capital. The perception of unfairness is sufficient to disrupt or break down markets. Markets can be perceived to be unfair for many reasons. Some investors may have better access to information than others. Certain investors may be able to exercise market power due to their size, access to information, domination, or volume of their transactions. Rational investors are frequently unwilling to execute transactions with counterparties who exploit their advantages; such perceived unfairness can easily lead to market failure. This chapter is concerned with the roles of trading and the impact that unfair trading activities can have on traders, markets, and institutions.

Sophisticated 19th-century English investors knew that the stock market tycoon Nathan Rothschild had pigeons and used them effectively to relay information. Then, as now, timely and accurate information was crucial to outperforming the market. In the early part of the 19th century, messenger pigeons were the fastest way to transmit news. For example, after the Battle of Waterloo, but before its outcome was publicly known in Britain, Rothschild's quiet and judicious (low-volume) selling activity was discovered by his countrymen who panicked and sold everything. However, Rothschild was merely manipulating the market. With prices down, and with a British victory over Napoleon at Waterloo, Rothschild actually bought huge quantities of stock at prices that his manipulative selling activity depressed. He then sold these shares at substantial profits when the news of the British victory finally reached England by more conventional news transmission.[1] Efficient acquisition and effective use of information along with appropriate manipulation of security prices were the trick to making stock market profits in the regulation-free 19th century. This case illustrates the importance of having better information than competing traders and acquiring the information sooner.

[1]At least parts of this account might be apocryphal.

Illegal insider trading is traditionally defined as the execution of transactions on the basis of material nonpublic information. We discussed this issue in Chapter 4. However, recall that there is no comprehensive statutory definition as to precisely what constitutes impermissible insider trading. Several statutes are generally relied upon to enforce prohibitions on insider trading. First, Section 10(b) of the Securities Exchange Act of 1934 prohibits the employment "in connection with the purchase or sale of any security registered on a national securities exchange or any security not so registered, any manipulative or deceptive device or contrivance in contravention of such rules and regulations as the Commission may prescribe as necessary or appropriate in the public interest or for the protection of investors." And SEC Rule 10b-5 prohibits "any act, practice, or course of business which operates or would operate as a fraud or deceit upon any person, in connection with the purchase or sale of any security."[2] These rules are extended to identify elements of a Section 10(b) or Rule 10b-5 insider trading claim:

**a.** Possession of material nonpublic information
**b.** Trading while in possession of that non-public information
**c.** Violation of a relationship of trust and confidence (Flannery, 1998: 1–2)

In addition, Section 14 of the Securities Exchange Act and Rule 14e-3 impose a "disclose or abstain from trading" obligation on any person who trades in securities that will be sought or are being sought in a tender offer, while that person is in possession of material nonpublic information that he knows or has reason to know has been acquired directly or indirectly from the offer or, the subject corporation, any of their affiliated persons (including officers, directors, partners, or employees or any person acting on behalf of either company). Thus, the Securities Exchange Act of 1934 (Section 14e) provided for the initial federal statutory insider trading restrictions, although a 1909 Supreme Court decision in Strong v. Repide interpreted inside trading by corporate officials without appropriately revealing that information to be a form of fraud. A 1980 Supreme Court decision (*Chiarella v. United States*) defined an insider as one who maintains a "relationship of trust and confidence with shareholders."[3] However, this definition can be rather broadly interpreted. As discussed in Chapter 4, the Insider Trading Sanctions Act of 1984 authorized penalties for illegal insider trading equal to three times the illegally obtained profits plus forfeiture of the profits. The Insider Trading and Fraud Act of 1988 was intended to help define exactly what constitutes an insider and to set penalties for illegal insider trading activity.

## Notorious Insider Trading Cases

A casual web search for "insider tips" will lead to many sites selling information for sports betting, where, like the stock market, the best information is the key to success. However, selling and acting on insider trading tips in securities markets are illegal.

[2]In an application of the "misappropriation theory," the U.S. Supreme Court in *United States v. O'Hagan*, 521 U.S. 642 (1997), held that a person can be held liable for violating Section 10(b) and Rule 10b-5 when misappropriating confidential information (in effect, stealing valuable information) for the purpose of trading securities.

[3]U.S. Supreme Court, *Chiarella v. United States*, 445 U.S. 222 (1980).

Nevertheless, investors require the best possible information for their investment decisions, and at least a few cross the line into illegal trading. The following represent just of a few of the high profile insider trading cases pursued by the SEC and other regulatory authorities (plus one that predates the SEC and insider regulations). There are many more such cases pursued by authorities, and we can only guess as to how many that have not been pursued or even suspected. One interesting aspect common to all of the individuals named in the cases that follow is that they were very successful in their businesses, and in most cases, quite wealthy—at least prior to the resolution of their cases.

### *William Duer*

William Duer was appointed Assistant Secretary of the Treasury in 1789 under Alexander Hamilton. Hamilton's and Duer's wives were cousins. Duer used information and connections obtained in his official position, along with substantial leverage to speculate in new U.S. debt and various bank stock issues. He resigned his position in 1791 after learning that Treasury officials were to be prohibited from speculating in Treasury securities, but continued to use his inside connections for speculative purposes. His speculation and subsequent failure was a major cause of the Panic of 1792.[4] Geisst (2004) wrote that "[t]he New York City economy crashed along with him, and Duer was nearly disemboweled by an enraged mob that chased him through the streets. He died in debtors' prison a few years later."

### *Dennis Levine, Ivan Boesky, and Michael Milken*

In 1985, Dennis Levine, a mergers and acquisitions specialist, was earning significant profits trading illegally on inside information through secret off shore accounts. He was a highly regarded managing director at Drexel, Burnham Lambert, once the fifth largest U.S. investment bank. Unfortunately for Levine, one of his trading account brokers, a Bahamian subsidiary of a Swiss bank, began "piggy backing" off his trades as did the bank's account executive at Merrill Lynch. Merrill Lynch became suspicious of these trades and notified the SEC. The SEC trail led back to Levine, who pled guilty in 1986 to securities fraud, tax evasion, and perjury. As part of his plea arrangement, he implicated fellow specialist Martin Siegel and famed arbitrageur Ivan Boesky, to whom he had passed illegal trading tips.

Boesky, considered the leading expert on merger arbitrage, had been paying Levine a percentage of his trading profits gained from Levine's tips.[5] Boesky agreed to a plea, whereby he would cooperate with authorities and secretly tape record conversations with his alleged confederates. Boesky, under the terms of his plea arrangement, implicated Michael Milken and Drexel Burnham, along with his longtime friend, John A. Mulheren Jr., the former head of Jamie Securities. This led to the SEC launching an investigation into all of them.

[4]The formation of the NYSE shortly followed, partly in reaction to the Panic of 1792 and the related market manipulation, an example of an early effort at market self-regulation as the charter members of the new exchange realized that the market needed to be perceived as having integrity in order to survive.

[5]In a line later adapted by Gordon Gecko in the movie *Wall Street*, Boesky told a 1986 UC Berkeley Business School audience that "[Greed ] is healthy. You can be greedy and still feel good about yourself."

Following up on his master's thesis at Wharton, Milken had innovated the 1980s junk bond market at Drexel. This led to extraordinary success for the firm, for which Milken was paid $550 million in 1987 alone. However, the investigation into the relationship between Boesky and Milken uncovered a $5.3 million payment in 1986 to Drexel that Boesky had characterized as a consulting fee. A significant amount of other evidence of insider trading was uncovered, but the bulk of the SEC's weak case against Milken and Drexel would be based on the testimony of Levine, Boesky, and other convicted felons. The SEC began to focus on Milken's brother Lloyd, who might have played a minor role in the insider trading activities (or at least would be subpoenaed to testify against his brother) and other relatives, including their 92-year-old grandfather. Milken agreed to a plea arrangement after the Department of Justice agreed not to pursue his brother. A codefendant of Milken, Alan Rosenthal, took his case to trial, whereby it was tossed by the judge before going to jury, lending significant credibility to the argument that the case against Milken was rather weak.

U.S. District Attorney Rudolph Giuliani threatened Drexel with an indictment under the Racketeer Influenced and Corrupt Organizations Act (RICO), which would have required Drexel post bond of $1 billion, a hefty amount for the heavily debt-financed firm. Even though company executives believed that the case against Drexel was weak, they decided that it would not be able to survive the costs and loss of reputation of a trial and agreed to pay a $650-million fine.

Levine received a two-year sentence, was fined $362,000, was disgorged of $11.5 million in illegal trading profits, and paid an additional $2 million in back taxes. Boesky served two years in Southern California's Lompoc Federal Prison, paid $100 million in fines, and was barred from the securities business for life. Milken received a 10-year sentence for fraud and illegal market manipulation, which was later reduced to 24 months; fined $600 million; and made restitution payments. Shortly after his release, he was diagnosed with terminal prostate cancer (but then he seemed much healthier 20 years later). Milken and other Drexel employees paid $1.3 billion into a pool to settle hundreds of lawsuits. Drexel was ultimately bankrupted in the aftermath of the scandal, fines, loss of reputation, and the collapse of the junk bond market.

### *Martha Stewart*

Martha Stewart is a well-known television talk show personality and majority shareholder of NYSE-listed Martha Stewart Living Omnimedia, Inc. and of other companies. In 2001, she sold approximately 3,928 shares of ImClone, which had just learned that its new prescription drug would not obtain Food and Drug Administration approval. After learning about the drug's setback, Sam Waskal, CEO of ImClone, quickly sold shares of his ImClone stock. His broker, Peter Bacanovic, who also served as Martha Stewart's broker, apparently notified her that Waskal was selling shares of his company's stock. The SEC investigated Bacanovic and Waskal, who were ultimately imprisoned. The SEC also began an investigation as to whether Stewart's selling was related to that of Waskal. Whether Stewart had engaged in illegal insider trading was not known at this point, and still is not completely clear. Even if Stewart had been completely forthright about the information that she had received and why she sold, the SEC's case against her would have been weak at best. Unfortunately for Stewart, she conspired with Bacanovic to fabricate a story about a stop order at $60. That is, Stewart falsely claimed to have placed a standing order to sell ImClone shares once its shares dropped to $60. This fabrication led to charges of conspiracy, obstruction of an agency proceeding, and making false statements to federal investigators. She was convicted and sentenced in 2004 to serve five months in federal prison followed by five months of incarceration in her Bedford home (she was allowed to depart for up to 48 hours with an electronic monitor) and a two-year period of supervised release. She also paid a fine and disgorged the reduction in short-term trading losses that she avoided.

After she was charged in the alleged insider trading incident involving ImClone, but before the general public knew of the investigation, Stewart sold shares of her own company, Martha Stewart Living Omnimedia, Inc. This exposed her to additional insider trading charges, based on the negative impact that her legal problems might be expected to have on her company. She was charged for manipulating the price of her company's stock. These charges did not result in convictions.

Stewart's case is rather perplexing. First, she was a billionaire, and the stock sale saved her only $45,673 in losses. So, if she did sell illegally, her forgone losses were only a tiny fraction of her wealth. Worse, she almost certainly was no better off lying to the SEC than she might have been had she honestly admitted to the circumstances of her trade rather than concoct the story about the stop order. Better yet, she could easily have invoked her Fifth Amendment right to silence. The SEC's insider trading case against her probably would not have merited further action or at least not merited a conviction. In fact, she was not even indicted on insider trading charges in the ImClone case. Lying to authorities about the preexisting order to sell at $60 essentially exposed her to all of the charges for which she was convicted. Finally, Stewart did possess a reasonable degree of financial sophistication, having been a billionaire, a CEO, and a stock broker early in her career. She should have known better than to respond to investigators as she did. Perhaps she fell victim to a level of hubris that seems to affect some particularly successful people. Nonetheless, a number of observers have commented that neither her crimes nor the strength of evidence on which her convictions were based warranted the sanctions that she suffered. On the other hand, the SEC and its crackdown efforts against illegal insider trading did receive substantial attention.

### *Raj Rajaratnam*

In December 2011, Raj Rajaratnam, billionaire and founder of the defunct hedge fund, the Galleon Group, began serving an 11-year sentence in the federal prison system after being convicted on 14 counts of conspiracy and fraud. This was the longest sentence ever imposed for illegal insider trading, although less than half of the term requested by prosecutors. Rajaratnam was also fined $92.8 million and will face civil and other actions. Rajaratnam had been accused of having taken more than $50 million in insider trading gains based on tips provided by fellow conspirators at Goldman Sachs, McKinsey & Co., Intel, and Google, among others. Among those implicated in the investigations were Roomy Khan (Intel), Anil Kumar (McKinsey), Danielle Chiesi (Bear Stearns), Zvi Goffer (Galleon), Rajat Gupta (McKinsey and Goldman Sachs), Robert Moffatt (IBM), and the extensive list continues. Many of these individuals have been charged, convicted, and served time in prison. Two interesting facets of this case were the large number of co-conspirators (49, more or less) and the use by authorities of wire and tapes to record conversations, including more than 40 wiretapped phone conversations between Rajaratnam and his accomplices.[6] Although pursuing illegal insider trading activities remains very difficult for authorities, its level of sophistication in the pursuit is improving. Furthermore, it seems interesting that such conspirator networks can be so large, given the conspirators' need to maintain secrecy.

### Monitoring Inside Trading Activity

It is usually very difficult for authorities to prosecute insider trading cases. Without substantial information from others—frequently codefendants—authorities often cannot prove who knew what and when, or what has motivated profitable trades. Thus, successful insider trading prosecutions usually require cooperation from codefendants or damaging information concerning other illegal behavior (such as tax evasion).

There have been recent improvements to enforcement efforts. First, surveillance techniques have improved significantly. For example, the SEC and all of the major markets and companies themselves are purchasing software systems to monitor for illicit activity. The SEC is making use of varied resources to monitor insider activity, including formation of special surveillance teams, wire tapping, and bounty payments to informants. The SEC currently contends with roughly 700,000 tips per year from informants. Markets such as the NYSE, Nasdaq, and CBOE are making greater use of technology to monitor trading activity for suspicious activity. For example, the NASD has been using an intelligent surveillance application known as the Securities Observation, News Analysis, and Regulation (SONAR) system to detect suspicious patterns. Regardless, insider trading enforcement remains difficult.

## 12.2 FRONT RUNNING AND LATE TRADING

Access to inside information clearly gives the trader a jump on the competition. So does access to information on other traders' activity, especially in the case of a broker with knowledge of her client's trades. Parasitic trading occurs when a broker uses knowledge of her client's trading activity to her own trading advantage, a practice that clearly violates professional standards and may itself constitute inside trading.

### Front Running and Parasitic Trading

*Front running* occurs when a broker uses his knowledge of a large pending order to buy (sell) the relevant security in front of the pending buy (sell) order so as to benefit from the market reaction to the large order. Thus, a broker might illegally front run a large buy order by purchasing shares of stock for her own account after receiving a large purchase order for that stock from a client. Front running is an example of securities fraud because

[6] Transcripts of many of these conversations can be found on the web.

the broker has taken advantage of her client, in whose interest she is obliged to act. For example, by front running a client buy order, the broker's own buy order may force the stock price up against her client's buy order. In addition, the front running broker may also be in violation of insider trading law, in that the she has nonpublic information about an order and violates her professional code of ethics by front running it. Front running can also occur when a broker passes on trade information to another client or trader.

In one front-running scandal, the U.S. Attorney's Office and the SEC accused brokers from Merrill Lynch of allowing certain clients to listen to conversations involving other clients through broadcasts on Merrill Lynch internal speaker systems. In this "squawk box scandal," some clients were privy in advance to other clients' trades. Favored clients then rewarded the brokers with business, commissions, and cash. Several former brokers from Merrill Lynch and Lehman Brothers were convicted and received probation or prison terms in 2010, as did several of their clients.

A similar, often legal, but frequently unethical practice is *tailgating*, a form of parasitic trading where the broker places an order immediately after the client's order. This practice is questionable because the broker is acting on the basis of the client's order, which itself might have been motivated by inside information or might precede additional client trading. Another type of ethically questionable parasitic order is *penny-jumping*, where the broker places a buy (sell) order one uptick above (downtick below) below the client's buy (sell) limit order, expecting to benefit either from the market's reaction to the client order or to limit his losses by transacting with the client. For example, if the client were to place a large buy order at 50.00, the broker would penny jump by placing her buy order at 50.01. The broker's order will execute ahead of the client's order due to price priority. If the client's order then executes, the broker will profit from any favorable price reaction due to the client's large buy order. If the price declines, the broker can quickly sell his shares to the client at a $.01 loss.

## Market Timing and Late Trading

We discussed in Chapter 3 the practice of *market timing*, which is the fund trading strategy intended to exploit stale security prices and NAV deviations from fundamental values. While market timing is not illegal, it can transfer wealth between fund shareholders and necessitate that funds maintain higher levels of cash to accommodate share redemptions. Market timing may increase fund transactions costs in response to shareholder redemptions. In addition, market timing could result in civil litigation due to prohibitions in the fund's prospectus or criminal penalties if a broker encouraged it to generate higher commissions for herself.

To limit these costs and problems, many mutual funds have announced in their prospectuses restrictions on the number of trades that customers may execute in and out of a fund per year. However, several scandals have erupted in recent years due to fund advisers having made undisclosed arrangements with favored customers to enable them to circumvent established trading restrictions. For example, in September 2003, New York State Attorney General Elliot Spitzer filed a complaint against the New Jersey–based hedge fund Canary Capital Partners, run by Edward Julius Stern, son of Leonard N. Stern.

Spitzer's complaint alleged that Canary Capital entered into illegal agreements with mutual fund companies to defraud investors. For example, Canary made a secret agreement with Security Trust to enable it to engage in market timing-related trades. In another case, PIMCO agreed to permit Canary a specified number of trades in exchange for fees to be earned on $25 million it would manage for Canary.

In addition, Spitzer's allegations went further than these market timing agreement allegations, accusing Canary of *late trading*. In these allegations of illegal late trading, Canary maintained arrangements with funds to purchase or redeem shares after daily NAV's were computed. Unlike market timing, late trading is always illegal. Late trading was described by Spitzer as "betting on a horse race after the horses have crossed the finish line." According to Spitzer's complaint, Canary engaged in schemes to purchase mutual fund shares after 4 PM exchange closing times with the assistance of certain Bank of America fund employees. Technically, Canary allegedly submitted trades in question prior to the 4 PM deadline so that they could be time-stamped before 4 PM. However, Spitzer alleged that the Bank of America employees would hold transactions until after the market closed, providing Canary the opportunity to "confirm" its trades. In fact, in 2001, Bank of America employees allegedly installed an electronic trading system in Canary's offices that allowed Canary to late trade by entering its orders directly, after the 4 PM deadline. Bank of America employees purportedly reconciled the "late" trades the following day. Canary Capital settled Spitzer's complaint for $40 million and was permitted to not admit guilt. Bank of America provided compensation to its mutual fund shareholders for related losses. Spitzer and the SEC also charged Janus, Bank One's One Group, and Strong Capital in other alleged incidences of late trading. In fact, the founder and chairman of Strong Mutual Funds, Richard Strong, was charged with late trading in his own fund.

## 12.3 BLUFFING, SPOOFING, AND MARKET MANIPULATION

The attraction of the securities markets to scoundrels can easily be likened to Jesse James's attraction to banks—*'cause that's where the money is*. Scam after scam has been created; most seem quite naive to us. However, we have the benefit of hindsight. There has always been a sense among investors that market prices do reflect information—hence, investors rely on the market for quality information. If an unscrupulous operator is able to manipulate the market, he manipulates the information to which investors react. Much as the market creates information for traders, traders can, through their trading behavior, create information for other traders. If an investor has sufficient resources to create a given type of appearance in the market, he can generate huge profits through the trading activities of his counterparts. As we discussed in Chapter 4, most forms of manipulation in the information marketplace are illegal, particularly if the manipulation involves actions in the securities markets.

### Bluffing

In Chapter 5, we discussed how uninformed traders react to the information gleaned from the activities of informed traders. *Bluffing* is the act of fooling other traders into making unwise trades by convincing them that the bluffer has superior material information about security values. Bluffing is a mechanism for manipulating the market. There are a number of ways that traders bluff, both legal and illegal. A trader can bluff the market by placing a bid or offer at a price or in a quantity that exaggerates his or her own true position, interest, or lack of interest in a security. For example, a bluffer might place a particularly attractive offer for a small quantity of shares, intending then to sell a much larger quantity of shares after a positive price response to the initial offer. As long as such orders are executed, they are usually perfectly legal. Bluffers may also simply spread rumors or false information about the value of a company's shares. Such false rumor spreading can represent deceit or fraud, illegal when used to manipulate markets, and perhaps otherwise as well.

## Spoofing

*Spoofing* is the act of placing a quote that is intended to be canceled prior to its execution. Spoofing might be considered a form of bluffing where the trader places a trade that she has no intent to execute. There are three primary motivations behind spoofing:

1. To overload the quotation system of a market, inhibiting its ability to execute trades
2. To delay a specific trader's trade execution by placing that trader's quotes behind a series of quotes with higher priority
3. To create the appearance of false market depth or direction, particularly by submitting then later cancelling multiple bids or offers. This type of spoofing is often referred to as *layering*. Layering is frequently accomplished through a high-frequency trading (HFT) program designed to submit many quotations that are canceled after an executed transaction.

Clearly, spoofing can be used to manipulate a market in an illegal manner. Orders, modifications, and cancellations are not considered to be spoofing if they were submitted as part of a legitimate, good-faith attempt to execute a trade.

### *Illustration: Spoofing*

In 2001, the SEC alleged that Alexander Pomper submitted a phantom limit order (an order that Pomper did not intend to execute) on NASDAQ to purchase 300 shares of the thinly traded Gumtech International ("GUMM") at \$11.375. This limit order improved the NBBO bid by \$0.3125 from \$11.0625, while the NBBO offer was \$11.4375 per share. Pomper improved the bid for GUMM, but with a bid that he apparently did not actually intend to fill. Nonetheless, this bid did seem to improve the liquidity for GUMM, tightening the spread and making the stock appear to be worth more. Then, Pomper placed an order to sell 2000 shares of GUMM at \$11.375 per share through another market making firm. Pomper's sell order was immediately executed at \$11.375 per share by this market maker because the best bid at \$11.375 seemed to suggest a higher value and more liquid market for GUMM. However, after executing its sell order, Pomper canceled his order to buy GUMM for \$11.375, realizing a profit of \$625 (2,000 × [\$11.375 − 11.0625]) relative to the initial bid for \$11.0625. In 2002, the SEC announced a settlement with Pomper, whereby without admitting or denying the allegations in the complaint (which also alleged other violations), Pomper agreed to pay \$9,800 in disgorgement and prejudgment interest and to pay a \$15,000 civil penalty.

## Buy, Lie, and Sell High

"Pump-and-dump" schemes occur when the market manipulator touts company's stock with false and misleading statements to the marketplace, causing the stock's price to rise before selling his own shares at inflated prices. Consider that it has been estimated that as much as 65% of e-mail traffic is unsolicited (spam), and that 15% of this spam was touting shares of stock (Frieder and Zittrain, 2008). Such spam operations have been linked to pump and dump operations, where operators tout shares of stock and then sell them. Frieder and Zittrain claim that stock volume for touted shares increases dramatically after spam is delivered. Frieder and Zittrain describe one scenario:

> In a well-known case brought by the U.S. Securities and Exchange Commission, stock touter Jonathan Lebed routinely purchased stock accounting for anywhere from 17% to 46% of the stock's market volume for a day, and sent spammed e-mail touts on the same day. He then lodged limit orders to sell for the next day's trading session, anticipating a rise in the stock price after the general public received his touts and some acted on them. Lebed's case and subsequent settlement with the S.E.C. focused on his failure to disclose his own financial interest in the securities he touted; as discussed below, stock touts today often include such disclosures (in Re Lebed, 2000).

Frieder and Zittrain found that on days prior to touting, and on days touting takes place, returns are positive. Returns after touting are negative. Two-day returns average −5.25%, worsening further when the intensity of touting increases. Surely no reader of these results would consider purchasing stock on the basis of unsolicited spam. Yet, someone must be. Who? Why? And why does this buying behavior continue to persist even after transaction returns are so consistently poor?

Jonathan Lebed, the stock touter described above, was a 15-year-old trader from Cedar Grove, New Jersey. In September, 2000, the SEC settled 11 cases of stock market fraud against this high school student that had resulted in gains ranging from $12,000 to $74,000 from September 1999 to February 2000. With interest, the SEC disgorged $285,000 in illegal profits. With his AOL connection and hundreds of Yahoo Finance postings under numerous fictitious names, Jonathan had apparently purchased shares in small companies and then posted numerous buy recommendations under fictitious names, increasing share volume from 60,000 to over a million per day in the affected companies. He also maintained a website, stock-dogs.com, where he published his opinions and recommendations. It was reported that Jonathan's father, Greg Lebed, had a heart attack and other heart issues during the period of Jonathan's trading and SEC battles. However, the ending of this story wasn't all bad for Lebed. In his settlement with the SEC, Lebed was permitted to keep over $800,000 in profits from other transactions. Lebed remains an active trader and distributes a newsletter, available on line through http://lebed.biz.

## Banging the Close

The CFTC defines *banging the close* as a "manipulative or disruptive trading practice whereby a trader buys or sells a large number of futures contracts during the closing period of a futures contract (that is, the period during which the futures settlement price is determined) in order to benefit an even larger position in an option, swap, or other derivative that is cash settled based on the futures settlement price on that day."[7] Consider the case involving the giant hedge fund Amaranth Advisors, LLC, which incurred $6.4 billion in losses in the early spring 2006. The fund's failure arose from losses in trading highly leveraged natural gas contracts on NYMEX. The CFTC later charged Amaranth and its former head trader, Brian Hunter, with trying to manipulate natural gas futures prices. More specifically, Hunter was accused of banging the close and flooding the then-open outcry NYMEX futures markets with "series of rapid and successive" orders for natural gas during the final minutes of trading before the close, thereby forcing prices down in this less active market as buying interest diminished. The actual intent of his selling activity, according to the CFTC, was to depress natural gas prices in the ICE, where Amaranth held much larger short positions through swap contracts.

## Corners and Pools

*Corners* involve the purchase a sufficient level of a given security to obtain market power over its price. The purpose of the corner is to manipulate the price of the security, an activity made illegal by the 1934 Securities and Exchange Act. Numerous corners have existed over the years in commodity and securities markets. For example, the Hunt brothers (Nelson and Lamar), two of the then-wealthiest men in the world, attempted to corner the silver markets in the early 1980s, taking billions of inherited dollars in long positions. Although they succeeded in bidding up the price of silver almost 10-fold through their purchases, the bottom fell out of the market before they could unload their holdings. They nearly went bankrupt. A *pool* is a common fund comprising participants who combine their resources to obtain a large position in a security in order to manipulate its price. Pools are typically used to facilitate cornering of a market, and were a common activity prior to the 1929 stock market crash.

### *Vanderbilt v. Drew*

One of the most interesting cases of market manipulation involved Commodore Cornelius Vanderbilt, a 19th century tycoon, and Daniel Drew, an operator with connections to Tammany Hall. As of the early 1860s, Vanderbilt had owned enough shares (with a cost as low as $8 per share) of Harlem Railroad Company stock to effectively control the company and its share price, bidding it up to $100. He intended to extend the railroad's service into Manhattan and required approval from the city to accomplish this. However, Daniel Drew, also a Harlem Railroad investor, sold his shares and shorted 137,000 shares, almost five times the number of outstanding shares. He used his influence to convince Boss Tweed to repeal the railroad's license to operate in New York City, with the intended effect of ruining the railroad. The price of shares fell from $100 to $72, with Vanderbilt purchasing shares as Drew sold. In fact, Vanderbilt had, in effect, purchased the company several times over by acting as counterparty on Drew's short sales, and had the market cornered. In time, the short selling peaked and Drew needed to cover his short positions by repurchasing the stock. But only one major investor owned shares—Vanderbilt.

[7]See http://www.cftc.gov/ConsumerProtection/EducationCenter/CFTCGlossary/glossary_b.

Vanderbilt, having cornered the market, set his price at $179 per share, a price calculated to be the maximum that Drew could afford to pay. Drew was forced to settle with Vanderbilt at his terms, Vanderbilt obtained his approval to extend the railroad into Manhattan with Drew's cooperation, and Drew was practically bankrupted in the process. Drew had fallen victim to a market *corner*, intended to *squeeze the short seller*[8]:

> He who sells
> What isn't his'n
> Buys it back
> Or goes to pris'n.

### *Modern Day Corners: Chase Medical, Porsche, and Solomon*

Such corners are not confined to "ancient" history. For example, two brokers employed by the now defunct firm Moore & Schley, Cameron & Company were accused in the late 1980s of acquiring shares of Chase Medical Group for the purpose of artificially inflating their prices.[9] In effect, these brokers were accused of cornering the market for these shares and engaging in phony transactions to prop up the share prices.

In the height of the financial crisis of 2008, the German automobile manufacturer Porsche revealed that it owned 42.6% of the stock of Volkswagen, along with call options on another 31.5% of its shares. A number of hedge funds had short sold Volkswagen stock, believing that it would drop once Porsche reached its target ownership level of 75%. Unfortunately, the state of Lower Saxony in Germany owned another 20% of the shares, which it did not want to sell, creating a shortage of shares in the market available for short sellers to cover their positions. This shortage of available shares caused the share price to rise from about 200 Euro to over 1000. In effect, without breaking German securities law, Porsche had, in effect, cornered the market for Volkswagen shares and squeezed hedge fund short sellers, earning significant paper profits on its shares.

The U.S. Treasury maintains a strict set of rules for trading its instruments intended to sustain a perception of fairness. For example, no bidder is permitted to bid for or obtain 35% or more of a given Treasury issue. These regulations are intended to prevent market corners. Nonetheless, it still might be possible to abuse trading and bidding rules to create an unfair advantage. For example, in summer 1991, the venerable investment bank Salomon Brothers created a huge scandal by routinely bidding on more than 35% of issues, illegally bidding on as much as 105% of certain new issues. To conceal their actions, many of their bids were placed under names of clients who were unaware of the activity. Bonds were "parked" in client accounts. Such overbidding enabled Salomon to corner the market and fix prices for new two-year treasuries, enabling the firm to generate substantial trading profits by engaging in short squeezing.

The Treasury responded to this scandal by expanding its list of primary market participants and changing bidding procedures. Salomon fired its CEO, John Geutfrend, and several key employees including John Meriwether and Paul Mozer, the primary instigator of

[8]This quote has been attributed to Drew.

[9]See Aggarwal and Wu (2002) and SEC, Litigation Release No. 11973, January 25, 1989 for details on this case.

the fraud.[10] Mozer subsequently pled guilty on two counts of lying to the Federal Reserve Bank of New York in his bid submissions, served four months in a minimum security prison, and was fined $30,000 and an additional $1.1 million in an agreement with the SEC that barred him from the securities business for life. Warren Buffet, who owned a substantial stake in the firm through his holdings in Berkshire-Hathaway, contributed significant credibility to the firm by taking over as interim CEO and is often credited with saving the firm, which has since consolidated with Smith-Barney into CitiGroup.

## Wash Sales

Unscrupulous market participants have always had an interest in manipulating market conditions to generate profits. For example, consider *wash sales*, which are sham transactions intended to create the appearance of sales where, in effect, no sales actually take place. The SEC defines a wash sale as a transaction that involves no change in beneficial ownership. Wash sales may be intended to manipulate security prices (e.g., conspirators execute transactions with one another to create records of sales prices to deceive other participants in the market). One may arrange to sell a security to a cohort at a fixed (as opposed to market-determined) price. The transaction and its price are revealed to the market, which is intended to accept this price as the market-determined value of the security. A series of wash sales at ever-increasing prices, known as a *jitney game*, can give other investors the impression that the value of the security is rising, leading investors to purchase the stock. The market manipulators benefit when investors are led to purchase from them the security at inflated prices. It is quite likely that the security's price will drop rapidly once investors realize that they had been tricked into purchasing the security. The market manipulators hope that they will no longer own the security when this happens. Wash sales may also involve the sale of securities for tax purposes with offsetting transactions to repurchase the securities or related instruments. The IRS defines a wash sale to be a sale and a re-purchase of the same security within 30 days. This sort of wash sale is not illegal, though any capital losses and associated tax write-offs generated by this activity will be disallowed by the IRS.

## Fishing

*Fishing* refers to a practice intended to obtain secret or hidden information concerning order sizes in dark pools. Fishing occurs when a trader (who might also be called a "gamer" in this setting) sends a series of small orders to a dark pool to detect whether there is a large order waiting in that pool. If the fishing results in successful order fills, the trader might infer that additional orders or a very large order await in the pool. Then, the trader can submit a much larger order at a size and price that reflects the information that he has obtained through his gaming activities. Suppose, for example, that an institutional trader has discretion reflected in his algo to buy shares at a price as high as 50.03 and places a bid at 50.00. Suppose that the current market for the shares is 50.00 bid/50.05

[10]We discussed Meriwether before in Chapter 6 with respect to his leadership of the hedge fund Long-Term Capital Management.

offer. Now, suppose that another trader, a prospective "fisher" or "gamer", detects this algo order, but does not know its reserve price to purchase shares. The gamer "pings" the algo by offering shares at 50.04. If the offer is not immediately executed, it immediately cancels. Then, the gamer offers 50.03 and the institutional algo buys. The gamer now realizes that it has found the institution's reserve price for the shares. The gamer now knows that it can probably sell many more shares at 50.03 rather than the 50.00 quoted bid. Thus, the gamer submits a much larger sell order at 50.03. This sort of gaming activity is often perfectly legal. In some cases, the gamer can manipulate the selling price of shares by entering small buy orders in the displayed market to force the displayed price up, say from 50.05 to 50.07. This might force the institutional seller to raise its bid to 50.05, at which time the gamer sells larger numbers of shares at this higher price.

As we discussed earlier, an important exception to the quote rule requiring that all market centers publicly disseminate their best bids and offers through the securities information processors allows an exception for quotes that are immediately executed or canceled, such as fill or kill orders. These quotes are often not publicly displayed, but may be displayed to select clients. These flash orders (see discussion from earlier chapter) can result in flash trading in advance of the public quote stream. Such flash orders can facilitate fishing and have been criticized as being very unfair to the majority of market participants.

*Predatory algo trading* strategies are designed to exploit other institutional algo orders. Suppose, for example, the predatory trader detects an institutional algo order to buy a large number of shares. Suppose that a small number of these shares are offered at 50.00, and the predatory trader suspects that the institution has pegged its order to the NBBO and is willing to pay as much as 50.25 per share. The predatory algo can seek to lock in a profit by artificially increasing the share price. Upon detection of this institutional order, the predatory trader places a small bid of 50.01, then continues placing small bids at successively higher figures as the institutional algo trader increases its bid with the NBBO. Ultimately, the predatory places a short sell order at 50.25, knowing that it created much of the apparent demand running the price up to 50.25. When the price falls, the predatory algo covers its short position.

## Other Quote Abuses

*Quote matching* occurs when a small trader places a quote one tick from that of a large trader so as to profit from the large trader's transaction price pressure, or to use the large trader as a counterparty should prices reverse. Quote matching exploits the option associated with a limit order. See end-of-chapter exercise 9 in Chapter 5 for an illustration of quote matching.

*Quote stuffing* is the placement of large numbers of rapid-fire stock orders, with most or all of which being canceled almost immediately, frequently for the purpose of clogging trading HFT and other algorithms and data computations. The purpose of quote stuffing is not to execute orders, but to sabotage algorithms of other traders. See the description of spoofing above, and note that this type of activity is likely to be illegal.

Many dealers are obliged to post quotes for even their least liquid securities. They sometimes fulfill their obligations by posting quotes that are very distant from any reasonable market price for the security (e.g., bid for $0.01 or offer at $100,000), not intending or expecting that these quotes would ever be executed. However, in a one-sided market, these "stub quotes" might be executed against as liquidity dries up, causing securities to trade at absurd prices. In many instances, the trades and profits realized with stub quotes were entirely unintended, but executed automatically by algorithms or due to stale quotes.

## 12.4 PAYMENT FOR ORDER FLOW

There has also been significant controversy over certain rebating practices that started on regional exchanges and ECNs and has since spread to the larger exchanges. When exchanges and their competitors sell virtually identical products, they compete for customer order flow, usually on the basis of prices or trading costs. Presumably, this competition enables customers to obtain better prices. However, many specialists, designated market makers (DMMs), and market makers work for brokerage houses, and many brokerage houses own alternative trading system (ATS) markets. This means that brokerage firms have a special incentive to send their orders to these ATS markets where possible—the firm will receive commissions on the trade, earn trading profits, and secure additional business for their own specialists and systems. In fact, markets might even pay brokers to direct their orders to them so as to enhance the liquidity of their markets and the profitability of their traders and market makers. In addition, markets usually have order imbalances, which means that certain additional orders will serve to create liquidity while others will consume liquidity in that market. It might make sense for such markets to charge higher prices on orders that consume liquidity than those that create liquidity. In fact, when imbalances are high enough, many exchanges and markets will provide rebates on orders that create liquidity, which essentially represents *payment for order flow*.

This system, also known as *make-or-take pricing*, refers to exchanges allowing patient traders to post standing limit orders that await execution until some other trader takes the other side. In effect, the patient trader is a market maker who receives payment from the exchange for making the market (liquidity rebate) and the market taker pays an access fee. Note the connection between this system and the "immediacy argument" of Demsetz described earlier in Chapter 5. A number of observers have noted that make-or-take pricing systems have reduced spreads and improved liquidity, although the liquidity rebates normally are not reflected in bid and offer quotations. This practice continues to grow more widespread, and as of February 2010, even the NYSE, which was the most vocal opponent of payment for order flow, has been making payments for order flow to providers of liquidity.

On the other hand, such payments and rebating for order flow might lead to market abuses, reduce price competition for securities, and reduce security price transparency. Some observers argue that the customer may lose the opportunity to obtain an unannounced better price from a broker on the national exchange floor. Regardless, as of November 2000, the SEC adopted Exchange Act Rule 11Ac1-6 (now SEC Rule 606), requiring broker-dealers to make available quarterly reports that present a general overview of their routing practices. These quarterly reports must identify the significant venues (exchanges or ATS markets) to which customer orders were routed and disclose the material aspects of the broker-dealer's relationship with such venues. In addition, the Rule requires broker-dealers to disclose, on customer request, the venues to which the customer's individual orders were routed.

## 12.5 FAT FINGERS, HOT POTATOES, AND TECHNICAL GLITCHES

In 2005, a novice trader in a subsidiary of Japan's second-largest bank, Mizuho Financial Group, attempted to sell one share of J-com stock on the Tokyo Stock Exchange for ¥610,000 ($5,041). By accident, he transmitted an offer to sell 610,000 shares at ¥1 each. In effect, he attempted to sell $3.075 billion worth of stock for $5,041. These 610,000 shares that he attempted to sell represented 41 times the total number of J-com shares issued by the Japanese recruitment company. Mizuho attempted to cancel and reverse the order, but not quickly enough, such that this incident (losses exceeding ¥27 billion) wiped out Mizuho's entire profit for the quarter. The absence of filters either at the bank or at the Tokyo Stock Exchange to prevent such an obviously erroneous trade played havoc with the market for J-com stock, and caused the entire Nikkei-225 to drop by 1.72%. The broader market reaction was largely in response to traders attempting to guess which firm had made the mistake, driving down share prices for nearly all Japanese financial institutions. Later litigation assessed a significant portion of the blame on the Tokyo Stock Exchange, and Mizuho recouped some of its losses.

Fat fingers seem to have led to many isolated incidents of sudden security price movements. For example, three years before the Mizuho incident, a trader at Bear Stearns seemed to have caused a 100-point drop in the Dow after inadvertently entering a $4-billion sell order instead of his intended $4 million buy order. Morgan Stanley made a similar mistake with a 2004 order for $10.8 billion rather than the intended $10.8 million. Another incidence involved Diebold Inc., which increased by 30% in six seconds on June 2, 2010 on NASDAQ and BATS exchanges. Washington Post Co. dropped by 99% in less than one second on June 16, 2010 on NYSE Arca, and Progress Energy Inc. increased by 90% in less than one second on September 27, 2010 on NASDAQ. Nikkei 225 futures contracts dropped by 1.1% on June 1, 2010 as a result of an unintentional algo order placed on the Osaka Stock Exchange. Each of these occurrences illustrates the need (and failures) for effective trade filters, even in the absence of automatic algo executions.

### The Flash Crash

One of the most worrisome market crashes occurred on May 6, 2010. This "flash crash" has often been blamed on HFT, but its cause remains unclear. The Dow Jones Industrial Average suffered its largest intraday loss ever, dropping by almost 1000 points in less than 30 minutes before recovering almost as quickly. Prices of over 300 stocks and ETFs changed by more than 60% relative to their prices of only minutes earlier. Trades were executed at absurd prices, ranging from less than one cent to over $100,000. Exchanges ultimately canceled over 20,000 executions. A SEC report noted that the crash was preceded by a rapid algo-initiated short, reportedly by mutual fund group Waddell & Reed (not an HFT), of a $4.1 billion block of E-Mini Standard & Poor's 500 futures contracts on the Chicago Mercantile Exchange.[11] However, HFT firms apparently were counterparties to these shorts, and immediately covered themselves by further shorting (turning the contracts into hot potatoes), drying up liquidity in these markets. Within 20 minutes of the start of the "crash," trading in the E-mini contract was halted for five seconds, which allowed the market to recover. When contract trading resumed, prices quickly recovered most of their losses. An important lesson from this and other mini flash crashes is that high trading volume and market liquidity are not the same, especially when hot potato volume is involved.

## Hot Potato Volume

One of the most important functions of a securities market is to convey information through the price aggregation process. Trading conveys information about securities, and higher volumes are often thought to convey more or higher quality information. However, hot potato trading, repeated passing of inventory imbalances among dealers, seems to actually dilute the information content of trading (Lyons [1997]). This type of trading tends to be more common in the presence of HFTs and where interdealer volume is high. On October 4, 2010, Gary Gensler, Chair of the CFTC, remarked that:

> Much of the volume on May 6 was just positions being moved back and forth over a matter of seconds between high-frequency traders and other market makers. This is what our economists refer to as "hot potato volume." For the large trader's order to actually be absorbed by the market, it had to find fundamental or opportunistic buyers who were willing to hold the position at least for more than a few seconds (Gensler, 2010).

## A Textbook for $23,698,655.93 (Plus $3.99 Shipping)

A trading algo program gone bad might seem more understandable when you consider Peter Lawrence's 1992 developmental biology textbook, *The Making of a Fly: The Genetics of Animal Design*. Michael Eisen, an evolutionary biologist at the University of California, reported that he sent one of his post-docs to purchase a copy on Amazon.com on April 18, 2011, who was shocked to see that Amazon listed 17 copies for sale: 15 used from $35.54, and 2 new from $1,730,045.91 (+$3.99 shipping) (See Rooney, 2011). The two new copies were offered by two booksellers, Profnath and Bordeebook. Their prices quickly increased from over $1.7 million to $2.8 million, and by the end of the day, to $3,536,675.57. Ultimately, the book's price topped out at $23,698,655.93, plus shipping.

How did this price manage to evolve to over $23 million? First, Profnath used an algorithm to undercut Bordeebook's price, at 0.9983 times Bordeebook's. However, Bordeebook used its algorithm that would set its own price at 1.270589 times Pronath's,

[11]See the joint report of the Commodities Futures Trading Commission and Securities and Exchange Commission (2010).

apparently seeking the larger markup. This was the recipe needed for the book price to explode: competing booksellers' price multiples exceeding one.

Such algo programs gone bad are not confined to markets for books, and they are not one-time isolated events. Consider the case of Hansen Transmissions (HSNTF.PK), a company that manufactures and supplies wind turbine gearboxes. On January 23, 2009, its stock price increased from $1.62, the prior close, to $143.32 on the trading of 100,000 shares, apparently on the news of an alternative energy speech given by President Obama. The next day, trading opened at $1.69. While this scenario itself was not a major market calamity, it does warn of potential meltdowns (e.g., the May 6, 2010 "flash crash") or other market disruptions that might occur with unfiltered or even filtered algo trading.

## 12.6 ROGUE TRADING AND ROGUE TRADERS

Markets can be perceived as unfair for many reasons. Some investors might have better access to information than others. Certain investors are able to exercise market power due to their size, access to information, domination, or transaction volume. Ultimately, investors lacking these advantages might be unwilling to trade with their advantaged counterparties; such perceived unfairness can lead to market failure. This chapter is largely concerned with the impact that unfair trading activities can have on traders, markets, and institutions. However, illegal trading activities are often less significant causes of market failure than trading misguided by poorly designed compensation systems. This scenario seems most apparent with failures associated with the financial market crises of the early 21st century. Perhaps, more than any other concept, the following scenarios illustrate *Darley's law*, named for John Darley, a professor of psychology at Princeton University who emphasized the importance of implementation and design of effective risk management systems to accompany objective incentive–based compensation systems:

> The more any quantitative performance measure is used to determine a group or an individual's rewards and punishments, the more subject it will be to corruption pressures and the more apt it will be to distort and corrupt the action patterns and thoughts of the group or individual it is intended to monitor.[12]

Rogue trading is usually characterized as systematic unauthorized trading, trading with unapproved counterparties, or trading with unapproved products. Rogue trading normally involves traders exceeding risk limits and/or loss limits set by their employers and is accompanied by efforts to conceal unauthorized actions from management and regulators. That is, rogue trading is often used as a cover for prior mistakes. In practically all instances, rogue trading is accompanied by poor internal control systems and supervisory failures that allow these deceptive actions to succeed. In most instances, rogue trading is motivated by what behavioral economists call an *irrational escalation of commitment*, which might be likened to "throwing good money after bad."

[12]Darley (1994), perhaps based in part on Campbell's law (Campbell, 1976) on "high-stakes" testing in the educational system.

## Rogue Traders

### *Nick Leeson and Barings Bank*

One of the most notorious rogue traders in history was Nick Leeson, chief derivatives trader at Barings' Singapore office. (See Waring and Glendon, 1998, for details.) In 1995, Leeson's trading activity singlehandedly brought down the centuries-old Barings Bank, forcing the sale of Britain's oldest bank to ING for £1. The proud bank, which had long served the English "upper crust," financed Napoleonic Wars, the Erie Canal, and the Louisiana Purchase, had been founded in 1762. Until its takeover, it had served as Queen Elizabeth's personal bank. Leeson incurred £880 million in trading losses, sufficient to bring down the entire bank. Leeson was authorized by the bank to execute futures and options orders for clients or for other units of Barings Bank and to arbitrage price differences between Nikkei futures traded on the SIMEX and the Osaka Exchange. Both were inherently low-risk activities and did not provide much latitude for exposing the bank to higher-risk speculative activity. However, to camouflage poor trading performance and his losses, Leeson created a fictitious trading account numbered 88888 (8 is a lucky number in Chinese numerology) into which he recorded fictitious trades offsetting his own trades. Leeson claimed that this account was initially created to hide an error made by a colleague; rather than purchase 20 contracts as a customer had ordered, the colleague sold them, costing Barings £20,000. Regardless, Leeson used this account to hide his own bad trades that followed.

When Leeson was discovered, he escaped Singapore to Malaysia aboard his yacht. The world followed as he then escaped to Thailand and then Germany, adding international intrigue to his story. Leeson served three years in a Singapore prison before being released for good behavior. He has since become somewhat of a celebrity ex-rogue trader, giving lectures to companies on risk management. He sold his story to a newspaper and, while in prison, wrote the book *Rogue Trader*, which became the basis for the movie of the same title starring Ewan McGregor. After being awarded time off for good behavior in prison, he went on to serve as the CEO of the Galway United Football Club in Western Ireland, to maintain an active schedule on the lecture circuit, and to write his second book, *Back from the Brink: Coping with Stress*.

Clearly, Barings' control systems were lacking. More than 20 of Barings' employees were implicated in failing to detect the fraud. Barings management was warned about the failure to segregate back office and trading operations, but they failed to implement remedial actions. Essentially, Barings failed to implement effective compliance mechanisms, proactive risk management measures, appropriate oversight, and sound management oversight.

What are the lessons to be learned from Leeson's fraud? The bank neglected the first and most important step in implementing risk controls: sufficient segregation of trading and back office (record-keeping) functions. This should be the first step in preventing and stopping trading fraud. In effect, Leeson was his own supervisor. Second, management did not react appropriately when it was warned of increased concentration of financial risks from a relatively small trading unit. A substantial proportion of this U.K. bank's profits were generated by a small trading unit in Singapore. In fact, higher-level managers might have intentionally overlooked this and other warning signs. Third, continued trading fraud, at least initially, is often committed not for personal gain, but to cover poor performance or losses. Each escalation is often an attempt to cover the previous failure. Fourth, incentive-based compensation contributes to trading fraud, not only motivating the perpetrator, but his supervisors as well. In fact, incentive-based compensation systems might have greater effects in failed supervisory systems than in rogue trading activity itself. Fifth, a single rogue trader can bring down even the largest and most venerable of financial institutions. Finally, the superstar trader should merit the closest observation, not only to ensure that his trading is legitimate, but to better understand the secrets to his success.

### *John Rusnak and AllFirst*

John M. Rusnak was a foreign exchange (FX) trader for the Baltimore-based AllFirst Financial Corp., which was owned by Allied Irish Banks PLC (AIB). Rusnak gambled incorrectly in 1997 that the U.S. dollar would fall against the Japanese yen. He used currency forward contracts to purchase yen as the dollar strengthened, inflicting several millions of dollars in losses on his employer. He hid these bad trades by attempting to trade out of them with larger trades, a doubling-up tactic used by many rogue traders. Second, Rusnak manipulated internal controls and entered fictitious trades and data into AllFirst's books and records, hiding the facts that he exceeded his trading limits and assumed excessive risks. Again, his activities illustrate the failure of financial institutions to maintain effective and independent control systems. In an effort to cover up his losses, Rusnak created a fictitious businessman with a mail drop at Mail Boxes Etc. in New York to confirm bogus currency trades with AllFirst's independent auditors. Over the next four years, as his trading losses mounted, Rusnak hid his losses with his fictitious account and other manipulations of his employer's control system. He wasn't caught until December 2001, by which time his losses had exceeded $691 million. Like Leeson, he disappeared and was later caught when his losses were revealed. Rusnak was not charged with stealing money, although he did earn $650,000 in bonuses related to his trading activity. He pled guilty on October 24, 2002, and received a 7-1/2-year jail term followed by five years of supervised probation, along with a $1000 per month restitution obligation. Earlier in 2002, AIB had sold majority control of AllFirst to M&T Corporation. Some of the same lessons from the Leeson case apply to Rusnak, except that from Rusnak, we learn that massive compensation levels are not a necessary condition for rogue trading.

### *Orlando Joseph Jett and Kidder Peabody*

Orlando Joseph Jett, an MIT graduate with a Harvard MBA, began trading strips (zero-coupon Treasury instruments) and other Treasury instruments for the well-regarded firm Kidder Peabody in 1991, failing to report significant profits in his "rookie" year and earning a bonus of $5000. Trading profits recorded by Jett in 1992 and 1993 were $32 million and $151 million, followed by $81 million in the first quarter of 1994. These apparent trading profits were realized on trading volumes of $25 billion, $273 billion, and $1.567 trillion for 1991, 1992, and 1993, and $1.762 trillion for the first 3 months of 1994. In 1993, Jett was named Kidder Peabody's "man of the year" and was awarded a $9 million bonus. His compensation awards were not merely a fixed proportion of his profits; compensation proportions were increased as his trading profits increased. Furthermore, Jett's supervisor,

Ed Cerullo, was awarded a $20 million bonus in 1993 for Jett's accomplishments. However, it was later revealed that Jett did not actually generate profits for his employer in those years; his desk actually lost $85 million. The "phantom" profits resulted from a mistaken entry in Kidder's internal accounting system where bond payments to be made later were not discounted; that is, future cash flows were being treated as though they were immediately realized. Ultimately, when the contracts settled, Kidder Peabody realized the losses, but Jett was able to cover these losses (on paper, with the help of the flawed internal accounting system) by increasing the size of his positions, realizing more phantom profits. Interestingly, Jett was ultimately cleared of criminal wrongdoing because it could not be proven that he knew about and intentionally exploited the glitch in the accounting system, even though he repeated transactions with almost identical results and with increasing frequency. In fact, Jett argued that Kidder ordered him to increase his risks to deceive Kidder's parent, GE, into believing that the Kidder unit was realizing its profit objectives. When GE became concerned about the ballooning sizes of Jett's trading volume, Jett was ordered to cut back on his holdings. He did so, but apparently entered offsetting transactions to exploit the faulty accounting system and to avoid having his bonuses cut. Ultimately, with his positions cut back, his trading losses were uncovered. Jett was ultimately fined $200,000 in 2007 and ordered by a judge to repay $8.2 million in losses. Kidder Peabody was sold to Paine Webber in 1994 shortly after the scandal broke, which later merged into UBS.

A significant contributor to Jett's losses at Kidder Peabody seems to have been lack of proper oversight by his supervisor, Ed Cerullo, who earned substantial bonuses based on Jett's phantom trading profits. Cerullo had a strong incentive to not adequately supervise his employee. Might Cerullo and his superiors have made a conscious decision to tolerate Jett's ballooning trading volume and probable risk limits simply because of his previous "successes" and their ballooning compensation levels? Might supervisors and higher-level managers have been complicit in the rogue trader's seeming success? A second contributor to many trading unit failures is that trading losses can often be covered with taking positions with increased risks, a cycle that often played out until the entire firm fails. Third, as we saw in the Leeson case, close monitoring of unusually high trading profits is probably as important as close monitoring of any unusual trading activity.

### *Jérôme Kerviel and Société Générale*

In 2008, Jérôme Kerviel of Société Générale confessed to a €4.9 billion fraud where he misappropriated computer access codes, falsified documents, and employed other methods to cover his activities. It was the largest discovered trading fraud in history until Bernard Madoff's detection (which was actually more of reporting and misallocation frauds than a trading fraud). Kerviel's case was particularly interesting because of how ordinary and unimpressive he seemed in almost all respects. Unlike Leeson and Jett, Kerviel was by no means a trading superstar. He apparently made very profitable, but unauthorized trades that he hid by intentionally executing transactions to create losses. He argued that the type of behavior that he engaged in was commonplace in trading units, but that employers turned a "blind eye" to these activities as long as the activities appeared to be profitable. Kerviel was formally charged in France in 2008 with abuse of confidence and illegal access to computers. He was ultimately sentenced to five years in prison (two years suspended) and to make full restitution of the lost €4.9 billion (he has no significant assets), and a permanent ban from employment in the financial services industry.

## 12.7 TRADING AND PONZI SCHEMES

Ponzi schemes are not trading schemes. However, Ponzi schemes have been used by rogue traders to mask illegal or unprofitable trading activity. For example, in December 2007, one of the most respected members of the Wall Street community, Bernard Madoff, revealed to his son that his investment firm, Madoff Securities, was a Ponzi scheme. Essentially, this meant that the Madoff lost or pocketed clients' money, and when asked or forced to meet client obligations, used funds raised from other clients to meet these obligations. This amounts to a sort of pyramid scheme to "rob Peter to pay Paul." Although Madoff was a trader and operated a well-respected trading firm, his Ponzi scheme was not a trading fraud per se. Madoff used the Ponzi scheme to cover his trading fraud. Essentially, Madoff lied to his investing clients about trades that he executed along with the profitability of those trades, and then used his Ponzi scheme to cover his trading fraud and associated losses, and to keep clients temporarily satisfied.

After the confession, Madoff's son promptly turned his father in to authorities, and investors in his fund realized that their losses totaled $50 billion to $65 billion (including profits that were never realized), far and away the largest Wall Street fraud incident ever. Madoff pled guilty to 11 counts of securities fraud on March 12, 2009. Previously, Madoff had maintained a highly successful trading and market-making business, accounting for as much of 12% of Nasdaq volume. He was an active securities market regulator, having served on the NASD and NASDAQ boards during much of the 1980s, and had even served in 1990–1991 as chairman of the board of Nasdaq. However, the fraud occurred in a business distinct from his trading operation, his investment advisory operation. Madoff accepted large sums of money from "feeder funds" such as Walter Noel's Fairfield Greenwich Group, Tremont Capital, Stanley Chais, and Avellino and Bienis as well as banks such as Santander. Madoff prohibited these funds from listing his fund in their prospectuses and was able to attract over 3,000 investment clients without registering with the SEC as an investment advisor (registration is required when the advisor's client base exceeds 15). This enabled Madoff to conduct his advisory operations outside of the purview of the SEC. Actually, the SEC had reviewed Madoff's operations repeatedly, overlooked the Ponzi scheme evidence, and focused on whether Madoff's investment advisory operation was obliged to register with the SEC. Madoff actually used the SEC reviews to bolster his credibility, maintaining that the SEC had regularly reviewed his operations and found nothing amiss.

Madoff regularly provided statements and trade confirmations to clients, apparently almost entirely fabricated. He claimed to be engaging in a trading practice known as "split strike conversion," a simple collar strategy involving the S&P 100. Madoff claimed to take long positions in a basket of stocks resembling the S&P 100, purchasing S&P Index 100 puts while writing S&P calls. In a Black-Scholes framework, his strategy should have produced a return comparable to the riskless rate, much less than the 14% to 20% that he actually "paid" to most of his investors. David Friehling, whose tiny accounting firm Friehling & Horowitz in Rockland County, New York, audited Madoff's records and was paid approximately $12,000 to $15,000 per month (after 2004), was also charged with securities fraud.

## Carlo Ponzi

The Ponzi scheme as we discuss it in this book is not so much a trading activity as it is an activity intended to cover up another crime. For example, Madoff used it to cover his failure to produce promised investment gains and to support his fraudulent reporting. The Ponzi scheme is named for an Italian immigrant to the United States, Carlo Ponzi, who in 1919 discovered an arbitrage opportunity for which he required financing. He had spent most of his working life as a dishwasher, waiter, clerk, and so on, but learned that he could trade postal coupons obtained for one cent in Spain for six cents of postal coupons in the United States. Hence, he proceeded to solicit investors to participate in this opportunity, promising returns of approximately 50% in 45 days. The scheme seemed simple enough and thousands of investors participated. Several government agencies examined Ponzi's operations, but found no illegal activity. Over several months, thousands of investors demanded their money back. Ponzi complied with each demand, enhancing his credibility. Essentially, each investor was paid from proceeds realized from the sale of securities from other investors and not enough investors demanded money back to render Ponzi insolvent. Payment from new investor proceeds was necessary because the red tape and various obstacles and expenses made the original arbitrage scheme unprofitable. When a Boston newspaper questioned the legitimacy of Ponzi's operations, state regulators investigated Ponzi's books and prohibited him from selling additional securities. Ponzi was still able to meet demands for cash, further enhancing his credibility. He invested company proceeds into a new bank, the Charles Ponzi Company, which brought in even more money. In time, bank auditors declared the bank to be bankrupt and it was revealed that Ponzi had served time in prison for an earlier fraud. This caused his operations to collapse and created widespread panic and even caused a number of other banks to fail. Ponzi was jailed for mail fraud and spent the remainder of his life in and out of prison for various types of fraud before dying in Brazil without enough money to be buried.

## Other Ponzi Schemes

Bernard Madoff's fund is by no means the only investment company that has turned out to be a Ponzi scheme. For example, a 2009 complaint filed by the SEC alleges that from at least February 1995 to 2009, Joseph S. Forte of Philadelphia had been operating a Ponzi scheme. Apparently, Forte fraudulently obtained approximately $50 million from roughly 80 investors through the sale of securities in the form of limited partnership interests in his firm and codefendant, Joseph Forte, L.P. Forte, who never registered with the SEC, apparently told investors that he would invest the limited partnership funds in a securities futures trading account in the name of Forte LP that would trade in futures contracts, including S&P 500 stock index futures. However, he continually lost money on the limited trading that he did, sustaining trading losses of approximately $3.3 million between 1998 and 2008. From the inception of the scheme, the SEC alleges that Forte and his firm lied to investors about the returns on the trading, reporting annual returns ranging from 18.52% to almost 38%. In addition, the SEC alleged that Forte stole significant portions of the funds entrusted to his care.

James Ossie of Atlanta was charged by the SEC along with his firm CRE after raising at least $25 million from over 120 investors offering "30-day currency trading contracts" that guaranteed a 10% return in 30 days. In addition, the SEC alleged that CRE and Ossie claimed to have generated profits sufficient to pay these guaranteed returns by trading U.S. and Japanese currency contracts as the exchange rate fluctuated. Apparently, Ossie told investors that his program involved very little risk because CRE had established a large, defensive reserve fund from which to pay back the 10% return on investment along with any principal that investors chose to redeem. The SEC alleged that Ossie and CRE never generated sufficient returns from currency trading to pay the promised returns, but was merely a Ponzi scheme.

Sir R. Allen Stanford and the Stanford International Bank based in St. Croix sold certificates of deposit that offered "unusually high and consistent returns" (double the market average, according to *Business Week*). C.A.S. Hewitt, the tiny Antiguan accounting firm that audited Stanford's books, was run by Celia Hewett, who went missing at about the time the scandal broke and Charlesworth "Shelly" Hewett, who died in early 2009. Stanford "managed" $51 billion, slightly more than the amount that Madoff managed, and seemed to be financing a lavish lifestyle on a Ponzi scheme. In early 2012, Stanford was convicted on 13 counts of fraud, conspiracy, obstructing justice, and violating U.S. securities laws, and was awaiting sentencing as of April 2012.

## Additional Reading

Chapter 2 of Kolb and Overdahl (2006) provide a nice discussion of market abuses and regulation in the futures markets. Lefevre's 1923 classic *Reminiscences of a Stock Operator* remains an entertaining and informative read, and is still the most widely referenced book on stock market scams. For a read on trading gone awry on an economy-wide level, MacKay's classic 1841 *Extraordinary Popular Delusions and the Madness of Crowds* is probably the most important reading material for bubbles and crashes during the first half of the 19th century. The 2001 *New York Times Magazine* article by Michael Lewis on the teenager Jonathan Lebed is a thoroughly entertaining read. Shiller's 2000 best-seller *Irrational Exuberance* remains a readable, relevant, and important book. Michael Lewis's *Liar's Poker: Rising through the Wreckage on Wall Street* (1989) and *The Big Short: Inside the Doomsday Machine* (2010) are entertaining reads on the Wall Street mindset. James Stewart's 1992 classic *Den of Thieves* remains among the most thorough and readable books on 1980s-era inside trading scandals. Finally, several relevant movies might be fun to watch. *Liar's Poker, When Genius Failed, Den of Thieves, Rogue Trader,* and *Wall Street* all are worth a watch.

## References

Aggarwal, R. K., & Guojun, W. (2002). *Stock market manipulation—theory and evidence.* Working paper. Dartmouth College: Tuck School of Business.

Campbell, D. T. (1976). *Assessing the impact of planned social change.* Dartmouth College: The Public Affairs Center.

Commodities Futures Trading Commission, Securities and Exchange Commission. (2010). Findings Regarding the Market Events of May 6, 2010: Report of The Staffs of the CFTC and SEC to the Joint Advisory Committee on Emerging Regulatory Issues, September 30.

Darley, J. M. (1994). Gaming, gundecking, body counts, and the loss of three British cruisers at the Battle of Jutland: The complex moral consequences of performance measurement systems in military settings. Speech to Air Force Academy, April 6.

Flannery, A. (1998). *Insider trading cases: Settlement criteria and recent developments*. Paper presented at Institute of Continuing Legal Education in Georgia, Fourth Annual Securities Litigation and Regulatory Practice Seminar, October 8.

Frieder, L., & Zittrain, J. L., (2008). *Spam works: Evidence from stock touts and corresponding market activity*. Berkman Center Research Publication No. 2006-11(2007), 13 Hastings Communications and Entertainment Law Journal 479.

Geisst, C. R. (2004). *Wall street: A history from its beginnings to the fall of Enron*. New York: Oxford University Press.

Gensler, G. (2010). Remarks, Swap Execution Facility Conference. Remarks, Swap Execution Facility Conference, Washington, DC, October 4.

Kolb, R. W., & Overdahl, J. A. (2006). *Understanding futures markets* (6th ed.). New York: Wiley-Blackwell Publishing.

Lefevre, E. (1923). *Reminiscences of a stock operator*. New York: George H. Doran Company.

Lewis, M. (1989). *Liar's poker: Rising through the wreckage on wall street*. New York: W.W. Norton.

Lewis, M. (2001). Jonathan lebed: Stock manipulator, S.E.C. nemesis—and 15. *New York Times Magazine*. February 21. Available at <http://www.cs.brown.edu/people/rbb/risd/Lebed.html> Accessed 25.08.09.

Lewis, M. (2010). *The big short: Inside the doomsday machine*. New York: W.W. Norton & Co.

Lyons, R. K. (1997). A simultaneous trade model of the foreign exchange hot potato. *Journal of International Economics*, *42*, 275–298.

MacKay, C. (1841). *Extraordinary popular delusions and the madness of crowds*. New york: Crown Publishers.

Rooney, B. (2011). For Sale: The Making of a Fly, Only $23,698,655.93 (Plus $3.99 Shipping. Tech Europe: The Wall Street Journal April 26) Available at <http://blogs.wsj.com/tech-europe/2011/04/26/for-sale-the-making-of-a-fly-only-23698655-93-plus-3-99-shipping/> Accessed 23.08.11.

Securities and Exchange Commission. (2001). Administrative Proceeding File No. 3-10631, November 5.

Securities and Exchange Commission. (1989). Litigation Release No. 11973, January 25.

Securities and Exchange Commission. (2001). SEC Charges Six Individuals with Spoofing, SEC Release 2001-129, Washington, DC, November 5.

Securities and Exchange Commission. (2002). Securities and Exchange Commission v. Alexander Mark Pomper, Civil Case Number CV-01-7391, SEC Litigation Release No. 17479, Washington, DC, April 19.

Securities and Exchange Commission. (2009). Securities and Exchange Commission v. Joseph S. Forte, et al., Civil Action No. 09-0063, SEC Litigation Release No. 20847, Washington, DC, January 8.

Securities and Exchange Commission v. CRE Capital Corporation and James G. Ossie, Civil Action No. 1: 09-CV-0114, SEC Litigation Release No. 20853, Washington, DC, January 15.

Shiller, R. J. (2000). *Irrational exuberance*. Princeton, NJ: Princeton University Press.

Stewart, J. (1992). *Den of Thieves*. New York: Simon & Schuster.

Waring, A., & Glendon, A. I. (1998). *Managing risk*. London: Thomson Learning.

## 12.8 EXERCISES

1. Most markets, including those for labor, commodities, and real estate, allow insider trading activity. Transactions in these markets are routinely based on unequally distributed information. Why should insider trading be common and legal in these markets?
2. Does insider trading violate the Securities Act of 1933? If so, what section? If not, why not?

3. In a release dated November 5, 2001, the SEC announced in a litigation release an action against Israel Shenker. In this announcement, the SEC provided the following example of a series of transactions executed by Shenker:

> 14:44:44—Shenker placed an order to buy 500 shares of the target security at \$34.0625, and directed that it be routed to the ECN. The order raised the NBBO bid price from \$31.50 to \$34.0625.
>
> 14:44:46—Shenker entered a limit order to sell 500 shares of the target security through SOES at a price of \$34.0625, and the order was immediately executed.
>
> 14:44:48—Shenker canceled his buy order, causing the NBBO bid price to drop from \$34.0625 to \$31.25.
>
> By manipulating the public quote to obtain a better execution price for his 500-share sell order, Shenker was unjustly enriched in the amount of \$1,281.25 (Securities and Exchange Commission, 2001).

a. What is the name of the type of market abuse alleged by the SEC?
b. Why were these manipulations not considered to be wash sales?
c. Why was the activity alleged by this announcement illegal?

# Mathematics Appendix

## A.1 A BRIEF OVERVIEW OF ELEMENTARY STATISTICS

### Mean, Variance, and Standard Deviation

The purpose of this appendix is to review several important elementary statistics concepts. To begin with, suppose that we wish to describe or summarize the characteristics or distribution of a single population of values (or sample drawn from a population). Two important characteristics include central location (measured by average, mean, median, expected value, or mode) and dispersion (measured by range, variance, or standard deviation).

In many instances, we will be most interested in the typical value (if it exists) drawn from a population or sample; that is, we are interested in the "location" of the data set. Mean (often referred to as average) or expected values (sometimes referred to as weighted average) are frequently used as measures of location (or central tendency) because they account for all relevant data points and the frequency with which they occur. The arithmetic mean value of a population $\mu$ is computed by adding the values $x_i$ associated with each observation $i$ and dividing the result by the number of observations $n$ in the population:

$$\mu = \sum_{i=1}^{n} x_i \div n \tag{A-1}$$

Variance is a measure of the dispersion (variability and sometimes volatility or uncertainty) of values within a data set. In a finance setting, variance is also used as an indicator of risk. Variance is defined as the mean of squared deviations of actual data points from the mean or expected value of a data set. Deviations are squared to ensure that negative deviations do not cancel positive deviations, resulting in zero variances. High variances imply high dispersion of data. This indicates that certain or perhaps many data points are significantly different from mean or expected values. Population and sample variances are computed as follows:

$$\sigma^2 = \sum_{i=1}^{n} (x_i - \mu)^2 \div n \tag{A-2}$$

$$s^2 = \frac{\sum_{i=1}^{n}(x_i - \overline{x})^2}{n-1} \tag{A-3}$$

Standard deviation is simply the square root of variance. It is also used as a measure of dispersion, risk, or uncertainty. Standard deviation is sometimes easier to interpret than variance because its value is expressed in terms of the same units as the data points themselves rather than their squared values. High standard deviations and high variances imply high dispersion of data. Standard deviations for populations and samples are computed as follows:

$$\sigma = \sqrt{\sum_{i=1}^{n}(x_i - \mu)^2 \div n} \tag{A-4}$$

$$s = \sqrt{\frac{\sum_{i=1}^{n}(x_i - \overline{x})^2}{n-1}} \tag{A-5}$$

## Co-movement Statistics

A joint probability distribution is concerned with probabilities associated with each possible combination of outcomes drawn from two sets of data. Covariance measures the mutual variability of outcomes selected from each set; that is, covariance measures the relationship between variability in one data set relative to variability in the second data set, where variables are selected one at a time from each data set and paired. If large values in one data set seem to be associated with large values in the second data set, covariance is positive; if large values in the first data set seem to be associated with small values in the second data set, covariance is negative. If data sets are unrelated, covariance is zero. Covariance between data set $x$ and data set $y$ may be measured as follows, depending on whether one is interested in covariance of a population or a sample or expected covariance:

$$\sigma_{x,y} = \sum_{i=1}^{n}(x_i - \mu_x)(y_i - \mu_y) \div n \tag{A-6}$$

$$\sigma_{x,y} = \frac{\sum_{i=1}^{n}(x_i - \overline{x})(y_i - \overline{y})}{n-1} \tag{A-7}$$

The sign associated with covariance indicates whether the relationship associated with the data in the sets are direct (positive sign), inverse (negative sign) or independent (covariance is zero). The absolute value of covariance measures the strength of the relationship between the two data sets. However, the absolute value of covariance can often be more easily interpreted when it is expressed relative to the standard deviations of each of the two data sets. That is, when we divide covariance by the product of the standard deviations of each of the data sets, we obtain the sample coefficient of correlation $\rho_{x,y}$ as follows:

$$\rho_{x,y} = \frac{\sigma_{x,y}}{\sigma_x \sigma_y} = \frac{\sum_{i=1}^{n}(x_i - \overline{x})(y_i - \overline{y})/(n-1)}{\sqrt{\frac{\sum_{i=1}^{n}(x_i-\overline{x})^2}{n-1}} \bullet \sqrt{\frac{\sum_{i=1}^{n}(y_i-\overline{y})^2}{n-1}}} \tag{A-8}$$

A correlation coefficient equal to 1 indicates that the two data sets are perfectly positively correlated; that is, their changes are always in the same direction, by the same proportions, with 100 percent consistency. Correlation coefficients will always range between −1 and +1. A correlation coefficient of −1 indicates that the two data sets are perfectly inversely correlated; that is, their changes are always in the opposite direction, by the same proportions with 100 percent consistency. The closer a correlation coefficient is to −1 or +1, the stronger is the relationship between the two data sets. A correlation coefficient equal to zero implies independence (no relationship) between the two sets of data.

The correlation coefficient may be squared to obtain the coefficient of determination (also referred to as $r^2$ or r-square in some statistics texts and here as $\rho^2$). The coefficient of determination is the proportion of variability in one data set that is explained by or associated with variability in the second data set. For example, $\rho^2$ equal to 0.35 indicates that 35% of the variability in one data set is explained in a statistical sense by variability in the second data set.

## Hypothesis Testing

In this section, we discuss the process of induction to form testable hypotheses or theories from specific observations. These hypotheses or theories are useful if they provide a means to make meaningful predictions. Normally, testing a theory involves the collection of additional observations to determine whether they support the theory's predictions. If the additional observations do not confirm the predictions, then one has grounds for rejecting the theory. The observations collected to test a theory are usually represented by numbers or data. In most cases, statistical inference concerns the generalization of sample results to a population.

In many instances, one might make use of statistical inference to test a hypothesis. By convention, a hypotheses test usually involves formulation of a *null* (or maintained) hypothesis along with a competing *alternative* (research or challenging) hypothesis. The null hypothesis $H_0$ usually is the claim that the population parameter equals some "maintained" value (note that null frequently implies no difference, no impact or nothing). The null hypothesis normally includes an equality sign or either ≤ or ≥ signs. The alternative hypothesis $H_A$ is the claim that the population parameter differs from the maintained value. The alternative hypothesis normally includes a strict inequality sign. Such tests are usually structured in a conservative manner such that the burden of proof is on the alternative hypothesis. One supports the research or alternative hypothesis by demonstrating the null hypothesis to be false (rejecting the null hypothesis). One rejects the null hypothesis only when the probability of its being true is sufficiently low (the conventional probability, known as a level of significance, is 0.05 or 0.01). In some instances, the appropriate level of significance for a hypothesis test can be based on the relative costs of rejecting the null hypothesis when it is true or accepting it when it is false.

One might list the steps of a typical statistical hypothesis test as follows:

1. Define the null hypothesis, $H_0$.
2. Define the alternative hypothesis, $H_A$.
3. Determine a level of significance, $\alpha$, for the test.
4. Determine the decision rule or test statistic along with acceptance or rejection regions or critical value based on $\alpha$.
5. Perform computations.
6. Form conclusions.

The *decision rule* or *test statistic* is a given function of a measurement drawn from the sample on which the statistical decision will be based. The *rejection region* consists of those values of the test statistic that will lead to rejection of the null hypothesis. The *critical value* marks the boundary between the acceptance and rejection regions.

An experiment involving a given sample drawn from a population has some probability of resulting in an erroneous conclusion. Thus, one's hypothesis test may lead to an incorrect acceptance of the null hypothesis (*Type I error*) or an incorrect rejection of the null hypothesis (*Type II error*). The *power of a test* refers to the probability of not committing a Type II error. This is equivalent to the probability of accepting the alternative hypothesis when it is correct. A test is considered to be superior when its power is higher.

Statistics are most useful for empirical studies in finance. This chapter provides, at best, a very superficial overview of a few of the applications of statistical methodology in finance. The reader is advised to consult a more comprehensive statistics text for a more detailed presentation of statistical methodology and its applications to financial problems.

## Hypothesis Testing: Two Populations

Here, we are concerned with comparing two means, $\mu_1$ and $\mu_2$ for populations 1 and 2 with standard deviations $\sigma_1$ and $\sigma_2$. We shall assume that our samples are independent and drawn from populations whose data are normally distributed. Our test will be based on samples of sizes $n_1$ and $n_2$. The samples will have means and variances equal to $\bar{x}_1$ and $\bar{x}_2$ and $s^2{}_1$ and $s^2{}_2$, respectively. We will base our testing methodologies on test statistics and distributions somewhat different from those used earlier. Suppose that we wanted to test whether the means of two populations were different based on samples drawn from those populations. Our hypotheses and test statistics might be as follows:

$$H_0: \mu_1 = \mu_2$$

$$H_A: \mu \neq \mu_2$$

$$t = \frac{(\bar{x}_1 - \bar{x}_2) - (\mu_1 - \mu_2)}{\sqrt{\left[\frac{(n_1 - 1)s_1^2 + (n_2 - 1)s_2^2}{(n_1 + n_2 - 2)}\right]\left[\frac{n_1 + n_2}{n_1 \cdot n_2}\right]}} \tag{A-9}$$

where $s^2_1$ and $s^2_2$ are the sample variances. If we are testing whether $\bar{x}_1$ and $\bar{x}_2$ are equal, then our hypothesized difference in means $\mu_1 - \mu_2 = 0$ is used for computing our test statistic. Our test statistic assumes that our data follows a student-*t* distribution.

A variety of other types of tests involving samples from two populations can be constructed as well. For example, tests can be developed to determine whether variances differ, other tests can be based on samples with matched pairs of observations, and so on. A statistics or econometrics text can be consulted to provide additional testing methodologies.

## Introduction to Simple OLS Regression

Regressions are used to determine relationships between a dependent variable and one or more independent variables. A simple regression is concerned with the relationship between a dependent variable and a single independent variable; a multiple regression is concerned with the relationship between a dependent variable and a series of independent variables. A linear regression is used to describe the relationship between the dependent and independent variable(s) to a linear function or line (or hyperplane in the case of a multiple regression).

The simple ordinary least squares regression (simple OLS) takes the following form:

$$y_t = \hat{b}_0 + \hat{b}_1 x_t + \hat{\varepsilon}_{i,t} \tag{A-10}$$

The OLS regression coefficients $\hat{b}_0$ and $\hat{b}_1$ are derived by minimizing the variance of errors in fitting the curve (or *m*-dimensional surface for multiple regressions involving *m* variables). Since the expected value of error terms equals zero, this derivation is identical to minimizing error terms squared. Regression coefficient $\hat{b}_1$ is simply the covariance between *y* and *x* divided by the variance of *x*; $\hat{b}_1$ and $\hat{b}_0$ are found as follows:

$$\hat{b}_1 = \frac{(\sigma_{x,y})^2}{\sigma_x^2} = \frac{\sum_{i=1}^{n}(x_i - \overline{x})(y_i - \overline{y})}{\sum_{i=1}^{n}(x_i - \overline{x})]^2} \tag{A-11}$$

$$\hat{b}_0 = \overline{y} - \hat{b}_1 \overline{x} \tag{A-12}$$

Appropriate use of the OLS requires the following assumptions:

- Dependent variable values are distributed independently of one another.
- The variance of *x* is approximately the same over all ranges for x.
- The variance of error term values is approximately the same over all ranges of x.
- The expected value of each disturbance or error term equals zero.

Violations in these assumptions will weaken the validity of the results obtained from the regression and may necessitate either modifications to the OLS regression or different statistical testing techniques.

A simple regression is concerned with the relationship between a dependent variable and a single independent variable. Regression coefficients $\hat{b}_0$ and $\hat{b}_1$ represent the vertical intercept and the slope in the statistical linear relationship between the dependent variable $y_i$ and the independent variable $x_i$. Thus the vertical intercept $\hat{b}_0$ represents the regression's forecasted value for $y_i$ when $x_i$ equals zero and the slope of the regression $\hat{b}_1$ represents the change in $\hat{y}_i$ (the value forecast by the regression for $y_i$) induced by a change in $x_i$. The error term $\hat{\varepsilon}_i$ represents the vertical distance between the value $\hat{y}_i$ forecasted by the regression based on its true value $y_i$; that is, $\hat{\varepsilon}_i = y_i - \hat{y}_i$. The OLS regression minimizes the sum or average of these error terms squared. The size of the sum of the squared errors (often called SSE or, when divided by $(n-2)$, the variance of errors $\sigma_{\hat{\varepsilon}}^2$) will be used to measure the predictive strength of the regression equation. A regression with smaller error terms or smaller $\sigma_{\hat{\varepsilon}}^2$ is likely to be a better predictor, all else held constant.

Once we have determined the statistical relationship between $y_i$ and $x_i$ based on our OLS, our next problem is to measure the strength of the relationship, or its significance. One of the more useful indicators of the strength of the regression is the coefficient of determination or $\rho^2$ statistic. The coefficient of determination (often referred to as r-square) represents the proportion of variation of variable $y$ that is explained by its regression on $x$. It is determined as follows:

$$\rho_{x,y}^2 = \frac{(\sigma_{x,y})^2}{\sigma_x^2 \sigma_y^2} = \frac{[\sum_{i=1}^{n}(x_i - \overline{x})(y_i - \overline{y})]^2}{[\sum_{i=1}^{n}(x_i - \overline{x})]^2 [\sum_{i=1}^{n}(y_i - \overline{y})]^2} \tag{A-13}$$

This coefficient of determination may also be expressed as either of the following:

$$\rho_{x,y}^2 = \frac{\text{Total Variation in } y \text{ Explained by the Regression}}{\text{Total Variation in } y} \tag{A-14}$$

$$\rho_{x,y}^2 = \frac{\sum_{i=1}^{n}(y_i - \overline{y})^2 - \sum_{i=1}^{n}\varepsilon_i^2}{\sum_{i=1}^{n}(y_i - \overline{y})^2} \tag{A-15}$$

The sum $\sum(y_i - \overline{y})^2$ represents total variation in $y$; the sum $\sum \hat{\varepsilon}_i^2$ represents the variation in $y$ not explained by the regression on $x$.

Assume that there exists for a population a true OLS regression equation $y_i = \beta_0 + \beta_1 x_i + \varepsilon_i$ representing the relationship between $y_i$ and $x_i$, without measurement or sampling error. However, we propose the regression $y_i = \hat{b}_0 + \hat{b}_1 x_i + \hat{\varepsilon}_i$, whose ability to represent the true relationship between $y_i$ and $x_i$ is a function of our ability to measure and sample properly. Our sampling coefficients $\hat{b}_0$ and $\hat{b}_1$ are merely estimates for the true coefficients $\beta_0$ and $\beta_1$ and they may vary from sample to sample. It is useful to know the significance of each of these sampling coefficients in explaining the relationship between $y_i$ and $x_i$.

Our estimate $\hat{b}_1$ for the slope coefficient $\beta_1$ might vary from regression to regression, depending on how our sample varies. Our estimates for $\hat{b}_1$ will follow a $t$-distribution if our sample of $y_i$'s is large or normally distributed; if our sample is sufficiently large, our estimates for $\beta_1$ may be characterized as normally distributed. One potential test of the significance of our coefficient estimate $\hat{b}_1$ is structured as follows:

$$H_0: \beta_1 \leq 0$$

$$H_A: \beta_1 > 0$$

Our null hypothesis is that $y$ is unrelated or inversely related to $x$; our alternative hypothesis is that $y$ is directly related to $x$. The first step in our test is to compute the standard error se($\hat{b}_1$) of our estimate for $\beta_1$ as follows:

$$se(\hat{b}_1) = \sqrt{\frac{1}{n}\frac{\sigma_{\hat{\varepsilon}}^2}{\sigma_x^2}} = \sqrt{\frac{\frac{\sum_{i=1}^{n} \hat{\varepsilon}_i^2}{n-2}}{\sum_{i=1}^{n} (x_i - \overline{x})^2}} \tag{A-16}$$

The standard error for $\hat{b}_1$ is, in a sense, an indicator of our level of uncertainty regarding our estimate for $\beta_1$. The numerator within the radical indicates the variability unexplained by the regression; the denominator indicates total variability. Our next step is to find the test statistic for $\hat{b}_1$. This is analogous to standardizing or finding the normal deviate in our earlier hypothesis tests:

$$t(\hat{b}_1) = \frac{\hat{b}_1}{se(\hat{b}_1)} \tag{A-17}$$

We next compare this test statistic to a critical value from a table representing the $t$-distribution.

The process for determining the statistical significance of the vertical intercept $\hat{b}_0$ is quite similar to that for determining the statistical significance for $\hat{b}_1$. We first designate appropriate hypotheses, such as:

$$H_0: \beta_0 = 0$$

$$H_A: \beta_0 \neq 0$$

The primary difference in the process is in determining se($\hat{b}_0$):

$$se(\hat{b}_0) = \sqrt{\frac{\frac{\sum_{i=1}^{n} \hat{\varepsilon}_i^2}{n-2} \cdot \sum_{i=1}^{n} x_i^2}{n \cdot \sum_{i=1}^{n} (x_i - \overline{x})^2}} \tag{A-18}$$

Next, we find our $t$-statistic as follows:

$$t(\hat{b}_0) = \frac{\hat{b}_0}{se(\hat{b}_0)} \tag{A-19}$$

We then compare the t-statistic to the appropriate critical value just as we did when testing the significance of the slope coefficient. This particular test involves two tails, since our alternative hypothesis is a strict inequality. Be certain to make appropriate adjustments to the critical value (for example, divide $\alpha$ by 2 for two-tailed tests) when making comparisons.

## A.2 ESSENTIALS OF MATRICES AND MATRIX ARITHMETIC

A *matrix* is simply an ordered rectangular array of numbers. A matrix is an entity that enables one to represent a series of numbers as a single object, thereby providing for convenient systematic methods for completing large numbers of repetitive computations. Such objects are essential for the management of large data structures. Rules of matrix arithmetic and other matrix operations are often similar to rules of ordinary arithmetic and other operations, but they are not always identical. In this text, matrices will usually be denoted with bold uppercase letters. When the matrix has only one row or one column, bold lowercase letters will be used for identification. The following are examples of matrices:

$$\mathbf{A} = \begin{bmatrix} 4 & 2 & 6 \\ 3 & 7 & 4 \\ 8 & -5 & 9 \end{bmatrix} \quad \mathbf{B} = \begin{bmatrix} 2 & -3 \\ 3/4 & -1/2 \end{bmatrix} \quad \mathbf{c} = \begin{bmatrix} 1 \\ 5 \\ 7 \end{bmatrix} \quad \mathbf{d} = \begin{bmatrix} \dfrac{3}{5} \end{bmatrix}$$

The dimensions of a matrix are given by the ordered pair $m \times n$, where $m$ is the number of rows and $n$ is the number of columns in the matrix. The matrix is said to be of *order* $m \times n$ where, by convention, the number of rows is listed first. Thus, **A** is $3 \times 3$, **B** is $2 \times 2$, **c** is $3 \times 1$, and **d** is $1 \times 1$. Each number or value in a matrix is referred to as an element. The symbol $a_{i,j}$ denotes the element in Row $i$ and column $j$ of matrix **A**, $b_{i,j}$ denotes the element in row $i$ and column $j$ of matrix **B**, and so on. Thus, $a_{3,2}$ is $-5$ and $c_{2,1} = 5$.

There are specific terms denoting various types of matrices. Each of these particular types of matrices has useful applications and unique properties for working with. For example, a *vector* is a matrix with only one row or one column. Thus, the dimensions of a vector are $1 \times n$ or $m \times 1$. Matrix **c** above is a column vector, of order $3 \times 1$. A $1 \times n$ matrix is a row vector with $n$ elements. The column vector has one column and the row vector has one row. A *scalar* is a matrix with exactly one element. Matrix **d** is a scalar. A *square matrix* has the same number of rows and columns ($m = n$). Matrix **A** is square and of order 2. The set of elements extending from the upper left-most corner to the lower right-most corner in a square matrix are said to be in the *principal diagonal*. For each of these elements $i_{i,j}$, $i = j$. Principal diagonal elements of square matrix **A** are $a_{1,1} = 4$, $a_{2,2} = 7$, and $a_{3,3} = 9$. Matrices **B** and **d** are also square matrices.

A *symmetric matrix* is a square matrix where $c_{i,j}$ equals $c_{j,i}$ for all $i$ and $j$; that is, the $i$'th element in each row equals the $j$'th element in each column. Scalar **d** and matrices **H**, **I**, and **J** below are all symmetric matrices. A *diagonal matrix* is a symmetric matrix whose elements off the principal diagonal are zero, where the *principal diagonal* contains the series of elements where $i = j$. Scalar **d** and matrices **H** and **I** in the following are all diagonal matrices. An *identity* or *unit* matrix is a diagonal matrix consisting of ones along the principal diagonal. Both matrices **H** and **I** following are diagonal matrices; **I** is the $3 \times 3$ identity matrix:

$$\mathbf{H} = \begin{bmatrix} 13 & 0 & 0 \\ 0 & 11 & 0 \\ 0 & 0 & 10 \end{bmatrix} \quad \mathbf{I} = \begin{bmatrix} 1 & 0 & 0 \\ 0 & 1 & 0 \\ 0 & 0 & 1 \end{bmatrix} \quad \mathbf{J} = \begin{bmatrix} 1 & 7 & 2 \\ 7 & 5 & 0 \\ 2 & 0 & 4 \end{bmatrix}$$

## Matrix Arithmetic

Matrix arithmetic provides for standard rules of operation just as conventional arithmetic. Matrices can be added or subtracted if their dimensions are identical. Matrices **A** and **B** add to **C** if $a_{i,j} + b_{i,j} = c_{i,j}$ for all $i$ and $j$:

$$\underset{\mathbf{A}}{\begin{bmatrix} a_{1,1} & a_{1,2} & \cdots & a_{1,n} \\ a_{2,1} & a_{2,2} & \cdots & a_{2,n} \\ \vdots & \vdots & \vdots & \vdots \\ a_{m,1} & a_{m,2} & \cdots & a_{m,n} \end{bmatrix}} + \underset{\mathbf{B}}{\begin{bmatrix} b_{1,1} & b_{1,2} & \cdots & b_{1,n} \\ b_{2,1} & b_{2,2} & \cdots & b_{2,n} \\ \vdots & \vdots & \vdots & \vdots \\ b_{m,1} & b_{m,2} & \cdots & b_{m,n} \end{bmatrix}} = \underset{\mathbf{C}}{\begin{bmatrix} c_{1,1} & c_{1,2} & \cdots & c_{1,n} \\ c_{2,1} & c_{2,2} & \cdots & c_{2,n} \\ \vdots & \vdots & \vdots & \vdots \\ c_{m,1} & c_{m,2} & \cdots & c_{m,n} \end{bmatrix}}$$

For example:

$$\underset{\mathbf{A}}{\begin{bmatrix} 2 & 4 & 9 \\ 6 & 4 & 25 \\ 0 & 2 & 11 \end{bmatrix}} + \underset{\mathbf{B}}{\begin{bmatrix} 3 & 0 & 6 \\ 2 & 1 & 3 \\ 7 & 0 & 4 \end{bmatrix}} = \underset{\mathbf{C}}{\begin{bmatrix} 5 & 4 & 15 \\ 8 & 5 & 28 \\ 7 & 2 & 15 \end{bmatrix}}$$

Note that each of the three matrices is of dimension $3 \times 3$ and that each of the elements in matrix **C** is the sum of corresponding elements in matrices **A** and **B**. The process of subtracting matrices is similar, where $d_{i,j} - e_{i,j} = f_{i,j}$ for $\mathbf{D} - \mathbf{E} = \mathbf{F}$:

$$\underset{\mathbf{D}}{\begin{bmatrix} d_{1,1} & d_{1,2} & \cdots & d_{1,n} \\ d_{2,1} & d_{2,2} & \cdots & d_{2,n} \\ \vdots & \vdots & \vdots & \vdots \\ d_{m,1} & d_{m,2} & \cdots & d_{m,n} \end{bmatrix}} - \underset{\mathbf{E}}{\begin{bmatrix} e_{1,1} & e_{1,2} & \cdots & e_{1,n} \\ e_{2,1} & e_{2,2} & \cdots & e_{2,n} \\ \vdots & \vdots & \vdots & \vdots \\ e_{m,1} & e_{m,2} & \cdots & e_{m,n} \end{bmatrix}} = \underset{\mathbf{F}}{\begin{bmatrix} f_{1,1} & f_{1,2} & \cdots & f_{1,n} \\ f_{2,1} & f_{2,2} & \cdots & f_{2,n} \\ \vdots & \vdots & \vdots & \vdots \\ f_{m,1} & f_{m,2} & \cdots & f_{m,n} \end{bmatrix}}$$

For example:

$$\underset{\mathbf{D}}{\begin{bmatrix} 9 & 4 & 9 \\ 6 & 4 & 8 \\ 5 & 2 & 9 \end{bmatrix}} - \underset{\mathbf{E}}{\begin{bmatrix} 5 & 0 & 6 \\ 2 & 1 & 6 \\ 5 & 0 & 9 \end{bmatrix}} = \underset{\mathbf{F}}{\begin{bmatrix} 4 & 4 & 3 \\ 4 & 3 & 2 \\ 0 & 2 & 0 \end{bmatrix}}$$

Now consider a third matrix operation. The *transpose* $\mathbf{A}^T$ of matrix $\mathbf{A}$ is obtained by interchanging the rows and columns of matrix $\mathbf{A}$. Each $a_{i,j}$ becomes $a_{j,i}$. The following represent matrix $\mathbf{A}$ and its transpose $\mathbf{A}^T$:

$$\underset{\mathbf{A}}{\begin{bmatrix} 1 & 8 & 9 \\ 6 & 4 & 25 \\ 3 & 2 & 35 \end{bmatrix}} \quad \underset{\mathbf{A}^T}{\begin{bmatrix} 1 & 6 & 3 \\ 8 & 4 & 2 \\ 9 & 25 & 35 \end{bmatrix}}$$

The transpose of a column vector is a row vector:

$$\underset{\mathbf{y}}{\begin{bmatrix} 9 \\ 6 \\ 3 \\ 7 \end{bmatrix}} \quad \underset{\mathbf{y}^T}{\begin{bmatrix} 9 & 6 & 3 & 7 \end{bmatrix}}$$

Similarly, the transpose of a row vector is a column vector. Note that the transpose $\mathbf{V}^T$ of a symmetric matrix $\mathbf{V}$ is $\mathbf{V}$:

$$\mathbf{V} = \begin{bmatrix} .09 & .01 & .04 \\ .01 & .16 & .10 \\ .04 & .10 & .64 \end{bmatrix} \quad \mathbf{V}^T = \begin{bmatrix} .09 & .01 & .04 \\ .01 & .16 & .10 \\ .04 & .10 & .64 \end{bmatrix} = \mathbf{V}$$

## Multiplication of Matrices

Two matrices $\mathbf{A}$ and $\mathbf{B}$ can be multiplied to obtain the product $\mathbf{AB} = \mathbf{C}$ if the number of columns in the first matrix $\mathbf{A}$ equals the number of rows $\mathbf{B}$ in the second.[1] If matrix $\mathbf{A}$ is of dimension $m \times n$ and matrix $\mathbf{B}$ is of dimension $n \times q$, the dimensions of the product matrix $\mathbf{C}$ will be $m \times q$. Each element $c_{i,k}$ of matrix $\mathbf{C}$ is determined by the following sum:

$$c_{i,k} = \sum_{j=1}^{n} a_{i,j} b_{j,k}$$

For example, consider the following product:

$$\underset{\mathbf{A}}{\begin{bmatrix} 7 & 4 & 9 \\ 6 & 4 & 12 \\ 3 & 2 & 17 \end{bmatrix}} \underset{\mathbf{B}}{\begin{bmatrix} 7 & 6 \\ 5 & 1 \\ 9 & 12 \end{bmatrix}} = \underset{\mathbf{C}}{\begin{bmatrix} 150 & 154 \\ 170 & 184 \\ 184 & 224 \end{bmatrix}}$$

[1]If it is possible to multiply two matrices, they are said to be conformable for multiplication. Any matrix can be multiplied by a scalar, where the product is simply each element times the value of the scalar.

Matrix **C** in the above is found as follows:

$$\begin{bmatrix} 7 & 4 & 9 \\ 6 & 4 & 12 \\ 3 & 2 & 17 \end{bmatrix} \begin{bmatrix} 7 & 6 \\ 5 & 1 \\ 9 & 12 \end{bmatrix} = \begin{bmatrix} (7\cdot 7)+(4\cdot 5)+(9\cdot 9) & (7\cdot 6)+(4\cdot 1)+(9\cdot 12) \\ (6\cdot 7)+(4\cdot 5)+(12\cdot 9) & (6\cdot 6)+(4\cdot 1)+(12\cdot 12) \\ (3\cdot 7)+(2\cdot 5)+(17\cdot 9) & (3\cdot 6)+(2\cdot 1)+(17\cdot 12) \end{bmatrix}$$

$$\mathbf{A} \qquad \mathbf{B} \qquad = \qquad \mathbf{C}$$

Note that the number of columns (3) in matrix **A** equals the number of rows in matrix **B**. Also note that the number of rows in matrix **C** equals the number of rows in matrix **A**; the number of columns in **C** equals the number of columns in matrix **B**.

## Inverting Matrices

An *inverse* matrix $\mathbf{A}^{-1}$ exists for the square matrix **A** if the product $\mathbf{A}^{-1}\mathbf{A}$ or $\mathbf{A}\mathbf{A}^{-1}$ equals the identity matrix **I**. Consider the following product:

$$\begin{bmatrix} 2 & 4 \\ 8 & 1 \end{bmatrix} \begin{bmatrix} \frac{-1}{30} & \frac{2}{15} \\ \frac{4}{15} & \frac{-1}{15} \end{bmatrix} = \begin{bmatrix} 1 & 0 \\ 0 & 1 \end{bmatrix}$$

$$\mathbf{A} \qquad \mathbf{A}^{-1} \qquad = \qquad \mathbf{I}$$

One means for finding the inverse matrix $\mathbf{A}^{-1}$ for matrix **A** is through the use of a process called the *Gauss-Jordan Method*. This method will be performed on matrix **A** by first augmenting it with the identity matrix as follows:

$$\begin{bmatrix} 2 & 4 & \vdots & 1 & 0 \\ 8 & 1 & \vdots & 0 & 1 \end{bmatrix} \qquad \text{(A)}$$

For the sake of convenience, call the above augmented matrix **A** temporarily. Now, a series of row operations (addition, subtraction, or multiplication of each element in a row) will be performed such that the identity matrix replaces the original matrix **A** (on the left side). The right-side elements will comprise the inverse matrix $\mathbf{A}^{-1}$. Thus, in our final augmented matrix, we will have ones along the principal diagonal on the left side and zeros elsewhere; the right side of the matrix will comprise the inverse of **A**. Allowable row operations include the following:

1. Multiply a given row by any constant. Each element in the row must be multiplied by the same constant.
2. Add a given row to any other row in the matrix. Each element in a row is added to the corresponding element in the same column of another row.
3. Subtract a given row from any other row in the matrix. Each element in a row is subtracted from the corresponding element in the same column of another row.

4. Any combination of the above. For example, a row may be multiplied by a constant before it is subtracted from another row.

Our first row operation will serve to replace the upper left corner value with a one. We multiply row 1 in **A** (row *1A*) by 0.5 to obtain the following:

$$\begin{bmatrix} 1 & 2 & \vdots & .5 & 0 \\ 8 & 1 & \vdots & 0 & 1 \end{bmatrix} \begin{matrix} 1A \cdot .5 = 1B \\ 2A \end{matrix}$$

where row $1B$ replaces row $1A$. Now we obtain a zero in the lower left corner by multiplying row 2 in **A** by 1/8 and subtracting the result from our new row 1 to obtain matrix **B** as follows:

$$\begin{bmatrix} 1 & 2 & \vdots & .5 & 0 \\ 0 & \frac{15}{8} & \vdots & .5 & \frac{-1}{8} \end{bmatrix} \begin{matrix} 1A \cdot .5 = 1B \\ 1B - (2A \cdot \frac{1}{8}) = 2B \end{matrix} \tag{B}$$

Next, we obtain a 1 in the lower right corner of the left side of the matrix by multiplying row $2B$ by 8/15:

$$\begin{bmatrix} 1 & 2 & \vdots & .5 & 0 \\ 0 & 1 & \vdots & \frac{4}{15} & \frac{-1}{15} \end{bmatrix} \begin{matrix} 1A \cdot .5 = 1B \\ 2B \cdot \frac{8}{15} = 2C \end{matrix}$$

We obtain a zero in the upper right corner of the left side matrix by multiplying row 2 above by 2 and subtracting from row 1 in **B**:

$$\begin{bmatrix} 1 & 0 & \vdots & \frac{-1}{30} & \frac{2}{15} \\ 0 & 1 & \vdots & \frac{4}{15} & \frac{-1}{15} \end{bmatrix} \begin{matrix} 1B - (2C \cdot 2) = 1C \\ 2B \cdot \frac{8}{15} = 2C \end{matrix} \tag{C}$$

The left side of augmented matrix **C** is the identity matrix; the right side of **C** is $\mathbf{A}^{-1}$. Because matrices cannot be divided as numbers are in arithmetic, one performs an analogous operation by inverting the matrix intended to be the "divisor" and postmultiplying this inverse by the first matrix to obtain a quotient. Thus, instead of dividing **A** by **B** to obtain **D**, one inverts **B** and obtains **D** by the product $\mathbf{AB}^{-1} = \mathbf{D}$. This concept is extremely useful for many types of algebraic manipulations.

## Solving Systems of Equations

Matrices can be very useful in arranging systems of equations. Consider, for example, the following system of equations:

$$.05x_1 + .12x_2 = .05$$

$$.10x_1 + .30x_2 = .08$$

This system of equations can be represented as follows:

$$\underset{\mathbf{C}}{\begin{bmatrix} .05 & .12 \\ .10 & .30 \end{bmatrix}} \underset{\mathbf{x}}{\begin{bmatrix} x_1 \\ x_2 \end{bmatrix}} = \underset{\mathbf{s}}{\begin{bmatrix} .05 \\ .08 \end{bmatrix}}$$

We are not able to divide **C** by $s$ to obtain **x**; instead, we invert **C** to obtain $\mathbf{C}^{-1}$ and multiply it by **s** to obtain **x**:

$$\mathbf{C}^{-1}\mathbf{s} = \mathbf{x}$$

Therefore, to solve for vector **x**, we first invert **C** by augmenting it with the identity matrix:

$$\begin{bmatrix} .05 & .12 & \vdots & 1 & 0 \\ .10 & .30 & \vdots & 0 & 1 \end{bmatrix} \qquad \text{(A)}$$

$$\begin{bmatrix} 1 & 2.4 & \vdots & 20 & 0 \\ 0 & .6 & \vdots & -20 & 10 \end{bmatrix} \quad \begin{matrix} RowB1 = A1 \cdot 20 \\ RowB2 = (10 \cdot A2) - B1 \end{matrix} \qquad \text{(B)}$$

$$\begin{bmatrix} 1 & 0 & \vdots & 100 & -40 \\ 0 & 1 & \vdots & \frac{-100}{3} & \frac{50}{3} \end{bmatrix} \quad \begin{matrix} RowC1 = B1 + -(2.4 \cdot C2) \\ RowC2 = B2 \cdot 5/3 \end{matrix} \qquad \text{(C)}$$

$$\mathbf{I} \qquad \mathbf{C}^{-1}$$

Thus, we obtain vector **x** with the following product:

$$\underset{\mathbf{C}^{-1}}{\begin{bmatrix} 100 & -40 \\ \frac{-100}{3} & \frac{50}{3} \end{bmatrix}} \underset{\mathbf{s}}{\begin{bmatrix} .05 \\ .08 \end{bmatrix}} = \underset{\mathbf{x}}{\begin{bmatrix} x_1 \\ x_2 \end{bmatrix}} = \underset{\mathbf{x}}{\begin{bmatrix} 1.8 \\ \frac{-1}{3} \end{bmatrix}} \qquad \text{(D)}$$

Thus, we find that $x_1 = 1.8$ and $x_2 = -1/3$.

## A.3 DERIVATIVES OF POLYNOMIALS

The derivative from calculus can be used to determine rates of change or slopes. They are also useful for finding function maxima and minima. For those functions whose slopes are constantly changing, the derivative is to find an instantaneous rate of change; that is, the change in $y$ induced by the "tiniest" change in $x$. Assume that

$y$ is given as a function of variable $x$. If $x$ were to increase by a small (infinitesimal—that is, approaching, though not quite, equal to zero) amount $h$, by how much would $y$ change? This rate of change is given by the derivative of $y$ with respect to $x$, which is defined as follows:

$$\frac{dy}{dx} = f'(x) = \lim_{h \to 0} \frac{f(x+h) - f(x)}{h} \quad \text{(A-20)}$$

One type of function that appears regularly in finance is the polynomial function. This type of function defines variable $y$ in terms of a coefficient $c$ (or series of coefficients $c_j$), variable $x$ (or series of variables $x_j$), and an exponent $n$ (or series of exponents $n_j$). Strictly speaking, the exponents in a polynomial equation must be non-negative integers; however, the rules that we discuss here still apply when the exponents assume negative or noninteger values. Where there exists one coefficient, one variable, and one exponent, the polynomial function is written as follows:

$$y = c \cdot x^n \quad \text{(A-21)}$$

For example, let $c = 7$ and $n = 4$. Thus, our polynomial is written as follows: $y = 7 \times ^4$. The derivative of $y$ with respect to $x$ is given by the following function:

$$\frac{dy}{dx} = c \cdot n \cdot x^{n-1} \quad \text{(A-22)}$$

Taking the derivative of $y$ with respect to $x$ in our example, we obtain $dy/dx = 7 \times 4 \times x^{4-1} = 28x^3$. Note that this derivative is always positive when $x > 0$; thus the slope of this curve is always positive when $x > 0$. Consider a second polynomial with more than one term ($m$ terms total). In this second case, there will be one variable $x$, $m$ coefficients ($c_j$), and $m$ exponents ($n_j$):

$$y = \sum_{j=1}^{m} c_j \cdot x^{n_j} \quad \text{(A-23)}$$

The derivative of such a function $y$ with respect to $x$ is given by:

$$\frac{dy}{dx} = \sum_{j=1}^{m} c_j \cdot n_j \cdot x^{n_j - 1} \quad \text{(A-24)}$$

That is, simply take the derivative of each term in $y$ with respect to $x$ and sum these derivatives. Consider a second example, a second-order (the largest exponent is 2) polynomial function given by $y = 5x^2 - 3x + 2$. The derivative of this function with respect to $x$ is: $dy/dx = 10x - 3$. This derivative is positive when $x > 0.3$, negative when $x < 0.3$, and zero when $x = 0.3$. Thus, when $dy/dx > 0$, $y$ increases as $x$ increases; when $dy/dx < 0$, $y$ decreases as $x$ increases; and when $dy/dx = 0$, $y$ may be either minimized or maximized. Also note that $y$ is minimized when $x = 0.3$; at this point, $dy/dx = 0$.

As suggested above, derivatives can often be used to find minimum and maximum values of functions. To find the minimum value of $y$ in function $y = 5x^2 - 3x + 2$, we set the first derivative of $y$ with respect to $x$ equal to zero and then solve for $x$. For our example, the minimum is found as follows:

$$\begin{aligned} 10x - 3 &= 0 \\ 10x &= 3 \\ x &= \frac{3}{10} \end{aligned}$$

In order to ensure that we have found a minimum (rather than a maximum), we check the second derivative. The second derivative is found by taking the derivative of the first derivative. If the second derivative is greater than zero, we have a minimum value for $y$ (the function is concave up). When the second derivative is less than zero, we have a maximum (the function is concave down). If the second derivative is zero, we have neither a minimum nor a maximum. The second derivative in the above example is given by $d^2y/dx^2 = 10$, also written $f''(x) = 10$. Since the second derivative 10 is greater than zero, we have found a minimum value for $y$. In many cases, more than one "local" minimum or maximum value will exist.

Consider a third example where our second order polynomial is given: $y = -7x^2 + 4x + 5$. The first derivative is $dy/dx = -14x + 4$. Setting the first derivative equal to zero, we find our maximum as follows:

$$\begin{aligned} -14x + 4 &= 0 \\ -14x &= -4 \\ x &= \frac{4}{14} \end{aligned}$$

We check second-order conditions (the second derivative) to ensure that this is a maximum. The second derivative is $d^2y/dx^2 = -14$. Since $-14$ is less than zero, we have a maximum at $x = 4/14$.

# A.4 REFERENCE TABLES

**TABLE A.1** Normal Distribution, *z*-values

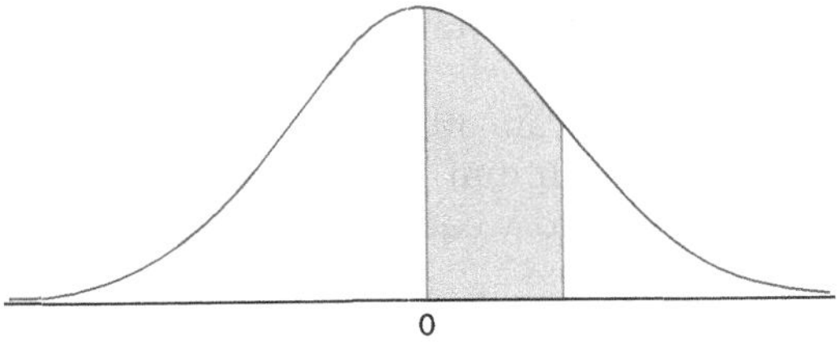


| z | 0.00 | 0.01 | 0.02 | 0.03 | 0.04 | 0.05 | 0.06 | 0.07 | 0.08 | 0.09 |
|---|---|---|---|---|---|---|---|---|---|---|
| 0.0 | 0.0000 | 0.0040 | 0.0080 | 0.0120 | 0.0159 | 0.0199 | 0.0239 | 0.0279 | 0.0319 | 0.0358 |
| 0.1 | 0.0398 | 0.0438 | 0.0478 | 0.0517 | 0.0557 | 0.0596 | 0.0636 | 0.0675 | 0.0714 | 0.0753 |
| 0.2 | 0.0793 | 0.0832 | 0.0871 | 0.0909 | 0.0948 | 0.0987 | 0.1026 | 0.1064 | 0.1103 | 0.1141 |
| 0.3 | 0.1179 | 0.1217 | 0.1255 | 0.1293 | 0.1331 | 0.1368 | 0.1406 | 0.1443 | 0.1480 | 0.1517 |
| 0.4 | 0.1554 | 0.1591 | 0.1628 | 0.1664 | 0.1700 | 0.1736 | 0.1772 | 0.1808 | 0.1844 | 0.1879 |
| 0.5 | 0.1915 | 0.1950 | 0.1985 | 0.2019 | 0.2054 | 0.2088 | 0.2123 | 0.2157 | 0.2190 | 0.2224 |
| 0.6 | 0.2257 | 0.2291 | 0.2324 | 0.2356 | 0.2389 | 0.2421 | 0.2454 | 0.2486 | 0.2517 | 0.2549 |
| 0.7 | 0.2580 | 0.2611 | 0.2642 | 0.2673 | 0.2703 | 0.2734 | 0.2764 | 0.2793 | 0.2823 | 0.2852 |
| 0.8 | 0.2881 | 0.2910 | 0.2939 | 0.2967 | 0.2995 | 0.3023 | 0.3051 | 0.3078 | 0.3106 | 0.3133 |
| 0.9 | 0.3159 | 0.3186 | 0.3212 | 0.3238 | 0.3264 | 0.3289 | 0.3315 | 0.3340 | 0.3365 | 0.3389 |
| 1.0 | 0.3413 | 0.3437 | 0.3461 | 0.3485 | 0.3508 | 0.3531 | 0.3554 | 0.3577 | 0.3599 | 0.3621 |
| 1.1 | 0.3643 | 0.3665 | 0.3686 | 0.3708 | 0.3729 | 0.3749 | 0.3770 | 0.3790 | 0.3810 | 0.3830 |
| 1.2 | 0.3849 | 0.3869 | 0.3888 | 0.3906 | 0.3925 | 0.3943 | 0.3962 | 0.3980 | 0.3997 | 0.4015 |
| 1.3 | 0.4032 | 0.4049 | 0.4066 | 0.4082 | 0.4099 | 0.4115 | 0.4131 | 0.4147 | 0.4162 | 0.4177 |
| 1.4 | 0.4192 | 0.4207 | 0.4222 | 0.4236* | 0.4251 | 0.4265 | 0.4279 | 0.4292 | 0.4306 | 0.4319 |
| 1.5 | 0.4332 | 0.4345 | 0.4357 | 0.4370 | 0.4382 | 0.4394 | 0.4406 | 0.4418 | 0.4429 | 0.4441 |
| 1.6 | 0.4452 | 0.4463 | 0.4474 | 0.4484 | 0.4495 | 0.4505 | 0.4515 | 0.4525 | 0.4535 | 0.4545 |
| 1.7 | 0.4554 | 0.4564 | 0.4573 | 0.4582 | 0.4591 | 0.4599 | 0.4608 | 0.4616 | 0.4625 | 0.4633 |
| 1.8 | 0.4641 | 0.4649 | 0.4656 | 0.4664 | 0.4671 | 0.4678 | 0.4686 | 0.4693 | 0.4699 | 0.4706 |
| 1.9 | 0.4713 | 0.4719 | 0.4726 | 0.4732 | 0.4738 | 0.4744 | 0.4750 | 0.4756 | 0.4761 | 0.4767 |
| 2.0 | 0.4772 | 0.4778 | 0.4783 | 0.4788 | 0.4793 | 0.4798 | 0.4803 | 0.4808 | 0.4812 | 0.4817 |
| 2.1 | 0.4821 | 0.4826 | 0.4830 | 0.4834 | 0.4838 | 0.4842 | 0.4846 | 0.4850 | 0.4854 | 0.4857 |
| 2.2 | 0.4861 | 0.4864 | 0.4868 | 0.4871 | 0.4875 | 0.4878 | 0.4881 | 0.4884 | 0.4887 | 0.4890 |
| 2.3 | 0.4893 | 0.4896 | 0.4898 | 0.4901 | 0.4904 | 0.4906 | 0.4909 | 0.4911 | 0.4913 | 0.4916 |
| 2.4 | 0.4918 | 0.492 | 0.4922 | 0.4925 | 0.4927 | 0.4929 | 0.4931 | 0.4932 | 0.4934 | 0.4936 |
| 2.5 | 0.4938 | 0.4940 | 0.4941 | 0.4943 | 0.4945 | 0.4946 | 0.4948 | 0.4949 | 0.4951 | 0.4952 |
| 2.6 | 0.4953 | 0.4955 | 0.4956 | 0.4957 | 0.4959 | 0.4960 | 0.4961 | 0.4962 | 0.4963 | 0.4964 |
| 2.7 | 0.4965 | 0.4966 | 0.4967 | 0.4968 | 0.4969 | 0.4970 | 0.4971 | 0.4972 | 0.4973 | 0.4974 |
| 2.8 | 0.4974 | 0.4975 | 0.4976 | 0.4977 | 0.4977 | 0.4978 | 0.4979 | 0.4979 | 0.4980 | 0.4981 |
| 2.9 | 0.4981 | 0.4982 | 0.4982 | 0.4983 | 0.4984 | 0.4984 | 0.4985 | 0.4985 | 0.4986 | 0.4986 |
| 3.0 | 0.4986 | 0.4987 | 0.4987 | 0.4988 | 0.4988 | 0.4989 | 0.4989 | 0.4989 | 0.4990 | 0.4990 |

**TABLE A.2** Student *t*-Distribution

| | Right Area, α | | | | |
|---|---|---|---|---|---|
| **df** | **0.100** | **0.050** | **0.025** | **0.010** | **0.005** |
| **1** | 3.078 | 6.314 | 12.706 | 31.821 | 63.657 |
| **2** | 1.886 | 2.920 | 4.303 | 6.695 | 9.925 |
| **3** | 1.638 | 2.353 | 3.182 | 4.541 | 5.841 |
| **4** | 1.533 | 2.132 | 2.776 | 3.747 | 4.604 |
| **5** | 1.476 | 2.015 | 2.571 | 3.365 | 4.032 |
| **6** | 1.440 | 1.943 | 2.447 | 3.143 | 3.707 |
| **7** | 1.415 | 1.895 | 2.365 | 2.998 | 3.499 |
| **8** | 1.397 | 1.860 | 2.306 | 2.896 | 3.355 |
| **9** | 1.383 | 1.833 | 2.262 | 2.821 | 3.250 |
| **10** | 1.372 | 1.812 | 2.228 | 2.764 | 3.169 |
| **11** | 1.363 | 1.796 | 2.201 | 2.718 | 3.106 |
| **12** | 1.356 | 1.782 | 2.179 | 2.681 | 3.055 |
| **13** | 1.350 | 1.771 | 2.160 | 2.650 | 3.012 |
| **14** | 1.345 | 1.761 | 2.145 | 2.624 | 2.977 |
| **15** | 1.341 | 1.753 | 2.131 | 2.602 | 2.947 |
| **16** | 1.337 | 1.746 | 2.120 | 2.583 | 2.921 |
| **17** | 1.333 | 1.740 | 2.110 | 2.567 | 2.898 |
| **18** | 1.330 | 1.734 | 2.101 | 2.552 | 2.878 |
| **19** | 1.328 | 1.729 | 2.093 | 2.539 | 2.861 |
| **20** | 1.325 | 1.725 | 2.086 | 2.528 | 2.845 |
| **21** | 1.323 | 1.721 | 2.080 | 2.518 | 2.831 |
| **22** | 1.321 | 1.717 | 2.074 | 2.508 | 2.819 |
| **23** | 1.319 | 1.714 | 2.069 | 2.500 | 2.807 |
| **24** | 1.318 | 1.711 | 2.064 | 2.492 | 2.797 |
| **25** | 1.316 | 1.708 | 2.060 | 2.485 | 2.787 |
| **26** | 1.315 | 1.706 | 2.056 | 2.479 | 2.779 |
| **27** | 1.314 | 1.703 | 2.052 | 2.473 | 2.771 |
| **28** | 1.313 | 1.701 | 2.048 | 2.467 | 2.763 |
| **29** | 1.311 | 1.699 | 2.045 | 2.462 | 2.756 |
| **30** | 1.310 | 1.697 | 2.042 | 2.457 | 2.750 |
| $\infty$ | 1.282 | 1.645 | 1.960 | 2.326 | 2.576 |

*Examples:* The $t$ value for $\infty$ degrees of freedom that bound a right-tail area of 0.025 is 1.960. The $t$ value for $\infty$ degrees of freedom that bound left- and right-tail areas (two tails) summing to 0.05 is 1.960.

# Glossary

**12(b)-1 fee:** Fee assessed shareholders by mutual funds for certain promotional expenses.

**Abnormal return:** The part of a security's return that was not expected; that is, it appears to be attributable to something other than time value of money or risk. Also called excess return or residual.

**Adverse selection:** Precontractual opportunism where one party to a contract (e.g., purchaser of insurance) uses his private information (e.g., information with respect to risk-taking) to the other counterparty's disadvantage.

**Agency issue:** A security issue by an agency of the U.S. federal government. Includes securities issued by GNMA (Ginnie Mae), FNMA (Fannie Mae), and SLMA (Sallie Mae).

**Alpha:** (1) See Jensen's alpha. (2) Model, program, or strategy intended to generate a profit.

**Agency trader:** Trader who acts as a commission broker on behalf of clients.

**Algo trading:** See algorithmic trading.

**Algorithmic trading:** (1) Automated trading with the use of live market data and rule-driven computer programs for automatically submitting and allocating trade orders among markets and brokers as well as over time so as to minimize the price impact of large trades. Also called automated trading, black box trading, and robotrading. (2) Alpha model automated trading that is used to make trade decisions to generate profits or control risk.

**Alpha model:** (1) Gauges the performance of a trading strategy relative to a benchmark on a risk adjusted basis. (2) Model that seeks to outperform a benchmark on a risk-adjusted basis.

**Alternative trading system (ATS):** A securities trading venue that is not registered with the SEC as an exchange.

**American depository receipts (ADRs):** Shares issued by banks evidencing ownership of shares of foreign company stock that are held by its sponsor through a trust.

**American option:** Can be exercised any time prior to expiry.

**Arbitrage:** (1) The simultaneous purchase and sale of the same asset. (2) The near-simultaneous purchase and sale of assets generating nearly identical cash flow structures.

**Arbitrage opportunity:** Arbitrage transaction producing a profit, by purchasing at a price that is less than the selling price.

**Arbitrageur:** Trader who seeks to profit from arbitrage opportunities.

**Arrival price (bid–ask midpoint or BAM):** The midpoint of the bid–offer spread at the time the order is received.

**Ask:** A solicitation to sell (also called an offer).

**ATS:** See Alternative trading system.

**Auction:** A competitive market process involving multiple buyers, multiple sellers, or both. An auction is the process of trading a security through bidding, then selling it to the winning bidder.

**BAM:** See Arrival price.

**Banging the close:** Flooding a market sell orders its final minutes of trading before the close, thereby forcing prices down as buying interest diminished. A form of wash sale intended to manipulate prices.

**Banker's acceptance:** Marketable security originated documenting a bank's acceptance of a responsibility to pay a client's loan or for assuming some other financial responsibility on behalf of a client.

**Bargaining:** The negotiation process over transaction contract terms that occurs between a buyer and a seller for a transaction.

**Basis point:** 0.0001 of a unit. Typically used in foreign-exchange and fixed-income market quotes.

**Basis:** The potential for a price to move in the direction anticipated by an arbitrageur, at least in the short run.

**Basis risk:** Risk that markets might move too slowly to profit from an apparent arbitrage, or that markets might move opposite to the arbitrageur's expectations, at least in the short run.

**Beta:** Coefficient that measures the risk of a security relative to the risk of some factor (usually the market).

**Bid:** A solicitation to buy.

**Binomial option pricing model:** Valuation model based on the assumption that the underlying stock follows a binomial return generating process.

**Binomial process:** The asset value takes on only one of two potential constant values at any given time period.

**Black-Scholes option pricing model:** A continuous time–space option pricing formula.

**Blockholder:** An owner of a significant number of shares of a firm. Sometimes refers to an owner of 10,000 or more shares.

**Block trade:** Transaction involving more than 10,000 shares or $200,000 of a security.

**Bluffing:** The act of fooling other traders into making unwise trades by convincing them that the bluffer has superior material information.

**Bond:** Financial security that makes fixed payment(s) at specified interval(s).

**Broker:** A security market participant who acts as an agent for investors, buying and selling on their behalf on a commission basis.

**Brownian motion:** A Newtonian nondifferentiable stochastic continuous time-space process whose increments are independent over time.

**Buy side traders:** Traders who buy liquidity services in the marketplace. Such traders often include individual investors, mutual funds, and pension funds.

**Call:** Security or contract granting its owner the right to purchase a given asset at a specified price on or before the expiration date of the contract.

**Call market:** Market where orders can be executed only at specific points in time, when orders are called (when buy orders are matched against sell orders or when orders are accumulated before being executed).

**Clearance:** Recording and comparison of records associated with a trade.

**Clearing:** See Clearance.

**Clearing firm:** Firm authorized by a clearing house to manage trade comparisons and other back office operations.

**Clearing house:** Institution that clears transactions for an exchange or other market.

**Closed-end investment company:** Investment company that issues a specified number of shares that can be traded in secondary markets such as the New York Stock Exchange.

**Coefficient of correlation:** A measure of the strength and direction of the relationship between two sets of variables. Ranges between −1 and +1 and may be regarded as a "standardized" covariance (dividing covariance by the product of the standard deviations of the two variable sets).

**Collar:** A portfolio consisting of a long position in a put and a short position in a call, collaring the underlying security selling price to lie between the exercise prices of the two options contracts.

**Co-location:** The practice by high-frequency traders to rent space from or very near market centers, such as the major exchanges ECNs and other and alternative trading systems for the purpose of co-locating their servers next to the market center's data servers to reduce latency and access to information. Also called proximity hosting.

**Common value auction:** Auction where all bidders place the same value on the item to be auctioned, and that value is known with certainty.

**Confirmation:** Verification of a trade.

**Consolidated tape:** High-speed electronic system for reporting transaction prices and volumes for securities on all U.S. exchanges and markets.

**Consolidated Quotations System:** Provides traders with price quotes from the various exchanges and FINRA and calculates the NBBO.

**Continuous market:** Market where orders can be executed whenever the market is open.

**Convexity:** (1) The slope of the slope of a function. (2) The sensitivity of the duration of a bond to changes in the market rate of interest.

**Corner:** The purchase of a sufficient level of a given security to obtain market or monopoly power over its price.

**Counterparty:** Person or institution with whom one trades.

**Counterparty risk:** The potential that a trade counterparty fails to fulfill their side of a transaction.

**Coupon:** The interest rate on debt as a percentage of its face value.

**Covariance:** A statistical measure of the co-movement between two sets of variables.

**Covered call writing:** Writing or selling a call while owning the underlying asset (or appropriate combination of other assets) needed to generate a hedge.

**Covered put writing:** Writing or selling a put while shorting the underlying asset (or appropriate combination of other assets) needed to generate a hedge.

**Crossed market:** Market where one or more bids exceeds one or more offer prices.

**Crossing network:** Alternative trading system that matches buyers and sellers with respect to agreed-upon quantities, and does not publicly display quotations, thereby enabling participants some degree of anonymity. Trades are priced by reference to prices obtained from other markets rather than by auctions. Traders using crossing networks announce their order sizes, which are matched at prices obtained auction markets such as the NYSE.

**Cumulative average residual (CAR):** The sum of abnormal returns or residuals over a period of time around an event.

**Current yield:** Measure of the annual interest payments made by a bond relative to the initial investment required by the bond.

**Custodian:** Holds assets on behalf of owners.

**Dark liquidity pool:** Broadly defined, any willingness to buy or sell that is not publicly displayed. Often refers to portions of large trades broken up into small trades to be executed in different markets and over time so as to minimize the price impact (slippage) of the trade. Sometimes refers to crossing networks.

**Dealer:** Securities market participant who trades directly with clients and brokers, seeking trade counterparties for clients, facilitating their trading process, posting and maintaining quotes, and buying and selling for their own portfolios on a profit basis.

**Delta:** Sensitivity of an option's price to changes in the price of the underlying security.

**Delta neutral:** Portfolio of options and underlying securities whose weighted average Black-Scholes delta is zero, and whose value is constant with respect to small changes in the value of the underlying asset.

**Depth:** A market's ability to process and execute a large order without substantially impacting its price.

**Derivative security:** Security whose payoff function is derived from the value of some other security, rate, or index.

**Designated market maker (DMM):** Exchange official and market participant charged with the responsibility to maintain a fair and orderly market in their stocks, quote at the NBBO a specified percentage of the time, and facilitate price discovery throughout the day as well as at the open, close, and in periods of significant imbalances and high volatility. The DMM provides price improvement and matches incoming orders based on a preprogrammed capital commitment schedule, which has been added to the NYSE Display Book and minimizes order latency. DMMs compete as market participants, trading on their own accounts.

**Direct access:** Trading systems that provide for direct access to markets bypassing brokers.

**Discount rate:** A rate used to discount (usually reduce) future cash flows to express their values relative to current cash flows.

**Discrete process:** A process whose variable can be assigned only a countable number of values.

**Diversification:** Holding multiple assets whose returns are not perfectly correlated.

**DKs (don't knows):** Trade reports filed with clearing firms or clearing houses with discrepancies resulting from recording errors, misunderstanding, and fraud.

**DMM:** See Designated market maker.

**Don't knows:** See DKs.

**Dow Jones Industrial Average (DJIA):** A price-weighted average of 30 actively traded blue chip stocks.

**Double auction:** Used for the trading of most publicly traded securities in secondary (resale) markets where buyers submit bids (maximum purchase prices) and sellers submit offers (minimum selling prices) that are ranked from best to worst. Also called bilateral auctions.

**Drift:** The predictable change component of a stochastic process.

**Duration:** Measures the proportional sensitivity of a bond value or price to changes in the market rate of interest.

**Dutch auction:** Auction that begins with the auctioneer calling out a high offer price, which is reduced until some participant submits the first, highest, and winning bid. Also called descending bid auction.

**ECN:** See electronic communication network.

**Efficient market:** A market where security prices fully reflect all available information.

**Electric communication network:** Virtual meeting place and screen-based system for trading securities.

**English auction:** Auction where participants bid openly against one another, with each successive bid higher than the previous one. Also called ascending bid auction.

**Equity:** Security that represents ownership in a business or corporation. Normally called stock.

**ETF:** See Exchange traded fund.

**European option:** Can be exercised only when it expires.

**Exchange:** A physical or electronic marketplace for trading securities.

**Exchange-traded fund (ETF):** Closed-end investment company whose shares are traded on an exchange.

**Execution:** The process of selling or buying a security.

**Execution speed:** The time it takes for an order to be executed.

**Exercise price:** See striking price

**Eurodollar:** Freely convertible dollar-denominated time deposit or debt instrument issued outside the United States and outside of the jurisdiction of the U.S. Federal Reserve.

**Exercise price:** Price at which an option can be exercised; that is, the price that the call owner has the right to pay for the underlying asset or put owner has the right to sell the underlying asset for. Also called striking price.

**Expectations theory:** See Pure expectations theory.

**Face value:** The principal or par value of debt.

**Federal funds rate:** The rate at which the excess reserves of one bank can be loaned to other banks for satisfaction of borrower reserve requirements.

**Filtration:** History, or indexed set of subobjects in a stochastic process.

**Financial Institutions Regulatory Authority (FINRA):** The largest independent regulator for all securities firms and exchanges conducting business in the United States. Formed by the merger of the NASD, and member regulation, enforcement, and arbitration operations of the New York Stock Exchange.

**FINRA:** See Financial Institutions Regulatory Authority.

**First-price sealed-bid auction:** All bidders simultaneously submit sealed bids so that no bidder knows any of the other bids. Does not allow for price discovery until the auction concludes. The winner submits the highest bid and pays the bid price.

**Fisher effect:** Defines the real interest rate as the ratio of the nominal rate to the inflation rate.

**Fishing:** Practice intended to obtain secret information concerning order sizes in dark pools. Occurs when a trader sends a series of small orders to a dark pool to detect whether there is a large order waiting in that pool.

**Flash order:** Quote that is immediately executed or canceled (within 500 milliseconds of the original quote), need not be publicly displayed, and may be displayed to select clients. Flash quotes are the basis for flash trading.

**Flash trading:** Trading motivated by private or select market participant receipt of quotes (flash orders) in advance of the public quote stream (also called prerouting displays). This means that the recipients of flash orders receive access to quotes before the public and can engage in flash trading on the basis of these quotes.

**FHLMA:** Federal Home Loan Mortgage Association. Founded in 1969 by the federal government of the United States to facilitate mortgage lending to prospective homeowners. It provides capital for the mortgage industry by selling securities backed by other mortgages issued by banks.

**FNMA:** Federal National Mortgage Association (Fannie Mae or FNMA). Founded in 1938 by the federal government of the United States to facilitate mortgage lending to prospective homeowners. It provides capital for the mortgage industry by selling securities backed by other mortgages issued by banks.

**Forward contract:** Instrument that obliges participants to either purchase or sell a given asset at a specified price on the future settlement date of that contract.

**Forward rate:** Locked-in interest rate on loans originating after time zero or in the future.

**Front running:** Using the information in another participant's order to set a bid or quote in a subsequent order with priority. An example of front-running might be where a broker with information about a client's order uses this information to set a bid or offer in her own order in setting a bid or offer so as to exploit the client's order.

**Futures contract:** Instrument that obliges participants to either purchase or sell a given asset at a specified price on the future settlement date of that contract. Normally traded on an exchange, with standardized contractual terms and providing for margin and marking to the market.

**Gamma:** Sensitivity of an option's delta to changes in the price of the underlying security.

**GNMA:** Government National Mortgage Association (Ginnie Mae or GNMA). Founded by the federal government of the United States to facilitate mortgage lending to prospective homeowners. It guarantees mortgage-backed securities issued by banks and other institutions.

**Greeks:** Sensitivities of options and portfolios of options to Black-Scholes pricing model inputs.

**Hedge fund:** A private fund that allows investors to pool their investment assets. To avoid SEC registration and certain regulations, hedge funds usually only accept funds from small numbers (often less than 100) of accredited investors, typically high-net-worth individuals and institutions.

**Hedge:** To take a position to reduce risk.

**Hedge ratio:** Defines the number of units of one security required to offset the position in one unit of another security in order to form or maintain a riskless portfolio.

**HFT:** See High frequency trading.

**High frequency trading:** The practice of rapid executions of multiple transactions for securities followed by extremely short holding periods, perhaps as short as fractions of seconds.

**Hot potato trading:** Repeated passing of inventory imbalances among dealers.

**Iceberg order:** Partially revealed order whose full size is not revealed. Also called hidden-size order.

**Immunization:** Strategies concerned with matching the present values of asset portfolios with the present values of cash flows associated with future liabilities. More specifically, immunization strategies are primarily concerned with matching asset durations with liability durations.

**Implementation risk:** Risk taken by arbitrageur that one or more arbitrage transactions might fail to execute or be executed at prices that differ from what the arbitrageur anticipated.

**Implementation shortfall:** The performance difference between hypothetical profits realized by a paper portfolio replicating an actual portfolio and the profits realized by the actual portfolio.

**Index:** A portfolio of stocks or other instruments intended to reflect performance of a particular market or sector.

**Infinitesimal:** Value approaching zero.

**Information asymmetry:** Scenario where agents have information that differs in quality.

**Inside information:** Material nonpublic information concerning the prospects of a security.

**Interest rate parity:** States that anticipated currency exchange rate shifts will be proportional to countries' relative interest rates.

**International Fisher effect:** By combining purchase power parity, interest rate parity, and the Fisher effect, the international Fisher effect demonstrates that different economies will have identical real interest rates.

**Investment company:** Institution that accepts funds from investors for the purpose of investing on their behalf.

**Intermarket trading system:** Displays quotes in different markets and links markets for trade executions to facilitate investors' access to the best quotes.

**Investment company:** An institution that accepts funds from investors for the purpose of investing on their behalf.

**Jensen's alpha:** Excess return on a portfolio over the CAPM-implied risk-adjusted return.

**Jitney game:** A series of wash sales at ever-increasing prices.

**Latency:** The amount of time that lapses from when a quote or an order is placed by a trader and when that order is actually visible to the market.

**Late trading:** An illegal fund trading strategy purchase or redeem shares after daily net asset values (NAVs) are computed.

**Law of one price:** States that securities or portfolios of securities offering the same cash flow characteristics or baskets offering the same commodities must sell for the same price.

**Leveraged buyout:** The purchase of a firm by private group of investors with substantial debt financing. It is usually a going private transaction; that is, a publicly traded company is transformed into a privately owned company in the transaction.

**Level I quotes:** Displays the best bid and offer prices (inside quote or BBO, best-bid-offer) and, in some cases, quote sizes.

**Level II quotes:** Display the best bid and offer prices, quote sizes along with other quotes in descending order for the best bids and ascending for the best offers with market maker symbols for each.

**Level III quotes:** Offered to Nasdaq members, provide the same information as Level II and enables traders to have direct access to enter and revise quotes.

**Limit order:** Sets an upper price for a purchase or a lower price limit for a sell, preventing the broker from paying more or accepting less for the security. The limit order restricts the price of the order.

**Liquidity:** An asset's ability to be easily purchased or sold without causing significant change in the price of the asset.

**Liquidity rebate:** See Payments for order flow.

**Load fund:** A mutual fund that charges a sales fee.

**Long:** (1) To have purchased or owned (2) position that obligates or enables the investor or participant to purchase a given or underlying asset on the expiration or settlement date of a derivative contract.

**Make-or-take pricing:** Refers to exchanges allowing patient traders to post standing limit orders that await execution until some other trader takes the other side, providing liquidity rebates to the patient trader making the market.

**Management buyout:** The purchase of a public firm by the management of that firm. It is usually a going private transaction.

**Market architecture:** The set of rules governing the trading process.

**Market impact:** The effect that a given transaction has on the market price of a security.

**Market microstructure:** Area of financial economics concerned with trading and market structure, market fairness, success and failure, and how the design of the market affects price formation and discovery. Market microstructure is concerned with costs of providing transaction services along with the impact of transactions costs on the short-run behavior of securities prices.

**Market on close:** The last price obtained by a trader at the end of the day relative to the last price reported by the exchange. Used for trader evaluation purposes.

**Market timing:** A fund trading strategy intended to exploit stale security prices and net asset value (NAV) deviations from fundamental values.

**Markov process (random walk):** A stochastic process whose increments or changes are independent over time.

**Mark to market:** Accounting for the fair value of an asset or liability based on its current market price, or, if unavailable, based on either similar instruments or an appropriate valuation model.

**Martingale process:** A Markov process whose increments have expected value 0.

**MOC:** See Market on close.

**Model risk:** Failure to fully understand the implications of a trading model.

**Multilateral Trading Facility:** European variation on the alternative trading system.

**Multiplicative movement:** The proportion by which an asset changes over a given time period.

**Mutual fund (open-end investment company):** An institution registered with the SEC under the Investment Act of 1940 that pools investors' funds into a single portfolio.

**Naked access:** Where algorithmic trade orders do not pass through pre–trade-risk controls, potentially leading to runaway executions.

**Naked call writing:** Writing or selling a call without owning the underlying asset (or appropriate combination of other assets needed to generate a hedge).

**Naked put writing:** Writing or selling a put without shorting the underlying asset (or appropriate combination of other assets) needed to generate a hedge.

**NASD:** See National Association of Security Dealers.

**National Association of Security Dealers (NASD):** Formerly the primary independent self-regulatory organization for the securities industry responsible regulation of the Nasdaq stock market and over-the-counter markets and for administrating competency exams for investment professionals. Merged with the member regulation, enforcement, and arbitration operations of the New York Stock Exchange to form FINRA.

**National best bid and offer (NBBO):** The highest bid and lowest offer prices available on a security at a given point in time.

**Nationally Recognized Statistical Rating Organization (NRSRO):** A credit rating agency whose ratings the U.S. Securities and Exchange Commission has designated as authoritative for certain regulatory purposes.

**NBBO:** See National best bid and offer.

**Negotiable certificate of deposit:** Tradable depository institution certificate of deposit with a denomination exceeding $100,000.

**Net asset value (NAV):** Market value of portfolio assets minus its liabilities at a particular point in time divided by the number of shares in the portfolio outstanding at that time.

**Netting:** The simplification process used by clearing institutions of adding all of a given firm's purchases of each security, adding the sales of each security, deducting sells from buys to determine the net change in holdings of that security for the firm, and computing the net cash flows associated with all transactions.

**Newsreader algorithms:** Electronic-based rules based on text mining and statistical techniques to analyze news sources, blogs, tweets, and other data to obtain relevant trading information and infer its impact on security prices.

**Noise trader:** Trades on the basis of what he falsely believes to be special information or misinterprets useful information concerning the future price or payoffs of a risky asset.

**No-load fund:** Mutual fund that accepts investments directly from investors without a sales charge.

**Novation:** The process whereby a clearing house assumes the settlement obligations of both counterparties to a transaction, in effect becoming the counterparty to both sides of the transaction.

**NRSRO:** See Nationally Recognized Statistical Rating Organization.

**OARS:** See Opening Automated Report Service.

**Offer:** A solicitation to sell (also called an ask).

**Opaque markets:** Markets that lack transparency.

**Open-end investment company:** See Mutual fund.

**Opening Automated Report Service:** (OARS) NYSE system that allows orders that have accumulated overnight or while the exchange is closed to be matched so that the designated market maker attempts to establish a market clearing price.

**Option:** Security that grants its owner the right to buy (call) or sell (put) an asset (underlying asset) at a specific price (exercise or striking price) on or before the expiration date of the option contract.

**Order-driven markets:** Markets where traders can trade without the intermediation of dealers.

**Order precedence:** Rules that determine which traders can place bid and offer quotations with greatest priority for execution and which can accept the quotations of other traders.

**Order Protection Rule:** Provision from the 2007 NMS legislation that provides intermarket price priority for quotations that are immediately accessible. Also known as the trade through rule.

**Out trades:** Trade reports filed with futures clearing firms or clearing houses with discrepancies resulting from recording errors, misunderstanding, and fraud.

**Over-the-counter (OTC) markets:** Securities markets other than those provided by exchanges.

**Pairs trading:** An arbitrage strategy that involves taking offsetting positions in two different stocks (perhaps options or index contracts) with correlated returns, one long and one short, such that gains in one position are expected to more than offset losses in the other position.

**Parasitic trading:** Broker trading on the basis of knowledge of her client's trading activity.

**Pattern day trader:** SEC definition for a trader who executes four or more round trip transactions in the same account within five consecutive business days.

**Payment for order flow:** Compensation received by brokers and other institutions from exchanges and alternative trading systems as payment for directing their order flow to those markets.

**Penny jumping:** A type of parasitic trading where the broker places a buy (sell) order one uptick above (downtick below) below the client's buy (sell) limit order, expecting to benefit either from the market's reaction to the client order or to limit his losses by transacting with the client.

**Ping:** To place a small order to detect the level of liquidity and possibility of large orders. If small orders are quickly executed, there might be significant interest in the security.

**Ping destination:** A pool, typically operated by a hedge fund or electronic market maker, that accepts only immediate or cancel (fill or kill) orders.

**Pip:** Basis point, or 0.0001 of a unit. Typically used in foreign exchange markets quotes.

**Precedence:** Which traders can execute bid and offer quotations and which can accept and execute the quotations of other traders. In most cases, the primary precedence is price priority; the participant with the highest bid or lowest ask has priority on an execution.

**Predatory algo trading:** Strategies designed to exploit other institutional algo orders.

**Prediction market:** A trading venue created to predict an outcome based on prices of specially created and traded securities that pay contingent on that outcome.

**Price discovery:** The process of determining the worth or price of an asset in the marketplace through the interactions of buyers and sellers.

**Price improvement:** Providing a better execution price than the quoted NBBO on market and limit orders; that is, providing a higher bid or lower offer price than the posted NBBO.

**Price priority:** Rule or rules dictating that the highest bids or lowest offers will be executed against in the presence of competing quotes.

**Priority:** Rule or rules dictating which quotations are to be executed in the presence of competing quotes.

**Private equity:** Refers to asset managers that make equity investments in companies that are not publicly traded.

**Program trading:** Defined by the NYSE as computer-initiated trades involving 15 or more stocks with value totaling more than $1 million.

**Prop shop:** See Trading arcade.

**Prop trader:** See Proprietary trader.

**Proprietary trader:** Trader *who* seeks profits by trading on his own account.

**Proprietary trading firm:** See Trading arcade.

**Proximity hosting:** See Co-location.

**Public Company Accounting Oversight Board (PCAOB):** Nonprofit corporation created by Sarbanes-Oxley to oversee public auditing firm practices.

**Pump and dump:** Market manipulator touts a security with false and misleading statements, causing the price to rise before selling their own holdings at the inflated prices.

**Purchase power parity:** States that commodities selling in different countries must sell for the same price after adjusting for exchange rates.

**Pure discount note:** A debt security paying no interest; it only pays its face value or principal.

**Pure expectations theory:** Term structure theory that states that long-term spot rates can be explained as a geometric mean of short term spot and forward rates.

**Put:** Security or contract granting its owner the right to sell a given asset at a specified price on or before the expiration date of the contract.

**Qualified institutional buyer (QIB):** Institution with an investment portfolio exceeding $100 million.

**Quote:** A solicitation to buy (bid) or solicitation sell (offer or ask).

**Quote-driven markets:** Markets where dealers post quotes and participate on at least one side of every trade.

**Quote matching:** Occurs when a small trader places an order one uptick (downtick) from that of a large trader so as to profit from the large trader's transaction upward (downward) price pressure, or to use the large trader as a trade counterparty should prices decrease (increase).

**Quote Rule:** Formally referred to as SEC Rule 602 of Regulation NMS, requires that all market centers publicly disseminate their best bids and offers through the securities information processors (such as the Consolidated Tape, Consolidated Quotations System, and the Intermarket Trading System).

**Quote stuffing:** The placement of large numbers of rapid-fire stock orders, with most or all of which being canceled almost immediately, frequently for the purpose of clogging trading HFT and other algorithms and data computations.

**Random walk:** A process whose future behavior, given by the sum of independent random variables, is independent of its past.

**Real estate investment trust (REIT):** A fund that invests in real estate and/or real estate mortgages, providing investors with opportunities to diversify into real estate with relatively small investment sums.

**Repo:** See Repurchase agreement.

**Repurchase agreement (repo):** Marketable security issued by a financial institution acknowledging the sale of assets and a subsequent agreement to repurchase at a higher price in the near term. This agreement is essentially similar to a collateralized short-term loan.

**Revenue equivalence theorem:** States that under specific restrictions, the auction type will not affect auction outcomes.

**Rho:** Sensitivity of an option's price to changes in the riskless return rate.

**Robotrading:** See Algorithmic Trading.

**Routing:** The process of executing the trade, involving broker selection, deciding which market(s) will execute the trade(s), and transmitting the trade(s) to the market(s).

**Rule 144A market:** Market specifically created for "qualified institutional buyers" to trade unregistered securities held by less than 500 shareholders.

**SDBK:** See Super Display Book System.

**Second-price sealed-bid auction:** All bidders simultaneously submit sealed bids so that no bidder knows any of the other bids. Does not allow for price discovery until the auction concludes. The winner submits the highest bid and pays the second-highest bid price (the highest losing bid). Also known as a Vickrey auction.

**Security:** Tradable claim on the assets of an institution or individual.

**Sell side traders:** Traders who sell side liquidity services, buying or selling when others need to execute transactions. Such traders normally include day traders, market makers, and brokers.

**Semistrong form efficiency:** Scenario where prices reflect all publicly available information.

**Settlement:** Physical or electronic actual delivery of the security and payment involved in a trade.

**Sharpe ratio:** Index of risk-adjusted portfolio performance, calculated as the portfolio's excess return to the riskless rate relative to its standard deviation.

**Short:** (1) To have sold or short sold (2) position that obligates or enables the investor or contract participant to sell a given or underlying asset on the expiration or settlement date of a derivative contract.

**Short sell:** To sell a security without actually owning it. Normally requires its purchase at a later date and may involve borrowing the security from another investor first, returning it when it is repurchased at a later date.

**Simple time slicing:** Order is split up and sent to markets at regular time intervals.

**Slippage:** Unwanted price impact as a trader's buy pressure forces the price up or his sell pressure forces the price down.

**Speculate:** To take a position of risk based on a forecast of the direction of a security price change.

**Speculator:** Trader who speculates.

**Sponsored access:** Where brokers loan their market participation identification numbers (MPIDs) to high-frequency trading traders, enabling them to gain faster, direct access to markets by bypassing the broker's trading systems.

**Spoofing:** Placing a quote that is intended to be canceled prior to execution.

**Spot rates:** Interest rates on loans originating at time zero or now.

**Spot transaction:** Occurs at the time of the agreement to make the exchange.

**Spread:** The difference between the best offer and bid prices.

**Stat-arb:** See Statistical arbitrage.

**Statistical arbitrage (stat-arb):** Strategies that seek to exploit mispricing of one or more assets based on their expected values. By using statistical methods, the arbitrageur takes positions in large numbers of trades, expecting to gain from expected mispricing through the law of large numbers.

**Stealth trading:** Trading with an effort to remain hidden or to hide intentions, often by spreading trades to different markets and at different times.

**Stochastic process:** A sequence of random variables $x_t$ indexed by time $t$. In other words, a stochastic process is a random series of values $x_t$ sequenced over time.

**Stop order:** Instructs the broker to place the buy order once the price has risen above a given level or place the sell order once the price of the security has fallen beneath a given level. The stop order triggers an order execution.

**Stop limit sell order:** Authorizes the broker to initiate the sell order once its price drops to the stop trigger, but only if the limit price can be realized for the sale.

**Straddle:** A combination of put and call options with identical exercise prices on the same underlying asset.

**Strike price:** See striking price.

**Striking price:** Price at which an option can be exercised; that is, the price that the call owner has the right to pay for the underlying asset or put owner has the right to sell the underlying asset for. Also called exercise price.

**Strong form efficiency:** Scenario where prices fully reflect all information, public or private.

**Stub quotes:** Quotes submitted with no intention of execution, often for the purpose of quote stuffing.

**Strip:** Single payment fixed income instrument issued through the U.S. Treasury's Separate Trading of Registered Interest and Principle Securities (STRIPS) program.

**Submartingale process:** A Markov process whose increments have expected value greater than 0.

**Supermartingale process:** A Markov process whose increments have expected value less than 0.

**Sunshine trading:** Occurs when traders announce their intentions, perhaps in an effort to increase the competition to act as counterparties on the same transactions, but when additional competition on the same side of the transaction is either unexpected or won't hurt the trader.

**Super Display Book System (SBDK):** The New York Stock Exchange ECN, order routing, and processing system.

**SuperMontage:** Nasdaq's automated exchange.

**Swap contract:** Instrument that provides for the exchange of cash flows associated with one asset, rate, or index for the cash flows associated with another asset, rate, or index.

**Tailgating:** A form of parasitic trading where the broker places an order immediately after the client's order.

**Tâtonnement:** A preliminary auction process to determine supply and demand levels at various prices.

**Technical analysis:** Concerned with finding situations where historical price sequences can be used to forecast price movements.

**Term structure of interest rates:** How interest rates on debt securities vary with respect to varying dates of maturity on the debt.

**Theta:** Sensitivity of an option's price to changes in the option's time to expiry.

**Tick:** The smallest unit of price change between successive transactions, 0.01 in some markets; 1/16, 1/8, or 1/4 in others.

**Time weighted average return:** Geometric mean of daily returns accounting for fund inflows and outflows.

**Trade:** A security transaction that creates a portfolio position based on an investment decision.

**Trade through:** The execution of an NMS stock trade at a price inferior to a protected quotation for that stock.

**Trade-through rule:** See Order protection rule.

**Trader:** Security market participant who trades, competing with others to generate profits, seeking compatible counterparties in trade, and seeking superior order placement and timing.

**Trading arcade:** Sometimes referred to as a proprietary trading firm or prop shop, is a location for traders to work and trade from.

**Trading floor broker:** NYSE member who work orders on behalf of clients.

**Trading rebate:** Payment for order flow.

**Transfer agent:** Processes orders to purchase and redeem a given security and maintains investor records.

**Transparency:** The extent to which a market quickly disseminates high-quality information to the public.

**Treasury bill:** Short-term zero coupon note issued by the U.S. Treasury. Considered to be relatively free of risk.

**Treasury bond:** Long-term (2 to 30 years) coupon-bearing debt instrument issued by the U.S. Treasury. Considered to be relatively free of default risk.

**Treasury note:** Intermediate-term (2 to 8 years) coupon-bearing debt instrument issued by the U.S. Treasury. Considered to be relatively free of default risk.

**Treynor ratio:** Index of risk-adjusted portfolio performance, calculated as the portfolio's excess return to the riskless rate relative to its beta.

**Triangular arbitrage:** Currency arbitrage transactions intended to exploit relative price differences between one currency and two other currencies.

**Underlying asset:** Security or asset on which an option is written.

**Unit investment trust:** An entity that invests its funds in some portfolio of securities when it is established and does not normally rebalance its portfolio. The shares of the trust are often publicly traded.

**Upstairs markets:** Markets where institutions trade securities directly among themselves. Also called fourth markets.

**Vega:** Sensitivity of an option's price to changes in the underlying security's standard deviation of returns.

**Venture capital (VC):** An alternative management vehicle that invests capital in private portfolio companies in development stages that have strong potential for rapid growth.

**Vickrey auction:** See Second-price sealed-bid auction.

**Volume weighted average price (VWAP):** The ratio of the total value traded to total volume traded over a given time horizon.

**VWAP:** See volume weighted average price.

**Walrasian auction:** A simultaneous auction where each buyer submits to the auctioneer his demand and each seller submits his supply for a given security at every possible price.

**Wash sales:** Transactions intended to create the appearance of sales where, in effect, no sales actually take place.

**Weak form efficiency:** Scenario where security prices reflect all information regarding historical prices.

**Winner's curse:** Problem occurring when the winning bidder bids the most, and is the most likely to have bid too much for the auctioned object.

**Term structure of interest rates:** How interest rates on debt securities vary with respect to varying dates of maturity on the debt.

**Yield curve:** Plotting of bond yields or market interest rates with respect to terms to maturity.

**Yield to maturity:** The internal rate of return for a bond.

**Zero coupon bond:** A bond that makes no interest payments.

**Zero cost collar:** A collar where the time zero proceeds from the call sale exactly offsets the cost of the put purchase. The options' exercise prices are set so that the call and the put have the same values.

# End-of-Chapter Exercise Solutions

## CHAPTER 1

1. Vigorous competition among professional short-term traders can itself lead to very important benefits for long-term investors, including narrower spreads and greater depth.
2. First, recall the definition of trading: "a security transaction that creates a portfolio position based on an investment decision." While the trade might indeed result from a decision to speculate, it might also result from a long-term investment decision or decisions to hedge or engage in arbitrage. While traders can be speculators who focus on profits derived from price changes, traders can also be arbitrageurs who focus on price discrepancies and hedgers who seek to control risk. Traders might even be executing transactions as an agent on a long-term investor's account, acting as a broker for that investor.
3. You should bid more than \$200, say, \$1000, because you will be able to obtain the object for \$10, the second-highest bid. No one will be willing to bid against you for more than \$200 to obtain the object for \$1000. Thus, it is important for second-price auction bids to be sealed.
4. **a.** $E[x_{MAX}] = 500{,}000 + (1{,}000{,}000 - 500{,}000) \times 2/(2+1) = 833{,}333$
   $E[x_{MIN}] = 500{,}000 + (1{,}000{,}000 - 500{,}000)/(2+1) = 666{,}666$, which is the second-highest bid.

   **b.** $E[x_{MAX}] = 500{,}000 + (1{,}000{,}000 - 500{,}000) \times 3/(3+1) = 875{,}000$
   $E[x_{MIN}] = 500{,}000 + (1{,}000{,}000 - 500{,}000)/(3+1) = 625{,}000$
   With only three draws from the distribution, the second highest bid is the mean of the highest and the lowest.
   $E[x_{2nd\ highest}] = 500{,}000 + (1{,}000{,}000 - 500{,}000) \times 2/(3+1) = 750{,}000$, which is the second-highest bid.

   **c.** $E[x_{MAX}] = 500{,}000 + (1{,}000{,}000 - 500{,}000) \times 999/(999+1) = 999{,}500$
   $E[x_{MIN}] = 500{,}000 + (1{,}000{,}000 - 500{,}000)/(999+1) = 500{,}500$
   The second-highest bid expected value is $E[x_{MAX}] - (x_2 - x_1)/(n+1)$
   $E[x_{2nd\ highest}] = 999{,}500 - (1{,}000{,}000 - 500{,}000)/(999+1) = 999{,}000$, which is the second-highest bid. Note that the second-highest bid increases as the number of bidders increases.

5. Obviously, the Treasury wants to sell as many bills as possible at the lowest possible prices. The bid-to-cover ratio in this illustration is \$34 billion/\$20 billion = 1.7. First, the \$2.5 billion in noncompetitive bids will be subtracted from the \$20 billion total to determine the stop-out price. Bids will be satisfied from the lowest yield (highest price) until \$17.5 billion in bills have been allocated to the competitive bidders. The stop-out price will be at a yield of 5.30% and all winners (Citigroup, Merrill Lynch, UBS, Deutsche Bank, noncompeting bidders) will pay this same price. Noncompeting bidders will be allocated \$2.5 billion and Deutsche Bank will be allocated \$5.5 billion.
6. **a.** The cost of placing each bid is its amount. The bidder that pays the most to place a bid receives the auctioned object. For example, the lobbyist that contributes the most has influence and the fans waiting for rock concert tickets receive them. The losers incur the costs of their bids, but receive nothing. In the case of the politician, all contributions are realized as revenue, not just the winning lobbyist's contributions. In the case of the \$1 bill, suppose one bidder opens with a bid for \$0.01. The second counters with a bid for \$0.02. It may seem reasonable for each of them to continue increasing their bids to a maximum of \$1. However, if the losing bid is \$0.99, it may seem reasonable to increase the bid to \$1.01. Any losing bid represents a sunk cost. To avoid the sunk cost, the bid has to be raised. Essentially, such an auction can be thought of as a war of attrition, where all but one bidder eventually realizes that he is better off abandoning his sunk cost and the winning bidder might end up paying far more for the auctioned item than it's worth.

   **b.** Essentially, from the perspective of the bidders, PennyCave offers an all-pay auction, or something quite close to it. Imagine that their auction results in a winner and a set of losers. Suppose that an object, worth \$100 ultimately sells for \$50, with bids starting at \$0 and increasing in \$0.01 increments until it reached a high of \$50. Assume that each bid costs \$1 to place. Although the \$100 object is obtained by the winning bidder for only \$50, the seller (who is also the auctioneer) receives $((50-0)/0.01 \times \$1) = \$5000$ in bidding fees, or \$5050 total. If, for example, there were only two bidders, the loser would have paid approximately \$2500 in bidding fees to receive nothing, while the winner would have paid \$2550 for the object worth \$100. Of course, this assumes naïve bidding strategies and no collusion on the parts of all bidders, but the outcome in this scenario could have been much worse, with bidding exceeding the value of the auctioned item as bidders seek to avoid losing sunk bidding costs. Keeping bid increments small (\$0.01) increases the number of bids placed in the auction. The auctioneer expects to earn more revenue from the bid activity than from the winning bid itself; it seeks to maximize the number of auction bids.
7. This answer depends on how many shares are being traded and applies only to a prospective purchaser of these shares. With respect to this particular investor's trade, in Market A, the investor will obtain 25,000 shares for \$100.00. The final price remains at \$50.00. In Market B, the investor will obtain 10,000 shares for \$100.00, 10,000 for \$100.01 and 5,000 for \$100.03. The final price in Market B rises to \$50.03, more than Market A. Thus, with respect to this order, Market B has less depth than Market A. However, this might not be the case for certain larger orders or even certain smaller orders.

# CHAPTER 2

1. a. The specialist system was intended to maintain a continuous, orderly, and liquid market for investors. Participants in a trading crowd on the NYSE trading floor are expected to contribute to this effort. Personal contact with each other enables the specialist and floor brokers and traders to better know each other and establish working relationships and trust.
   b. The NYSE was a very old exchange with well-established practices that worked very well over the years. In many respects, it is more expensive to change a way of doing business to make it more efficient than it is to create a new one without any history. In addition, the exchange was owned by its members, who had invested their capital and careers into working on the floor of the exchange. It is very difficult to induce members with such heavy investments in this manner of doing business to give up such a large investment.
2. A limit order sets an upper price for a purchase or a lower price limit for a sell, preventing the broker from paying more or accepting less for the security. A stop order instructs the broker to place the buy order once the price has risen above a given level or place the sell order once the price of the security has fallen beneath a given level. The limit order restricts the price; the stop order triggers the order execution.
3. This stop-limit order triggers the buy once the price rises to 50, but is executed only if the stock can be purchased for no more than 50.10. Stop orders to buy are often placed when the investor wants to buy the stock on upward price momentum, but the limit is typically placed when the investor wants protection from paying more than she wants for the stock.
4. a. Yes; more francs will be required to purchase a dollar: 2.5 rather than 2 now
   b. No; fewer dollars will be required to purchase a franc: 0.4 rather than 0.5 now
   c. The percentage revaluation (devaluation) of francs relative to dollars is determined: $\%\text{reval} = [(S_1 - S_0) \div S_0] = [(0.4 - 0.5) \div 0.5] \times 100 = -20\%$
   d. The percentage revaluation of the dollar in terms of francs is 25%: $\%\text{reval} = [(2.5\text{-}2) \div 2] \times 100 = +25\%$
5. a. The value of \$1 is equal to the value of £.6. Thus, the value of £1 must be \$1/0.6 = \$1.6667. Since the value of \$1 is ¥108, the value of £1 must be 1.6667 × ¥108 = ¥180. Thus, we could have solved as follows: £1 = (\$1 ÷ 0.6) × ¥108 = ¥180.
   b. The value of \$1 is equal to the value of ¥108. Thus, the value of ¥1 must be \$1/108 = \$0.0092593. Since the value of £1 is \$1.6667, the value of ¥1 must be 1 ÷ (1.6667 × 108) = £.0055556. Thus, we could have solved as follows: ¥1 = 1 ÷ (1/0.6 × ¥108) = £0.0055556.
   c. \$1500 = £.6 × 1500 = £900; \$1500 = ¥108 × 1500 = ¥162,000.

# CHAPTER 3

1. First, the order can be parsed/sliced and distributed a number of ways to a number of markets. Slices of the order can be submitted to exchange or OTC markets, and broken

into small quantities during the day. Algorithms can be used to efficiently slice the order and to minimize the transparency and price impact of the orders. Pieces of the order can be shopped or submitted through other brokers and through other markets, including crossing networks and other block trading facilities. Finally, the dealer can use its own capital to take up any unsold shares by the end of the day.

**2. a.** First, total the transactions costs $B$ and set the derivative of total transaction costs with respect to the number of slices equal to zero and solve for $X$:

$$B = nF + nv\left(\frac{X}{n}\right)^m = 10n + .0001\frac{500,000^2}{n} = 10n + 25,000,000n^{-1}$$

$$\frac{dB}{dn} = \frac{d\left[nF + nv\left(\frac{X}{n}\right)^m\right]}{dn} = F - mv\frac{X^m}{n^m} = 10 - 2(.0001)\frac{500,000^2}{n^2} = 10 - \frac{50,000,000}{n^2} = 0$$

$$n = \sqrt[m]{\frac{mvX^m}{F}} = \sqrt{\frac{2(.0001)\cdot 500,000^2}{10}} = 2,236$$

Thus, we find that the optimal number of slices or transactions is $n = 2236$, with $X/n$, the size of each transaction equal to 500,000/2236 = 224. One note here: First, noninteger numbers of transactions should probably be prohibited; hence, we have rounded our figures.

**b.** Total slippage costs equal $nv(X/n)^m = 0.2236 \times 224^2 =$ \$11,180. Note that fixed administrative transactions costs total to \$22,360 = 2236 × 10 (again, figures are rounded). Total trading costs are 33,540.

**c.** First, we write the total slippage cost function as $n \times B/n$ as follows:

$$B = nrn^s + nv\left(\frac{X}{n}\right)^m = rn^{s+1} + nv\left(\frac{X}{n}\right)^m = .1n^{1.5}$$

$$+ .0001\frac{500,000^2}{n} = .1n^{1.5} + 25,000,000n^{-1}$$

Next, we solve for $n$, the optimal number of order slices to execute as follows:

$$\frac{dB}{dn} = \frac{d\left[nrn^s + nv\left(\frac{X}{n}\right)^m\right]}{dn} = r(s+1)n^s - mv\frac{X^m}{n^m} = .15n^{.5} - \frac{50,000,000}{n^2} = 0$$

Unfortunately, solving for $n$ requires substitution. We substitute and iterate to find that $n = 1944$. Since $X = 500,000$, the optimal order size is 500,000/193 = 257 (allow for rounding to obtain integer values).

**3. a.** Beagle can observe slice sizes only. Based on its market impact model, these individual execution sizes $c = 214 = X/n$ do not reveal either $X$ or $n$. We need to find $n$ to solve for $X$. Beagle cannot observe the number of orders $n$ until the purchase program is complete; therefore it cannot infer total or latent demand for the stock. Optimal slice or execution size will not vary with the size of the total demand with the given slippage cost function.

**b.** Based on its own revised market impact function, Beagle will assume that the total slippage for the stock purchase program is determined from the following:

$$B = nrn^s + nv\left(\frac{X}{n}\right)^m = rn^{s+1} + nv\left(\frac{X}{n}\right)^m = .1n^{1.5} + .0001\frac{X^2}{n} = .1n^{1.5} + .0001X^2n^{-1}$$

Total slippage is minimized when the derivative of the market impact function $B$ is minimized with respect to $n$. Thus, we will find and set equal to zero the derivative of $B$ with respect to $n$:

$$\frac{dB}{dn} = \frac{d\left[nrn^s + nv\left(\frac{X}{n}\right)^m\right]}{dn} = r(s+1)n^s - mv\frac{X^m}{n^m} = .15n^{.5} - .0002 \cdot \frac{X^2}{n^2} = 0$$

Since slices or orders of size 214 shares were observed by Beagle, who will assume that these slices are of optimal size, $c = X/n = 214$. Now, we can solve for $n$ in the following to obtain the optimal number of orders in this purchase program:

$$.15n^{.5} - .0002.214^2 = 0$$

$$\mathrm{n} = \left(\frac{\left(\frac{\mathrm{X}}{\mathrm{n}}\right)^{\mathrm{m}} \cdot \mathrm{mv}}{\mathrm{r} \cdot (1+s)}\right)^{1/s} = \left(\frac{.0002(214)^2}{.15}\right)^2 = 3,728$$

Answers might vary from 3720 to 3735 based on rounding to integer values. Thus, 3728 slices with 214 shares each indicates a total or latent demand for $3{,}728 \times 214 = 797{,}896$ shares, again, subject to rounding errors.

4. Arnuk and Saluzzi (2009) note that it "appears that 'fairness' and the equalization of market data speed among co-located firms is an important 'must' for the exchanges, but not so when it comes to all other institutional and retail investors." The implication here is that exchanges providing co-location facilities and equal amounts of connecting cable to all co-location participants reflects some degree of hypocrisy. Does this practice mean that exchanges know that they are providing, for a fee, opportunities for their tenants to obtain advance quote and trading information?
5. In general, flash orders are communicated to certain market participants and either executed immediately or withdrawn immediately after communication. Immediate or cancel orders are generally displayed to the general public.
6. Flash orders can give HFTs the order flow information that they need to front run large incoming orders.

## CHAPTER 4

1. While even insiders do not have perfect information concerning the stock valuation of their companies, their information is likely to be superior to that of the general public. If insiders are able to buy and sell shares on the basis of their inside information, they

will convey this information to the general public through their trading activity and resulting price changes. The general public will buy and sell stock to reflect this information. Thus, share prices will more quickly and accurately reflect the best and most recent information relevant to the pricing of shares. Markets will more closely resemble the theoretical strong-form efficient market where prices fully reflect all information.

2. Insider trading is not specifically mentioned in this rule. This rule is rather broad in its scope, and provides regulatory authorities and firm operating and compliance officers significant judgment in ensuring that anti-fraud objectives are being fulfilled.
3. Regulations can apply only to members who voluntarily join the regulated body. Regulations will not help entities (e.g., the general public) damaged by contracts in markets if they are not participants of the regulated body. Private regulators might be subject to more conflicts of interest than their government counterparts. Self-regulation can easily be created to serve as barriers to entry in the market, reducing competition. Private regulators do not have as much power to enforce regulations as does a government. For example, private regulators cannot imprison their members or enforce subpoena power.
4. The Securities Act of 1933 does not contain merit tests (e.g., tests as to whether the securities are valuable) as did earlier "blue skies" legislation, but instead provides for full disclosure of all material facts. This "sunlight theory of regulation" is based on the assumption that if investors are provided with all necessary and relevant information, they will make wise investment decisions. Presumably, firms that are forced to provide this information will pay attention to the merits of the securities that they sell.
5. **a.** Rules based: Do not exceed 55 miles per hour. Principles based: Do not drive faster than is necessary to maintain safety and fuel economy.
   **b.** In setting speed limits, rules-based regulations might need to specifically distinguish between driving conditions, road conditions, light conditions, vehicle type, driver experience, visibility, road surface conditions, traffic, and so on. Such conditions complicate the rule-setting process, and lead to more complicated sets of rules.
   **c.** Enforcement officers and traffic-court judges will need to interpret vague rules contingent on situations and conditions, and likely leave it to case law or drivers themselves to determine speed levels that are safe.

# CHAPTER 5

1. Perhaps there are many reasons for this, but the most relevant to this chapter is that members of the tribal society share in the catch of fish whereas modern fishermen compete against one another to harvest the catch.
2. Kyle's informed demand function $x$ is as follows:

$$x = \alpha + \beta v = -\frac{E[v]}{\sqrt{\frac{\Sigma_0}{\sigma_u^2}}} + \frac{v}{\sqrt{\frac{\Sigma_0}{\sigma_u^2}}}$$

where $\beta = 1/\sqrt{\frac{\Sigma_0}{\sigma_u^2}}$ and the expected value or price of the asset is $E[v] = p_0$. Thus, we can rewrite the informed trader's demand function as a function of the informed trader's per share profit as:

$$x = -\frac{E[v]}{\sqrt{\frac{\Sigma_0}{\sigma_u^2}}} + \frac{v}{\sqrt{\frac{\Sigma_0}{\sigma_u^2}}} = \beta(v - p_0).$$

**3. a.** Given:

$$v = 100; \sum_0 = 60; \sigma_u^2 = 10,000; E[v] = 100$$

$$x = -\frac{\mathrm{E[v]}}{\sqrt{\frac{\Sigma_0}{\sigma_u^2}}} + \frac{v}{\sqrt{\frac{\Sigma_0}{\sigma_u^2}}} = -\frac{100}{\sqrt{\frac{60}{10{,}000}}} + \frac{100}{\sqrt{\frac{60}{10{,}000}}} = 0$$

That is, if the private information does not change the informed trader's expected value of the stock from the market value, he will not trade. His demand for the stock at the current price is zero.

**b.** Given:

$$v = 100; \sum_0 = 60; \sigma_u^2 = 10,000; E[v] = 90$$

$$x = -\frac{\mathrm{E[v]}}{\sqrt{\frac{\Sigma_0}{\sigma_u^2}}} + \frac{v}{\sqrt{\frac{\Sigma_0}{\sigma_u^2}}} = -\frac{90}{\sqrt{\frac{60}{10{,}000}}} + \frac{100}{\sqrt{\frac{60}{10{,}000}}} = \frac{10}{.07746} = 129.1$$

That is, the private information increases informed demand for the stock by or to 129.1 shares.

**c.** Given $\sum_0 = 60$, and $\sigma_u^2 = 10,000, E[\pi] = \sqrt{\sum_0 \sigma_u^2} = 774.60$, or 6 per share.

**d.** Assume that $E[v] = 90, \sum_0 = 60, \sigma_u^2 = 10,000, x = 129.1$, and $u = 0$.
First, we will calculate $\alpha$ and $\beta$:

$$\alpha = -\frac{E[v]}{\sqrt{\frac{\Sigma_0}{\sigma_u^2}}} = -\frac{90}{\sqrt{\frac{60}{10{,}000}}} = -1161.895$$

$$\beta = \frac{1}{\sqrt{\frac{\Sigma_0}{\sigma_u^2}}} = \frac{1}{\sqrt{\frac{60}{10{,}000}}} = 12.91$$

Next, we calculate the price set by the dealer:

$$p = E[v] + \left[\frac{\beta\Sigma_0}{\beta^2\Sigma_0 + \sigma_u^2}\right][x + u - \alpha - \beta E[v]]$$

$$= 90 + \left[\frac{12.91 \cdot 60}{12.91^2 \cdot 60 + 10,000}\right][129.1 + 0 + 1161.895 - 12.91 \cdot 90]$$

$$= 90 + .0387 \cdot 129.1 = 95$$

Similarly, since the dealer sets the price at $p = \mu + \lambda(x + u) = E[v] + \lambda(x + u)$, and $\lambda$ is calculated as follows:

$$\lambda = \frac{1}{2}\sqrt{\frac{\Sigma_0}{\sigma_u^2}} = \frac{1}{2}\sqrt{\frac{60}{10,000}} = .0387$$

The dealer sets the stock price at $p = 90 + 0.0387(129.1 + 0) = 95$ based on the total demand for shares. Ultimately, the informed trader makes 5 per share buying from the dealer and the dealer makes 5 per share by buying shares from uninformed traders who pay 95 for shares that are known to informed traders to be worth 100. The dealer loses 5 per share relative to the 100 intrinsic value of the stock by selling to informed traders at 95.

4. The Kyle model suggests that informed traders have two ways to attempt to exploit their informational advantage. First, informed traders can choose to trade in large volume, earning small returns on large transactions as dealers adjust their spreads to reflect the suspected informed trader order volume. Second, informed traders could choose to trade in small volume, earning large returns on small transactions since dealers will not suspect informed trader presence. To avoid dealer spread adjustment, informed traders will tend to avoid large transactions. But many small transactions will also alert dealers. Thus, informed traders are rather likely to camouflage themselves by neither executing large transactions nor large numbers of transactions, and medium sized transactions are more likely to be undertaken by informed traders, and ultimately move markets.
5. Unbalanced order arrivals indicate the presence or likelihood of informed trader orders. This causes the dealer to bias the bid downwards or offer upwards to reflect the possibility of increased informed trader activity.
6. Solve as follows: $Pa - Pb = \pi(P_H - P_L)$; $14.1 - 12.9 = \pi(3)$; $\pi = 0.4$.
7. Transactions costs tend to increase dealer spreads. In the absence of new information, execution prices often tend to bounce between bid and ask prices. For example, after a trade at the bid price, the next trade would be either at the same price or at the offer. After a trade at the offer, the next trade would be either at the same price or the bid. That is, price changes would tend to be either zero or at the opposite side of the spread. Thus, execution prices will tend to be either unchanged or to change in the opposite direction from the most recent transaction. Thus, transactions costs tend to induce negative serial correlation in asset prices.
8. In the event of a transaction at the bid, the risk-averse dealer would adjust quotes to promote inventory equilibrating trades. For example, after a transaction at the bid (which implies that the dealer purchased additional securities), both bid and ask quotes would fall so that the dealer would be able to liquidate this additional inventory, or at least not as readily increase it. That is, the dealer would want to discourage subsequent sales and to encourage purchases by traders so as to not significantly imbalance her portfolio. Similarly, after a transaction at the offer (which implies that the dealer sold additional securities), both bid and ask quotes would rise so that the dealer would be able to more easily purchase or replenish recently sold inventory, or at least not as readily further decrease it. That is, the dealer would want

to discourage subsequent purchases and to encourage sales by traders. Over time, transactions prices and dealer quotes would tend to exhibit negative serial correlation.

9. **a.** If the trader's \$10.01 limit order executes, and if the stock price continues to decline, he will have to option to sell his shares to the institutional investor at \$10.00, losing \$0.01 per share. However, if the trader's \$10.01 limit order executes, and the stock price rebounds, the trader has unlimited profit potential.
   **b.** The institutional investor's large limit order has provided a put option to the trader. First, if the stock price drops to \$10.01 and eventually rebounds, the institutional investor will lose out on the trade (the trader took it at the higher limit) and not profit from the increase. Alternatively, the stock price can drop to \$10.00 and continue to drop, meaning that the institutional investor purchases the stock for \$10.00 (200,000 shares from the trader should he choose to sell) and loses money on the transaction.
10. Models discussed in this chapter shed light on this relationship between the dealer spread and security risk:
    - In the Stoll (1978) model, increased dealer spreads will result from increased security uncertainty. Increased security uncertainty increases (decreases) the Arrow-Pratt risk premium associated with the security sales (purchase) price due to the dealer's risk aversion, as indicated by her ARA (absolute risk aversion coefficient). Increased uncertainty might also affect inventory size, which in itself will not affect the size of the spread (the difference between bids and offers), but will affect the levels of these quotes.
    - In the Glosten and Milgrom (1985) model, the spread is a function of the likelihood that there exists an informed trader in the market and the uncertainty in the value of the traded asset. The greater the uncertainty in the value of the traded asset, and the greater the likelihood that a trade has originated with an informed trader, the greater will be the spread. Thus, increased spreads result from asymmetric information availability and the associated adverse selection problem.
    - In the Copeland and Galai (1983) model, an options pricing model can be used to value the implied put and the implied call associated with the dealer spread. The values of both options increase as uncertainty increases. The implied premium associated with this dealer spread is paid by liquidity traders who trade without information. Thus, in the Copeland and Galai option-based model, the spread widens as the uncertainty of the security price increases.
    - The Demsetz (1969) argument might imply the Stoll (1978), Glosten and Milgrom (1985), and Copeland and Galai (1983) models as well.

# CHAPTER 6

1. **a.** $\overline{R}_R = 0.062$
   $\overline{R}_B = 0.106$
   $\overline{R}_M = 0.098$
   **b.** $\sigma_R^2 = 0.000696$ (Remember to convert returns to percentages.)
   $\sigma_B^2 = 0.008824$ (Square roots of these variances are standard deviations)
   $\sigma_M^2 = 0.001576$

c. Assuming variance and correlation stability, the forecasted values would be the same as the historical values in parts a and b.

2. a. Since probabilities must sum to 1, the probability must equal 0.15.
   b. First, note that there is a 0.25 probability that the return will be 0.05 (0.10 + 0.05 + 0.10) and 0.20 and 0.55 probabilities that the return will be 0.15. Thus, the expected return is $0.05 \times .25 + 0.10 \times 0.20 + 0.15 \times 0.55 = 0.115$. The variance is $0.25 \times (0.05 - 0.115)^2 + 0.20 \times (0.10 - 0.115)^2 + 0.55 \times (0.15 - 0.115)^2 = 0.001775$, which implies a standard deviation equal to 0.04213.

3. Standardize returns by standard deviations and consult "z" tables: $(R_i - E[R])/\sigma = z$. Only use positive values for $z$ here.
   a. $(0.05 - 0.15)/.10 = z(\text{low}) = 1$; $(0.25\text{-}0.15)/.10 = z(\text{high}) = 1$
   From the z table (Table A.1 on page 368), we see that the probability that the security's return will fall between 0.05 and 0.15 is 0.34. The value 0.34 is also the probability that the security's return will fall between 0.15 and 0.25. Therefore, the probability that the security's return will fall between 0.05 and 0.25 is 0.68.
   b. From Table A.1 on page 368, we see that the probability is 0.34.
   c. 0.16
   d. 0.0668

4. Simply reduce the standard deviations in the z scores in Problem 3 to 0.05.
   a. 0.95
   b. 0.47
   c. 0.0228
   d. 0.0013

5. a. The traditional sample daily variance estimator for this stock based on these returns equals 0.00317.
   b. The monthly variance would be $0.095 = 0.00317 \times 30$.
   c. The Parkinson measure results in a variance estimate equal to 0.022465:

$$\sigma_p^2 = .361 \cdot \left[\ln\left(\frac{HI}{LO}\right)\right]^2 = .361 \cdot \left[\ln\left(\frac{38.5}{30}\right)\right]^2 = .022465$$

6. a. First, calculate returns as follows:

| | Company X | Company Y | Company Z |
|---|---|---|---|
| Date | Return | Return | Return |
| 1/09 | – | – | – |
| 1/10 | 0 | 0 | 0.00207 |
| 1/11 | 0.00249 | 0.00625 | −0.00413 |
| 1/12 | 0 | 0.00621 | −0.00207 |
| 1/13 | 0.00248 | 0.00617 | −0.00207 |
| 1/14 | −0.00248 | 0 | 0.00208 |
| 1/15 | 0.03980 | 0.04907 | 0.04158 |

| | | | |
|---|---|---|---|
| 1/16 | 0.00239 | −0.00584 | −0.02994 |
| 1/17 | −0.00238 | 0.00588 | 0 |
| 1/18 | 0.00239 | 0.00584 | 0.00205 |
| 1/19 | 0.00238 | −0.00581 | 0 |
| 1/20 | −0.00238 | 0.00584 | 0 |

**b., c.**

| Stock | Average Return | Standard Deviation |
|---|---|---|
| X | 0.004064 | 0.011479 |
| Y | 0.006693 | 0.014150 |
| Z | 0.000869 | 0.015537 |

**7.** The variance estimate is computed as follows:

$$\sigma_p^2 = .361 \cdot \left[\ln\left(\frac{HI}{LO}\right)\right]^2 = .361 \cdot \left[\ln\left(\frac{50}{25}\right)\right]^2 = .173444$$

The standard deviation is the square root of this value, or 0.416466.

**8.** If investors have used the Black-Scholes options pricing model to evaluate this call, the following should hold:

$8.20 = 75 \times N(d_1) - 80 \times e^{-0.1 \times 0.5} \times N(d_2)$

$d_1 = \{\ln(75/80) + (0.1 + 0.5\sigma^2) \times 0.5\} \div \sigma\sqrt{0.5}$

$d_2 = d_1 - \sigma\sqrt{0.5}$

Thus, we wish to solve the above system of equations for $\sigma$. There exists no closed form solution for $\sigma$. Thus, we will substitute and iterate to search for a solution. We first arbitrarily select $\sigma_1 = .35$. We find that this estimate for sigma results in a value of 6.90 for $c_0$. Since this call price is less than the market value 8.20, we know that $\sigma$ is larger than 0.35. Thus, we try a larger value for $\sigma$, repeating the process until finding that $\sigma = 0.411466$. We have estimated the implied value with a greater degree of accuracy than is needed for most applications.

**9.** Implied volatilities are given as follows:

**a.** $X = 40$; $\sigma = 0.2579$
**b.** $X = 45$; $\sigma = 0.3312$
**c.** $X = 50$; $\sigma = 0.2851$
**d.** $X = 55$; $\sigma = 0.2715$
**e.** $X = 60$; $\sigma = 0.2704$

These values are obtained through a process of substitution and iteration. That is, readers should select trial values for $\sigma$ to substitute into the Black-Scholes formula, and then compute the trial call value. A closer trial value for the call to the actual market price leads to a closer computed volatility to its Black-Scholes implied value. Each reader will probably use a process that will differ at least slightly from those used by others.

# CHAPTER 7

1. With matrices, the weights are found by solving for $b$ as follows:

$$\begin{bmatrix} 50 & 80 & 110 \\ 50 & 80 & 1110 \\ 1050 & 1080 & 0 \end{bmatrix} \begin{bmatrix} \#_A \\ \#_B \\ \#_C \end{bmatrix} = \begin{bmatrix} 30 \\ 30 \\ 1030 \end{bmatrix}$$

$$\mathbf{CF} \quad \times \; \mathbf{b} \; = \; \mathbf{p_0}$$

Alternatively, without matrices, we set up and solve the following system:
$50b_A + 80b_B + 110b_C = 30$
$50b_A + 80b_B + 1110b_C = 30$
$1050b_A + 1080b_B = 1030$
First, subtract the second equation from the first equation. We obtain the equation: $1000b_C = 0$. Next, solve for $b_C$: $b_C = 0$.
Now, substitute $b_C = 0$ in the original second equation:
$50b_A + 80b_B = 30$
Now, we have an equation with two unknowns. Combine with our original third equation:
$50b_A + 80b_B = 30$
$1050b_A + 1080b_B = 1030$
Now, solve this $2 \times 2$ system for $b_A$ and $b_B$. First, solve the first equation for $b_A$:
$50b_A = 30 - 80b_B$
$b_A = 0.6 - 1.6b_B$. Divide both sides by 50.
Now, substitute this equation for $b_A$ in the second equation:
$1050(0.6 - 1.6b_B) + 1080b_B = 1030$
Simplify by combining similar terms:
$600b_B = -400$
Now, we know $b_B$:
$b_B = -0.666666$
We substitute $b_B$ into our original third equation to obtain $b_A$:
$1050b_A + 1080 \times -0.666666 = 1030$
Finally, we obtain $b_A$:
$b_A = 1.666666$
We find that $b_A = 1.666666$, $b_B = -0.666666$, and that $b_C = 0$. This means that bond $D$ is replicated by a portfolio consisting of 1.666666 of bond $A$ and −0.666666 of bond $B$.

2. a. Its annual interest payments:
$i_y = \text{Int}/F$
$\text{Int} = i_y(F); = (0.12)(1000) = \$120$

**b.** Its current yield: $cy = \text{Int}/P_0 = 120/1200 = 0.10$
**c.** Through substitution, we find yield to maturity to be 0.04697429 or 4.697429%.
**3. a.** Its annual interest payments: \$120, or \$60 every six months.
**b.** $120 \div 1200 =$ current yield $= 0.10$ or 10%.
**c.** Its yield to maturity $y$ is found by substitution and eventually arriving at:
$-1200 + 60/[1+(y/2)]^1 + 60/[1+(y/2)]^2 + \cdots + 60/[1+(y/2)]^5 + 1060/[1+(y/2)]^6$
$y = 0.0476634$
**4.** The following matrix system may be solved for $b$ to determine exactly how many of each of the bonds are required to satisfy the fund's cash flow requirements:

$$\begin{bmatrix} 1100 & 100 & 110 & 120 \\ 0 & 1100 & 110 & 120 \\ 0 & 0 & 1110 & 120 \\ 0 & 0 & 0 & 1120 \end{bmatrix} \begin{bmatrix} b_1 \\ b_2 \\ b_3 \\ b_4 \end{bmatrix} = \begin{bmatrix} 30,000,000 \\ 15,000,000 \\ 25,000,000 \\ 35,000,000 \end{bmatrix}$$
$$\mathbf{CF} \times \mathbf{b} = \mathbf{P_0}$$

First, we invert matrix **CF** to obtain $\mathbf{CF}^{-1}$:

$$\begin{bmatrix} .000909 & -.000083 & -.00008 & -.000079 \\ 0 & .000909 & -.00009 & -.000087 \\ 0 & 0 & .00090 & -.000096 \\ 0 & 0 & 0 & .000892 \end{bmatrix}$$
$$\mathbf{CF}^{-1}$$

We then post-multiply $\mathbf{CF}^{-1}$ by $\mathbf{P_0}$ to obtain **b**. Alternatively, without matrices, we set up and solve the following system:
$1100b_1 + 100b_2 + 110b_3 + 120b_4 = 30000000$
$1100b_2 + 110\,b_3 + 120b_4 = 15000000$
$1110b_3 + 120b_4 = 25000000$
$1120b_4 = 35000000$
First, solve the fourth equation, we obtain $b_4$:
$b_4 = 31{,}250$
Now, substitute $b_4 = 31{,}250$ in the original third equation:
$1110b_3 + 120 \times 31250 = 25{,}000{,}000$
Solving this equation, we find that $b_3 = 19{,}144.14$. Now, substitute $b_3$, $b_4$ into the original second equation:
$1100b_2 + 110 \times 19{,}144.14 + 120 \times 31{,}250 = 15{,}000{,}000$
Solve this equation. We know that $b_2 = 8312.858$. Substitute $b_2$, $b_3$, $b_4$ into the original first equation:
$1100b_1 + 100 \times 8312.858 + 110 \times 19{,}144.14 + 120 \times 31{,}250 = 30{,}000{,}000$
Finally, we find that $b_1 = 21{,}193.5$. Note that we were able to use the bootstrapping method to solve his system. We find that the purchase of 21,193.5 bonds 1, 8,312.858 bonds 2, 19,144.14 bonds 3, and 31,250 bonds 4 satisfy the insurance company's exact matching requirements.
**5. a.i.** First, find the yield to maturity ($ytm$) of the bond:

$$0 = NPV = \sum_{t=1}^{n} \frac{CF_t}{(1+ytm)^t} - P_0; \quad \text{yield to maturity} = ytm$$

$$0 = NPV = \sum_{t=1}^{n} \frac{1000}{(1+ytm)^1} - 900;\ \text{solve for } ytm$$

$ytm = 0.111$

**a.ii.** Use $ytm$ from part i in the duration formula:

$$Dur = \frac{\sum_{t=1}^{n} t \cdot \frac{CF_t}{(1+ytm)^t}}{P_0}$$

Note: Negative signs are omitted.

$$Dur = \frac{1 \cdot \frac{1000}{1.111}}{900} = Dur = 1 \text{ year}$$

**b.i.**

$$0 = NPV = \sum_{t=1}^{n} \frac{CF_t}{(1+ytm)^t} - P_0 = \frac{1000}{(1=ytm)^t} - 800$$

$ytm = 0.118$

**b.ii.**

$$Dur = \frac{\sum_{t=1}^{n} t \cdot \frac{CF_t}{(1+ytm)^t}}{P_0} = \frac{2 \cdot \frac{1000}{1.118^2}}{800} = 2$$

**c.** $ytm = 0.126;$

$$Dur = \frac{3 \cdot \frac{2000}{(1.126)^3}}{1400} = 3$$

**d.** There are several ways to work this problem. First, consider the cash flows of the portfolio:

$$P_0 = 900 + 800 + 1400 = 3100$$
$$CF_1 = 1000;\ CF_2 = 1000;\ CF_3 = 2000$$

$$0 = NPV = \frac{1000}{(1+ytm)^1} + \frac{1000}{(1+ytm)^2} + \frac{2000}{(1+ytm)^3} - 3100;\ ytm = 0.122$$

$$Dur = \frac{\sum_{t=1}^{n} t \cdot \frac{CF_t}{(1+ytm)^t}}{P_0} = \frac{\frac{1 \cdot 1000}{1.122} + \frac{2 \cdot 1000}{(1.122)^2} + \frac{3 \cdot 2000}{(1.122)^3}}{3100}$$

$Dur = 2.161$ years

Second, note that the portfolio duration is a weighted average of the bond durations:

$(900/3100) \times 1 + (800/3100) \times 2 + (1400/3100) \times 3 = 2.161$

6. The duration of a pure discount bond equals its maturity.
7. a. First, find the bond's *ytm*:

$$0 = NPV = \frac{100}{(1+ytm)^1} + \frac{100}{(1+ytm)^2} + \frac{100+1000}{(1+ytm)^3} - 900; \quad ytm = 0.143$$

Now, use *ytm* to find duration:

$$Dur = \frac{\frac{1 \cdot 100}{1.143} + \frac{2 \cdot 100}{(1.143)^2} + \frac{3 \cdot 1100}{(1.143)^3}}{900} = 2.722$$

b.

$$0 = NPV = \frac{120}{(1+ytm)^1} + \frac{120}{(1+ytm)^2} + \frac{1120}{(1+ytm)^3} - 900; \quad ytm = 0.165$$

$$Dur = \frac{\frac{1 \cdot 120}{1.165} + \frac{2 \cdot 120}{(1.165)^2} + \frac{3 \cdot 1120}{(1.165)^3}}{900} = 2.672$$

c.

$$0 = NPV = \frac{100}{(1+ytm)^1} + \frac{100}{(1+ytm)^2} + \frac{100}{(1+ytm)^3} + \frac{1100}{(1+ytm)^4} - 900$$

$ytm = 0.134$

$$Dur = \frac{\frac{1 \cdot 100}{1.165} + \frac{2 \cdot 100}{(1.165)^2} + \frac{3 \cdot 100}{(1.165)^3} + \frac{4 \cdot 1100}{(1.134)^4}}{900} = 3.456$$

d.

$$0 = NPV = \frac{100}{(1+ytm)^1} + \frac{100}{(1+ytm)^2} + \frac{1100}{(1+ytm)^3} - 800$$

$ytm = 0.194$

$$Dur = \frac{\frac{1 \cdot 100}{1.194} + \frac{2 \cdot 100}{(1.194)^2} + \frac{3 \cdot 1100}{(1.194)^3}}{800} = 2.703$$

8. a. $\%\Delta P_0 = Dur \times \%\Delta(1 + r)$; $\%\Delta P_0 = 2.722 \times 0.10 = 0.2722$
$\%\Delta P_0 = 0.2722$; $\Delta P_0 = 0.2722 \times 900 = 244.98$
The new price is $900 + 244.98 = 1144.98$
b. $\%\Delta P_0 = 2.672 \cdot 0.10 = 0.2622$; $\Delta P_0 = 235.98$; price $= 1135.98$
c. $\%\Delta P_0 = 3.456 \cdot 0.10 = 0.3456$; $\Delta P_0 = 311.04$; price $= 1211.04$
d. $\%\Delta P_0 = 0.2703$; $\Delta P_0 = 216.24$; new price $= 1016.24$

9. $$Dur = 20772 \cdot \frac{900}{3500} + 2.672 \cdot \frac{900}{3500} + 3.456 \cdot \frac{900}{3500} + 2.703 \cdot \frac{800}{3500} = 2.893$$

**10.** Durations and convexities are as follows:

**a.** $Dur = 4.203743015$; Con = 20.31015, calculated as follows:

| Dur A | Con A |
|---|---|
| 92.59259258 | 158.7664481 |
| 171.467764 | 441.0179114 |
| 238.1496722 | 816.6998358 |
| 294.0119409 | 1260.339253 |
| 3743.207581 | 19255.18302 |

Add and then divide by $P_0 = 1079.8542$ to obtain:

| | |
|---|---|
| −4.203743015 | 20.31015527 |

**b.** $Dur = 4.0373493$; Con = 17.86, calculated as follows:

| Dur B | Con B |
|---|---|
| 107.1428571 | 170.8272595 |
| 191.3265306 | 457.5730164 |
| 256.2408892 | 817.0946722 |
| 305.0486776 | 1215.914691 |
| 3177.590392 | 15198.93363 |

Add and then divide by $P_0 = 1000$ to obtain:

| | |
|---|---|
| −4.037349347 | 17.86034327 |

**11. a.** $P_{1A} = 995.7906904 = 1079.8542 - 4.203743 \times [(0.1 - 0.08)/(1.08)] \times 1079.8542$
$P_{1B} = 1072.095524 = 1000 - 4.037349 \times [(0.1 - 0.12)/(1.12)] \times 1000$

**b.** $P_{1A} = 1000.1770910 = 1079.8542 - 4.203743 \cdot [(0.1 - 0.08)/(1.08)] \times 1079.8542 + 0.5 \times 1079.8542 \times 20.3101 \times (0.1 - 0.08)^2$
$P_{1B} = 1075.667592 = 1000 - 4.037349 \times (0.1 - 0.12)/(1.12) \times 1000 + 0.5 \times 1000 \times 17.86 \times (0.1 - 0.12)^2$

**c.** $P_{1A} = 1000.00 = (100/0.1) \times (1 - 1/(1.1)^5) + 1000/(1.1)^5$
$P_{1B} = 1075.815735 = (120/0.1) \times (1 - 1/(1.1)^5) + 1000/(1.1)^5$
The new bond values given in part c are more precise. Note how much better the bond convexity model in part b estimates revised bond prices than the duration model in part a.

**12.** According to the pure expectations theory, we compute the two-year spot rate as follows:

$$(1+y_{0,2})^2 = \prod_{t=1}^{2}(1 + y_{t-1,t}) = (1 + .05)(1 + .08) = 1.134$$

$$y_{0,2} = [(1+.05)(1+.08)]^{1/2} - 1 = \sqrt{1.134} - 1 = .0648944$$

**13.** The three-year rate is based on a geometric mean of the short-term spot rates as follows:

$$(1+y_{0,3})^3 = \prod_{t=1}^{3}(1 + y_{t-1,t}) = (1 + .05)(1 + .06)(1 + .07) = 1.19091$$

$$y_{0,3} = [(1+.05)(1+.06)(1+.07)]^{1/3} - 1 = \sqrt[3]{1.19091} - 1 = .0599686$$

**14.** The three-year rate is based on a geometric mean of the short-term spot rates as follows:

$$(1+y_{0,3})^3 = (1.07)^3 = 1.22504 = \prod_{t=1}^{3}(1 + y_{t-1,t}) = (1 + .05)(1 + .07)(1 + y_{2,3})$$

We solve for $y_{2,3}$ as follows:

$$1.22504 \div [(1 + .05)(1 + .07)] - 1 = y_{2,3} = 0.0903$$

**15.** **a.** First, we set up discount functions used by investors to value the bonds:
$1010D_1 = 1005$
$50D_1 + 1050D_2 = 1040$
$40D_1 + 40D_2 + 1040D_3 = 1020$
$40D_1 + 40D_2 + 40D_3 + 1040D_4 = 990$
Next, solve for, in order, $D_1$, $D_2$, $D_3$, and $D_4$:
$D_1 = 1005/1010 = 0.99505$
$D_2 = (1040 - 50 \times 0.99505)/1040 = 0.943093$
$D_3 = (1020 - 40 \times 0.99505 - 40 \times 0.943093)/1020 = 0.906225$
$D_4 = (990 - 40 \times 0.99505 - 40 \times 0.943093 - 40 \times 0.906225)/990 = 0.842524$
Finally, solve for $y_{0,1}$, $y_{0,2}$, $y_{0,3}$ and $y_{0,4}$:
$y_{0,1} = 1/D_1 - 1 = 1/0.99505 - 1 = 0.004975$
$y_{0,2} = (1/D_2)^{1/2} - 1 = (1/0.943093)^{1/2} - 1 = 0.029729$
$y_{0,3} = (1/D_3)^{1/3} - 1 = (1/0.906225)^{1/3} - 1 = 0.033367$
$y_{0,4} = (1/D_4)^{1/4} - 1 = (1/0.842524)^{1/4} - 1 = 0.043769$

**b.** Use $y_{0,n}$ and $y_{0,1}$ to solve for each $y_{1,n}$ as follows:
$y_{1,2} = (1 + y_{0,2})^2/(1 + y_{0,1}) - 1 = 0.055092$
$y_{1,3} = [(1 + y_{0,3})^3/(1 + y_{0,1})]^{1/2} - 1 = 0.035191$
$y_{1,4} = [(1 + y_{0,4})^4/(1 + y_{0,1})]^{1/3} - 1 = 0.05703$

**c.** Use $y_{0,n}$ and $y_{0,2}$ to solve for each $y_{2,n}$ as follows:
$y_{2,3} = [(1 + y_{0,3})^3/(1 + y_{0,2})^2] - 1 = 0.040683$
$y_{2,4} = [(1 + y_{0,4})^4/(1 + y_{0,2})^2]^{1/2} - 1 = 0.058001$

**d.** Use $y_{0,4}$ and $y_{0,3}$ to solve for $y_{3,4}$ as follows:
$y_{3,4} = [(1 + y_{0,4})^4/(1 + y_{0,3})^3] - 1 = 0.075607$

**16. a.** First, assume that bonds are priced with the following present value functions:

**Equation Set A**

$$964.3227 = 70D_1 + 70D_2 + 1070D_3$$
$$1010.031 = 80D_1 + 1080D_2 + 0D_3$$
$$938.4063 = 60D_1 + 60D_2 + 1060D_3$$

We will call this first set of equations Equation set A. This set contains three equations with three unknown values for which we need solutions. Note that the coefficient for $D_3$ in the second equation in Set A equals zero. If we can produce another equation with a zero coefficient for $D_3$, we will be able to solve for two unknowns in a two-equation system. We will call this next set of equations Equation Set B. If we multiply Equation 1A by (1060/1070), the coefficient for $D_3$ Equation 1B will match the coefficient for $D_3$ in Equation 3A (which will be rewritten as Equation 2B).

**Equation Set B**

$69.34579D_1 + 69.34579D_2 + 1060D_3 = 955.3103$ *1060/1070 × Equation 1A = Equation 1B*
$60D_1 + 60D_2 + 1060D_3 = 938.4063$ *Equation 3A = Equation 2B*

Next, subtract Equation 2B from Equation 1B to eliminate $D_3$ and its coefficient 1060. The result of this subtraction is the first equation in Equation Set C. The second equation in Equation Set C is the second equation in Equation Set A multiplied by (9.345794/80). This multiplication will enable us to subtract later to eliminate unknown $D_1$:

**Equation Set C**

$9.345794D_1 + 9.345794D_2 + 0D_3 = 16.90401$ *Equation 1B − Equation 2B = Equation 1C*
$9.345794D_1 + 126.1682D_2 + 0D_3 = 117.9943$ *Equation 2A × (9.345794/80) = Equation 2C*

When we subtract the second equation in Equation Set C from the first, Variable $D_1$ will be eliminated:

$0D_1 + -116.822D_2 + 0D_3 = -101.09$ *Equation 1C − Equation 2C*

Now, we can easily solve for $D_2 = -101.09/(-116.822) = 0.865333$. Now, using Equation 1C, we can solve for $D_1 = (16.90401 - 9.345794 \times D_2)/9.345794 = 0.943396$. Finally, we use Equation 1A to solve for $D_3 = (964.3227 - 70 \times D_1 - 70 \times D_2)/1070) = 0.782908$. Now that we have solved for our three discount functions $D_1$, $D_2$, and $D_3$, we can obtain spot rates:

$$\frac{1}{D_1} - 1 = 0.060 = y_{0,1}$$

$$\frac{1}{D_2^{1/2}} - 1 = 0.075 = y_{0,2}$$

$$\frac{1}{D_3^{1/3}} - 1 = 0.085 = y_{0,3}$$

Obtain the one- and two-year forward rates on loans originated in year 1 as follows:

$$y_{1,2} = \frac{(1+0.075)^2}{(1+0.06)} - 1 = 1.0902123 - 1 = .0902123$$

$$y_{1,3} = \sqrt{\frac{(1+.085)^3}{1+.06}} - 1 = \sqrt{1.2049897} - 1 = .097720228$$

The one-year forward rate on a loan originated in two years is computed as follows:

$$y_{2,3} = \frac{(1+0.085)^3}{(1.075)^2} - 1 = 1.052799 - 1 = .1052799$$

**17. a.** First, solve the following system for the discount functions $d$:

$$\begin{bmatrix} 50 & 50 & 1050 \\ 80 & 80 & 1080 \\ 110 & 1110 & 0 \end{bmatrix} \begin{bmatrix} D_1 \\ D_2 \\ D_3 \end{bmatrix} = \begin{bmatrix} 878.9172 \\ 955.4787 \\ 1055.4190 \end{bmatrix}$$

$$\mathbf{CF} \quad \times \mathbf{d} \quad = \quad \mathbf{p_0}$$

We find that $D_1 = 0.943396$, $D_2 = 0.857338$, and $D_3 = 0.751314$. The spot rates are obtained as follows:

$$\frac{1}{D_1} - 1 = \frac{1}{.943396} - 1 = .06$$

$$\frac{1}{D_2^{\frac{1}{2}}} - 1 = \frac{1}{.857338^{\frac{1}{2}}} - 1 = .08$$

$$\frac{1}{D_3^{\frac{1}{3}}} - 1 = \frac{1}{.751314^{\frac{1}{3}}} - 1 = .10$$

**b.** The weights are found by solving for $\mathbf{w}$ as follows:

$$\begin{bmatrix} 50 & 80 & 110 \\ 50 & 80 & 1110 \\ 1050 & 1080 & 0 \end{bmatrix} \begin{bmatrix} w_A \\ w_B \\ w_C \end{bmatrix} = \begin{bmatrix} 30 \\ 30 \\ 1030 \end{bmatrix}$$

$$\mathbf{CF} \quad \cdot \mathbf{w} \quad = \quad \mathbf{p_0}$$

$$\begin{bmatrix} -.03996 & .00396 & .002666 \\ .03885 & -.00385 & -.001660 \\ -.00100 & .00100 & 0 \end{bmatrix} \begin{bmatrix} 30 \\ 30 \\ 1030 \end{bmatrix} = \begin{bmatrix} w_A \\ w_B \\ w_C \end{bmatrix}$$

$$\mathbf{CF}^{-1} \quad \cdot \quad \mathbf{p_0} \quad = \quad \mathbf{w}$$

We find that $w_A = 1.666666$, $w_B = -0.666666$, and $w_C = 0$, which means that bond $D$ is replicated by a portfolio consisting of 1.666666 of Bond A and −0.666666 of Bond B.

**18.** USD2.30 × (CAD1/USD0.64) = USD2.30 × 1.5625 = CAD3.59375

**19. a.** CHF1.5÷(CanD1/USD0.64) = CHF1.5/1.5625 = CHF0.96/CAD1
CHF9.6 are required to purchase 10 Canadian dollars. In Switzerland, one Big Mac should cost CHF1.5 per USD times 2.30 USD per Big Mac or CHF3.45 when purchase power parity holds.

**20. a.** The value of \$1 is equal to the value of £0.6. Thus, the value of £1 must be \$1/0.6 = \$1.6667. Since the value of \$1 is ¥108, the value of £1 must be 1.6667 × ¥108 = ¥180. Thus, we could have solved as follows: £1 = (\$1÷0.6) × ¥108 = ¥180.
The value of \$1 is equal to the value of ¥108. Thus, the value of ¥1 must be \$1/¥108 = \$0.0092593. Since the value of £1 is \$1.6667, the value of ¥1 must be \$1÷(1.6667 × ¥108) = £0.0055556. Thus, we could have solved as follows: ¥1 = \$1÷(1/0.6 × ¥108) = £0.0055556.
\$300 = £0.6 × 300 = £180;\$300 = ¥108 × 300 = ¥32,400

**21.** First, we will consider the alternative of doing nothing.
*Unhedged alternative:*
Strategy: Wait six months and then sell ¥15,000,000 for dollars at the then-prevailing spot rate.
Result: All ¥15,000,000 is at risk. The expected value of the transaction is \$144,230.77.
*Forward market hedge:*
Strategy: Sell ¥15,000,000 forward for dollars at once.
Result: \$144,230.77 will certainly be received in six months. Transactions costs at time zero will total \$500. Forgone interest over six months totals \$12.50. The total amount (net of transactions costs and forgone interest) to be received in six months is \$143,718.27. This amount is certain.
*Money market hedge:*
Strategy: Borrow ¥14,354,067 in Japan for six months at 9% per year; exchange ¥14,354,067 for \$136,705.40 now; invest \$136,705.40 for six months at 5% per year.
Result: Yen loan is repaid by receipts from sale in six months. \$140,123.03 are obtained from U.S. investment. This amount is certain in the absence of default risk. Note that this strategy is inferior to the forward market hedge.

# CHAPTER 8

**1. a.** $c_T = MAX[0, S_T - X]$; $c_T = \$0$ or \$15
**b.** \$100/\$90 − 1 = 0.1111
**c.**

$$\alpha = \frac{c_u - c_d}{S_0(d - u)}$$

$$\alpha = \frac{15 - 0}{50(.6 - 1.4)} = -.375$$

**d.**

$$c_0 = \frac{-(1+r_f)\alpha S_0 + C_d + \alpha d S_0}{(1+r_f)}$$

$$c_0 = \frac{(1+.1111) \cdot .375 \cdot 50 + 0 - .375 \cdot .6 \cdot 50}{(1+.1111)} = 8.625$$

**e.** $p_0 = c_0 + X/(1+r_f)^T - S_0 = 8.625 + 55/(1.111111) - 50 = 8.125$

**2.** First, find the hedge ratio:

$$\alpha = \frac{c_u - c_d}{S_0(d-u)}$$

$$\alpha = \frac{8-2}{12(.83333 - 1.3333)} = -1$$

Now, value the call:

$$c_0 = \frac{-(1+r_f)\alpha S_0 + c_d + \alpha d S_0}{(1+r_f)}$$

$$c_0 = \frac{-(1+.125) \cdot (-1) \cdot 12 + 2 - 1 \cdot .83333 \cdot 12}{(1+.125)} = 4.88889$$

**3.** The statement for this problem leaves open a few ambiguities, primarily how jumps and riskless returns should be compounded over the course of the relevant time periods. Thus, depending on compounding methodologies, there should be several ways to complete each of these problems, but all should yield fairly similar solutions. First, we will estimate from the annualized volatility ($\sigma$) values for $u$, $d$, and $p$ in the two-, three-, and eight-time-period cases:

$$u = e^{.6 \times \sqrt{.75/2}} = 1.444; \quad u = e^{.6 \times \sqrt{.75/3}} = 1.350; \quad u = e^{.6 \times \sqrt{.75/8}} = 1.202$$

$$d = \frac{1}{1.444} = .692; \quad d = \frac{1}{1.35} = .741; \quad d = \frac{1}{1.202} = .832$$

$$p = \frac{e^{.08 \cdot .75} - .692}{1.444 - .692} = 0.449689; \quad p = \frac{e^{.08 \cdot .75} - .741}{1.35 - .741} = 0.564; \quad p = \frac{e^{.08 \cdot .75} - .832}{1.202 - .832} = 0.475$$

For the two-time-period framework, call valuation calculations proceed as follows:

$$a = INT\left[MAX\left[\frac{\ln\left(\frac{80}{50 \cdot .692^2}\right)}{\ln\left(\frac{1.444}{.692}\right)}, 0\right]\right] + 1 = 2$$

$$c_0 = \frac{.449^2 \times .551^{2-2} \times [1.444^2 \times .692^{2-2} \times 50 - 80]}{(1+.08 \cdot .75/2)^2} = 4.62$$

Put values are found with put-call parity. The following are call and put values for the two-, three-, and eight-period frameworks:

| n | $c_0$ | $p_0$ |
|---|---|---|
| 2 | 4.62 | 30.13 |
| 3 | 3.91 | 29.42 |
| 8 | 3.86 | 29.37 |

The calls are easily valued in the two- and three-step models because the maximum number of up-jumps (two and three) are required for exercise. Call value calculations are summarized as follows for the three-period framework, where calls will not be exercised with two or fewer up-jumps:

$$[0.0965 \times (122.98015 - 80)]/(1 + 0.08 \times 0.75/3)^3 = 3.91$$

In the eight-period framework, at least 6 up-jumps were required for exercise. Call value calculations are summarized as follows for the 8 period framework, where calls will not be exercised with 5 or fewer up-jumps:

$$\{[0.0883 \times (104.258 - 80)] + [0.02279 \times (150.55 - 80)] + [0.00257 \times (217.395 - 80)]\}/(1 + 0.08 \times 0.75/8)^8 = 3.86$$

**4.** $S_0 = 50$, $X = 60$, $T = 0.75$, $r_f = 0.081$, $u = 1.2776$, $d = 0.7828$
$p = 0.501295527$, $(1 - p) = 0.498704473$, $a = 2$, $T/n = 0.375$, $r_f \times T/n = 0.030375$ (adjust $r_f$)

$$c_0 = \frac{c_{u^2}p^2 + 2p(1-p)c_{ud} + (1-p)^2 c_{d^2}}{(1+r_f)^2} = \frac{21.61309 \cdot .251297 + 0 + 0}{(1+.030375)^2}$$

$c_0 = \$5.10$; based on put-call parity, $p_0 = \$11.61$

**5. a.** $d_1 = 0.6172$; $d_2 = 0.1178$; $N(d_1) = 0.7314$; $N(d_2) = 0.5469$
$c_0 = 11.05$; with put-call parity: $p_0 = 4.34$

**b.** Use $X = 30$; $d_1 = 0.925$; $d_2 = 0.4245$; $N(d_2) = 0.6644$
$1 - N(d_2) = 0.3356$

**6.** Value the calls using the Black-Scholes model:
$c_0 = S_0 N(d_1) - Xe^{-rT} N(d_2)$
$d_1 = [\ln(S \div X) + (r + 0.5\sigma^2)T] \div \sigma\sqrt{T}$
$d_2 = d_1 - \sigma\sqrt{T}$
Thus, we will first compute $d_1$, $d_2$, $N(d_1)$, and $N(d_2)$ for each of the calls; and then we will compute each call's value. We will then use put–call parity to value each put. First find for each of the 15 calls values for $d_1$:

| X | Aug | Sep | Oct |
|---|---|---|---|
| 110 | 2.833394 | 1.129163 | 1.162841 |
| 115 | 1.417978 | 0.617046 | 0.658904 |
| 120 | 0.062811 | 0.126728 | 0.176418 |
| 125 | −1.237028 | −0.343571 | −0.286369 |
| 130 | −2.485879 | −0.795423 | −0.731003 |

Next, find for each of the 15 calls values for $d_2$:

| X | Aug | Sep | Oct |
|---|---|---|---|
| 110 | 2.801988 | 1.042362 | 1.074632 |
| 115 | 1.386572 | 0.530245 | 0.570695 |
| 120 | 0.031405 | 0.039928 | 0.088208 |
| 125 | −1.268433 | −0.430371 | −0.374578 |
| 130 | −2.517284 | −0.882222 | −0.819212 |

Now, find $N(d_1)$ for each of the 15 calls:

| X | Aug | Sep | Oct |
|---|---|---|---|
| 110 | 0.997697 | 0.870585 | 0.877553 |
| 115 | 0.921901 | 0.731398 | 0.745021 |
| 120 | 0.525041 | 0.550422 | 0.570017 |
| 125 | 0.108038 | 0.365584 | 0.387298 |
| 130 | 0.006462 | 0.213184 | 0.232388 |

Next, determine $N(d_2)$ for each of the 15 calls:

| X | Aug | Sep | Oct |
|---|---|---|---|
| 110 | 0.997461 | 0.851378 | 0.858730 |
| 115 | 0.917214 | 0.702029 | 0.715897 |
| 120 | 0.512527 | 0.515925 | 0.535145 |
| 125 | 0.102322 | 0.333463 | 0.353987 |
| 130 | 0.005913 | 0.188828 | 0.206333 |

Now use $N(d_1)$ and $N(d_2)$ to value the calls and put–call parity to value the puts.

CALLS

| $X$ | Aug | Sep | Oct |
|---|---|---|---|
| 110 | 10.165 | 11.494 | 11.942 |
| 115 | 5.305 | 7.616 | 8.030 |
| 120 | 1.593 | 4.586 | 4.930 |
| 125 | 0.193 | 2.488 | 2.741 |
| 130 | 0.008 | 1.211 | 1.375 |

PUTS

| $X$ | Aug | Sep | Oct |
|---|---|---|---|
| 110 | 0.003 | 0.701 | 0.666 |
| 115 | 0.134 | 1.787 | 1.685 |
| 120 | 1.415 | 3.721 | 3.537 |
| 125 | 5.009 | 6.587 | 6.290 |
| 130 | 9.816 | 10.274 | 9.866 |

The options whose values are underlined are overvalued by the market; they should be sold. Other options are undervalued by the market; they should be purchased.

7. Zero. This is because the futures contract can be replicated with a long position in a call and a short position in a put with the same exercise terms. The gammas of the call and the put are the same. A long position in a futures contract is replicated with a single long position in a call and a single short position in a put. Thus, the gamma of the long call position offsets the gamma of the short put position.
8. **a.** Tanker Company calls expiring in three months with an exercise price equal to 25 are currently worth 6.5725. This value is based on $d_1 = 0.799405189$, $d_2 = 0.499405189$, $N(d_1) = 0.787972249$, and $N(d_2) = 0.691253018$.
   **b.** Greeks for the call are computed as follows:
   Delta = 0.787972249
   Gamma = 0.032206303
   Theta = −6.070521207
   Vega = 4.347657115
   Rho = 4.266663344
   **c.** $N(d_2) = 0.691253018$
   **d.** $p_0 = 1.261959101$
   **e.** Delta = −0.212027751
   Gamma = 0.032206303
   Theta = −9.503750259
   Vega = 4.347657115
   Rho = −1.905697909

9. a. Tanker Company calls expiring in three months with an exercise price equal to 30 are currently worth 3.7442. This value is based on $d_1 = 0.019166667$, $d_2 = -0.10833333333$, $N(d_1) = 0.575998341$, and $N(d_2) = 0.456865641$.

b. Greeks for the call are computed as follows:
Delta = 0.575998341
Gamma = 0.043524258
Theta = −7.727401147
Vega = 5.875513
Rho = 3.383927737

c. $N(d_2) = 0.456865641$.

d. Portfolio settings are determined by solving the following:

$$\begin{bmatrix} delta_P \\ gamma_P \\ \#_S \end{bmatrix} = \begin{bmatrix} delta_S & delta_{C1} & delta_{C2} \\ gamma_S & gamma_{C1} & gamma_{C2} \\ \#_S & 0 & 0 \end{bmatrix} \begin{bmatrix} \#_S \\ \#_{C1} \\ \#_{C2} \end{bmatrix}$$

$$\mathbf{r} \quad = \quad \mathbf{Y} \quad \#$$

$$\begin{bmatrix} delta_P \\ gamma_P \\ \#_S \end{bmatrix} = \begin{bmatrix} 0 \\ 0 \\ 1 \end{bmatrix} = \begin{bmatrix} 1 & .787972 & .575998 \\ 0 & .0322 & .0435 \\ 1 & 0 & 0 \end{bmatrix} \begin{bmatrix} \#_S \\ \#_{C1} \\ \#_{C2} \end{bmatrix}$$

$$\mathbf{r} \quad = \quad \mathbf{Y} \quad \#$$

$$\begin{bmatrix} \#_S \\ \#_{C1} \\ \#_{C2} \end{bmatrix} = \begin{bmatrix} 1 \\ -2.7643 \\ 2.045477 \end{bmatrix} = \begin{bmatrix} 0 & 0 & 1 \\ 2.7643 & -36.5826 & -2.7643 \\ -2.04548 & 50.04546 & 2.04548 \end{bmatrix} \begin{bmatrix} 0 \\ 0 \\ 1 \end{bmatrix}$$

$$\# \quad = \quad \mathbf{Y}^{-1} \quad \mathbf{r}$$

Thus, for each underlying share of stock purchased, a delta-gamma neutral portfolio requires a short position in 2.7643 calls with \$25 exercise prices and a long position in 2.045477 calls with \$30 exercise prices.

e. First, investment amounts in the stock and each of the options are computed as follows:
$\#c_{25}$: $-2.7643 \times 6.5725 = -18.1684$
$\#c_{30}$: $2.045477 \times 3.7442 = 7.6586$
$\#S$: $1 \times 30 = 30$
Total investment: $(-2.7643 \times 6.5725) + (2.045477 \times 3.7442) + (1 \times 30) = 19.4903$
Investment weights are computed as follows:
$Wc_{25} = -18.1684/19.4903 = -0.9322$
$Wc_{30} = 7.6586/19.4903 = 0.39294$
$W_S = 30/19.4903 = 1.53923$
Thus, the portfolio theta is computed as follows:
$Wc_{25} \times \theta c_{25} + Wc_{30} \times \theta c_{30} + W_S \times \theta_S$
$\theta_p = -0.9322 \times -6.0705 + 0.39294 \times -7.7274 + 1.53923 \times 0 = 2.622$

**10.** To answer this question, we first calculate $d_1$:

$$d_1 = \frac{\ln\left(\frac{.7e^{-.06 \cdot 2}}{.65e^{-.04 \cdot 2}}\right) + \left(.06 - .04 + \frac{.3^2}{2}\right) \cdot 2}{.3\sqrt{2}} = .1983$$

Next we calculate $d_2$:

$$d_2 = d_1 - \sigma\sqrt{T} = 0.1983 - 0.4242 = -0.226$$

Next, find cumulative normal density functions (z-values) for $d_1$ and $d_2$:

$$N(d_1) = N(0.1983) = 0.5786$$
$$N(d_2) = N(-0.226) = 0.4106$$

Finally, we value the call as follows:

$$c_0 = 0.65(0.5786) - [0.7 \times .8869] \times (0.4106) = \$0.1128$$

We can evaluate a put for this European currency option series using Equation (4) as follows:

$$p_0 = c_0 + Xe^{-r(d)T} - S_0e^{-r(f)T} = 0.1128 + 0.65e^{-0.06 \times 0.5} - 0.7e^{-0.04 \times 0.5} = 0.092$$

**11.** The two relevant options market hedging strategies are the put hedge strategy and the conversion. These are described as follows:

*Put Hedge*

Strategy: Purchase a six month put option on ¥15,000,000 with an exercise price of \$0.009/¥ and a premium of \$150. Time zero brokerage costs total \$750 (15 contracts at \$50 per contract—pretty high, given the premiums involved). Thus the total time zero cash outlay is \$900. Expressed in terms of future value, the total cash outlay is \$922.50 since interest forgone on the sum of the premium and brokerage costs totals \$22.50.

Result: Receive one of the following in six months:

An unlimited potential maximum less the \$922.50 premium and brokerage fees. The dollar value of this strategy increases as the value of the dollar drops.

A minimum of \$135,000 less \$922.50 for a net of \$134,077.50. This minimum value to be received might be unacceptably low for some managers; however, there is upside cash flow potential.

*Conversion or Call and Put Hedge*

Strategy: Through the combination of short call and long put positions, total risk can be eliminated. Consider the writing of a call with an exercise price of \$0.009 expiring in six months along with the purchase of a put with the same terms. The time zero cash flows are summarized as follows:

| | | | |
|---|---|---|---|
| Put premium | −\$150 | Call premium | +\$1500 |
| Put brokerage fee | −\$750 | Call brokerage fee | −\$750 |
| Net time zero cash flows | −\$150 | | |

Result: The forgone interest on the net time zero outlay is \$3.75. If the six-month exchange rate is less than \$0.009/¥, the exchange rate of \$0.009/¥ is locked in by the put. If the exchange rate exceeds \$0.009/¥, the obligation incurred by the short position in the call is activated. Thus, the exchange rate of \$0.009/¥ is locked in no

matter what the exchange rate is. The cash flows in six months are summarized as follows:
Put cash flows (¥15,000,000 × MAX[0.009 − $S_1$,0])
Call cash flows (¥15,000,000 × MIN[0.009 − $S_1$,0])
Total of option transactions:
(¥15,000,000 × (0.009 − $S_1$) = \$135,000 − (¥15,000,000 × $S_1$)
Exchange of currency = (¥15,000,000 × $S_1$)
Time zero cash flows = −\$150
Interest on time zero flows = \$3.75
Total time one cash flows = \$134,846.25

# CHAPTER 9

**1. a., b.** See following table.

| Date | Investor Contributions | Investor Withdrawals | Fund Dividends | Assets | Number of Shares | Net Asset Value | $r_t$ |
|---|---|---|---|---|---|---|---|
| 2/1 | 1,000,000 | 0 | 0 | 1,000,000 | 20,000 | 50.00 | N/A |
| 2/2 | 0 | 0 | 0 | 1,030,000 | 20,000 | 51.50 | 3.00% |
| 2/3 | 0 | 0 | 30,000 | 1,030,000 | 20,000 | 51.50 | 2.91% |
| 2/4 | 0 | 0 | 0 | 980,000 | 20,000 | 49.00 | −4.85% |
| 2/5 | 0 | 49,500 | 0 | 940,500 | 19,000 | 49.50 | 1.02% |

**c.**

$$\bar{r}_{g,p} = \sqrt[n]{\prod_{t=1}^{n}(1 + r_t)} - 1 = \sqrt[4]{(1.03)(1.0291)(0.9515)(1.102)} - 1 = .004676$$

**2. a.** NAV and DIV data for Fund A are followed by return calculations:

| Date | $t$ | $NAV_t$ | $NAV_{t-1}$ | $DIV_t$ | $r_t$ | NOTES |
|---|---|---|---|---|---|---|
| June 30 | 2 | 50 | 0 | 0 | — | First month |
| July 31 | 2 | 55 | 50 | 0 | 0.100 | (55÷50) −1 = 0.10 |
| Aug 13 | 3 | 50 | 55 | 0 | −0.091 | (50÷55) −1 = −0.091 |
| Sep 30 | 4 | 54 | 50 | 0 | 0.080 | (54÷50) −1 = 0.08 |
| Oct 31 | 5 | 47 | 54 | 2 | −0.092 | ex-\$2 dividend; [(47 + 2)÷54)] − 1 = −0.092 |
| Nov 30 | 6 | 51 | 47 | 0 | 0.081 | (51÷47) − 1 = 0.081 |

**b.** Monthly returns for Fund B beginning with July are 0.60, −0.50, 0.50, −0.50, and 0.50.

**c.** Geometric mean returns are calculated for Funds A and B (including their dividends) as follows:

$$\bar{r}_{g,A} = \sqrt[n]{\prod_{t=1}^{n}(1+r_t)} - 1$$
$$= \sqrt[5]{(1+.10)(1-.091)(1+.08)(1-.092)(1+.081)} - 1$$
$$= .0117$$

$$\bar{r}_{g,B} = \sqrt[n]{\prod_{t=1}^{n}(1+r_t)} - 1$$
$$= \sqrt[5]{(1+.60)(1-.50)(1+.50)(1-.50)(1+.50)} - 1$$
$$= -.0208$$

**d.** Fund internal rates of return from part c are time-weighted returns.

**3. a.** Average historical returns (in decimal format) are as follows:

$$\overline{R}_p = .062$$
$$\overline{R}_L = .106$$
$$\overline{R}_M = .098$$

**b.**

$$\sigma_P^2 = 0.000696$$
$$\sigma_L^2 = 0.008824$$
$$\sigma_M^2 = 0.001576$$

**c.** COV[P,M] = [ (0.04 − 0.062) • (0.15 − 0.098) + (0.07 − 0.062) • (0.10 − 0.098) + (0.11 − 0.062) • (0.03 − 0.098) + (0.04 − 0.062) • (0.12 − 0.098) + (0.05 − 0.062) • (0.09 − 0.098) ] ÷ 5 = −0.000956

$$\rho_{P,M} = \frac{COV[P,M]}{\sigma_P \sigma_M} = \frac{-.000956}{.0264 \cdot .039} = -.912$$

**d.** COV[L,M] = [ (0.15 − 0.098) • (0.19 − 0.106) + (0.10 − 0.098) • (0.04 − 0.106) + (0.03 − 0.098) • (− 0.04 − 0.106) + (0.12 − 0.098) • (0.21 − 0.106) + (0.09 − 0.098) • (0.13 − 0.106) ] ÷ 5 = 0.003252

$$\rho_{L,M} = \frac{COV[L,M]}{\sigma_M \sigma_L} = \frac{-.003252}{.039 \cdot .094} = .872$$

**e.** Stock or fund beta is COV[S,M]/VAR[M]. The two fund betas are:

$$\beta_P = \frac{COV\{P,M\}}{VAR[M]} = \frac{-.000956}{.001576} = -0.61$$

$$\beta_L = \frac{COV\{L,M\}}{VAR[M]} = \frac{-.003252}{.001576} = 2.06$$

**f.** The Treynor Index for the market is $T_M = (0.08 - 0.03)/1 = 0.05$.
The Treynor Index for the Patterson Fund was $T_P = (0.10 - 0.03)/(-0.61) = -0.1148$.
The Treynor Index for the Liston Fund was $T_L = (0.14 - 0.03)/(2.06) = 0.0539$.

**g.** The Treynor Index for the market is always simply the market's risk premium. Thus, there is nothing particularly noteworthy here other than the standard by which we compare the performance of the two funds. The Treynor Index for the Patterson Fund is negative, which would normally compare unfavorably to that of the market Treynor Index. However, since the risk premium for Patterson is positive while its beta is negative, this negative risk premium actually indicates strong risk-adjusted performance. Thus, Patterson outperformed the market on a risk-adjusted basis. Liston also outperformed the market on a risk adjusted basis since its Treynor Index of 0.0539 exceeded that of the Liston Fund.

**4. a.** First, calculate risk premiums for both the fund and the market as follows:

| $t$ | $R_p$ | $R_m$ | $r_f$ | $R_p - r_f$ | $R_m - r_f$ |
|---|---|---|---|---|---|
| 1 | 0.35 | 0.28 | 0.05 | 0.3 | 0.23 |
| 2 | 0.04 | 0.05 | 0.05 | −0.01 | 0 |
| 3 | 0.1 | 0.09 | 0.05 | 0.05 | 0.04 |
| 4 | −0.01 | −0.02 | 0.05 | −0.06 | −0.07 |
| 5 | 0.38 | 0.32 | 0.05 | 0.33 | 0.27 |
| 6 | 0.31 | 0.25 | 0.05 | 0.26 | 0.2 |
| 7 | 0.33 | 0.26 | 0.05 | 0.28 | 0.21 |
| 8 | 0.42 | 0.3 | 0.05 | 0.37 | 0.25 |
| 9 | 0.07 | 0.14 | 0.05 | 0.02 | 0.09 |
| 10 | −0.02 | −0.06 | 0.05 | −0.07 | −0.11 |
| 11 | −0.07 | −0.15 | 0.05 | −0.12 | −0.2 |
| 12 | −0.11 | −0.21 | 0.05 | −0.16 | −0.26 |
| 13 | 0.42 | 0.26 | 0.05 | 0.37 | 0.21 |
| 14 | 0.01 | 0.04 | 0.05 | −0.04 | −0.01 |

| | | | | | |
|---|---|---|---|---|---|
| 15 | 0.05 | 0.08 | 0.05 | 0 | 0.03 |
| 16 | 0.07 | 0.11 | 0.05 | 0.02 | 0.06 |
| 17 | −0.01 | −0.03 | 0.05 | −0.06 | −0.08 |
| 18 | −0.12 | −0.37 | 0.05 | −0.17 | −0.42 |
| 19 | 0.33 | 0.3 | 0.05 | 0.28 | 0.25 |
| 20 | 0.05 | 0.13 | 0.05 | 0 | 0.08 |

Next, run a simple ordinary least squares regression of $(R_p - r_f)$ on $(R_m - r_f)$. The fund's beta is the slope term in the regression and the fund's alpha is its vertical intercept:

| | | | | | |
|---|---|---|---|---|---|
| SUMMARY OUTPUT | | | | | |
| Regression Statistics | | | | | |
| Multiple R | | 0.910030353 | | | |
| R Square | | 0.828155243 | | | |
| Adjusted R Square | | 0.818608312 | | | |
| Standard Error | | 0.079179681 | | | |
| Observations | | 20 | | | |
| ANOVA | | | | | |
| | df | SS | MS | F | Significance F |
| Regression | 1 | 0.543845407 | 0.543845407 | 86.74570346 | 2.63657E-08 |
| Residual | 18 | 0.112849593 | 0.006269422 | | |
| Total | 19 | 0.656695 | | | |
| | Coefficients | Standard Error | t Stat | P-value | |
| Intercept | 0.045004834 | 0.018088349 | 2.488056431 | 0.022868369 | |
| X Variable 1 | 0.895978331 | 0.096199656 | 9.313737352 | 2.63657E-08 | |

Thus, the fund beta is 0.8959.

**b.** The fund alpha is 0.04. Since the alpha is statistically significant at the 5% level, we can conclude that the fund has outperformed the market.

c. Risk premiums and relevant squared values are given as:

| $t$ | $R_p - r_f$ | $R_m - r_f$ | $(R_m - r_f)^2$ | $t$ | $R_p - r_f$ | $R_m - r_f$ | $(R_m - r_f)^2$ |
|---|---|---|---|---|---|---|---|
| 1 | 0.3 | 0.23 | 0.0529 | 11 | −0.12 | −0.2 | 0.0400 |
| 2 | −0.01 | 0 | 0.0000 | 12 | −0.16 | −0.26 | 0.0676 |
| 3 | 0.05 | 0.04 | 0.0016 | 13 | 0.37 | 0.21 | 0.0441 |
| 4 | −0.06 | −0.07 | 0.0049 | 14 | −0.04 | −0.01 | 0.0001 |
| 5 | 0.33 | 0.27 | 0.0729 | 15 | 0 | 0.03 | 0.0009 |
| 6 | 0.26 | 0.2 | 0.0400 | 16 | 0.02 | 0.06 | 0.0036 |
| 7 | 0.28 | 0.21 | 0.0441 | 17 | −0.06 | −0.08 | 0.0064 |
| 8 | 0.37 | 0.25 | 0.0625 | 18 | −0.17 | −0.42 | 0.1764 |
| 9 | 0.02 | 0.09 | 0.0081 | 19 | 0.28 | 0.25 | 0.0625 |
| 10 | −0.07 | −0.11 | 0.0121 | 20 | 0 | 0.08 | 0.0064 |

Regression results are given as follows:

| | | | | | |
|---|---|---|---|---|---|
| SUMMARY OUTPUT | | | | | |
| Regression Statistics | | | | | |
| Multiple R | | 0.910030353 | | | |
| R Square | | 0.828155243 | | | |
| Adjusted R Square | | 0.818608312 | | | |
| Standard Error | | 0.079179681 | | | |
| Observations | | 20 | | | |
| ANOVA | | | | | |
| | df | SS | MS | F | Significance F |
| Regression | 1 | 0.543845407 | 0.543845407 | 86.74570346 | 2.63657E-08 |
| Residual | 18 | 0.112849593 | 0.006269422 | | |
| Total | 19 | 0.656695 | | | |
| | Coefficients | Standard Error | t Stat | P-value | |
| Intercept | 0.045004834 | 0.018088349 | 2.488056431 | 0.022868369 | |
| X Variable 1 | 0.895978331 | 0.096199656 | 9.313737352 | 2.63657E-08 | |

Since the regression coefficient for the squared market risk premium is positive and statistically significant at the 1% level, the Ripco Fund does present evidence of market timing ability.

**d.** Risk premiums and interaction terms are given as follows:

| $t$ | $R_p - r_f$ | $R_m - r_f$ | $D(R_m - r_f)$ | $t$ | $R_p - r_f$ | $R_m - r_f$ | $D(R_m - r_f)$ |
|---|---|---|---|---|---|---|---|
| 1 | 0.3 | 0.23 | 0 | 11 | −0.12 | −0.2 | −0.2 |
| 2 | −0.01 | 0 | 0 | 12 | −0.16 | −0.26 | −0.26 |
| 3 | 0.05 | 0.04 | 0 | 13 | 0.37 | 0.21 | 0 |
| 4 | −0.06 | −0.07 | −0.07 | 14 | −0.04 | −0.01 | −0.01 |
| 5 | 0.33 | 0.27 | 0 | 15 | 0 | 0.03 | 0 |
| 6 | 0.26 | 0.2 | 0 | 16 | 0.02 | 0.06 | 0 |
| 7 | 0.28 | 0.21 | 0 | 17 | −0.06 | −0.08 | −0.08 |
| 8 | 0.37 | 0.25 | 0 | 18 | −0.17 | −0.42 | −0.42 |
| 9 | 0.02 | 0.09 | 0 | 19 | 0.28 | 0.25 | 0 |
| 10 | −0.07 | −0.11 | −0.11 | 20 | 0 | 0.08 | 0 |

Regression results are given as follows:

| | | | | | |
|---|---|---|---|---|---|
| SUMMARY OUTPUT | | | | | |
| Regression Statistics | | | | | |
| Multiple R | | 0.974705741 | | | |
| R Square | | 0.950051281 | | | |
| Adjusted R Square | | 0.944174961 | | | |
| Standard Error | | 0.043925789 | | | |
| Observations | | 20 | | | |
| ANOVA | | | | | |
| | df | SS | MS | F | Significance F |
| Regression | 2 | 0.623893926 | 0.311946963 | 161.6745344 | 8.65879E-12 |
| Residual | 17 | 0.032801074 | 0.001929475 | | |
| Total | 19 | 0.656695 | | | |
| | Coefficients | Standard Error | t Stat | P-value | |
| Intercept | −0.014398622 | 0.013629095 | −1.05646213 | 0.305539994 | |
| X Variable 1 | 0.984588481 | 0.055112431 | 17.86508898 | 1.87737E-12 | |
| X Variable 2 | 1.58370714 | 0.245876938 | 6.441056058 | 6.09187E-06 | |

Since the regression coefficient for the interaction term is positive and statistically significant at the 1% level, the Ripco Fund does present evidence of market timing ability.

5. The daily VWAP for stock X is calculated as follows:

$$\text{VWAP} = \frac{\sum_j Q_j P_j}{\sum_j Q_j} = (30,000 \times 100.00 + 10,000 \times 100.00 + 40,000 \times 100.02 + 10,000$$
$$\times 100.01 + 10,000 \times 100.05 + 10,000 \times 100.03 + 20,000 \times 100.06$$
$$+ 20,000 \times 100.04 + 30,000 \times 100.07 + 40,000 \times 10.05 + 10,000$$
$$\times 100.09 + 40,000 \times 100.05)/(30,000 + 10,000 + 40,000 + 10,000$$
$$+ 10,000 + 10,000 + 20,000 + 20,000 + 30,000 + 40,000$$
$$+ 10,000 + 40,000 = 27,010,700/270,000$$
$$= 100.0396296$$

The VWAP excluding the broker's transactions were:

$$\text{VWAP} = \frac{\sum_j Q_j P_j}{\sum_j Q_j} = (30,000 \times 100.00 + 40,000 \times 100.02 + 10,000 \times 100.05 + 20,000$$
$$\times 100.06 + 30,000 \times 100.07 + 10,000 \times 100.09)/(30,000 + 40,000$$
$$+ 10,000 + 20,000 + 30,000 + 10,000)$$
$$= 100.0392857$$

Since $100.0396296 > 100.0392857$, meaning that the average price paid in the market with the broker's transactions were higher, the broker was outperformed (slightly) by the market. The broker's VWAP without the rest of the market was 100.0396, higher than that of the market.

# CHAPTER 10

1. **a.** $E[U_{w,\ No\ Gamble}] = ln(2) = 0.693147$

   **b.** Solve the following for $G$, where $G$ is the cost of the gamble and $x$ is its winnings:

$$E[U_{w,\ With\ gamble}] = \sum_{i=1}^{\infty} p_i U(w + x_i - G) = \sum_{i=1}^{\infty} [.5^i \ln(2 + 2^i - G)] = .693147$$

$$G = 3.34757$$

Note: A spreadsheet may be useful to solve this infinite series. The value $G$ is the payment for the gamble, the initial wealth level is 2, winnings are $2^i$ where $i$ is the number of tosses before the first head. The value of $G$ is obtained by iteration. The following is the first 13 rows of spreadsheet calculations for this problem:

| | $p^i$ | $(2-G+2^i)$ | $(p^i)(2-G+2^i)$ | $\text{SUM}(p^i)(2-G+2^i)$ |
|---|---|---|---|---|
| 1 | 0.5 | −0.42705 | −0.213525713 | −0.213525713 |
| 2 | 0.25 | 0.975476 | 0.24386905 | 0.030343338 |
| 3 | 0.125 | 1.894982 | 0.236872775 | 0.267216113 |
| 4 | 0.0625 | 2.684606 | 0.167787887 | 0.435004 |
| 5 | 0.03125 | 3.422712 | 0.106959748 | 0.541963748 |
| 6 | 0.015625 | 4.137602 | 0.064650039 | 0.606613787 |
| 7 | 0.0078125 | 4.841447 | 0.037823801 | 0.644437588 |
| 8 | 0.00390625 | 5.5399 | 0.021640233 | 0.666077821 |
| 9 | 0.00195313 | 6.235689 | 0.01217908 | 0.678256901 |
| 10 | 0.00097656 | 6.930155 | 0.006767729 | 0.68502463 |
| 11 | 0.00048828 | 7.623961 | 0.003722637 | 0.688747268 |
| 12 | 0.00024414 | 8.317437 | 0.002030624 | 0.690777892 |
| 13 | 0.00012207 | 9.010749 | 0.001099945 | 0.691877837 |

A trial value $G$ is entered elsewhere in the spreadsheet and this cell is referenced for all other cells where $G$ is used. The value for $G$ is iterated until the sum is sufficiently close to the natural log of 2. In this table, the value 3.34757 is used, where this value was obtained by trial and error in an effort to obtain 0.693147 (or some sufficiently close value) for the sum in the 13th row.

**c.** First, find the utility of \$1000: $ln(1000) = 6.907755$.
Now, solve the following for $G$, where $G$ is the cost of the gamble:

$$E[U_{w,\ With\ gamble}] = \sum_{i=1}^{\infty} p_i U(w + x_i - G) = \sum_{i=1}^{\infty} [.5^i \ln(2 + 2^i - G)] = .6907755$$

$G = 10.954$

Note: See the following table excerpted from a spreadsheet used to solve the infinite series, iterating for $G$. The key column, "Contribution to Utility", equals Probability $\times$ $ln(1000 +$ "Gamble Payoff" $- G)$. The column is then summed such that the sum equals the utility of \$1000:

| Toss | Probability | Gamble Payoff | Log of Post-Gamble Wealth | Contribution to Utility | Contribution to Wealth |
|---|---|---|---|---|---|
| 1 | 0.5 | 2 | 6.898761 | 3.449380476 | 1 |
| 2 | 0.25 | 4 | 6.900777 | 1.725194247 | 1 |

| | | | | | |
|---|---|---|---|---|---|
| 3 | 0.125 | 8 | 6.904797 | 0.863099613 | 1 |
| 4 | 0.0625 | 16 | 6.912789 | 0.432049287 | 1 |
| 5 | 0.03125 | 32 | 6.928583 | 0.216518215 | 1 |
| 6 | 0.015625 | 64 | 6.959442 | 0.108741284 | 1 |
| 7 | 0.0078125 | 128 | 7.018443 | 0.054831586 | 1 |
| 8 | 0.00390625 | 256 | 7.126928 | 0.027839562 | 1 |
| 9 | 0.00195313 | 512 | 7.313917 | 0.014284995 | 1 |
| 10 | 0.00097656 | 1024 | 7.607404 | 0.007429106 | 1 |
| 11 | 0.00048828 | 2048 | 8.018641 | 0.003915352 | 1 |
| 12 | 0.00024414 | 4096 | 8.534059 | 0.002083511 | 1 |
| 13 | 0.00012207 | 8192 | 9.124896 | 0.001113879 | 1 |
| 14 | 6.1035E-05 | 16384 | 9.762675 | 0.000595866 | 1 |
| 15 | 3.0518E-05 | 32768 | 10.42694 | 0.000318205 | 1 |
| 16 | 1.5259E-05 | 65536 | 11.10533 | 0.000169454 | 1 |
| 17 | 7.6294E-06 | 131072 | 11.79102 | 8.99583E-05 | 1 |

**d.** Solve the following for $G$, where $G$ is the cost of the gamble:

$$E[U_{w,\ \mathit{With\ gamble}}] = \sum_{i=1}^{\infty} p_i U(w + x_i - G) = \sum_{i=1}^{\infty}[.5^i \ln(2 + 2^{2i-1} - G)]$$
$$= (2 + 1 - G) + (2 + 8 - G) + (2 + 32 - G) + (2 + 64 - G) + \cdots$$

For any finite value of $G$, expected utility must equal $\infty$. Thus $G = \infty$, and an investor would be willing to pay any finite sum for this gamble. That is, this illustration shows how an investor, with diminishing marginal utility of wealth (log utility function) and risk aversion would still be willing to pay an infinite sum of money for a gamble. This example might be referred to as a "Super St. Petersburg Paradox."

**2.** In a pairwise choice between ice cream and cake, ice cream would be preferred by two out of three traders. In a pairwise choice between ice cream and cookies, cookies would be preferred by two out of three traders. In a pairwise choice between cake and cookies, cake would be preferred by two out of three traders. Thus, the social preferences, as indicated by the votes taken by traders, would be cookies > ice cream > cake > cookies. Obviously, the social preferences, as determined by majority vote, are not transitive (rational).

**3.** **a.** Based on expected value, the actuarial value of this policy is $0.05 \times \$20{,}000 = \$1{,}000$.

**b.** $\$1{,}200 - 1{,}000 = \$200$

$\$1{,}000 - 1{,}200 = -\$200$; \$200 expected loss to the consumer

The sale is a rational transaction if the insurance company intends to increase its wealth (more is preferred to less).

The purchase is a rational transaction to the consumer if she is sufficiently risk-averse.

4. a. There should be no statistically significant difference
   b. Selling prices will exceed purchase prices. Kahneman and Tversky actually performed this experiment and found that the median selling price was $5.79 and the median purchase price was $2.25, a ratio of more than 2. On the possibility that this result might have been due to "wealth effects"—subjects given mugs were simply wealthier than those not given mugs, and this might drive the price differences. But the experiment was repeated where selling prices of one group were compared to the "choosing" prices of the other. In this scenario, subjects selected from listings of money amounts whether they would prefer to have a mug or money. Choosers are in precisely the same wealth position as sellers—they choose between a mug and money. The only difference is that sellers are "giving up" a mug they "own," whereas choosers are merely giving up the right to have a mug. The results were consistent. The median choosing price was half the median selling price ($3.50 vs. $7.00). Similar experiments have been performed in many markets with consistent results.
   c. Selling prices are likely to exceed buying prices by larger amounts. Investors will be more reluctant to sell stock that they already own and would be reluctant to purchase shares.
5. Option sets i and ii establish that people are impatient and associate a time value with money and good meals. However, this impatience and positive time value is inconsistent with the preference revealed in decision set iii. Apparently, in this scenario, people look forward to improved meals, as though they would give up time value to see an upward trend. This experiment was conducted by Lowenstein and Prelec (1993).
6. Each contestant has his own method for estimating the number of jelly beans, based on his abilities, experiences, visual and quantitative skills, etc. Each contestant, who possesses each of these and other attributes to at least a degree, incorporates all of these attributes into his best estimate. Since each contestant makes every effort to incorporate all of these attributes into the estimation process, there will be at least some systematic and correlated individual strengths in the estimation process of the population or consensus. However, each contestant also incorporates his weaknesses and biases in the estimation process, despite his best efforts not to. If these weaknesses in the estimation process are uncorrelated, and then consensus estimates will be unbiased.
7. First, since a 0.66 probability of a $2400 payout is being shifted to 0 from A and *B* to A* and B*, we will rewrite the statement of gamble payoffs as follows:

   Gamble $A$: 0.33 probability of receiving 2500, 0.66 of receiving 2400 and 0.01 of receiving 0

   Gamble $B$: 0.34 probability of receiving 2,400 and 0.66 of receiving 2400

   and

   Gamble $A*$: 0.33 probability of receiving 2,500, 0.01 of receiving 0 and 0.66 of receiving 0

   Gamble $B*$: 0.34 probability of receiving 2,400 and 0.66 of receiving 0

The investor is indifferent between Gambles A and B. Recall that the strong independence axiom states that if $x_j \succ x_k$, and then for any $\alpha \in [0,1]$, $\alpha x_i + (1-\alpha) x_k \sim \alpha x_j + (1-\alpha)x_k$. This strong independence axiom implies that for any $\alpha \in [0,1]$:

$$\alpha(\text{0.33 prob. of receiving 2500 and 0.01 of receiving 0}) + (1-\alpha)(\text{0.66 prob. of receving 2400}) \sim \alpha(\text{0.34 prob. of receiving 2400}) + (1-\alpha)(\text{0.66 prob. of receving 2400})$$

which implies that:

$$(\text{0.33 prob. of receiving 2500 and 0.01 of receiving 0}) \sim (\text{0.34 prob. of receving 2400})$$

The same decomposition for Gambles A* and B* results in:

$$\text{Gamble } A*: \alpha(\text{0.33 prob. of receiving 2500 0.01 of receiving 0}) + (1-\alpha)(\text{0.66 prob. of receiving 0})$$

$$\text{Gamble } B*: \alpha(\text{0.34 prob. of receiving 2400}) + (1-\alpha)(\text{0.66 prob. of receiving 0})$$

which, by the same strong independence axiom, reduces to a comparison between:

$$\text{Gamble } A*: (\text{0.33 prob. of receiving 2500 and 0.01 of receiving 0})$$

$$\text{Gamble } B*: (\text{0.34 prob. of receiving 2400})$$

We know from our statement above concerning Gambles A and B, (0.33 prob. of receiving 2500 and 0.01 of receiving 0) $\sim$ (0.34 prob. of receiving 2400), that the investor must be indifferent between Gambles A* and B*.

**8.** **a.** This is a simple example of the framing problem discussed by Kahneman and Tversky.
**b.** The first set of choices is framed in terms of lives saved, or gains. The second set is framed in terms of lives lost, or losses. Framing the problem in terms of lives saved triggers risk aversion, while framing the same problem in terms of lives lost triggers risk seeking. Again, this is consistent with Kahneman and Tversky's prospect theory.

**9.** **a.** $0.5(300{,}000 - 100{,}000) + 0.5(0 - 100{,}000) = 50{,}000$
**b.** $[0.5(200{,}000 - 50{,}000)^2 + 0.5(-100{,}000 - 50{,}000)^2]^{.5} = 150{,}000$
**c.** $5 \times 50{,}000 = 250{,}000$
Alternatively, in five wagers, with 120 (5!) possible win/loss scenarios, there is one scenario in which five consecutive losses totaling 500,000 occur with a probability of $0.5^5$, five scenarios in which four losses and one win occur with a net loss of 200,000, and a probability of $5 \times 0.5^5$ and so on:
$1 \times 0.5^5 \times (-500000) + 5 \times .5^5 \times (-200000) +$
$10 \times .5^5 \times 100000 + 10 \times .5^5 \times 400000 + 5 \times .5^5 \times 700000$
$+ 1 \times 0.5^5 \times 1000000 = 250{,}000$
**d.** $(1 \times 0.5^5 \times (-500000 - 250000)^2 + 5 \times 0.5^5 \times (-200000 - 250000)^2$
$+ 10 \times 0.5^5 \times (100000 - 250000)^2 + 10 \times 0.5^5 \times (400000 - 250000)^2$
$+ 5 \times 0.5^5 \times (700000 - 250000)^2 + 1 \times 0.5^5 \times (1000000 - 250000)^2)^{.5} = 335{,}410.2$

Alternatively, since payoffs from each of the five wagers are independent of one another, this standard deviation of five gambles can be computed as follows: $(5 \times 150{,}000^2)^{.5} = 335{,}410.2$

e. Obviously, the set of five wagers described in parts c and d has the higher expected value.

f. Obviously, the set of five wagers described in parts c and d has the higher standard deviation. However, note that this higher standard deviation is less than five times the individual wager standard deviation.

g. The answer to this depends on how you evaluate the wagers and your own individual preferences. However, the reward to risk ratio for the single wager 50,000/150,000 = 3 is much greater than the reward to risk ratio of the set of 5 gambles 250,000/335.410.2 = 0.746. This suggests that as the number of gambles increases, the reward to risk ratio will also increase due to diversification. However, consider the response to the next part of this question.

h. Suppose that you find the individual wager described in parts a and b unacceptable. Then, if after having wagered four times (the first four of five wagers described in parts c and d), you have the opportunity to wager a fifth time, you should decline, since you find any single wager of this type to be unacceptable. Then, by the same logic, after having wagered three times, you would find the fourth wager unacceptable, and so on. Thus, any person finding the single wager described in parts a and b to be unacceptable should also find the set of five wagers to be unacceptable. Hence, diversification over time or over a series of sequential gambles would not mitigate risk. This is the substance of Paul Samuelson's "law of large numbers" fallacy (Samuelson, 1963).

## CHAPTER 11

1. New information arrives randomly; otherwise it is not news. Thus, price reactions to news will be random.
2. Three-day moving averages are computed as follows:

| t | $P_t$ | $MA_t$ |
|---|---|---|
| 1 | 50 | NA |
| 2 | 51 | NA |
| 3 | 52 | 51 |
| 4 | 58 | 53.67 |
| 5 | 56 | 55.33 |

Our three-day moving average would suggest that investors sell the stock on each of days 3, 4, and 5.

3. The five-day simple weighted average is computed as follows:

| | | | | | | | | | | | |
|---|---|---|---|---|---|---|---|---|---|---|---|
| NA | NA | NA | NA | 6 | 7 | 7.6 | 9 | 10.8 | 11.6 | 12.8 | 14.6 |

4. No: Seasonal cycles are anticipated by shareholders who anticipate and discount cash flows accordingly. However, unanticipated changes in sales revenue would affect share prices.
5. Ten spin-offs provides for a very small sample set. Did stock returns increase for the year? Since returns were collected for only one year, and that year may not have both longer periods of decline and longer periods of increase, the returns might simply have been normal market returns. This scenario is especially likely if stock returns have not been adjusted for normal market returns.
6. Either service can be used equally well to time market decisions.
7. **a.** Acquiring company daily stock returns, $(P_t/P_{t-1}) - 1$, are computed as follows:

| Day | Company X Return | Company Y Return | Company Z Return |
|---|---|---|---|
| −6 | NA | NA | NA |
| −5 | 0 | 0 | 0.00207 |
| −4 | 0.00249 | 0.00625 | −0.00413 |
| −3 | 0 | 0.00621 | −0.00207 |
| −2 | 0.00248 | 0.00617 | −0.00207 |
| −1 | −0.00248 | 0 | 0.00208 |
| 0 | 0.03980 | 0.04907 | 0.00831 |
| 1 | 0.00239 | −0.00584 | 0.00206 |
| 2 | −0.00238 | 0.00588 | 0 |
| 3 | 0.00239 | 0.00584 | 0.00205 |
| 4 | 0.00238 | −0.00581 | 0 |
| 5 | −0.00238 | 0.00584 | 0 |

**b.** Excess returns (residuals) are computed in the following table:

| Day | Company X Residual | Company Y Residual | Company Z Residual | Average Residual |
|---|---|---|---|---|
| −5 | −0.000465 | −0.000520 | 0.001988 | 0.000333 |
| −4 | 0.002028 | 0.005729 | −0.004214 | 0.001181 |

| | | | | |
|---|---|---|---|---|
| −3 | −0.000465 | 0.005690 | −0.002156 | 0.001022 |
| −2 | 0.002021 | 0.005652 | −0.002161 | 0.001837 |
| −1 | −0.002947 | −0.000520 | 0.002001 | −0.000488 |
| 0 | 0.039335 | 0.048559 | 0.008233 | 0.032042 |
| 1 | 0.001926 | −0.006368 | 0.001979 | −0.000820 |
| 2 | −0.002852 | 0.005361 | −0.000082 | 0.000809 |
| 3 | 0.001926 | 0.005327 | 0.001975 | 0.003076 |
| 4 | 0.001920 | −0.006334 | −0.000082 | −0.001498 |
| 5 | −0.002846 | 0.005327 | −0.000082 | 0.000799 |

**c.** Average residuals for the stocks on each date along with standard deviations and normal deviates are computed as follows from Part b:

| Day | Average Residual | Standard Deviation | Normal Deviate |
|---|---|---|---|
| −5 | 0.000333 | 0.00143 | 0.23248 |
| −4 | 0.001181 | 0.00503 | 0.23501 |
| −3 | 0.001022 | 0.00413 | 0.2475 |
| −2 | 0.001837 | 0.00391 | 0.46985 |
| −1 | −0.000488 | 0.00247 | −0.1972 |
| 0 | 0.032042 | 0.02113 | 1.5165 |
| 1 | −0.00082 | 0.0048 | −0.1707 |
| 2 | 0.000809 | 0.00418 | 0.19362 |
| 3 | 0.003076 | 0.00195 | 1.57778 |
| 4 | −0.001498 | 0.00431 | −0.3479 |
| 5 | 0.000799 | 0.00416 | 0.1922 |

We shall assume the residuals follow a t-distribution and we will perform a one-tailed test with a 95% level of significance. Given $1 = 3 - 2$ degrees of freedom, the critical value for each test will be 6.314. Based on our computations above, we find that none of the residual t-statistics (normal deviates) exceed 6.314. Thus, we may not conclude with a 95% level of confidence that any residual differs from zero.

**d.** Cumulative average residuals are based on the following formula:

$$CAR_t = \sum_{i}^{t} AR_i$$

e. Cumulative average residuals are computed in our example as in either of the two following tables:

| Day | Average Residual | Cumulative Average Residual |
|---|---|---|
| −5 | 0.000333 | 0.000333 |
| −4 | 0.001181 | 0.001514 |
| −3 | 0.001022 | 0.002537 |
| −2 | 0.001837 | 0.004375 |
| −1 | −0.000488 | 0.003886 |
| 0 | 0.032042 | 0.035929 |
| 1 | −0.000820 | 0.035108 |
| 2 | 0.000809 | 0.035917 |
| 3 | 0.003076 | 0.038993 |
| 4 | −0.001498 | 0.037495 |
| 5 | 0.000799 | 0.038294 |

| Day | Cumulative Residual, X | Cumulative Residual, Y | Cumulative Residual, Z | Cumulative Average Residual |
|---|---|---|---|---|
| −6 | NA | NA | NA | NA |
| −5 | −0.00046 | −0.00052 | 0.00198 | 0.000333 |
| −4 | 0.00156 | 0.00520 | −0.00226 | 0.001514 |
| −3 | 0.00109 | 0.01089 | −0.00438 | 0.002537 |
| −2 | 0.00311 | 0.01655 | −0.00654 | 0.004375 |
| −1 | 0.00017 | 0.01603 | −0.00454 | 0.003886 |
| 0 | 0.03950 | 0.06459 | 0.00369 | 0.035929 |
| 1 | 0.04143 | 0.05822 | 0.00567 | 0.035108 |
| 2 | 0.03858 | 0.06358 | 0.00558 | 0.035917 |
| 3 | 0.04050 | 0.06891 | 0.00756 | 0.038993 |
| 4 | 0.04245 | 0.06257 | 0.00748 | 0.037495 |
| 5 | 0.03958 | 0.06790 | 0.00739 | 0.038294 |

f. Standard deviations and normal deviates are computed in the following table:

| Day | Standard Deviation | Normal Deviate |
|---|---|---|
| −5 | 0.001432 | 0.23307 |
| −4 | 0.003717 | 0.40749 |
| −3 | 0.007742 | 0.32775 |
| −2 | 0.011599 | 0.37720 |
| −1 | 0.010778 | 0.36056 |
| 0 | 0.012468 | 3.77089 |
| 1 | 0.021347 | 1.66432 |
| 2 | 0.023212 | 1.56549 |
| 3 | 0.024538 | 1.60622 |
| 4 | 0.022204 | 1.70760 |
| 5 | 0.024190 | 1.60047 |

g. Normal deviates do not exceed the critical value of 6.314. Thus, if our hypotheses concerning each date $t$ in our testing period were given as follows:
$H_0$: $CAR_t \leq 0$ $H_A$: $CAR_t > 0$,
We would not be able to reject the null hypothesis that $CAR_t >$ with 95%confidence for any date.

8. a. Average residuals, standard deviations, and normal deviates are given in the following table:

**Average Residuals**

| $AR_t$ | $\sigma_t$ | Normal Deviate |
|---|---|---|
| 0.006628066 | 0.010006 | 0.662407616 |
| 0.009156222 | 0.023227 | 0.394210557 |
| 0.025319415 | 0.023516 | 1.076709668 |
| 0.095348093 | 0.017464 | 5.459552045 |
| 0.006292193 | 0.025738 | 0.244470407 |
| 0.003757852 | 0.018872 | 0.199125429 |
| 0.000728706 | 0.02107 | 0.03458566 |

b. Cumulative average residuals for each stock follow:

**Cumulative Average Residuals for Individual Stocks**

| Day | Stock 1 | Stock 2 | Stock 3 | Stock 4 | Stock 5 | Stock 6 | Stock 7 | Stock 8 | Stock 9 | Stock 10 |
|---|---|---|---|---|---|---|---|---|---|---|
| −3 | 0.003279 | −0.00814 | 0.008945 | −0.00255 | 0.011395 | −0.00797 | 0.011223 | 0.014037 | 0.020344 | 0.015708 |

| | | | | | | | | | | |
|---|---|---|---|---|---|---|---|---|---|---|
| −2 | 0.007719 | −0.0281 | 0.026009 | 0.001244 | 0.059814 | 0.009998 | 0.000247 | −0.01064 | 0.044042 | 0.047514 |
| −1 | 0.03971 | −0.00554 | 0.012505 | 0.027555 | 0.1298 | 0.05721 | 0.012878 | 0.027403 | 0.059544 | 0.049967 |
| 0 | 0.131334 | 0.080815 | 0.10067 | 0.105526 | 0.258151 | 0.169602 | 0.082141 | 0.116799 | 0.167306 | 0.152173 |
| 1 | 0.174439 | 0.109783 | 0.128434 | 0.112295 | 0.209142 | 0.158994 | 0.092843 | 0.107061 | 0.172755 | 0.161694 |
| 2 | 0.181154 | 0.121328 | 0.142789 | 0.125576 | 0.182949 | 0.125532 | 0.119173 | 0.110469 | 0.188128 | 0.167919 |
| 3 | 0.16173 | 0.116801 | 0.135713 | 0.124435 | 0.178023 | 0.154783 | 0.111341 | 0.077968 | 0.213058 | 0.198455 |

Cumulative average residuals, standard deviations, and normal deviates follow:

**Cumulative Average Residual Statistics**

| **Day** | $CAR_t$ | $\sigma_t$ | **Normal Deviate** |
|---|---|---|---|
| −3 | 0.006628 | 0.010006 | 0.662408 |
| −2 | 0.015784 | 0.027937 | 0.565002 |
| −1 | 0.041104 | 0.037577 | 1.09386 |
| 0 | 0.136452 | 0.053544 | 2.548386 |
| 1 | 0.142744 | 0.037887 | 3.76762 |
| 2 | 0.146502 | 0.030352 | 4.826832 |
| 3 | 0.147231 | 0.041947 | 3.509878 |

**c.** Average residuals are statistically significant at the 1% level only on day 4, the event day. Cumulative average residuals are statistically significant at the 1% level on days 5 through 7, and at the 5% level on day 4.

**9.** The Hollywood Stock Exchange can provide information about the potential success for the movie, where that success will likely impact the film company's stock price and be of interest to prospective investors. These prices may also provide useful information on other film company offerings as well as trends useful to the film industry. Such information will also be useful to managers of firms in the industry, helping them to determine and plan movie ideas to explore and movies to produce and to distribute.

## CHAPTER 12

**1.** This is really a rhetorical question. Nonetheless, consider the following:

- Inside information is often considered to be the property of the firm's owners. Trading on inside information can violate the insider's fiduciary duties that the firm's officers and directors owe to their shareholders. No such fiduciary duties are violated in real estate and other markets, nor is there a violation of a relationship of trust and confidence.

- Inside traders in real estate and other markets do not obtain their inside information through illegal means or the breach of professional ethics.
- Because officers and directors control the production and disclosure of inside information, they can use this information to transfer wealth from shareholders to themselves. The sellers of real estate and other assets are the beneficiaries of their own inside information.
- The primary economic rationale advanced for prohibiting insider trading is that such trading can adversely affect securities markets. Prohibiting insider trading in labor and real estate markets would probably destroy those markets.

**2.** Insider trading does not violate the Securities Act of 1933. It violates the Securities and Exchange Act of 1934, which deals with secondary markets for securities.

**3.** **a.** Shenker was accused of *spoofing*, placing buy and sell orders that he had no intent of executing. These orders were placed for the purpose of manipulating the prices of the affected securities to obtain better executions on larger orders. Actually, this case was related to the Pomper case discussed in the text section on spoofing.

**b.** The actual transactions were not used to manipulate the market; only quotes that he intended to cancel were used to manipulate the market.

**c.** Any attempt to manipulate securities prices in secondary markets is illegal.

# Index

Note: Page numbers followed by "f", "t" and "n" refer to figures, tables and notes, respectively.

## B

## D

## E



## F

## Q

Edwards Brothers Malloy
Ann Arbor MI. USA
March 31, 2016